# PIONEERS TO PARTNERS

THE HISTORICAL SERIES OF THE REFORMED CHURCH IN AMERICA
NO. 75

# PIONEERS TO PARTNERS
The Reformed Church in America and
Christian Mission with the Japanese

**Gordon D. Laman**

WILLIAM B. EERDMANS PUBLISHING COMPANY
Grand Rapids, Michigan / Cambridge, UK

Wm. B. Eerdmans Publishing Co.
2140 Oak Industrial Drive SE, Grand Rapids, Michigan 49503
PO Box 163, Cambridge CB3 9PU UK
www.eerdmans.com

Printed in the United States of America

**Library of Congress Cataloging-in-Publication Data**

Laman, Gordon, 1934-
  Pioneers to partners : the Reformed Church in America and Christian
mission with the Japanese / Gordon Laman.
      p. cm. -- (The historical series of the Reformed Church in America
; no. 75)
  Includes bibliographical references (p.      ) and index.
  ISBN 978-0-8028-6965-4
  1. Reformed Church in America--Missions--Japan--History. 2.
Missions--Japan--History. 3. Japan--Church history.  I. Title.
  BV2580.L36 2012
  266'.57320952--dc23
                              2012038323

*Dedicated to the memory of*
*Evon Janice (Southland) Laman,*
*1935 – 2011,*
*best friend for sixty-one years,*
*faithful and loving wife for fifty-four years,*
*partner in Christ's mission with the Japanese*
*for forty-three years,*
*always "the wind beneath my wings."*

## The Historical Series of the Reformed Church in America

The series was inaugurated in 1968 by the General Synod of the Reformed Church in America acting through the Commission on History to communicate the church's heritage and collective memory and to reflect on our identity and mission, encouraging historical scholarship which informs both church and academy.

www.rca.org/series

General Editor
> Rev. Donald J. Bruggink, PhD, DD
> Western Theological Seminary
> Van Raalte Institute, Hope College

Associate Editor
> George Brown Jr., PhD
> Western Theological Seminary

Copy Editor
> Laurie Baron

Production Editor
> Russell L. Gasero

Commission on History
> Douglas Carlson, PhD, Northwestern College, Orange City, Iowa
> Hartmut Kramer-Mills, MDiv, DrTheol, New Brunswick, New Jersey
> David M. Tripold, PhD, Monmouth University
> Audrey Vermilyea, Bloomington, Minnesota
> Linda Walvoord, PhD, University of Cincinnati
> Lori Witt, PhD, Central College, Pella, Iowa

# Contents

# Illustrations

# On Japanese Names and Transliteration

All Japanese names have been presented in the Japanese word order; that is, the surname comes first, followed by the given name. All Japanese words and place names have been transliterated into the Roman alphabet. However, in the nineteenth century, the manner of transliteration was not at first solidified in a consistent system. When quotations have required presentation of early spellings, in first citings the later standardized transliteration has been added in brackets.

Some readers may wish to sound out Japanese words. Pronunciation of Japanese words transliterated into Romanized script is relatively simple once several basic factors are understood. There are only five vowel sounds in Japanese; *a* as in father, *i* as in in, *u* as in full, *e* as in egg, and *o* as in obey. Technically speaking, there is no Japanese alphabet, but rather two syllabaries consisting of fifty Japanese syllables each (the second syllabary is for words of foreign origin) and thousands of ideographs, all of which, for purposes of pronunciation, can be transliterated into Romanized script. A syllable is always either a vowel or one or two consonants followed by a vowel. There are no silent letters in Romanized Japanese, and words are pronounced with little or no accent.

# Foreword

The Reverend Dr. Gordon Laman informs us in the very first line of his preface, "The story I have written is intended to promote a greater understanding and appreciation for Christ's mission in Japan." He is uniquely qualified to fulfill that purpose for his North American readers. In the opening pages we learn that, as a boy during World War II, he saw Japanese people being portrayed as evil, cartoonish enemies of America. Such caricatures changed with growing knowledge and faded from memory as he and his wife, Evon, entered Japan as missionaries in 1959, sent by the Reformed Church in America to serve as evangelistic missionaries in communion with the United Church of Christ in Japan (Kyodan). By the time of their retirement in 2002, the Lamans had been thoroughly assimilated into Japanese life and language and gained a profound appreciation for Japanese culture in general and for the rich relationships they enjoyed during their ministry in Japan.

Gordon Laman's perspective on the history of Christianity in Japan has been shaped by his more than twenty years' experience serving in an equal collegial relationship with Japanese pastors and evangelists in the prefectures of Saga and Nagasaki. Memories of the devastation of World War II, culminating in the dropping of atomic bombs on Hiroshima and Nagasaki, were still fresh when the Lamans arrived there. During his final ten years in that area, Laman was asked by Japanese church leaders to take responsibility for evangelistic outreach in the northern part of Nagasaki Prefecture and to serve as pastor of a preaching station on the off-shore island of Hirado.

His ministry in Hirado helped shape Laman's perspective on the position of Christianity in Japan, because there he encountered descendants of Christians converted by Jesuit missionaries in the sixteenth century. Laman provides a brief history of that Jesuit mission, which resulted in the conversion of more than 500,000 Japanese. Many of them were martyred by crucifixion and other excruciating methods when the imperialistic aims of the Jesuits' European allies became known to the political authorities in Japan. In their opposition to that coming of Christianity, the Japanese authorities did not stop at severely persecuting the Christian converts and closing Japan to outsiders. They erected placards forbidding the Christian religion. Laman contends that their annual ceremony that required people to trample on the cross as a sign of rejection of Jesus Christ has left a deep mark on the Japanese psyche to the present day.

The modern Protestant missionary movement became possible in 1859, after Commodore Perry forced Japan to open several ports to foreign trade and refueling sites. Reformed Church missionaries Guido F. and Maria Verbeck, Samuel R. and Elizabeth Brown, and James H. and Margaret Ballagh were permitted to reside in Japan, although under severe restrictions and only in places reserved for foreigners. They had to obtain visas for inland travel in Japan and keep authorities informed of their movements. Laman makes clear that even by nineteenth-century missionary standards, missionary life was extraordinarily difficult in Japan. Disease and death threatened constantly. The Japanese language is one of the most difficult for North Americans to learn. Missionaries often lived in isolation from each other with little psychological support. Moreover, the Reformed Church Board of Foreign Missions was always short of funds, particularly in years of American financial panic such as 1873 and 1893, with the result that the missionaries' meager salaries and work funds were cut back even more drastically.

As a consequence of spending more than twenty years in Kyushu in southwest Japan, followed by more than two decades in the Tokyo area, as well as through extensive research, Laman is able to provide the reader with a balanced perspective. We read that in 1899, just when it was hoped that Japan would become more democratic and allow more freedom of religion, the government not only increased its surveillance of religion but also ruled that Shinto ceremonies and rites such as bowing to symbols of the emperor were acts of patriotism rather than religious acts. We learn that Christians in Japan in the first half of the twentieth century were forced to deal with political ambiguities and faith decisions similar to those faced by Christians in the first centuries under Roman rule, when they were expected to bow down to images of Caesar. In view of the mythical claim that the emperor was a descendent and representative of the great original goddess of Japan, Christians could not help but see the religious roots of the demand that all teachers and students participate daily in bowing to the emperor as a sign of their loyalty. As the militarism of Japan prior to World War II became ever more evident, the dilemma for the Japanese churches and missionaries became more pressing as they had to defend themselves against the charge that the Christian faith was a foreign religion.

From his vantage point as a pastor and evangelist, as well as a theological university professor of Asian mission and communication and the seminary's director of field education, Laman provides a clear overview of the ecumenical and theological issues that have faced the church in the course of the decades. He details how the Japanese church and the six cooperating missions with whom the Reformed Church missionaries were associated struggled to work out policies of cooperation. They sought, on the one hand, to further the independent role of the Japanese church and, on the other hand, to provide space for the missionaries to carry out their ministry in evangelistic outreach and educational institutions. He follows the changing patterns of cooperation from before the beginning to the end of the twentieth century.

He also introduces us to several of the theological controversies that threatened to divide Christians, especially the Uemura-Ebina Controversy of 1901-1902. The debate between Uemura Masahisa and Ebina Danjo developed because Ebina emphasized the role of Jesus Christ as teacher and example rather than as redeemer through his sacrifice on the cross. Ebina did not believe in the incarnation of Christ and consequently denied Christ's divinity and the doctrine of the Trinity. Uemura defended the traditional evangelical doctrines on these matters, with the result that the debate in Japan roughly paralleled the American division between nineteenth-century liberals and evangelicals. Laman also introduces us to the intense controversy about liberation theology, which maintained that the world sets the agenda for the church. Influenced by radical liberation theology, some students went so far as to engage in violent activity and at times took over Christian university buildings, as well as Tokyo Union Theological Seminary, in their opposition to American capitalism and its military presence in Japan during the Vietnam War.

Gordon Laman has written a book that is filled with his passion for the gospel of Jesus Christ and with his passion for the spiritual and numerical growth of the church in Japan. He holds the strong conviction that North American Christians and Japanese Christians are not called to carry out mission apart from each other. They are called to share their spiritual gifts across the broad stretches of the Pacific Ocean. Ecumenical missionaries working across national boundaries must remain a vital force in the twenty-first century, but they are likely to be effective only to the extent that they carry with them an awareness of the historical context of their work. Thus, the following words from his preface tell us why we must read this book as we support those who serve in the church in Japan. It is well to take note of his conviction that, for the future as well as for the past, mission

> ...is always carried on in a unique cultural and historical setting, in an encounter with a particular religious, sociological, and political context. I believe we can begin to grasp the realities of the Christian mission to Japan through the study of Japan's history and its early encounters with Christianity. In fact, without examining this earlier history, it will not be possible to understand the experience of the Reformed Church in America as it entered into its mission with the Japanese in the middle of the nineteenth century.

Eugene P. Heideman

# Preface

The story I have written is intended to promote greater understanding and appreciation for Christ's mission in Japan. This book is intended for North American readers, and many of the resources used are the records of missionaries and their activities. As a consequence, the book may give the regrettable and false impression that it is primarily the missionary that is important in the story. Despite this shortcoming, it is hoped that, especially in its discussion of the early period, Japanese Christians may find this narrative enlightening with regard to the roots of their faith, their churches, and their schools. The life and work of the pioneer missionaries I found to be not only intriguing, but also formative for the subsequent development of mission with the Japanese. Writing this record has been for me a labor of love, for it is not only a portrayal of past events but also the record of a mission in which I have been personally involved for virtually my entire adult life.

During my lifetime, my image of Japan and the Japanese people gradually changed. My first memory related to Japan goes back to my early childhood in the late 1930s; it seems that I complained about the food Mom had prepared. As I remember it, in response to my impertinence, Dad took my plate, scattered the food on it in the back yard, put grass on my plate in its place, plunked it down in front of me, and told me that if I didn't like the good food Mom had prepared I could eat grass like the Chinese, whose food was being taken away by the Japanese (a fact: in the late 1930s the food produced by Chinese, Taiwanese, and Korean farmers was being confiscated to feed the Japanese military).

Later, I remember such things as Pearl Harbor, the "Japs" as our enemies, cartoon caricatures of Japanese as stupid, buck-toothed people, and Japanese people as the cruel conquerors of much of Asia. I subsequently also came to see the Japanese people as the first and only nation to experience the atomic bomb directly, and Japan as a defeated, destroyed, and destitute nation occupied by the Allied Command under General Douglas MacArthur, with its leaders being tried as war criminals. A bit later I heard of Japan as the producer of cheap toys and clothes, but also as a nation of remarkably resilient people and as an exotic Asian country. It was years later before I gradually came to see Japan as a nation with an ancient history, a rich culture, and an extremely difficult language—and at the same time as a modern nation; an economic power that produced quality cameras, motorcycles, electronics, and cars; and America's chief ally in Asia.

Ki Bum Han, my Korean roommate at Hope College, was the source of my first direct information on Japan. Having spent nine years of his childhood in Japan, he had suffered the double ignominy of living in Japan as a despised Korean national and as the son of a Christian minister before and during World War II. At that time Korea was a cruelly subjugated part of the Japanese Empire, and Christians in Japan were suspect as believers in the religion of the enemy. I had first felt a call to be a missionary at the age of thirteen, but, ironically, it was through my college roommate who had suffered under the Japanese that I was attracted to Asia and to Japan. I gradually learned that the Christian church in Japan was a small, struggling minority, that the percentage of Christians among the Japanese population was less than 1 percent, and that there was something unique about Japanese attitudes toward Christianity and outsiders.

My wife, Evon, and I arrived in Japan as missionaries August 31, 1959, and we immediately began studying the language and acclimating to Japanese life and culture. That year in October we attended the celebration of the hundredth anniversary of the beginning of Protestant mission in Japan. With the realization that we were second-century

Protestant missionaries to Japan serving in partnership with Japanese Christians, and gradually growing into a colleagial relationship with them, we worked in Japan almost forty-three years. We have always looked for, worked for, and hoped for the growth and progress of Christ's church in Japan, but to date, while the church in Japan has matured in many ways, we have hoped in vain for any great ingathering. The statistics remain virtually unchanged in 2011.

I stand firm in the conviction that Jesus Christ is "the way, the truth, and the life." Nevertheless, in our experience, most of the people around us in Japan did not have "ears to hear." As I considered most of my neighbors during those many years, I gained an increasing appreciation for Jesus' words in Matthew 23:37. He gazed at the unreceptive city and said, "O Jerusalem, Jerusalem, you who kill the prophets and stone those sent to you, how often I have longed to gather your children together, as a hen gathers her chicks under her wings, but you were not willing."

From the beginning I have been haunted by a question, as I am even now: Why is Japan so resistant to the Christian faith? Mission never takes place in a vacuum, sheltered from outside influences. It is always carried on in a unique cultural and historical setting, in an encounter with a particular religious, sociological, and political context. I believe we can begin to grasp the realities of the Christian mission to Japan through the study of Japan's history and its early encounters with Christianity. In fact, without examining this earlier history, it will not be possible to understand the experience of the Reformed Church in America as it entered into its mission with the Japanese in the middle of the nineteenth century.

In uncovering and telling the story of the Reformed Church's involvement in mission in Japan, I am indebted to many. I am especially grateful to the general editor of this series, Donald J. Bruggink; the Reformed Church archivist, Russell Gasero; Eugene P. Heideman; copy editor Laurie Baron; the staff of the Joint Archives of Holland; and my many colleagues in mission in Japan for assistance, encouragement, guidance, and wise counsel in this process. May Christ's mission be advanced, and to God be the glory.

# A Sketch of Japan's Historical and Cultural Background

Mythology and tradition in Japan have taught that Japan is the "god-country," ruled by an unbroken line of emperors going back to the seventh century BCE, who could claim descent from the sun-goddess, *Amaterasu Omikami*. Actually, over the centuries the emperors of Japan sometimes reigned, but they have never truly ruled over Japan. Nevertheless, given the mythology associated with them, and given the fact that the emperors carry out a priestly function in Shintoism, Japan's primitive folk religion, the emperors have always fulfilled a symbolic and unifying role. Furthermore, the historical reality of early Japan is that, unlike China with its highly developed culture going back several thousand years before the time of Christ, even in the sixth century of the Christian Era Japan was still in the process of becoming what could be called a nation. It was at that time made up of tribal groups gradually forming a loose connection and hierarchy.

Although numerous earlier influences from the Asian continent are apparent, in the sixth century Japan had as yet no system of writing, and of course no recorded history, and it lagged far behind Korea and China in cultural development. However, for several centuries the leading clans had been influenced by an influx of Korean and Chinese refugees into the Japanese islands from wars on the Asian continent. The superior culture and the religion of these immigrants were implemented by the Japanese clans, who made use of some of the newcomers as teachers, scribes, accountants, interpreters, and craftsmen. For a time, Korea served as the filter through which China's rich material and intellectual achievements were transmitted to Japan.

In the mid-sixth century the king of Paekche, one of three Korean kingdoms at the time, sent Japan's Emperor Kinmei an image of Buddha, as well as Buddhist scriptures and religious articles, and recommended the Buddhist religion. This is considered the official introduction of Buddhism to Japan. Subsequently, widespread propagation of Buddhism was assured when Japan's most powerful Soga clan supported the imperial clan in fostering Buddhism, building temples, and sending delegations directly to China beginning in the year 600 to investigate the sources of Buddhism and Chinese culture.

> Having thus established direct ties with China, the Japanese Court proceeded in the next decades to import Chinese culture wholesale, adopting a Chinese-style government and legal system, Chinese writing, Chinese art, Chinese dress, Chinese science, and Chinese philosophy, all primarily through the medium of Buddhism. Within the next century Japan underwent a cultural transformation of astonishing proportions.[1]

It was only after this influx of Chinese culture that Japan's first literary efforts appeared. In the eighth century the first accounts of Japan's early times were produced. The *Kojiki* ("Record of Ancient Matters") was compiled in 712, and the *Nihon Shoki* ("Chronicles of Japan") was compiled in 720. They contain myriad myths and legends designed to enhance the prestige of the ruling family and create the image that Japan had long had centralized rule and national respectability like ancient China. Some of the later material in these writings has a measure of historical validity. However, it is interesting to note that in these early traditions, a Prince Shotoku is credited with numerous very remarkable, but at the same time not really believable, accomplishments in the nation's development. Prince Shotoku has been revered in popular tradition as the great Japanese innovator of the

---

[1]    Charles S. Terry, "Legend and Political Intrigue in Ancient Japan," Murakami Hyoe and Thomas J. Harper, eds., *Great Historical Figures of Japan* (Tokyo: Japan Culture Institute, 1978), 11.

seventh century, and his visage has long been featured on the 10,000 yen note of Japanese currency.

Early in the ninth century, Japanese monks Kukai and Saicho, returning from pilgrimages to China, established the Shingon and Tendai sects of Japanese Buddhism, with Buddhist centers on Mt. Koya and Mt. Hiei respectively, and Buddhism began its deeper assimilation into Japanese culture. During Japan's Kamakura period (1185-1333), new forms of Japanese Buddhism emerged, but Shintoism, with its myriad shrines and cultic practices and with countless spirits or gods, continued to be practiced alongside Buddhism.

INTRODUCTION

# Japan's Exposure to Christianity Before the Nineteenth Century

## The First Encounter

Very little is known about the first encounter of Christianity with Japan. Nestorian missionaries from the Middle East traveled six thousand miles on foot to the interior of China as early as the seventh century and established a Christian mission there, but by the ninth century almost all traces of this earliest Chinese Christianity had been eliminated. Sometime during this early Chinese experience with Christianity, it seems also to have reached the shores of Japan. However, there are no historical records of this initial contact between Christianity and the Japanese islands, and only very meager archaeological evidence survives to substantiate that there was in fact a limited very early encounter with Christianity.

In this regard, the *Nihon Shoki* compiled in 720 contains an account of the unusual birth of the Prince Shotoku. While it is obvious that the intent of these "Chronicles of Japan" was to enhance the prestige of the prince, the story is an intriguing one.

The empress-consort, on the day of the dissolution of her pregnancy, went round the forbidden precinct, inspecting the different offices. When she came to the Horse Department, she was suddenly delivered of him without effort. He was able to speak as soon as he was born, and was so wise when he grew up that he could attend to the suits of ten men at once and decide them all without error. He knew beforehand what was going to happen. Moreover he learned the Inner Doctrine (Buddhism) from a Koguryo priest named Hye-cha (a Korean), and studied the Outer (Confucian) Classics with a doctor called Hak-ka. In both of these branches of study he became thoroughly proficient.[1]

Some have suggested that this story, with its description of the birth of Prince Shotoku at the stable door, could have been inspired by the Christian narrative of Jesus' birth. This is plausible in light of the presence of Nestorian Christians in China at the time, and their beliefs may have crept into Buddhist lore brought by Chinese priests to Japan. Furthermore, a ninth-century elaboration of the story speaks of a priest shining with a golden light appearing to Prince Shotoku's mother-to-be on the auspicious first day of the year to announce that he is actually the Bodhisattva Guze Kannon ("World-saving Kannon"). He persuades her to let him reside in her body for a while so that he can be born a human being. The origin of such an annunciation legend might be either Christian or Buddhist.[2]

In any case, from whatever level of encounter that occurred between Nestorian Christianity and Japan, no apparent influence is observable today. This was not to be the case with the next Christian encounter with Japan.

## The Early Roman Catholic Mission to Japan

### A. The Historical Setting

Christianity's encounter with Japan cannot be understood apart from Japan's history and the situation in Japan at the time Roman Catholic missionary activity began there in the middle of the sixteenth century. Japanese society and the Japanese people at that time were very different from the society and people encountered by the later Westerners who arrived to begin Protestant mission work in the nineteenth century, and different beyond imagination from

---

[1]     Ibid., 4.
[2]     Ibid., 4.

the Japanese of today. Japan and the Japanese people were not only radically transformed by their encounter with the superior culture of China, they were also greatly changed a millennium later as a result of their encounter with Roman Catholic Christianity in the sixteenth and seventeenth centuries.

The feudal system had been established in the islands of Japan from the twelfth century. However, it was not yet a fully unified nation with an effective central authority, but a land made up of about 260 fiefdoms ruled by feudal lords (*daimyo*). By the middle of the fifteenth century any unity or order in the nation had broken down completely. Japan had entered a period of chaotic political confusion known as the *sengoku jidai*, or the age of the country at war. During the sixteenth century the whole country was in a state of war. As the century progressed, the political unification and tight control of Japan was accomplished mainly under the leadership of three military dictators. They were Oda Nobunaga, Toyotomi Hideyoshi, and Tokugawa Ieyasu. The destiny of early Christianity in Japan was determined largely by its interaction with these three dictators and their policies.

Despite the political confusion, there had been a considerable flowering of Japanese culture, including the arts and literature, during several centuries. The Buddhism of the nobility that had been imported from China and Korea from the seventh century had been assimilated, but it had also degenerated. Subsequently, several indigenous and unique branches of Buddhism, called Kamakura Buddhism, developed and prospered during the twelfth and thirteenth centuries. Most prominent were the *Jodo-shinshu* ("New Pure-land") Sect founded by Shinran, and the *Nichiren* Sect named after founder Nichiren. No longer the religion or philosophy only of the nobility, these sects had penetrated somewhat into lower elements of the society. However, by the sixteenth century, major Buddhist sects had become not only religious but also political and even military forces that challenged the growing authority of the dictators.

This period of Japanese history was a time of perpetual war, of repeated rebellions and treasons, of power struggles, of political chaos and confusion. Bloodshed was commonplace. Life was cheap. The lot of the peasants was pitiful. It was an age of cruelty, poverty, and starvation. Into this land of immeasurable misery, toward the end of the longest period of military strife and general disorder in Japanese history, Christianity entered significantly for the first time at the mid-point of the sixteenth century.[3]

---

[3]     Richard H. Drummond, *A History of Christianity in Japan* (Grand Rapids: Eerdmans, 1971), 20-21.

### B. Christianity Enters Japan

The period from 1549 to 1639 is sometimes called Japan's Christian century. The events that transpired during that time had a profound effect not only on the progress of the Christian faith in Japan, but upon the very destiny of the nation. It is important to understand the manner of Christianity's entrance into Japan, as well as the nature and extent of its penetration.

Portuguese traders were the first Europeans to make contact with Japan, in 1542. It actually happened by accident, when they were driven off course by a storm. They commenced trade with Japan, and soon missionaries were able to take advantage of these traders' ships to reach Japan. On August 15, 1549, Francis Xavier, one of the founders of the Jesuit Order, arrived in Kagoshima, Japan, with two Jesuit assistants to begin missionary work. Xavier was a deeply committed and remarkable missionary. However, Xavier was also a typical sixteenth-century European. In other words, he did not separate particularly the cause of Christ and the cause of Portugal as a colonial power. Xavier established in Japan the Jesuit policy of working from the top down, always attempting to gain the favor, permission, and support of the feudal lords for his activities wherever he went. He was unequivocal in his goal. He came to convert Japan. And he didn't hesitate to use political and economic means in order to achieve his missionary goals.[4]

Francis Xavier was in Japan for a mere two years and three months. His accomplishments were remarkable. He and his colleagues spoke no Japanese and knew nothing about Japanese culture and religion. Yet, through a semiliterate Japanese refugee they had brought back to Japan, who served as their interpreter, they immediately began missionary activity. They boldly attempted propagation, despite ignorance, obstacles, and misunderstandings. Amazingly, Xavier baptized 150 people at Kagoshima during his first ten months in Japan.[5] During the remainder of his brief time in Japan, Xavier also established mission work on the island of Hirado, and at Yamaguchi and Oita, all regions in the southwest of Japan. When he left Japan, the two Jesuits he had brought with him were left behind to carry on the work, and the Jesuit mission was gradually enlarged.[6]

---

[4]   George Elison, *Deus Destroyed: The Image of Christianity in Early Modern Japan* (Cambridge: Harvard Univ. Press, 1973), 25, 252.

[5]   G. B. Sansom, *The Western World and Japan: A Study in the Interaction of European and Asiatic Cultures* (Tokyo: Charles E. Tuttle, 1977), 117.

[6]   Drummond, *History of Christianity*, 41-44.

### C. The Era of the Patronage of the Missionaries

The first part of Japan's Christian century, from 1549 to 1587, may be described as the era of patronage. Because the nation was disunited and in social and political chaos, the Jesuit missionaries were able to approach individual feudal lords, urge permission for propagation, and impress them with the advantages involved. These missionaries often gained the cooperation or allegiance of feudal lords, or even their conversion to Christianity, by suggesting advantages to be realized by Portuguese trade or military aid. Jesuit missionaries used their connections with the traders, often functioning as interpreters as they gained Japanese language skill, and Japan's local rulers benefited.[7] Feudal lords were eager for profits to be gained from trade, and to acquire Portuguese weapons.

Especially on the island of Kyushu and in the Kyoto region, Japanese of all classes began to embrace Christianity in large numbers. By the year 1580, it is estimated that 150,000 Japanese had become Christians.[8] This remarkable growth took place despite very small numbers of mission personnel. Jesuit missionary personnel numbered six in 1561, and still only eighteen in 1570. They depended heavily on assistance from Japanese catechists and interpreters to carry on the work.[9]

As we consider the progress of Christianity during this period of patronage, we must not overlook the role of the most powerful person in Japan at the time. Oda Nobunaga began his military career in 1549 at the age of fifteen, and before long he had set about the task of unifying the country. He became the most powerful ruler in the land by subjugating others. He made use of the Neo-Confucian teaching of the ideal of absolute subordination, but it was by his military ability and ingenuity that he enforced it. Nobunaga is hailed in Japanese history as a great leader and unifier, but the fact is that he rose to power and enforced his authority by ruthless murders, massacres, espionage, trickery, and betrayal, not only of his many enemies, but also of his own family members, other relatives, and allies.[10] His ruthlessness makes King Herod, who massacred the baby boys of Bethlehem, look like a choirboy.

---

[7]   Elison, *Deus Destroyed*, 27-28.

[8]   Edwin O. Reischauer, *Japan: The Story of a Nation* (Tokyo: Charles E. Tuttle, 1970), 92.

[9]   Sansom, *Western World and Japan*, 125.

[10]   Billy J. Cody, "Unifiers of Japan: Nobunaga, Hideyoshi, and Ieyasu," Murakami Hyoe and Thomas J. Harper, eds., *Great Historical Figures of Japan* (Tokyo: Japan Culture Institute, 1978), 154-57.

Some Buddhist sects had gained considerable power, especially in the Kyoto and Osaka regions. The political and military activities of Buddhist warrior monks posed a major threat to Nobunaga. They were his enemies, not for religious but for political reasons. Monks of the Tendai Buddhist sect on Mt. Hiei in Kyoto opposed him. He attacked their headquarters in 1571, burned its more than four hundred buildings to the ground, and killed its three thousand inhabitants. Nobunaga threatened the Shingon Buddhist sect with the same fate if they opposed him. His struggle against the Jodo Shinshu Buddhist sect lasted ten years and culminated in the destruction of the Osaka Honganji main temple. More than sixty thousand adherents were massacred.[11]

Incredibly, from 1569 the Jesuit missionaries eagerly sought and gained and held the favor of this Nobunaga. Consequently, the success of the Jesuit missionaries during this period was made possible by cultivating the favor of this ruthless dictator. Nobunaga found the Jesuits useful for his purposes. He respected the men, the products, and particularly the guns of Europe, but he feared none of them. However, Nobunaga was not aware of the facts of Portuguese and Spanish colonialism.[12] During the period from 1569 to Nobunaga's death in 1582, his patronage of the Jesuit missionaries was most significant. The mass conversions on the island of Kyushu and elsewhere began after Nobunaga's welcome of the missionaries became known.

After Nobunaga's death, his able general, Hideyoshi, soon took his place as the undisputed ruler of central Japan. The unification of Japan subservient to one military dictator or shogun that had begun under Nobunaga continued, and Hideyoshi subdued all of the islands of Shikoku and Kyushu, thus gaining control of all of western Japan. Hideyoshi seemed favorable toward the Jesuits at first, and the missionary work flourished more and more under his rule.[13] Like his predecessor, his policy toward the missionaries and the church was lenient, while his attitude and actions toward militant Buddhism were hostile and oppressive. Some of Hideyoshi's most trusted advisors and generals and *samurai* soldiers were prominent Christians.

The Roman Catholic missionaries no doubt felt optimistic about the future of the church and of their goal to convert Japan.

---

[11]   Ibid., 154.
[12]   Elison, *Deus Destroyed*, 25-26; Edwin O. Reischauer and Albert M. Craig, *Japan: Tradition and Transformation* (Tokyo: Charles E, Tuttle, 1981), 77.
[13]   Tomonobu Yanagita, *A Short History of Christianity in Japan* (Sendai, Japan: Seisho Tosho Kankokai, 1957), 19.

Sketch of Oda Nobunaga at Chokoji
Temple, Toyota City, Aichi, Japan

However, these early Roman Catholic missionaries and their policies were sometimes extremely unwise. For example, a leading Jesuit priest fraternized directly with military dictator Hideyoshi. The priest involved himself in deliberations over whether he would arrange for Portuguese warships to assist Hideyoshi's forces in controlling the Japanese feudal lords or in the conquest of the Korean peninsula.[14]

Another serious problem had to do with mission economics. By the 1580s, the Jesuit mission in Japan was supporting and providing residences for five hundred mission personnel, including not only the missionaries but also their numerous Japanese assistants. They had more than two hundred churches, as well as educational and social work institutions to maintain. Financial support from Portugal and the Jesuit order was totally inadequate for such a large program. In order to support this vast enterprise, the Jesuit mission got involved in the lucrative Portuguese silk trade and was reaping enormous profits.[15]

Hideyoshi wanted to continue to trade with the Europeans. However, because the nation's stability and his hegemony over the feudal lords were crucial for him, and possibly for economic reasons, he began to view Christianity with disfavor.[16] Dictator Hideyoshi issued his famous Edict of Expulsion July 24, 1587, which demanded that all the foreign missionaries leave Japan within twenty days. This edict was a total surprise to the naive and pretentious Jesuit missionaries,

[14]  Drummond, *History of Christianity*, 76-78.
[15]  Elison, *Deus Destroyed*, 102.
[16]  Reischauer and Craig, *Tradition and Transformation*, 79.

with whom Hideyoshi had been carrying on negotiations in a cordial manner only hours before. But this was no sudden and erratic reversal. It was a rational political decision. Expelling the priests was simply part of Hideyoshi's program of establishing his central authority. He demonstrated that his control of Japan was to be absolute, with no room for pretensions to power or for participation in the profits of commerce on the part of the Jesuits. From this time, the missionaries were seen as a possible threat comparable to that of the Buddhists. Christianity was seen as an external force engaged not only in religious activity but also in political intrigue, and it could not be ignored by a dictator like Hideyoshi.[17]

### D. The Era of Antagonism

The second part of Japan's so-called Christian century, from 1587 to 1614, may be described as the period of antagonism. The situation had changed. The era of patronage had clearly come to an end. Hideyoshi's Edict of Expulsion required all foreign missionary priests to leave Japan within twenty days. If this had been fully implemented, the mission work would have at that point come to an end, for the Jesuit missionaries had not up to that time trained or ordained any Japanese priests. They had retained all church authority for themselves and relied on Japanese catechists and interpreters working under them to carry on their work. In any case, the Edict of Expulsion was not actually enforced.

Nevertheless, its impact may be seen in a necessary change in missionary policy. While the foreign priests did not leave Japan, they had to assume a lower posture in order to continue their work, and they had to try more cleverly to avoid offending dictator Hideyoshi. As evidence of increased suppression, some of the churches and schools were destroyed and church lands in Nagasaki were confiscated by the central government, and at least one Christian feudal lord lost his property, but no thoroughgoing persecution was carried out at that time. The head of the Jesuit mission, Valignano, was even able to appear before Hideyoshi in 1591. The purge directive was not rescinded, but the Jesuits were able to continue with certain conditions. Though unobtrusively, great progress was achieved with thousands of new converts. But then the course of events changed suddenly.[18]

---

[17] Elison, *Deus Destroyed*, 85, 115-19.
[18] Yanagita, *Short History*, 19-20.

Rivalries among Roman Catholics brought about their own doom. Despite the fact that the pope had given the Jesuit order the exclusive right to do missionary work in Japan, Spanish Franciscans arrived in 1592. They came ostensibly to work out plans for Spanish trade and stayed to enter rather ostentatiously into missionary activity, having obtained permission from dictator Hideyoshi for both. The end result was protracted bickering between Jesuits and Franciscans, as well as discordant political and commercial rivalry between Portuguese and Spanish traders. Such behavior deepened the suspicions of Hideyoshi toward the missionaries. He became increasingly aware of the association of the missionaries with European soldiers in colonial outposts such as Manila.[19]

Then a specific incident seems to have triggered a tragedy. In July of 1596, a Spanish ship, the *San Felipe*, filled with valuable cargo, ran aground on the Japanese island of Shikoku in a storm. In an effort to save the ship's cargo from confiscation, one of the ship's officers told local Japanese officials of the power of Spain, showing them a map of Spain's colonial possessions. When asked how Spain had gained such an empire, he responded, "The kings of Spain begin by sending out teachers of our religion, and when these have made sufficient progress in gaining the hearts of the people, troops are despatched who unite with the new Christians in bringing about the conquest of the desired territory."[20] It is certain that this remark had a great influence upon Hideyoshi, to whom it was reported. While the *San Felipe* incident was not the only factor involved, it was certainly a turning point. After this, Hideyoshi's attitude toward the missionaries became one of implacable but restrained hostility.[21]

Taking advantage of the trouble over the *San Felipe*, Hideyoshi immediately issued a warrant for the arrest of all the Franciscans in the Kyoto and Osaka areas. Six Spanish Franciscans, a Japanese Jesuit brother, and nineteen other Japanese converts were condemned to death, publicly humiliated, and forced to walk in chains hundreds of miles under guard to Nagasaki as a vivid public demonstration of the peril of embracing the Christian religion. On a hill in Nagasaki they were all crucified on February 5, 1597. These people are known around the world today as the Twenty-six Martyrs of Japan.[22]

---

[19]  Drummond, *History of Christianity*, 83-85; Reischauer and Craig, *Tradition and Transformation*, 80.

[20]  Otis Cary, *A History of Christianity in Japan: Roman Catholic, Greek Orthodox, and Protestant Missions*, Vol. I (Tokyo: Charles E. Tuttle, 1976), 124.

[21]  Drummond, *History of Christianity*, 86.

[22]  Yanagita, *Short History*, 21.

Sketches of Tokugawa Ieyasu (left) and Toyotomi Hideyoshi
at Kodaiji Temple, Kyoto, Japan

Some other Christians were killed, too, at that time, and many were sent into exile. They included not only Franciscan but also Jesuit missionaries. Churches and seminaries for training Japanese lay assistants were also burned. The remaining missionaries went into hiding for a while or worked very cautiously.[23] Remarkably, many Jesuits did in fact continue their missionary activity, and the number of believers continued to grow. All persecution ceased temporarily at the death of Hideyoshi in 1598. In any case, by the end of the sixteenth century the number of Christians in Japan had grown to more than 300,000.[24]

Tokugawa Ieyasu came to power as the new ruler of Japan in 1600. He became the first of a long line of Tokugawas to rule Japan by military dictatorship. Once again the new ruler was quite tolerant of Christianity for a while, and missionary work continued more or less unhindered. Scattered local persecutions did take place, however, and there were 132 recorded martyrdoms between 1600 and 1612. Thousands more of the Japanese Christians were stripped of their property and banished, and from 1613 overt persecutions increased.[25]

The policy of dictator Ieyasu had been tempered by the fact that he was interested in trade, especially with the Spanish. However, in 1609 the Dutch established a trade center on the Japanese island of Hirado. Dictator Ieyasu learned from the Dutch envoy that the Netherlands was not a Roman Catholic country, but had become Protestant. Furthermore,

23    Sansom, *Western World and Japan*, 131.
24    Reischauer and Craig, *Tradition and Transformation*, 75.
25    Sansom, *Western World and Japan*, 132.

the Dutch were aware of the antagonism toward the Roman Catholic missionaries, and being motivated primarily by profit from trade, they refrained from religious involvement in Japan. Ieyasu concluded that by trading with the Dutch instead of Spain and Portugal he could avoid having to patronize Roman Catholic Christianity. Out of this unique utilitarian conclusion came an outbreak of renewed hostility toward the Catholics.[26]

No doubt the religious and political rivalries of Europe that were reflected so virulently before the eyes of Ieyasu strengthened his determination to banish all missionaries and drive the Christian faith out of Japan. But this does not mean that Ieyasu really feared external military aggression against Japan. What he, like his two predecessors, feared was the subversion, the undermining of his quest for absolute power and authority over all of Japan. This quest brought about the further development of suspicion, hostility, and repressive action. It was a process that ended finally in the Great Edict of Annihilation promulgated on January 27, 1614. The dictator Ieyasu had become determined to stop all Christian missionary work in Japan, and then to abolish the faith from among his subjects.[27]

### E. The Era of Martyrdom

The third part of Japan's Christian century, from 1614 to 1638, may be described as the era of martyrdom. By this time there were perhaps as many as 500,000 Christians in Japan.[28] It seems apparent, therefore, that while the mode of penetration and some of the policies of the missionaries may have been unwise or highly questionable and their behavior sometimes repulsive, nevertheless many Japanese had sincerely embraced Christian faith. In fact, the percentage of Christians in the Japanese population in 1614 was probably about three times what it is today. Despite its many converts, however, the Japanese Roman Catholic church had remained totally dominated by the foreign clergy. Efforts by the missionaries to train a Japanese clergy were too little and too late. Nothing was done during the first thirty-one years, despite the vision of Xavier at the beginning for a self-perpetuating Japanese Christianity. The first two Japanese priests were finally ordained in 1601, after fifty-two years. And when the general persecution broke out in 1614, there were still only fourteen Japanese priests.[29]

[26]   Yanagita, *Short History*, 22-23.
[27]   Drummond, *History of Christianity*, 90-94.
[28]   Reischauer and Craig, *Tradition and Transformation*, 75.
[29]   Elison, *Deus Destroyed*, 70-71.

At that time there were fifty-five Jesuit missionary priests, as well as some Franciscans, Dominicans, and Augustinians. In addition there were perhaps fifty Japanese lay brothers and several hundred Japanese catechists.[30] Though these many catechists had little formal training and no place of authority in or influence on the policy of the Catholic hierarchy, they had been remarkably effective as evangelists and lay teachers, a crucial factor in the spread of Christianity. It was no doubt helpful that the movable press brought to Japan by the Jesuits in 1590 was used to print numerous materials in simple Japanese, such as devotional tracts, for use in the propagation of the faith.[31] Unfortunately, the Bible had not been translated and published in Japanese because the Roman Catholic policy of that time did not allow lay people to read or interpret the Bible on their own.

The period of martyrdom that began in 1614 was very different from the sporadic persecutions that had preceded it. But it is important also to note that both the style of ministry and the nature of the Christian constituency had changed considerably during the previous fifteen years. Those who were merely Christians of convenience had apostatized. No longer able to use patronage and political intrigue for their purposes, and possibly chastened by their experiences, the missionaries and their colleagues concentrated more on their catechetical and pastoral work. Believers became more deeply rooted in the faith. They were also encouraged and prepared to accept martyrdom rather than apostatize, or give up their faith. They were thus not easily defeated by the intense persecution that followed.[32]

As a direct result of the Great Edict of Annihilation of 1614, more than four hundred missionaries and their Japanese associates were assembled at Nagasaki, put on several foreign ships, and sent away as exiles to Manila and Macao.[33] However, at least thirty-eight foreign priests had gone into hiding and managed to escape being sent off.[34] Christianity was forced to go underground, but it continued to carry on despite the burning down or confiscation of all churches. Twenty Jesuits and many other foreign priests managed to slip into the country by various infiltration plots to help carry on the work in secret.

After the death of dictator Ieyasu in 1616, under successive shoguns, or military dictators, of the Tokugawa Clan, a much more

---

[30]  Sansom, *Western World and Japan*, 174.
[31]  Elison, *Deus Destroyed*, 20.
[32]  Drummond, *History of Christianity*, 95.
[33]  Yanagita, *Short History*, 23.
[34]  Drummond, *History of Christianity*, 96.

thorough and brutal persecution was carried out. It became more and more widespread and intense, but Christianity was not easily stamped out. From 1617, the Christians were searched out, and public executions of both foreign priests and Japanese Christians increased. Most of the more ostentatious and large-scale persecutions took place at Nagasaki and Omura by beheading or burning at the stake. The martyrdom reached its peak in 1622. But despite this public display of the consequences of refusing to give up Christian faith, and despite the step-by-step annihilation of all the church's leaders, the persecution was not achieving its desired effect. While some of the upper-class Christians apostatized, most of the believers, especially the peasants, courageously accepted martyrdom rather than recant.

More extreme measures were adopted. The government's administrator in Nagasaki from 1626 to 1633 developed extremely excruciating types of torture. To the beheading and burning at the stake were added methods such as sawing asunder with a bamboo saw, stabbing to death with a spear, torture to death by being gradually lowered into boiling hot springs, burying alive, and finally *ana tsurushi* (hanging the victim bound upside down in a pit with his head just above fume-producing excrement until death). This last torture, *ana tsurushi*, was the most painful and horrible. Victims remained conscious throughout such torture and usually lasted anywhere from one day to a week or more.[35] These unmatched anti-Christian horrors were implemented in an effort to elicit an apostasy by whatever means might be necessary.[36]

As to the methods used to force apostasy, there was always an effort toward a kind of intellectual persuasion, but also an ultimate reliance on torture. In the classical mode, an interrogator would switch jarringly from a soft, pliable manner to a harsh, threatening tone. Assaults with rhetoric followed any signs of a disoriented mind. And in the end, apostasy in writing was demanded.[37] On October 18, 1633, the then head of the Jesuit mission, Father Ferreira, who had been hunted down and discovered, was subjected to the *ana tsurushi*. After leaving Ferreira five hours upside down in the pit, his torturers were successful in forcing the priest's apostasy. From then on, this horrible method became the mainstay of torture. After his apostasy, Ferreira was used as a tool of the government to help force others to apostatize. The demonic inquisitor, whose name was Inoue Chikugo, was determined

---

35   Yanagita, *Short History*, 24-26.
36   Elison, *Deus Destroyed*, 188.
37   Ibid., 208.

to destroy the image that Christianity was insuperable. He didn't want martyrs. He wanted apostates in order to attest to the impotence of Christianity.[38]

As a result of the persecution, Christianity in Japan became an increasingly underground movement. In order to abolish Christianity, the Tokugawa rulers had to develop means for ferreting out the remaining believers. Tokugawa Iemitsu, shogun from 1623 to 1651, initiated a plan that involved Buddhism. It is important to remember that the military dictator unifiers of Japan, Nobunaga and Hideyoshi, had ruthlessly massacred thousands of Buddhists in the sixteenth century, totally subjugating them. Ironically, in the seventeenth century Tokugawa Iemitsu proceeded to use Buddhism for his purposes. Initiating a plan that involved Buddhism directly in the process of persecuting Christianity, he established the system known as the *danka seido*, which required that every Japanese household register its affiliation with a Buddhist temple. This made Buddhism in effect a state institution and a part of the government's system of social control. Buddhism was thus changed from a voluntary, minority religion to *ie no shukyo*, the required religious affiliation of each household.[39] The chief priest of each temple had to evaluate the religious conformity of the parishioners and report regularly to the government. In effect, the Buddhist priests became spies for the government in its anti-Christian edict enforcement program.[40] In addition, the general populace was divided into groups of five families, called *gonin gumi*, for mutual surveillance. In other words, people had to spy on their neighbors to verify that they were not related to what the government labeled the subversive religion of Christianity.[41]

Related to the whole system of surveillance was the infamous practice of *ebumi* ("picture trampling"). According to information at the Shrine of the Twenty-six Martyrs in Nagasaki, "Every year, from 1627 to 1858, all citizens of Nagasaki and other parts of Japan were forced to step on a holy picture or bronze medal (*fumie*), as a proof that they were not Christians." Especially in Kyushu, this became a regular part of New Year celebrations. The ceremony was conducted either at homes, at town offices, or at Buddhist temples, and record books were kept to verify compliance with the laws requiring this test. Of this use

---

38    Ibid., 187, 191.
39    Suzuki Norihisa, "Christianity," Hori Ichiro, ed., *Japanese Religion: A Survey by the Agency of Cultural Affairs* (Tokyo: Kodansha International. Ltd., 1972), 72.
40    Drummond, *History of Christianity*, 96.
41    Elison, *Deus Destroyed*, 3.

Examples of fumie, which were at first sacred pictures on paper but later were made of wood (left) or bronze (right). The bronze fumie of the Madonna and child shows faces worn smooth by trampling.

of the *fumie*, historian Richard Drummond says, "This practice was only part of the extensive system of surveillance carried on throughout the country, but perhaps more than anything else it symbolized the government's hostility toward Christianity, from which in turn an abhorrence of the faith as an evil thing developed among the general populace."[42]

As a part of the calculated anti-Christian campaign, two related derogatory terms came to be used by the government to designate Christianity, namely, *jakyo*, which means evil sect or diabolical religion, and *jashumon*, meaning the evil faith. These terms were used on edict boards, the large wooden signboards put up all over the country stating the prohibition of Christianity. The missionaries and their converts suffered an inescapable fate. Their only choice was between martyrdom and apostasy.[43] The program to eradicate Christianity was ruthless and total. Tokugawa Ieyasu and his successors had made certain that organized religion would have no power in the Japanese state. They reduced Buddhism to obedience and suppressed Christianity, and they went on to enforce their rule over the people using Confucian teachings interpreted to their own taste.[44] But it is interesting to note here the difference in the fates allotted to Buddhism and to Christianity. "Buddhism had set deep roots in Japan and adapted to Japanese conditions. Christianity could do neither, and was an alien religion.

[42]    Drummond, *History of Christianity*, 111.
[43]    Elison, *Deus Destroyed*, 253.
[44]    Sansom, *Western World and Japan*, 179-88.

That was the crucial difference. Buddhism could not be erased and was used; Christianity could not be used and was erased."[45]

That is to say, by the middle of the 1630s Japanese authorities had concluded that they had erased Christianity. In the winter of 1637-38, however, Shimabara, on the island of Kyushu, became the scene of one additional horror. Christian peasants of Shimabara and Amakusa rose in rebellion as a result of the cruel and intolerable economic and political oppression of their terribly greedy landlords. The Shimabara Uprising, however, was without question religious in nature. No Portuguese and no priests, foreign or Japanese, were involved, but the peasants were spurred on by quasimessianic hopes and proclaimed their Christian faith and their readiness to die for it. Thirty-seven thousand peasants, including their families, assisted by a small number of disaffected samurai, captured Hara Castle on the Shimabara peninsula and set up their defenses. It took five months and more than one hundred thousand samurai sent by the government to quell the rebellion. The end result was the total slaughter of all of the thirty-seven thousand insurgents.[46]

It had been twenty-four years since Tokugawa Ieyasu had issued his Great Edict of Annihilation. It had been fourteen years since Tokugawa Iemitsu had begun to demonstrate his grisly intent to exterminate what was repeatedly called the evil faith. His government was shocked when it realized that Christianity in Japan still had the vitality to give the spiritual impulse for a major peasant revolt. On August 4, 1639, making reference to the Shimabara Uprising and accusing the Portuguese of continuing to smuggle Catholic priests into Japan, the government issued its final *sakoku* edict. *Sakoku* was the national policy of isolation or exclusion and is a key to understanding Japanese history.[47]

The government had announced already in 1636 that no Japanese was permitted to leave the country. This final *sakoku* edict prohibited all foreigners from entering Japan. Any caught entering would be executed. The only exception to this rule would be a small number of Dutch traders, who would be allowed to live on a small man-made island called Dejima in the Nagasaki harbor and to maintain a trading house there. These Dutch traders were from that time allowed the visit of only one ship per year for trade, and they were kept under strict surveillance.[48] Chinese trading ships were also permitted to visit Nagasaki. Furthermore, by

---

45    Elison, *Deus Destroyed*, 253.
46    Yanagita, *Short History*, 27; Elison, *Deus Destroyed*, 3.
47    Elison, *Deus Destroyed*, 192-93.
48    Yanagita, *Short History*, 27.

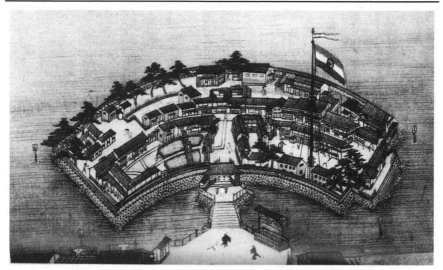

The island of Dejima as depicted in a painting of Nagasaki harbor
by Maruyama Okyo (1733-1795) in 1792

the law of exclusion and isolation any Japanese who went abroad and was caught returning to Japan would be subject to capital punishment by decapitation. It was forbidden for Japanese ships of ocean-going size to be built or used. This total isolation policy was strictly enforced by the Tokugawa shoguns until the middle of the nineteenth century.

### F. The Era of Isolation

Japan's isolation was one of the consequences of early Roman Catholic mission. *Sakoku*, i.e., Japan's period of enforced isolation from the rest of the world, lasted from 1639 to 1858. The architects of this isolation policy wanted to ensure that nothing disturb the balance of what still seemed to them a perilously organized nation.[49] What motivated the closing of Japan was fear. It was not really fear of external conquest, nor was it fear of the contamination of national customs. It was fear of domestic rebellions against themselves, of subversion. The policy of the rulers was designed to guard against revolt and in that way assure the permanence of their rule.[50] They justified their policy of isolation by means of a nurtured alarm about Christianity as the external threat, i.e., using Christianity as a scapegoat. But there is also

[49]    Elison, *Deus Destroyed*, 2.
[50]    Sansom, *Western World and Japan*, 170, 178.

clearly a causal relationship between the coming of Christianity to Japan as it did and the isolation policy of the government.[51]

A subtle change took place as the nation moved from the period of war (sixteenth century) to the period of isolation (seventeenth to nineteenth centuries). The period of war was an age of power. By brutal use of power the nation had been unified. The period of isolation was the age of authority. The dictators, or shoguns, developed a well-calculated program to use whatever means necessary to enforce their absolute authority over Japan.

After the Shimabara Uprising, the search within Japan for any remaining Christians was intensified, and the expanded dragnet reached into previously neglected areas, as far north as the Tohoku (the northeastern part of Japan's largest island of Honshu). Between 1638 and 1640, the last few missionaries who had survived or been smuggled into Japan and remained secretly active fell victim to the persecution. In 1647 the permanent position of inquisitor was established by the government for the purpose of carrying out a well-coordinated, nation-wide implementation of the anti-Christian policy. Many of the peasant-class Christians had apostatized verbally but were still practicing their faith in secret. Periodically some of them were discovered by the thorough techniques of the government officials. For example, in 1667, 608 Christians were discovered in Omura on the island of Kyushu, and 411 of them who refused to apostatize were executed.[52]

It is impossible to know with any certainty the extent of the martyrdom or the total number of martyrs. The Roman Catholic Church officially recognized 3,125 martyrs. However, the church defines martyrdom rather narrowly. To be officially declared a martyr by the Roman Catholic Church requires that there be witnesses, identifying names, and dates. Martyrdom of the well-known Christians was quite well documented. But most of the faithful believers were literally nameless peasants, and their martyrdom could not have been documented. Japanese statesman and historian Arai Hakuseki claimed that between 200,000 and 300,000 Christians perished in Japan by 1650.[53] This may be an exaggeration, but it gives some idea of the thoroughness and ruthlessness with which the proscription of Christianity was enforced.

Another significant development during the period of Japan's enforced isolation was the use of a carefully orchestrated anti-Christian

---

[51]  Elison, *Deus Destroyed*, 1, 3.
[52]  Ibid., 195, 204.
[53]  Sansom, *Western World and Japan*, 173.

propaganda program. It served the purposes of the rulers well to use Christianity continuously as a scapegoat. They demanded loyalty and obligation to the shogun, who took credit for having choked off the threat of the "barbarians" of this "pernicious faith" Christianity. This diversion of anxieties to the outside, a typical ploy of dictators, reinforced the homogeneity that was already strong in Japan. Tokugawa Japan under the shoguns was thus molded into a single organism. It was fused into a social whole. The shut-in populace became malleable. To assist in this integration of the nation's allegiances, a calculated anti-Christian propaganda campaign was waged.

The image of Christianity as an evil faith threatening Japan was impressed upon the populace by means of a very skillfully devised propaganda campaign using literature. There was an abundance of this popular literature; at least 113 items of seventeenth-century anti-Christian literature are extant and may be seen at the archives of Kyoto University. Blood, brocade, and gold are constantly repeated images in this literature, in which the priests dazzle with exotic finery and buy allegiance with their wealth. And the end result is death. Much of this material, in the manner of a cheap novel, was written in simple Japanese and was aimed at the semiliterate among the populace.[54] There were also other works that were major polemical efforts to discredit Christianity. These were produced with the forced assistance of prominent apostate priests.

During the course of the eighteenth century, the emphasis on a Christian threat seemed to fade for a while. Anti-Christian propaganda had come to seem almost irrelevant to the rulers. But about the beginning of the nineteenth century, amid a sense of impending foreign crisis, it was emphasized again. Nationalists raised the cry of *sonno-joi*, which means "revere the emperor, repel the barbarians." These patriots again used the image of the Christian peril, of Christianity as a pernicious foreign religion that was a threat to the wellbeing of Japan. Vilification of Christianity was a basic part of their nationalistic program. They did not distinguish between a Christian peril and the threat of colonial conquest.[55]

### G. The Overall Effect of Japan's Early Christian Encounter

Looking back over all that happened as a result of the early Roman Catholic mission to Japan, it can be said that many individual

---

[54] Elison, *Deus Destroyed*, 212-13.
[55] Ibid., 241-43.

Japanese accepted Christianity, but Japan rejected it. What a paradox! The significance of its coming to Japan was not in the triumph of Christianity but in the effect of its defeat.[56] Japan's Christian century had run its course, and what remained? Estimations are that approximately one million Japanese people had been baptized. Allowing for deaths from natural causes, the numbers of those who apostatized or emigrated, and the thousands martyred, one historian has estimated that there were perhaps as many as a hundred thousand Christians left in Japan practicing their faith in concealment at the midpoint of the seventeenth century.[57]

One of the utterly remarkable facts, discovered in March of 1865, is that throughout more than two centuries, some of these believers had persisted in passing on their faith in secret, for seven generations. These people who maintained and transmitted their faith in secret are called the *kakure-kirishitan*, or, the "hidden Christians" of Japan. During the latter third of the nineteenth century, Roman Catholic missionaries were once again able to engage in mission activity in Japan. A small number of the hidden Christians came out into the open at that time and returned to the fold of the Roman Catholic Church, but they had to be retaught in order to bring them in line with orthodox Roman Catholic belief and practice.

Others of the hidden Christians on some of the offshore islands of Nagasaki Prefecture such as Ikitsuki, Hirado, and Goto refused affiliation and persist even today as a separate religion. The nature of the faith of the scattered groups of secret believers during those long years of prohibition must have varied greatly. But, in general, it could be said that the hidden Christians "continued guarding in deepest secrecy a faith which gradually deteriorated and merged with the grass roots of native popular religion."[58]

The author had an experience that illustrates that struggle to pass on the Christian faith to the next generation. One day while distributing Christian literature door to door on the island of Hirado, I entered an antique store and presented literature to the woman who was the proprieter. As I turned to leave, I noticed something surprising. There on a shelf was a very unusual cross, with an image of Buddha protruding at its transept. I asked where it had come from and learned that it had come from the wall of an old house torn down on the neighboring island of Ikitsuki. I bought it, and further investigation

56     Ibid., 1.
57     Sansom, *Western World and Japan*, 173.
58     Elison, *Deus Destroyed*, 253.

Cast iron cross of the hidden Christians (*kirishitan*), with protruding Buddha image at the transept (actual size, 8" by 10").

uncovered the meaning behind it. Hidden Christians, to avoid being discovered but wishing to have a focal point for their secret worship, apparently made these cast-iron crosses and imbedded them in the red clay plaster walls of their homes. If authorities came searching, they would see only the Buddha protruding through the plaster on the wall. However, in secret, behind closed shutters, they could point to that place and tell their children that a cross, the symbol of their faith, was hidden there. Thus, hidden Christians tried to pass on faith to succeeding generations. Sadly, without the church's ministry, without clergy, and without the Bible, most such efforts failed.

The hidden Christians who no longer recognize their origin or relationship to the Catholic Church persist in isolation to this day. While some continuity in form or practice with the Christianity learned from missionaries four hundred years before is observable, basically this faith became a Japanese folk religion in which the basic tenets of the Christian faith are totally absent. The people survived by adapting, by ceasing to be Christians.[59] We must conclude that what remained from Japan's Christian century, in terms of a Christian church or the Christian community, was very little indeed. The prohibition and annihilation and isolation policies had been eminently successful in eradicating Christianity from Japan.

However, that does not mean that when Christianity encountered Japan once again in the nineteenth century it could begin as though the

[59]   Ann M. Harrington, "The Kakure-Kirishitan and Their Place in Japan's Religious Tradition," *Japanese Journal of Religious Studies*, VII/4 (Dec., 1980), 318-36.

first encounter had never happened. As indicated earlier, the significance of Christianity's coming to Japan in the sixteenth and seventeenth centuries is in the effect of its defeat. By means of all that happened during the period of persecution, Japan had been effectively inoculated so as not to contract the disease called Christianity. And if the original period of persecution served as the initial inoculation, then perhaps we could draw out the metaphor further and say that subsequent Japanese history has provided repeated booster shots.

What, then, has been the effect of Christianity's defeat? What impact has the period of persecution and isolation and everything associated with it had on Japan and on subsequent Christian mission in Japan? In the words of Edwin Reischauer:

> The two centuries of strictly enforced peace under the watchful eye and firm hand of the Edo government have left an indelible mark upon the people. The bellicose, adventurous Japanese of the sixteenth century became by the nineteenth century a docile people looking meekly to their rulers for leadership and following without question all orders from above. They grew accustomed to firmly established patterns of conduct. A thousand rules of etiquette, supplementing instructions from their rulers, governed all their actions. As a result of this rigid regimentation of society, the Japanese became a people who lived together in their cramped islands with relatively few outward signs of friction.[60]

And in the words of a Japanese church historian:

> The horrible persecution of Catholic Christians in the sixteenth and early seventeenth centuries was Japan's answer to the first Christian challenge, but the country did not escape the consequences of the bloodiness of that answer. Of her own volition, for two and a half centuries Japan cut herself off from the rest of the world....By restricting themselves in this way to their own narrow civilization, the long isolation implanted an insular spirit in the Japanese people and destroyed their concepts of the dignity and freedom of the individual. The semifeudal and surprisingly unenlightened thinking of many Japanese even today can be traced to that national isolation policy of the Shogunate. The anti-Christian spirit in the country, therefore, not only is

---

[60]     Reischauer, *The Story*, 97.

linked to these characteristics, but also has been accentuated by them.[61]

The consequences of those three hundred years had been immense. Japan and the Japanese had been transformed. Persecution, surveillance, and propaganda had implanted an anti-Christian and antiforeign feeling deeply into the minds and hearts of the Japanese populace. A kind of folk memory of aversion and fear of both the Christian faith and its adherents had been created.

---

[61]  Yanagita, *Short History*, 31.

PART I

# The Period of the Protestant Pioneers

CHAPTER 1

# The Beginning of Protestant Mission to Japan

## The First Protestant Attempts To Enter Japan

In the early nineteenth century, Japanese sailors caught in storms were occasionally swept out to sea far from their homeland and carried to the shores of North America or to Pacific islands. Because of Japan's strictly enforced isolation policy, they had no way to return to their homeland. Three such sailors were rescued near the mouth of the Columbia River and sent to China in the hope of finding a way to return them to Japan. Dr. Karl Gutzlaff, a missionary to the Chinese in Macao, took the sailors into his home. He became keenly interested in them and learned some simple conversation in Japanese from them. Soon after this, four more Japanese sailors shipwrecked in the Philippine Islands joined the first three at the home of Gutzlaff. Mr. King, an American merchant living in China, offered to take all of them back to Japan on his ship, the *Morrison*. It sailed for Japan July 4, 1837, having taken precautions to avoid suspicion and indicate its peaceful purpose by leaving its guns behind. Since King shared the hope of many for the opening of Japan to the gospel, he took three Protestant missionaries working in China along on the voyage. They included Gutzlaff of Macao; S. Wells Williams, an American Presbyterian missionary operating a mission press in Hong Kong; and Peter Parker, a medical doctor who hoped to offer his professional services in Japan.

Documents for presentation to the Japanese government were prepared in advance of the voyage. One of these included the names of the Japanese sailors, the stories of their rescue, and a request that an officer be sent to the ship to receive them. A list of the presents they had brought, as well as a list of the merchandise on board that might be considered for trade with Japanese merchants, were included. These documents could not even be delivered. The *Morrison* anchored in Tokyo Bay July 30, 1837, and small boats brought numerous curious Japanese, who came aboard, but no officer appeared. Letters were sent ashore with the visitors requesting an opportunity to confer with someone in authority. The Americans expected an official the next morning, but instead they were greeted at dawn by cannon balls fired from the shore. The ship was only slightly damaged, and at the advice of the Japanese sailors on board, they decided to go to Kagoshima, on the southern island of Kyushu. However, at Kagoshima the ship was again fired upon. King offered to try to leave the sailors with the Dutch at Dejima in Nagasaki harbor, but the sailors were afraid to be turned over to officials of their own country and begged to be taken back to China. Four of these sailors were later employed by Gutzlaff and Williams, who learned rudimentary Japanese from them. Gutzlaff and Williams made primitive attempts at translating the Bible, rendering portions of Genesis, Matthew, John's Gospel, and the Epistles of John into Japanese.

This unsuccessful early attempt of Protestant missionaries to begin work in Japan illustrates once again the persistent impact of the legacy of the encounter of Japan with the Roman Catholic missionary activity of the sixteenth and seventeenth centuries. Nevertheless, missionaries on board that voyage of the *Morrison* proved to have an influence on the later, more successful entrance of missionaries of the Reformed Church in America into Japan.

The Reverend Samuel R. Brown, who later became a pioneer missionary of the Reformed Church in America to Japan, went to China as a missionary teacher in 1839. At that time, he lived for seven months in the home of S. Wells Williams, where he would have learned of the aborted attempt to enter Japan. Furthermore, in 1849 and 1850 Gutzlaff traveled extensively in Europe, speaking about mission in Asia. The young Guido F. Verbeck, who would become another of the Reformed

Church's pioneer missionaries to Japan, heard Gutzlaff speak in the Netherlands and was greatly moved by what he heard about Japan.

## Japan's Isolation Broken

From 1639 to the middle of the nineteenth century, that little island in Nagasaki harbor called Dejima had been the only point of contact between Japan and the rest of the world. The Dutch had been allowed to maintain a trading post on that island throughout the long period of Japan's isolation, and not only Dutch but also Chinese ships had been allowed to come for trade. The island of Dejima had been for more than two centuries Japan's only open door, not only for trade, but also for information. Consequently, it was through the Dutch at Dejima that Japan became somewhat aware of European and American advances in science and technology, medicine, astronomy, and the arts and literature. Intellectuals in Japan had gained an increasing appetite for this Western learning which, because of their source of that knowledge, came to be called *ran-gaku*, "Dutch learning." This interest in "Dutch learning" would prove to be very important in later developments.

By the middle of the nineteenth century, Japan had also become aware of the outside pressures for world trade and of her lack of defense, since no large ships were allowed under Japanese law. There was also some fear of aggression by other nations, such as Russia and England. However, it was the United States government and American traders that forced the issue. When American ships, whaling or trading in the north Pacific, were sometimes driven onto the shores of Japan, shipwrecked sailors were poorly treated. And as we have noted, even American ships trying to repatriate Japanese sailors they had rescued at sea were ill treated and repulsed.

The United States government approached Japan repeatedly with efforts to improve relations and establish trade, but it was rebuffed. On July 8, 1853, Commodore Perry entered a Japanese harbor with four navy ships and succeeded in inducing local authorities to convey documents to the Japanese government. They consisted of a letter from United States President Fillmore, Perry's own official credentials as a representative of the U.S. government, and a letter which made it clear that, although his country had friendly intentions, it would insist upon carrying out its policy of securing good treatment for distressed sailors and facilities for navigation and trade. Perry indicated that he would return the next spring with more ships and hoped for a favorable response.

Commodore Perry's famous Black Ships returned to Japan the next winter. Missionary to China S. Wells Williams was persuaded to accompany Perry as an interpreter. On March 31, 1854, a treaty between the two countries was successfully negotiated, according to which two ports would be opened (Shimoda, on the Izu Peninsula, and Hakodate, in Hokkaido) and diplomatic relations would be established. Japan was thus brought to agreement without bloodshed but by a demonstration of power. Similar agreements between Japan and Great Britain, Russia, and Holland followed by the end of the next year. In 1858, Townsend Harris of the United States was able to negotiate a more adequate treaty. According to that treaty, beginning July 4, 1859, Americans would be permitted to reside in two designated ports opened for trade, Nagasaki and Kanagawa. They would be required to live in restricted foreigners' quarters, where they could exercise a limited freedom. As a result of Harris's strong insistence, the foreigners would be allowed to practice their religion within their quarters and even erect churches. Nevertheless, it was made clear that for Japanese to become Christians remained strictly forbidden.

### Renewed Hope for Protestant Mission in Japan

In 1858, three American Protestant ministers and missionaries met at the newly opened port of Nagasaki. They were Presbyterian Williams, who had attempted contact with Japan in 1837 and visited Japan in 1854 as Commodore Perry's interpreter, and the Episcopalian Reverend E. W. Syles, both missionaries to China who were visiting Nagasaki, and the Reverend Henry Wood, who was chaplain on the U.S. Navy ship *Powhatan* visiting at the port. In Nagasaki these three men met the Dutch envoy, Donker Curtius, who had just signed a treaty. He reported to the Americans that Japanese officials had declared themselves ready to allow foreigners all trading privileges if a way could be found to keep opium and Christianity out of the country. The Americans were shocked to hear opium and Christianity being spoken of together in this way, and the three prayed together and agreed to write to the directors of the Presbyterian, Episcopal, and Reformed mission boards urging them to appoint missionaries for Japan who could teach the people true Christianity. Remarkably, within the next year all three mission boards responded by appointing and sending missionaries to Japan. In that first year, 1859, one Presbyterian couple, two Episcopalian clergy, and three Reformed Church missionary families arrived in Japan to begin Protestant mission work.

The first Reformed Church missionaries were the Reverend Samuel R. Brown; Duane B. Simmons, M.D.; and the Reverend Guido F. Verbeck. Simmons left the mission in 1860, but he practiced medicine in Japan until 1882. In 1861 the Reverend James H. Ballagh joined the Reformed Church mission. The wives of these pioneers were a significant part of the work, but in those early days the women were classified as assistant missionaries. The stories of these first missionary families warrant consideration at some length. We shall see how the Lord had been preparing these pioneers for their unique roles in the challenging task of beginning Protestant mission in Japan.

# CHAPTER 2

# The Reformed Church Pioneers

## Samuel R. and Elizabeth Brown

Samuel Robbins Brown was certainly a person prepared by the Lord for his pioneering role in Japan, as well as for his relationship to the Reformed Church in America. He was born June 16, 1810, to Timothy and Phoebe (Hinsdale) Brown in East Windsor, Connecticut. His mother was descended from pilgrims who came on the *Mayflower* and was an early American hymn writer, composer of many hymns, including "I love to steal awhile away, from every cumbering care." Phoebe was not only a devout Christian and active in a Congregational church, but she took part in a group that prayed for the realization of foreign missions. It was reported that Samuel was thirteen days old when his mother learned that the American Board of Commissioners for Foreign Missions had been formed. Hearing of the founding of this missionary sending agency, Phoebe Brown took her infant son in her arms and in a thrill of rapture dedicated him to the Lord to proclaim his Good News of love to distant lands.

The American Board of Commissioners for Foreign Missions, the first American foreign missionary sending agency, was established in 1810 by a group of laymen from Congregational, Presbyterian, and Reformed churches, and Reformed Church members served on its governing council from its inception. In 1832, the Reformed Church formed its own first Board of Foreign Missions and negotiated a plan of cooperation with the American Board, a formal agreement by which Reformed missionaries were sent out under the American Board. From 1857, after twenty-five years of sending out missionaries under this arrangement, the Reformed Church's own Board of Foreign Missions assumed full responsibility for its mission program. This development reflected in part the denominational self-consciousness of that era in America. It was hoped that this change would help increase denominational support for world missions, as well as guarantee greater supervision in the Reformed Church's foreign mission work.[1]

In 1818 the Browns moved to Monson, Hampden County, Massachusetts, where there were better prospects for Timothy Brown's work as carpenter and printer, but also because of educational opportunities afforded Samuel by the Monson Academy. In Brown's own words, "From my early childhood I had had one chosen line of life before me, to study for the sacred ministry, and then to be a missionary to some heathen people."[2]

After graduating from Monson Academy at seventeen, Brown taught school for brief periods and assisted in his father's business. Although accepted as a student at Amherst College, he could not actually enter for lack of funds. The offer of a friend of his mother to assist her son at New Haven deflected his educational course from Amherst to Yale, which he entered in the class of 1832. Musically gifted, with a fine tenor voice, he earned his expenses teaching vocal and instrumental music, as well as by serving as a waiter and the college bell-ringer. After completing his studies at Yale University, he taught school for three years at the Institution for the Deaf and Dumb in New York City, in part to help pay off family debts.

In 1835 Brown entered the Presbyterian Theological Seminary in Columbia, South Carolina. During his study there he supported

---

[1]    Herman Harmelink, III, "World Mission," in James W. Van Hoeven, ed., *Piety and Patriotism: Bicentennial Studies of the Reformed Church in America, 1776-1976*, Historical Series of the Reformed Church in America, no. 4 (Grand Rapids: Eerdmans, 1976), 80-81.

[2]    William Elliot Griffis, *A Maker of the New Orient: Samuel Robbins Brown* (London: Revell, 1902), 31.

himself teaching vocal and instrumental music at Barhamville Ladies' Seminary. One of the reasons he had decided to go south was to recover in a warmer climate from a severe bout with pneumonia. There his health was restored, and after two years at Columbia Seminary he returned to the Northeast. He became engaged to the minister's daughter in East Windsor, Connecticut, and he was attracted to the newly established Union Theological Seminary in New York, where he became a member of the first full class. He had been offered a teaching position with a good salary at the New York Institute for the Deaf and Dumb, and he also directed the choir at the Allen Street Presbyterian Church. Supporting himself in this way, Brown completed his theological education.

When Brown graduated from Union Seminary, he applied to the American Board, desiring to go to China as a missionary. At that time, the American Board still served as the sending agency on behalf not only of the Congregational, but also of the Reformed and Presbyterian churches, and Brown was associated with the Presbyterian Church at that time. Because there had been a financial panic in 1837 from which the country had not yet recovered, there was no money for mission boards to send out missionaries when Brown completed his theological education in the spring of 1838. Fifty applicants were ahead of him. Consequently, for the time being, he continued teaching the hearing impaired.

Meanwhile, Robert Morrison, founder of the Protestant mission to China in 1807, had died August 1, 1834. In his honor, men involved in trade in Hong Kong began that year to form and fund what they named the Morrison Education Association. Its object was to support schools in China where young people would be taught not only Chinese but also to read and write in English. The schools would make use of the Bible and books on Christianity. In the fall of 1838, this association decided to bring out a teacher from America to China, and a representative visited Yale University seeking a recruit. Yale faculty members immediately recommended Brown, who not only had a missionary calling and a theological education, but also already had broad teaching experience.

Brown was offered the position on October 4, 1838. The ship named *Morrison* was scheduled to sail from New York October 16. Brown's fiancee, Elizabeth Goodwin Bartlett, daughter of the Reverend Samuel Bartlett of East Windsor, was willing to go, and they prepared to leave. During those twelve days Brown obtained release from his teaching; visited New Haven, Connecticut, Monson, Massachusetts, and East Windsor, Connecticut; he and Elizabeth were married October 10; he was ordained at the Allen Street Presbyterian Church in New York

City October 14; and the couple gathered their baggage and boarded the ship.

On Wednesday morning, October 17, the *Morrison* set sail for Macao, a voyage of 123 days by way of the Cape of Good Hope, the Indian Ocean, and the Dutch East Indies. The ship arrived February 18, 1839. The Reverend David Abeel, the Reformed Church's pioneer missionary to China, was also aboard during that four-month voyage, returning to China from America. The *Morrison*, of course, was the same ship that had visited Japan in 1837 in an unsuccessful attempt to return shipwrecked Japanese sailors to their homeland. It was during this time in China that the Browns stayed for seven months in the home of S. Wells Williams, who had also been aboard the *Morrison* in 1837 and who would go to Japan with Commodore Perry in 1854.

Brown took charge of the school for Chinese boys, first in Canton and then in Hong Kong, teaching there until 1847, when Elizabeth's health compelled their return to America. His intention was to remain in the United States for two years to allow for his wife's recovery. Returning to the States, Brown took over responsibility for an academy in Rome, New York. In 1851, Elizabeth's health not yet sufficiently recovered to allow a return to China, Samuel accepted a call to become pastor of a small, struggling church in upstate New York, the Reformed Dutch Church of Owasco Outlet, near the town of Auburn. Thus began S. R. Brown's formal relationship with the Reformed Church in America.

However, the Owasco Outlet church was too small and weak to support its new pastor, so Brown bought a seventy-acre farm. In addition to farming he subsequently founded a boarding school to aid in his own support. The school soon flourished, while the church also grew into an independent church that was able to build a new sanctuary, dedicated July 27, 1855. A proponent of higher education for women, Brown was one of the founders of Elmira College, the first chartered women's college in America.

Nevertheless, the call to be a missionary implanted in Brown's heart in early childhood had never waned, and on December 11, 1858, still hoping for an opportunity to return to Asia, he sent a letter of application to the Board of Foreign Missions of the Reformed Church, offering himself for missionary service to either China or Japan. He was aware of the developments that had occurred vis à vis Japan: the beginning of diplomatic relations, the opening of ports of trade, and the new ability of foreigners to reside in the treaty ports and practice their religion.

Letters from Henry Wood and S. Wells Williams appealing for

The Reformed Church at Owasco Outlet, built during
Brown's pastorate, in 1855

missionaries to be sent to Japan reached New York, and the Board of
Foreign Missions of the Reformed Church began to consider the matter.
Forthwith, the board began seeking three missionaries. One should be a
medical missionary, and two should be ordained ministers, one of those
an "Americanized Dutchman." Even before the necessary financial
support could be arranged for by the board, Brown not only showed his
readiness to go but began to seek a companion in the venture. In mid-
January, 1859, the Reverend Charles Hawley of the First Presbyterian
Church of Auburn introduced to Brown as a potential candidate Guido
Verbeck, who was in his last year at the Auburn Theological Seminary
and a Dutch immigrant,.

On January 30, 1859, in a sermon on Isaiah 54:2-3 given at the
South Dutch Church of New York City, Brown urged, "It will not do to
send out one man or one missionary to Japan. The day for such stinted
operations is passed. We require many workers in this promising
field. Let it be seen by the Japanese how Christianity affects the family
relations—what it is to the training of the young—how it fosters
education—and how it administers to the sick and suffering, and in
every way ministering to human wants. Let us present Christianity
favorably to the Japanese."

The Reverend John M. Macauley, pastor of South (Reformed)
Church, followed Brown's sermon with an appeal for funds to send not

only two ordained missionaries, but also a medical missionary.[3] The above-mentioned appeals for missionaries were repeated at a monthly prayer meeting for the spread of the gospel held at this South Church on Fifth Avenue and Twenty-First Street in New York City. The result was that Thomas C. Doremus and another gentleman, both elders of South Church, each offered eight hundred dollars annually for five years, and the congregation pledged the same amount, thus facilitating the commencement of mission to Japan by the sending of three missionaries and their families.[4]

### Guido F. and Maria Verbeck

The young man who was introduced to Brown, Guido Fridolin Verbeck, was also a person uniquely prepared by God for the particular situation to be faced by Protestant missionaries in the mid-nineteenth century. Because the only contact the Japanese had had with Western learning and technology during its long period of seclusion was through Dutch traders, there was an openness to "Dutch learning" in Japan. This openness was seen as a possible bridge to future missionary endeavors. Verbeck, the "Americanized Dutchman," could be part of that bridge.

Guido Verbeck was born January 23, 1830, in Zeist, Utrecht, Holland. He was educated at a Moravian academy, where he grew up learning to speak and write Dutch, German, English, and some French, all taught by native speakers. This broad linguistic background, and his later study of Chinese, proved to be an invaluable preparation for his future work in Japan. Furthermore, his experiences at the Moravian school prepared him for the missionary call he eventually received. To the influence of those days Verbeck himself ascribed "whatever of true missionary spirit I imbibed in youth and retained through life. I still hold in dear remembrance my early attendance at missionary meetings, and can vividly recall the deep impressions received in hearing missionary reports and addresses, among others especially those of Gutzlaff, the Apostle of China."[5]

Verbeck's family had decided on a career in engineering for him, and for this he prepared. Then he went to America and worked four years as an engineer. He had two married sisters living in America: Minna, Mrs. P. C. Van Laer of Auburn, New York; and Selma, wife of the Reverend

3    *Christian Intelligencer*, Feb. 10, 1859.
4    Henry N. Cobb, *A Century of Missions: Reformed Church in America, 1796-1896* (New York: Board of Foreign Missions, 1900), 12-13.
5    Martin N. Wyckoff, "Re. Guido Fridolin Verbeck," *Japan Evangelist* 16 (Sept. 1909), 330.

George Van Deurs of Brooklyn. Through family connections he worked as an engineer in Wisconsin but left after one winter. Then he took a position in Arkansas. The following summer he barely survived in an emaciated condition amid an epidemic of cholera. This illness proved to be a turning point in Verbeck's career. During that life-threatening ordeal he promised God that if he recovered, he would consecrate his life in service as a missionary. He moved back to Wisconsin, where his sister Selma and her husband were temporarily living, and once again worked as an engineer. During a lonely winter there after his family had left, the way became clear. Feeling a call to preach the gospel, he entered the theological seminary in Auburn, New York, in 1856.

In response to the request from the three men who had met in Nagasaki, the Reformed Church sought a missionary for Japan familiar with the Dutch language, an "Americanized Dutchman," because of the unique Dutch history related to Japan. Ironically, no such person was at that time available at the Reformed Church's New Brunswick Theological Seminary. Through Brown, Verbeck was found in the graduating class at Auburn. In mid-January, 1859, he was approached and on January 20 sent his letter of application to become a missionary of the Reformed Church. He immediately made plans to go with the Browns to New York to meet with the Reformed mission board on January 31, at which meeting they were all appointed as missionaries to Japan. Back in Auburn, Verbeck was licensed and ordained as a minister by the Presbyterian Church. The next day, March 23, he was received by Cayuga Classis as a minister of the Reformed Church in America.

Verbeck spent March 28-31 in Albany, New York, in an unsuccessful effort to gain American citizenship. By virtue of having left the Netherlands at the age of twenty-two, he had lost his Dutch citizenship. As a result, Verbeck would leave for Japan without citizenship papers anywhere, legally a man without a country. On April 18 he and his fiancee, Maria Manion, a member of the congregation where Brown was pastor, were married by Verbeck's brother-in-law Van Deurs in Philadelphia, and Verbeck and his nineteen-year-old bride prepared for departure to Japan.[6]

### Duane B. Simmons, M.D.

Duane B. Simmons was born August 13, 1832, in Glens Falls, New York. He began his medical education in 1852 in Glens Falls and

---

[6]     William Elliot Griffis, *Verbeck of Japan: A Citizen of No Country* (New York: Revell, 1900), 62-64.

attended lectures in Albany. He went to New York in 1854, where he graduated from the College of Physicians and Surgeons in 1855. After serving as an assistant surgeon at King's County Hospital, he opened his own practice in Brooklyn, New York. Simmons, perhaps based on the Reformed Church's pioneer medical missionary experience in India and China, was recruited as a medical missionary to Japan. It had already become an accepted principle among those promoting world mission that mission should be holistic, ministering to spirit, mind, and body. The appointment of Simmons was announced in the *Christian Intelligencer*, February 24, 1859. It was reported that he was an accomplished surgeon, with training and experience in hospitals in both America and Europe, who relinquished brilliant professional opportunities and a growing and successful practice in Brooklyn, New York, to accept appointment as a medical missionary to Japan. "Dr. Simmons, actuated by those higher motives which mark the truly Christian spirit, has accepted a mission of difficulty and hardship, in the hope of making his science a handmaid to evangelical truth."

At a send-off meeting at a New York church, Simmons related how "for a long time past, he had felt an unsatisfied longing to labor for the good of his fellow-men in the vineyard of the Lord. This desire had been gratified by the call which had been made upon him to connect himself with this mission; he felt that he was walking in the path of duty, and trusted that the prayers and sympathy of God's people, and the Divine blessing, would accompany himself and fellow-laborers in their enterprise."[7]

## Departure and Arrival of the Pioneers

Samuel R. Brown, the forty-nine-year-old experienced teacher and Reformed Church minister, was appointed senior missionary of the group to be sent to Japan. Twenty-one years after they had first sailed for China as newlyweds, once again the Browns prepared to sail to the Far East. As preparations were being made, to arouse missionary zeal and to provide for future reinforcements, Brown visited some of the churches, as well as New Brunswick Theological Seminary. James H. Ballagh was a seminary student at New Brunswick, and Ballagh's sense of calling to mission in Japan grew out of his encounter with Brown at that time.

On May 7, 1859, Brown, Verbeck, and Simmons and their families, including three daughters of the Browns, sailed out of New York harbor aboard the ship *Surprise*, with flags flying and cannons firing, bound for

[7]    *Christian Intelligencer*, May 5, 1859.

The three pioneers in 1859, l-r: Verbeck, Brown, and Simmons

Shanghai, China. From New York to Tokyo today is a twelve-hour non-stop flight, but in 1859 it required months under sail for these pioneers to reach their destination. They sailed by way of the Cape of Good Hope around the southern tip of Africa. Delays occurred when they ran aground and were stuck for six days in the Banka Strait (between Sumatra and Java) and when they spent five weeks for ship repair in Hong Kong en route to their initial destination of Shanghai. There they were very pleased to meet the very three men who had appealed the previous year for missionaries to be sent to Japan, i.e., Syle, Williams, and Wood. Realizing the potential for danger, the new missionary men left their families temporarily with Syle in Shanghai and sailed by separate ships, Brown and Simmons to Kanagawa and Verbeck to Nagasaki. The men arrived at their ultimate destinations on November 1 and 7, after 178 and 184 days, respectively. Their families were able to join them in Kanagawa and Nagasaki December 29, 1859.

On October 27, 1859, as their ship had come within sight of the islands of Japan, Simmons made an effort to express his feelings. "Think you that pen can trace, tongue describe my feelings, as I stood looking for the first time upon these islands, surrounded by so much natural beauty, and with all their associations of the past, and my earnest hopes and anticipations for their future."[8]

<hr />

[8]    "Letter from Dr. Simmons of Japan," Kanagawa, November 9, 1859, *Christian Intelligencer*, Feb. 9, 1860.

The clipper ship
*Surprise*, on which
the pioneers and
their families sailed to
Asia in 1859[9] *(Used
by permission of San
Francisco History
Center, San Francisco
Public Library)*

The long and arduous journey of this group of missionaries had been spent in useful endeavors. After getting past an initial period of seasickness, they had begun preparing for the adventure ahead. Throughout the many weeks aboard ship, they not only observed Sunday worship but also held group family worship each evening. The long voyage was also an opportunity to begin language study. At that time, not even one English-speaking person could really speak and write the Japanese language. Some aids to learning Japanese had been prepared by the Roman Catholic missionaries from Portugal and Spain early in the seventeenth century, but the Protestant pioneers were unaware of their existence. Also, both Gutzlaff and Williams, in preparation for the earlier attempts at Protestant missionary activity in Japan in 1837, had tried to learn rudimentary Japanese. Moreover, during his earlier service in China, Brown had gained considerable knowledge of Chinese, and of course the Japanese had adapted the Chinese characters for use in creating written Japanese. Brown's knowledge of Chinese characters would serve as valuable preparation for learning Japanese.

In any case, the missionaries on board the *Surprise* in 1859 had in hand a vocabulary list of Japanese words. Using the primitive language study materials available, Brown led in the study of Japanese, and at the end of the voyage the group had memorized 250 Japanese words and learned to write the fifty basic syllables of Japanese script. It was a beginning in the extremely difficult task of learning Japanese without the aid of textbooks, dictionaries, or trained instructors. How formidable that task was is verified by the conclusion of more recent linguistic scholars that, if we include reading and writing as well as

9    Built in Boston in 1850. Its dimensions were 183'3" x 38'8" x 22', 1066 tons.

speaking Japanese, it is still considered the most difficult language in the world for an English-speaking foreigner to learn. In addition to their preliminary Japanese study during the voyage, Verbeck taught the men Dutch, so that they could talk a little and read more in that language. This was important because of Japan's long years of contact with Western learning through the Dutch traders and because some educated Japanese had attempted to learn Dutch.

The arrival in Japan of the first Reformed missionaries was preceded several months earlier by the transfer of the two unmarried Episcopalian missionaries from China to Nagasaki, John Liggins and Chandler M. Williams. Presbyterian missionaries Dr. and Mrs. James C. Hepburn, MD, arrived in Kanagawa October 18, 1859, two weeks before the Reformed missionaries. In any case, the Reformed Church in America sent three of the first six Protestant missionaries and their families to Japan.

When Christianity thus encountered Japan once again, it could not begin as though the earlier encounters had never occurred. When Protestant missions to Japan were initiated in 1859, the missionaries experienced directly the aversion and fear that had been implanted in the hearts and minds of the Japanese people. The Verbecks served in Nagasaki their first ten years. In a letter, Verbeck described the situation he and his wife first encountered.

> We found the natives not at all accessible touching religious matters. When such a subject was mooted in the presence of a Japanese, his hand would, almost involuntarily, be applied to his throat, to indicate the extreme perilousness of such a topic. If on such an occasion more than one happened to be present, the natural shyness of these people became, if possible, still more apparent; for you will remember that there was then little confidence between man and man, chiefly owing to the abominable system of secret espionage, which we found in full swing when we first arrived and, indeed, for several years after.... By the most knowing and suspicious, we were regarded as persons who had come to seduce the masses of the people from their loyalty to the "god-country" and corrupt their morals generally.[10]

Other accounts of those first years substantiate this experience. They refer repeatedly to the prevalence of hatred toward foreigners and Christianity. Missionaries found that people were very suspicious of

---

[10]    Guido F. Verbeck, "History of Protestant Missions in Japan," *Proceedings of the Osaka Conference of Missionaries in Japan: 1883* (Yokohama: Meiklejohn, 1883), 31.

them. Not only were they themselves watched closely, but also people who came into contact with them came under strict surveillance. Language teachers might turn out to be government spies. Missionaries could feel the hatred of some of the samurai and were sometimes insulted or even threatened or assaulted. They could not go for a walk in the town without armed guards, and they felt obliged to carry revolvers with them because of the animosity of renegade young samurai. Verbeck reported that while the upper and official classes expressed bitterness and hatred toward foreigners in general and Christianity in particular, the lower classes showed a curiosity about foreigners but widespread and deep-seated fear of Christianity. Such was the extremely challenging situation under which the first Protestant missionaries began their lives in Japan.[11]

### The Pioneers in Kanagawa

One of the striking characteristics of the first Protestant missionaries was their mutual respect and cooperation across denominational lines. Their sense of oneness in Christ was clear from the beginning. When Brown and Simmons and their families arrived in Kanagawa November 1, 1859, they were met by Presbyterian missionary Hepburn, who had arrived in Japan just two weeks earlier. The Hepburns and Browns had known each other when they were missionaries among the Chinese many years before. The Hepburns had served two years in Singapore, then three years in Amoy, China, from 1841 to 1846. In the intervening years, both families having returned to the United States for health reasons, they had been in private medical practice and Reformed Church pastoral ministry, respectively, in America. Once again they had become fellow workers in missionary endeavor.

The Brown and Simmons families were also met by U.S. Consul Dorr, who had already arranged with the Japanese government for the newcomers to rent, strange as it may seem, a Buddhist temple building as their first home in Japan. The building was located in Kanagawa, a small seaport just inside Tokyo Bay, about three miles from what was to become the city of Yokohama.[12] A portion of the building had been set aside for the foreigners' residence and a wooden partition erected to mark the space. Buddhist images, incense burners, and temple furniture had simply been stowed beside the main altar behind the partition. It was little more than a roof over their heads, but with the help of some

---

[11]   Ibid., 30-33.
[12]   Yokohama in 1859 was nothing more than a narrow strip of land beside a marsh, in the process of development as a center for foreign trade.

Brown's temple home in Kanagawa

Japanese carpenters Brown was soon able to transform it into the semblance of a residence. When the women arrived at the end of the year, it was transformed into a home. They found their temple home delightful in summer, but dreadfully drafty in other seasons, remarking that living in that building was almost like living outdoors.

The Japanese rulers didn't really want foreigners to learn their language or about their people. All of the native Japanese who came in contact with the missionaries at the beginning, whether teachers, servants, or hucksters selling fish or vegetables, were actually also spies. Furthermore, in their early days in Kanagawa, Japanese officials visited the homes of the missionaries regularly to make certain they were not dangerous, but after a while these visits ceased. However, the Japanese government erected a strong, high fence around the missionaries' home and posted a guard of four soldiers at the gate.[13] Under the circumstances, for their convenience and safety, the American government minister, Townsend Harris, gave some of the missionaries nominal appointments to the American legation—Hepburn as physician, and Brown as chaplain.

During his first several months in Kanagawa, Brown had been unsuccessful in finding a suitable language teacher. On March 6, 1860, at the invitation of Harris, who was still in Japan negotiating with the Japanese on behalf of the U.S. government, Brown went to Edo (what is now Tokyo, often spelled Yedo in documents of the time). In the company of Consul Dorr and accompanied by an armed guard, he

[13]   William Elliot Griffis, *Hepburn of Japan and His Wife and Helpmates: A Life Story of Toil for Christ* (Philadelphia: Westminster, 1913), 80-81.

went there on horseback to seek the help of the American legation in obtaining a language teacher. He found Harris also living in a Buddhist building, on the grounds of the Zenpukuji Temple. There Brown heard a dozen priests of the Jodo Shinshu sect chanting the *sutras* (Buddhist scriptures) interspersed with music on the *shakuhachi* (bamboo flutes) and was reminded of the Christian Gregorian chants. This first visit of Brown to Edo afforded an opportunity to see the enormous, fortified Edo Castle, home of the shogun, five miles in diameter, with its moats, causeways, drawbridges, and massive stone walls. Thousands of wild geese, ducks, and cranes swam in the moats. He also was able to move about the region, seeing the storehouses for the wealth of the shogun, the mansions of the various feudal lords, numerous temples, and the superb mausoleums of the Tokugawa shoguns.

During this one-week trip, on Sunday, March 11, at the request of the head of the American legation, Townsend Harris, a faithful Episcopalian, and with nine men of the British and American legations present, Brown conducted the first ever Protestant Christian worship service in what was to become Tokyo, using Harris's Bible and preaching on Genesis one.[14] However, Brown had been conducting English worship services in Kanagawa from the beginning. From the second Sunday after his arrival on November 1, 1859, Brown had held worship services daily at the Hepburn home in the same temple grounds where the Browns lived.[15] During the first eight months, many English-speaking foreigners came from the foreign concession in Yokohama to attend the services. From the beginning Brown pleaded for a church building, requesting one thousand dollars to build the first Protestant house of worship in Japan.[16] In July of 1860, Brown crossed the bay to Yokohama at the request of English-speaking merchants and preached to a group of eight of them. The following week he was asked to conduct continuing public worship in Yokohama. A meeting room was arranged, and services there averaged thirty in attendance. These Sunday morning services were attended by Scotch, English, and Americans, and, interestingly, included Jews as well as Gentiles.

Out of this group a committee of businessmen was formed with the responsibility to purchase land and raise money to build a sanctuary and provide the salary for a chaplain. At that time, the British presence in Yokohama—diplomatic, business, and military—was especially dominant. Four thousand dollars was raised and a church building

---

[14]   Griffis, *A Maker*, 152-57.
[15]   Ibid., 166.
[16]   Ibid., 161.

erected by the foreign residents. However, the committee stipulated that the clergyman for what soon became the British Consular Chapel was to be from the Church of England. Consequently, despite Brown's ecumenical service to this group, including drawing up the building's plans, specifications, and contract, he was never asked, or even allowed, to preach in the building he had planned.

However, even while crossing the bay each Sunday morning to conduct services in Yokohama before the British Consular Chapel was built, Brown had also continued to hold evening services on weekdays and Sundays in the missionaries' residential compound in Kanagawa. The American community, and also some British who didn't approve of the direction things had taken at Yokohama, insisted that the union service continue even after the arrival of an Anglican chaplain and the beginning of services in the new chapel. Brown's ministry to the English-speaking community thus continued and ultimately led to the formal organization of the Yokohama Union Church, an English-language congregation established to minister to expatriates in Yokohama.

In 1861 Brown was surprised by a remarkable gift. Chaplain Wood of the USS *Powhatan*, while visiting missionaries and Christians in Honolulu, had collected an offering for the building of a church in Japan, a large gift of two hundred pounds sterling (equivalent to about $1,000 USD at that time). This gift from the early Christians of Hawaii became the nest egg for the eventual construction of a sanctuary for the first Japanese Protestant church in Japan. The Reformed Church missionaries invested the money at interest in preparation for the future building project.[17]

In Kanagawa, acquiring a language teacher was a persistent problem at the beginning. After his trip to Edo in 1860, Brown evidently was provided with a teacher, but the first one turned out to be a government spy. "A proposal to translate the Scriptures caused his frightened withdrawal."[18] Despite the obstacles, Brown pursued his acquisition of the Japanese language, in both its oral and written forms. He gradually came to realize that, despite the use in written Japanese of Chinese characters and the many words borrowed from Chinese, "the genius of the two languages is so different that it is a marvel to me that the one should have ever been thus wrought into the other...yet these two languages which seem scarcely to have any ground for affiliation are mixed and compounded into one."[19] In fact, the linguistic labors

---

[17]   Ibid., 171-72.
[18]   Verbeck, "History," 30-31.
[19]   Griffis, *A Maker*, 164.

of Brown, and also of Hepburn and Verbeck, were nothing short of amazing and provided resources for later generations of missionaries to learn the language.

Duane Simmons did not remain long in the missionary ranks, and consequently medical mission did not continue to be a part of the Reformed Church's contribution in Japan. Simmons severed his formal relationship with the Reformed mission board in 1860 after serving just one year in Kanagawa. It had become apparent that Mrs. Simmons was an extreme Unitarian, in great contrast to the clearly Calvinistic faith of both Brown and Hepburn. Furthermore, the Simmonses soon became active in the ostentatious social life of the ex-patriot community developing in Yokohama, including dance parties and card playing in their home. These activities were an affront to the piety of their colleagues. The formal relationship with Simmons ended when he resigned as a missionary. However, in a demonstration of his personal integrity, Simmons reimbursed the cost of his outfitting, including medical equipment, as well as the cost of his and his wife's passage to Japan to the treasury of the Board of Foreign Missions.[20] Furthermore, Simmons maintained good relations with the missionaries and frequently assisted with their medical needs.

Dr. and Mrs. Simmons remained in Japan, and the doctor was successful in private medical practice as a physician for the expatriate community in Yokohama until 1882. He also entered directly into the medical service of the Japanese, helping organize hospitals, including serving as the first administrator of the Yokohama Juzen Hospital, and contributing to the development of medical science in Japan. Under his leadership small pox was almost completely eradicated through immunization, and Western methods of prevention and treatment of cholera were introduced. Simmons was looked upon with favor by Fukuzawa Yukichi after Fukuzawa recovered from an illness Simmons had treated. Fukuzawa was an influential Japanese scholar and publisher and the founder of Keio University. Simmons taught for a time at Keio University and also left his mark through invaluable study of Japanese private law. Simmons died in Japan November 19, 1889.[21]

---

[20]   Samuel R. Brown to Board of Foreign Missions, Dec. 31, 1860; Apr. 8, 1861; Aug. 16, 1861; and Feb. 26, 1862, Archives of the Reformed Church in America, Gardner Sage Library, New Brunswick Theological Seminary, New Brunswick, New Jersey (hereafter Archives of the RCA). From this point, many footnotes refer to correspondence between missionaries on the field and representatives of the mission board and are located in the archives. From the second citation, the correspondents are identified by their initials and, unless identified otherwise, are missionaries or mission board staff.

[21]   Griffis, Verbeck, 65; Griffis, Hepburn, 158; Cary, History II, 49.

## James H. and Margaret Ballagh

James Hamilton Ballagh, while still a student at New Brunswick Theological Seminary, was among those present at the departure from New York of the first missionaries to Japan on May 7, 1859.[22] Ballagh and his wife, Margaret, would become the next of the pioneers to depart for Japan. James H. Ballagh was born September 7, 1832, in Hobart, New York, of Irish immigrant parents. He graduated from Rutgers College in 1857 and New Brunswick Seminary in 1860. Margaret Tate Kinnear, a native of Virginia, and Ballagh were married the next year on May 15, and the newlywed couple sailed almost immediately for Japan, on June 1, 1861. Two other Reformed missionary couples (sailing to Amoy, China) were among the forty-two passengers and crew on board. Despite long bouts with seasickness, the Ballaghs made good use of their months aboard ship. They learned some of the Chinese characters from returning missionary Elihu Doty before the ship dropped off the two Amoy Mission couples in China.

After a long and arduous voyage, the Ballaghs finally arrived in Shanghai September 27. No ship to Japan being immediately available, they stayed with Episcopal missionaries in Shanghai for three weeks. Finally finding passage on a small brig, they boarded the ship but found their accommodations less than desirable. Margaret Ballagh described the scene.

> I do not think I have ever seen Mr. B as much disheartened; What with the filth that is quite perceptible, ants, cock-roaches, and rats scampering over and into everything; a little low dark cabin, no deck, a corpse on board, inefficient and small crew; the promise is anything but flattering for a pleasant voyage; and I confess that my heart went down into my shoes at the first glance, but I try not to show it, and talk cheerfully to my husband of how nice we can fit up our room for I see that he is annoyed exceedingly, only on my account.[23]

In any case, after almost five and a half months en route, the Ballaghs finally arrived at their destination. They were warmly welcomed by their missionary colleagues in Kanagawa November 11, 1861, Margaret Ballagh's twenty-first birthday. Their first home in Japan was in the Jobutsuji temple compound, which the missionaries were renting

---

22    Griffis, *Verbeck*, 65.
23    Ballagh, *Glimpses*, 20.

Margaret and James Ballagh, about the time they went to Japan

for twelve dollars per month. The Browns lived in a building next door, which had been the priest's house; a Baptist missionary, Mr. Goble, lived in another small house; and the Ballaghs lived in the temple building itself with Presbyterian missionary Hepburn, whose wife had temporarily returned to America.

In a letter written three days after their arrival, Margaret Ballagh contemplated the tasks of learning the language without adequate study aids and of beginning missionary work where there were as yet no Japanese Christians, and where Christianity was proscribed. "And who are to do it? How good of God to pick up a poor weak instrument like me for instance, and bring me safely half way around the globe and give me an interest in this work. Is it not just like Him though to make something out of nothing! If He only empties my heart of all worldliness, and puts his spirit to fill the vacuum what may I not become! I hope to be a vessel that He can use."[24]

Although their careers began two years after the first missionaries, we shall see that the Ballaghs deserve to be listed among the pioneers. Their life at that temple home comes alive in one of Margaret's letters to America, written in March of 1862.

> Oh! the noises and smells that assail us…what word can describe them?…the ceaseless buzzing, chirping, and whirring of bats,

<hr />

[24]    Ibid., 33.

birds, and insects, and the yelping of hungry, wolfish dogs, and the cawing of black, cunning crows which are very daring in robbery, so that a servant going to market dare not bring his basket home on his head....The cawing of the crows, the chiming of the bells in the temples, the endless chanting of the priests, and the monotonous sound of the scholar as he says his i-ro-ha (child memorizing Japanese abc's), are the varied sounds that meet us in the morning on awakening; and then begins our round of study. First comes Mr. Ballagh's bald-pated teacher; their study is a little room off the verandah in front of the house; then Dr. H has his stern, melancholy teacher in the center of the house, while I have my frisky little baldheaded priest at the back of the house. Any one to look in on us, would be amused to see the various methods to which we severally resort, in pumping, and jerking and holding tight to the little we can get from these native teachers, who have no more idea how to teach us, or what we wish to learn than my pussy cat which purrs softly at my feet. With no books as helps, and being able to speak but a very few words, it is wonderful that the poor creatures understand as well as they do, what we want to know.[25]

## Efforts amid the Gathering Storm

By mid spring of 1861, both Brown and Hepburn were working separately on a translation of the Gospel of Mark into Japanese. After repeated revisions of Mark, they began to translate the Gospel of John.[26] At the same time, they were endeavoring to prepare materials for other missionaries to learn Japanese and thus to facilitate progress in the next stage of missionary outreach to the Japanese.

Meanwhile, the United States had entered into its Civil War, and the missionaries had begun to feel its effect. Confederate warships had brought shipping to a standstill in the Pacific and left the missionaries without financial support from America. Within Japan, too, the political situation following the forced opening of the country had gradually worsened, as the struggle between those favoring international relations and foreign trade and those fearing foreign influence and power escalated. It was a threatening situation for all foreigners. The Brown, Ballagh, and Hepburn families were still living in the Jobutsuji

25    Ibid., 58-59.
26    Griffis, *A Maker*, 172.

Buddhist temple compound in Kanagawa, while most Westerners involved in trade or representing their governments were residing in the expanding foreigners' settlement across the bay in Yokohama.

On January 1, 1862, a young man from the British consulate in Yokohama visited the Brown residence. He conveyed a document from the British consul and twenty-four other men, British, American, and Dutch. It read:

> The friends of Rev. S. R. Brown having learned that he will be required to give up his premises at Kanagawa and remove to the foreign settlement at Yokohama, and that no funds are provided to build him a suitable residence, have in consideration of the high esteem they entertain toward Mr. Brown and his family, and in consideration of the valuable services rendered by them since two years passed, resolved to present Mrs. Brown with a house and lot, toward which we subscribe the sum set opposite our respective names.[27]

This New Years present of $1,450, an enormous sum at the time, was offered in appreciation for Brown's preaching, as well as his help preparing for the building of the British Consular Chapel during the previous two years. As a result, when it later became necessary for the Browns to leave Kanagawa, the Reformed mission board did not need to provide the funds to build a house for them.

The political situation was growing progressively worse. William Griffis described the environment.

> Things outwardly beheld were these: A military despotism in Yedo whose beginning had been in the twelfth century; the anachronism in the nineteenth century of a perfected system of feudalism; an iron-handed ruler, called by foreigners the Tycoon [Shogun], holding nearly three hundred daimios, or landed feudal barons in leash, treating diplomatically with western nations which gradually found that the signatory of their treaties had not power to enforce his decrees or fulfill his promises, and that the centre of authority in Japan must be elsewhere, even in Kioto [Kyoto]; all critical study and investigation of scholars laid under interdict, an embargo put on foreign ideas, death the penalty for going abroad, or believing in Christianity; patriots and scholars imprisoned or beheaded; the whole nation given to

---

[27]   Ibid., 174-75.

lying; officials abnormally numerous and fattening on the people by oppression; feudalism made spectacular, brilliant, divided, so that the common people might be kept contented and the daimios might be kept poor; the Mikado's [Emperor's] court isolated, and politically a shadow; Buddhism subsidized and used as an engine of inquisition and despotism; harlotry made legal, and sensualism encouraged in order to lull the intellect; one grade of people beyond the pale of humanity [the outcasts or *buraku-min*, then called the *eta*]; the mercantile and agricultural classes with no rights which the samurai or sword-bearers were bound to respect; with no process of law known for the punishment of the murder of people in certain classes, and even local government that of "despotism tempered by assassination." In a word, Japan lay socially and politically in primitive barbarism, her civilization outwardly glossed with art and learning, but inwardly a mass of rottenness. The two and a half centuries of perfect peace, which the genius of Ieyasu had secured to his country, had become moral corruption and political paralysis. It was the calm of ice, the quiet of the stagnant pool, not the stillness of water that runs deep.[28]

In those trying historical circumstances, the missionaries endeavored to build trust and to dispel the suspicion and hostility toward foreigners. However, as a consequence of the influx of Westerners into Japan, troubles developed between fervent samurai activists and some Western diplomats and traders. Already in 1859 there had been several assassinations, and in 1861 Harris's Dutch interpreter, Heusken, was attacked and killed. In the same year the British legation in Edo was attacked. In 1862 four Britishers were attacked near Yokohama and one of them, Richardson, was killed. In 1863 the British legation in Edo was burned down. Also in 1863, in retribution for the murder of Richardson, the British bombarded Kagoshima, home of the samurai who had killed him. The Japanese atrocities resulted in demands for heavy indemnities, straining the finances of the already precarious shogunate. It was caught between demanding foreign powers and intransigent Japanese isolationists, whose policy was "honor the emperor" and "expel the barbarians."[29]

---

[28]   William Elliot Griffis, *The Rutgers Graduates in Japan* (New Brunswick: Rutgers College, 1916), 7.

[29]   John K. Fairbank, Edwin O. Reischauer, and Albert Craig, *East Asia: Tradition and Transformation* (Boston: Houghton Mifflin, 1973), 489-90, 496; Reischauer, *The Story*, 124.

By 1863 the situation had become so disturbed that for their safety the Browns and Ballaghs, as well as the minister-resident of the United States, Robert H. Pruyn, were suddenly required to move from Kanagawa to Yokohama.[30] On June 20, 1863, on the ship's boats of the U.S. naval ship *Wyoming*, the missionary families were evacuated across the bay to Yokohama, to live in the foreigners' settlement. The Browns moved into a hastily rented temporary house, and the Ballaghs accepted as a temporary solution the offer of two rooms at the American consulate.[31]

Meanwhile, at the court in Kyoto, under the influence of the radical isolationists, June 25, 1863, was the date set for the expulsion of all foreigners from Japan. While the emperor and his court in Kyoto were powerless to carry this out, radicals took matters into their own hands, and forts in the Straits of Shimonoseki started firing on foreign ships passing through the straits. In response, the *Wyoming* sank two Japanese gunboats and damaged shore batteries on July 16, 1863. Four days later, French warships sent landing parties ashore, which destroyed the forts and their ammunition.[32] Such was the turmoil amid which the missionaries were attempting to prepare for the day when direct witness and evangelism might become possible.

The pioneers continued to develop aids for learning the Japanese language with more ease and less time, for themselves and all future missionaries. In this regard, in 1863 S. R. Brown published a book of 255 pages, *Colloquial Japanese and Dialogues in English and Japanese*. The one thousand dollars necessary for the printing of this book was provided by a Scottish merchant in Yokohama, and Brown's passage to and from Shanghai to oversee the publication was given by a Jewish gentleman.[33]

In August of 1863 Brown wrote about the class of interpreters in a government school where he and Ballagh, as well as Presbyterians Hepburn and the Reverend David Thompson, who had come to Japan in 1863, taught on alternate days. The class had grown to fifteen, and, though teaching English, the missionaries would quote scripture in lieu of illustrations. At first, professional spies from the government were always in the classroom. Failing to find any incitation to treason

30    Pruyn, in effect the first U.S. ambassador to Japan, was a Reformed Church member and graduate of Rugers College, class of 1833, appointed to his post in 1861 by President Lincoln.

31    Griffis, *Rutgers*, 5.

32    Fairbank, et al., *East Asia*, 496-97.

33    Stephen Willis Ryder, *A Historical Sourcebook of the Japan Mission of the Reformed Church in America (1859-1930)* (York, PA: York Printing, 1935), 25; Griffis, *A Maker*, 167.

or subversion, they ceased coming after 1864. As Griffis, biographer of the pioneer missionaries, describes them,

> The pupils were males of all ages and there was or could be little school discipline of the strict sort, though the pupils were polite enough. All wore two swords and pulled out their tiny pipes for a whiff or two of tobacco at any time and at all hours. Dutch, which had hitherto been the one European language of culture and communication, was now giving way to English, the world-language.[34]

The missionaries looked for opportunities to engage some of the students in private Bible study and dialogue as a means of Christian witness.

On January 4, 1864, the governor of Yokohama granted the missionaries use of a plot of land by a lease. It was near the harbor in the center of Yokohama, a lot 200 by 114 feet. There was no money for construction of a building at the time, but this land later became the site not only of a missionary residence but also of the sanctuary of the first Japanese Protestant church building in Japan.[35]

By the beginning of 1866, the government English school in Yokohama, called Shubunkwan, had been put in the charge of the missionaries. Brown, Ballagh, Hepburn, and Thompson took turns teaching for several hours each day. Enrollment had increased to one hundred males of various ages. Small groups of young men were also coming unobtrusively to the missionaries' homes to read the English Bible. Many Japanese were coming to Hepburn's clinic, where the Ten Commandments and other scripture verses were exhibited on the walls in Japanese, and where Thompson began to preach to those waiting at the dispensary.[36]

Margaret Ballagh, in poor health and expecting another child, returned to America with their two children to be with her family in Virginia, while her husband continued alone in Yokohama. James Ballagh, despite the prohibitions, quietly began a worship service for the Japanese on the first Sunday in August of 1866. At first only two people came, his former teacher and a house servant. In the fall, attendance grew to ten or twelve. However, this service was temporarily interrupted when Ballagh lost almost all his possessions, including all

[34]  Griffis, *A Maker*, 186-89.
[35]  Ibid., 188.
[36]  Ibid., 202, 208; Verbeck, "History," 48.

his books and his manuscripts from two years' work of Bible translation into Japanese, in a disastrous house fire November 26. Ballagh lived temporarily in Hepburn's dispensary, which was not open at that time. Ballagh resumed the Japanese worship services as soon as possible. The attendance was less than before, but Ballagh was encouraged by the courageous, diligent participation of several of the seekers. There being as yet no Japanese Bible translation, those who were able read the Bible in English or Chinese, along with Ballagh and his former teacher, explained the meaning in Japanese. This was one of the earliest efforts in worship for the Japanese seekers.[37]

Ballagh labored in loneliness and anxiety for his wife and children then in America. Communication was still very slow. It was several months before he knew his son had been born at the home of his wife's family in Virginia, and of his wife's very serious health condition. Ballagh wrote, "It was with dread, and yet faith and resignation, I trust, that I read the letter that would make known unto me what was her condition. That letter, by the mercy of God, told me she was alive and that I felt was enough, notwithstanding the paralytic symptoms which the Dr. could not determine upon as to whether they were likely to be transient or permanent. God has had great compassion upon me. He knows that whatever by His grace I might be able to stand I could not stand this and continue His work. Now I can work on cheerfully and heartily for him. My wife is spared to me and my children."

In this same letter, Ballagh told of his ongoing efforts, despite the prohibition against Christianity, to nurture the little group of common folk who attended his seekers' meeting each Sunday. And he told of an additional ministry.

> I have a still lower class of twenty to thirty beggar boys whom by the aid of money collected by Mr. Brown from our American merchants I have been feeding for the last month and am now trying to get them established in gardening in hopes they can be self-supporting, to these I go on Sabbath afternoons, tell them the Commandments, man's sin, and the great love of the Saviour. They afford encouragement; the Gospel is wonderful to them. The eyes of one of the most intelligent of their number filled with tears when he heard the manner of the death of Jesus. I found afterwards he had communicated the same to some new beggars I had not before met." Ballagh continues, "And then the prisoner

---

[37]    James H. Ballagh to SRB; Feb. 5, 1867; JHB to John M. Ferris, Jan. 5 and 28, 1867.

and the prostitute, what a state these are in and how destitute of mercy! The heart sickens and is oppressed with the load of the infirmities of this people. The Gospel, the Gospel, the only salvation of men. 'The glorious Gospel of the blessed God!' Such are the feelings of man's misery and God's sovereign remedy stirred in the heart when one contemplates the state of Japanese society."[38]

It was in January of 1867 that regular steamship service to Yokohama apparently began. This marked the first step in the improvement, in terms of time and safety, for transoceanic travel and communication. Whereas the first missionaries to Japan arrived at their destination after almost six months aboard sailing ships, the new steamers would reduce trans-Pacific transit of passengers, mail, and cargo to less than a month. James Ballagh remarked, "How good it seems to be able to speak of events without several months interval elapsing."[39]

James Hepburn spent the winter of 1866-67 in Shanghai, to oversee the publication at the mission press there of his monumental, forty-thousand-word *Japanese-English and English-Japanese Dictionary*. This dictionary and its later revised versions would prove to be one of the most important literary productions of the early missionaries, and an indispensable tool for learning the Japanese language.[40]

As the 1860s progressed, like all the missionaries, Brown had also met quietly with small groups at his home reading the Bible. Five days each week Brown taught half of the day at the government school (physics and grammar), and all of Saturday was spent preparing his Sunday sermon for the English-speaking community. He longed to relinquish some of these duties in order to concentrate more on his translation work, especially the translation of the Bible into Japanese. By 1865 and 1866, he had already prepared first drafts of portions of the New Testament.[41]

In June of 1866, the Japanese government announced a policy change. Japanese would now be allowed to go abroad, whereas formerly the punishment for trying to leave the country had been decapitation. With this change, Brown promptly began to arrange for Japanese youth to study in America. The first left for Monson Academy, Brown's alma

[38]   JHB to JMF, March, 1867.
[39]   JHB to JMF, Jan. 28, 1867.
[40]   Verbeck, "History," 41.
[41]   Griffis, *A Maker*, 202-03.

mater, in Massachusetts in August of 1866, and by the next year six were studying there. Simultaneously, the missionaries arranged for others to be sent to the Reformed Church's Rutgers College in New Brunswick, New Jersey.[42] A few years later two Japanese students began study at Hope College in Holland, Michigan. These examples mark the beginning of a long line of Japanese foreign students introduced by missionaries who studied at Reformed educational institutions.

S. R. Brown was also involved in ministry to the many foreign seamen who came to Yokohama, a work he continued for many years. Many seamen attended Bible readings or prayer meetings at the Brown home, and at times a separate center for what came to be called the Seaman's Friend Society was maintained.[43]

In a letter dated February 18, 1867, Brown wrote to John Ferris, "I am longing to have the gospels published in Japanese. I have revised and rewritten the gospel of Matthew four times, and am now going over Mark the third time, to make it as faithful, correct, and idiomatic as possible. I shall treat every book which I undertake to translate in this same way. The gospels of Luke and John are awaiting my revision now. Also the book of Genesis."[44]

After residing thirteen months at various temporary quarters following their sudden move from Kanagawa in 1863, the Browns had moved into a house built for them on the bluff in Yokohama in the summer of 1864.[45] This home served their needs for almost three years, but on April 26, 1867, tragedy struck. As in the case of Ballagh only five months before, a house fire, very possibly involving arson, resulted in the loss not only of the home built for them and some of their household possessions, but in the reduction to ashes of Brown's library, the Bible Depository, the mission account books, many manuscripts, and the notes and records of many years. Only his Bible translation manuscripts of Matthew and Mark and a box of sermons were saved from the flames.[46]

This event resulted in the Browns' return to the United States, an intermission in their missionary service. It was, however, appropriate timing for the family, since their son, Robert Morrison Brown, was a student at Rutgers College, and Brown wished to take this opportunity to enroll his daughter Hattie in a school. The University of the City of

---

[42]    Ibid., 204-06.
[43]    Ibid., 187-88.
[44]    SRB to JMF, Feb. 18, 1867.
[45]    Griffis, *A Maker*, 191.
[46]    JHB to JMF, Apr. 30, 1867.

New York having granted him an honorary Doctor of Divinity degree in June of 1867, he returned to his home country as Dr. Brown. This travel was less time-consuming than in 1859. They crossed the Pacific by steamer, traversed the Isthmus of Panama, and sailed up to New York. Soon after his return to America, Brown was again called to serve his former congregation, the Reformed Church in Owasco Outlet, near Auburn in upstate New York. Hattie was enrolled in Auburn High School, and Brown reassumed pastoral duties, saying, "I shall try to be faithful to the people while I am with them, be it a longer or shorter time."

Brown, however, expressed disappointment. He had expected that the Board of Foreign Missions would have implemented him upon his return from the field to present the claims of foreign missions in the churches. He wrote to Ferris, "It is, I am persuaded, a mistaken policy that keeps returned missionaries from work among the churches. A live man among them fresh from heathendom will awaken an interest in the subject of missions which is as much more effective than a printed page, a *Sower* even, as a living preacher who is in earnest is better than a printed sermon. Who does not know this? It is so obvious that it seems a waste of time to write it." Furthermore, Brown addressed what seemed to him the inertia of the churches and the Board of Foreign Missions.

> Our Board will never thrive until some more stirring measures be adopted to give the people of our churches information about the fields of their operation. It is distressing to me to think of our present condition. I hear it hinted from New Brunswick that Misters Stout & Davis have received no reply to their request to be sent to the heathen. Do not let them be kept in suspense. It will be death to the missionary spirit in the Seminary. I know others there who are seriously debating whether it be not their duty to go on a mission to the heathen, and if they see those who have first offered themselves held back in doubt about the Board's acceptance of them, it will chill the ardency of the rest, and most surely defeat the great object we have in view, viz., to awaken a spirit, and keep alive a spirit of missions in the Seminary.[47]

### The Verbecks' Initial Experiences in Nagasaki

Meanwhile, Reformed Church missionaries had also initiated work in western Japan, 750 miles southwest of Yokohama. Guido

[47]    Griffis, *A Maker*, 213-14; SRB to JMF, Jan. 28, 1868.

Verbeck had departed from Shanghai for Nagasaki November 5, 1859, leaving his wife, Maria, with missionaries in Shanghai until he could make suitable arrangements for her to join him. She was expecting their first child. In a letter to Isaac Ferris, Verbeck told of his initial experiences. He arrived in Nagasaki late at night on November 7. The next day he visited the American Episcopal missionaries, both single men. Liggins and Williams welcomed him warmly and invited him to stay with them until he could arrange lodging for his family.

Verbeck then sought the U.S. consul's protection and assistance in finding suitable lodging. In principle, all foreigners permitted by the treaties to enter Japan were to reside in special areas set aside as the foreign concessions. This arrangement facilitated not only their protection but also their surveillance. However, there was no suitable place in the Nagasaki foreign concession, where the resident merchants and diplomats already had taken up residence, and Verbeck was obliged to seek housing in the city proper, among the Japanese. He was actually pleased with this prospect, as it would allow more interaction with the people, and after days of foot-dragging and empty promises on the part of the Japanese authorities, he eventually acquired a house to rent about a mile from the foreign quarter. He moved into their new home December 5, having written to his wife urging her to join him by the next ship from Shanghai. She arrived December 29, 1859, the same day that the families of Brown and Simmons arrived in Kanagawa.[48]

Verbeck immediately commenced his study of the language. In contrast to the situation in Kanagawa, he was able to engage a language teacher immediately who was not only a relatively educated man, but could even understand a little Dutch. He also learned of and obtained what appeared to be an excellent Dutch-Japanese grammar, which he immediately began to translate into English and to send valuable portions to Brown and Simmons. He planned to complete an English translation of the book in the next six months, to be of assistance to the other missionaries learning Japanese. As it turned out, this research on Japanese grammar proved more difficult and time-consuming than originally anticipated, and the Dutch-Japanese grammar less adequate than at first thought. Nevertheless, his research of Japanese grammar ultimately resulted in the publication of Verbeck's *Synopsis of All the Conjugations of the Japanese Verb*.[49]

Verbeck learned that Episcopal missionary Liggins was to leave Nagasaki for health reasons after only nine months in Japan and

[48]    Guido F. Verbeck to Isaac Ferris, Jan. 14, 1860.
[49]    Ryder, *Historical Sourcebook*, 25.

took over from him the task of selling scientific and religious books in Chinese to educated Japanese. In his annual reports during the first years, Verbeck recorded this activity, by which he served as the source of literature in Chinese for the highly educated class. He thus sold hundreds of volumes in Chinese on science, history, geography, and religion and gave away when possible copies of the Chinese translations of the Bible or New Testament and of Christian pamphlets.

However, Verbeck's next letter to Ferris conveyed a message of mingled joy and sorrow.

> On the 26th January we were rejoiced by a dear little daughter, the first Christian infant in Japan since its reopening to the world. After one week of apparent health, and another of ailing and drooping, the Lord in His wisdom took her little soul to Himself, on the 9th instance - On the Sabbath before her death, I baptized our daughter, "Emma Japonica," the first Christian baptism in Japan for centuries!—Our sorrow at this sudden bereavement is deep indeed! How many hopes disappointed and prospective joys turned into mourning! The harder to bear in a heathen wilderness and solitude! And still we rejoice to know that our daughter is happier with her Saviour than we or this world could ever make her; that the Lord doth all things well, and knows what is best for us all.[50]

The grave of Emma Japonica Verbeck may still be seen in a cemetery on a hillside in Nagasaki. A year later, on January 18, 1861, the Verbecks rejoiced in the birth of their first son. After two years in Nagasaki, Verbeck's report to the board was upbeat:

> We have by this time gained a firmer footing in the country, obtained the confidence of the people and authorities, as well as vindicated the peaceableness and disinterestedness of our aims by living among them; we have considerably enlarged the circle of our acquaintance, consequently influence. Taking these and many other past favors of our God as a pledge for future and greater ones, we look with more courage than ever upon our field as a permanent and eventually successful one....The opening process is a slow one, but none the less a sure one, and to judge from present appearances, it seems clearly evident that the prejudices and exclusiveness of the Japanese must ere long vanish before

[50]  GFV to IF, Feb. 17, 1860.

foreign influence, like "darkness before the rising sun." And then, may we not confidently trust that such a change will usher in not only a day of commercial prosperity, scientific progress and civil development, but also a day of the Lord, radiant with His marvelous light? Shall this people receive perishing things, many of which are evil, at the hand of foreigners, and shall they not receive that which is good above all things?[51]

Verbeck persisted in his acquisition of the Japanese language. He affirmed after two years something with which missionaries to Japan ever since can identify. "My principle progress made during the year is in the language, and the language will necessarily be our chief study for some time to come; for without a good knowledge of it we can do next to nothing, even if there were no other obstacles to be overcome."[52]

He also continued to teach an English class of seven students, three of whom were government interpreters, and the others officers and scholars sent to Nagasaki by their superiors to learn English. These were not children, but young men. Despite possible repercussions under the prohibition, Verbeck didn't hesitate to give them English and Chinese New Testaments, urging his students to study and compare them. During the course of 1862, Verbeck began to teach the Bible to several of these students of English, who came privately alone or two or three together to ask for help in understanding the Bible.[53] During the first several years it appeared that Nagasaki was the better place to begin mission in Japan, since it was peaceable and more conducive to learning the language than Kanagawa/Yokohama and Edo, which were at the center of the political storm gradually descending upon Japan.

There were also negative experiences in Nagasaki, however. The Verbeck home was burglarized as they slept. Six months later one of Verbeck's students saw "Guido F. Verbeck" on a telescope at a pawnshop, leading to the recovery of the telescope, as well as a clock and silverware.[54] Verbeck later referred to this experience with good humor saying, "We had thieves in our house, carrying off some valuable things from the very room where we slept, within reach of the bed. Japanese thieves are however not dangerous, except to inanimate articles."[55]

---

[51]   Guido F. Verbeck, "Annual Report of the Year Ending December 31, 1861" Archives of the RCA.
[52]   Ibid.
[53]   Verbeck, "Annual Report," 1862.
[54]   Griffis, *Verbeck*, 94-95.
[55]   GFV to JMF, Oct. 19, 1867.

There were other difficulties as well. In the summer and fall of 1862, Nagasaki was visited by epidemics of measles, small pox, and cholera that killed hundreds of people. The Verbecks were grateful to have been spared. Fortunately, in November of 1861, they had been able to move into another house up the mountainside in a healthier location, at the advice of a doctor.[56] Furthermore, the ban against Christianity was still posted publicly in Nagasaki and throughout Japan. The 1862 version read, "The Christian religion has been prohibited for many years. If anyone is suspected, a report must be made at once." The signs spelled out the various rewards to be given for informing on priests, Catholic brothers, Christians who had previously recanted, Japanese lay catechists, a family sheltering a Christian, or one's own family. The rewards ranged from three hundred to five hundred pieces of silver, large sums in that day. Verbeck harbored no illusions as to what would happen to his Bible students if they were found out. He wrote later about Japanese law enforcement in those early days:

> How dirty the prisons were, words fail to describe. *Gomon* (examination by torture) was always employed. It was at a certain night during my sojourn at Nagasaki, that I heard a plaintive cry, the remembrance of which is still a shock to me. Wondering what that was, I stole out of my house, and looked down, a musket in hand, far beneath, when I found that several warders were whipping the prisoners, who were the subjects of that cry. I, who was yet young was about to aim at the cruel officials with my musket, but was restrained from this by myself.[57]

Under such circumstances, Verbeck knew that his students showed remarkable courage in coming to study the Bible. He remarked, "In view of all this we must bridle our expectations and be patient, but persevere."[58]

In the spring of 1863, Verbeck was warned secretly at night of a plot by radicals to assassinate him. On May 13 he and his family evacuated Nagasaki, crossing the East China Sea to Shanghai. They remained there several months, until it appeared safe to return. During their time in Shanghai, Verbeck had his first Christian tract in Japanese printed at the Presbyterian mission press. He had prepared it with the help of his language teacher in Nagasaki.

---

[56]  Verbeck, "Annual Report," 1862.
[57]  Griffis, *Verbeck*, 95-96.
[58]  Verbeck, "Annual Report," 1862.

Eager to return, the Verbecks set sail from Shanghai July 1. However, a few miles downriver toward the ocean, the ship met the American steamer *Pembroke* arriving from Japan. That ship had been fired upon by two Japanese gunships in the Inland Sea of Japan. Deeming the risk too great, Verbeck's ship returned to Shanghai. Japan was in turmoil. The conflicts with other nations were not resolved, and neither was the internal struggle for hegemony between those resigned to opening Japan to the West and the recalcitrant samurai who wanted to drive out foreigners and close Japan's ports once again.

By autumn, seeing that the situation had improved somewhat, the Verbecks returned to Nagasaki, arriving October 13. However, they did not yet believe it safe to return to their house in Nagasaki. After a brief stay with Episcopal missionary Williams in his home on the edge of the foreign quarter, the Verbecks rented a house temporarily from the Dutch on the island of Dejima and resumed their lives.[59] One day two young men who had been studying with Verbeck visited him in an excited state. They brought with them two black suckling pigs as a thank-offering for his teaching. They had surpassed all competitors in an examination before the governor and had received the highest prizes.[60] In the summer of 1864 Verbeck accepted the role of superintendent and teacher of a government school called Seibikan in Nagasaki. He was told "that the Governor of Nagasaki was so much pleased with the proficiency of my two pupils, who I used to teach a little English when I first came here (in 1860), who have been twice promoted in office, that on the Governor's return to Yedo he proposed to the Government to try to secure my taking charge of their school for languages and foreign science at Nagasaki."[61]

Verbeck's letters of 1864-65 indicate that he was pleased with the progress at this school, and he was being paid for his services. The government built a new school building, which in 1865 enrolled about a hundred students from various parts of Japan. Verbeck taught only the advanced students. When Lord Nabeshima of Hizen, i.e., Saga, learned of this school, he asked Verbeck also to teach promising young men of the Saga Clan. Consequently, Chienkan, a Saga Clan School (of English and Western learning) was also opened in Nagasaki in 1866, and Verbeck taught at the two schools on alternate days. Among Verbeck's students at the two schools were Okuma Shigenobu, Soejima Tane-omi, and two sons of court noble Iwakura Tomomi. Verbeck didn't hesitate to

59    GFV to Philip Peltz, July 21, Aug. 4, Sept. 4, Oct. 4, Nov. 14, 1863.
60    Wyckoff, "Re. Guido Fridolin Verbeck," 333.
61    GFV to PP, Aug. 22, 1864.

Verbeck with his students at the government school
in Nagasaki, March 1869

use the English New Testament and the United States Constitution as textbooks.[62] By teaching young men from influential families, Verbeck not only ingratiated himself with a number of Japanese leaders but also began to exercise his influence on men who would later come to prominence. Furthermore, the trust he developed with his students proved to be of crucial significance for his future work and for the Christian mission in Japan.

In the fall of 1866, two Japanese young men unexpectedly appeared at the New York office of the Reverend John M. Ferris, secretary of the Board of Foreign Missions of the Reformed Church. They presented a letter of recommendation from Verbeck, in which he stated simply that they were of good family and worthy of attention. They gave their names as Ise and Numagawa (false names, for their personal safety) and said that they wished to study navigation and to learn how to build large ships and make big guns in order to prevent European powers from taking over their country. These young men were in fact two nephews of an influential samurai named Yokoi Heishiro of Kumamoto and had studied for several months under Verbeck in Nagasaki. They had left their homeland at great personal risk, for punishment by decapitation upon return of any Japanese who dared to leave Japan was still the law of the land.

Ferris treated the young men kindly and accompanied them to New Brunswick, New Jersey, where he arranged for their care and education.

[62]   Griffis, *Verbeck*, 124-25.

He introduced them to two gracious Christian ladies, Mrs. Van Arsdale and Mrs. Romeyn, who took them in as if they were their own children, and he arranged for their education at the grammar school in New Brunswick. The two young men would also face financial difficulties, for they had arrived in America with one hundred dollars, expecting that the cost of living would be similar to Japan. Ferris organized a group of Reformed lay people, who provided not only hospitality but also financial aid to these and subsequent students from Japan. During Japan's political unrest, when funds for their maintenance were not forthcoming from Japan, these members of Reformed churches gathered a fund for the students' support. In many cases, this financial aid was accepted and later reimbursed by the Japanese.

Ise and Numagawa were the first of about five hundred students from Japan who were aided in some way by Ferris and the Reformed Board of Foreign Missions during the next ten years. Furthermore, Ferris was in communication with the missionaries in Japan (Verbeck, Brown, and Ballagh), who fostered the cause of this wave of foreign students. The missionaries trusted in the impact American Christians would make upon these young men, who would, in turn, make valuable contributions toward their nation's future. A number of these students studied at the Reformed Church's Rutgers College. More than anyone else, it was Verbeck who promoted this flood of foreign students.[63]

**First Fruits among the Japanese**

Meanwhile, in Japan, it was Ballagh who baptized the first Japanese Protestant Christian convert. Ballagh himself told the story.

> Yano Riuzan, a shaven-headed Buddhist, a *yabu-isha* or quack doctor, who held an inferior position, was selected by the Shogun's Council of State for a language teacher for Dr. S. R. Brown. On my arrival, November 11th, 1861, he became my teacher. With him I undertook the translation of St. John, more to translate the Gospel into him than for the use of others. In the summer of 1864 he became quite weak. I was impressed with a failure of duty and asked him if he would be willing for me to seek a blessing upon our translation. On his consenting, I made my first impromptu Japanese prayer, which seemed to impress him much and which made a remarkable impression upon me. One day, while explaining a picture of the baptism of the Ethiopian

63    Griffis, *Rutgers*, 32-35; Cary, *History* II, 68-69; Griffis, *Verbeck*, 124.

eunuch, he suddenly said to me: "I want to be baptised; I want to be baptised because Christ commanded it." I warned him of the law against Christianity and the fact that, even should he escape, his son might not. The son, being consulted, said that whatever would please his father should be done. On the first Sabbath in November his baptism took place in the presence of his wife, son, and daughter.[64]

Yano was bedridden at the time of his baptism at Yokohama, and he died a few weeks later, never knowing another Japanese Christian.

During his almost ten years of work in Nagasaki, Verbeck was unable to witness openly or preach publicly. He had applied himself diligently to learning the Japanese language, acquired an intimate understanding of Japanese culture, and cultivated crucial relationships with influential people. The missionaries had all at first concentrated on learning the language and preparing for the day when they could evangelize openly. Although that day was slow in arriving, they had found among the educated class a keen interest in learning English and in the study of Western science and technology.

This way had, of course, been opened by Japanese contact with Dutch traders during the more than two centuries of Japan's self-imposed isolation. Reformed Church missionaries enjoyed acceptance based on their Dutch heritage. Verbeck, born and raised in the Netherlands and a gifted linguist, was especially well received by the Japanese. In Japan's state of transition, missionaries took advantage of the renewed interest in education to form classes and teach many young people, whenever possible using curriculum that stimulated interest in Christian values. Some missionaries, like Verbeck, taught English privately, using the Bible as a text, in spite of the prohibition against Christianity. However, in terms of actual missionary activity, the most Verbeck and others had been able to do was to secretly nurture the faith of several men.[65]

The events that led to the conversion and baptism of Murata Wakasa and his brother Murata Ayabe make a fascinating and remarkable story, and at the same time illustrate the situation in which the pioneer missionaries labored. The Muratas' story begins before the arrival of the first Protestant missionaries. Murata Wakasa was born in 1815 in the province of Hizen to a family of samurai. As an adult he rose to the position of first minister, second in command under

[64]  Ballagh, "25th Annual Report of the Council of Missions," Archives of the RCA, 154.
[65]  GFV to IF, Jan. 14, Feb. 17, March 2, 1860; Verbeck, "Annual Report," 1861, 1862.

the *Daimyo* (feudal lord) of Saga, capital of Hizen, on Japan's southern island of Kyushu. Following the signing of the treaties of 1854, foreign ships began to call at the treaty ports. When some of the first American and English ships anchored in Nagasaki harbor in 1854, some Japanese people found a little book floating in the harbor. This book came into the hands of Murata Wakasa, who was in command of a patrol watching the activity of the foreign ships. It was a book printed in a foreign language, and Murata was eager to find out what it was. All he could figure out was that it was different from any book that had ever come to Japan, and that it was about God and Jesus Christ. It was in fact an English New Testament. Being highly educated, he was able to read Chinese characters, and when he learned there was a Chinese translation (in about 1860), he sent a young officer under his command by ship to Shanghai to purchase a copy secretly. Despite the fact that Christianity was strictly forbidden, Murata began to read the Bible and persuaded four others to study it with him, including his younger brother Ayabe, his young junior officer Motono, and a relative of the feudal lord of Saga.

Verbeck, who arrived in Nagasaki in 1860, had Chinese translations of books and Bibles from the Presbyterian mission press in China at his disposal. In May of 1861, he sent some of these books, as well as several New Testaments and a Chinese translation of Martin's *Evidences of Christianity*, to Saga. Verbeck's first contact was apparently with the samurai officer Motono. Verbeck was not aware of the little group reading the Bible together, but in the autumn of 1862 the younger brother Murata Ayabe appeared at his door in Nagasaki to ask questions about the Bible. Ayabe became a regular inquirer and diligent Bible reader. In the spring of 1863, it was Ayabe who had come secretly with a message from Murata Wakasa warning Verbeck of the plot to assassinate him. Since a new shipment of books arrived from the Presbyterian mission press in Shanghai just before the Verbecks' sudden departure, Verbeck had sent more than a hundred of the books and pamphlets to Saga.

When the Verbecks returned to Nagasaki in October of 1863, S. R. was disappointed to learn that Ayabe had been promoted and transferred elsewhere. However, not long afterward the little group in Saga sent a messenger; the young officer Motono appeared. He had instructions to read with Verbeck the parts of the New Testament they found difficult, obtain any available new books, and inquire about certain points of doctrine. Motono traveled back and forth the two-day journey between Saga and Nagasaki on behalf of the remote Bible class for more than two years, without any conclusive result. But on May 14, 1866, a messenger appeared at Verbeck's door and reported that some high officials of Hizen had arrived in Nagasaki and wished to set a time for an interview. They were to visit in two groups, and Verbeck agreed to meet them on the 15th and 17th.

The first group consisted of about thirty men, including the member of the class who was a prince in the Saga clan, a relative of the feudal lord. He was the primary inquirer, and proceeded to raise serious questions. In Verbeck's words, "I could hardly bring him and his attendants to dwell on the higher topics of faith, hope and love; for my august visitor insisted on reasoning concerning the unprofitable subjects of the origin of evil in the world, the mysterious permission of the continuance of evil, the justice of God, or the apparent want of it, under various aspects, and more of the like."

Verbeck was disappointed in this encounter, for as he said, "He had made up his mind, I think, beforehand, that for him the convenient season had not yet come. But we parted as good friends."

The second interview proved to be quite different. Although he recorded the encounter in detail, he could not even report it to mission personnel in America for several years, because of the potential danger to those involved. His visitors included Murata Wakasa, first minister of state in the government of Hizen Province; his two sons, young men of twenty and twenty-two; his younger brother Ayabe; and Motono, the junior officer who had filled the role of messenger between them for more than four years. Verbeck met Wakasa for the first time, and Verbeck's report reveals Wakasa's exuberant joy.

> His eyes beamed love and pleasure as I met him. He said he had long known me in his mind, had long desired to see and converse with me, and that he was very happy that now, in God's Providence, he was permitted to do so....These men, like those of Berea, in the Apostles' time, had received the Word, with all readiness of mind, and did not come to puzzle themselves or me, with unprofitable controversies, but asked several quite natural and sensible questions, to gain additional light on some points of reference, principally, to Christian character and customs. They had been taught of the Spirit.
>
> They showed great familiarity with their Bibles, made several pertinent quotations, and when, during the conversation, I referred them to sacred passages, they readily identified them, and always accepted them as conclusive proofs. They were prepared to believe all that Jesus said, and to do all that He required.

After this delightful afternoon and just when Verbeck expected his guests to leave, Wakasa took him by surprise. He requested that Verbeck baptize him and his brother. Verbeck had assumed that even though these members of his remote Bible study group had obviously become believers, they would find it impossible to be baptized as long as the threat of capital punishment hung over any Japanese taking such a step. However, after serious consideration of both the meaning of the sacrament and all the implications in their situation, they insisted they wished to be baptized; they only requested that it be done and kept in secrecy.

At the appointed hour of the following Lord's Day, the Day of Pentecost, May 20, 1866, Murata Wakasa and his brother Ayabe were baptized by Guido Verbeck. He reported:

> The retinue, consisting of eight followers, was dismissed at our door, with orders to return in an hour. I had arranged everything beforehand, to avoid unnecessary detention. The shutters were closed, the lamps lit, a white cloth spread on the centre-table, a large, cut-glass fruit dish, for want of anything better, prepared to serve as a font. Besides Motono, my wife was the only witness present, so that there were but five persons in the room." In this secret and solemn setting, Verbeck conducted the service; he read scripture, gave explanation and exhortation, and offered prayer in English and Japanese. He then administered the sacrament of baptism, using the R.C.A. liturgy and translating it into Japanese. After the conclusion of the service, Wakasa said, "Now I have that which since long I have heartily wished for."[66]

Wakasa, who was fifty-one years old at the time of his baptism, returned to Saga and actually informed Lord Nabeshima of what they had done. Seeing the firmness of their faith and out of his great respect for Wakasa, the feudal lord left them unquestioned, but the shogun in Tokyo got word of their conversion and ordered Nabeshima to punish them. The order was not enforced, although some of Wakasa's books were confiscated and burned. In a letter to John Ferris, Verbeck reported, "From our brother Wakasa at Saga I have good news. I am rejoiced to hear that having resigned his office in favor of his first-born, he is at liberty to move about, and intends coming to this port on a visit

---

[66]   Margaret E. Sangster, ed., *A Manual of the Missions of the Reformed (Dutch) Church in America* (New York: Board of Publications of the Reformed Church in America, 1877), 301-09.

Murata Wakasa (seated, center) with his two sons
and his samurai retainers, 1866

next spring. Our interview is longed for on both sides."[67] Wakasa retired
quietly to the village of Kubota near Saga, where it is said he worked on
translating the Bible from Chinese into Japanese, and where he lived
until his death in 1874. As was discovered many years later, he was a
quiet, faithful witness to the end of his life. Ayabe went to Tokyo and
was able later to live openly as a Christian and church member.

Verbeck also baptized a young Buddhist priest named Shimizu
on June 13, 1868. The next year this man was put in prison for his faith,
and for the next five years endured suffering in various prisons before
finally being released.[68] Also, on December 19, 1868, Verbeck baptized
one of Wakasa's sons and a samurai doctor that he brought to Verbeck
at Nagasaki.[69] These baptisms were exceptional events. And while it
is true that Verbeck made preparations that would prove extremely
valuable for the future of mission work in Japan, he was unable to
lay any lasting foundations for a Christian congregation in Nagasaki
during his ten years there.

The experience of the other missionaries was similar. While
struggling to learn the Japanese language under difficult circumstances,
they devoted considerable time and care to teaching inquirers in small

---

[67] GFV to JMF, Oct. 17, 1867. This writer has found no evidence that Murata Wakasa
was able to go to Nagasaki.

[68] He was later a member of Kojimachi Church in Tokyo.

[69] GFV to JMF, Dec. 19, 1868.

English classes at their homes, clandestinely using the Bible as their textbook, despite the prohibitions. S. R. Brown and James Ballagh in Yokohama, Presbyterians David Thompson and C. Carrothers in Tokyo, and Episcopalian C. M. Williams in Nagasaki also reported teaching such small classes. As a result, several more secret baptisms did take place.[70] However, in the spring of 1872, after thirteen years of Protestant missionary labors in Japan, only twelve people, five in the North and seven in the South, had received Christian baptism. Many missionaries felt discouraged by this meager fruit from all their efforts. Clearly, despite the opening of Japan to international commerce and the obvious eagerness of many educated Japanese to learn from Western civilization, the ongoing prohibition of Christianity in Japan rendered any major progress extremely difficult.

### James Ballagh's Trials

Ever since James Ballagh's family, Margaret and the children, had gone to the United States in 1866, he had labored on alone in Yokohama. Their home having burned down, he lived with other families or in temporary quarters. Although the prohibition against Japanese becoming Christians was still in effect, Ballagh and David Thompson held Sunday afternoon services in Japanese for seekers. From November 11, 1867, the sixth anniversary of the Ballaghs' arrival in Japan, Ballagh also began Bible study classes three nights a week at Hepburn's dispensary, with attendance of twelve to fifteen. He described the scene:

> I have my stove put up for their comfort & have couple of kerosene lamps for light. We read tonight 5th chapter of Genesis. It is very delightful meeting with them. I open with prayer. Ask questions on previous night's readings & then as I have no translation made of Genesis...I read a verse in English & call on one of the young men to read it in Chinese. They all have either English or Chinese Bibles in their hands. I then explain the verse familiarly [in Japanese] & answer all questions. I hold it just an hour. Our Sabbath service in Japanese held by Mr. Thompson and myself alternately is attended by about same no. of persons but different hearers for the most part. We are rereading the Gospel of Matthew

---

[70]    Bishop Williams baptized Shiomura in 1866. In May of 1868, Ballagh baptized Awazu Komei. In February of 1869, Thompson baptized Ogawa Yoshiyasu, who later became a highly respected pastor, Suzuki Kojiro, and an elderly woman, who died shortly afterward. In 1871, Episcopalian Ensor baptized a man named Nimura.

with them, trying the new translation on which we have got as far as 17th of Matthew completed.[71]

Laboring in loneliness was not the only trial Ballagh faced. Not only his wife and children, but also the Browns were in America, leaving him in sole charge of the Reformed Church mission in Yokohama. He had not yet even met colleague Verbeck, 750 miles away in Nagasaki. Ballagh taught his Bible classes, preached in Japanese for his Sunday service for seekers, and continued to work on Bible translation in cooperation with Presbyterians Hepburn and Thompson. He corresponded regularly with Board Secretary Ferris and had custody of the mission treasury.

This latter responsibility made him custodian of the mission property, in particular the land near Yokohama harbor set aside for a future church and mission house, for which the Reformed Church had received clear title and deed. This property had become available to the Reformed missionaries several years before with the help of Robert H. Pruyn, then the U.S. government's representative in Japan. The new U.S. consul at Yokohama, a man apparently not as sympathetic to the missionary cause, wanted the property for his own purposes and tried to force the mission to accept an exchange of property. However, the proposed new property was only partially reclaimed swamp and in an undesirable location.

Driven by a sense of righteous indignation, Ballagh fought for the mission property rights. The resulting clash with the U.S. consul and delicate deliberations with the Japanese government and local authorities concerning these property rights proved to be a persistent source of aggravation for Ballagh. To consolidate the legal right to hold and use the property, Ballagh went ahead with construction of a small stone chapel that was later to become the educational wing of the church. He also had the foundation for the future church building laid and fences erected, leaving a portion of the property for the eventual construction of a missionary residence. However, the need to resolve this property dispute was a great emotional strain on Ballagh and forced the postponement of his return to America for a furlough and to bring his family back to Japan by almost a year.[72] He was finally able to leave Yokohama for his first furlough in America in December 1868.

[71]  JHB to JMF, Dec. 4, 1867.
[72]  JHB to JMF, letters written in 1867 and 1868.

## Political Change, Renewal of Persecution, and Prohibition

In 1859 and for the next few years it had appeared to the missionaries that Nagasaki was less restrictive and more promising as a place for learning the language and establishing rapport with influential people than the Kanagawa/Yokohama area, where the Browns, Simmonses, and Ballaghs had begun their work. Verbeck had even suggested in his earliest correspondence that it might be well to have a coworker sent to Nagasaki.[73] This perspective seemed to be supported by subsequent experience, such as the difficulty of acquiring language teachers and violence against foreigners in the Edo/Yokohama area. However, as the decade progressed, despite the ongoing official prohibition of Christianity, the atmosphere seemed to be changing and pressure easing somewhat in the Edo/Yokohama area, while there were new and sinister developments in Nagasaki.

Roman Catholic missionaries had also come to the newly opened ports of Japan, where they built church buildings for the foreign residents. French missionaries had a church built in the foreigners' quarter in Nagasaki. It was there that descendants of early Roman Catholic believers who had survived for seven generations as hidden Christians (the *kakure-Kirishitan*) came out into the open on March 17, 1865. The French priests discovered that groups of them in Nagasaki and nearby islands had passed on Roman Catholic teachings, albeit compromised to varying degrees. During the next two years, the French priests began to teach them clandestinely and to administer the sacraments. Father Petitjean estimated that there were as many as twenty thousand such hidden Christians in Japan.[74]

In 1867, these Roman Catholic Christians who had come out of hiding became bolder and refused to accept the compulsory Buddhist funerals for their relatives. This triggered the first renewal of persecution in Nagasaki and nearby Omura, with arrests, interrogations, imprisonments, punishment by hard labor in coal mines, torture, and some deaths from beatings and starvation in prison. Once again Japanese authorities attempted to force apostasy by torture. The French government representative in Japan became involved in an effort to defuse the situation, but with little effect.

During this same period Japanese political turmoil and intrigue was moving toward a climax. The shogun, or military dictator of Japan, could no longer maintain his authority and control over Japan's more

---

[73]   GFV to PP, March 2, 1860.
[74]   Cary, *History* I, 281-92.

than 260 autonomous feudal regimes. For more than two centuries the shoguns had enforced their authority by the infamous practice of requiring each feudal lord to maintain a residence in Edo and reside there for half of each year, and to leave family members as hostages at Edo during their alternate periods of residence at the castles in their fiefdoms. Gradually, amid the struggle between radical isolationists and those who accepted the inevitability of international relations and trade, the shogunate lost that control.

The mid-1860s was a period of civil war, during which feudal lords and samurai from southwestern Japan gradually gained the upper hand in the internal power struggle. Verbeck was in the unusual position of having developed trusting relationships with the several parties involved in the conflict. Verbeck had taught in the school established in the open port of Nagasaki by the central government at Edo, and then also in the school for young men from Saga, Hizen. Also, in the years immediately preceding the revolution, he had become friends with leading clansmen of Satsuma, Choshu, Tosa, and Hizen, who traveled back and forth via Nagasaki discussing plans that were eventually realized in the coup of January 3, 1868.[75] It had been with a view to really opening Japan and to breaking down the barriers against Christianity that Verbeck had begun in 1866 sending Japanese young men to study in America. This proved to be one of his very valuable contributions to the cause of the mission; however, it also ingratiated him further with some of those who would become influential in changing Japan.

The *coup d'etat* that occurred in Kyoto January 3, 1868, overturned the shogunate with relatively little bloodshed. It brought to an end more than two and a half centuries of rigid rule under military dictatorship. In what came to be called the Meiji Restoration, a new government was established that claimed to restore authority to the emperor of Japan. In reality the country came under the control and leadership of an oligarchy of relatively young samurai, mostly from southwestern Japan.[76] This new government found itself in a difficult position. Its dilemma was that two ideas had motivated the samurai who toppled the military dictatorship: one was the restoration of the emperor as head of the nation, and the other was an idea inculcated by long years of indoctrination—the expulsion of foreigners.

Nevertheless, in the spring of 1868 the emperor met at Kyoto with representatives of the foreign nations that had opened relations with Japan and signed the treaties that had formerly been recognized only

---

[75]   Wyckoff, "Re. Guido Fridolin Verbeck," 333.
[76]   Reischauer, *The Story*, 120-22, 125.

by the shogunate. On April 6, 1868, in the presence of the court nobles and leading feudal lords involved in forming the new government, the emperor took an oath to establish the foundation of the empire of Japan on five principles, as follows:

1. Government based on public opinion.
2. Social and political economy to be made the study of all classes.
3. Mutual assistance among all for the general good.
4. Reason, not tradition, to be the guide of action.
5. Wisdom and ability to be sought after in all quarters of the world.

This last principle made education the basis of the nation's progress and resulted in a quest for talent and learning from Western nations. It opened the way for foreign teachers, engineers, physicians, scholars, and experts in many fields to enter and influence the new Japan.[77] More than anyone else, Verbeck was positioned and prepared to respond to this new situation. He corresponded with John Ferris, and perhaps others, and began to arrange for Christian men to teach in Japanese government schools.

During the political turmoil of 1868, foreign residents experienced well-grounded fears for their safety. They were threatened with arson and attacks and expulsion from the country by the sword-wielding, masterless samurai, ruffians called *ronin*, who strongly opposed the opening of Japan. However, Verbeck wrote,

> As to ourselves, except in a general outbreak, I did not fear any personal violence, as I had numerous good friends on both sides of the question, and as our pacific character and calling are too well understood by all....All I did at the critical time was to reload an old revolver, so as to be ready for common thieves and robbers...but especially did I commend ourselves to Him who is mightier than any that might be against us....On the whole we hope that all these great changes in the empire will lead to more liberal views on the part of the authorities, especially in regard to our religion.[78]

With this change of government and the anticipated accelerated modernization of Japan, the missionaries hoped that the age-old prohibitions forbidding Japanese to embrace Christianity would be

---

[77]    Griffis, *Verbeck*, 148-49.
[78]    Griffis, *Verbeck*, 137-38; GFV to JMF, Feb. 26, 1868.

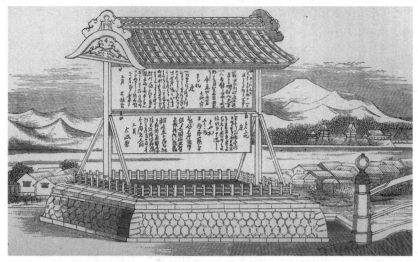

Drawing by Ozawa Nankoku of the edict board (*kosatsu*) at Nihonbashi in Tokyo reasserting the prohibition of Christianity, erected in April 1868. The prohibition was posted on public edict boards throughout the country, though most were less ostentatious than this one at the center of Tokyo.

abrogated. However, the new Meiji government immediately reaffirmed the edicts against Christianity. Despite the fact that the new leadership included some who had been students of Verbeck in Nagasaki, as well as some former students of Brown and Ballagh in Yokohama, fresh signs prohibiting Christianity were posted throughout the country. The signs read, "The evil sect called Christian is strictly prohibited. Suspicious persons should be reported to the proper officers, and rewards will be given."[79]

New arrests, interrogations, and threats ensued. Repeated protestations by representatives of Britain, France, America, and the Netherlands, and their resultant confrontations with the Imperial Council, including some of Japan's new leaders,[80] proved unproductive. Persecution, exile, and imprisonment of hidden Christians who had come out into the open continued. The Protestant missionaries and those associated with them also felt the impact.[81] For example, the former Buddhist priest named Shimizu baptized by Verbeck was thrown into prison.

[79]  Cary, *History* II, 66.
[80]  Leaders such as Okuma, Kido, Iwakura, Sawa, and Terashima.
[81]  Cary, *History* I, 306-26.

Despite continuing protests from representatives of the Western powers, on June 7, 1868, the Meiji Government's Supreme Council ordered the dispossession of property and deportation of 4,010 formerly hidden Japanese Roman Catholic Christians of the Nagasaki area to thirty-four regions of the country, and their deportation was begun. This renewed persecution was called the *Urakami Kuzure*. These descendants of the early Japanese Roman Catholics were consigned to slave labor in mines and other hard occupations and to living in the forest until they should apostatize. In many cases families were broken up and sent to different locations. Torture and starvation rations were used in an effort to elicit recantations. Authorities claimed they were simply enforcing the law, stated that all Japanese were obligated to adhere to the Shinto religion, and insisted there was no cruelty involved. In fact, while conditions faced by these exiles varied according to location, many suffered indescribable torture. Persecutions continued until December of 1871. Only 3,404 were officially recorded as having been sent into exile. Apparently about 500 apostatized under torture, at least outwardly. Only 1,981 were later reported as returned from exile.[82]

The Meiji Government was from its inception in 1868 unhappy with what it considered unequal treaties Japan had been pressured into accepting in 1858. The new leaders tried repeatedly to renegotiate them, but each time they were rebuffed by the Western powers. Foreign government representatives pointed to the persecution of Christians as evidence that Japan was barbarian in its refusal to grant freedom of religion.

The missionaries became increasingly frustrated by the apparent intransigence of the government regarding in-country travel and residence restrictions and the lack of religious tolerance that prohibited public witness to their faith. They entertained the hope that the anti-Christian edicts might be removed when the treaties between Japan and the several Western nations were reviewed in 1872. Their concern intensified, however, when they became aware of the attitudes of the British and German representatives in regard to these matters.

S. R. Brown wrote to Ferris, explaining the situation and appealing not only for understanding but also for American Christians to press for change. The Prussian minister, or German representative in Japan, had taken an anti-Christian position and was promoting his pet scheme, i.e., the opening of Japan to all foreigners except missionaries. Furthermore, the British representative, Harry Parker, favored the

---

[82]  Cary, *History* I, 306-33.

status quo for foreigners and foreign trade, since the British had gained a virtual monopoly of commercial interests and were reaping enormous profits. The development of Japan's infrastructure, such as railroads, telegraph, and lighthouses, was also supervised by British civil engineers and built with British capital. Brown reported,

> In Sir Harry's dispatch to his government about the Christian question he states that the Minister of Foreign Affairs at Yedo offered to let the Ministers of the respective treaty powers go to the places whither the poor Roman Catholics of Nagasaki have been banished, and see for themselves, how humanely they are treated. Mr. DeLong [U.S. minister, i.e., ambassador, to Japan] told me today that he never heard of such an offer till he read it in the dispatch. Had it been made, as no minister can go into the interior without first notifying the government and having an armed escort, it would be quite easy for the powers that be to send an express in before & have all things about the prisons of the Christians put in fine order for inspection on the ministers' arrival....The Japanese are quite as expert at such things. How charming was the naivete of the Jap. Minister of foreign affairs, in his suggestion that inasmuch as the 3000 persecuted Christians had been sent to 19 different places, it was an excellent plan for the propagation of Christianity in Japan! And Earl Granville and the then French foreign minister at Paris were mightily pleased with the liberal measures advanced by the Jap. government. As if the Mikado's ministers intended to favor the propagation of Christianity! They mean to kill off all these Roman Catholics as fast as they can by every refinement of cruelty. I am happy to find that the U.S. minister is for progress & freedom here. He does not fail to relate on these themes to the Secretary of State. Now, let the good people of America take hold of the matter and make the Secretary of State and the President see that they are in earnest for the liberty of the Japanese – let them advocate such a change in the treaty next year, as I have suggested, basing their pleas upon the same ground that Commodore Perry took, viz., that it is for humanity's sake, and if they are really in earnest about the matter, the U. S. gov't. will have no insuperable difficulty— in accomplishing the repeal of the anti-Christian laws, that now insult all Christian nations, and bind this nation in absolute slavery to a small minority of the people, the daimios and their retainers. It is this class that oppose progress in the enlightenment of the

common people. They cannot abuse & defraud an enlightened people as easily as they can the ignorant peasantry, who now groan under the weight of the tyranny of their rulers, but know no way of escape from it.[83]

Not only Brown and Verbeck, but James Ballagh also pleaded for agitation by American Christians for the removal of the bans against Christianity.[84] Furthermore, in support of a proposed trip by the Presbyterian David Thompson, representing the missionaries, to visit the various treaty nations to raise awareness of the issues and to urge Christians to act,[85] virtually all of the almost thirty missionaries and Christian teachers then in Japan—Reformed, Presbyterian, Congregational, and Baptist, and including Brown, Ballagh, Verbeck, Stout, and Wolff of the Reformed Church—signed the following resolution and appeal:

> Yokohama, Japan, 22 May, 1871.
>
> The undersigned members of the Protestant Missions to Japan most earnestly solicit united and vigorous efforts on the part of all Christians to secure religious liberty to the people of this country. We believe that the recent revival of hostility to Christianity exhibited by the Japanese government is in no small degree attributable to the feebleness of the remonstrances made by the treaty powers. The ministers representing these powers at the court of the Mikado are not authorized to take effective measures against the persecution of Christians, and consequently their faint protests are utterly disregarded by the government. Hence, too, the old laws, against Christians, that were suffered [allowed] to remain inoperative for more than nine years following the opening of Japan, have not only been reaffirmed, but put in execution with terrible severity. These laws are odious and cruel. Odious, because insulting to every socalled Christian nation: & calculated to prejudice the Japanese against all foreigners, and cruel, because bitterly tyrannical & oppressive to native Christians. But, however much a foreign minister might desire the repeal of these laws, he is so hampered by his instructions, that his appeals to the Japanese government are necessarily so unintensified, that the rulers of Japan feel that they may disregard them with impunity.

---

[83]   SRB to JMF, May 19, 1871.
[84]   JHB to JMF, Oct. 23, 1871.
[85]   JHB to JMF, May 20, 1871.

What therefore is wanted, is the force of public opinion pressing upon the governments that have treaty relations with Japan, to demand the repeal of the anti-Christian laws that are so insulting and prejudicial to themselves. Such a demand would be no violation of international comity, and if successful, as we believe it would be, if the Japanese should see fixed determination behind it, it would at the same time gain an inestimable boon for this nation, freedom to worship God.

In the hope that Christians at home will consider this subject, and bring their influence to bear upon their governments, so as to induce them to instruct and empower their respective ministers to use all proper means to achieve the revocation of these laws and edicts against Christianity, we commend our brother and fellow laborer the Rev. David Thompson to all who love our Lord Jesus Christ everywhere. May the good Lord whose is the kingdom under the whole heaven prosper our brother in his endeavors to awaken an interest in this matter. May he also have his reward in seeing deliverance even for the oppressed and persecuted, and religious liberty secured to all the dwellers in this land.[86]

---

[86]   SRB to JMF, May 22, 1871.

CHAPTER 3

# Period of Change and Promise

## Verbeck Moves to Tokyo

In Nagasaki, significant changes had occurred for the Verbecks. In a letter of October 16, 1868, Guido Verbeck remarked, "For five years I have not been outside of a circle of a radius of 4 miles & very seldom to the periphery of that." Such had been their isolation. Verbeck expressed his pleasure that at long last he would gain a Reformed Church colleague, saying, "I also had a letter of Bro. Stout. We were glad to hear of his coming, & we shall give him & his good wife a hearty welcome."[1]

Verbeck requested and received permission from the Board of Foreign Missions to visit the Kyoto, Osaka, Kobe area, a region subsequently spoken of as the Kansai. Kyoto was the traditional capital, and the emperors had resided there for centuries. Osaka was Japan's center for business and industry. Kobe was newly opened as a foreign port. Verbeck set out October 18, 1868. His trip, sailing past Hirado Island and through the Inland Sea, was his first opportunity to see other parts of Japan. With the exception of the Verbecks' emergency

---

[1]    GFV to JMF, Oct. 16, 1868.

trip to Shanghai under threat of assassination in 1863, they had never left the city of Nagasaki during nine years.

Several purposes were served by this trip to central Japan. Verbeck needed to visit the new government authorities (those controlling the country since the coup nine months before) on behalf of the Japanese students studying in America under the auspices of the Reformed Church. The Yokoi brothers, who had been studying at Rutgers, and four other young Japanese were applying to the U.S. Naval Academy, and Verbeck needed to negotiate their official appointment and support from the Japanese government. Such negotiations with top officials, including Soejima and Komatsu, deepened the trust between Verbeck and people in positions of power in the new government. During his meeting with Komatsu, he was told that the government wanted to establish a school in Edo for three hundred students, with three teachers besides Verbeck, one of the departments being for the study of Dutch. This was the first intimation that new possibilities were developing.[2]

Verbeck was also surveying the scene for possible mission work in the Kansai area. The Browns were in America at the time, and Ballagh and the Verbecks were the only Reformed Church missionaries in the country. Verbeck (and Brown as well) had repeatedly asked for more colleagues. James Ballagh, whose wife and children were still in America, also came down to the Kansai by ship from Yokohama, and thus the only two Reformed missionaries in Japan met on the field for the first time there. Regarding this trip, Verbeck had also written, "If a favorable opportunity offers, I shall not fail to impress upon leading men the reasonableness and importance of toleration of our faith in Japan."[3]

Verbeck returned to Nagasaki and soon after made another trip. This time he traveled to Saga, in Hizen, where Murata Wakasa lived and where he had developed good relationships with local rulers by teaching in their school in Nagasaki. He was welcomed and treated royally, and he was delighted to see Murata once again. During this visit to Saga, Verbeck secretly baptized Murata's elderly mother.[4]

Yokoi Heishiro, a trusted counselor to the daimyo of the province of Echizen and uncle of the first two students introduced by Verbeck for study in America, had become a counselor of the emperor at the time of the Meiji Restoration. After obtaining a Chinese Bible from Shanghai, impressed with its contents, Yokoi reportedly wrote to a friend, "In a

---

[2]   Griffis, *Verbeck*, 169.
[3]   Ibid., 153.
[4]   Ibid., 179.

few years Christianity will come to Japan and capture the hearts of the best young men."[5] He was said to have urged that men be allowed the freedom to follow whatever religion seemed to them to be true.

In a letter to Secretary Ferris dated November 4, 1868, and received in New York March 23, 1869, Yokoi wrote the following:

> Dear Sir,
>
> I pen a few lines. My nephews, Ise Sabaro and Numagawa Saburo, write me very often that, ever since they arrived in America, they have been treated so kindly that they can scarcely express their feelings. Hence I am exceedingly grateful to you, and my mind is satisfied. I send to you, for them, by this mail, three hundred dollars. Please hand this amount to them. Thanking you for your kindness shown to these lads and begging also to send you my kind regards, I remain dear Sir, Yours most sincerely, Yokoi Heishiro.[6]

While this letter was on its way, on February 15, 1869, while returning from the emperor's palace in Kyoto, Yokoi was assassinated. The reason given for this act was the suspicion that he harbored "evil opinions," meaning, of course, sympathy with Christianity.[7]

Edo, long since the actual political capital of Japan, had been in September of 1868 renamed Tokyo (meaning eastern capital), and the emperor and his court were in 1869 moved there to the great Edo Castle of the shoguns, transforming it into the emperor's palace. Not only the Meiji emperor and his court, but also all the functions of government were soon transferred to Tokyo. However, the new government was formed of a coalition of court nobles, certain of the feudal lords, and a large number of young men of the samurai class, many of whom had been students of Verbeck at the two schools in Nagasaki. Perhaps it was only natural that, facing the challenge of building the new Japan, several of the older leaders, and many of the young ones rising to power, turned to their respected foreign teacher for help.

Unexpectedly, Verbeck found himself facing a new opportunity. In Verbeck's words to the mission board,

> There came to me a high official of the Imperial government, now located at Yedo, who had been specially sent to this port to call me to the Eastern Capital, Yedo. As far as I know now, the chief

5    Cary, *History* II, 68-69.
6    Griffis, *Rutgers*, 35.
7    Cary, *History* II, 69.

object is to get me to establish a university, or something of the kind. I am not, however, given to understand much of the detail of the object of my call; only I am assured that some of my former pupils, now in the new government, are to meet me there and to arrange matters satisfactorily. As you see from the enclosure, the government wants me forthwith, next month, and I did not feel justified to refuse the invitation....and under these circumstances it would never do to let such an opportunity as is now offered me pass by unnoticed or unprofited.

Verbeck responded to the call as follows:

To Yamaguchi Hanzo, Esq.,
    Dear Sir:
    Having duly considered the proposition of the Imperial government in regard to my going to the Eastern Capital by the middle of next month, which you kindly transmitted to me, I have the pleasure to communicate to you that I shall be happy to accept the same."[8]

Guido Verbeck moved to Tokyo in March of 1869. The manner of his departure, as told by his successor in Nagasaki, Henry Stout, reveals a great deal about Verbeck and his missionary motivation.

When I first met Dr. Verbeck, he was under appointment to go to Tokio to assist in establishing a school for the Western languages and sciences, and so we were together but ten days as associates of the Mission in South Japan. For him, those days were filled with engagements with officials and old friends, made up of dinners and visits of ceremony for the exchange of courtesies and leave-taking, from which little time could be found for preparation for his going to his new position and for his family's returning to America. But the morning of the day the steamer was to sail, was spent, from immediately after breakfast till a late lunch, closeted with a Buddhist priest. The explanation given at the lunch was that the priest was eager to have certain questions with regard to the Truth answered before his teacher should leave. Whatever else was neglected, this opportunity must not be lost. Lunch having been served, hasty final preparations were made for leaving. Bearers were called for the luggage and the start was about to be made. But some things yet unpacked must be taken. A blanket was spread upon the floor of the sitting-room, and upon it went books, curios, a clock, cushions, shoes, a great medley of the last odds and ends of things, when the corners of the blanket were drawn together and tied, making a huge bundle, which was hoisted upon the back of the last man in the line of bearers hastening to the wharf. This was the scant consideration his personal affairs received. No wonder he found afterward that some of his most valuable belongings had been forgotten.[9]

Verbeck sent his family to America for a time, and his letter of March 31, 1869, written soon after his arrival in Tokyo, reveals a very uncertain situation. The ultimate goal of his invitation was to develop an imperial university. In the meantime, however, he was expected to act as an advisor to the highest officials of the government as they consulted with the most powerful of the feudal lords on improving government structures and revising foreign treaties. Verbeck's convictions were firm.

> Whatever happens, I am convinced that I am not called here by a mere chance, and that I have work to do, in the doing which, being quite aware of my insufficiency, I look to the Master for counsel and guidance. This confidence removes mountains of difficulty.[10]

Verbeck faced a delicate and daunting task. While he had earned the respect and trust of many, the forced opening of Japan and agreement to what the Japanese considered humiliating and unequal treaties with Western nations had affected the pride of many among the upper and ruling classes.

## Verbeck's Early Government Service

Verbeck was in the employ of the Japanese government, while at the same time keeping in close contact with missionary colleagues and John Ferris, secretary of the mission board. From March of 1869 Verbeck was connected with the school called Kaiseijo, which later developed into Tokyo Imperial University. He superintended all matters related to teachers and instruction in the foreign studies department of the school, including relations between the twenty foreign teachers and the government. He continued in this role until 1873. At the same time, he was held in such high regard that government officials, from the prime

---

9    Ibid., 184-85.
10   Ibid., 186.

minister on down, constantly called on him for advice in all matters of foreign relations. Albeit behind the scenes, Verbeck became the most influential foreigner in Japan, helping mold new directions in the Meiji Restoration Government. On November 17, 1871, Verbeck even "had the honor of an audience with the Emperor."[11] Emperor Mutsuhito visited the university where Verbeck had responsibility, and Verbeck himself decorated the hall in preparation. He brought in one of the best parlor chairs from his home and wrapped it in his wife's India shawl to serve as a temporary throne for the Emperor.[12]

In a letter to the board in 1869, Verbeck had conveyed his feelings about the ongoing prohibitions against Christianity.

> Often I feel a spirit of impatience rise up within, & after a long and weary siege of well-nigh ten years, I sometimes feel like risking a storm in open force. But yet on due reflection & a survey of the whole position, it seems as if an open attack might be, very certainly would be, anticipating the gradual developments of Providence, & the resolution to labor, wait, & pray a little longer is reluctantly come to again.[13]

Verbeck, not only demonstrating great restraint but also showing insight into the psyche of the Japanese, remained in the shadow and ultimately exercised a large influence on the situation. Asked by the board secretary for material for publication, on June 22, 1872, Verbeck wrote, "My usefulness in this country would be at an end, if I made a show of what I do. It is just because these people know that I do not, like many, tell all about what I do and know about them, that they have implicit confidence in me."[14] As part of his government service, in connection with some Japanese associates, Verbeck translated constitutions, laws, and legal documents from English, German, and French into Japanese. Verbeck was also asked to write memoranda for some members of the government, on education, religious liberty, and other topics.[15]

Western medicine had been seized upon as superior to Oriental medicine. As there was no Western medical literature in the Japanese language, Japanese doctors were questioning what should be the language of their science of medicine, and there was considerable

[11]    GFV to JMF, Nov. 21, 1971.
[12]    Griffis, *Verbeck*, 266-67.
[13]    GFV to JMF, Aug. 28, 1869.
[14]    Griffis, *Verbeck*, 258.
[15]    Wyckoff, "Re. Guido Fridolin Verbeck," 334.

difference of opinion. At the time of Verbeck's death in Japan in 1898, Japan's surgeon-general, Ishiguro, remarked:

> I was not invited to attend the funeral, but I went to the church and attended anyway. Toward the year 1870 or so, many agreed to the opinion that education should be English and American, and that English and American teachers should be employed. In those times, Drs. Iwasa, Sagara, Hasegawa, and I held the view that the science of medicine should be German. How we were ridiculed and criticised by the public! Dr. Verbeck was already in those times respected and believed in by the people. One day, Dr. Sagara got an interview with him, and talked about the necessity of enforcing our opinion about the science of medicine. With our view this American teacher expressed his sympathy. It was through his advice to the government that German professors of this science came to be employed. The present prosperity of the science owes a great deal to the deceased doctor. This is the reason why I attended his funeral.[16]

Verbeck had advised that, in the case of medicine, the language to be acquired for professional study should be German, since at that time German medical science was the most advanced in the world. As a result, German terminology and its transliteration into Japanese became predominant in the medical field in Japan and remained so until after World War II.

Verbeck's memoranda and advice even extended into areas such as national defense and military development. In 1870, Verbeck was approached by Iwakura and other officials of the Meiji Government for advice as to whether Japan should give serious effort to forming a national army and navy for defense. Verbeck was asked to provide the rationale for his views, and the result was a meeting of several hours.

> Mr. Verbeck believing that Japan, then weak and divided, was in the presence of the continually growing power of the great aggressive European nations, Russia, France, and Great Britain, advised military and naval development and defense of the coast. For this he gave two reasons, first and greatest of all, to secure national unity and the development of the resources of the empire, and second to preserve the very existence and integrity of the Japanese nation.[17]

[16]   Griffis, *Verbeck*, 210-11.
[17]   Ibid., 275-76.

Ironically and tragically, the result for Asia and for the world of the subsequent Japanese military build-up and Japan's imperialistic ambitions gradually became apparent in the early twentieth century.

Verbeck himself came to see one particular memorandum as his most valuable service to the Japanese government. This document proved also to be of crucial significance for the progress of missionary work. The paper was originally submitted in June of 1869 to Okuma Shigenobu, Verbeck's former student and at the time a leading young government official.[18] In this memorandum Verbeck had suggested that the Japanese government send an official delegation, called an embassy, to America and Europe in an effort to better understand the West, and as a step toward the eventual revision of the treaties. But something he believed more significant was on Verbeck's mind. In his words, "It is my hope and prayer that the sending of this mission may do very much to bring about, or at least bring nearer, the long longed-for toleration of Christianity."[19]

Actually, Okuma had done nothing with the memorandum and its recommendations at the time he received it. He had been afraid to show it to anyone, as it might endanger his high position in the government, for 1869 was a time of intense antiforeign feeling. Okuma, as a former student and continuing friend of Verbeck, had already been suspected by some conservatives of being a Christian convert. However, Okuma eventually showed Verbeck's memorandum to his friends and colleagues, and it did its work quietly.

In October of 1871, only three days after he had learned of the paper, Iwakura Tomomi, the prime minister and most powerful member of the new government, came to see Verbeck about it. It must be remembered that Verbeck had a very close relationship with Iwakura. Not only was Verbeck his trusted advisor, but also Verbeck had arranged for Iwakura's three sons to study at the Reformed Church's Rutgers College, and the Japanese sense of indebtedness and obligation following a genuine favor is very strong. Iwakura and other government leaders were apparently in a quandary as to how to proceed, as they contemplated the approach of the scheduled date for the revision of the foreign treaties, July 5, 1872. In a confidential letter to Ferris, dated June 22, 1872, Verbeck described his meeting with Iwakura and its outcome, the departure of a Japanese embassy to America and Europe

---

[18]    Okuma of Saga was to hold numerous important positions in government, including that of prime minister, and later founded Waseda Univerity.
[19]    GFV to JMF, Nov. 21, 1871.

late in December of 1871. Apparently, the men went over Verbeck's memorandum clause by clause, and Verbeck reported:

> At the end he told me it was the *very* and the *only* thing for them to do, and that my programme should be carried out to the letter. A number of interviews followed, some of them till late in the night.
>
> The embassy is organized according to my paper (that I had sown in faith more than two years before). It sailed in two months from the date of my paper becoming known to Iwakura and the emperor. How could they get over the perplexity of the near revision of the treaties? If Iwakura was not on the spot, no revision could take place at all. How could they qualify themselves for the great task? By carrying out my program. I had the appointment of two of the members of the embassy, though not chief members. I laid out the route for them to follow. But all this is nothing, compared to that which lies nearest our hearts. I count all parts but loss for those that touch on *our cause* and toleration. If the Master on this and other occasions has given me an opportunity to show this people what toleration really is, and what is expected of them in regard to it, this is what makes me say: "Bless the Lord, Oh my soul!" And that the men on whom it most depends, had mistaken it, and understand it now, I have had many proofs of since.[20]

At the end of his letter, Verbeck again emphasizes,

> Now all this I only write to *you* and *not* to the *public*; for, as I said before, publishing such things would be directly contrary to my invariable principles of operation, would ruin my reputation, and make me lose the confidence of the people, which it has taken me twelve years to gain in a small degree. Besides, there is a tacit understanding between Iwakura and myself, that I shall leave the outward honor of initiating this embassy to themselves. And who cares for the mere name and honor, if we are sure to reap the benefits, toleration and its immense consequences, partly now, but surely after the return of this embassy.[21]

The embassy, led by Iwakura himself and consisting of a party of forty-eight officials, departed Japan for America December 23, 1871, and did not return until September 13, 1873. Eight or nine members

[20]   Griffis, *Verbeck*, 260-61.
[21]   Ibid., 261-62.

Leaders of the embassy to America and Europe: Prime Minister Iwakura Tomomi (in Japnese dress), surrounded by (l-r) Kido Takayoshi, Yamaguchi Naoyoshi, Ito Hirobumi, and Okubo Toshimichi

of the delegation were Verbeck's former students. This embassy also included the other two most prominent members of the government, Kido Koin and Okubo Toshimichi, as well as rising stars such as Ito Hirobumi. The Iwakura mission went first to the United States, and then visited various countries in Europe.

The embassy's goal was to observe the West at first hand and then to persuade the foreign powers to modify the unequal treaties inherited from the shogunate. They were particularly offended by the extraterritoriality clauses, by which foreign residents were exempted from the application of Japanese laws, and by which treaty nations could exercise jurisdiction over their own subjects within Japan. The resulting international experience proved to be of great educational benefit to the members of the embassy, who came to understand fully Japan's weakness compared to the West. However, the delegation failed in its efforts to persuade the Western powers to make the desired modifications to the treaties.[22]

The reason is clear. Wherever the delegation traveled, first in the United States, and later in nation after nation in Europe, it met with the same reaction. For example, Iwakura presented Emperor Mutsuhito's letter to the U.S president: "We expect and intend to reform and improve" the treaties "so as to stand upon a similar footing with the most enlightened nations, and to attain the full development of public right and interest." However, the U.S. secretary of state responded that "before permitting citizens of the United States to come under the jurisdiction of Japan it would be necessary to consider the laws of that country, and he proceeded to ask about religious liberty and the edicts against Christianity."[23]

---

22    Fairbank, Reischauer, and Craig, *East Asia*, 510.
23    Cary, *History* II, 80.

Okuma Shigenobu (left) and Ito Hirobumi at Ito's villa. The picture reveals the eclectic mix of Japanese and Western dress of Meiji Era gentlemen.

The persecution of Christians and the prohibitions against Christianity were an offense everywhere the embassy went. The situation it faced was communicated to officials in Japan by telegraph. Ito Hirobumi, a member of the embassy and later Japan's leading statesman, wrote to his government that everywhere he encountered strong appeals on behalf of the Japanese Christians in exile as a result of the renewed persecutions, as well as the demand for religious toleration in Japan. He was certain that friendly concessions would be impossible unless the exiles were released and religious toleration initiated.[24]

It became absolutely clear that in proposing and organizing this Japanese embassy to the outside world, Verbeck was able, albeit in anonymity, to have a profound impact not only on Japan's international relations but also on the future of the Christian movement in Japan. It is also clear that not only the Reformed Church missionaries in Japan, but also Ferris and the Board of Foreign Missions itself contributed to the stock of goodwill between America and the Japanese. While the Japanese delegation was in America, an acknowledgment was sent to Ferris, as a representative of the Reformed Church Board of Foreign Missions, by the leaders of the group:

> Secretary's Office of the Japanese Embassy
>      Boston, August 5, 1872
>      Rev. J. M. Ferris, D.D.
>
> Dear Sir - The Ambassadors, being on the eve of their departure from the United States, desire again to convey to you

---

[24]   Ibid., 81.

this expression of their thanks for the interest which you have (for many years) invariably manifested in their people and country.

The kind assistance and encouragement which were so generally extended by you to the Japanese students who studied in this country during a crisis of such importance in our national history, will long be remembered by us. These students are now far advanced in knowledge, and are very useful to our country, and the Ambassadors feel it is mainly due to your instrumentality.

Until recently an impression has prevailed in Japan, that many foreign nations did not entertain kindly feelings toward our people.

The generous conduct exhibited by yourself and other gentlemen in this instance, as well as in all matters of educational interest pertaining to the Japanese youth, will do much to correct this impression, and will do more to cement the friendly relations of the two countries than all other influences combined.

Please extend to the gentlemen this renewed assurance of the Ambassadors' high appreciation of their kindness, and they will likewise, on returning to Japan, explain the matter satisfactorily to our government

We remain yours very truly,
TOMOMI IWAKURA
TOSHIMITI OKUBO.[25]

Another area in which Verbeck made a valuable contribution during this period was his arrangement for and recruitment of foreign teachers, not only for the college in Tokyo for which he had responsibility, but also for schools in other parts of Japan where local leaders were developing Western studies. He was convinced that Christian men in these teaching positions in government-related schools could make a valuable contribution. Verbeck recruited these teachers through the Reformed Church mission board; several of them were graduates of Rutgers College. One of the earliest of these graduates was William E. Griffis, an ordained minister of the Reformed Church. Griffis taught first at Fukui and then at Tokyo and later became well known as a scholar of Japan and missionary biographer. Another was Griffis's successor at the Fukui school, Martin N. Wyckoff, who would make a great contribution in Japan as a missionary educator.

---

[25]    Griffis, *Rutgers*, 36.

**The Stouts Arrive in Nagasaki**

Henry and Elizabeth Stout had volunteered to serve with the Verbecks in Nagasaki. But, as we have seen, Guido Verbeck's situation had changed. Since his new opportunities developed while the Stouts were sailing to Japan, they in effect succeeded the Verbecks as the Reformed Church missionaries in Nagasaki.

Henry Stout was born January 19, 1838, and grew up on a farm near Raritan in Somerset County, New Jersey. He made a Christian commitment at the age of twenty and entered Rutgers College at the age of twenty-three. Feeling it his duty and calling, he went on to prepare for the ministry at New Brunswick Theological Seminary. During Stout's seminary days, the first of many Japanese students introduced by Verbeck had begun studying at New Brunswick. Furthermore, it was a time of great interest in world missions at New Brunswick Seminary. During his senior year, Stout came to believe that he was called to become a missionary, and he applied to the Reformed Church's Board of Foreign Missions to be appointed and sent. The board did not at first even respond to his request[26] and was apparently financially unable to act. Stout's determination and his efforts to realize his calling are revealed in a letter to the board from the Raritan Classis.

> The Classis of Raritan convened today to hear the report of Mr. Henry Stout, Licentiate, when the following minute was adopted.
>
> Whereas Mr. Henry Stout, in accordance with the request of this classis has visited the churches within its bounds, and presented to them the claims of the Board of Foreign Missions, and made report of the result of his efforts,
>
> Therefore, Resolved that the Stated Clerk notify the Board, that the sum of at least Fifteen Hundred & Forty Seven Dollars has been pledged annually by the members of these congregations towards his support as missionary in Japan,
>
> Classis also have made arrangements for the ordination of Mr. Stout as missionary, on Wednesday October 14th...[27]

Henry Stout graduated from the seminary in May of 1868 at the age of thirty, and the next month he married Elizabeth Provost. They were appointed by the mission board, corresponded with Verbeck, made their final preparations, and, despite the financial struggles of the

---

[26]  SRB to JMF, Jan. 28, 1868.
[27]  John F. Mersick to JMF, Sept. 15, 1868.

Henry Stout at about the time
of his departure for Japan

board, were able to depart for Japan as missionaries of the Reformed
Church. In January, the Stouts sailed south from New York, crossed the
Isthmus of Panama overland, took another ship to San Francisco, and
then crossed the Pacific on a side-wheel steamer, arriving in Nagasaki
after almost two months on March 11, 1869.

The Stouts were welcomed warmly by the Verbecks upon their
arrival in Nagasaki. However, since they had expected to adjust to their
new life and ministry under the Verbecks' guidance, the Stouts must
have been surprised and disappointed to learn that the Verbecks were
packing to leave Nagasaki Station. Guido Verbeck did his best in their
ten days together to introduce Henry Stout and arranged for him to take
over teaching responsibilities at the government school, where Stout
taught for the next three and one-half years. When they arrived, the
Stouts had moved into rented rooms in Daitokuji, a Buddhist temple
building. Later, for $1,600, they purchased a house, originally built by
a foreign merchant, to use as a residence. It was located in Nagasaki's
foreign concession, where foreigners were required to reside.

The Stouts took students from the government school into their
home as boarders. Henry could witness discreetly to these students in the
privacy of his home. Stout also made friends with some of the Japanese
teachers at the school. Sometimes he was able to get a few people,
including one or more teachers, to come secretly for Bible study at his
home.[28] The work of Brown, Verbeck, and Hepburn in the preparation

---

[28]    Henry Stout, *Sketch of the South Japan Mission* (New York: Board of Foreign Missions,
RCA, 1899), 10.

of dictionaries and grammars must certainly have been a great boon for the language study of missionaries arriving ten years later, such as the Stouts. However, the fact remains that they had to learn Japanese without the benefit of a formal language school or qualified teachers. During their first two or three years they put forth prodigious effort, for Stout gained a high level of proficiency in this extremely difficult language.

Ten years had passed since the coming of the first Protestant missionaries, but the situation had not improved. In fact, when the Stouts arrived, persecution was in progress in Nagasaki against hidden Christians who had come out into the open, and young nationalist patriots continued to call for the expulsion of foreigners, calling them the "outside barbarians." The missionaries had hoped for a new, more lenient policy toward Christianity, but their dilemma remained. Since the new government had re-enacted the law that prohibited Japanese becoming Christians, antagonism, suspicion, and fear of Christianity were being intensified, especially in Nagasaki, as evidenced by the arrest and exile of the hidden Christians and the imprisonment of Protestant convert Shimizu.

By the path up the bluff leading to the Stout home stood one of the new signs erected in 1868 by order of the Meiji Government. The sign read, "The evil sect called Christians is strictly prohibited. Suspected persons should be reported to the proper officers, and rewards will be given." What courage must have been required even to approach the missionaries' residence! Such were the local conditions when the Stouts began their work and under which all the missionaries still labored.

## The Browns Return to Japan

Less than a year after S. R. Brown's temporary resumption of pastoral work in upstate New York, he showed his eagerness to go back to Japan in a letter to the board[29] in which he proposed the family's return in the summer of 1869. His desire was to give all his time to the translation of the scriptures into Japanese. He continued to negotiate with the board regarding the return to Japan, and the Classis of Kingston offered to pay his salary. Brown also recommended to the board the appointment of Mary E. Kidder to serve as a missionary teacher in Japan. She had been a member of his church in Owasco Outlet and had taught in his school there. Subsequently, she had been teaching

---

[29]    SRB to JMF, Jan. 9, 1869.

in a school in Brooklyn, New York, but she had come to feel a call to missionary service.

Then a totally unexpected opportunity arose, which would realize Brown's desire to return to Japan without placing a great burden on the board's treasury. The opportunity came in the form of a letter of invitation from Brown's son-in-law, J. C. Lowder, who was acting British consul at the newly opened port of Niigata on the west coast of Japan's main island of Honshu. Some Japanese authorities, former students of Brown in Yokohama, wanted Brown to open a school in Niigata and serve as its principal. They would pay him a salary of three thousand dollars a year (about three times the usual missionary salary) and provide travel expenses to Japan. The board approved, and Brown accepted the offer. He also suggested that the support from the Classis of Kingston could be used to send another missionary to Japan. The Browns crossed the United States on the newly opened transcontinental railroad and sailed from California via steamer on August 4, arriving once again in Yokohama August 26, 1869.[30]

The Browns returned to a Japan considerably changed in their absence. Edo, the seat of the shoguns, had become Tokyo, the capital of Japan and the seat of power of Japan's emperor. The civil war had ended, and the leaders were embarked on the path of nation building. Brown recognized more than twenty of his former students among those working in the new government. One of them urged him to teach at the newly forming Tokyo University, another wanted him to open a school in Yokohama. Brown was determined to go to Niigata as planned, and he made preparations to travel there by land, traversing the main island of Honshu from the Pacific coast to the Japan Sea. Before departing Yokohama for Niigata, Brown made arrangements for the portion of the Yokohama Mission property set aside for a missionary residence to be leased out for income for a period of seven years.[31]

There was at that time no actual road traversing the island, and the party traveled in palanquins carried by four to six bearers each. The group included, besides the Browns, a retinue of six armed guards, an interpreter, and fifty bearers carrying baggage. This journey of 284 miles from Yokohama to Niigata, via Takasaki, Annaka, Ueda, Nagano, and Naoetsu through the beautiful central mountain region and historic rural towns, took sixteen days. The Browns arrived in Niigata October 24, 1869, and soon moved into a house prepared for them on the edge of the city near the ocean.

[30]   Griffis, *A Maker*, 216-17; SRB to JMF, Jan. 29, Feb. 28, Apr. 29, and June 15, 1869.
[31]   SRB to JMF, Nov. 9, 1869.

A nearby Buddhist temple served as a school building, and Brown took up his teaching with thirty diligent students. There were no other Americans in the city. When he wasn't teaching, Brown began to pursue his real goal in returning to Japan, the translation of the scriptures into Japanese. According to Otis Cary, "Though the engagement was for three years, at the end of eight months Dr. Brown was recalled, the local government professing inability to pay his salary. Since another teacher was at once employed at nearly the same sum, the real reason for the change was probably because Dr. Brown on Sundays taught the Bible to those who cared to study it."[32] In any case, the isolation first seen as an asset had turned out to be a liability. With a desire to be close to his fellow translator, Hepburn, and to the books and conferences necessary for making a standard translation of the New Testament, a return to Yokohama seemed wise.

Consequently, when authorities in Yokohama sent word in the early summer of 1870, asking Brown to take charge of their new school, he accepted the invitation. The Browns returned to Yokohama July 16, and the new school opened September 11 with thirty-two students. Twenty-six of Brown's Niigata students had followed him to Yokohama. The Browns bought a house on the bluff in Yokohama, where among their first callers were the Verbecks from Tokyo.[33]

The missionaries were welcomed and popular as teachers, as a means to acquire the languages and knowledge of the West. But Japan continued to be intolerant of Christianity, and freedom of religion for Japanese people remained elusive. In the past, it had been the Buddhists that had cooperated with the government under the shoguns in the persecution of Christians. The new Meiji government, with the restoration of the emperor, had become pro-Shinto, with the emperor implemented as a kind of high priest, and once again Christianity was being made a scapegoat. Brown hated such bigotry and did not hesitate to speak and write openly against the persecution of the Roman Catholic Christians, which was in full swing in 1870 under the new government.[34]

As soon as Brown had returned to Yokohama in 1870, he had again been prevailed upon to serve as pastor of the Yokohama Union Church, the English-language church serving the foreign community there.[35] However, more than anything else, Brown was eager to see

32   Cary, *History* II, 70.
33   Griffis, *A Maker*, 217-30.
34   Ibid., 236.
35   Ibid., 238.

the Bible translated into Japanese. While he expended great effort in this endeavor, he was at the same time still, at first, almost supporting himself by his teaching at the government school in Yokohama.

## Mary E. Kidder, First Woman Missionary to Japan

Secretary Ferris received the following letter, dated March 1, 1869.

Being desirous to make myself useful among those who have not many teachers, and feeling as I told you on Saturday that I had been led by Providence to think of this foreign mission work again and again, all hindrances of a personal character now being removed, I offer myself I believe unresolvedly to the work, feeling strong but knowing that I am weak, yet believing that in trying to help others I may be really strengthened and fitted for duty as it comes. I should like much to be sent out to Japan with the Rev. S. R. Brown, D.D. and it is this request that I present to the Reformed Church Board of Foreign Missions. My pastor will send you a letter and some others have promised to say a word for my fitness seemingly, for this work.

Dr. Brown has left a letter here to be sent with mine but I fear he says too much in my praise. Had I seen him when he left it I should have asked him to restate it. Please make allowance for the opinion of a very partial friend.

I hope I may soon know what your Board think of my request.

Very Respectively Yours,
Mary E. Kidder

Mary E. Kidder was duly appointed as the first single woman missionary to Japan.[36] As a single missionary, her salary was about half that of the married male missionaries, six hundred dollars per year. Kidder sailed to Japan with the Browns, arriving in Kanagawa August 26, 1869. She lived with them in Niigata, where Brown had contracted to teach, and Kidder at first occupied herself studying the Japanese language. She moved with the Browns to Yokohama the following summer, arriving there with them July 16.

On September 23, 1870, Kidder took over teaching a class of two girls and one boy at Hepburn's dispensary from Mrs. Hepburn. In a letter written a month later, Kidder told of her efforts in language study and

---

[36] Wives were not appointed as missionaries in those days, but considered to be assistant missionaries.

Mary E. Kidder (1834 – 1910)

about her pupils. She reported that she had been reading a half chapter of Matthew to them each day [in English, even though they couldn't understand]. She herself had read Hepburn's translation of Mark in Japanese, and she was having her language teacher hand copy it for use by her pupils. They had already learned to repeat the Lord's Prayer in English and Japanese, which they did daily after reading scripture.[37] At the close of the first year she had six girls in her class. She had hopes of establishing a school exclusively for girls as soon as possible. That hope was realized September 8, 1871, with seventeen girls and women, and Mary E. Kidder became the founder of what came to be called Ferris Seminary, a mission school for girls. The school met at Hepburn's dispensary, and Kidder requested and Brown urged that the Reformed Church's mission board provide her with a school building.[38] The brief attempt by Caroline Adriance a decade earlier having been unsuccessful, this may be considered the humble beginning of Christian education for women in Japan.[39]

Kidder's school immediately began to attract young girls and women. During the second year her pupils increased to twenty-two, including not only young girls but also the vice-governor's wife, two married women whose husbands were attached to Japanese embassies in Europe, and a young woman from 250 miles north. This growth

[37]   Mary E. Kidder to JMF, Oct. 22, 1870.
[38]   MEK to JMF, Oct. 21, 1871; SRB to JMF, Nov. 17, 1871.
[39]   Griffis, *A Maker*, 217, 231.

necessitated a move from the room lent to her by the Presbyterians at Hepburn's clinic to a house in the part of the city of Yokohama called Ise Yama. The move was arranged without cost to the mission through the kindness of Mr. Oe, governor of Yokohama. Governor Oe also provided Mary with a very pretty enclosed carriage, to be pulled by coolies, saying "that the distance was too great to walk, and he would do himself the pleasure of giving me a conveyance." This *jin-riki-sha* ("person-pulled-vehicle") was a mode of human transport that was gaining in popularity at the time.[40]

To assist Kidder in developing the school for girls, the mission board sent out Miss S. K. M. Hequembourg in November 1872. Upon arrival, Hequembourg described her initial impressions of the school in a letter home.

> As we enter the room a little before nine, each pupil is in his place, quiet and orderly. Without rising they greet us with a low bow and pleasant "Good Morning." School opens at nine with a hymn from "Children's Praises," a little book published by the American Tract Society Presbyterian Board. This is followed by a portion of the Gospel of Saint Mark in Japanese, Dr. Hepburn's translation. Each pupil reads a verse, which is explained by Miss Kidder. The girls ask questions very freely, and are encouraged to do so.

Hequembourg went on to comment,

> The time seems to be right to establish a permanent institution in the form of a boarding school. Miss Kidder's school now consists of 29 pupils, all girls of the higher class, and eager to be educated, and also to learn our ways of living. Having them with us constantly and away from their own homes, they could be taught the beauties of the Christian home life, and thus be prepared to spread that influence in homes of their own as they leave school.[41]

Hequembourg later wrote, "Japanese of position and culture have great confidence in Miss Kidder as an instructress and thorough lady. No school in Japan has the reputation that hers has for girls, and the Japanese consider it a privilege to send their wives and daughters to us. The school now numbers 42 girls and women."[42]

---

[40]   Sangster, *Manual*, 260-61; Griffis, *A Maker*, 251.
[41]   Ryder, *Historical Sourcebook*, 83; S. K. M. Hequembourg to JMF, Nov. 6, 1872.
[42]   Ibid., 83; SKMH to JMF, Dec. 23, 1872.

Early in 1873, Mary Kidder became engaged to marry the Reverend Edwin Rothsay Miller, a new missionary of the Presbyterian mission who was studying the Japanese language in Yokohama. Mary and E. R. Miller were married July 10, 1873, and the board approved her continuing with the mission.[43] Kidder was committed to continue developing the school in partnership with Hequembourg, who was a fine addition to the mission and popular among the students. However, Hequembourg's health was not good. She was unable to teach from the fall of 1873, which hampered development of the school. She apparently had a serious case of tuberculosis and was forced to resign and return to America in very precarious health.[44]

Mary struggled to keep the work going, but, with prospects for the boarding school unclear, enrollment began to dwindle. Even so, during its first few years, this educational work bore fruit in the Christian commitment and baptism first of Okuno Hiza, daughter of one of the first elders in the Yokohama Church, and then of Okada Ko. In July of 1875 E. R. Miller joined the Reformed Church Japan Mission.[45] While continuing his language study, Miller assisted his wife at Ferris Girls' School.

**Maintenance of the Reformed Church's Japan Mission Staff**

Reinforcement of the missionary personnel in Japan was an issue from very early. Missionary correspondence to the board repeatedly called for additional appointees. Financial support seems often to have been insufficient even for the support of those already on the field, without considering an increase in personnel. The board repeatedly sank seriously into debt, only to be bailed out periodically by major gifts from generous individuals.

During much of the Verbecks' time in Nagasaki, Guido Verbeck received income from teaching in government schools, reducing the financial burden for the board. Later, during his ten years in the employ of the Japanese government, the Verbecks received no financial support from the Reformed Church.

In 1868, some time after the disastrous fire that destroyed their home, James Ballagh returned to America for his first furlough. During his time in America, Ballagh raised $2,373.83 toward the construction of a church for the Japanese in Yokohama, even though there was as yet no congregation. However, the mission board's treasury was so low that

---

[43]   MEK to JMF, April 19 and August 22, 1873.
[44]   SRB to JMF, Dec. 5, 1873.
[45]   Verbeck, "History," 27, 72.

the board had to borrow a portion of the church building fund Ballagh had raised to send the family back to their field in Japan in 1870. The Browns returned to Japan in the summer of 1869 at their own expense, and S. R. Brown was for some time virtually self-supported by his teaching.

In 1869, in response to the pleas of the missionaries, the Stouts had been sent to take up work in Nagasaki, having in essence raised their own support from the Classis of Raritan churches. Verbeck having gone to Tokyo under the employ of the Japanese government, the Stouts worked alone in Nagasaki for many years, and the missionaries in Yokohama were also overburdened with work. The missionaries on the field continued to ask for additional colleagues.

Eventually, the mission board paid off its debt to the Yokohama church building fund and, in 1871, the board appointed the Reverend Charles H. H. and Mrs. L. Wolff as missionaries to Japan. Charles Wolff was born in the Netherlands but had lived in the United States for fourteen years and graduated from Auburn Seminary.[46] The Wolffs arrived in Japan to augment the Reformed mission force in February of 1871.

The Wolffs settled in Yokohama, where Charles taught English to classes of Japanese young men while he and Mrs. Wolff immersed themselves in language study. However, after several months, Mrs. Wolff gave up the study of Japanese and took up teaching English, too. Someone had remarked to her, "What is the use of your studying Japanese? By the time you know enough of the language to do some good, all Japanese will speak English."[47] As generations of missionaries since could bear witness, this assumption was entirely off the mark. Learning the language well has always been and remained crucial to significant relationships and ministry in Japan.

On November 22, 1872, the Reformed Church missionaries in Yokohama met to discuss their financial dilemma. The board's support was so inadequate that they were forced to teach classes of English in government schools in order to pay the high house rents. The only solution seemed to be to reduce the Japan mission budget on the field by reducing staff.[48] Consequently, early in 1873 the Wolffs were obliged to move to Hirosaki in the far north of the main island. There, on a one-year contract, Wolff taught in the government school, thus earning their own support teaching English classes five hours a day.

[46]   Charles H. H. Wolff to JMF, Jan. 20, 1870.
[47]   CHHW to JMF, Sept. 1, 1871.
[48]   CHHW to JMF, Nov. 23, 1872.

After describing this temporary solution to the financial crisis, James Ballagh pleaded in an eloquent, twelve-page letter for the Reformed Church, pioneer in sending the first missionaries to Japan, to faithfully and adequately fulfill its calling to preach the gospel and establish the Christian mission in Japan by sending more personnel and properly supporting them.[49]

While in Hirosaki, the Wolffs endeavored to carry on a Christian witness by holding Bible study classes on Sundays. One of the other teachers in the school was a former student of Ballagh in Yokohama. Although this Japanese teacher was not yet a Christian, he had told others about Christianity, arousing their interest even before the arrival of the Wolffs. During their one-year contract in Hirosaki, reassured by correspondence from the board that the Reformed Church would more adequately support its missionaries on the field, the Wolffs looked forward to the day when they would be able to return to actual missionary service.[50] However, they would have continued their work in Hirosaki, as desired by the local officials and students, if it had not been for another development. The Japanese government issued orders that local school officials were not allowed to hire missionaries as teachers. Consequently, the Wolffs left Hirosaki January 1, 1874, after only one year. Wolff expressed his desire to go to Nagasaki to work with Henry Stout. But Wolff was in need of medical care, and the couple traveled overland for twenty-four days in winter to reach Yokohama. Later, they proceeded to Nagasaki to take up work with the Stouts.[51]

Over the course of many years, correspondence between the missionaries on the field and the Board of Foreign Missions spoke repeatedly of the shortage of personnel for effectively carrying out the mission on the one hand and the struggle of the board to raise the necessary funds—or even to get out of debt—on the other. Until the women of the Reformed Church became directly involved in promoting foreign missions, this situation persisted.

**The Woman's Union Missionary Society**

The Woman's Union Missionary Society, a separate but significant development in missionary activity in Japan, deserves inclusion in this narrative. Although it was an ecumenical movement from the beginning, the union originated from challenges presented by the man known as

---

[49]  JHB to JMF, Jan. 22, 1873.
[50]  CHHW to JMF, Apr. 21, 1873.
[51]  CHHW to JMF, March 26 and Dec. 30, 1873; JHB to JMF, Jan. 16, 1874; Cary, *History* II, 106.

the Reformed Church's pioneer missionary to China, the Reverend David Abeel. After Abeel's initial missionary experiences in Southeast Asia from 1829 to 1833, he traveled through Europe, pleading the cause of missions. In England, his appeal to Christian women to reach out to the women of Asia resulted in the formation in 1834 in London of the first ever mission organization by and for women. During the next twelve years, this women's society sent forty missionaries to various foreign fields.

Returning to New York City in 1834, Abeel met with a group of women gathered by Sarah Doremus (1802-1877), wife of Thomas C. Doremus, an elder in the South Reformed Church. An enthusiastic supporter of foreign missions, Sarah Doremus had boarded the ship to bid Abeel farewell in 1829, when he left for China the first time, and she had welcomed him in her home upon his return. Abeel urged these American Christian women to form a mission organization, similar to that in England, for the salvation of the women of Asia. Although considerable interest was shown, the actual inauguration of such work was postponed due to opposition from Rufus Anderson, secretary of the American Board of Commissioners for Foreign Missions, with which the Reformed Church was cooperating. One of the women involved, Joanna Bethune, responded, "What! Is the American Board afraid the ladies will get ahead of them?" David Abeel's reaction was a fervent plea. "What is to become of the souls of those who are ignorant of the offers of mercy and of the Bible?"[52] In any case, in the words of Mary Chamberlain, "His [David Abeel's] is the name associated more than any other with the beginnings, in every denomination, of woman's work for women in Eastern lands....His was the first clear call to the women of the Church to organize in the interests of the women of heathen lands."[53]

On February 1, 1861, twenty-seven years later and long after Abeel had died at the age of forty-two, the Woman's Union Missionary Society of America for Heathen Lands was organized. It was thanks to the diligent efforts of Sarah Doremus of the Reformed Church, who served as its first president, that this interdenominational missionary society came into being. This first American women's missionary sending agency was thus inspired by a Reformed Church missionary and finally brought into being under the leadership of a Reformed Church lay woman.

---

[52]    Mary E. A. Chamberlain, *Fifty Years in Foreign Fields: China, Japan, India, Arabia: A History of Five Decades of the Woman's Board of Foreign Missions, Reformed Church in Ameica* (New York: Woman's Board of Foreign Missions, 1925), 7.

[53]    Ibid., 3, 5.

In the 1860s, women in America did not have the right to vote or hold property, so it was no small accomplishment that the Woman's Union Missionary Society developed a program for long-term financial support of women missionaries. The society's vision was realized through the efforts of many small groups of prayerful, diligent Christian women who were organized to gather their pocket change and hold bazaars to sell their handwork. The society began a periodical to publicize its activities and sought out qualified single women or widows to send as missionaries. By 1869, the society had sent women for educational, medical, and evangelistic work to Burma, India, and China.

The society's decision to begin work in Japan was the direct result of the pleas of James Ballagh, during his first furlough in America in 1869. Ballagh appealed to American Christian women to respond to two needs he had observed in Japan: girls and women had little or no opportunity for education, and Eurasian children fathered by Western men at the port of Yokohama and born to Japanese women were despised and rejected by Japanese society. The Woman's Union Missionary Society embraced this calling, and, in answer to Ballagh's appeal and the prayers of society members, three gifted women volunteered to go to Japan as missionaries and establish the society's mission there.

The first to volunteer was Mary Putnam Pruyn (1820-1885), of the First Reformed Church in Albany, New York. Mary Pruyn was a widow and grandmother and vice-president of a local chapter of the Union Missionary Society. She became the leader and founder of the mission. Two other women, Julia N. Crosby (1833-1918) of Poughkeepsie, New York, also a member of the Reformed Church, and Louise Henrietta Pierson (1832-1899), a highly educated woman from Kentucky whose husband and four children had all died, were recruited to go with Pruyn. These devout and courageous Christian women departed from New York May 18, 1871, by transcontinental railroad and sailed for Japan, arriving in Yokohama June 25, 1871. They were welcomed and assisted by James Ballagh and the other Reformed and Presbyterian missionaries in Yokohama and began to lay the foundations for their work in female education and with the despised Eurasian children. In October of 1872 they opened their boarding school, which came to be known as the American Mission Home. Pruyn also opened their home for Bible study and worship services in English for the larger community.[54]

---

[54] Verbeck, "History," 29; *Yokohama Kyoritsu Gakuen: Hyakunijunen no Ayumi* (Yokohama: Yokohama Kyoritsu Galuen, 1991), 22-26.

Mary Pruyn (top), Julia Crosby (bottom left), and Louise Pierson, first missionaries to Japan from the Woman's Union Missionary Society

## Japan's First Protestant Church

Following their return from America in November of 1870, the Ballaghs worked quietly but diligently in Yokohama, teaching small classes of interested young people. The classes and other meetings were held in the small building on the mission property (the education wing of the future church building) that Ballagh had erected before going to America. Ballagh's course of study included one hour each day of Bible study. Ballagh was especially known as a man of prayer, and he prayed openly for Japan in the presence of his students. After about nine months, this pattern of ministry began to bear fruit.

In November 1871, Ballagh reported that the little chapel/schoolroom was full at Sunday services in Japanese, and that the

English-language services held at Mary Pruyn's house on Sunday afternoons and Wednesday evenings were well attended not only by the foreign residents of Yokohama but also by numerous Japanese students and community people. Even though the prohibition of Christianity was still in effect, Ballagh expressed his desire to build the long-planned church building in order to accommodate more people.[55]

During the first week of January 1872, missionaries and some other interested foreigners in Yokohama held special prayer meetings to read through the book of Acts and pray for Japan, and a number of Japanese young men who were students in the various classes of the missionaries chose to attend. The scripture was translated extemporaneously into Japanese for them, as there was as yet no published Japanese version of the Bible. These young men began to participate actively in the meetings, which continued until the end of February, praying that God would give his Spirit to Japan as to the early church.

> After a week or two the Japanese, for the first time in the history of the nation, were on their knees in a Christian prayer-meeting, entreating God with great emotion, with the tears streaming down their faces, that he would give His Spirit to Japan as to the early church and to the people around the Apostles....Half a dozen perhaps of the Japanese thus publicly engaged in prayer; but the number present was much larger. This is the record of the first Japanese prayer-meeting.[56]

One day James Ballagh set aside an hour during his day of teaching for special prayer. After the prayer meeting, Ballagh told his students, "If any one of you desires to become a Christian let him place a card with his name on my table." The students didn't discuss the matter among themselves, but the next morning Ballagh found the names of nine of his students on his table.[57]

As a direct result of these prayer meetings, the first Protestant Japanese Christian church was organized March 10, 1872, in Yokohama with eleven members. They included nine young men who were baptized that day, students of James Ballagh, and two middle-aged men who had previously become Christians: Ogawa, baptized by Thompson, and Nimura, baptized by George Ensor, in Nagasaki. Since there was as yet no Japanese ordained minister, James Ballagh became the church's

---

[55]   JHB to JMF, Nov. 22, 1871.
[56]   Verbeck, "History," 52-53.
[57]   Allen R. Bartholomew, *Won By Prayer, or The Life and Work of Rev. Masayoshi Oshikawa* (Philadelphia: Reformed Publishing House, 1889), 46.

The stone chapel Ballagh had constructed on the church building site in Yokohama, where the first Japanese Protestant church was organized March 10, 1872, in the thirteenth year after the arrival of the first Protestant missionaries

first pastor. This was seen as a temporary arrangement until a qualified Japanese pastor was prepared to take over the role. Mr. Ogawa was chosen as an elder, and Mr. Nimura as a deacon of the young church.[58]

The members gave their church a catholic name to indicate that it was nonsectarian: The Church of Christ in Japan. They also drew up a church constitution—a simple evangelical creed, together with some rules of church government, according to which the government was to be in the hands of the pastor and elders, with the consent of the members.[59]

This step was taken in spite of the fact that the law prohibiting Christianity had not yet been rescinded. This was a courageous step, to be sure, but at the same time one taken in the belief that a crack was opening in the wall of resistance, and that the moment was imminent for overt evangelistic activity by the missionaries. In fact, although this infant congregation was kept under surveillance by Japanese government spies, it was not subjected to overt persecution. Perhaps the communications from the Iwakura Embassy in America were already beginning to have their effect on the Japanese government's will to implement its prohibitions against Japanese becoming Christians.

The young congregation continued to prosper. Three months after its inception, it had already added twelve new converts to its membership. However, the strain of overwork was beginning to take its toll on James Ballagh's health. In his words, "I have become very

58    Cary, *History* II, 76-77.
59    Verbeck, "History," 53.

nervous not only but very much troubled with a pain in my head, which makes me very irritable and almost violent. I am now almost unfitted for any spiritual service. At the time I enjoy it much, but about 24 hours after an attack comes on that will last one or two days." Besides his service as pastor of this first Japanese congregation, Ballagh taught a daily Bible study class and held morning and afternoon Sunday services in Japanese. He had also been leading the English-language gathering for Japanese and foreigners at Mary Pruyn's home. Furthermore, in part to earn his rent, he was temporarily teaching English three hours daily to one hundred students in a government school.

S. R. Brown showed great concern for Ballagh's health and thought that ideally he should have a year's furlough in America to recuperate. Brown took over Ballagh's responsibility for the Bible study/prayer meeting in English on Sunday evenings, but Brown also was already overworked. With new possibilities finally opening up after so many years of preparation and prayer, Ballagh could not think of leaving Japan. He hoped that a summer vacation in the country of two or three months would help him recover his health. His health did improve, and in the summer of 1873 Brown concurred that Ballagh could not be spared from the work of the mission and that any furlough plans ought to be postponed.[60]

Brown himself expressed his desire to quit teaching in government schools to earn his support and to return to support by the mission board, so that he could devote himself to Bible translation work. He requested annual support from the board in the amount of $2,200 for his salary and house rent. Brown's estimate was treated as excessive, and he saw that there was no prospect of board support. However, he resigned from the time-consuming teaching at the government school and accepted the offer of a Japanese merchant to open a school at Brown's home for ten young men, his salary being paid by the merchant and the students. This allowed Brown, while still self-supporting, to spend half his time on Bible translation. At the same time, a number of the young men who were members of the newly organized church were beginning their training for the ministry. Ballagh had been teaching them as best he could. Other missionaries looked to Brown as the best person to teach them, and he took up that responsibility. However, citing the fact that he himself and Verbeck and Wolff were self-supporting, already in 1873 Brown pleaded with the board to send a young man to take responsibility for teaching theology.[61]

---

[60]   JHB to JMF, June 22, 1872, July 7, 1873; SRB to JMF, June 24, 1872, June 1, 1873.
[61]   SRB to JMF, Nov. 19, 1873.

### The Vision of Ecumenical Mission

Until the midpoint of the nineteenth century, the American Board of Commissioners for Foreign Missions had been the ecumenical agency through which Congregational, Reformed, and Presbyterian churches had begun to send out foreign missionaries. However, by mid-century, the various denominations had formed their own sending agencies, or mission boards. The Reformed Church's denominational mission board had been formed in 1857, and the American Board had become the sending agency of only the Congregational churches. This American Board began sending Congregational missionaries to Japan in 1869. At the beginning, the Congregational missionaries were concentrated in the newly opened Kobe/Osaka/Kyoto region of central Japan.

With regard to Christian unity, S.R. Brown was a pioneer and held strong convictions. He wrote the following to the mission board:

> Now, from the ingathering of converts from this land, it seems as if all who love the Lord Jesus must wish to see such a foundation laid as that the Church here shall be one and undivided, the "Church of Christ in Japan," rather than a church here of one name, others of another, confusing the heathen by its divisions, and weakening the power of the church thereby.[62]

On another occasion Brown wrote, "May God incline all who are interested in the progress of Christianity in Japan to the same catholicity of sentiment and unity of aim, so that the divisions that mar the beauty of the Church in Christendom may as far as possible be excluded from this country."[63]

On September 28, 1872, just six months after the first Protestant church was organized, a convention for all of the missionaries then working in Japan and a few other interested parties was held in Yokohama. While the Episcopalians declined to come, a total of forty-three people attended. Included among them was the first Japanese elder (already functioning as a lay evangelist), Ogawa Yoshiyasu, who was seated as a member of the convention. The missionary representatives were of the Reformed, Presbyterian, Congregational, and Baptist denominations.

Among the resolutions passed at the convention was the following: "Whereas in the work of Foreign Missions the native element must constitute the chief means for prosecution—Resolved—That we

---

[62]    Griffis, *A Maker*, 243-44.
[63]    Ibid, 244.

deem it of the utmost importance to educate a native Ministry as soon as possible."[64] The two other key issues considered at this conference were the translation of scripture into Japanese and the union of the churches of Christ in Japan. S. R. Brown played a leading role at this conference. On the issue of unity, when dialogue was at an impasse, his compromise proposal resolved the conflict, gaining unanimous approval.

> Whereas the Church of Christ is one in him, and the diversities of denominations among Protestants are but accidents which, though not affecting the vital unity of believers, obscure the oneness of the Church in Christendom and much more in pagan lands, where the history of the divisions cannot be understood; and whereas we, as Protestant missionaries, desire to secure uniformity in our modes and methods of evangelization so as to avoid as far as possible the evil arising from marked differences; we therefore take this earliest opportunity offered by this Convention to agree that we will use our influence to secure as far as possible identity of name and organization in the native churches in the formation of which we may be called to assist, that name being as catholic as the Church of Christ, and the organization being that wherein the government of each church shall be by the ministry and eldership of the same, with the concurrence of the brethren.[65]

The Reformed Church had already accepted the idea of establishing national churches on its mission fields, with the understanding they were not to be overseas branches of the Reformed Church in America. This issue had been resolved in connection with the Amoy Mission, in relation to the formation of the Church of Christ in China, as revealed in the Reformed Church's General Synod minutes of 1857 through 1863.

The movement called the Evangelical Alliance also undoubtedly had its impact upon the missionaries in Japan. Originating in England in 1846, the purpose of the alliance was to draw together evangelicals of all denominations for fellowship and prayer. The American branch of the Evangelical Alliance was formed in 1867, under the leadership of church historian Philip Schaff, a professor at Union Theological Seminary in New York, where Brown had completed his theological

---

[64]　"Report taken from the Minutes of the Convention of Protestant Missionaries in Japan, held at Yokohama, September 20th–25th, 1872," Archives of the RCA.

[65]　Griffis, *A Maker*, 241-43.

education. The influential Schaff exerted a great effort to further unity among Christians, and under his leadership the most notable of a series of world gatherings of the alliance took place in 1873.[66] Correspondence of the Reformed Church missionaries indicates that they followed this movement with great interest and appreciation.

In any case, it is clear that the Protestant church in Japan began as an evangelical and ecumenical church, with the vision of establishing a united community of Christ's followers, without denominational labels, and the Reformed Church's missionaries were leaders who persuaded others to embrace this vision. This ecumenical spirit was exemplified by James Ballagh, who unavoidably served as the first pastor of the Yokohama church. A Ballagh letter referred to Joseph Hardy Niishima, who had become a Christian and studied for the ministry under the Congregationalists in America. Niishima graduated from Andover Theological Seminary and was ordained in Boston in 1874, the first Japanese to become an ordained Protestant minister. Ballagh's letter stated, "We hoped to get Niishima for the Yokohama Church.... Thus this first church would have stood forth in its true character as a church officered and governed all by its own people. We desire such a boon soon for the Church of Christ in Japan."[67]

Niishima did return to Japan in the fall of 1874, but he worked as a missionary of the American Board, founding the school at Kyoto called the Doshisha. Ballagh's letter also indicated that many of the missionaries in Japan found it hard to overcome their denominationalism and reticence in relinquishing control.

> It is just here where our Presbyterian brethren, or some of them, differ with us, and the wishes of the native church....The Presbyterians want to be ex-officio rulers in the church, but the Japanese think it better before their jealous government not to invite the foreign missionaries to a share in their government. This we think is wise.[68]

## S. R. Brown and Bible Translation

The missionaries realized from the beginning that translating the Bible into the vernacular Japanese would be essential for the propagation

[66]    Kenneth Scott Latourette, *A History of Christianity* (New York: Harper, 1953), 1171, 1268, 1340.
[67]    JHB to JMF, June 18, 1874.
[68]    Ibid.

of the faith in Japan. Consequently, the several early missionaries all attempted translations. They were hampered by the fact that it was extremely difficult to find Japanese who would or could assist in Bible translation, as well as those who would be willing to publish Christian materials. Nevertheless, already in 1865 and 1866, S. R. Brown had prepared first drafts of portions of the New Testament, only to have many of the manuscripts lost in the fire that consumed his house in 1867. In the meantime, James Hepburn was working on translations of Mark and John. In 1867 he began working with James Ballagh and David Thompson on a translation of Matthew. After Brown returned to Yokohama in 1870, he worked with Hepburn to revise Mark and John. Then with Hepburn and later with Thompson, Brown completed the Gospel of Matthew, which was published in 1873. These represent the cooperative efforts of the Reformed and Presbyterian missionaries.

This translation work required the assistance of qualified Japanese scholars. Working with some of the earliest of these men, who were, of course, not Christians, sometimes bore fruit. In June of 1872, Brown reported,

> Today my teacher, who assists me in the translation of the gospels, asked me if I would baptize him. He is a man of superior attainments in his country's learning and literature, and was formerly an officer in the...Shogun's government. He has been putting into Japanese a work of the Rev. Dr. Martin's on the evidences of Christianity, and the study of this and the gospels of Matthew, Mark and John, seems to have produced a decided effect upon his mind & I hope also upon his heart. I have of course had much conversation with him on religious subjects, and have been pleased to see the change coming over him from time to time. The Japanese have lived with such a system of government, that it is no wonder that they should at first tremble with fear at the consequences that might follow their embrace of Christianity. But there is a heroic vein in them, after all, & such stuff as martyrs are made of often shows itself in persons who might before have been accounted timid.[69]

An important outcome of the missionary conference held in September of 1872 was the formation of the New Testament Translation Committee. Brown was chosen to chair the committee, and after the translators began to gather regularly for this joint project in 1874,

[69]    SRB to JMF, June 24, 1872.

Brown gave himself almost completely to this work for about five years. James Hepburn of the Presbyterian Mission, and others of missions that had subsequently begun work in Japan, were also included on the working committee. This ecumenical Bible translation project, which elicited the collaboration of all the Protestant missions working in Japan and of course also enlisted the help of some of the first Japanese converts, was of crucial importance for the communication of the Christian faith. Brown and Hepburn's prior experience in China, and their consequent familiarity with the Chinese ideographs that had been adapted by the Japanese for their written language, as well as the two men's thorough study of Japanese literature, were great assets in this undertaking. Helpful materials, such as copies of Chinese Bibles, were provided, and the Japanese assistants to the translators were supported financially in part by the American Bible Society. Later the British and Foreign Bible Society also contributed to the eventual publication of the scriptures in Japanese.[70]

A daughter of James Ballagh, writing under the penname, "Harold Ballagh," described the Bible translation scene at the Brown home from her childhood memories.

> Now and then we would steal in with overpowering awe, to watch the learned translators of the Scriptures. We knew that the seventy had translated the Old Testament very, very many years before, and we wondered if these men were as great as the 70's.
>
> A large, long table extended down the room and a bay window let in floods of light; under the window the pomegranates blushed at the frivolity of their existence, while such momentous work was going on. The table was piled high with books and the chairs were reserved for the same occupants—much as editors' chairs on metropolitan newspapers are. Japanese assistants with long white beards filled me with the same awe that the venerable domines did. There was a large buffet in the room, and I often wondered if these good men ever condescended to refresh themselves like ordinary mortals.
>
> The daily sessions were opened with prayer. All discussions were conducted with well-bred formality and in low tone.
>
> I have been told that the translation of the Scriptures took years to perform, and the fact that these many lives were spared

---

[70]    Edward Tanjore Corwin, *A Manual of the Reformed Church in America: 1628-1902* (New York: Board of Publication of the Reformed Church in America, 1902), 266; Verbeck, "History," 42-44.

daily to conduct this work, impressed me powerfully. Each man worked upon a different portion of the Bible, and I used privately to wonder which had the most difficult task.

My sister and I would tip-toe from the room and whisper, until we got well out of range of the bay window. The awe of that chamber was in my mind associated with the individuals who worked there. I was afraid to laugh in their presence, even in the garden.[71]

## Public Witness Possible at Last

From the beginning of Protestant mission in Japan, the missionaries had hoped and prayed for the early removal of the prohibitions against Christianity. In a letter dated March 12, 1860, only a few months after his arrival in Japan, Brown had written, "It will not be long, in my opinion, before the ancient edict against Christianity will be revoked."[72] However, such was not the case. It was more than thirteen years later that at least outward change was finally realized.

It was the proposal and careful planning of Guido Verbeck in relation to the new leaders of the Japanese government that ultimately bore significant fruit. Under pressure from foreign governments, and while Japan's embassy to America and Europe was still in progress, on February 24, 1873, the Japanese government finally ordered the removal throughout the country of the notice boards prohibiting Christianity. However, attached to the order sent to local government authorities (and not at first known by the missionaries or reported to outsiders) was an explanation stating that the prohibition against Japanese becoming Christians was so well understood already that any further public notice had become unnecessary, and that, consequently, the edict boards were to be removed. Furthermore, in another example of submission to outside pressure, in March and April of 1873, hundreds of formerly hidden Japanese Roman Catholic Christians who had been exiled were released and allowed to return to their homes.

In effect, the Japanese government had adopted the policy of tacitly permitting the practice of the Christian faith by Japanese people. This was not, however, a positive acknowledgment of the principle of religious freedom. It was primarily an effort to improve its image among Western nations, who had been persistently critical of Japan's religious intolerance. The intent was to facilitate Japan's renegotiation of more

---

[71]  Griffis, *A Maker*, 276-77.
[72]  *Christian Intelligencer*, June 28, 1860.

equal treaties and ultimately to attain equality with the West. In any case, at last the Protestant missionaries had the outward freedom to proclaim the gospel in Japan.[73] Verbeck was ecstatic. In a private letter, he wrote, "The great and glorious event of the day is that, about a week ago, the edicts were removed by command of the government from the public law-boards throughout the country! It is equivalent to granting toleration! The Lord be praised!"[74]

Few people ever knew that, more than anything else, it had been the prayers, planning, and quiet efforts of Guido Verbeck that lay behind the realization of even this limited measure of religious freedom. But Verbeck had become not only hopeful, but also confident that the first fissure in the wall of intolerance was opening up. Anticipating the time when Christianity would be tolerated, and revealing his genius for seizing the opportunity with sensitivity, Verbeck reported,

> Hoping for the approach of this good time, I handed to his Excellency, the Minister of Religious Affairs—quite privately, as I usually manage such business with my native friends—a "Rough Sketch of Laws and Regulations for the Better Control of Church Affairs in Japan," a few days before the removal of the edicts. My object was to show what might, rather than what ought to be done in this direction.[75]

Verbeck's optimism proved premature. The Japanese government had in fact ordered that the notice boards be removed. But it wasn't long before the missionaries realized that their problems were not over. The government's departments of Religion and Education issued an order to expel all missionaries from teaching positions at public and private schools. This order affected people such as Charles Wolff. And, in the words of Ballagh,

> The Dept. of Religion have their licensed preachers out in every direction to counteract Xty & these make the local civil officials trouble all who receive or favor Xty. This has been the case in the several villages in which the Elders preached last fall. The people with whom they stopped and at whose houses they preached have been very much annoyed by the Shinto priests & the local authorities. No actual violence has yet been committed, but it is very painful to those thus beset & they have written repeatedly

73    Verbeck, "History," 54-55.
74    Griffis, *Verbeck*, 265.
75    Ibid., 265-66.

for information and instruction to our Elders....The Gov't's notification to foreign powers of the repeal of the edicts against Xty is a matter of infinite joy; yet the Gov't's failure to notify their own people of the same, together with the decrees of the Education & Religion Departments, & the recent attempt at intimidation of the people we consider as very difficult of reconciliation with Gov't's professed toleration of Xty.[76]

Nevertheless, with the removal of the public prohibitions against Christianity, at long last Japan's self-imposed isolation was truly broken. The centuries-long persecution and prohibition of Christianity and the virtual brainwashing of the Japanese people that had implanted an antipathy toward Christianity would have its long-lasting impact. Even so, the missionaries already in Japan commenced public evangelistic efforts in several regions, and missionary ranks began to swell. Twenty-eight missionaries of the several denominations were working in Japan in 1872, but during 1873 twenty-nine new ones arrived. The reason for this sudden influx is clear. In the words of Verbeck, "The unmolested rise and growth of a native Christian church at Yokohama unmistakably announced to a grateful Christendom that God had indeed opened a door of faith to this family of the Gentiles also."[77]

During 1873, public worship services were begun in Tokyo, under the leadership of Presbyterian David Thompson, who had moved there from Yokohama. Thompson baptized the first convert in Tokyo, Takahashi Toru. The elder of the Yokohama church, Ogawa Yoshiyasu, moved to Tokyo and assisted in this ministry, and Ogawa and six other members from the Yokohama congregation helped form a nucleus for this sister church. The first church in Tokyo was organized September 20, 1873, a year and a half after the organization of the first Protestant congregation in Yokohama. Later, it was called the Shin-sakae-bashi Church. This second Protestant church in Japan, like its sister church in Yokohama, was organized as a congregation of the non-sectarian Church of Christ in Japan, and on the same doctrinal and ecclesiastical basis. Following a suggestion by mission secretary John Ferris, passed on through Ballagh, founding pastor Thompson led the new church also to adopt the Nine Articles of the Evangelical Alliance as its confession of faith.[78]

As a result, this doctrinal basis of the Evangelical Alliance, drawn up in London in 1846 and adopted at the organization of the American

[76]   JHB to JMF, Dec. 22, 1873.
[77]   Verbeck, "History," 57.
[78]   JHB to JMF, Jan. 16, 1874; Verbeck, "History," 59.

branch of the Evangelical Alliance in January 1867, became the first official creedal statement of the nonsectarian Church of Christ in Japan. The Nine Articles are as follows:

· The Divine inspiration, authority, and sufficiency of the Holy Scriptures.
· The right and duty of private judgment in the interpretation of the Holy Scriptures.
· The Unity of the Godhead, and the Trinity of the persons therein.
· The utter depravity of human nature in consequence of the Fall.
· The incarnation of the Son of God, his work of atonement for the sins of mankind, and his mediatorial intercession and reign.
· The justification of the sinner by faith alone.
· The work of the Holy Spirit in the conversion and sanctification of the sinner.
· The immortality of the soul, the resurrection of the body, the judgment of the world by the Lord Jesus Christ, with the eternal blessedness of the righteous, and the eternal punishment of the wicked.
· The divine institution of the Christian ministry, and the obligation and perpetuity of the ordinances of Baptism and the Lord's Supper.

While the Yokohama Church provided seven members to the new Tokyo congregation, it also continued to prosper in Yokohama. On March 2, 1873, Okuno Masatsuna was ordained elder, and Maki Shigeto was baptized. Of Maki, Ballagh wrote,

Last night it was Dr. Brown's and my unspeakable pleasure to examine Maki, a pupil of his who followed him from Niigata to Yokohama 3 yrs. ago, & who has been under Dr. Brown's instruction thereof [in English] ever since....He feels he must be a preacher, to tell the people of the true God & of faith in Jesus Christ. Besides, he says, his people are very fickle & unprincipled, and he desires them to have the strongest, broadest & most immoveable foundation.[79]

During 1873 the Yokohama church grew to a membership of sixty-two communicants and thirteen baptized children. The early Japanese church leaders, Elder Okuno of the Yokohama church and

[79]   JHB to JMF, Jan. 16, 1874.

Elder Ogawa of the Tokyo church, had made a preaching tour to several villages in October of 1873, and they began regular evening preaching meetings in Yokohama and Tokyo respectively. The meetings were well attended by very interested listeners.[80]

## Developments in Nagasaki

Meanwhile, Henry and Elizabeth Stout had been faithfully carrying on the mission in Nagasaki. Henry Stout's words best show the vicissitudes of their situation.

> After about three and a half years connection with the government school at this place, it was believed the way was opening for more direct mission work. A private boys' school was therefore established at the mission residence, with the Bible as the principal textbook, but with other English studies as a further inducement to pupils to attend.
>
> In connection with teaching, both in the Government and private schools, opportunity had offered to present and urge the subject of female education upon the parents, and finally a request was made that a school for girls should be opened by Mrs. Stout. This was gladly acceded to, and in the spring of 1873 the school was begun. But it soon overgrew the limits of private rooms, and it was arranged that both schools should be removed to the native city. It was a distinct understanding, that while the school should be under native patronage, the teachers should have entire control of all instruction, leaving the way thus clear to make the school entirely Christian, when the time should come to do so. It was felt that this could not be done while the edicts against Christianity were still in force. In the course of a few weeks about 50 girls and 30 boys were in regular attendance. Common English branches only were taught in the city, but a Bible-class, at the mission residence, was regularly attended by a large number of the older boys in the evening. In the meantime, however, the edicts against Christianity were removed, and it was believed the time had come to make the school openly Christian. The Bible was, therefore, introduced into the boys' department. An attempt at intimidation was made by those who had been most active in establishing the school, by assuring the young men, that while the edicts were removed, the laws against Christianity were not abrogated. They, however, seemed to be but little disconcerted,

---

[80]    JHB to JMF, Dec. 22, 1873.

and the Bible-class was continued. But popular sentiment against the innovation was intensely excited, and the only remedy left the patrons was to close the school, which was done in a summary manner. In the course of a few days a number of the pupils, both boys and girls, came again to beg for instruction. The school went on, therefore, as at the first, at the mission residence, with the best elements of what had constituted the school in the city.

Shortly after this, in connection with Mr. Bonnell, the teacher in the Government school, a Sunday School was established, consisting of young men both from the Government and private schools. For the work thus carried on, private rooms were found too strait [small and limiting]. But by the kindness of Captain Janes, a Christian gentleman teaching in Kumamoto, a commodious school-house was built in 1873 and the schools carried on there. This building was well filled with an interested school, especially on Sundays. There also the first baptisms took place, in 1873, the first native prayer-meeting was held, and the Gospel first publicly preached, in this part of the empire."[81]

Out of these efforts of the Stouts laboring alone in Nagasaki, the evangelistic work of southwestern Japan began to bear fruit, and the groundwork was laid for two of the mission schools of the Reformed Church. However, getting these schools on a firm foundation proved to be a daunting task with many setbacks along the way.

In 1874, following the completion of his teaching contract at Hirosaki, Charles Wolff and his wife moved to Nagasaki to work with the Stouts. However, Wolff's service there did not continue long. In January of 1876, Wolff resigned from the mission and became a teacher in government schools, serving as a teacher in that self-supporting capacity until 1882. The Stouts were left to labor on alone. Of Wolff's departure, Ballagh remarked, "Want of success at Nagasaki I consider no criterion of a man's fitness or usefulness in the mission field. I do not feel that Brother W. is happily constituted for a preacher. But he certainly is diligent and moderately successful as a teacher. He succeeds also in enlisting the friendship of the people....Nagasaki has a very discouraging aspect....I believe Bro. Stout is the only man who could hold on there and keep up his spirits."[82]

Like his colleagues in Yokohama, very early in his work Stout led early converts from among his students to aspire to the Christian

81    Verbeck, "History," 60-62.
82    JHB to JMF, Dec. 31, 1875.

ministry. Soon after the baptism of Segawa Asashi and Yamada Yozo in September of 1873, Stout began (by December of the same year) biblical and theological education in Nagasaki, a small class for the ministerial training of Segawa and Yamada.[83] Unfortunately, Yamada, a close friend of Segawa and a young man of deep faith who, along with Segawa, had pledged himself to Christian service, became ill and died. Despite this setback, in the spring of 1874 Stout was able to begin public preaching services in Nagasaki (in Japanese, of course), with Segawa preaching alternately. These first public services were held in the schoolroom built on the corner of Stout's residence lot. However, Stout believed the location was a problem. In order to attend, Japanese people had to come into the middle of the area of the city set aside as the foreigners' concession, which was under constant surveillance by the authorities. It was not permissible for a foreigner to obtain property in the regular Japanese community, so Stout did the next best thing.

In the summer of 1874, Stout believed that the time was right for open and active evangelistic work. He arranged for the building of a chapel (twenty-four by thirty-six feet) at the edge of the foreign settlement (rather than in the middle, where he resided), hoping to make it more accessible to the Japanese public. Unfortunately, when the building was nearly completed, on the night of August 20, 1874, a severe typhoon struck Nagasaki, almost completely destroying the new structure, along with the surrounding houses. Undeterred, reconstruction was begun immediately, and the first evangelistic services were held in the new building on the first Sunday in December. Using this new facility, Stout and Segawa began aggressive evangelistic activity. This could be called the first truly public evangelism in Nagasaki. Immediately crowds came. During the first two years of meetings there, attendance was so great that the preachers felt very excited about the prospects of the work. Audiences reached as many as two and even three hundred people. Even after the novelty of hearing a foreigner preach wore off, large numbers attended, especially on Sunday nights.

In 1875, those who had been baptized, though not yet an organized congregation, extended the ministry to a rented house in the middle of the city of Nagasaki. Rented in Segawa's name, this house in Sakaya Machi in Nagasaki served as an additional preaching place. The results were similar there. Whenever the doors were opened for meetings at these two locations, the rooms were filled with people. Frequently, during the winter, they held a series of nightly meetings for a week,

[83]    JHB to JMF, Dec. 22, 1873.

and always they had a large attendance. But despite these promising beginnings, lasting results proved to be meager indeed. Many people visited the meetings; few continued for very long.

Church organization was considered soon after the first baptisms, but Stout was waiting for the formation of a structured organization and appropriate rules for the young Japanese churches. Since these were not forthcoming, however, he decided to go ahead and organize a church in Nagasaki on the basis of a few temporary regulations. On December 23, 1876, the nucleus of believers in Nagasaki was organized as a congregation, with a membership of ten adults and two children. This first Protestant church in southwestern Japan was given the name, *Nagasaki It'chi Kyokai* ("Nagasaki Union Church"), in line with the churches in Yokohama and Tokyo.[84]

**The Kumamoto Band**

Meanwhile, by way of Secretary Ferris, Verbeck had recruited Captain L. L. Janes, a West Point graduate and former army officer and a devout Christian, to teach in Kumamoto (previously called Higo), a neighboring district to Nagasaki on the island of Kyushu.[85] Captain and Mrs. Janes arrived in Nagasaki, where they were assisted by the Stouts, and then went on to Kumamoto, where he began teaching at the new government school of occidental learning in October 1871. This was of course not a Christian school, and Kumamoto was one of the centers of agitation against the new foreign presence in Japan. Furthermore, the students had been predisposed to suspect Christianity. At first Janes cautiously avoided speaking about Christianity, but he soon won the respect and admiration of his students. After a year or two, Janes offered to teach the Bible at his home to any who wished to study it. The responses of the students varied. Many thought they should avoid contact with the book that taught what they had been told were the evil doctrines of Christianity. A few thought they should accept the invitation out of courtesy to their kind teacher. Others thought that since knowledge of the enemy is essential for victory, they should learn what they could in order to oppose Christianity intelligently and prevent its spread among the people.

At first ten students attended the Bible study, and they were soon joined by others. Before long some became convinced of the truth of Christianity. Eventually attendance at Janes's Bible class increased to

84    Verbeck, "History," 69, 80-81.
85    Leroy Lansing Janes to JMF, Sept. 11, 15, and 26, 1871.

about forty. During about three years of this Bible study, Janes never suggested that any of his students should become Christians. However, his influence upon them eventually became apparent. At dawn on the first Sunday in January of 1876, thirty-five of them climbed a hill called Hana-oka and there pledged their Christian commitment. They promised to follow Christ as their Lord, emancipating their nation by preaching the gospel, even if it meant the sacrifice of their own lives. This group nurtured by Janes came to be known as the Kumamoto Band. When their Christian commitment became known, it caused an uproar in the school and community. Although the young men were persecuted by fellow students and many became estranged from their families, about thirty of them remained firm in their commitment. In the fall of 1876 the school was abruptly closed, and in October Janes escaped from Kumamoto and took refuge with the Stouts in Nagasaki only hours before he would have been slaughtered in his bed. Janes was unable to return to his teaching in Kumamoto.

At that time Niijima Jo, in connection with the American Board, was struggling to establish a Christian college called the Doshisha, in Kyoto. Janes introduced his Kumamoto Band of Christians to Niijima, and they infused new life into Niijima's school. Most of them prepared for Christian service. Among them were Ebina Danjo, Kozaki Hiromichi, and others who became prominent Christian leaders.[86] Although L. L. Janes came to Japan through the Reformed Church Board of Foreign Missions and its missionaries, the Kumamoto Band that resulted from his witness became the nucleus for Japanese leadership in the churches that developed in relation to the missionaries of the American Board, which by this time came primarily from American Congregational churches.

**Verbeck's Later Government Service**

Exhausted from his labors in Tokyo, in 1873 Guido Verbeck took a leave of absence of six months. With the exception of the brief refuge he took in Shanghai in 1863 under threat of assassination, it was the first time he had left Japan in fourteen years. He traveled to Europe, returning to his hometown of Zeist in the Netherlands for his first visit since emigrating.[87] Following meetings in London on school business,

---

[86]    Charles W. Iglehart, *A Century of Protestant Christianity in Japan* (Tokyo: Charles E. Tuttle, 1959), 50-52; Cary, *History* II, 123-24; Drummond, *History of Christianity*, 169-70; Kuroki Goro, *Baiko Jo Gakuin Shi* (Shimonoseki, Japan: Baiko Jo Gakuin, 1934), 83, 85.

[87]    GFV to JMF, July 10, 1873.

Verbeck with the first science class of
Tokyo Imperial University, 1874

Verbeck sailed to New York. After a few days there seeing friends and mission staff, he crossed the continent by train and sailed from San Francisco for Japan on October 1.[88]

After returning to Japan, from 1873 to 1878 Verbeck worked for the Daijokwan (which functioned as the Department of State), and then for the senate, as an advisor and translator, while at the same time continuing some college teaching. To meet all these demands, he spent his evenings in serious reading and study, and his daytime hours orally advising and teaching. His son, Col. William Verbeck, said of him, "My father was an omnivorous reader with the wonderful faculty of remembering all he read. In referring to books read many years before, he could turn to the exact page of which he was in search, even associating the location on the page."[89]

During Verbeck's last year in government employment, eager to return to his first calling, he at the same time taught part time at a newly organized union theological school and preached extensively in the young Japanese churches. Exhausted, he resigned from all government responsibilities, and on July 31, 1878, sailed with his large family to California for a year of rest and recuperation.[90]

During many of the ten years of Verbeck's ministry in Nagasaki, he had received payment from the Japanese government for his teaching,

88    Griffis, *Verbeck*, 268.
89    Wyckoff, "Re. Guido Fridolin Verbeck," 334.
90    Griffis, *Verbeck*, 289, 297. Besides Emma Japonica, who died in infancy in Nagasaki, and son Guido, who died at the age of sixteen, the Verbecks had five sons and two daughters.

Tokyo Imperial University building, 1874

thus reducing the cost of his support. And during the ten years that Verbeck worked for the Japanese government in Tokyo, he received no income from the mission board. Nevertheless, Verbeck always saw himself as a missionary of Jesus Christ and of the Reformed Church in America. Despite his incredibly heavy responsibilities, he maintained his relationship with missionary colleagues, was in continuous correspondence with the board secretary, and, most importantly, never ceased to be involved in some missionary activity. A colleague said of him,

> During all the time of his government service Dr. Verbeck did direct missionary work as opportunity offered, and during the latter part of this period he was accustomed to preach at least once every Sunday and frequently two or more times. He therefore felt that, as there were open doors for missionary work and as the Government was so well supplied with specialists that his services were no longer so important as before, it was his duty to devote himself exclusively to the active work of a missionary. He rejoined his mission as a full-time, active member in 1879.[91]

---

91   Wyckoff, "Re. Guido Fridolin Verbeck," 334.

CHAPTER 4

# Foundations Laid

## Leadership for a Growing Church

In just a few years, remarkable progress was evident not only in Yokohama and Tokyo and Nagasaki, but also elsewhere. By Japanese law, foreigners, including missionaries, were still not allowed to travel freely about the country. However, additional treaty ports had been opened, such as Hyogo (now the port of Kobe) in central Japan and Niigata on the western Japan Sea coast. In addition to the treaty ports, foreigners had been given permission to reside not only in Tokyo, but also in Osaka, already a center of manufacturing and trade. Visits to other areas of the country had also become possible, but these trips required special government permits, called "passports," for travel into the interior. Despite these limitations, during the 1870s numerous additional missionaries of various denominations arrived in Japan to begin work. For several years the newcomers were primarily focused on acquiring language skills.

The more experienced missionaries, with the help of Japanese converts, at last were able to launch openly evangelistic efforts, and additional churches were organized not only in Tokyo, Yokohama, and Nagasaki, but also in Yanagawa, Kobe, Osaka, Kyoto, Hirosaki, and Ueda. Protestant missionaries of the nineteenth century did not make the mistake of the sixteenth-century Roman Catholic missionaries. From the very beginning they gave high priority to training native leadership for the Japanese churches. Happily, a remarkably large proportion of first-generation Japanese converts felt called to the Christian ministry. Some sources have indicated that the first theological training was that initiated by S. R. Brown in Yokohama in 1872. This class for theological instruction, however, grew out of the class of students that had been taught by James and Margaret Ballagh, and which had borne fruit in the organization of the first Japanese Protestant church. Already in 1871 Ballagh was training young Christian Japanese in theology and enlisting their help in conducting Christian meetings. Ballagh reported:

> Dr. Brown has offered to take all candidates for the ministry into his English classes & so their mental training in this respect will be cared for. I will continue my exegetical exercises held for the past two years, & now confined to one hour from seven to eight in the morning. This has been to afford all those supporting themselves by teaching, Biblical instruction at the only hour in the day at their disposal. Hereafter, however, I will give in addition, two hours in the P.M. to this study, or to Church History.[1]

This training had been taking place, therefore, even before the organization of the first Japanese church in 1872, but Ballagh was happy to turn over his group of future ministers to Brown for more study. In 1874 he wrote, "What I do must be by example. I was never designed for a professor's chair or a doctorate of divinity. My call and ordination is a simple one—to be an evangelist—to be Jesus Christ's man—to the heathen, that is all."[2]

Brown, a seasoned educator and already in his sixties, saw his calling differently. One of his early theological students, Oshikawa, remarked,

> He always said to us: "I believe that the best plan for the evangelization of Japan is to educate Japanese young men. Just think!" he would say; "twenty Japanese preachers educated in my school! That means twenty Browns sent out into the world. How

1    JHB to JMF, Dec. 22, 1873.
2    Ryder, *Historical Sourcebook*, 68; JHB to JMF, Sept. 24, 1874.

much better and greater a work will they perform than I could! They will understand the habits and customs of the people, and can speak in their mother tongue, while I have an imperfect knowledge of the people and of their language. For these reasons I educate young Japanese."[3]

The theological class developed by Brown met in a small room attached to Brown's home at 211 Bluff, Yokohama. This early class, which came to be called the Yokohama Band during 1874, consolidated into an informal theological school.[4] Brown reported,

> I now have eight young men who have been selected by vote of the church, in my school, studying English as a preparation for theological study. There are two more to join the school in a few days, making the number ten in all. One of them Mrs. Pruyn provided for, through friends in Albany, one is supported by myself, and the rest divide the appropriation of the Ref. Ch. Board of Missions among them, according to their several necessities. I trust that in this way I may do something to perpetuate the Church of Christ here while I have the ability to work, & when I can do no more, may be able to see a native ministry prepared to preach the Gospel when I am laid aside.[5]

Brown assumed the main responsibility for teaching these theological students while at the same time continuing his New Testament translation work, and the other Reformed missionaries in Yokohama assisted in the students' training. Ballagh not only continued his biblical studies one hour each morning but also taught Old Testament history four hours each week. Miller taught five hours each week in various subjects.[6] Even so, Brown's health began to deteriorate.

In response to the pleas of the missionaries, the Reverend James L. Amerman, a classmate of Henry Stout at New Brunswick Seminary, was recruited by the mission board to assist in theological education. He arrived with his wife, Rebecca, in 1876. Amerman began to assess the situation and assume some responsibility for coordinating training of the theological students, but he was at first necessarily engaged in Japanese language study. From September of 1876, James Ballagh

---

3   Griffis, *A Maker*, 280.
4   Ibid., 266, 268.
5   SRB to JMF, Feb. 19, 1874. The mission board subsidized five students. Others had private aid, but many of these and later students endeavored to be self-supporting.
6   JHB to JMF, Dec. 9, 1875.

continued teaching, and Edwin Miller taught the courses, "Biblical Introduction," "Harmony of the Gospels," and "Exegesis of Romans." Amerman reported that seven of the students might complete their studies in one year, and six or seven more might be finished in two years. However, there were no other candidates coming after these, and Amerman stressed the need for a preparatory course of study to ensure future candidates for the ministry.[7]

Brown continued to teach the students Greek and some biblical studies, and he was assisted in ordinary subjects by his daughter Hattie and his niece, Harriet Louise Winn, who had been living with the Browns in Japan since 1874. In the spring of 1877, in failing health and in need of rest and recuperation, Brown accepted an invitation for an extended sea voyage to points in Southeast Asia and China, revisiting scenes of his work more than thirty years before. During his absence, his daughter and niece taught the subjects they could in English and kept the English-language training going for his thirteen seminary students. The students made good progress under the instruction of the two young women, passing with fine records their examinations in English, history, geology, algebra, and geometry, after being taught all of these subjects in the English language.[8] Ten young men from Brown's early theological class—his "Yokohama Band"— were eventually ordained as ministers for the Japanese churches.[9]

Presbyterian missionaries David Thompson in Tokyo and James Hepburn in Yokohama had also been nurturing small classes of students for the ministry. The three classes in Yokohama and Tokyo were joined late in 1877 to form the Tokyo Union Theological School, a joint seminary of the Reformed, American Presbyterian, and Scottish Presbyterian Missions. Thirteen of the twenty-six students were from Brown's class, and they were said to be the most advanced. Each mission contributed a member for the new faculty, the Reformed representative being James Amerman,[10] who taught systematic theology, church history, and the biblical theology of the New Testament.[11]

[7]    James L. Amerman to JMF, July 21, 1876; E. Rothsay Miller to JMF, Feb. 10, 1877; Henry Stout to JMF, June 25, 1877.

[8]    Griffis, *A Maker*, 271, 297.

[9]    Griffis, *A Maker*, 268. Their names were Maki, Oshikawa, Honda, Ibuka, Uemura, Ito, Kawakatsu, Yamamoto, Furusawa, and Fujiu.

[10]   The other faculty membera were S. G. MacClaren (Scottish Presbyterian) and William Imbrie (American Presbyterian).

[11]   Griffis, *Verbeck*, 294; James L. Amerman to JMF, Oct. 12, 1877. Guido Verbeck, during his last year in Japanese government service, began to assist in theological education part time, teaching Christian evidences and homiletics at the newly

On the day that the Nagasaki church was organized in December of 1876, Tomegawa Ichiro was one of those baptized. Tomegawa entered into biblical and theological study and began learning to preach under Stout's tutelage along with Segawa. Like Ballagh and Brown in Yokohama, Stout had begun to train some of the first converts in Nagasaki for pastoral and evangelistic leadership. Accordingly, not only in Yokohama and Tokyo but also in Nagasaki, from very early in the life of the Protestant church in Japan, able ministers were being prepared to take responsibility for the church's ministry. When the Tokyo Union Theological School was established in 1877, Stout sent Segawa for further training for one year. He returned as a licensed preacher and became Stout's closest colleague in establishing churches and extending theological training in southwestern Japan. After Segawa's return to Nagasaki, Stout sent Tomegawa to complete his theological training at the Tokyo school as well.

Japanese converts were deeply involved in witness and evangelism from very early. Not only did these converts assist the missionaries, but as early as 1873, Ogawa Yoshiyasu and Okuno Masatsuna, the first elders at the Yokohama and Tokyo churches, began pioneer evangelistic efforts of their own. James Ballagh reported:

> Some months ago the two elders set out on a preaching tour as I informed you. They returned with joy having experienced nothing but mercy on their journey. Since then, however, threatened persecution has set in of the persons who rec'd them. This persecution has arisen from the local officials & priests of the Shinto religion there & in Yedo and Yokohama. No real violence has yet taken place but all that can be done to intimidate and annoy has been done.[12]

The courage and commitment of the first Japanese church leaders was self-evident. Both Ogawa and Okuno later became well-qualified and very effective ministers. The Japanese Christians had the advantage of being able to move about freely in the country without the special permits required for missionary travel in the interior. Despite continuing resistance official and unofficial, not only the first elders, who were in fact serving as preaching elders, but also the theological

---

formed theological school. E.R. Miller of the Reformed Church lectured once a week on church polity, and Presbyterian Thompson gave lectures in Old Testament studies. Ibuka Kajinosuke was the first Japanese to share in the teaching responsibilities.

12   JHB to JMF, Dec. 3, 1873.

Okuno Masatsuna (left)
and Ogawa Yoshiyasu

students became increasingly engaged not only in the preaching ministry at newly formed churches, but also in evangelistic preaching tours.

Foreigners were for four decades restricted in their travel away from the treaty ports and major cities, required to carry "passports" for travel into the interior. Technically, such passports could only be granted for "health" or for "scientific investigation," perhaps with the intention of preventing foreigners from traveling to the interior for trade purposes and thereby reaping great profits. The question for missionaries was whether it was proper to use passports worded in this way for missionary purposes. Furthermore, the application had to state the exact route to be taken, and the passports were often valid for only two weeks. The Foreign Department of the Japanese government refused to change the form of the documents, but it sometimes gave unofficial assurance that missionaries might use the passports for religious work in the interior. Residence of foreigners in the interior was only permitted for those employed by Japanese, usually as teachers, with written contracts approved by both local and national government officials. This led some missionaries to take teaching positions, in which cases they were often able also to carry on some religious work.[13]

---

[13]    Cary, *History* II, 129, 253.

**Church Formation and the Vagaries of Ecumenical Cooperation**

In the words of one of S. R. Brown's early seminary students,

They (the Yokohama Band) were Christians, but they belonged to no particular denomination. Indeed the existence of denominations was unknown to them. The converts of missionaries sent out by the Dutch Reformed Church, or by the Presbyterian Church, or by the American Board, all mingled together, unconscious of any ecclesiastical distinction between them. All they thought about themselves was that they were Japanese Christians.[14]

As we have seen, the second Protestant church in Japan had been organized in Tokyo in 1873 under the leadership of David Thompson. It was directly related to the first Protestant church, often called the Kaigan Church, in Yokohama, organized under the leadership of James Ballagh. Both Ballagh and Thompson shared the vision agreed to by all the missionaries in September of 1872 and enthusiastically supported by the Japanese Christians. The goal then set had been to establish a Church of Christ in Japan that was not organically related to any foreign denomination and did not emphasize denominational affiliations.

However, the Japanese Christians gradually came to realize that in America there were various denominations, and that some of the new converts were expected by the missionaries who had nurtured them to belong to or be associated with the American denomination under whose missionary they had been converted. This circumstance caused great consternation among some young converts. Confused young Japanese Christians in Yokohama and Tokyo turned to several older and highly respected Japanese Christian leaders among them, especially elders Okuno and Ogawa, for advice. They considered whether they should become members of a foreign denomination or organize their congregations into an independent church, without any sectarian character. After numerous meetings and thorough debate, the Japanese Christians decided to organize their two congregations and future additional churches into an independent Japanese church, and a constitution was formulated. The church was named *Nihon Kirisuto Kokai* ("Japan Church of Christ"), and it was composed of the original two churches in Yokohama and Tokyo, where for lack of any Japanese ordained ministers, Ballagh and Thompson still served as the pastors.[15]

---

[14]    Griffis, *A Maker*, 268-69 (quoting Fujiu in *Japan Evangelist*, Dec., 1895).
[15]    Ibid., 269.

Not only did the Japanese themselves form this independent church structure, but they also demonstrated a healthy sense of pride and self-reliance in the decision of some of the seminary students studying under Brown to decline any longer to receive the customary financial support from the missions. Many students engaged in manual labor for their income half of the day, in order to be able to study theology the other half.[16]

The original vision of 1872 of one united, evangelical, nondenominational Japanese church encouraged and supported by all the missionaries of the several denominations was never realized. Even some of the mission boards and missionaries with the most in common, who had worked together from the beginning, sometimes did not seem to grasp fully the implications of their own clearly stated vision. Presbyterian missionaries in Tokyo and Yokohama (with the exception of Thompson and E. R. Miller) apparently following instructions from America, organized a presbytery on December 30, 1873. In so doing, they violated their own rules. The constitution of the Presbyterian Church in the USA defined a presbytery as composed of the ministers and elders of the churches in a given district. However, there were at that time no Presbyterian churches in Japan, and only several Presbyterian ministers and one elder, Hepburn, who actually was an elder of the 42nd Street Presbyterian Church in New York City.

James Ballagh wrote, "I am sure if you knew fully the status of things here you would feel we had great cause to be gratefully proud of our old Catholic Dutch Church." He went on to relate the frustration all the Reformed Church missionaries felt as they were confronted with the crass denominationalism even Hepburn and some of the other Presbyterian missionaries had belatedly exhibited, following Hepburn's return from a furlough in America. Without any intimation to any of the missionaries of the other missions, and in utter contradiction of the unanimous agreement of all the missionaries only fifteen months before, these colleagues had betrayed the original vision and were insisting upon the establishment of Presbyterian churches in Japan. Hepburn proceeded to deny the use of his dispensary on Sundays for worship by the Yokohama (Kaigan) Church, of which Ballagh was pastor, and began separate "Presbyterian" services there on Sunday mornings. As to the feelings of the Japanese Christians of the two original churches in Yokohama and Tokyo in regard to this action of the Presbyterians, Ballagh reported, "They are united to a man in deploring the movement.

---

16    Ibid., 270.

They are to hold a special meeting today to announce their adherence to their original position. No missionaries are to be invited."[17]

The two Japanese churches held their special joint meeting January 16, 1874, and the clear result was communicated in a letter from Ballagh to John Ferris, secretary of the mission board.

> Their first action was to unite in a declaration of their adherence to their non-denominational platform. They drew up a paper to show to all the missionaries here stating that all who would labor for this object should be welcome by them as their teachers, etc. Their next action was to decide about receiving help for candidates for the ministry. Their decision was if receiving help was to necessitate their belonging to the denomination furnishing the support they could not accept it. But if it was given with the clear understanding it was to aid an united cause in Japan they would most gladly receive it. Eleven candidates made known their desire to the churches to be prepared for the ministry. They have consulted me on the point of church allegiance. I showed them your letter, where no mention is made of denominationalism, and they were satisfied. They have heard, however, from other sources, that is from some Presbyterians, that if our Board educated them they would have to belong to the Dutch church.
>
> I leave this question with you & the Board to decide. In view of the above facts no young men could be educated by or on a denominational basis. If they offer themselves to us we will take up 5 on the express grounds they are to belong to "the Church of Christ in Japan" to labor for its extension. If we receive instructions to the contrary from you we will have to discontinue them. This alternative I sincerely hope we may not be compelled to adopt. Yesterday, Sabbath, I thought would be a somewhat critical day with us, as the Presbyterians expected to open their chapel and begin their services. They put them at the conclusion of the native A.M. service. How well it may have been attended I do not know. The native A.M. service (of the Yokohama Church) was large. The P.M. service in the theatre at 4 P.M. was unexpectedly so from the presence of many strangers....
>
> Another important decision of the native churches at their recent meeting was that the elder of the Yokohama church could not give Dr. Hepburn more than 1/2 of his time & that, if possible he should give the whole of his time to labor for the

[17]   JHB to JMF, Jan. 16, 1874.

(already organized Yokohama) church. They also decided it was important he should remove now from the Drs. premises (where he had been boarding) to prevent misunderstandings arising in the future. In respect to preaching by the elder for the Dr. to his patients assembling in the dispensary it would only be done on the condition that converts should be free to join the union native church.

Thus the Lord is caring for his own work, & this attempt we feel assured will only lead to build up His cause stronger & stronger in Japan. The native brethren all feel very much broken in spirit & yet most hopeful & thankful to God for His great deliverance, in which we most heartily & gratefully join them.[18]

The integrity and self-reliance of these first two Japanese congregations was self-evident and highly commendable. Furthermore, the disappointment of the Reformed missionaries in some of their Presbyterian colleagues, and their own conviction in support of a nondenominational, evangelical, and independent Japanese church was also apparent. The position of the Reformed missionaries in support of the union movement whereby all Japanese Protestant churches being formed should be part of one Japanese Christian church without denominational identity received firm support from Ferris and the Reformed Church's mission board, for which the missionaries were grateful. They believed that the Reformed Church was setting a good example for other missions.[19] This was notwithstanding the fact that, not only among American Presbyterians but also in the Reformed Church in America, there was at that time a rising tide of denominationalism.

In any case, during the next three or four years all three new congregations organized under the leadership of missionaries of the Presbyterian Mission in Japan were brought under the care of this presbytery in Japan of the Presbyterian Church in the United States of America, instead of being organically related to the first two churches in Yokohama and Tokyo.[20] It seems that the Presbyterian Church in the USA was especially emphatic about its denominational identity at this time, and that most of its missionaries in Japan were especially influenced by one of their number, the Reverend C. Carrothers, an

---

[18]  JHB to JMF, Jan. 19, 1874.
[19]  JHB to JMF, Apr. 13, 1874.
[20]  Verbeck, "History," 60, 67. The three congregations were Sumiyoshi-cho in Yokohama (1874, begun by Hepburn, later called Shiloh Church), the Choro Church at Tokyo (1874), and the Hoden Church east of Tokyo (1876).

extremely partisan Presbyterian. As a result they briefly departed from the ecumenical position taken jointly by all the missionaries in Japan in 1872 and embraced by the first Japanese Christians. Subsequently all the Presbyterians except Carrothers once again showed support for the union movement,[21] and fortunately at least the rift between the Reformed and Presbyterian missionaries was gradually resolved amicably.

On April 7, 1874, a committee of the Presbyterian Mission (Thompson, Loomis, and Green) reportedly approached the Reformed and American Board (Congregational) missions with regard to a union in mission work. This committee later reported that no definite result could be reached. However, the Annual Meeting of the Congregational Mission, meeting in Kobe May 24, 1874, passed the following action:

> "Resolved, That we as a mission declare that we are unequivocally in favor of Union; that we have never for a moment wavered from our unanimous desire for union as expressed at the Convention in Yokohama in September, 1872, and that we are organizing and shall continue to organize our churches on the basis adopted at that Convention." And an expression of what they considered a specific church structure made on the basis of the 1872 agreement was drawn up. In July of the same year they reiterated the action of the annual meeting and sent copies of the same to the Presbyterian, Reformed, and Scottish Presbyterian Missions.[22]

However, to the great surprise of the church members and missionaries in Yokohama and Tokyo, when the first churches related to the Congregational Mission were organized in Kobe and Osaka in 1874, they adopted different rules for church government. They were obviously influenced by the congregational principle that each congregation was completely autonomous, while the first churches in Yokohama and Tokyo were influenced by the presbyterian principle that some authority, and the status of church, is recognized in a classis or presbytery or synod. The original vision of a full union of all the Protestant churches in Japan resulting from the pioneer work of the various missionaries was thus undermined by the different understandings on the part of the missionaries as to what constituted a church. These differences proved to be irreconcilable. When this reality was grasped, the several churches growing out of the work of

---

[21] JHB to JMF, Apr. 13, 1874.
[22] Verbeck, "History," 85-86.

the Reformed Church missionaries, namely those in Yokohama, Tokyo, Ueda, and Nagasaki on the one hand, and the several churches that had been established by the Presbyterian missionaries and organized as a separate presbytery on the other, began to consider forming one organization. The Japanese church leaders clearly saw themselves as a group of Japanese Christian churches and not as branches of Western denominations.

Looking back in 1913 upon the realities they had experienced, Japanese Christians expressed their lament. "It was the hope and intention of both missionaries and Japanese Christians at that time that the church to be built up in this land should be non-sectarian, and should be one, not only in spirit and name, but also in faith and organization. It was a distinct disappointment to many that in later years this high ideal failed of accomplishment."[23] In the later decades of the nineteenth century, the ideal of one evangelical and ecumenical church for Japan embraced by the early Japanese Protestant Christians was undermined, misinterpreted, dishonored, rejected, or ignored successively by Congregationalists, Episcopalians, Baptists, Methodists, Lutherans, and others. Consequently, as the Church of Christ in Japan developed, its mission partners were at first three, and eventually six Reformed and Presbyterian Japan missions.

To this end, on June 21, 1876, negotiations between the Presbyterian Japan Mission (of the Presbyterian Church in the United States of America) and the Reformed Japan Mission (of the Reformed Church in America) bore positive results. They also invited the United Presbyterian Church of Scotland Japan Mission, which had begun work in Japan in 1874, to join them. The "Council of the Three Missions" was formed as a basis for their cooperation.[24] Later, three other Japan missions joined this cooperative arrangement, those of the Presbyterian Church in the United States (Southern Presbyterian) in 1885, the Reformed Church in the United States (German Reformed) in 1886, and the Cumberland Presbyterian Church in 1889.[25] Consequently, the partners of the Japanese churches that had come into being with the intent of becoming *the* evangelical and ecumenical church of Japan were actually only the six Reformed and Presbyterian missions.

At the time of the formation of the Council of the Three Missions, the three congregations under the care of the Presbyterian Mission had already been provided with a full set of church government rules

23    Ryder, *Historical Soucebook*, 55 (quoting *Handbook of the Church of Christ in Japan*), 91.
24    Verbeck, "History," 86-87.
25    Ryder, *Historical Soucebook*, 55.

translated from the "Form of Government of the Presbyterian Church in America." Meanwhile, the two original Japanese churches in Yokohama and Tokyo had been revising their original simple rules of government. A committee of elders met with E. R. Miller in an effort to draft rules and regulations to govern church structures. They adopted language from the Japanese educational system, i.e., *shokai* (for consistory), *chukai* (for classis or presbytery), and *daikai* (for synod). Ballagh remarked, "In the vernacular they are short names and so preferable to any names we could give them."[26] During the following year, rules of church government were worked out cooperatively based on those used by the home churches represented by the Council of the Three Missions, with alterations, additions, and omissions to adapt them to the situation of the churches in Japan, and these rules were translated into Japanese. The three missions received the full consent of their respective mission boards for the formulation of the union church, and the rules for its establishment and governance were submitted for approval to the Japanese churches. Its narrowing perspective, as well as its ecumenical spirit, were apparent in the opening words of the Rules of Government adopted by the newly structured Japanese church at its fall meeting in 1876 (English translation of original).

> The Government of the Church and the Several Assemblies.
>
> It is necessary that there should be an orderly government established in the Church. We believe it is in accordance with Scripture and eminently proper that the government of the Church be by means of Great, Middle, and Little Assemblies (*Daikai, Chukai, and Shokai,* i.e., Synod, Classis, and Elders Meetings, a presbyterian form of church government). Nevertheless believers in Christ who do not hold these views and have not the same form of government are to be beloved and held as in fellowship with us.[27]

Since the missionary partners all not only had experience in a presbyterial form of church government but were Reformed in theology, and since the missionaries wielded considerable influence at this formative stage, it is perhaps not surprising that the standards of doctrine agreed upon for the Japanese church being formed were the Westminster Shorter Catechism, the Heidelberg Catechism, the Westminster Confession of Faith, and the Canons of the Synod of Dort. These doctrinal standards were each adopted by the Japanese

---

[26]   JHB to JMF, March 25, 1876.
[27]   Archives of the RCA.

churches and were to be translated into Japanese. Stout, of Nagasaki Station, made the initial translation of the Heidelberg Catechism into Japanese. Brown and Miller revised this translation and prepared for its publication.

From the early days of the work in Japan, sacred music was an issue. Japanese traditional musical instruments and singing were generally associated with either Shintoism or Buddhism and deemed by Japanese Christians inappropriate or unadaptable to Christianity. The missionaries had made an effort to introduce group hymn singing, but this had presented a decided challenge, since there was nothing really comparable in Japanese culture. Samuel Brown, a gifted musician himself and one of the most knowledgable concerning the Japanese language, after nineteen years in Japan relayed the following insights.

> The Chiukwai [*Chukai*, or classis] at its spring session in Tokio appointed me & two Japanese as a committee to prepare a hymnbook for use in the native churches. Hitherto the hymn books used have been gotten up by various missionaries on their own responsibility, and it is a singular fact that those who have been the shortest time in the country, & have therefore but a very limited knowledge of the language have frequently tried to make themselves useful by writing hymns. The consequence is that many, indeed most of the hymns now in use, are unidiomatic in expression and unpoetical in structure. There is no such thing as rhyme in Japanese poetry, but our poetasters [would be poets] have thought it necessary to introduce rhyme into their hymns, in order to do which they have frequently inserted a monosyllabic word that is meaningless at the end of the lines. Such syllables are used solely to rhyme with others that precede them, and give the lines in which they stand the required number of syllables for certain meters. The hymns we have are largely encumbered with these words, & besides, to a Japanese ear, if intelligible they are little more than the most prosaic prose. It is no small undertaking to prepare a hymn book that shall be not only free from these blemishes, but accord with the Japanese poetic taste & be fitted to give expression to the emotions and desires of a Christian heart. For myself, I do not expect to be able to write Japanese hymns, though I can probably be serviceable to my native friends in the committee in helping them to compose hymns of a devotional spirit, & arranging or composing tunes for them. Having little time that I can devote to this work, I have, in the past year

with my native assistant's help, translated a few Psalms, & set them to chants, and five or six hymns, from themes furnished in the "Hymns of the Church." These have been printed in... "Yorokobashiki Otodzure," [*Glad Tidings*] from month to month, & I have taught my Sunday school scholars to sing the hymns. In this way I hope in time to be able to get a collection of hymns & tunes & chants, that shall be an improvement on those now in use in the churches. When it is done, it must be mainly a collection of new hymns, for in the present state of Japanese hymnology mere compilation is impossible. In everything missionaries do here, we are at work on the beginnings of things. Such work makes little show, but I trust those who come after us will find that we have prepared in some measure the way for their future success.[28]

The position of the foreign missionary in the new church structure was an important issue to be resolved. Some missionaries wished to have no vote, but simply to sit as observers and advisors. When the Japanese churches adopted the rules, following a motion by one of the Japanese elders, it was decided that all missionaries, whether ordained or not, would be recognized as members of the *chukai* by virtue of the office of missionary. However, the Japan missions (the official organizations on the field of the missionaries of each denomination) were given neither voice nor place in the governmental structures of the Japanese church.

Another issue to be resolved was the matter of a name for the united church. Finally, agreeing to derive the name from the nature of their formation into one church, the name decided upon by the Japanese churches was *Nippon Kirisuto It'chi Kyokai* (United Church of Christ in Japan). The first meeting, at which this union was consummated, was held in Yokohama October 3, 1877. Present were eight or nine elders representing the churches and twelve missionaries of the three cooperating missions. The church was formed with nine congregations, with a total membership of 623, among whom were twenty-five students studying for the ministry.[29] At this inaugural assembly of the United Church of Christ in Japan, from among those who had been studying for the ministry and serving as elders, the first three Japanese candidates were ordained.[30] It was also in October of 1877 that the

---

[28]  SRB to JMF, Dec. 31, 1879.

[29]  Verbeck, "History," 87-88; Yanagita, *Short History*, 40; Ryder, *Historical Sourcebook*, 55. The nine congregations were Kaigan Church (Yokohama), Shinsakae Church (Tokyo), Tsukiji Church (Tokyo), Sumiyoshi-cho Church (Yokohama), Hoden Church (Shimosa), Ueda Church (Shinano), Shinagawa Church (Tokyo), Omori Church (Shimosa), and Nagasaki Church.

[30]  Ogawa Yoshiyasu, Okuno Masatsuna, and Toda Tada-atsu.

Tokyo Union Theological School was established by the Council of the Three Missions.

Already in these formative stages of the United Church and of theological education in Japan, different perspectives were apparent. Should the missionaries maintain authority and control over theological education, or should the program of theological education be under the jurisdiction of the newly organized Japanese church organization, the *chukai*? How willing would the missionaries be to truly recognize the independence of the Japanese Christians? Ballagh wrote,

> Theological education has been taken up by the three Missions, and at present is to be independent of the *chukai*. Preparatory schools are also to be independent of the same. This is to be regretted, since the one want of the Christian Church in Japan is a Common Christian Educational Institution. This to some of us as well as to many of the native brethren was the chief if not the sole cause for desiring the union of the churches. Here was a point in common where combined action would lead to the greatest economy of forces & greatest influence for good. We do not despair of the step being yet taken, but an effort will be required in bringing it about involving not a little labor on the part of those who would see it accomplished.[31]

The United Church was comprised, as has been stated, only of churches organized through the missionaries of the Reformed and Presbyterian missions. The missionaries of other denominations gradually formed their separate Episcopal, Congregational, Baptist, Methodist, and other denominational churches in Japan. However, among the Japanese Christians there was for some time no real sense of denominational identity. This is exemplified by the fact that entirely apart from any foreign influence a kind of movement had begun, and in Tokyo, Yokohama, Osaka, Nagasaki, and perhaps other places, Japanese Christians of all denominational connections had begun to gather monthly for what they called *shinbokkai*, meetings for the cultivation of Christian fellowship. Further, they organized and held a *Daishinbokkai*, or Great Fellowship Meeting, in Tokyo for three days, beginning July 15, 1878. It encompassed Japanese Christians from thirteen localities, representing nearly all organized congregations from throughout Japan. Although entirely planned and carried out by the Japanese Christians, they invited one missionary speaker for each day. This *Daishinbokkai*

---

[31]    JHB to JMF, Oct. 11, 1877.

demonstrated not only the evangelical and ecumenical spirit of the first Japanese Christians, but also their considerable organizational ability. Amerman said, "This meeting was in spirit if not in name an Evangelical Alliance of the Christians of Japan."[32]

The Reformed Church missionaries of the pioneer period, and no doubt virtually all of the Protestant missionaries of this era, had been profoundly influenced by the evangelical piety of their day. Their faith embraced the conservative evangelical convictions regarding the Trinity and the divinity of Christ, the centrality of the cross and the resurrection, and a high view of scripture. However, it also included a strong Sabbatarian strain, an emphasis upon the strict observance of Sunday as the Sabbath. The correspondence of Ballagh, Miller, and Amerman all contain repeated references to Japanese believers whose requests for baptism as Christians were denied or postponed because of inability or unwillingness to "observe the Sabbath." Gainful employment or conducting one's business on Sunday was deemed unacceptable for a Christian. This conviction reflected one of the basic emphases of the Evangelical Alliance movement that had spread from England and Europe to America, and it would prove to impede the spread of Christianity and its image in Japan.

### Expansion of Evangelistic Outreach—Tokyo/Yokohama Station

Already in 1873, though there were as yet no ordained Japanese ministers, as elders, Ogawa and Okuno had begun evangelistic work at their own initiative. Others in training for the ministry were also very active in evangelism. When in July of 1874 Brown discontinued theological classes for a two months' vacation, Ballagh reported, "I have been organizing as many of the young men that are left into a band of evangelists—to go and herald the Gospel in neighboring provinces." Twelve candidates offered to go out. The church selected five of them to support, and the others were given permission to go out as representatives of the church, but at their own expense. It was decided that the seven less experienced should accompany the five selected. Consequently, already in the summer of 1874 five of the theological students from Brown's class[33] took responsibility for evangelistic efforts. In this way, early outreach into outlying areas away from the port cities where the foreign missionaries were required to live was also in large part accomplished by Japanese Christians.[34]

---

[32]  JLA to JMF, July 29, 1878.
[33]  Shinozaki, Oshikawa, Ikeda, Honda, and Amenomori.
[34]  JHB to JMF, July 18 and Sept. 24, 1874; Yanagita, *Short History*, 40.

In both 1874 and 1875, James Ballagh followed up the witness of the theological students, who had encountered some opposition instigated by Shinto priests, with his own evangelistic tours to the Hakone area and even out onto the Izu Peninsula. However, he was able to travel only part way onto the peninsula before being stopped by government authorities. They informed him that his passport would only allow going that far. Furthermore, he could only go to the region once a year. Even so, the trips by Ballagh resulted in groups of seekers and several requests for baptism.

This period was, however, a time of deep personal trial for James Ballagh. On April 1, 1874, Margaret Ballagh, who was expecting their fourth child, had returned to America with the children. Her physician, Dr. Simmons, "gave it as his opinion that it was necessary for her to go to America or somewhere for a change soon." She left rather suddenly when favorable travel arrangements materialized, including lower travel costs and a young woman returning to America who could help her with the children en route.[35] But not only was James Ballagh left to labor on alone without his family, he was clearly under a cloud.

Sometime after Margaret's departure, the Reformed board sent a letter to Ballagh ordering his recall from the field and demanding that he report to the office in New York by June of 1875, in effect firing him. On February 12, 1875, Brown wrote to the board in Ballagh's defense. He argued that there must be some misunderstanding, because although there had been questions as to Ballagh's physical and mental health eighteen months previously, after country touring, etc., he was now in fine health. Furthermore, his work was essential for the future of the Japan mission.[36] Margaret Ballagh also wrote to Secretary Ferris. She had been away from Japan and her husband for eight months and reported that her health was restored. She also requested reconsideration of the mission board's recall of her husband.[37]

James Hepburn, MD, of the Presbyterian Mission, had obviously been consulted regarding Ballagh. It is clear from his letter that it had been intimated to him that the board had judged James Ballagh to be insane, which Hepburn insisted was not the case. Hepburn described Ballagh's nature or personality:

> (He is) constitutionally a man of highly nervous temperament, very easily excited and carried beyond the bounds of moderation,

---

[35]    JHB to JMF, Apr. 13, 1874.
[36]    SRB to JMF, Feb. 12, 1875.
[37]    Margaret Ballagh to JMF, Feb. 12, 1875.

when he is led to say and do things that cooler and less excitable people are surprised at, and cannot help deprecate....I regard Mr. Ballagh as a truly Christian man with kind and Christian impulses, but very deficient in calm, sound judgment. He is unquiet, restless and mostly driving at something new and extravagant, and it has often seemed to me a great pity that such a man should have such an influence in directing the first sprouting of Christian life in this country. But there is no denying that he has, and in so doing, has entailed trouble upon the church of which he is now pastor.

Hepburn added that Ballagh's health was good, much better than two or three years ago.[38] Margaret Ballagh appears to have remained in the United States through the end of 1875, but Ballagh's letter of March 22 and the mission's annual report of March 25, 1876, indicate that Margaret was by then back in Japan.

Despite these personal troubles and any shortcomings James Ballagh may have had, the Yokohama (Kaigan) Church prospered during the six years of Ballagh's ministry as its pastor, accompanied as it was by the gifted and energetic lay leadership and witness of many Japanese Christians, as well as the work of the other missionaries in Yokohama. Prior to the formal organization of the church on March 10, 1872, there had been a nucleus of four baptized Christians. Baptisms at this church during the next four years were as follows: 1872 = 21, 1873 = 36, 1874 = 57, and 1875 = 56, a total of 154 baptisms. During that time 2 people were received from other churches, 28 were dismissed to other churches, and 2 died, and the membership on March 10, 1876, was 136. This was a remarkable record, as baptism was not taken lightly. Ballagh reported on the church's situation as of March 1876.

> It is the rule of the church officers to baptize none, unless urgent cases, under three months from their application. This is to afford time for their trial and further instruction. It is offence at the delay that has turned away some. The additions to the church membership, all adults, are more in the aggregate than I was prepared to expect, and represents the results of the labors of the Woman's Union Mission, and the lady and other missionary laborers of our Mission at this place....
>
> In systematic administration of the church affairs there has been very marked advance made the past year. The eldership

---

[38]    James C. Hepburn to JMF, Feb. 17, 1875.

has been increased from one elder to five, and two new deacons have been added. All of them are competent men able to teach as well as to govern and administer the charities and consolation of the Gospel. In church work they take a responsible part. They conduct the Wednesday evening prayer meetings and instruct the four companies or class-meetings of the church members. On Sabbath P.M. they take turns in preaching at Kanagawa, and at the evening meeting at the Woman's Union Mission School Room. One of them also holds Sabbath supplementary services at the Ferris Seminary (girls' school). The Sabbath A.M. church service falls to me and a P.M. service for inquirers.

The Yokohama church also had a Sunday school, with a Japanese superintendent, assisted by Mrs. Ballagh and several Japanese teachers, two or three of whom also started a branch Sunday school at Kanagawa. Each of these endeavors had an attendance of about twenty pupils. At each of these Sunday schools, and also at another held at the Ferris Seminary, a Japanese catechism based on the Westminster Shorter Catechism was used in nurturing Christian faith. Elizabeth Brown and Margaret Ballagh also taught in the Sunday school at the foreigners' Yokohama Union Church. In this way, the missionary wives, although classified as assistant missionaries, participated actively in the work[39]

The Japanese evangelists, from before any of them were ordained ministers, worked both independently and in tandem with the missionaries to reach out beyond their churches. The early theological students also were especially active in evangelistic work. Verbeck told of Miller's 1876 evangelistic tour, working in partnership with Japanese lay evangelists and theological students.

Late in the year a church was organized at Uyeda [Ueda] in Shinshiu, situated about 115 miles to the N.W. from Tokiyo. Mr. Miller gave an interesting account of the origin of the church at the time, from which the following facts are gleaned. Having learned that a deep interest in Christianity had spontaneously— as far as any missionary agencies were concerned—sprung up at Uyeda and that a number of enquirers were anxiously looking for the visit of a foreign missionary, Mr. and Mrs. Miller set out, early in August, for the foot of the great smoking volcano Asama

---

[39]    JHB to JMF, March 22 and 25, 1876.

Yama, near which the town lies in a valley, intensely hot at that time of the year. They were heartily welcomed on their arrival by those who had been awakened, chiefly through the faithful labors of Mr. Suzuki, a member of the Yokohama Church, on his visit there in the summer of 1875, and of Mr. Inagaki, then a resident of the place....Mr. Miller, with the help of Mr. Maki Shigeto, who had accompanied him from Yokohama, at once set to work, opening Sunday preaching services, a Sunday-school, and two daily meetings, while Mrs. Miller, in the intervals of these, had several meetings with the women. The daily and Sunday meetings were attended by from 50 to 100 attentive hearers. On his second and last Sunday, Mr. Miller baptized 10 men, two of them men in middle life and the remainder young men, 4 widows past middle age, and 1 young girl,—in all 15....I am confident that none of those whom I baptized had ever heard a foreigner preach before I went there. There were in Uyeda but three baptized Christians....Before the close of the year, Mr. Ballagh, passing through Uyeda on a return trip from Niigata, baptized a similar company of believers, and with these and the former company of 18, organized a church. Mr. Maki Shigeto eventually became the pastor of the Uyeda Church, and continued to labor there and in the neighborhood for several years.[40]

As this example illustrates, even before any could be licensed or ordained as pastors, witness by Japanese Christians had helped widen the scope of evangelistic activity. Systematic evangelistic work, sometimes but not always under the guidance of the missionaries, was initiated by the native Christians and theological students already in 1875. Outreach activity of the Reformed Church missionaries and theological students working together continued to result in the establishment of numerous preaching stations, and not long after in organized churches in several cities and towns remote from the treaty ports.[41]

Several of Brown's students, members of the Yokohama Band, were prominent in the early outreach activity of the 1870s. As we have seen, Inagaki Akira was instrumental in the beginning of the church at Ueda, and Maki Shigeto became its first pastor. One of the students, Amenomori Nobushige, was an example of the courage of these budding evangelists, boldly preaching at Niigata, despite opposition from Buddhist priests and a near riot.[42] Some members of Brown's

---

[40]   Verbeck, "History," 79-80.
[41]   Ibid., 72.
[42]   JHB to JMF, Dec. 9, 1875.

Yokohama Band also provided key leadership in the work of the Japan missions of other denominations.

Another early convert nurtured by Reformed missionaries who was active in evangelism is Oshikawa Masayoshi. A member of the Yokohama Church and a student in Brown's theological class, he was present at a prayer meeting at which Ballagh prayed that an evangelist be provided for the work begun in Niigata, where Amenomori had preached amid great opposition. Oshikawa felt he was called to that ministry, volunteered, and was commissioned by the Yokohama Church to begin work in Niigata.[43] En route there, Oshikawa spent several days in Nagano, where he taught an interested group. As a result, a representative of this group went to Yokohama to ask the church there to send someone to teach them. Another elder of the Yokohama Church and member of Brown's Yokohama Band, Shinozaki Keinosuke, responded to that call, and the result was the opening of work and eventual forming of a church at Nagano.

Oshikawa Masayoshi walked thirteen days and reached Niigata January 2, 1876. He was instrumental in establishing a church there, the first one on the west coast of Japan. He served the Niigata church for four years. During that time he also made exploratory tours to Yamagata, Yonezawa, and Sendai, preaching and distributing Bible portions. After three successive great fires destroyed nine thousand houses—most of the city of Niigata—leaving him without a meeting place and a community totally distracted by rebuilding, he moved his base of evangelistic operations to Sendai.[44] He later became closely associated with the German Reformed Japan Mission.

Another member of the Yokohama Band, Honda Yoichi, organized a church in Hirosaki, far to the north, where Charles Wolff had taught in a government school for a year and held Bible study classes. Wolff's successor in that English teaching position was a Methodist missionary, John Ing. Honda, who had been ordained by the Yokohama Church as an elder, went to Hirosaki as an evangelist, supported financially by the Yokohama Church. The newly formed Hirosaki Church applied to the Yokohama and Tokyo churches to be organized and accepted as a congregation associated with the nondenominational union movement. However, Hirosaki Church, influenced by Ing, suddenly switched its affiliation and became related to the Japanese Methodist Church. As a result, Honda Yoichi became a prominent leader and eventual bishop in the Japan Methodist Church.[45]

43    Bartholomew, *Won By Prayer*, 70-71.
44    Ibid., 76.
45    ERM to JMF, June 9, 1877; Griffis, *A Maker*, 278-79.

Ballagh's temporary role as pastor of the Yokohama Church continued for six years, until April 20, 1878, when he was able to turn that responsibility over to Inagaki Akira, who was later ordained and formally installed as pastor April 20, 1879.[46] However, long before turning the pastorate over to Inagaki, Ballagh had begun to implement his calling as an itinerant evangelist. Although limited by government restrictions, he traveled widely throughout central Japan, witnessing and preaching to all who could be persuaded to listen. When his itinerating led to the formation of a nucleus of seekers or believers, a Japanese theological student or evangelist might be sent to nurture the group. In such cases, Ballagh would follow up with visits to assist and encourage. Sometimes the initiative for beginning a new preaching station was taken by Japanese evangelists. In these cases, too, Ballagh would visit to assist and encourage. The following episodes, shared by his grandson, illustrate Ballagh at work.

> It was the power of prayer...that won a high naval officer in Yokosuka for Christ. No hotel was allowed to take foreigners in except in the four treaty ports; so Dr. Ballagh would wait under the eaves of a hotel near the wharf in Yokosuka for the late night sailboat to get back to Yokohama. One cold January night when mixed snow and rain was falling, this naval officer looked out to see this foreigner shivering and eating his lunch under the eaves. Against the advice of his wife, who warned against "foreign devils," he invited him in out of the cold to wait for the boat.
>
> Each week thereafter, Dr. Ballagh waited in that home and ate his sandwiches. The officer had made a condition that nothing was to be said about Christianity, a condition Dr. Ballagh had accepted and scrupulously observed. However, before eating he invariably offered thanks with bowed head in silent prayer. This finally brought a question from his host, whereupon Dr. Ballagh warned that to answer would involve an explanation of Christianity. The officer told him to go ahead and explain; he did so and this finally resulted in the officer's conversion and baptism and consequent expulsion from the navy for his faith.
>
> Dr. Ballagh's intense passion for souls caused him to range, on foot, far and wide all over Japan from Tokyo to Nagoya, on both coasts and down the central part of Japan on the old "Naka Sendo" Central Highway. Crossing the central range north of Toyohashi at Tsugu, on the road from Iida, he climbed the top

---

[46]  JLA to JMF, Apr. 19, 1879.

of the pass from which he could look into Nagano, Aichi, and Gifu Prefectures and there prayed earnestly for the winning of central Japan for Christ. This happened not once, but on several occasions.

He walked all the way from Yokohama to Nagoya on three different occasions for a double purpose. The first was to preach Christ to those he met who would stop and listen and to those going in his direction as they walked along. The second purpose was to donate the rail fare thus saved to the purchase of a lot for the group in Seto, ten miles out of Nagoya, which he had started. This story was told the people of Seto Church by one of the original group on the occasion of the 50th anniversary of the church in May 1950. Though the speaker was concerned with only the second part, he could have added that there are churches all along the way now where Dr. Ballagh stopped—at Odawara, Gotemba, Mishima, and Okazaki, to mention but a few.

The church at Mishima began when a lantern-maker by the name of Hambei was impressed by the earnestness of Dr. Ballagh. No one would dare come to hear the foreigner who hung a lantern at the *torii* [shrine entrance gate] in front of the great Mishima Jinja shrine and would preach in a loud voice to passersby on the main highway. From time to time a rock would come flying out from the dark, but Dr. Ballagh would continue unperturbed.

Since the hotel would not admit him, he would sleep on the ground, a stranger who had nowhere to lay his head! This earnestness and devotion caused the lantern-maker, Hambei San, to dare custom and neighbors to come seeking the answer. And Dr. Ballagh caught another fish for the Master. Through the lantern-maker, Date Kakutaro also became a Christian, and was later the pastor of Mishima Church.[47]

Similarly, after their application, acceptance, and transfer to the Reformed Church Mission in July 1875,[48] the Millers also became involved in evangelistic work in the interior of the country. For several years, until their first furlough in 1879, the Millers lived in Yokohama, where Mary retained responsibility at Ferris Girls' School. Nevertheless, E. R. and Mary Miller gradually became associated with the expansion of evangelistic outreach and the organization and nurture of churches in the region to the northwest and north of Tokyo.

47    J. A. McAlpine, "The Rev. James Hamilton Ballagh, D.D.," *Japan Christian Quarterly* (April, 1955), 169-70.
48    ERM to JMF, Feb. 25 and Oct. 26, 1875.

On April 24, 1878, the Millers set out on a tour to visit the Ueda region, where E.R. had presided over the organization of the Ueda Church in December of 1876. His twenty-seven-page letter reporting on the tour portrays vividly this early travel and ministry in support of the pioneer Japanese evangelists who served in the interior of the country. Miller humorously described the trip as a picnic, with lots of baggage. They took along not only much of their food and camping utensils, but also a Japanese servant as a cook. Miller remarked,

> Indeed traveling in Japan is only a picnic indefinitely extended, what would be exceedingly pleasant for a day or two soon becomes tiresome for you must remember that this picnicing [*sic*] extends not only to the eating but to the living and sleeping also, there being no chairs, tables, or bedsteads, so that we not only have to "hang up our hats on the floor," but ourselves also, disposing of our awkward limbs as best we can, not having the power to sit on them quietly for hours together as the Japanese do.

After going from Yokohama to Tokyo, where they stayed with foreign friends, the Millers departed at 5:00 A.M. by a kind of stagecoach, arriving some sixty miles north in Takasaki twelve hours later. There they met the Reverend Okuno, a recently ordained Japanese minister, and theological student Amenomori, both related to the Reformed Mission, who had begun work in that place. Miller held a preaching service that evening at the home of one of the five new converts there, attended by about fifty people. Miller noted, "While on this trip I found that all the evening meetings were very late,...generally not till after nine, and continuing indefinitely till the preacher was tired out, or if he tired out too soon, till two preachers were tired out."

The next day the Millers walked about eight miles to Annaka. There a church of thirty members had been organized by Niijima Jo of the American Board Mission. The believers in Annaka had never heard a foreigner preach and asked Miller to do so. About 100 attended an afternoon meeting, and 150 or more came to the evening meeting, many of these people hearing the gospel for the first time.

The following day the Millers proceeded on toward their destination, walking to a village at the foot of the mountains. There they hired *jinrikisha* pulled by two men to take them up the narrow, winding mountain road called the Usui-toge, past the smoking Mount Asama volcano to the village of Karuizawa, where they spent the night. Early the next morning they set out again by *jinrikisha*, covering the thirty miles to Ueda and arriving on Saturday afternoon. Despite pouring rain and mud, Pastor Maki and some of the Christians came out to meet them a mile or so before they reached the town. At Ueda they stayed at lodgings belonging to one of the believers, many of whom visited the lodging place that evening to welcome them.

Maki, a licensed preacher but not yet ordained, was very tired from his heavy work load and was pleased to have the missionary visit and assist in his ministry. He presented Miller with his usual schedule of meetings and urged Miller to undertake all or as much of it as he could during the several weeks of his visit. The work schedule was as follows: Sunday (at the church): 8 A.M. Bible Class in John; 9 A.M. Morning Preaching Service; 1 P.M. Bible Question Class in Acts; 2 P.M. Sunday School; 8 P.M. Evening Preaching Service. Wednesday: 8:30 P.M. Preaching Service held in the town. Thursday: 8:30 P.M. Old Testament Bible Class at Maki's house. Friday: 10 A.M. Preaching Service at Tanaka, a village seven miles from Ueda, held at a believer's home. Saturday: 9 P.M. Preaching Service at Yazawa, a village four miles from Ueda. In addition to this schedule, Maki, who had learned English from the missionaries, taught English classes daily to earn part of his own support. During his visit of several weeks, the missionary took over part, and, from the second week, after Mary Miller returned to Yokohama for her own teaching responsibilities at Ferris, all of this preaching schedule. However, it was the long hard work and courageous witness of Maki that was bearing fruit at Ueda and the surrounding region. The following quotations from Miller's letter give a glimpse into the challenges of this life and ministry.

> The second Sunday I was at Ueda, being the first Sabbath of the month, we celebrated the Lord's Supper and so the Thursday before had an examination of the candidates Mr. Maki had been instructing preparatory to baptism. There were five women and five men, three others being detained, one on account of sickness and two on account of a school examination. Of the ten who were examined it was thought best to postpone the baptism of two of the men. Some of the women were so extremely timid that they could hardly summon up courage to answer the questions put to them. Everything was done to put them at their ease, but the wife of one of the elders was so very diffident that we were obliged to put off the examination for a day or two and see her at her own house where she was more comfortable though still embarrassed.
>
> The examinations were probably more rigid and exacting than is generally the case at home, but on the other hand they

serve to prevent after trouble and sorrow to the church. I was greatly aided by the native elders, on whose judgment of Japanese character I relied much more than on my own opinions.

On the Sabbath I baptized the five women and three men whose examinations had been approved, and for the second time since the church was organized, we celebrated the Lord's Supper.... Two of the men are from Yazawa, the village where service is held on Saturday evening. Of one of these I heard the following interesting account.

His wife and the whole family are extremely opposed to his Christianity and have done their utmost to make him give it up. This he refused, so that finally all the family and relations came together to consult about it, and the father was so angry that he said he would turn him out of doors without a penny. To this the son replied that though he would be very sorry if they did so, yet as there was no help for it he would have to submit [accept the fact of being disowned]. One of the relations then suggested that as he had a wife it would be well to consult her as to whether she was willing to go with her husband should he be turned out of the father's home. So they called her and on putting the question to her, she replied, like a true wife, that when she came to that home it was to be the wife of Nochigoro, and should he leave, whether with money or without, she would certainly go with him. They were all so completely surprised by this answer, because they knew that she hated Christianity as much as any of them did, that for a while they did not know what to do. Finally one of them turned to Nochigoro and asked him if he were willing in case all the property were made over to him, to care for and support his parents as long as they lived even should they live in illness. He could not imagine why they asked such a question, since they had just determined to turn him out of doors, but he replied that of course he was willing to do what was his simple duty. Then the one who asked the question turned to the father and said, would it not be better for him to give now his business entirely to his son and not trouble himself about it any further since his son promised to give him all he needed and to care for him as long as he lived. The old father thought this was a very reasonable proposition. And so instead of the son's being turned out of doors for his Christianity, he will be virtually the head of the household.

On the Saturday after we had celebrated the Lord's Supper together, the two young men who had been detained from coming the week before were examined. One of these was received into the church. I also made a point of talking to some of the church members about infant baptism. They were all very willing to receive instruction on the subject and readily agreed to the basic arguments. The next Sabbath I had the pleasure and privilege of baptizing four of the lambs of Christ's fold together with the one young man whom we had examined. So that in all there were thirteen baptisms of whom four were babies.

Just before the baptismal service I ordained three elders and two deacons some of whom had been elected and indeed acting previously but were waiting for an opportunity to be ordained.[49]

Members of the Ueda Church lived in towns somewhat scattered about the region. Maki used this dispersion to extend his ministry. In that year (1878) he had begun meetings in Komoro, to the East of Ueda. Since several of the Ueda Church members were also then living in Nagano, about twenty-three miles beyond Ueda, Miller decided to visit them there for preaching services during this tour. However, his government passport did not allow him to go beyond Ueda, so Maki went to Nagano while Miller maintained the services at Ueda. After about a month of sharing the work of the Ueda area, Miller returned to Yokohama. In this manner, the missionaries gradually developed a pattern of periodic touring in the interior in support of their Japanese colleagues. They also established the practice of sending theological students into the interior of the country on evangelistic tours during their summer vacation time.[50]

Preaching services were begun in Tokyo by the Reformed Mission in the summer of 1877. As a result of this initiative, involving cooperation between Okuno and theological students as well as Amerman and Verbeck, the Kojimachi Church was organized in Tokyo November 3, 1877.

Amerman's main responsibility was to teach at the new Tokyo Union Theological School. However, he also had some involvement in outreach through the theological students. Three members of the Yokohama Church and one or two members of churches related to the Presbyterian missionaries were living in the vicinity of the town of Wado, about thirty miles northeast of Tokyo. In the spring of 1878,

49   ERM to JMF, June 6 and 18, 1878.
50   ERM to JMF, June 17, 1878.

Amerman arranged for a theological student to be sent there once a week to preach. The believers provided the student's food and lodging, and the Reformed Mission paid for the student's transportation. During the summer vacation of the theological school, Amerman sent a well-qualified student there for two months, and in the fall he resumed sending students for weekly preaching visits. Several applicants for baptism resulted. One man came to Tokyo for several days to be instructed in preparation for baptism. Okuno and Elder Ibuka went to Wado to examine others. The group gathering there increased and asked to be organized as a church.

Okuno and Amerman visited the place, and the Wado Church was organized on Saturday, October 26, 1878, with thirteen members. Another adult and an infant were baptized the next day and several more were candidates. Several preaching services were held that weekend in Wado and a nearby village. Amerman remarked, "The Japanese display a wonderful capacity for listening to sermons." During the five services held that weekend, Okuno preached five times and gave a separate address at the Communion, while Amerman administered the sacraments and preached twice, and a visiting elder also gave a speech. Throughout these services, the attendees remained eager and attentive. Amerman added, "and with the continued helping of the Master we hope to see their numbers continually growing and the people becoming increased in Christian graces. From the beginning they will endeavor to defray all their expenses except the traveling expenses of their supplies [preachers]."[51]

At the end of the first year of the theological school, nine of the most advanced students became licensed preachers, and five of them passed part of their ordination examinations as well. Nine of the advanced students withdrew from the school in the fall of 1878 to take advantage of long-awaited evangelistic opportunities opening up in many places, but most hoped to return later for further study.

Concerning developing self-supporting Japanese churches, Amerman informed the board,

> The native church is being taught to stand alone as rapidly as can be & when it has learned to stand it will doubtless learn to walk and run. We are exerting ourselves in this matter but the matter depends on the condition of the people as well as on our exertions. And there are few rich or moderately able men financially in any of the churches, and in our Kojimachi Church here in Tokyo

[51] JLA to JMF, Nov. 4, 1878.

there are none. I succeeded however in persuading them—those who could give anything to give 25 sen per month [about $.50] towards their expenses so that they are now paying half their rent. By and by I shall try to have them do more and in God's good time I trust we shall have a thoroughly self-supporting church here.... Be assured however that we do not encourage the Christians here to believe that they may depend upon the church of America any more than is absolutely needful, and we do constantly endeavor to inculcate lessons of piety, energy, independence, & courage as of first importance.[52]

During the summer of 1878, S. R. Brown and his family went to the Hakone area for "health and recreation." Despite failing health and exhaustion, during his supposed vacation Brown participated for a week in the itinerant evangelistic work in the Hakone region. Accompanied by two of his advanced theological students (Ito and Amenomori, already licensed preachers), he visited Yamanaka, Mishima, Daiba, and Numazu, visiting and encouraging scattered believers, holding numerous preaching services in homes, and examining and baptizing converts. Evangelist Ito had taken six months off from theological study to develop the outreach at Mishima, and Brown remarked about him,

> The faithful labors of Ito in that region, where, at my advice he concluded to remain a year longer, before going back to the theological school, are not likely to be fruitless. They have not been so hitherto, though he has met with vigorous opposition in the past of a traveling Buddhist lecturer, and the Shinto priests. At one time almost all his Sunday school children were withdrawn from the school in his house, but they begin to return to some extent, & probably now that the Buddhist lecturer has departed from Mishima, Ito will soon recover his pupils. He has met all this opposition patiently, kindly & prayerfully, and I cannot but think a better day is dawning upon him. He is a man of marked humility, kindness of manner, & perseverance. He was not born to rank, nor an heir to wealth, but he came up from among the common people, is not ashamed to do any honest work, but ready to turn his hand to whatever occasion may require. May the Lord crown his labors at Mishima & its vicinity with abundant success.[53]

---

[52]    JLA to JMF, Aug. 14, 1878.
[53]    SRB to JMF, Dec. 31, 1878.

By the end of 1878, through the labors of these Japanese evangelists and the partnership of the three missions, the ministry of the United Church had grown significantly. It had eighteen organized congregations and forty-one preaching places related to the churches, besides three mission stations not yet organized as churches. During 1878 there had been 300 adult and 55 infant baptisms. Total membership had reached 970 adults and 119 children. Of these ministries, those affiliated with the Reformed Church's Japan Mission included five organized congregations, eleven preaching places related to churches, and the three mission stations not yet organized as churches.[54]

Amerman relates the story of one of the preaching places related to the Reformed Mission, describing the pattern implemented of cooperation among the mission, Japanese church leaders, and theological students:

> In March of last year a preaching station was opened in the district called Shitaya [present-day Ueno district], where a location has been found after protracted and discouraging search, where after all we had only a small house in a back street, but it was the best and only place we could find to rent and was about three fourths of a mile from the nearest scene of Christian work. The design was to have a place where our young men in the theological school could exercise their gifts in preaching, etc., in such a way that the results if any could be properly cared for....From the beginning the church in Kojimachi, with its acting pastor and consistory, gave the enterprise all possible aid, and during the past year Rev. Mr. Okuno has conducted the service regularly on Sunday afternoons....At first the audiences were small and our efforts met with little encouragement; even novelty of Christian preaching did not attract as in other places, but we were thankful that there were no direct obstacles for us to contend with. After a few weeks the people of the neighborhood began to attend in small numbers. The place was small, the entire available space inside being twenty feet by twelve including the porch, but the usual lattice extended across the house front, and when the paper screens were removed twenty or thirty people could stand outside and see and hear all that was going on within. The usual audience during the past year, in pleasant weather, has been from twenty to forty, but on a few occasions I have counted as many as seventy....

---

[54]    JLA to JMF, Jan. 27, 1878.

The organization took place on Saturday afternoon, Nov. 8, [1879]....Hereafter regular preaching services will be held on Sunday mornings and afternoons and on Wednesday evenings; Sunday School after the morning service and prayer meeting Sunday evenings. Rev. Dr. Verbeck, in addition to his other work will preach here on Sunday afternoons; the remaining services being in charge of a licensed helper, Uyemura [Uemura] Masahisa, who is also an elder of the church.[55]

In this way, by means of the partnership of the young Japanese church and the mission, Shitaya Church was formed and organized as a congregation and its further nurture provided for.

## Expansion of Evangelistic Outreach—Nagasaki Station

The Nagasaki Station of the Reformed Church Japan Mission, at which the Nagasaki Church was organized in December of 1876, was limited by the shortage of personnel. Even so Henry Stout found opportunities to enlarge the work in the vicinity of Nagasaki and actually to reach out to the southern part of the island of Kyushu. During the first two years after the organization of Nagasaki Church, with the assistance of the two young men he was training for the ministry, Stout held regular preaching services at two locations in the city. This ministry resulted in a number of adult baptisms, and during those two years Nagasaki Church membership grew from the original twelve to twenty-two. Of one of the new converts, Morita Sono, a widow who became a Christian at the age of sixty-seven, Stout said that she was a "marked example of the power of the Spirit to change, and of Christ to save even despisers of God and his word." Morita died at the age of seventy-two, and hers was the first Protestant Christian funeral in Nagasaki.[56]

When the Stouts joined the other Reformed missionary families for the first time for a much-needed vacation in the mountains north of Tokyo in the summer of 1877, Amerman noted how the years of work in isolation from the other missionaries had taken its toll on the Stout family's health.

I need not say that I was specially glad to spend awhile near Bro. Stout....The nine years that have passed since we studied together

---

[55] JLA to JMF, Nov. 14, 1879.
[56] Henry Stout, "First Christian Funeral at Nagasaki," *Sower and Mission Monthly* (April, 1881).

have wrought changes in both of us. Some of that I trust for the better. He has suffered in health, however, and while there is the same man with his good nature & good humor & solid sense and earnestness I could not fail to see the evidences of depressing influences. Mrs. Stout's health, too, is far from good, indeed at times she is exceedingly weak, and while she may possibly be able to bear another winter here, can hardly bear another summer even if she should come north.[57]

Refreshed by the summer vacation with the other missionaries, in addition to the regular work in Nagasaki, Stout attempted to reach out to the surrounding region. In so doing, eighteen years after the arrival of the first missionaries, he encountered directly the age-old anti-Christian resistance. He reported,

I have just returned from a trip of a week into Shimabara. In one village quite an interest seemed to be felt to hear the truth, when on Sunday night a Shinto priest broke up the meeting by threatening to inform against the farmer, at whose home I was stopping and meeting the people. It seems the priest subsequently carried the matter to the officials, and that the old farmer had to give security [post bail] for his appearance whenever required. The affair has been referred to superiors and we are anxious to see what will come of it.[58]

While some progress was evident in the evangelistic work of the Nagasaki Station, it soon became clear that exuberant optimism was not warranted. By the end of 1878, audiences at preaching services in Nagasaki had dwindled considerably from the two hundred or more who had attended earlier. Though fewer in number, non-Christians continued to come. Stout, in any case, remained positive, describing the situation in his Nagasaki Station Annual Report for 1878.

The regular services have been attended as usual, by the church members and strangers in the city. For some reason missionary effort fails for the most part to reach the residents. And those who identify themselves with the churches are quite cut off from association and live in the place almost literally as "pilgrims and strangers." And yet the field is in many respects a very encouraging one, for visitors are constantly in the city, a natural center for

---

57   JLA to JMF, Sept. 4, 1877.
58   HS to JMF, Dec. 7, 1877.

communication, and come to hear the preaching and so, though those who sow the seed are stationary, it is scattered far and wide. The fruit will doubtless be found perhaps at no very distant day.[59]

The Meiji Restoration of 1868 had removed Japan's shogun from power and disinherited the samurai class, who lost their place in Japanese society. In the words of Edwin Reischauer,

> It was not possible...to disinherit so large a privileged class [about 6 percent of the population] without some turmoil. Irreconcilable conservatives among the samurai often defied the new government in its first decade of rule. Significantly, these troubles occurred largely in the same western domains from which the new leaders had come....The most serious as well as the last of the samurai revolts came in Satsuma [Kagoshima] itself. There some 40,000 discontented conservatives rallied around Saigo, who had withdrawn from the government in dudgeon [anger] four years earlier. In bloody fighting, the government's new peasant conscripts managed to crush the rebels, proving even to the diehards that the old order had indeed passed.[60]

The turmoil and rebellions in southwest Japan had taken place in the regions surrounding the Reformed Church's Nagasaki Station, and since the rebels there were opposed to the government opening Japan to foreign influences, the uprisings had their impact on the progress of mission work in the region. With the defeat of the rebellion at Kagoshima, one hundred miles south of Nagasaki on the island of Kyushu, Stout saw there sheep without a shepherd and an opportunity to expand the outreach of the Nagasaki Station. In the fall of 1878, he sent his closest Japanese associate, Segawa, recently returned from a year of study at the new Tokyo theological school, along with the student Tomegawa Ichiro, on a preaching tour to Kagoshima. They returned with reports of a positive response, and Stout decided to open an outstation there.

Segawa and his wife, Tsuya (Fujiyama Tsuya, who had studied for three years at Ferris Seminary), moved to Kagoshima in December of 1878 to take up that work, traveling there by boat and *jinrikisha*. Tsuya had taken along a little reed organ, very rare then, and her playing and singing added much to the attractiveness of the meetings. At first as

---

59    HS to JMF, Jan., 1879.
60    Reischauer, *The Story*, 128-29.

many as sixty or seventy attended the meetings, including five or six interested school teachers. Stout was enthused about the possibilities in Kagoshima, and of his Japanese colleagues he remarked, "Mr. and Mrs. Segawa, who have charge of it, are earnest and diligent, and if natural abilities, training and piety are qualifications from which good results may be expected, there is reason to look for favorable reports from them."[61]

During the 1878-79 school year, the Verbecks and the Ballaghs were in America on a much-needed furlough. Verbeck had brought his service to the Japanese government to a close, and he planned to return to full-time missionary work after the furlough. In the absence of Ballagh, Miller went out on tours not only to Ueda, in his own area of responsibility, but also to Ballagh's territory, Nagoya and the Izu peninsula region, to encourage the evangelists in the field.[62] Anticipating the return of Verbeck and Ballagh, the Stouts and the Millers were to go to America just when their colleagues would be returning to the field. Under these circumstances, the mission was very short-handed and all were overworked.

The missionaries were concerned about the future of the work of the Nagasaki Station, where the Stouts had borne the responsibility virtually alone for ten years. Their health was at the breaking point, and they needed to return to America to rest, but someone would need to keep the station going. New personnel were repeatedly pleaded for, but the possibility of the Ballaghs going to Nagasaki after furlough was also considered. Hearing that Ballagh might be willing to go there if necessary, Amerman remarked, "He is always willing to go where there is most work to do."[63] And Amerman lamented, "There seems to be no one else to go. My hands are full here [teaching at the theological school], & Dr. Brown cannot go. His health is so feeble now that he cannot always meet the Translation Committee, and I should not be surprised to hear at any time that his labors are closed. Cannot the church do something more for this people?"[64]

Twenty years had passed since the first Protestant missionaries arrived in Japan. However, all missionaries continued to be restricted in their travel into the interior and were still required to reside in the treaty ports. Government regulations still required the special "passports" that limited travel in the interior to that for purposes of "health" or

---

[61] HS to ERM, Dec. 5, 1878.
[62] ERM to JMF, May 5, 1879.
[63] JLA to JMF, Apr. 19, 1879.
[64] JLA to JMF, March 25, 1879.

"scientific investigation." Even though authorities often permitted a broad interpretation of the two purposes, and missionaries regularly received passports for touring to visit churches and preaching stations in the interior, these regulations nevertheless limited missionary activity.

On April 10, 1879, an interdenominational Christian gathering of foreigners considered a proposed memorandum to the foreign ministers of Western nations who were negotiating with the Japanese government regarding revision of their treaties. The missionaries hoped to secure greater freedom of movement in the country. The memorandum had to do with foreigners' travel and residence in the interior and was presented by the Reformed Church's Amerman and the Methodist Mission's Maclay to the American government representative, Mr. Bingham, in October 1879. It contained the signatures of more than eighty American citizens in Japan, of whom more than half were not missionaries.[65] Despite such appeals, the restrictions remained intact.

### Developing Mission School Education—Tokyo/Yokohama

From the time the first missionaries arrived in 1859, the one area of service open to all of them had been the teaching of English and Western knowledge. At first they had been asked by the Japanese government to teach classes of interpreters, who were needed to deal with foreigners at the opened ports. Gradually the new leaders of Japan came to realize that education was the essential ingredient required to transform Japan into a modern and prosperous nation. Consequently, missionaries could capitalize on the area of education as an opportunity to break into Japan's otherwise closed society. However, the missionaries were not interested in education for education's sake. This was apparent in the earliest developments in both Yokohama and Nagasaki. Their primary purpose from the beginning was evangelism. It was for that reason that as soon as and whenever possible, they used the Bible as a textbook. As we have seen, in the early years they taught both in government schools and in private classes at their homes or in small classrooms attached to their homes. In the 1870s, the missionaries gradually replaced their teaching at government schools with the further development of the small private classes. The first to take concrete and more permanent form as an actual mission school was the school for girls in Yokohama.

---

[65]    JLA to JMF, Apr. 10 and Oct. 27, 1879.

The first Ferris Seminary building, completed in 1875

*Ferris Seminary (School for Girls)*

Mary Kidder, since marriage in 1873 Mrs. E. R. Miller, had continued to entertain the vision of a boarding school for girls in Yokohama, in order to nurture the girls in an atmosphere like a Christian home. However, she was hampered by the lack of an assistant after Hequenbourg's departure in poor health, and by inadequate facilities. Prospects began to change in November of 1874 when, with the help of Governor Oe of Yokohama and the American consul-general, she finally obtained the lease of the desired land from the government.

During that same month, the Reformed Church appropriated money to construct a building on the site, and Emma C. Witbeck arrived to assist Mary in the development of what came to be called the Ferris Seminary for Girls. The boarding school was opened in its new building June 1, 1875. At the end of 1875, nineteen girls were enrolled. The girls were given a well-rounded education, and at the same time were daily taught the Bible and to sing hymns and to pray. A large percentage of them became Christians in the early days of the school. During 1876, enrollment increased to thirty-four students, of whom thirty were boarders. Miller believed that the school was finally established on a good foundation. Witbeck taught English, while Miller not only served as the school administrator, but also taught the Bible and gave spiritual and pastoral guidance to the students.

Mary Miller continued to be responsible for the school until she returned to the United States in 1879 for her first furlough, after ten years in Japan. However, during the four years they worked together, the relationship between Witbeck and Miller had become strained. Witbeck evidently did not learn the Japanese language and did not seem to share Miller's enthusiasm and efforts to nurture Christian faith in the students. Furthermore, Witbeck was apparently jealous of the confidence and intimacy Miller enjoyed with the Japanese associates and students, and was not only unreceptive to any advice, but also very annoyed when anyone referred to her as Miller's assistant. Asked later to tell of their working relationship, Miller said, "In the first place my work with Miss Witbeck was up hill work, any influence I had in the school was in spite of her influence opposing me." Miller never spoke of the difficulty of this relationship to anyone but her husband at the time. However, she came to believe that the constant tension had contributed to the breakdown of her own health.[66]

When Mary Miller and her husband departed to America for their first furlough in the summer of 1879, Emma Witbeck was left in charge of the school. By this time the board had made clear that Harriet L. Winn, Brown's niece, was a duly appointed missionary of the Reformed Church. Since neither Witbeck at the girls' school, nor Winn, teaching Brown's boys' classes in Yokohama, could carry on the work adequately alone, Winn was asked by the mission to assist Witbeck in teaching at Ferris Seminary. By the teaching and guidance of these two women, the educational program for girls continued. However, representing the Japan Mission, Amerman asked for more teachers for Ferris Seminary, for it was clear that Witbeck would not be able to stay in Japan much longer.[67]

### Sen-shi Gakko, A Male Preparatory School

Educational efforts for boys and young men in Yokohama by the Reformed missionaries were very fruitful in the beginning, but lacked clarity of purpose for a time. Small classes taught by Brown and Ballagh, assisted by their wives and daughters, had produced a nucleus of converts for the first organized congregation in 1872 as well as most of the first class of candidates for the ministry. Amerman had been sent out by the Reformed Church in 1876 to assist in theological education, and he became the Reformed Church representative on the faculty of the joint theological school established in 1877. However, it had gradually become clear that a preparatory course of Christian

[66]    Sangster, *Manual*, 262-63, 268-69; Mary E. Miller to JMF, Jan. 19, 1882.
[67]    JLA to JMF, Sept. 19, 1879, Dec. 20, 1880.

education was necessary, not only for purposes of evangelism, but also to continue to raise up future church leaders and students for the theological course. Although there was no properly organized boys' school at the time, the two young women, Hattie (Harriet) Brown and her cousin Harriet Winn, despite receiving no missionary salary, had continued a modest educational effort for boys and young men. In the fall of 1876, Winn, pointing out that she had taught in Brown's school for two years without pay, requested appointment as an assistant missionary to Japan under the Reformed mission board.[68]

Fifteen months later, Winn had received no reply from the board, and S. R. Brown wrote to Secretary Ferris to express his dismay and speak on her behalf. He asked nothing for his daughter but believed it unjust that Winn's valuable work had been neither recognized nor remunerated. Brown heard indirectly that the board had appointed her as an assistant missionary, but neither Winn nor the Japan Mission had been informed. Brown went on to plead for the establishment of a preparatory school for boys, pointing out that without it, future candidates for the theological school would be very difficult to acquire.[69] There was some discussion of a joint preparatory boys' mission school in Yokohama, in partnership with the Presbyterians. However, the Presbyterians were looking toward moving their small school to Tokyo. This would preclude the Reformed Church's Winn and Hattie Brown teaching in a joint school.[70]

During the second year of the Tokyo Union Theological School, Amerman reported progress in the joint effort for theological education. Not only was education taking place in the classroom, and a small library being gathered, but also almost all the students had gone out during the summer to different parts of the country "preaching the Word of life." Seven new students entered the first-year class, but not one of them was related to the Reformed Mission. Amerman, too, showed his concern that without a proper preparatory school for boys and young men, it would be difficult to recruit future candidates for the theological school.[71]

Hattie Brown returned to the United States with her parents in the summer of 1879, and since Winn was unable alone to carry on the preparatory classes for boys and young men, those classes were not resumed in the fall. As we have seen, the Millers were in America,

---

[68]   Harriet L. Winn to JMF, Oct. 21, 1876.
[69]   SRB to JMF, Jan., 1878.
[70]   ERM to JMF, Apr. 10, 1879.
[71]   JLA to JMF, Jan. 27, 1879.

leaving Witbeck alone at Ferris Seminary, so Harriet Winn began to work with her. On behalf of the Japan Mission, Amerman insisted that it was essential for the mission board to send teachers and provide the necessary facilities for a preparatory school for male students.

The Ballaghs returned to Japan from furlough late in the fall of 1879, and, despite heavy responsibilities for evangelistic work, they endeavored to reinstate the preparatory classes for boys and young men. James and Margaret reopened the preparatory school on January 16, 1880, the classes meeting in rooms at their home, renovated at a cost of $500. There were twenty-two students, two of whom were schoolteachers studying English with hopes of entering the theological school. Of the other twenty students, about half were boys of eight to twelve years, and five or six of these were children of foreign fathers and Japanese mothers (outcasts in Japanese society), who boarded with the Ballaghs.[72]

James Ballagh continued teaching the preparatory school classes for a year and a half. He lamented in a letter to Ferris, "You have kindly intimated your conviction I should be in the evangelistic work, and I have realized the same myself and deplore the loss of time I feel it to be that I am engaged in teaching, not that the latter is devoid of interest or barren of results. I feel confident 4 or 5 pupils of my school are inquiring the way of life. But I cannot concentrate my heart on this work enough to make it a success, nor can I go to the stations as often as I would wish." At the annual mission meeting, Ballagh had been asked to keep the classes going until the board could send an educational missionary to develop male education, so he was delighted to learn that a teacher, Martin N. Wyckoff, would be sent in time for fall classes in 1881.[73]

The whole Reformed Japan Mission was convinced of the importance of a preparatory school for the future of the work and had continued to urge the board to send missionaries to develop male education properly. In response to these pleas, the Reformed Church

[72]  JHB to JMF, Apr. 15, 1880.
[73]  JHB to JMF, Apr. 20 and July 20, 1881. A native of Middlebush, New Jersey (born April 10, 1850), Martin Wyckoff was a graduate of Rutgers College, and not only a well-trained educator but also experienced in teaching in Japan. At the time of his college graduation in 1872, he had been recommended by the Rutgers faculty to succeed Griffis as teacher in the government school in Fukui, Japan. After teaching two years in Fukui, two years in Niigata, and one year in Tokyo in government schools, Wyckoff had returned to America in 1877. He taught one year at Rutgers, after which the Rutgers College faculty asked him to open a preparatory school in Summerville, New Jersey, which he conducted for three years. It was at that point, urged by the missionaries in Japan, that the Reformed Church board had appointed Wyckoff as an educational missionary to Japan.

decided to send Professor Martin N. Wyckoff to Yokohama as an educational missionary. Amerman wrote, "We are glad to hear your announcement concerning Bro. Wyckoff. We know him and shall be glad indeed to see him at the head of our preparatory school."[74] The Wyckoffs, Martin and his wife, Anna Catherine Wyckoff, and their children, arrived in Yokohama September 25, 1881, and Martin took over and formalized the classes taught by the Ballaghs. This Reformed Mission boys' school in Yokohama was called *Sen-shi Gakko*, meaning "First a Purpose School." The name, while an awkward one in English translation, came from a maxim of Confucius. "First form a purpose, then afterwards look for results."[75] While this boys' school proved short-lived, Wyckoff's arrival facilitated an important step forward in the development of mission school education for boys in Japan.

When Wyckoff opened the school on October 3, just one week after arriving in Japan, it began with thirteen students. Early in November the enrollment had already increased to twenty-eight in the day school, and Wyckoff had initiated evening classes for young men working in the daytime, with ten students. He obviously saw his missionary vocation as more than teaching English, and, in order to become an effective missionary, he was eager to build on knowledge of the Japanese language gained during his previous five years in Japan. Wyckoff reported,

> I teach them an hour and a half each evening, and give them a half hour of Scripture extra. Some of them are boarding with the regular scholars, and we thus have a better opportunity for imparting religious instruction. I am obliged to do all my Bible work in Japanese, with the exception of a Saturday evening class, which I formed last week from the most advanced of the boarding pupils. On Sabbath afternoons I have a Bible class in the schoolroom, which anyone whether a pupil or not may attend.
>
> I am obliged to use my Japanese tongue more here than I ever did in the government schools. I know it is badly mangled language, but I found myself in deep water, without a support, and I was obliged to swim. I do not find as much difficulty in speaking and reading as I expected, but my ears, or rather the faculties that make the ear useful, need training badly, before I will be able to understand well. Perhaps however I understand quite as well as I speak, but do not realize my deficiency so much

[74]   JLA to JMF, Nov. 6 and Dec. 20, 1880.
[75]   Martin N. Wyckoff to JMF, Sept. 27, 1881; JHB to JMF, Oct. 8, 1881.

Martin N. Wyckoff (left)
and James L. Amerman

in that direction....I find all my time for study now occupied with the Japanese New Testament, in preparing for the scholars. I hope soon to be able to undertake something in the direct study of the language.[76]

With the preparatory school under Wyckoff's leadership and with Amerman teaching at the theological school, it appeared that at long last the Reformed Church Japan Mission was on track to provide future leadership for the churches that were forming and growing in central Japan in connection with the mission.

### Early Educational Efforts in Nagasaki

Meanwhile, in Nagasaki, classes of both boys and girls had been taught by the Stouts from the fall of 1872. Henry Stout had taught the classes for boys and young men, assisted for a brief period by Charles Wolff. When the girls' school classes were first opened there, the Stouts had sent the mission board urgent requests for women teachers. They received only indefinite encouragement in the matter, but in the hope of help being sent out, the classes were continued. However, in the summer of 1874, suffering from sheer exhaustion, Elizabeth Stout was forced to discontinue temporarily the small school that she had kept going for almost two years. Henry Stout continued his classes for boys and young men, both as a means of evangelism and as training for future Japanese church leaders. In the spring of 1877, having been assured by the recently formed Woman's Board of Foreign Missions of the Reformed Church that they would endeavor to send women teachers to Nagasaki, and frequently having had requests for such instruction, Elizabeth Stout once again undertook responsibility for a class of girls.[77]

---

[76]   MNW to JMF, Nov. 8, 1881.
[77]   Verbeck, "History," 69, 91.

However, Henry Stout had become quite discouraged with the work of Nagasaki Station. While the Reformed Mission personnel had been reinforced repeatedly in Yokohama and Tokyo, the work in Nagasaki had essentially rested on one couple, first the Verbecks and then the Stouts, for more than eighteen years. Stout came to feel that unless the board could staff the Nagasaki Station sufficiently, so that male and female education and the training of church leaders could be properly developed, the work there ought best be abandoned to others. He was ready to resign. The Stouts had not had a furlough since their arrival in March of 1869, and health concerns dictated their departure for America in the spring of 1879. The Woman's Board had decided to send two women teachers for Nagasaki, but Stout believed it would be disastrous to the Nagasaki Station to leave the entire work in the hands of two newly arrived women teachers. On the other hand, if the board was really committed to staffing Nagasaki Station adequately, and to sending further reinforcements before their departure, the Stouts were ready and willing to return to Nagasaki in the future and commit their lives to its prosperity.[78]

In August of 1878, the hope of developing education for girls seemed finally to be realized with the arrival of sisters from the Reformed Church of Fishkill, New York. Elizabeth F. Farrington and Mary J. Farrington were sent by the Woman's Board to more formally develop a girls' school in Nagasaki. When they arrived, Elizabeth Stout handed her class of six girls over to them. However, only weeks later, Henry Stout wrote, "The Misses Farrington arrived in due time, and we find them very pleasant. They certainly possess qualities that should make them successful missionaries. But the health of the elder is a cause for apprehension."[79] A month later, Stout informed the board,

> The health of the elder Miss Farrington continues so poor that we have serious apprehensions she will not be able to remain here. It is quite evident she has not the strength necessary for one at the head of a boarding school. Their physician has told us there is little hope of her ever being strong in the East. In fact, I ought to say, doubtless, that these young ladies are, both of them, mentally and physically weak. They have some fine qualities, and I have no doubt the younger, with care, and with some good strong person to lean upon, would become useful as a teacher in a school. But nothing more can be expected.[80]

[78]   HS to JMF, March 28, 1878.
[79]   HS to JMF, Oct. 17, 1878.
[80]   HS to JMF, Nov. 15, 1878.

Unfortunately, in January of 1879, due to the serious failure of the older sister's health, after only five months the sisters were forced to abandon the work they had barely begun. They left Nagasaki and went to Yokohama to seek medical advice and treatment. The older sister seemed at first to be improving in health, and the younger sister briefly assisted Witbeck, teaching at Ferris Seminary in the spring of 1879. However, the Farrington sisters never went back to Nagasaki but instead, on the advice of doctors in Japan, they returned permanently to America in the summer of 1879.[81]

Once again, the structured development of mission school education for girls in Nagasaki had to be postponed. As to these classes for girls, Miller suggested that the little work begun in Nagasaki might be left in the hands of Kikutake Hatsui [also called Ohatsu] till the Stouts were able to return there.[82] This young woman, who had studied at Ferris Seminary, did in fact teach the class for girls until the summer of 1879. However, she married a young man who worked as an assistant to the Anglican missionaries and moved to another city.[83] Consequently, the class for girls at Nagasaki Station was once again temporarily discontinued.

Stout was able to make a trip to Kagoshima to visit the Segawas at the outstation there and encourage them in their work. Given the shortage of personnel and the persistent shortfall in board support for its Japan Mission, Stout felt sadness and anxiety as he prepared to return to the United States. He thought that the Reformed Church might abandon the Nagasaki Station and he might never be able to return there.[84] When the Stouts left Nagasaki in May of 1879 after more than ten years on the field, they had to leave the work of the Nagasaki Station of the Japan Mission in the hands of young Japanese converts. Nagasaki Church and the various other classes for boys and young men in Nagasaki, and the work of the outstation in Kagoshima, were all taken over by Stout's Japanese assistants, Segawa, Tomegawa, Tsuge Takenori, and Hirayama Taketomo, while the classes for girls were kept going by Miss Kikutake.

With the loss of the Farrington sisters, Henry Stout suffered not only the disappointment of having to postpone development of female education in Nagasaki, but also the ignominy of an unjust scandal with regard to the Farringtons. It appears that the sisters blamed Stout, and

---

81    Verbeck, "History," 100, 106; SRB to JMF, June 10, 1879.
82    ERM to JMF, March 26, 1879.
83    JLA to JMF, March 3, 1880.
84    HS to JMF, Apr. 4, 1879.

also Amerman and the Japan Mission in general, for their inability to fulfill their mission. After their return to America, critical rumors were circulated and published in the August, 1879, issue of the *Mission Monthly*. Their pastor, the Reverend Asher Anderson, also got involved on their behalf, supposedly in an effort to "vindicate the character" of Elizabeth and Mary Farrington. He sent questioning letters to Reformed Church and other missionaries in Japan, and even to one of Stout's assistants in Nagasaki, Pastor Tomegawa. The health problems of the sisters were blamed on Stout's arrangements for their housing. Since the Stout family lived in a four-room house, Stout had rented a separate Japanese style house next door for the sisters' use.[85]

A subsequent visit to Nagasaki by L. H. Gulick, M.D., of the American Bible Society, indicated that Stout had provided them with more healthful housing than his own. Letters from Amerman clarified that medical doctors and all the members of the mission on the field had concluded that the sisters were seriously ill and lacked the physical and mental vigor required for missionary work. After thorough investigation, the Reformed Church Board of Foreign Missions determined that there was no reason for further action, but the inappropriate and unjust action taken by the women and their pastor was detrimental to Stout's reputation and to the cause of missions.[86]

### The Church Building in Yokohama

A building fund for the future construction of a church building in Yokohama had been initiated already in 1861, before there were any Japanese Protestant Christians, as the result of the generous gift of $1,000 from Christians in Hawaii. Others had added to this building fund. Townsend Harris, first minister of the United States government to the Japanese government of the shogun when the first missionaries arrived, had contributed another $1,000 (given to Brown in December of 1861 as a Christmas present, "to build a church in connection with your Mission"); Harris's successor, Robert H. Pruyn, a Reformed Church member, had contributed $500; and some British seamen had given $50. Ballagh himself later contributed $559, his income from teaching at the government school three months out of the year. This building fund had been invested at interest, waiting for the day when its purpose could be realized.

---

[85]   HS to JMF, May 31, 1878.
[86]   JLA to JMF, Oct. 29 and Nov. 20, 1879; Eugene S. Booth to HS, Dec. 26, 1879; L. H. Gulick to JMF, Dec. 20, 1879.

Early in the history of Protestant mission to Japan, the Japanese government had agreed to the lease of a valuable plot of land, centrally located near the harbor in Yokohama, to the Reformed Church Mission. It was seen as an ideal future church building site. The mission paid an annual fee for the lease of this property. During the 1860s, no public worship was as yet possible, and there was in any case no congregation. However, in part to protect the property rights, in 1868 Ballagh erected a small building toward the back of the lot to be used as a schoolroom, with the idea that it might eventually form a wing of a church building. A small portion of the building fund was used for this purpose, and the rest continued to be invested at interest, looking toward the day when a church building might be required.

During Ballagh's first visit back to the United States (December 1868 to November 1870), he raised $2,373.83 to be added to the church building fund. In the meantime, in 1869, while Ballagh was in America, newly returned Brown received what appeared to be a very favorable proposal from two wealthy merchants who desired to live at that fine location for several years. These men wished to build a home for their families on part of the site, with the understanding they would need it for only seven years. They bound themselves to give the house to the mission at the end of that time. They also agreed to pay the annual fee for the land lease. The proposal seemed fair and very beneficial to the mission. The merchants proceeded to build a large and elegant house and moved in with their families.[87] However, the merchants encountered a series of calamities. One of them set out on a voyage, and, since the ship was never heard from again, it was assumed sunk in a storm. The other merchant died suddenly, and consequently their families left Japan. True to the original agreement, the property reverted to the mission, but much sooner than expected. Furthermore, because the building on the property came into their possession so soon, the mission was obligated to pay off the $2,000 balance of the mortgage on the house to retain possession. The $6,000 house and outbuildings thus became mission property, and the beautiful home stood vacant and available on the lot leased to the Reformed Mission.[88]

The Ballaghs received an annual allowance from the mission board in lieu of rent for a house. Ballagh decided to make use of the vacant house on the Mission property as his family residence, and to pay the annual rent allowance into the church building fund. Furthermore, during three months of the year Ballagh was able to rent the house to

87    SRB to JMF, Nov. 9, 1869.
88    SRB to JMF, Sept. 19, 1872.

silkworm merchants, and the large amount they were willing to pay was added to the church building fund. During those three months each year the Ballaghs found temporary quarters wherever they could, undoubtedly a great inconvenience for the Ballagh family. Nevertheless, in this way the mortgage was paid off and the building fund was built up.

For several years the Ballaghs lived in this large house during much of the year, while next door, at the back of the lot set aside for the future church building, stood the small building used as a classroom. It was in that small building that the first Protestant church in Japan met and was organized with eleven members on March 10, 1872. Unfortunately, the large missionary residence next to a small building used temporarily for the church gave rise to scandalous rumors by those who were eager to disparage the missionary movement. The slander was that a missionary was living in a magnificent home, while the Japanese Christians were relegated to an insignificant church built from the surplus bricks, which was labeled "The Sacred Dog Kennel." Pictures of the two buildings were also publicized by westerners unsympathetic to the work of the missionaries. This slander had, of course, no foundation.

In July of 1874 Ballagh reported having laid the foundation for a church building on the Yokohama property, with three feet of concrete beneath the first tier of stones. The main part of the building was seventy by thirty-six feet, with a tower for the belfry, but no steeple. The beautiful new church building was formally dedicated July 10, 1875, with a seating capacity of 450, and the original small building became the attached educational wing. The total cost for the main building and educational wing was approximately $8,000. Additional gifts were received from the United States, including stained glass windows by the South Dutch Reformed Church of New York City, a church bell by Mr. Cowenhoven of Long Island, and a silver Communion set by Miss Jane Van Schaick of Albany.[89]

For thirty-five years after its completion, this beautiful sanctuary served the needs not only of the Japanese congregation for which it was built, but also of the Yokohama Union Church serving the English-speaking community. The Japanese congregation worshiped at 9:00 a.m. and the English-speaking congregation at 11:00 a.m. In 1910, Yokohama Union Church moved to a new building on the Bluff in Yokohama.

---

[89]   Sangster, *Manual*, 255-57; Verbeck, "History," 73-74; Ryder, *Historical Soucebook*, 52-53; Ballagh, "Statement," Archives of the RCA, 1-6.

The church building in Yokohama (Kaigan Kyokai) dedicated
July 10, 1875. The building in the left foreground became
the missionary residence.

## Publication of the Bible in Japanese

S. R. Brown lived to see the completion, if not the publication, of
his translation work. Since his return to Japan in 1869, Brown's primary
goal had been to focus his time and energy on translating the Bible
into Japanese. He was often frustrated by the need to spend much time
teaching English to support himself. He lamented, "I feel the effect of
years [sixty-five] and hard work. If I have accomplished little in life, it is
not because I have been idle. I want to accomplish something for Japan,
that shall live after me, when I am gone. This incites me to work at
the translation of the S.S. [Sacred Scriptures]. In the good providence
of God, I have a little property getting me some income, & this with
what I can earn by teaching half of each day, enables me to live, and do
something for the cause of missions. I have just finished the revision
of Luke's gospel."[90] From 1874, as chair of the translation committee,
Brown was able for the next five years to make this his primary work. Of
course it had become a team effort.

The four missionaries who, in fulfillment of the plan set forth at
the missionary meeting of September 20, 1872, contributed most to
the project were Brown (Reformed), Hepburn (Presbyterian), Greene
(American Board), and Maclay (Methodist). They could not have fulfilled
their responsibilities, however, without the assistance of their Japanese

90    SRB to JMF, Dec. 5, 1873.

The mature Samuel R. Brown and Okuno Masatsuna

colleagues, chosen from among the first Christian converts. Okuno Masatsuna, one of the first elders and one of the first three ordained Japanese ministers, had more to do with the first efforts at translation than any other. He worked with the committee more than two years. Takahashi Goro, Ibuka Kajinosuke, and Miwa also participated in the translation work. However, it was of Matsuyama Takayoshi that Hepburn said,

> He was our chief dependence, assistant, and arbiter in all cases of difficulty. Whatever virtue there is in our Japanese text, is mainly, if not altogether owing to his scholarly ability, the perfect knowledge he has of his own language, his conscientious care, and his identifying himself with the work. As a Committee we feel especial obligation to him, and extend to him our hearty thanks.
>
> It may safely be said that there is no foreigner in this country who has such a knowledge of the language as to qualify him alone to bring out an idiomatic and good translation, without the aid of a native scholar. And the literary merit of a translation will depend principally upon the ability and scholarship of the native assistant.[91]

As the work of New Testament translation had progressed, the various completed portions had been published piecemeal, for Japanese

[91]    Verbeck, "History," 113-7; Cary, *History* II, 149.

Christians eagerly awaited the publication of the scriptures in their own language and missionaries and Japanese evangelists desperately needed this resource. The translated portions were cut on wooden blocks and printed for publication and distribution. Brown's health had begun to deteriorate already in 1877. At that time he had written, "My disease is neuralgia and affects my heart. If I can keep up the school for the theological students, by the aid of my daughter and niece, and work at the translation of the Scriptures, I shall be happy."[92] However, Brown was forced to discontinue his work on the translation of the last two chapters of Revelation and on the final revision of the New Testament in the summer of 1879. His health had deteriorated to the point that he could not sit still because of discomfort. He was seen by a Dutch doctor in Tokyo and was under the care of Simmons in Yokohama for what was described as a bladder condition and as an old man's disease. Brown was likely suffering from prostate problems. He wrote to Ferris, "I have no desire to give up my work in Japan (it is home to me), but it may be the only way to recover my health. So I wish now to go to the U. States for a change I think. I desire to do God's will in the matter, not my own."[93]

Unable to continue their work, the Browns sailed to America for the last time July 27, 1879. On May 11, 1880, the veteran translator received a letter in America from Japan announcing the meeting that had taken place April 19, 1880, at the Shinsakae-bashi Church in Tokyo to celebrate the completion of the translation of the New Testament into the Japanese language. Brown died a month after receiving the letter, on June 19, 1880, at the age of seventy, knowing that his final life goal had been accomplished. He died at Monson, Massachusetts, his childhood home, and was buried there beside his parents.[94]

In 1880, almost twenty-one years after the arrival of the first Protestant missionaries, at last the entire New Testament was available to the Japanese people in their own language. It was a significant milestone for the spread of Christianity in Japan. Concerning Brown's chief work, the translation of the New Testament into Japanese, Stout wrote in 1901: "If the length of time during which the first translation has been the accepted standard version by all classes in Japan—some portions for nearly thirty years and the whole book over twenty—be a test of excellence, then that translation must have been the product of careful, conscientious scholarship. As the work went on his health failed.

[92]   Griffis, *A Maker*, 271.
[93]   SRB to JMF, June 10, 1879.
[94]   Griffis, *A Maker*, 301-02, 316-17.

He prayed that he might live to see it completed, and to accomplish this seemed to be the first ambition of his last days. He had the satisfaction of seeing the New Testament complete in print."[95] This fine translation was recognized as the authorized translation of the New Testament until a revision was undertaken in 1917.

Meanwhile, in May of 1878, a broader ecumenical basis for the promotion of Bible translation had been worked out at a convention of missionaries. In the interim since 1872, when the original translation committee had been agreed upon, many additional agencies or mission boards had sent missionaries to Japan. Furthermore, in addition to the work of the New Testament translation committee based in Yokohama, missionaries of several denominations in Tokyo had begun translation of the Old Testament in 1876. At the convention of 1878, missionaries representing ten mission boards and three Bible societies—the American Bible Society, the British and Foreign Bible Society, and the National Bible Society of Scotland—worked out a cooperative agreement. The result was the first organized measures for the translation of the Old Testament, as well as wider cooperation in overseeing the final stages of the translation and revision of the New Testament. Consequently, when the full New Testament was published, and later when the whole Bible was published, it was done with the authorization of all Protestant missionaries in Japan.[96]

Guido Verbeck became deeply involved in this revision and translation after he resigned his government work. Upon his return to Tokyo from a furlough in 1879, he resumed part-time teaching at the Tokyo Union Theological School and preached and taught weekly in the churches, especially at the Koji-machi Church in Tokyo. However, the decade of the 1880s was the period of Verbeck's most intense commitment to Bible translation. For several years he spent five or six days a week engrossed almost exclusively in Bible translation. This task made use of his prodigious linguistic gifts and depth of biblical and literary scholarship. He completed his translation of the Psalms on July 19, 1887, a gift to the Christians of Japan for which he was to be long admired and remembered.[97]

The daunting task of translating the Old Testament into Japanese was initiated by the missionaries. However, from 1884 Matsuyama Takayoshi, Uemura Masahisa, and Ibuka Kajinosuke became members of the translation committee. Without their participation in this

---

[95]    Ibid., 318-19.
[96]    Verbeck,"History," 95-98, 115.
[97]    Griffis, *Verbeck*, 320.

endeavor, this first Japanese translation of the whole Bible could never have achieved the literary quality for which it became renowned. The Old Testament translation was completed and the whole Bible at last published in Japanese by the end of 1887, a translation task spanning twenty-eight years from the arrival of the first missionaries. The Old Testament translation was of such high quality that it came to be recognized by the churches and biblical scholars of Japan as the authorized text until 1955.[98]

### The Future of Nagasaki Station

The Japan Mission was plagued not only by the continuing shortage of missionary personnel but also by the related persistent shortfalls in financial support of the work by the Reformed churches. The mission board would approve an annual budget for the Japan Mission, but then not actually send all the approved funds to the treasurer of the Japan Mission on the field. Consequently, the Japan Mission treasurer was forced repeatedly to borrow money at high interest rates in Japan in order to pay missionary salaries and other expenses.

Furthermore, although all the Japan missionaries strongly desired that not only the Yokohama/Tokyo Station but also the Nagasaki Station be adequately staffed and properly supported, they began to discuss whether it would be possible to continue work at both places. What to do especially about the inadequately staffed Nagasaki Station had become a critical issue for the Japan Mission. Amerman, working in Tokyo, stated, "I am not opposed to the Nagasaki work, quite the contrary. I should rejoice to see well supported work in both places, but it is becoming more and more distasteful and repulsive to me and to many others to see half-supported work anywhere."[99] The missionaries had pleaded repeatedly for more personnel but encountered repeated disappointments.

They had asked the board to make a clear decision concerning Nagasaki and been assured that the board wanted the work continued there. However, Amerman felt impelled to write the following from the field. "You will not be surprised that I do not regard the question respecting the abandonment of Nagasaki settled. The Board said we were to continue our work there, but the church do not [sic] sustain the Board. The matter cannot be settled by saying 'we will not give it up.' It can be settled only by <u>doing</u> either the one thing or the other."[100]

[98]    Yanagita, *Short History*, 34.
[99]    JLA to JMF, June 27, 1879.
[100]    JLA to JMF, July 24, 1879.

The Verbecks and the Ballaghs returned from furlough in the fall of 1879, the Stouts and the Millers had left Japan for furlough in late spring of that year, the Farrington sisters departed for America that summer, and the Browns also left Japan during the summer because of the failing health of Dr. Brown. Consequently, the Amermans and Misses Witbeck and Winn were in fact the only Reformed Church missionaries left in Japan in the summer of 1879. Clearly, the time had come for the mission board and the Reformed Church constituency to act decisively in regard to its Japan Mission.

During that summer there was a cholera epidemic in many parts of Japan, and travel within the country was restricted to prevent the further spread of disease. Amerman maintained the work of the mission by regular correspondence with the Japanese pastors, evangelists, and theological students working at all of the outstations and Nagasaki. He believed that the work would not suffer irreparably while so short-handed during the summer months. But he urged, "The work will suffer however if help does not come before the middle of September, and it will suffer specially of course in Yokohama in the schools. I should make an exception in what I have said, in reference to the work in the city of Nagasaki. There the work must suffer anyhow. We have not even a licensed helper to send there."[101]

In response to the repeated requests of the missionaries, the board sent the Reverend Eugene S. and Emilie Booth as new missionaries in the fall of 1879. Eugene Booth was a graduate of Rutgers College (1876) and of the New Brunswick Theological Seminary (1879). The young missionary couple was assigned to Nagasaki. Amerman continued to be concerned about the future of Nagasaki Station. He reported,

> If the station is to be properly maintained he can not be there too soon. Already the eyes of others are upon the place. By Bro. Stout's advice, Mr. Tsuge, who was left in charge of the chapel and its services, began to attend a school conducted by one of the members of the English Church Mission, and has since had strong pressure brought to bear on him to "go over" to the work of that body, and the A. M. E. Mission [Methodist], I am credibly informed, are about starting a girls' school on the lot adjoining that on which Bro. Stout and the Misses Farrington lived.[102]

Obviously, even while carrying on monthly fellowship meetings across denominational lines and ostensibly recognizing the legitimacy

[101]  JLA to JMF, Aug. 6, 1879.
[102]  JLA to JMF, Aug. 30, 1879.

of each other's ministries, the missionaries of these other denominations that did not join the union church movement were not above "sheep stealing" and blatant competition.

On December 19, 1879, an important meeting was held at the home of S. R. Brown in Orange, New Jersey. Those present at the meeting were the Browns and the Japan missionaries then on furlough, Henry Stout and E. Rothsay and Mary Miller. In a letter to Ferris, Miller reported:

> In view of the well understood opinions of the members of the Japan Mission as a whole relative to the station at Nagasaki, those of the mission at present in this country, in order to bring these views before the Board of Foreign Missions, met at the home of Dr. S. R. Brown....
>
> After full discussion and comparison of views it was the unanimous opinion of the members of the mission there present that:
>
> 1st. In order to carry on the work at Nagasaki effectively, it must be made a full station, with Preparatory school and a Theological class, and to do this there must be at least <u>three</u> men there. The reasons for this are:
>
> · Nagasaki is so far removed from Yokohama and Tokyo, being some 750 miles, or five days by steamer.
> · The students who go to Tokyo to study, after seeing the work and Christianity there seem to lose interest in Nagasaki and wish to remain in the capital.
> · All the time these young men are studying in Tokyo their work is lost to Nagasaki, for even during the summer vacation they could hardly be expected to return on account of the distance and expense, and did they do so there would be no one to carry on the work they might thus begin.
> · We have in a sense to compete with other missions because the natives incline to go to the strong missions where the work is carried on effectively.
>
> 2nd. If the Board cannot carry out the plan of manning Nagasaki efficiently, we would advise to give up the Nagasaki station at once without more waste of time and money and to concentrate on Yokohama & Tokyo....Mr. Miller was appointed to present this matter before the Board at its next meeting in January, with the understanding that Dr. Brown was also to be present if possible.

Consequently, it is clear that there was unanimity among the Japan Reformed missionaries in regard to the work at Nagasaki, in which the Verbecks and Stouts had each labored for ten years. They were at one in their conviction that the mission work there ought to be adequately supported and developed, and if that could not be done, it would be wise to abandon that effort and to focus the Reformed Church Mission's limited resources in Yokohama and Tokyo. In fact, the American Board Japan Mission had offered to take over the inadequately supported work centered in Nagasaki, and to receive the Stouts into their Mission.[103]

During the absence of the Stouts from Nagasaki (from May of 1879), Japanese assistants carried on the ministries of the Nagasaki Station to the best of their abilities for several months. Eugene and Emilie Booth arrived in Yokohama October 24, 1879, and proceeded soon afterward to Nagasaki, their assigned destination, arriving there by ship on December 9. The Japanese assistants had gained a certain level of English, and, in the absence of the Stouts, Eugene Booth, despite his inexperience, was to give them a measure of supervision while studying the Japanese language.

There was discussion of sending Ballagh, who had just returned from America, to Nagasaki for a few months to introduce Booth to the work and help him get started. Instead, at the urging of Verbeck and Ballagh, it was Amerman who was sent to Nagasaki. His colleagues pointed out that he had had only one week of vacation in two years, and that his visit to give moral support and counsel to the Booths could also be a time of rejuvenation for himself. Amerman was away from his seminary teaching in Tokyo on his trip to Nagasaki from January 21, 1880, for thirty-six days, and he gave a thorough evaluation of the situation of the Nagasaki Station. He wrote in part,

> I found Rev. & Mrs. Booth well and settled in the house formerly occupied by Mr. Stout. I was much pleased with the intelligent zeal and effectiveness with which he begins his study of the language and his oversight of our work. I was gratified too by what I saw and heard of Christian work in Nagasaki, specially our part of it. It has been represented as discouraging, and it is.... Notwithstanding great labor,...few of those who live in the city are affected by the truths of the Gospel, and with a few exceptions the various audiences at the preaching are made up from those

[103]   JLA to JMF, Sept. 6, 1879.

who come in from the outlying villages. Yet our part of the work in this city is at least equally fair & promising with that of the other two Missions represented. It is more prosperous when we consider their greater number of workers....The attendance does not vary in the different churches. It is ordinarily 12-15 on Sunday morning & 30 Sunday evening. The number of scholars in the Sabbath School varies from 6-18. There will be on one Sunday 6 or 8 new scholars, who receive one session's instruction & take away with them the little books from which they study. But before the next Sunday the little books will be sent back with the message that they will not be allowed to attend....

Our helper Mr. Tsuge is working well, and seems anxious to do all that he can....He was ordained as an elder and Mr. Kamitaro, formerly in Bro. Stout's employ, was ordained as deacon while I was with them, Rev. Mr. Segawa assisting in the service....

I will tell you of the effort we made to secure a stall for the sale of Scriptures, etc., at the annual exhibition....The application was made in due form in the name of Mr. Tsuge, with frank avowal of the character of books which would be exposed for sale. The officials replied that they could not give permission to sell Christian books, but we could have assigned a place to sell books and then we could sell what we pleased, only requiring that a catalogue should be sent by the middle of March, the exhibition opening April 1. The location of the stall is peculiar. Adjoining the exhibition ground in the Nagasaki Park at the south of the city is a temple called the Suwa Sha [actually a Shinto shrine]. It is on the hillside and is approached by an ascent of over 250 stone steps. The principle exit from the exhibition ground will be through the precincts of this temple, and there on the thoroughfare in the quadrangle before the temple is the spot assigned for the sale of books. And there for the space of 50 days if nothing occurs to deprive us of the permission now in Mr. Tsuge's possession Japanese & Chinese Bibles & portions and other Christian books will be exposed for sale. Pray for our brethren there that the Lord will bless and prosper them in this enterprise & make it a seed sowing whose harvest will be speedy and joyous.[104]

During Amerman's Nagasaki visit, Segawa came up from Kagoshima and was able to give a firsthand account of the progress at that outstation. What had appeared at first to be wonderfully promising

[104] JLA to JMF, March 3, 1880.

had turned out to be quite disappointing. Amerman reported that after the Satsuma rebellion,

> the people formerly the most exclusive of all this exclusive race suddenly appeared to be specially open to the influences of Christianity....Helpers were sent down to preach, and found large audiences, 250 I am told was not unusual. But now alas, the novelty has worn away, and the crowds melted. 8 or 10 come to Sunday morning service and 20 in the evening, 20 also on Wednesday evening of whom 4 or 5 stay to attend a prayer meeting afterward. Many who were baptized have fallen away. Bro. Stout's policy (& it is the policy of the whole Mission) was the true one. When others were baptizing many he would baptize none...not satisfied that the applicants were sufficiently prepared. We have in Kagoshima but 4 baptized persons but these are all steadfast in the faith and one of them renders much assistance to the Rev. Mr. Segawa. Souls are to be saved no more easily in Kagoshima than anywhere else in Japan. As a field of labor it is no worse nor yet is it any better than a multitude of other localities....
>
> In this connection let me say that the action of the members of the Japan Mission now in America giving certain advice in reference to the maintenance or discontinuance of Nagasaki work meets with the approval of the members of the Mission here. Either sustain it well, or give it up.[105]

In his first letter to the board from Nagasaki, Booth shared his quite positive observations of the work there and showed his concern that the possibility of abandoning the Nagasaki Station was being considered. He appealed "to the churches that they will...by their prayers & material strength reinforce & strengthen the field." He added, "The influences working against Christianity as you know are peculiar here. But shall we acknowledge that we are baffled by them & be driven from the field?...The work is God's and not our own. Let us then have faith in Him to speedily give us a rich harvest in the place of strong prejudice and terrible idolatry." He also quoted James Ballagh, who had said, "I think the agitation of giving up Nagasaki field exceedingly unfortunate."[106] In the summer of 1880, word of the board's decision regarding Nagasaki Station finally reached missionaries on the field. Booth responded, "We were delighted to hear through Mr. Amerman

---

[105]   Ibid.
[106]   ESB to JMF, Feb. 2 and March 24, 1880.

'Nagasaki is not to be given up at present,' and 'an effort is to be made to sustain it.'"[107] Later Booth wrote, "We are greatly rejoiced by the news from home, received last mail. Bro. Stout writes that they will leave in the early autumn for <u>Nagasaki</u>, and also that the Board promises another man, for this station, who will follow speedily. My greatest wish is he might accompany Bro. Stout."[108]

## Surprising Developments in Saga

The Booths still represented the mission alone in Nagasaki when surprising developments came to light. With the aid of the Japanese assistants, services continued at the Nagasaki Church, with an average attendance of fifteen in the morning and twenty-five in the evening. The work at the outstation in Kagoshima also continued. However, during the absence of the Stouts a remarkable encounter brought about a significant discovery. The witness of the samurai from Saga, Murata Wakasa no Kami, who had been a member of Verbeck's distant Bible class and baptized secretly by him in 1866, was still having an impact fourteen years later, some six years after his death. With great excitement, on May 13, 1880, Booth wrote the following from Nagasaki to Verbeck.

An incident occurred here last week, in connection with the mission, which I am sure you will be deeply interested in, and I take the first opportunity to write you about it.

On Sunday last I noticed two ladies at preaching, whom I had never seen there before. I noticed them particularly because of the marked interest they took in every word spoken, & several times I could see tears flowing freely.

The next day I received word that they wished to see me. They came accordingly and introduced themselves as O. Kumashiro and O. Miyanaga. The former was none other than the daughter of Wakasa, whom you baptized fourteen years ago. The latter was her old nurse. This old servant had wished to be baptized for a long time, but was too poor to come all the way from Saga where she has been living ever since. The daughter, too, had desired to be baptized, but had failed in her purpose; for when four years ago she came with her husband to Nagasaki, she found that you had left this place long ago, nor did she know of any other missionaries here. But her father's faithful teaching has

[107]   ESB to JMF, July 1, 1880.
[108]   ESB to JMF, Aug. 13, 1880.

remained with them both. It appears, however, that her husband is soon to be removed to Osaka, & she felt that she must be baptized before leaving this place for good. She wrote therefore to her old nurse to come from Saga, in order to go with her in search of a man of the true God. The nurse came & for several days they went together looking for your successor, if he could be found. They chanced one day to pass our bookstore, and seeing the books, they stopped to examine them. And there they found the Scriptures translated into Japanese & in a style which they could read. The Word of God which they had heard read by the father & master they could now read for themselves! The young man in charge of the bookstore says their joy at the discovery was unbounded. Their search had not been in vain; they staid a long time at the store asking the young man about Christianity; they evidently had found "the pearl of great price."

When they came to me they asked for baptism, saying they could remain a few days only. I put them off, but they importuned me with tears. I then explained to them the nature of baptism, all of which they seemed to know before; they had come well prepared & were not to be refused. They had truly been taught of the Spirit. I learned from the daughter, in the course of our conversations, that she had for years been accustomed to daily go into her husband's godown [storage building] to pray. When I asked her for the reason of this, she said that her children & others would disturb her when she tried to pray in her house. She said they believed Jesus Christ to be their only Saviour, & they wished to be baptized because Wakasa had taught them from the Bible that if they believed in Jesus they should be baptized. I therefore set a time for the ceremony. They came at the appointed time and, indeed, accompanied by O. Kumashiro's husband, who seemed quite willing that she should be baptized & asked many intelligent questions, expressing a desire to know more about Christianity.

Yesterday these ladies called upon me to say goodbye, as they leave here for Osaka today. I gave them letters to native Christians & also a few lines to an American missionary at Osaka. They expressed deep regret at being compelled so soon to separate from us. They have purchased the whole of the N. T. Scriptures in Japanese [just recently published]. I was very happy to be able to --- with them the N. T. complete. They have taken besides a large budget of tracts, saying they wished them to give to their friends, many of whom are anxious to learn about Christianity.

The man who years ago picked up the English N. T. in Nagasaki Bay still lives....He is a kindman [relative] of the old nurse, & she says she will lend him her Japanese N. T., which she thinks he will be delighted to read. I also send him a number of tracts.

Mrs. Kumashiro's husband said you would probably remember him. They all asked to be remembered to you.

You can better imagine the fullness of our hearts than we can describe it. God is truly good to give us the privilege we have enjoyed in welcoming these people to the visible church of our Lord, Jesus Christ. He kept them all these years, though we knew it not. I shall live in daily expectation of "more to follow."[109]

Historian Otis Cary later related the following:

The nurse soon returned to Saga, where she resumed her work of teaching a small school for girls. She also organized a Bible-class for women, and its members soon became the teachers of a Sunday school. Though she is no longer living [1909], the influence of her work still remains in Saga. Among the believers there was a son of Wakasa. The daughter, who removed to Osaka and later to Tokyo, became prominent in religious and philanthropic work. Her husband also became a Christian.

At the close of a meeting held in Tokyo about 1883, a man stepped forward and said to Dr. Verbeck: "I am Ayabe [brother of Wakasa, also baptized by Verbeck in 1866]. Since my baptism I have been in the army and also employed in surveying. During all these years I have always carried the Bible with me, and I have been accustomed to read it daily." The next day he came with his only daughter, about fifteen years old, asking that she be baptized. At one time he was a local preacher in the Methodist Church.[110]

In this manner, the hitherto unknown influence of the Murata family of Saga gradually came to light. Wakasa had faithfully taught the people around him, and he had translated the Lord's Prayer and a few portions of the gospels from the Chinese Bible he had obtained, and had written these out for them in the simple *kana* form of Japanese.[111]

---

[109]    ESB to GFV, May 13, 1880.
[110]    Cary, *History* II, 60-61.
[111]    ESB to JMF, May 14, 1880.

Wakasa's daughter was called Orui (Kumashiro Rui). The one who had been her nurse (woman employed for child-care) was called Osuga (Miyanaga Suga).

During Stout's absence, many changes had occurred. Shortly before the Booths arrived in Nagasaki, on October 5, 1879, Segawa Asashi was ordained the first Japanese minister of western Japan. He continued in his ministry in Kagoshima. Tomegawa left Nagasaki to complete his theological education at the seminary in Tokyo. During 1880, lay preacher Tsuge Takenori preached at Nagasaki Church but also undertook some itinerant preaching out from Nagasaki. From May, for about six months, he went twice each month to conduct preaching services in Omura. Despite opposition from local Buddhist priests, an average of twenty-five people attended. Tsuge also made one more extensive preaching tour in 1880, visiting Amakusa, Shimabara, and Saga. Amakusa and Shimabara had been the scenes of horrendous persecution and martyrdom of Christians in the seventeenth century. In Amakusa the reception Tsuge received was decidedly cool. No opportunity to preach developed, but he went from house to house with tracts and spoke to some individuals about Christianity. In Shimabara, however, audiences of about one hundred gathered to hear him preach. The experience in Saga was even more exciting.

In Saga, not only did audiences of about one hundred gather to hear Tsuge preach, but also an important encounter took place. Two women, to his great surprise, expressed an interest in being baptized. They had been taught Christianity by the old woman from near Saga called Osuga (Miyanaga Suga), who had recently been baptized in Nagasaki. Tsuge learned that Osuga was diligently studying the Bible she had acquired in Nagasaki in the spring and that she was teaching the gospel to her friends. Booth commented, "Thus the Lord is opening a work for us in Saga, which we are in no condition, at present, to look after & care for. We need a native helper there very much."[112] Later, additional remarkable stories came to light about the faith and witness of the first converts baptized by Verbeck in 1866.

---

[112]   ESB to JMF, Sept. 24, 1880.

CHAPTER 5

# The Most Promising Years of Protestant Mission

## Henry Stout's Enlarged Vision

The Stouts returned to Japan in time for the Japan Mission meeting in Yokohama early in December 1880, and they returned to Nagasaki Station December 19. They brought with them promises from the board that provision would be made to enlarge the work on the island of Kyushu. Stout now had a colleague in Eugene Booth. His closest associate, Segawa, had become an ordained minister, and his second protégé, Tomegawa, would soon return from a year of study at the Tokyo theological school. The work in Kagoshima had continued under the Segawas, with help from Tomegawa and then from the lay preacher, Tsuge. Kagoshima Church was organized July 23, 1881, with a membership of eighteen adults and thirteen children, mostly from six families, and the Kagoshima work included outstations in Sendai and Taramizu.[1]

Having been reassured by the mission board of the sure prospect of increased support for Nagasaki Station after a year or so, Stout and

[1]    HS to JMF, Sept. 2, 1881.

Booth formulated plans and proposals for enlarging the work and began what they could immediately. Stout served as secretary and Booth as treasurer of Nagasaki Station, and another missionary was to be appointed to join them. Their plans for the station included the development of a school for boys and young men under Booth's leadership. He opened this preparatory school in February 1881, and during the spring session attendance averaged seventeen or eighteen. He was assisted in the school by two Japanese men. One served as an interpreter of English textbooks while the other taught Japanese and Chinese classical literature. This program began as a day school, but Booth hoped to develop it into a boarding school in order to nurture Christian faith and life in the students more effectively.

The classes for girls had been temporarily suspended for lack of teachers, but the proposed plan envisioned a boarding school for girls as well. In contrast to the school recently begun in Nagasaki by Methodist missionaries, at which education was in English and tuition free, Stout and Booth held that the school should avoid denationalizing the students and should expect parents to share the cost of education. Clarifying their vision, they said, "It seems to us it would be better to establish a boarding school in a number of Japanese houses grouped together, and differing not materially from what the girls would occupy when settled in life. There they could be taught not only English and Japanese branches of learning, but to be useful as wives and members of society when they leave the school." Three Christian young women, two who had been educated at Ferris Girls' School and one who had been taught by Mrs. Hepburn, lived in Nagasaki and could serve as assistants in such a school. They hoped that women missionary teachers for this school would be provided by the Reformed Church soon.[2]

Stout took responsibility for evangelistic work and oversight of the churches and outstations. In August of 1881, the church work of Nagasaki Station included the two organized churches and several outstations. Kagoshima Church activity included a small day school as well as the outreach to Taramizu and Sendai. Segawa was in charge there and Tsuge assisted him. Nagasaki Church work encompassed regular itinerant services in Saga and Omura. The licensed preacher, Tomegawa, was in charge of the work in Saga, although not resident there.

At the same time, Stout was beginning to formalize a program of theological education and training of candidates for the ministry in Nagasaki. He had, of course, already for several years been teaching

---

[2]    HS to JMF, Aug. 19, 1881.

Segawa and Tomegawa, as well as Tsuge. In the summer of 1881, when the plan for Nagasaki Station was proposed, Segawa was already an ordained minister and Tomegawa was a licensed preacher, to be examined for ordination in the spring of 1882. However, the development of the work of Nagasaki Station would require many Japanese evangelists. This need began to be met in an unexpected manner.

An Anglican missionary, H. Maundrell, had worked briefly in Saga and had baptized a number of people there. Among them were Yoshidomi Yasada[3] in 1877, and Kawasaki Toshio, Mine Shinzo, and Ohara Masao, with some members of their families, in 1879. In November of 1877 Maundrell had initiated a class of four students in Nagasaki to train candidates for the ministry. In 1881 these four men from Saga requested transfer to Nagasaki Church and the tutelage of Henry Stout. Although baptized by the Church of England missionary, Stout reported that the men "found the government [of that mission] as administered here quite intolerable, so that for some time they had contemplated a change of church relations, and about a week ago they were received by us."[4]

Saga was the very place where the first fruits of witness in western Japan had been realized in the baptism of Murata Wakasa and his brother Ayabe by Verbeck fifteen years before, and where Murata's influence continued to be felt. These four men wanted to become ministers, and thus a group of candidates for the ministry was providentially provided. Kurihara Kemmei, a member of Kagoshima Church, also joined the group of theological students, and Stout began to formalize theological education. Yoshidomi had already had considerable preparation, but the other four were beginning students. Segawa was brought up from Kagoshima to Nagasaki in the fall of 1881 to be pastor of Nagasaki Church and assist Stout in the development of a theological school. Of Segawa it was reported, "He is a fair scholar in English, and with Mr. Stout's help will make a translation of the essential points of a theological system, and prepare lectures for the class by reading English textbooks. In this way it is hoped that a more serviceable course can be given to the students, and that the way may be made clear to pass this work eventually into native hands."[5]

Stout and Booth did not believe that teaching the candidates English thoroughly first and then providing a theological education with English as the medium, as at first practiced by Brown, was the best

---

3    Yoshidomi married Kikutake Hatsui, the young woman who kept the class for girls going in Nagasaki after the Farrington sisters left.
4    HS & ESB to Japan Mission Tokyo/Yokohama Station, Nov. 3, 1881.
5    HS Nagasaki Station Report, Aug. 10, 1881.

way to prepare men for the ministry. Furthermore, the Tokyo Union Theological School was 750 miles away, five days in good weather by ship. The distance and travel expense would preclude fieldwork by such students in their native region and transfer their affections to the big city areas. Stout was convinced that it was best to train candidates for the ministry on the island of Kyushu in close proximity to the places where they would serve. He unveiled his vision of training for the ministry, in which the academic aspect of theological education would be interspersed with practical evangelistic training and experience. His plan integrated theological education with evangelistic outreach into the interior of the island of Kyushu.

> We have arranged a plan of study and work which is to carry the students through a four year course of preparation for the ministry. So important do we consider it to train these men, who are of the samurai or two-sworded class, to habits of work as well as study, that in connection with six months of study here, we shall require them to go in turn to the outstations for four months, two months at a time, for work. During the two months summer vacation, they will all be out, and being able to assist each other the work will be lighter. By this arrangement we shall have an assistant with the regular workers at Kagoshima, and one man to look after the interests of Saga.[6]

The plan for Nagasaki Station proposed by Stout and Booth also included establishing a Christian hospital there. They urged, "We are more and more persuaded of the great utility of medical work for this place. The prejudice against the Christian name is terrible, —fruit of Jesuit sowing. Something to bring the people into contact with Christians and to show what they are, is of absolute necessity to the success of missions here."[7] The board gave positive consideration to this proposal, and Stout urged, "Something is needed to break the terrible prejudice against the Christian name."[8] However, the proposal was never acted upon, and, except for Simmons in Yokohama for one year (from 1859), the Reformed Church never implemented medical mission work in Japan.[9]

---

[6]    HS to JMF, Aug. 10, 1881.
[7]    Ibid.
[8]    HS to JMF, Jan. 2, 1882.
[9]    HS to JMF, Dec. 30, 1880, Aug. 10, 1881; ESB to JMF, Feb. 24 and Aug. 19, 1881; Cary, *History* II, 132; Nishi Yutaka, *Nagasaki Kyokai no Sosoki, Jo: Shiryo to Kaisetsu* (Shizuoka, Japan: Kirisutokyo Shidankai, 2003), 16-18.

Stout was encouraged by reassurances from the board that some priority was to be given to enlarging the work of Nagasaki Station. However, he could not hide his disappointment when Booth had to depart for Yokohama to recover his health in the fall of 1881. Booth had seemed committed to the work in Nagasaki but appeared to Stout to lack the stamina required for that work. Stout determinedly continued the classes of the little preparatory school, with help from Elizabeth and Japanese assistants.

Not only the particularly resistant environment of the Nagasaki area but also the lack of provision for facilities by the Reformed Church Board of Foreign Missions played a part in the attrition among missionary personnel. But repeatedly, issues of health also contributed to the problem. The climate in Kyushu was clearly more difficult. The summer weather in particular was more debilitating than farther north in Japan, both heat and humidity being extremely high. After an unusually dry hot spell, Henry Stout jokingly remarked, "It has been intensely hot and very dry. But last night we had a fine rain. However, this does not increase our personal comfort. One becomes more limp under boiling than by roasting."[10]

Regarding education for girls, he wrote, "As to the girls' school, it is indeed a hope deferred and a subject of great disappointment, so far, but none the less eminently desirable, difficult as it may now be to establish, under the shadow of the great Methodist, free institution. But judiciously managed and headed by talant [sic], it will win in the end."[11]

Stout believed firmly in the validity of the master plan for Nagasaki Station and pleaded determinedly for the personnel necessary for its realization. Stout was promised reinforcements but disappointed again and again. The latest disappointment was that Booth did not return. Stout, carrying on virtually alone, showed growing discouragement, impatience, and irritation, perhaps even anger at what he perceived to be the low priority given to the work in Nagasaki. In the fall of 1882 he wrote to Ferris, saying,

> I am going to make a confession....I have felt for a long time that there was a very lukewarm feeling in the Board towards Nagasaki. It has seemed to me that there was no real expectation, nor intention, perhaps, to do much more for the place, unless the circumstances of the Board were changed in some very marked

---

[10]   HS to JMF, Aug. 10, 1883.
[11]   HS to JMF, Jan. 2, 1882.

manner....I had therefore some months ago decided to wait the action of the Board in the Autumn, and if no more favorable disposition appeared towards Nagasaki, to offer my resignation, asking the Board either to take me home, or to give me a letter to some other Board, so that I might make arrangements to work in the field to which I am attached by many ties. It was hard to reach such a conclusion, for my life is bound up in the Refd. Church and her mission. But there are no doubt times when we ought to sacrifice feeling, in order that we may, as we believe, serve our Master better.

You may therefore imagine my pleasure in reading your letter. If I have waited and worked alone nearly fourteen years, I can certainly wait one more, being assured that steps are actually taken for relief.[12]

His hope had been buoyed by a letter from the secretary indicating that something would really be done to augment the missionary force in Nagasaki. Consequently, Stout sent information that might be used to persuade others in America of the great possibilities and opportunities of Nagasaki Station. He continued to advocate enthusiastically for the enlargement of mission work there, and he also continued to feel that if the missionary personnel could be increased at Nagasaki, it would be more practical and economical for Nagasaki Station to become organized as a mission, separate in organization from the work centered in Yokohama and Tokyo.

Meanwhile, as of January 1883, the work of Nagasaki Station was being carried on by the Stouts and the two ordained Japanese colleagues, Segawa and Tomegawa, in Nagasaki, Kagoshima, and Saga. Besides general oversight of the station, Stout was involved in preaching, teaching the class of theological students (church history and biblical studies), and the translation of theological works into Japanese for use in theological education. Elizabeth Stout worked with the women of the church, and did some informal teaching of young girls. Segawa served as pastor of Nagasaki Church, taught the theological students (theology), and also translated materials for the theological curriculum. Tomegawa served as pastor of Kagoshima Church, while also overseeing a small school there and preaching at outstations. No pastor was available to send to Saga, but the lay leaders there were assisted by a Bible colporteur resident in Saga for a time, and Stout, Segawa, and the

---

12    HS to JMF, Oct. 2, 1882.

theological students regularly visited Saga to preach. In this way, the work at the three sites was maintained, but Stout and his colleagues waited and yearned for the means to reach out more effectively and to act on larger opportunities they saw before them.

Stout's vision at last began to be realized late in 1883 with the appointment of the Reverend Nathan H. and Annie Demarest. Upon arrival, Demarest began language study in preparation for evangelistic work. In May of 1884 the force was further augmented by the arrival of the Reverend Howard and Lizzie B. Harris, Mary E. Brokaw, and Clara B. Richards for educational work. The Nagasaki Station report for 1884, written by Demarest, reflected an optimism scarcely imaginable before. "Such a large reinforcement...is...unprecedented, and we hope it will be the means of new vigor and under God's blessing of much ingathering in this Station for twenty-five years held by a single man."[13]

In 1885, the board in America clearly reaffirmed the plan to develop both evangelistic and educational work in Kyushu (Nagasaki Station). However, before Stout could fully orient the new missionaries, once again their number was depleted. Only months after her arrival in Nagasaki, Clara Richards resigned to become the wife of Professor J. M. Dixon, an American teaching at the Imperial University in Tokyo. Howard Harris helped by teaching the regular English studies for boys for almost a year, sharing the small schoolroom built next to the Stout home with Mary Brokaw, who was using it for a small class of girls. Appropriations from the board for proper school buildings were not forthcoming. Having accepted the call to do educational missionary work at Nagasaki, Harris felt frustrated by the lack of facilities and any structured school at which to serve. Some missionaries in Tokyo and Yokohama were not in sympathy with the board's decision to develop the work in Nagasaki. While not objecting to lower level mission school education, they took the position that "a school for advanced academical instruction and theological school are entirely unnecessary" in Nagasaki.[14]

Influenced at least in part by the attitudes of missionaries in Tokyo, Harris soon showed a lack of enthusiasm for developing the mission schools in Nagasaki and apparently did not get along well with Stout. Harris actually sent a private letter to the board in which he stated, "There is no hope of building up a school there, nor is there an opportunity to teach the Bible. This would have but little weight with me—knowing the desire of the Church to carry on educational

[13]   Nathan H. Demarest to Henry N. Cobb, Nov. 30, 1884.
[14]   JLA to HNC, Aug. 31, 1885.

work there—if I could work in harmony with one who has been there for many years. I find that he who goes there must keep quiet on certain questions and not differ with opinions already entertained, or else he's in deep water. I do not hesitate to say, that as things are going on in Nagasaki at present no one can go there and succeed & for this reason I hesitate."[15] Invited by Wyckoff to assist in the teaching in his school, Harris petitioned the mission for a transfer to Tokyo, and it was granted.[16]

Happily, with the arrival of Mary Brokaw, permanence for the education of young women in Nagasaki was finally assured. Nevertheless, until an associate to replace Richards and the resources to provide a school building could be provided, the school had to remain small. Demarest was studying the language in the hope of concentrating on evangelism, especially outside of the city of Nagasaki. After Harris left, necessity required that Demarest assist in teaching the English subjects at Stout's small school. Demarest was in total agreement with Stout that development of educational work was essential for the future of the Japan Mission's work on the island of Kyushu, but it is clear that they did not have full support in this from missionaries of the Tokyo-Yokohama Station. Friction and disagreement festered within the mission regarding the need for schools in Nagasaki, and when Stout was attacked in a letter from the Tokyo-Yokohama Station intimating he was stubbornly fixated on his own plans and insensitive to the needs of the mission as a whole, Demarest argued in support of the school plans and also came to Stout's defense.

> I am exceedingly surprised and mortified that a brother's candor and honor be thus boldly and recklessly impugned. I think it not only unkind but very uncalled for. For over a year I have worked most intimately with Mr. Stout and our relations have always been of the pleasantest. His plans I have always found well considered and any suggestions I have made have been kindly received. A pleasanter or more thoughtful and faithful companion I could not desire. Such imputations do him much wrong.[17]

The mission board was having great difficulty raising the necessary funds for its gradually more extensive mission work in India, China,

---

[15]    Howard Harris to HNC, Oct. 2, 1885.
[16]    Henry Stout, *Sketch of the South Japan Mission* (New York: Board of Foreign Missions, 1899), 15; HH to HNC, Feb. 14, 1885.
[17]    NHD to HNC, Apr. 19, 1885.

and Japan. In fact, in 1885 there was some talk of retrenchment, and Madanapalle, India, and Nagasaki, Japan, were pointed out as possible places where that could be accomplished.[18] Stout repeatedly made the case that not only evangelistic work but also educational work was essential to the success of Nagasaki Station. But as late as the spring of 1886, the funds promised for the erection of school buildings had not yet arrived on the field. Stout, known as a man of patience in his dealings with students and Japanese colleagues, was losing his patience with the Japan Mission and the board as he felt the fulfillment of his duty and calling, as well as his long cherished and repeatedly approved plans, thwarted again. In desperation, he fought for the future of the work centered in Nagasaki.

In an effort to force things to happen, Stout attempted new approaches. In an April 13, 1886, letter written confidentially to the new secretary of the Board of Foreign Missions, Henry N. Cobb, he suggested that the solution to the financial pressure might be a cutback on personnel in the Tokyo-Yokohama area, where they had the advantage of union work with other Reformed and Presbyterian missions.

A month later, Stout tried another unusual tactic. He composed two lengthy letters addressed to mission board leaders with whom he was personally acquainted in the Reformed Church in the United States (German Reformed) and the Presbyterian Church in the United States (Southern). The virtually identical letters appealed to these other mission boards for help in Nagasaki. However, Stout did not send the letters directly to the addressees, but to his own board secretary, Cobb. He included with them also a letter to the Reformed Church Board of Foreign Missions and a cover letter to Cobb. These four letters reveal Henry Stout's vision, tenacity, unswerving commitment, sense of disappointment, growing impatience, courage, and willingness to fight for his cause.

In the letter to his own board dated May 14, 1886, Stout wrote,

> Dear Brethren: We were greatly encouraged by the action you took last year on two occasions with regard to the work to be done at Nagasaki. And we were led to hope that measures would soon be taken for the execution of the plans decided upon. But the delay enjoined upon us has been disheartening, and is becoming most trying especially in view of the temporary and uncertain condition

---

18   HS to JLA, March 14, 1885.

in which our work is placed. Is it therefore asking too much that the Board take measures at once to proceed in accordance with the decision of last year? We must be perfectly frank and say that we feel unwilling to continue waiting for an indefinite period longer, hoping against hope in view of past experience.

To this letter Nathan Demarest and Mary Brokaw added their signatures. In the cover letter to Cobb, dated May 13, 1886, Stout said about the letter to the board, "The delay to which we are subjected together with the uncertainty which apparently attends the whole matter, is becoming most distressing. We all feel that in some way this suspense must be brought to a close. That is our reason for writing as we have." He went on to explain about the letters to the other mission boards, which he was sending to Cobb for forwarding to the addressees with recognition that it would not be right to take matters into his own hands and initiate basic change without the approval of his own mission board, and also because he hoped the board would approve and pursue such cooperative proposals as he was suggesting. He went on to say, in justification of his aggressive new approach,

> When I see the open doors and consider the demands that are being made, when I go over the field as I have lately done over a portion of it and look at the opportunities, and begin to consider how utterly inadequate our Board appears to be to meet the demands and improve [act on] the opportunities, I feel ready to do almost anything so that the work may go forward. My mind is set a-going first in one direction and then in another, thinking what can be done. These letters are the latest result.

In the letters he prepared for the other mission boards, Stout very diplomatically stated his case, urging cooperative mission work to reach the people of Kyushu with the gospel. He explained how his Japan Mission's Nagasaki Station had continued since 1859 and that marvelous opportunities were opening up, but that the Reformed Church in America had not been able to staff the station adequately. He pointed out that six million people, one-sixth of Japan's population, lived in Kyushu. And that since only two other missions, the Episcopalians and the Methodists, were at work in Kyushu, reaching one-third of that population, or two million people, was the responsibility of the Nagasaki Station. His letter pleaded for their partnership in this task.

Such intense advocacy certainly succeeded in arousing a response from the Reformed Church board. However, as it turned out, Stout's assessment was seen as unnecessarily pessimistic. Moreover, the German Reformed and Southern Presbyterian mission boards never saw the letters. Mail took two or three months to go back and forth. While they were in transit, ironically, positive steps had already been taken by the Reformed Church. Both the Board of Foreign Missions and the Woman's Board had really taken action to implement the promised plans.

A new couple, the Reverend Albert and Alice Oltmans, had been appointed to Nagasaki for the development of the boys' school, and funding for construction of school buildings for both the boys' and girls' schools had finally been provided for through the two mission boards. Stout acknowledged in a letter to Cobb that, in view of the actions the boards had already taken at the time, albeit unknown to Stout in Nagasaki, his strong letters had been unfortunate.[19] In any case, at long last it seemed that Henry Stout's unremitting advocacy was resulting in a more adequate provision for Nagasaki Station.

## The Japan Missions and the Japanese Church

Churches that had organized as a result of the cooperative evangelistic outreach of the Japanese pastors and evangelists and the missionaries of the Reformed and Presbyterian Japan missions became part of the United Church of Christ in Japan. Japanese Christians to be trained at the Tokyo Union Theological School entered the school on the recommendation of their respective churches and were under the supervision of the United Church while preparing for the ministry. As the Japanese church began to grow and mature, and Japanese elders and pastors increased in number, the relationship between the several Japan missions and the United Church began to change. The self-reliance and independence of the church leaders was apparent and, to a large extent, appreciated by the missionaries.

The self-support and self-government of the Japanese churches was a matter of mutual concern. Nevertheless, Amerman's report reveals the difficulty some missionaries had in relinquishing control and trusting the spiritual maturity and wisdom of the Japanese Christians.

Another special meeting of the Council of the Three Missions was held last week, when the matter of requiring churches to assume the entire support of their pastors was discussed at length. It was finally decided however that this should <u>not</u> be required; a

[19]   HS to HNC, Sept, 2, 1886.

schedule, however, was adopted,...providing that according to the number of members in any church, viz., under 25, 25-50, from 50 to 75, & from 75-100 the church must pay 1/4, 1/3, 1/2 & 3/4 of its pastor's salary,...the balance being the maximum of help to be given in any case. Churches having more than 100 members are expected to pay their pastor's entire salary....

Another matter, which provoked lengthy discussion at this meeting of the Council, was the proposition that as missionaries we should withdraw from any formal connection with the native church and assume a position purely advisory. The reasons advanced in favor of this were; 1st, We only became members (ex officio) in order to train them to manage affairs for themselves and this they can now do after 3 years of training, as they have men who are fully competent to fill all the offices and who are familiar with the rules of government and methods of procedure. 2nd, We would still be at least as influential with them as now, because the native members of the Chukuwai [*chukai*] already outnumber the missionaries and can refuse our advise [*sic*] and even outvote us if they please, and this reason has force from the manifestation at the spring meeting of a spirit, in some of the younger men especially, of opposition to foreigners as such, which led to some unpleasant scenes. And 3rd, Our position would be more dignified and our relation to the church as its advisors and fosterers more clearly exhibited. The brethren were not however ready to take the proposed action, and the proposal was finally tabled.[20]

With the obvious influence of the missionaries, four doctrinal standards, all with origins in the Reformed and Presbyterian traditions, had been adopted in June 1876 by the young Japanese church. Consequently, it seems to have taken the missionaries a bit by surprise that in the fall of 1880, when the Japanese translations of these documents were completed, Japanese church leaders discussed throwing out the Canons of Dort and the Westminster Confession as required doctrinal standards. The Heidelberg Catechism and the Westminster Shorter Catechism were not an issue and evidently their retention not in question.[21]

The four-day spring assembly (*chukai*) of the United Church of Christ in Japan was held in April 1881. Inagaki had presided over the

---

[20]    Ibid.
[21]    JLA to JMF, Oct. 2, 1880.

previous session, but the *chukai* elected James Ballagh, to his surprise, to preside over this assembly. As it turned out, the assembly decided not to throw out the Canons of Dort and the Westminster Confession of Faith. Actually at issue were the Japanese translations of these documents, the English versions having already been approved when the United Church was formed in 1877. The *chukai* first decided to appoint a committee to consider amending the documents so as to make them more appropriate for the Japanese church, but before the end of the last session it voted to accept the translations. Another issue was whether or not to ordain women as deaconesses. It was decided that women would not be ordained to church offices by the laying on of hands, but that any church would be permitted to select women helpers, and that they would be free to call them by such titles as they thought fitting.

The *chukai* meeting reflected the maturity of the young church in that it dealt very carefully with issues related to preparation for the ministry. The delegates examined candidates who wished to enter into theological study under the care of the *chukai*, candidates for the office of licensed preacher, and candidates for ordination to the ministry. Ballagh reported, "The native ministers are very strict with candidates, and carry on the examinations with rapidity, point, and particularity. Of seven or eight candidates for licensure, only three passed, and none of the three for ordination, though it is true one of them was not examined owing to some informality in his call. A great deal of instruction is obtained by the elders and church members at these examinations. Notebooks and pencils are freely in use, and the examiners also keep a list of failures for a guide to their decision." The preaching ability of candidates was also evaluated. Trial sermons were delivered before a large audience, "The sermons showed great variety of treatment, and were remarkably well delivered. They were unsparingly criticized as to style, analysis, substance, and delivery by the native pastors present."

Since the organization of the United Church of Christ in Japan in 1877, it had consisted of only one *chukai*, but as the number of organized churches began to grow, it was thought that the time had come to develop church structures further. At this assembly in 1881, it was decided that the original single *chukai* should be divided into three, and that for general oversight of the churches there should be the *Daikai* (General Synod or General Assembly). To avoid cliques and eclecticism, the three *chukai* were formed not according to the three cooperating missions with which the several churches and their pastors were affiliated, but according to geographical region, and named *Hokubu* (North) *Chukai*, *Tobu* (East) *Chukai*, and *Nishi* (West)

*Chukai*. This new organization having been decided upon, as presiding officer Ballagh preached the sermon at the closing worship service and dissolved the single *chukai* that had served as the governing body of the United Church of Christ in Japan during its first four years.[22]

*Seibu* (West) *Chukai* was organized July 8, 1881. When the Tokyo Union Theological School had been formed under the Council of the Three Missions in 1877, it was made independent of the Japan United Church of Christ formed at that time, and was linked to the Reformed and Presbyterian Japan Missions. However, when theological education was formalized in Nagasaki in 1881 under Henry Stout's leadership, the theological school there was placed under the care of the newly organized *Seibu Chukai*. Furthermore, five men applying to begin theological study were examined before the *chukai*. Stout reported that these decisions were taken "so as to secure the interest and cooperation of that body."[23]

Within the Reformed Church's Japan Mission, there was apparently some difference of perspective regarding not only the role and authority of the missionary within the Japanese church structures but also the ideal pattern of ministerial training. The Tokyo/Yokohama missionaries tended to be more reticent to relinquish authority, and also tended to emphasize the academic preparation of pastors at the Tokyo Union Theological School. Stout clarified his position.

> One of the chief aims, no doubt, of missions should be to develop independent churches, and this can only be done by training natives for the work....I have been privileged to do more for the ultimate success of the work in Kiushiu [Kyushu] by training the few men who have been under my care than if I had engaged in evangelistic work only....In training men responsibility must be put upon them. I believe most thoroughly in the principle clearly set forth at the time it was proposed to give the franchise to the negro. "In order that he may learn how to vote, he must vote." Upon this principle, from the very first establishment of the United Church in Japan, and quite alone, I opposed the plan for making the missionaries members of the deliberate bodies of the Church, either "ex officio" or otherwise. The missionaries should be present at the meetings, and by their sympathy and advice assist the natives in their deliberations. They may be called "corresponding members," and should have the privileges granted

[22]    JHB to JMF, Apr. 9, 1881.
[23]    HS to JMF, July 19, 1881.

to such persons at home, but nothing more. Consequently, I never vote in the *Chiukai* & *Daikai*, though the constitution makes me an "ex officio member," an anomalous position surely. For the same reason I do not baptize, in fact do no part of the work that belongs to the Church proper. It might be supposed that in this way I had unnecessarily deprived myself of influence, which I ought to exert upon the young Church. On the contrary, however, I believe my influence in directing its policy has been greatly increased. Men are more willing to listen to friendly advice than to official dictation.[24]

Already during the period of the missionary pioneers, as the Japanese church leadership grew in maturity, the role and identity of the foreign missionary necessarily began to change. The missionaries exercised no authority in Japanese church government and continued to encourage self-reliance and self-support on the part of the Japanese Christians. On the other hand, the missionaries continued to maintain a separate organization, the Japan Mission of the Reformed Church in America, with its own areas of authority and responsibility. It was the mission that related to and was accountable to the mission board in America. In January 1882, Amerman sent a letter to the board on behalf of the Japan Mission, in which several important issues were raised.

The first issue was in response to information from the board indicating that two Japanese students at New Brunswick Seminary had applied to the Reformed Church Board of Foreign Missions to be sent to Japan as missionaries. These young men, Ohgimi Moto-ichiro and Kimura Kumage, had spent nine years in Holland, Michigan, after having been befriended and taken in by Hope College President Philip Phelps. They had graduated from Hope College in 1879, the first foreign students to do so, and were about to graduate from New Brunswick Theological Seminary in 1882. However, their application to be sent to Japan as Reformed Church missionaries raised serious questions, and the response of the missionaries on the field was unequivocal.

> It is the unanimous desire of your Mission here that the Board <u>will not accept</u> the offer of these two brethren....We rejoice with you and with the Board that the Lord has put it into the hearts of these brethren to devote themselves to the work of the ministry, and to labor for the evangelization of their own countrymen, and we hope most sincerely that so much of their desire may be

---

[24]   HS to HNC, May 2, 1885.

thoroughly fulfilled, but we fear that it will be utterly impossible for them to come to Japan as foreign missionaries. Should they be so sent by our Board they would of course become members of our Mission, and as such they would hear and take part in all of our discussions, not only in reference to various items of missionary policy, but in reference also to the expenditure of funds. Their sympathies could not be as our sympathies are, they would be either with the foreigner or with the native, or there would be—pardon me if I say so—dissembling [pretended agreement] with both. They would fail to be trusted either by one side or by the other side, and probably would not enjoy the full confidence of either side....Moreover these two brethren who are now asking to be sent to us, would receive if accepted by the Board, what would be for the Japanese immense incomes....from 6-10 times as much as other men equally well educated and educated abroad are now actually receiving under the most favorable circumstances. This state of things would not inspire confidence among the people. Many many years will pass before any native congregation will [be] able to give one sixth part of this sum to a pastor, or a worker of any sort. There would be dissatisfaction too among our native pastors, some few of whom are no doubt equally well furnished for their work as are these brethren....In saying this we do not in the slightest degree disparage the quality of instruction given in our institutions at New Brunswick, and we do not doubt the Christian character and pure motives of these brethren, but we have before us our own experience of Japanese character and such a knowledge of difficulties as the Board can not possibly have, and we all agree that the appointment of these men by the Board would be the occasion of trouble and embarrassment to us and calamity to the native church. If the two brethren in question desire to come to Japan to labor here for Christ and for the souls of their countrymen we are of decided opinion that they should come as Japanese and not as foreigners, and they should come ready to live as Japanese live, and work as Japanese work.[25]

The position of the Japan Mission was reiterated in subsequent letters. In Amerman's words, "The Board should have no direct relations with the men. They should be solely in Mission employ as our other helpers are. Any other arrangement will result in trouble."[26] The mission

25   JLA to JMF, Jan. 14, 1882.
26   JLA to JMF, Feb. 21, 1882.

board apparently decided to send them as missionary coworkers. The missionaries objected, "We cannot agree with the opinion expressed by you that these brethren will be worth more than Japanese helpers educated here, and we are sure that in almost every respect as evangelists they will be worth less....If the Board are not satisfied with arguments already adduced, kindly urge them to ask for more light on any point and we will endeavor to satisfy them, but do not I beg of you do us the great harm of sending these men as proposed."[27] In fact, Kimura and Ohgimi were ordained as ministers of the Reformed Church in America and the board sent them to Japan in the fall of 1882. Difficulties over their salaries as employees of the mission arose immediately. Both Kimura and Ohgimi demanded higher salaries than those paid to the other Japanese "helpers."[28] Booth pointed out that if the Japan Mission paid Kimura the salary he demanded, the board would have to raise the salaries of all the native workers by 300 percent to avoid trouble.[29]

The assimilation and reintegration of returning Japanese Christians educated abroad continued to be a difficult issue not only for the missionaries but also for the Japanese churches. At the same time, the disparity between the cost of living for foreigners living in Japan and Japanese living in their own country, and also the issue of the Japan Mission employing and paying Japanese pastors and evangelists who served as coworkers of the missionaries, proved to be serious challenges for a long time. For the missionaries personally, who necessarily had taken the initiative and responsibility for all mission activities on the field at the beginning, and even more for the Board of Foreign Missions in America, overcoming a paternalistic mindset would not be easy.

When the first Reformed Church missionaries went to Japan, each one's basic connection to the sending church was maintained directly by correspondence with the board secretary. With time, and with the increase in the number of missionaries, the Japan Mission gradually gained stature and identity as the body on the field representing or advocating for the missionaries to the mission board in America. In 1882, the Japan Mission proposed a detailed plan for more equitable financial support of the missionaries. Two characteristics of the proposed plan are of particular interest. The missionaries proposed that "unmarried ladies" be paid the same salaries as unmarried men. Furthermore, they proposed that all of the missionaries and all of the regularly appointed unmarried women, who were classified by the

---

27    JLA to JMF, Apr. 11, 1882.
28    ERM to JMF, Jan. 13, 1883.
29    ESB to JMF, Sept. 25, 1882.

board as assistant missionaries, the same as the wives of missionaries, be required to study the Japanese language and to pass language exams after the first and second years on the field. They urged that newcomers not be considered full missionaries until the language exams were passed satisfactorily, and that until that time they should receive the smallest salary on which they could manage to live.[30] It is noteworthy that thirty-eight years before women's suffrage was achieved in the United States (in 1920), although the male missionaries did not ask for full missionary status for the women, they expected them to learn the Japanese language, and they urged equal pay for equal work.

The mission also was concerned that newly arrived career missionaries were generally pressed into service almost immediately to teach English, which infringed upon their language study time. They therefore proposed the idea that unmarried men be sent for three-year terms to teach English at the preparatory schools, presumably in both Tokyo and Nagasaki, without the two years of language study. They judged that three such men could be sent for the equivalent expense of one career missionary family.[31]

As we have observed, the original vision of 1872 of one united, evangelical Protestant church in Japan was never realized, and only the three, and later six, Reformed and Presbyterian missions were associated with the United Church of Christ in Japan. The others formed their several denominations in Japan (Episcopal, Congregational, Baptist, Methodist, etc.). Nevertheless, by the early 1880s, where several denominations had congregations in a locality, there were often joint prayer meetings or special services. Furthermore, through the work of the Bible Societies and the annual meetings of the Evangelical Alliance the missionaries were able to cooperate and experience a measure of mutuality across denominational lines. Similarly, Japanese Christians found a venue for interdenominational cooperation and mutual edification and inspiration in their annual *Daishimbokkai* ("Great Fellowship Meeting"). Though divided organizationally into the United Church of Christ in Japan and the several denominations directly identified with those in the West, the Japanese Christians also found much to bind them together in a mutual faith.

During April 16 to 22, 1883, a general conference of Protestant missionaries in Japan was held in Osaka. Most of the Protestant missionaries in Japan at the time were in attendance, and a fine spirit of mutual respect and cooperation was exhibited. For this conference

30  JLA to JMF, Jan. 14, 1882.
31  Ibid.

the Reformed Church's Guido Verbeck was asked to prepare a major presentation, entitled "History of Protestant Missions in Japan," which was later published in the conference's book of proceedings. This historical record remains one of the most valuable resources available on the first quarter century of mission work in Japan.

In 1883, there were 208 foreign missionaries in Japan, representing nineteen missionary sending agencies. Only 62 of these missionaries represented the Reformed or Presbyterian mission agencies that cooperated with the United Church. Despite their separation into various denominations, the missionaries displayed a remarkable unanimity about the nature of their evangelical faith and missionary goals, and they experienced a beneficial ecumenicity. Martin Wyckoff remarked,

> The conference at Osaka was very enjoyable, and we think profitable to us all. The harmony of the meeting not disturbed by the slightest disagreement. Of course there were differences of opinion, and they were freely expressed; but even in cases of disagreement good feeling was preserved. We were undoubtedly kept by the Holy Spirit, for humanly speaking, it was impossible for that body, composed of persons of strong convictions, different nationalities, diverse education and ecclesiastical training, to consider and discuss so many different subjects, about which their opinions must necessarily differ, without friction.[32]

During the next month, the Japanese Christians held a similar conference in Tokyo. Their annual interdenominational *Daishimbokkai* was especially fruitful, not only very interesting and profitable, but also exhibiting evidences of a great influence of the Holy Spirit and a new hope and confidence among the Christians. Several weeks after the meetings, Miller reported, "We are happy to say that the results of the meetings are still felt and the people all over the city & indeed almost throughout the country seem anxious to know what Christianity is & all the preaching places are filled with inquirers & the Christians themselves are much stirred up."[33] As an example of the new openness to Christianity, Inagaki of the Yokohama Kaigan Church baptized forty new converts during the first five months of 1883 and had more inquirers preparing for baptism.[34] This surge in the number of conversions was

---

[32]  MNW to JMF, May 14, 1883.
[33]  ERM to HNC, May 31, 1883.
[34]  MNW to JMF, May 30, 1883.

apparent in many churches. At the fall meeting of the *Tobu Chukai*, the thirteen churches reported 150 baptisms since its spring meeting,[35] and at its next spring meeting reported another 100 baptisms.[36]

Reformed Church missionaries, working with the United Church, believed they must take care not to try to hold onto authority within the Japanese church structures and that they must be clear in their role as foreign missionaries. In Amerman's words,

> In the mind of some of us the time has fully come when all that is anomalous should be done away in the various courts of that body. It would not be anomalous for the foreign missionary to be an advisory member of these bodies but a full <u>voting</u> connection is no longer needed. They can fill all their offices & committees satisfactorily without us. They can outvote us at any time if they please and a close vote, if on a matter of importance which may be decided by the action of a few foreigners would not be desirable. They have passed the educational stage in <u>this</u> matter and unless we <u>sever</u> our relations with home classes & presbyteries we ought not to be full members of the church assemblies here.[37]

It became the unanimous position of the Reformed missionaries that they should no longer be voting members within the Japanese church organization and should have no more than an advisory role. On the other hand, Amerman noted that at that juncture the American Presbyterian missionaries still unanimously desired to remain *ex officio* voting members.[38]

In the fall of 1883, the missionaries of the Council of the Three Missions initiated a proposal to the *Daikai* for the formation of a joint Committee on Domestic Missions for carrying out the expanding work of evangelism and church planting. It was to be composed of ten Japanese members and ten foreign missionaries, with Japanese and foreign secretaries and treasurers, and funds to carry out its work were to be contributed both from the Japanese and the three missions. The proposed committee was to oversee and administer a more unified plan for establishing new churches and supporting pastors, evangelists, and theological students involved in the work. It was intended that the Japanese Christians would gradually take more responsibility for this outreach.

[35]   JHB to JMF, Oct. 3, 1883.
[36]   JHB to JMF, April, 1884.
[37]   JLA to HNC, March 10, 1884.
[38]   JLA to HNC, Apr. 24, 1884.

According to this proposal, at the beginning the three missions were each to provide one yen for each yen raised by the Japanese, with the understanding that as contributions by Japanese Christians increased, the number of missionaries on the committee would be reduced. The Committee on Domestic Missions was to function under supervision of the *Daikai*, and Japanese Christians were gradually to take over responsibility for evangelism and church planting. Unfortunately, after deliberation, "the native brethren thought it best to postpone it for a while." Japanese church leaders thought the church was not yet prepared to contribute so largely as suggested, and the plan was not brought before the synod for discussion. Miller added hopefully, "It will probably come up again before long."[39]

The missionaries affiliated with the Council of the Three Missions (Reformed, Presbyterian, and Scottish Presbyterian) then drew up and agreed upon a plan, entitled "Union in Evangelistic Work." The Japanese church leaders were requested to send corresponding members, but they were not to be given the right to vote until the churches contributed to the funds of the committee.[40] The plan included a uniform salary support system, proportioned to the number of church members, to assist the pastors, evangelists, and theological students of congregations not yet strong enough to be self-supporting. It was intended as a temporary solution to resolve inequities, avoid duplication, and foster efficiency in evangelistic outreach. In this regard, Miller reported, "We hope that this action on our part will incite the Japanese to more energetic work for Home-Missions so that they will be ready to adopt some such action as we recommended at the time of the meeting of the Dai-Kuwai [*Daikai*] next autumn."[41] This plan was soon implemented and cooperative work among the missionaries and representative Japanese pastors increased. Reformed and Presbyterian missionaries began touring together, both to observe established outstations and to explore and pioneer new work. Miller described a providential opening for evangelism at Kochi on the island of Shikoku that was initiated jointly:

> There has been a very favorable opening for work in the province of Tosa in the south of the island of Shikoku. Mr. Itagaki, the head of the liberal party [Japanese political group], and whose home is in Kochi of that province, has been staying in Tokiyo and in some way became interested in Christianity and would

[39]    ERM to HNC, Feb. 29, 1884.
[40]    ERM to HNC, Nov., 1885.
[41]    ERM to HNC, July 3, 1884.

like to see it introduced in his province. He thinks that it is only by Christianity that the lower classes can be elevated so as to be able to govern themselves. Possibly he may have thought formerly that Christianity could be used as a political agent, but if so he knows better now. He does not want to be identified with the Christians, however, but is anxious to have the first impression made as favorable as possible, and so we are going down there on his invitation. Dr. Verbeck and Mr. Thompson have gone already, and if they report favorably Mr. Knox and myself will go about the first of December.[42]

The pioneering work in Kochi was the first joint project that implemented the union in evangelistic work. Kochi Church was organized May 15, 1885, and continued to grow rapidly, primarily through the extended tours of Verbeck, Miller, Presbyterian missionaries, and experienced Japanese pastors such as Uemura, then affiliated with the Reformed Japan Mission. In the summer of 1885, the newly ordained Reverend Yamamoto Hideteru, another pastor nurtured and trained by Reformed Church missionaries, became the first pastor of Kochi Church.[43] The Millers and Ballagh continued extended tours to assist in the work in 1886. Organized with twenty-two members, Kochi Church showed remarkable growth. In less than two years it had more than two hundred members. This successful beginning in cooperative evangelism bode well for adoption of the earlier plan for shared responsibility with the Japanese churches.

The Japanese churches in the Tokyo area had in the meantime formed a Home Mission Society and begun gathering funds, but were lacking personnel, since those who had finished theological training were either pastors of established churches or employed by one of the Japan missions. The Japanese ministers had also in the meantime fully discussed among themselves the original proposal for a joint Committee on Home Missions. They had prepared a document that contained the original proposal with a few modifications, all of which were acceptable to the missionaries. At the United Church's biannual *Daikai* in 1885, this plan was fully and frankly discussed. The *Daikai* adopted the proposal, forming the joint Home Mission Board. Miller reported,

The question which raised the most discussion was whether the salaries of pastors should in any way come under this Board.

42    ERM to HNC, Nov. 4, 1884.
43    JHB to HNC, Sept. 16, 1885.

Some of the pastors were very strongly of the opinion that no church which was fully organized should receive any help, but must support its own pastor entirely. It was seen, however, that, for the present at least, this rule must have exceptions and the Board was so formed as to be able to take under its jurisdiction all kinds of evangelistic work, the support of evangelists, pastors or theological students; but it was understood that, for the present and until the churches could give more largely to this Board, the support of the students would be left to the several missions, while at the same time the Board could, if it wished, undertake their support also....

The proportion to be contributed by the churches was fixed as had been proposed by the missions two years ago, namely one-fourth, while the three missions are to give three-fourths....

The native pastors feel very sanguine over the results as we do ourselves and think that the next two or three years will witness a great change in the character of the Japanese churches, that is that they will be much stronger and more self reliant.[44]

The Reformed Japan Mission consistently fostered ecumenical cooperation. For example, James Ballagh had initiated the work in Nagoya by evangelistic touring in 1879, and a Japanese evangelist, a Reformed Church missionary protégé, was the first evangelist there. Ballagh continued to give oversight in Nagoya, and by 1887 it had grown to a church of more than eighty members.[45] When Southern Presbyterian missionaries first arrived in 1885 (the Reverends R. Bryan Grinnan and Robert E. McAlpine), Ballagh took them with him on evangelistic tours to both Nagoya and Kochi to introduce them to possible fields of work. Later the work centered in Kochi and then that centered in Nagoya were turned over to the Southern Presbyterian Mission, which partnered with Japanese Christians in evangelism and in establishing mission schools there.

During Oshikawa's first five years as a pioneer evangelist in Sendai, without missionary connections, he had established three churches in that region with two hundred members. Desiring to expand evangelistic outreach and establish mission schools, he approached his mentors among Reformed Church missionaries and church leaders in Tokyo, and Verbeck, Ballagh, and the Millers toured the region to give some assistance. However, the Reformed Church Japan Mission,

---

[44]     ERM to HNC, Nov., 1885.
[45]     JHB to HNC, May 23, 1887.

under whom Oshikawa had been trained, was unable to provide him with permanent personnel or funds. Instead, Oshikawa was introduced to a newly arrived missionary, the Reverend W. E. Hoy of the Reformed Church in the United States (German Reformed). Thus began in 1886 a fruitful cooperative relationship and expansion of mission work in the Tohoku District, centering around Sendai.[46]

The German Reformed Japan Mission not only assisted Oshikawa in evangelism, but also eventually developed mission schools and theological education in Sendai. Once again, the Reformed Church in America missionaries demonstrated their spirit of cooperation with other evangelical Christians. Both the Southern Presbyterian and German Reformed Japan Missions agreed to join the partnership with the United Church of Christ in Japan, and they joined the Council of Three Missions, which was then called the Council of the United Missions. Later, in the fall of 1889, the Cumberland Presbyterian Japan Mission became the sixth member of the Council of the United Missions, and at that time the nine churches organized by the Cumberland Presbyterians in Japan were joined to the United Church of Christ in Japan.[47]

The implications of the ecumenical cooperation and partnership pioneered by the missionaries and their Japanese colleagues were not always adequately understood in America. The Reformed Church General Synod of 1885 asked the mission board to prepare statistics of the Japan Mission's Japanese churches and their membership so as to include these as part of the statistics of the Reformed Church in America. The request suggested not only that these churches were part of the Reformed Church, but also that the progress or success of its Japan Mission might be described by the number of converts won and churches formed by its missionaries in Japan. This request presented the missionaries with a dilemma.

From the beginning they had labored to help form an independent and united Japanese church. The Japanese congregations and pastors had at first been associated with whichever of the three original missions had nurtured them, and it had been possible to identify particular churches and pastors or evangelists as related to the Reformed Church

46    Bartholomew, *Won By Prayer*, 84-85.
47    JHB to HNC, Dec. 4, 1885. The 1885 *Daikai* increased the number of *chukai* to five. The four independent churches in the Sendai area, established under Oshikawa's leadership, were admitted to the United Church and formed the northern *Miyagi Chukai*. Furthermore, four churches in central Japan, in Osaka, Nagoya, Kanazawa, and Kochi, formed the *Naniwa Chukai*, and *Seibu Chukai* became *Chinzei Chukai*. These changes reflected the church growth of the mid-1880s.

missionaries. But each of the organized churches had joined the United Church of Christ in Japan, an independent and self-governing church. The larger of these congregations were already self-supporting. Furthermore, the missionaries assisted at various churches without regard to the mission with which they had at first been associated.

In addition, Reformed and Presbyterian missionaries were increasingly carrying on mission outreach and church-planting projects together. In order to develop new work in partnership with and with joint support from the Japanese church, they had organized the Home Mission Board. Thus it was no longer possible to identify unique statistics for the work of the Reformed Church's Japan Mission. Rather, the mission was part of the Council of the United Missions working to build up a united Japanese church. Amerman made the issue clear.

> There is great danger of misunderstanding and there are seeds of trouble in the action of the Synod. <u>The Japanese Church will have fraternal relations but no more intimate connection with any Church in another land</u>. We promised them at the outset that this should be so, and yet the last General Synod <u>claims</u> them. So far as they have been connected with the work of our Mission the Synod puts the names of their ministers on its roll and includes ten of their churches among the five hundred and thirty-four which are reported to the world as belonging to it. If this were generally known to our Japanese brethren the effect would be very unhappy. Surely I need not enlarge upon this for you well know the suspicious jealousy of their independence of foreign control which has characterized the Japanese Church from the beginning. And the roots of this feeling go back to the time when the Jesuits were expelled from the country because of the suspicion that through them the effort was being made to bring the land under the power of the Pope.
>
> The Japanese Christians are naturally sensitive in this matter. They have in some cases even objected to being reported as belonging to the Mission to whose work they owe their existence as churches. And once they attain to the condition of self-support they are disposed to repudiate any idea of further connection or accountability to any Mission or missionary. They are not unmindful of their history, nor are they ungrateful for past aid, but when able to take care of themselves the thought that they are claimed and reported by any Mission is offensive, and it is by no means a wise policy that ignores this.[48]

[48]   JLA to HNC, Apr. 10, 1886.

The missionaries of the Tokyo-Yokohama Station unanimously passed a resolution urging the Reformed Church's General Synod to reverse its 1885 action with reference to the publication of the statistical tables of the Japan Mission as part of the statistics of the synod.[49]

Beginning in November 1885, efforts for further church union of the United Church of Christ in Japan and other denominations that had been established there were initiated. On February 6, 1886, Amerman wrote, "There are rumors in the air of a desire for union between the churches established by our missions and those established by the American Board. So far as I can learn the matter has been mooted in the first place by the Japanese Christians." A consultation of ministers of the United Church with the Congregational churches (American Board related) held in January initiated dialogue to that end.[50]

At the United Church *Daikai* held in May 1887, there was strong support and enthusiasm for union with the *Kumiai* (association of Japan's Congregational churches). A committee of five United Church leaders was appointed and instructed to meet with a similar committee of the *Kumiai* organization and discuss a basis of union between the two churches. Each committee included four Japanese representatives and one missionary.[51] It became clear in the original negotiations that church government and theology would be crucial issues for the United Church leaders. The Congregationalists subsequently appeared to accept a Presbyterian form of church government, but there was still concern as to theological agreement, since some sensed that "the theology taught in the institution of the Cong. Church [*Doshisha*] differs widely from our accepted standard." Nevertheless, Demarest observed, "What will be the action concerning theology we cannot say, but there seems a reasonable probability that our wishes in this respect will be met."[52] Ballagh and a few other missionaries and Japanese pastors were concerned that the *Kumiai* tendency toward a loose view of doctrinal matters might prove to be a problem.[53]

Also in 1887, after three Anglican missions working in Japan joined forces,[54] their General Conference of Missionaries passed a resolution proposing church union with the other church bodies

49    ERM to HNC, Apr. 23, 1886.
50    JLA to HNC, Feb. 6, 1886.
51    United Church committee members were Ibuka, Oshikawa, Uemura, and Presbyterian missionary William Imbrie.
52    NHD to HNC, May 3, 1887.
53    JHB to JMF, May 12, 1887.
54    The Protestant Episcopal Church of America, The Society for the Propagation of the Gospel, and the Church Missionary Society.

in Japan. While it was hard for Amerman to imagine this Anglican proposal being taken very seriously by either Japanese churchmen or other Protestant missionaries, it appeared to him that consultations looking toward the union of the United Church and Congregational churches might be more fruitful.[55]

The movement for union of the United Church and the *Kumiai* clearly looked promising. A Basis of Union having been approved by both parties, as a next step a larger committee of ten members each was appointed to prepare standards of government and doctrine to be submitted for approval by their respective churches. The committee of the United Church included five Japanese pastors, one Japanese elder, and four missionaries, each of whom represented a different mission in the Council of the United Missions.[56] Amerman, the Reformed Church Mission representative, reported, "For the fuller information of the Boards an explanatory letter has been adopted by the Council of the United Missions. We do not feel that we have need to persuade the Board to consent to what is proposed but as a matter of course we wish all the steps in the transaction with the reasons therefore to be before the Boards for their better knowledge of the situation."[57] In regard to standards of doctrine, Miller noted,

> The Board gave its consent to our joining in the establishment of the first churches in Japan when they had only the Nine Articles of the Evangelical Alliance for a creed and we do not suppose that they will oppose this greater union, to which we feel drawn not only by our inclinations but also by the conviction that it will be for the best interests of the churches which have been committed to our care by the great Head of the Church, for we feel that in all this we have been led by the hand of our Good Father and we do not wish to oppose that which would in the end shew us to have been fighting against God.

[55]  JLA to HNC, March 18, 1887. The Episcopal/Anglican missionaries expressed their "desire for the establishment in Japan of a Christian Church which by imposing no non essential conditions of communion shall include as many as possible of the Christians of this country." However, their communications referred to other churches in Japan as "Christian bodies," in effect not recognizing them as legitimate churches. Furthermore, it was made clear that while expressing the hope for such a union, they would require that any ordained ministers of other "Christian bodies" coming into such a union would have to be reordained. Amerman could not resist noting that there was not a single self-supporting church and not a single ordained Japanese minister in the newly organized Anglican Church in Japan.
[56]  ERM to HNC, May 13, 1887.
[57]  JLA to HNC, May 23, 1887.

It may seem to many at home that to take only the Apostles' Creed, the Nicene Creed and the Nine Articles of the Evangelical Alliance is giving up a great deal, but we must look at it also from a Japanese view-point, as the Rev. Professor Ibuka has well said, for a Japanese church to accept such standards and to promise to teach nothing contrary to these creeds is a strong position to take before their countrymen and every Japanese will see that it is so.[58]

Ibuka and several other original members of the first Japanese Protestant church, founded in Yokohama in 1872 (Kaigan Church), were fifteen years later key Christian leaders in Japan, and they still cherished the ideal of one united Christian church for Japan. Negotiations continued between representatives of the United Church and the *Kumiai* churches. The proposed Constitution, By-laws, and Appendix were completed, and after six months' consideration, they were presented for approval to simultaneous meetings of the United Church *Daikai* and the Congregational Council in November of 1888. The United Church accepted the proposed documents, despite concern expressed by two Japanese ministers that important doctrines were not sufficiently safeguarded. However, there was considerable dissent at the Congregational Council. Some resisted having any rules of governance and feared that the liberty of the local churches would be lost.[59] Amerman summed up the situation.

As the matter stands now we have adopted the proposed Constitution with a very few small amendments on condition of union, and the Congregational churches have postponed final action until next May. Meantime, under the stimulus of these meetings at Osaka, the intelligent desire for union will doubtless increase more and more. This is especially probable because each body has given the matter in charge to a large and representative committee pending their next regular meetings, which are to be held in May. One thing we wish to be clearly understood by our friends at home,...the desire for this union here in Japan is not a matter of mere sentiment, but among foreign missionaries and Japanese Christians alike it is the development of a strong conviction that only after such union can the great work of the Church, as respects the unevangelized millions of Japan, be most effectively accomplished.[60]

---

[58]   Ibid.
[59]   Cary, *History* II, 193-94.
[60]   JLA to HNC, Dec. 4, 1888.

Miller also spoke hopefully. "I am so thankful that the prospect for union is so bright. It will give a great impetus to the work."[61] However, these hopes were betrayed. After the scheduled May meeting Ballagh wrote, "Our body did everything possible to facilitate the union, and were in an enthusiasm for union more than was seemly or called for. My previous experience at union efforts with the Congregational body was of such a kind as to render me almost unwilling to entertain the subject further....The experience of the Committee however has been useful in enlightening themselves and the whole Daikai in the almost futile hope of a union.[62] The reason for the futility of such a hope gradually became clear. Amerman stated,

> Of course we are greatly disappointed that the union was not consummated last week. We were more than disappointed. I frankly own that I was to no small extent disgusted, not with the fact but with the means. The United Church has taken a dignified stand & foreign missionary & Japanese minister alike have labored & labored together, to secure the union. Each time that a conference committee reported certain amendments there was a hearty effort to take the amendments if we could conscientiously do so, & each time the other side seemed to make our concession the basis of a demand for more....The original "basis of union" was ignored, the principle amendments suggested being in violation of it, and one of their ministers remarked to me, what was suggested was not even congregationalism but rank independency....Some at least of their best men foreign & Japanese are ashamed of what was done & the manner of doing it. If union means that a large section of the united body is to be subject to the vagaries of a set of school boys, of course we do not want union on any terms.[63]

The Congregational Council had in fact been dominated and manipulated by a minority group of radicals, mostly students of the Doshisha, the university founded by Niijima Jo and the American Board Mission, over which church leaders could not exercise control. It became clear that negotiation and cooperation in good faith were not possible, because the congregational mentality did not allow for any church authority beyond the local congregation. Without church authority, neither sound doctrine nor good government could be

---

61    ERM to HNC, May 26, 1889.
62    JHB to HNC, June 5, 1889.
63    JLA to HNC, June 6, 1889.

maintained. It is not surprising, therefore, that this union movement, for which so much time and energy had been expended, and in which so much hope for unity in the evangelization of Japan had been placed, ended in failure.

## Reformed Church Mission Schools Take Form

### Ferris Seminary

When Mary Miller had returned to the United States for furlough in 1879, Ferris Seminary, the Reformed Church Mission's girls' school in Yokohama, was left in the hands of Emma Witbeck, assisted by Harriet Winn. By the fall of 1881, it had become clear that for health reasons Witbeck would soon be leaving Japan and that this would be the termination of her work. Meanwhile, Eugene Booth, in Nagasaki, was also having health problems. Having understood that Booth's health was such that he must either have an entire change for the present or be forced to return to America in a year, Witbeck asked whether he might not be able to give some oversight at Ferris Seminary. She thought it would be the best thing for him and for the school, and the mission recommended it.

The Booths moved to Yokohama. The intent was that Eugene Booth would take charge of the girls' school part time, teach the Bible classes, and continue his Japanese language study. He was to be assisted by Winn in the teaching, by Emilie Booth in household management, as it was a boarding school, and by Ballagh's daughter Carrie, teaching part time.[64] Carrie E. Ballagh had returned to her parents' home in Japan in 1881, and though at that time she was not officially a missionary, she was eager to help with the teaching. She taught music and some English, while at the same time studying Japanese. She later applied for assistant missionary status.[65] The situation of the school began to improve almost immediately under the leadership of Booth.[66] However, his correspondence indicated that his role at Ferris was a temporary arrangement.

> You will remember that I intimated in a former letter the probability of our coming here for a year or so on account of my health, which has suffered somewhat from the climate in Nagasaki. It is needless for me to say that it was with deep regret

---

[64]    ERM to JMF, Sept. 24, 1881.
[65]    Carrie E. Ballagh to JMF, March 17 and June 1, 1882.
[66]    HLW to JMF, March 27, 1882.

that I finally determined, with the advice of a physician & the assent of Mr. Stout, to accept the cordial invitation extended me by the Yokohama & Tokyo members of the Mission & proceed to Ferris Seminary.

It seemed to me like throwing away the labor of two years and yet it was extremely doubtful if I could have carried it on through the year had I remained.

I hope it will be quite well understood that it is my desire to return to Nagasaki as soon as my health will warrant it. I have no disposition to abandon my post. And the three weeks I've already spent warrant me I think, judging from the benefit I've already experienced, in saying that I shall be quite able to return in the Fall of '82. I do hope that by that time the Board will be in condition to give us the Boys School in Nagasaki. Between this time and that, however, two ladies should be sent out to Ferris Seminary or it will I fear be without a teacher.[67]

Booth's letter also exhibited aspects of his educational philosophy for mission schools. It ran counter to views expressed earlier by Brown and others, who urged teaching the Japanese to master English, and then to teach Western learning in the English language. The pioneers' first students and converts had been mostly exceptionally bright young men of the elite educated class, and this method had been quite successful at the beginning. Booth's views reflected the perspective of someone arriving in Japan twenty years after the pioneers, and they were more in line with ideas expressed by Stout based on his experience in Nagasaki.

The time and strength spent in teaching the Japanese English as the medium for instruction in other branches cannot be compensated for by any advantage real or imaginary accruing therefrom. Although it is the prevailing system at present yet I believe it is a wrong one. It requires a protracted course of study, running over a period of six to eight years to complete. And two evils arise. One is that not one pupil in ten is able or willing to complete the course, except he be supported by foreign money. And consequently the second evil arrise [sic], viz., a self-supporting school under the present system is quite impossible. Whereas if the foreign teacher could handle the native tongue as well as his own the same curriculum could be accomplished in half the time and I believe 9/10 of the pupils who enter would finish the course

---

[67]    ESB to JMF, Nov. 22, 1881.

and a large proportion would be able to pay the current expenses of the school....If our schools can be made wholly self-supporting a great advantage will have been gained over the present system of working mission.[68]

Emma Witbeck left Japan early in 1882. Ferris Seminary had not prospered under her leadership, and the number of students had dwindled. She had no doubt diligently taught the students English, but she had made little effort to provide meaningful Bible study or give religious instruction. Winn had taught the students well but evidently seldom saw or spoke to any of them outside of class, not being conversant in the Japanese language. According to what Mary Miller later learned and reported concerning the students, "No one knew or seemed to care anything about their personal joys and sorrows. I think this has been one of the greatest obstacles to the prosperity of the school." Although Miller was living in Tokyo, in the matter of the mission board's recruitment of new teachers for Ferris Seminary, she wrote, "If ladies are sent out from home to take charge of the Seminary who desire my assistance I shall be glad to do all I can. In selecting those ladies I would suggest that it be very definitely ascertained whether they have been earnestly engaged in Christian work at home; if not it is much to be feared they will have little heart for the work here, and anyone who finds nothing to do there had better not be sent here for experiment."[69]

The temporary transfer of the Booths to Yokohama and the consequent leadership Booth began to give to Ferris Seminary proved to be of great benefit to the school. While recouping his health and continuing his language study, Booth was able not only to give oversight for needed repairs and maintenance of the school building, but also to guide the reorganization of the school, structuring it into well-defined courses and departments. He prepared and published the first brochure for parents, explaining the objectives and courses of study. In Ballagh's words, "Bro. Booth's work at the Ferris Seminary is very timely and efficient....I think therefore our Bro. Booth's coming here has been very providential, and with the competent help native and foreign he has secured, the school is in a most hopeful state for increasing and continued usefulness."[70]

Among the innovations Booth introduced was the practice of holding public year-end examinations of the students, administered by

[68]  Ibid.
[69]  MEM to JMF, Jan. 19, 1882.
[70]  JHB to JMF, Feb. 6, 1882.

Second Ferris Seminary school building, dedicated in 1884

qualified outsiders, some Japanese Christians and some missionaries. This custom began to bring recognition of the quality of this mission school's education.[71] Ferris Seminary began to grow and prosper as never before. Booth held firmly to the principle that mission schools should not be charitable institutions, but as self-supporting as possible. Needy students were admitted (about one-fifth of the pupils), but in Booth's words, "they return us an equivalent in teaching or other services."[72] This was in contrast to other mission schools, such as those of the Methodists, where most students received a free education.

By the spring of 1883, one-third of the girls enrolled at Ferris Seminary had become Christians, and the school had outgrown its facilities. Booth planned to construct an addition, so that the school would not only have additional classrooms, but also a music room and more dormitory space and be adequate for one hundred students.[73] Funds were provided by the Reformed Church's Woman's Board of Foreign Missions, and the new building project was completed and dedicated on April 28, 1884.

M. Leila Winn, a cousin of Harriet Winn, arrived December 26, 1882, to begin her missionary career. She lived with the Booths and primarily studied the language at the beginning. Carrie Ballagh, for health reasons and because of her upcoming marriage to an

[71]  ESB to JMF, Oct. 1, 1882.
[72]  ESB to HNC, Jan. 25, 1883.
[73]  ESB to JMF, March 21, 1883.

Episcopalian missionary, resigned from the mission and from teaching at Ferris Seminary as of the spring of 1885. Fortunately for Ferris, Carrie's younger sister, Anna H. Ballagh, after an absence from Japan of nine years, had returned to be with her parents and was able to help teach the younger girls. Anna made application to the mission board to be appointed as a missionary, and, although this was not accepted, she was approved to serve as a temporary employed teacher.[74] It seems that there was some misunderstanding on the part of the board, and they may have been seeking an older and experienced missionary teacher. In any case, the Ballagh's second daughter, Anna, taught full-time at the school and was greatly appreciated by Principal Booth.[75]

Booth's leadership at Ferris Seminary changed by mission decision from a temporary assignment to a permanent position. Anticipating a furlough, Booth expressed his goals and vision for the future of the school.

> I need the opportunity of acquainting myself with some of the new methods of teaching which are being now so successfully applied in the States. Please do not misunderstand me. I appreciate fully your remark that "the end of our work is spiritual & not educational in the ordinary sense" and I have this ever before me. And it is really that this end may be the most fully realized possibly, that I seek to make the educational features of the school equal at least to any in Japan. I cannot content myself to a course which will require us to pay a few pupils for the privilege of filling them with spiritual truth, and who would have no higher appreciation of this privilege than the "loaves and fishes" they were receiving. If however we can make this a popular educational center, we can, by the blessing of God, make a spiritual power that will revolutionize the whole social fabric in Japan.
>
> The hope of Japan is the character of the mothers of the coming generations....That school [a particular government school for girls in Tokyo] makes the mistake that all un-Christian systems of education are liable to make, that woman is an ornament in society rather than a factor of society. The time will come when the Japanese will appreciate the distinction.
>
> My object is to afford the best possible facilities for physical & intellectual training & Christian culture of the largest possible

---

[74]    Anna H. Ballagh to HNC, June 5, 1885.
[75]    ESB to HNC, Oct. 2, 1885.

number of girls. That some may not reach our expectations may be expected, but the large majority of them will not disappoint us.[76]

The Booths returned to America for furlough in April of 1886, leaving the school under the care of cousins Harriet and Leila Winn and Anna Ballagh, with nominal oversight by Amerman. The school was continuing to grow and in need of more property. The properties on two sides of the school building were occupied by undesirable neighbors. On one side dairy cows were kept, a mere nuisance, but on the other side were small shanty-like houses used for prostitution and patronized by foreign men. Furthermore, the activity at the latter property was visible to the pupils from the windows of their rooms. The proposed solution was to purchase these properties for the expansion of Ferris Seminary.[77]

During the absence of the Booths, Harriet Winn left Ferris and the mission to be married. Amerman wrote of his concern for the school, which would be left very short-handed. He noted that Mary Miller, the school's founder, had volunteered to commute from Tokyo to Yokohama in the interim to assist Leila Winn and Anna Ballagh. He thouht that to accept her offer would be impractical and unwise. Not only would this be potentially risky due to Mary Miller's not very robust health, but also it would be ill conceived to send the person formerly in charge into a changed situation. Amerman noted, "In confidence I may say & without any disparagement to Mrs. Miller in her proper work, that she does not <u>assist</u>, she <u>directs</u>."[78] Fortunately, in the summer of 1887, Anna DeForrest Thompson was sent to teach at Ferris Seminary, and the Booths returned to resume their ministry there. Enrollment continued to grow, and Booth gave oversight to the construction of additions to the school facilities.

The Woman's Union Missionary Society, although an independent missionary sending agency separate from the Reformed Church's mission boards, had early ties with women in the Reformed Church, and its missionaries in Japan cooperated with Reformed Church missionaries and with the United Church of Christ in Japan. Its work in Japan was centered in Yokohama. Begun as a ministry to unwanted Eurasian children, as well as female education, it had developed into a boarding school for young girls, called the American Mission Home. This mission had continued its school for girls but also expanded into

---

[76]   ESB to HNC, Apr. 27, 1885.
[77]   JLA to HNC, March 29, 1886.
[78]   JLA to HNC, Dec. 10, 1886.

Eugene and Emilie Booth. Eugene Booth served
as principal of Ferris Seminary from 1881 to 1922.

a training program for women involved in ministry to women and children. These lay church workers came to be called Bible women.

In March 1887, the Reformed Church missionaries of the Tokyo-Yokohama Station met to consider a proposal Booth had brought. He proposed to unite Ferris Seminary and the American Mission Home, and, convinced that the time had come for higher education of women in connection with the girls' schools, the missionaries unanimously supported the idea.[79] However, the proposal was ultimately rejected by the missionaries of the American Mission Home, who saw no advantages in such a union.[80] The American Mission Home continued to maintain its high-quality boarding school for girls at Yokohama, and its training course for Bible women made a valuable contribution not only to the evangelistic outreach of the United Church in Japan, with which it continued to cooperate, but also to Reformed Church women missionaries, by training their Japanese assistants. The school was later named Yokohama Kyoritsu Gakuen.

The Ballagh's second daughter, Anna, resigned from her teaching position at Ferris to be married to the Reverend Robert E. McAlpine, a Southern Presbyterian missionary, on October 7, 1887. The McAlpines took over the work begun by Ballagh in Nagoya from that fall of 1887. However, once again Booth found himself very shorthanded at Ferris at a time the school was growing and adding facilities. He pleaded for help. The Booths and Leila Winn and Anna Thompson, with the help

---

[79]     ERM to HNC, March 18, 1887.
[80]     ESB to HNC, Sept. 27, 1887.

of their Japanese assistants, managed to carry on the work. At the end of the school year, Eugene Booth commented,

> Our school closed on the 11th July, after the most successful year in the history of the school. The pupils have done more in all the various lines than ever before. And what is very gratifying to us is the awakening of a hearty school spirit among the pupils. Not only this but it would do your heart good to see the care and solicitude of the older Christian girls toward the younger ones. The earnestness with which they try to lead them to the Saviour affords an example worthy of imitation by inmates of schools in Christian lands.[81]

The Reformed Church responded to the need for teachers later in 1888, sending Mary Deyo to teach at Ferris Seminary. Still shorthanded, and in need of a music teacher, Booth was fortunate to find Julia Moulton and recruit her as a teacher. She was the sister-in-law of the pastor of Yokohama Union Church and already in Yokohama, having come to Japan with her sister. Booth subsequently appealed to the board on her behalf, and she was appointed as a career Reformed Church missionary.[82] Ferris's new building was named VanSchaick Hall, in honor of Miss VanSchaick, a member of the Reformed Church from Albany whose generous gift had made it possible.[83] Unfortunately, six weeks after taking up her responsibilities at Ferris Seminary, Mary Deyo became seriously ill with typhoid fever. She was delirious with fever for twenty-eight days, and all feared for her life. She was fortunate to recover without serious disabilities but required many months of rest to regain her strength.[84]

### Meiji Gakuin

Martin Wyckoff, though without proper school facilities, worked to develop Sen-shi Gakko, the Reformed Church's preparatory school for boys in Yokohama. Encouraging results followed. In February of 1882, enrollment in Wyckoff's classes had risen to forty students, taxing the limits of space in the available rooms. Erection of a school building in Yokohama was being contemplated and plans made. A Mrs. Sandham of the Reformed Church pledged to give a large sum for this building

---

81   ESB to HNC, Aug. 7, 1888.
82   ESB to HNC, Feb. 18, 1889.
83   ERM HNC, Aug. 10, 1887.
84   ESB to HNC, Nov. 27, 1888; HLW to HNC, Dec. 7 and 18, 1888.

project. Meanwhile, Wyckoff's efforts at the school in Yokohama were bearing promising fruit. Since Wyckoff opened Sen-shi Gakko in the fall of 1881, eleven of the students had become Christians.[85]

However, on July 4, 1882, Wyckoff reported, "We are discussing union in educational work."[86] And Miller wrote for the Japan Mission, "The union in the Theological School has been of such benefit to us and been productive of only good, that we may hope for the same in preparatory work."[87] In 1883, it was decided finally that mission school education for boys in the Tokyo/Yokohama area could best be developed in partnership with others of like mind. Accordingly, Wyckoff's Sen-shi Gakko was moved to Tokyo, forming a union school with two Presbyterian schools there. The new school opened in September of 1883, the amalgamation of the Reformed Church's Sen-shi Gakko and Tsukiji College, a school in Tokyo already having brought together early educational efforts of two missionaries of the Presbyterian Church USA. The Presbyterians already had school buildings, located in Tsukiji, the Tokyo foreign settlement. The plan was for the Reformed Church to build "Sandham Academy" next door, creating a blended school with academic and preparatory departments. The Reformed and Presbyterian school thus formed met temporarily in the Presbyterian mission's school buildings and was called Tokyo Union College. During its first year as part of Union College, the preparatory department under Wyckoff's tutelage showed significant growth. Wyckoff reported that the total number of students enrolled had reached 147, with an average attendance of ninety-five, and forty-five of the students were Christians.[88] During the next school year enrollment in the academy reached 187, and fifteen students were baptized during that school year.[89]

Subsequently, in 1886, this Union College, the previously established (1877) Tokyo Union Theological School, and the Tokyo Japanese-English Preparatory School, founded in 1884 by Prof. Hattori, a Japanese Christian, were united to form one institution, and it was named Meiji Gakuin. By this union, a new era of Christian education began, involving cooperative efforts between the United Church of Christ in Japan and the Japan missions of the Reformed and Presbyterian churches. Furthermore, property for Meiji Gakuin was purchased on the hill of Shirokane, in the southern suburbs of Tokyo, outside and

85    MNW to JMF, March 22, 1883.
86    MNW to JMF, July 4, 1882.
87    ERM to JMF, July 12, 1882.
88    MNW to JMF, July 22, 1884.
89    MNW to JMF, Aug. 4, 1885.

distant from the foreign settlement, and there the new campus began to develop.[90]

The Plan of Organization of Meiji Gakuin stated, "It shall be the aim of the institution to furnish a thorough Christian education, and especially to train young men for the ministry of the Church."[91] The rationale of the missionaries was that preparatory Christian education was essential for the recruitment of candidates for theological education and consequently for Christian ministry. Meiji Gakuin as first structured consisted of three departments: a four-year general arts course, a two-year preparatory course, and a three-year theological course.[92] These later became the *Chugaku-bu* (middle school), a five-year course approximating the American seventh through eleventh grades, the *Koto-bu* (high school), a three-year literature department approximating the American twelfth grade and two years of college, and the *Shingaku-bu* (theological department), a three-year course of study in preparation for the Christian ministry. To this union school the Reformed Church contributed Martin Wyckoff, professionally trained and experienced as an educator, for administration and teaching, and Howard Harris as instructor at the preparatory school, as well as James Amerman as a full-time member of the theological faculty. Reformed Church pioneer Guido Verbeck taught part time in the theological school from its inception, and E. R. Miller also shared some of the teaching responsibilities. Amerman was elected to serve as the first president of the faculty of Meiji Gakuin. In this regard, Amerman subsequently wrote,

> I may say for your information that I have resigned the position of President of the Faculty of the Meiji Gakuin. Dr. Hepburn has come nearly to the end of his work on Bible translation and has talked of going home. Some of us thought that there was work still for him to do in Japan, and that being known especially, all over the country, by his Dictionary the 3rd Edition of which was issued last year he could be of use in our Educational work here in Tokyo. I offered at once to make the inducement as large as possible for him & to resign in order that he might be elected to the position which I held. This has been done, and so far as anyone can be recognized as at the head of the institution he will be.[93]

90    Albert Oltmans, *Meiji Gakuin Semi-Centenial:1877-1927* (Tokyo: Meiji Gakuin, 1927), 8; Gordon J. Van Wyk, *Eighty Years of Concern: Meiji Gakuin, 1877-1957* (Tokyo: Meiji Gakuin, 1957), 7.

91    Oltmans, *Meiji Gakuin*, 11.

92    Van Wyk, *Eighty Years*, 7.

93    JLA to HNC, April 14, 1887.

Meiji Gakuin's Sandham Hall (above), completed in 1887,
and (below) the Meiji Gakuin Theological Department building

After the formation of Meiji Gakuin as a union school, with Mrs.
Sandham's permission her original gift for a Reformed Church boys'
mission school, as well as her additional gift, were used for a building
to serve Meiji Gakuin in Tokyo. Sandham Hall, completed in 1887 with
seven classrooms, a chapel seating 250, and a library and reading room,
served as the main building of the Academic Department of Meiji
Gakuin.

In the fall of 1887, enrollment at Meiji Gakuin reached 190 in the
Academic Department and thirty-three in the Theological Department.
Meiji Gakuin was growing. Wyckoff was enthusiastic about its future
and did not hesitate to ask for financial support, saying, "For awhile

now I suppose our wanting something in connection with this work, will be chronic, but it is a good investment, and it will not be long ere the church in Japan from being helped will take its place among the helpers in carrying on the Master's work in the earth."[94]

The plan of organization for Meiji Gakuin established that the care and supervision of the school would be shared equally by Japanese church leaders and missionaries. Foreigners were not permitted to own land in Japan; consequently, seven Japanese Christians formed a legal holding body, the Board of Trustees, to hold ownership of the school property.[95] These seven Japanese, along with seven missionaries representing the Reformed and Presbyterian Japan missions, formed the Board of Directors, the governing organization for Meiji Gakuin. It was clearly stated that the purpose of the Reformed and Presbyterian Japan missions was the establishment of an institution of Christian learning and education in connection with the *Nippon Itchi Kirisuto Kyokai* (United Church of Christ in Japan), and further that they hoped the day would speedily come when Japanese Christians could assume the entire educational and financial responsibility for the institution.

In 1888, Wyckoff reported, "Quite a number of our pupils have gone out to do evangelistic work during the summer vacation. They are for the most part working in connection with workers sent out by the Home Mission Board, so their results, if there are any, will be gathered up at once."[96] Not only were a large percentage of these college students becoming Christians, but also many of them were actively participating in the evangelistic outreach of the United Church.

In this period when the popularity of Christianity was apparently rising, mission school educators were hopeful and confident of great success. Howard Harris claimed, "It is quite the thing for parents to place their children in Christian schools, while not one of the hundreds of young people attending Christian schools objects to the study of the Bible."[97] Gordon VanWyk later noted,

> These two men, Dr. Hepburn and Dr. Verbeck, while exceptional in their influence, are nonetheless representative of many of the missionaries of the early period, who while in many cases not particularly trained in educational methods, gave their primary

---

[94]    MNW to HNC, Oct. 8 and Nov. 28, 1887.
[95]    The original trustees were Ibuka Kajinosuke, Hattori Ayao, Ishimoto Sanjuro, Ohgimi Motoichiro, Uemura Masahisa, Kumano Yushichi, and Nakajima Nobuyuki.
[96]    MNW to JMF, July 27, 1888.
[97]    HH to HNC, Nov. 24, 1886.

attention to the establishment of a sound system of Christian education for Japan. When we remember that nine out of every ten educated men and women in Japan before 1890 received their first instruction from missionaries, we are struck with new appreciation for the importance of this teaching phase of their ministry.[98]

### Nagasaki Mission Schools

Stout and Segawa continued to teach theological classes in Nagasaki. Looking toward developing this aspect of the work of Nagasaki Station, they both worked at translating materials so that theological education could be carried out effectively in the Japanese language. Greatly influenced by his professor at New Brunswick Seminary, Dr. Samuel M. Woodbridge, Stout translated and adapted Woodbridge's works on sacred history and church history for use in their Japanese theological curriculum. These textbooks were published in the mid-1880s and widely used in Japan.

Despite the objections of most of the missionaries in Tokyo and Yokohama, the mission board "declared in favor of the educational work (in Nagasaki) being sustained in full."[99] Accordingly, the appointment of the Reverend Albert and Alice Oltmans to Japan and Nagasaki was a significant step in the realization of the long-held educational plans for Nagasaki Station. Albert Oltmans was born in the Netherlands in 1855 and had emigrated to America in 1873. After graduating from Hope College in 1883 and New Brunswick Theological Seminary in 1886, he married Alice Voorhoorst, and they made ready and departed for Japan, arriving in October 1886. Oltmans was the first of many American Hope College graduates to be sent to Japan as missionaries. Stout eagerly anticipated a blossoming of boys' education under Oltmans. At the same time, the arrival of Oltmans would free Demarest to oversee the evangelists at the outstations and for evangelistic outreach into new areas to which Stout was committed.

There were of course two mission boards associated with the Reformed Church. In addition to the church's Board of Foreign Missions, the Woman's Board of Foreign Missions, backed by the women's missionary societies in the various congregations, took particular interest in overseas missionary work related to women. The Woman's Board dedicated itself to the development of the girls' school

---

[98]    Van Wyk, *Eighty Years*, 11.
[99]    HH to HNC, Aug. 15, 1885.

in Nagasaki. The board had sent Mary Brokaw and would also send subsequent teachers for the school. Alice Oltmans offered to assist Brokaw in getting the school program going until the second single woman teacher could be recruited and sent by the Woman's Board. The Woman's Board and its related societies also worked diligently to raise money for the girls' school building.

In 1886 construction of the long-awaited school buildings for both the boys' and girls' schools became financially feasible. These two building projects, each requiring about five thousand dollars, became possible because of two very significant gifts from America. The president of the Woman's Board was Mrs. Jonathan Sturges, wife of a prosperous New York businessman and known as a person of deep faith and high character who offered dedicated service in her church and community. The Woman's Board's goal of five thousand dollars for the building fund was met through many small gifts and one large gift of three thousand dollars from Mrs. Sturges. The Woman's Board decided to name the girls' school in Nagasaki the Jonathan Sturges Seminary in honor of the benefactor. The president of the Reformed Church's Board of Foreign Missions at the time was William H. Steele. A little before this time Steele had been grieved by the death of his seventeen-year-old son William Henry. Steele gave five thousand dollars, money he had saved for his son's education, so that Japanese youth might be educated and the goals in education for boys in Nagasaki might be realized. Accordingly, the boys' school was named Steele Memorial Academy.

Even before these funds were in hand, Stout and his colleagues went into action to realize their long-held educational goals. On their own responsibility, Stout, Demarest, and Brokaw negotiated for and purchased land on which to build.[100] In consultation with missionary and Japanese colleagues, Stout designed and drew plans for the buildings for both mission schools. When the money came through, they were able to proceed immediately. The girls' school property was adjacent to the Stouts' residence, and the boys' school property was several hundred yards away. Construction was carried on simultaneously at the two sites from the fall of 1886, and the work was completed in the summer of 1887. Stout not only served as architect, but also supervised the construction.

The girls' school, Sturges Seminary, consisted of a two-story wooden building that contained an auditorium, classrooms, dormitory,

[100]    HS to HNC, Sept. 2, 1886.

Sturges Seminary
in Nagasaki,
completed in 1887

and foreign teachers' residence, all under one roof. It was not large, but it was described as very functional, attractive, and blending well with its surroundings. The boys' school, Steele Academy, included a two-story main school building, a separate dormitory, and a small gymnasium for use on rainy days. These buildings, too, were all of wooden construction.[101]

Steele Academy opened in its new buildings September 26, 1887. Albert Oltmans was the principal. Almost immediately he found himself short of teachers. The small classes Oltmans had been teaching in temporary facilities grew immediately to a student body of more than sixty students. Oltmans did much of the teaching, as did his wife, Alice, but she was expecting a baby and would not be able to continue for many more months. Stout's son, Provost, who was seventeen years old at the time, helped out temporarily by teaching a couple of classes. A Japanese teacher was also hired.

Albert Oltmans, faced with the necessity of teaching ten hours a day, sent a letter to the board requesting a young male teacher to assist him.[102] Stout also sent an urgent request in a letter to Secretary Cobb. He asked the board immediately to recruit and send a single man fresh out of college to teach on a two- or three-year contract. Stout concluded his plea humorously by writing, "Do send someone, as they say, 'by return mail.'"[103] Demarest and Oltmans also wrote letters to the board to plead that a teacher be sent out immediately.[104] Amazingly, this request was fulfilled almost literally. Harmon Van Slyck (H. V. S.) Peeke, a twenty-one-year-old minister's son who graduated from Hope

---

[101]    The original main building of Steele Academy may still be seen. It has been moved to a park in Nagasaki and restored as a historic building of fine quality.
[102]    Albert Oltmans to HNC, July 2, 1887.
[103]    HS to HNC, Oct. 5, 1887.
[104]    NHD to HNC, Oct. 24, 1887; AO to HNC, Jan. 10, 1888.

Steele Memorial Academy buildings, completed in 1887

College in 1887, was recruited. He left the United States in December of 1887 and arrived in Nagasaki to begin teaching at Steele Memorial Academy January 21, 1888.[105]

As a structured institution, Steele Academy was for some years very crude, but in terms both of religious impact and actual education, it was effective. One characteristic of the school in the early years was a great deal of coming and going. As many as one hundred new students came each year, while the enrollment hardly varied at all. From 1887, when the school entered its new buildings and began to grow, the theological classes taught by Stout and Segawa were incorporated into the school. It was organized with two departments, the Academic Department and the Theological Department. The Academic Department was developed as a six-year program, including two years of preparatory school and a four-year academic course. The three-year theological training course, for which the academic course was a prerequisite, prepared young men for evangelism and pastoral work through biblical and theological study and a program of practical training for ministry. Stout was happy to be able to put the administration of the school in the hands of Oltmans and to concentrate his efforts on theological education.

By late 1888, Peeke could report, "Our school is getting along nicely. We have 59 in the preparatory department, 36 in the academic

---

[105]    Harmon Van Slyck Peeke to HNC, Jan. 21, 1888. Peeke could perhaps be called the first Reformed Church "J3" missionary to Japan, a title that would later be used to describe short-term teachers sent to teach English at the mission schools.

and 5 in the theological, a total of one hundred. We have over sixty boarders & our accommodations are strained to their utmost limit. We ought to have another house for the accommodation of about sixty more. That would enable us to take nothing but boarders." The students had Bible instruction every day except Monday, when they had a prayer meeting instead. The latter was a worship service at which the students lustily sang Japanese translations of gospel hymns. Their lack of experience singing Western style music resulted in what was "a trifle painful to the ears" for the missionaries, but certainly expressed their sentiment and enthusiasm.[106]

Sturges Seminary opened in its new building September 14, 1887. Brokaw was the principal, and two Japanese teachers, Mr. Saito and Mr. Natsuyama, worked with her. The month after the school opened in the new facilities, on October 8, 1887, Rebecca L. Irvine arrived to work in partnership with Brokaw and the Japanese teachers. The enrollment was less than twenty that school year, but a four-year course of study was set up, and the little school was established on a firmer foundation for the future than had been possible before.[107]

Newly arrived Rebecca Irvine shared her early impressions.

Am now studying the language, devote most of my time to it while the school is small. Have taken charge of the knitting and sewing, and teach one English class. My interest in the girls daily grows stronger, and I am thankful that I can love them so well and that each day they become dearer to me. They are very bright, interesting and affectionate and seem so grateful for the instruction they receive from me. I am very happy in this pleasant home and look forward to the future, hoping we may be able to accomplish much. What a glorious work it will be to help raise the women of Japan from their degraded condition and to lead them to their Savior. I must speak of our school building. It is so comfortable and convenient, and the location is very beautiful, indeed the Mission could not possibly have selected more suitable grounds for a girls' school. I really think we have the best location in Nagasaki. We are secluded and see nothing of the degrading scenes which are daily visible in the streets of this city. We are near Mr. Stout and Mr. Demarest who are so kind and willing to assist and guide us. All the members of the Mission are and have been so very kind to me since here that I know that I can be happy with them.[108]

---

[106]    HVSP to HNC, Nov. 9, 1888.
[107]    Mary E. Brokaw to HNC, Sept. 9 and Oct. 29, 1887.
[108]    Rebecca L. Irvine to HNC, Dec. 19, 1887.

However, despite realizing the long-held dream of a proper building and teachers for the girls' school, Sturges Seminary did not grow as had been anticipated. As of early October 1889, there were only eighteen students, fifteen of them boarding students. Brokaw and Irvine, as well as the other missionaries in Nagasaki, were very discouraged at the school's lack of success and in a quandary as to what to do. During the two years since opening the school in its new facilities, Brokaw had been in charge and the main foreign teacher, while Irvine had been studying Japanese and teaching part time. After considerable deliberation, all the missionaries in Nagasaki agreed that a change of missionary teachers was the only solution.[109]

By way of background, it is important to note that in May 1887, while the school buildings were still under construction, Brokaw had reported her engagement to an Anglican missionary. She assured the board that she would fulfill her obligation as an appointed assistant missionary to administer the girls' school and teach there for at least two years.[110] However, during those next two years her engagement did not go smoothly, and it was eventually broken off. The distraction in her personal life, added to the fact that she was extremely strict with the girls, apparently contributed to the school's failure to attract students as expected. Irvine believed that, while she might be thought to share responsibility for the situation, as a part-time teacher during her first two years she had not really had an opportunity to contribute much to the success of the school. She still felt a strong call to the work and entrusted her future as a missionary to the discretion of the mission and the board.[111]

Feeling responsible for the school's lack of success but hoping for a new opportunity to serve, Brokaw requested a transfer to Yokohama, to teach under Booth at Ferris Seminary.[112] Representing all the missionaries in Nagasaki, Peeke reaffirmed the necessity of properly developing Sturges Seminary and urged the board to act immediately to provide teaching staff for the school.[113] Severing her relationships in Nagasaki, Brokaw transferred to Yokohama and took up teaching at Ferris Seminary under Booth.

---

[109]    HVSP to HNC, Oct. 17, 1889.
[110]    MEB to HNC, May 7, 1887.
[111]    RLI to HNC, Oct. 18 and 21, Nov. 6, 1889.
[112]    MEB to HNC, Oct. 18, 1889.
[113]    HVSP to HNC, Nov. 9, 1889.

## Church Growth and Missionary Itineration

The objectives missionaries were expected to hold were laid out clearly in a letter of Henry Stout.

> Our object in mission work should be, 1. To evangelize, 2. To establish churches, 3. To provide what is essential to independent church life, and 4. To make the churches a means for the further propagation of the truth. In order to do this, it may not be wise to arrange our mission policy so that the best apparent results may be obtained immediately, but looking to the end, so plan that the Church will be in the best possible condition, when our work as missionaries is done.[114]

The 1880s, a period when great effort was expended toward realizing these lofty goals, proved to be a time of very promising evangelism and church formation. Gifted and well-trained Japanese men were one by one completing their theological educations and taking the main responsibility for the preaching stations and newly forming churches. The role of the evangelistic missionaries was becoming one of encouragement, nurture, support, and supervision. Organized churches were expected to become self-supporting and encouraged to work toward that end. However, the pastors and evangelists who were serving at the various preaching stations and involved in pioneer work were, as a general rule, supported by the mission. All the Reformed Church missionaries worked cooperatively with pastors and evangelists at churches and preaching stations in or close to Yokohama, Tokyo, and Nagasaki. The ordained missionaries all shared preaching, lecturing, and Bible teaching duties with their Japanese colleagues. Evangelistic touring became an increasingly valuable aspect of the missionaries' work. Missionary correspondence presents a vivid picture of the progress of this work.

### Tokyo-Yokohama Station

The Millers lived in Tokyo to take responsibility for the evangelistic work of the Reformed Mission in Tokyo itself and to the north and northwest. Upon their return from furlough in the spring of 1881, Mary Miller began her own work among women in the churches. She began to meet with women at Shitaya Church and Kojimachi Chapel, where she also worked with the Sunday school, teaching singing and a

---

[114]    HS to JLA, March 14, 1885.

class. She gathered former Ferris Seminary students at her home each month to further nurture seeds of faith planted at the mission school. Mary also took up a unique literature ministry. In her own words,

> I have also just begun editing *"Yorokobi no Otodzure"* ["Glad Tidings"], a small monthly for women and children. I think this paper was first issued in 1878. It has been partly supported by subscribers and partly by a donation of $800. per year from the Brooklyn S.S. Association. 2730 copies are printed per month, of which over 2000 are subscribed for by the Japanese and the missionaries of all denominations, who use them in their Sunday School. About 400 are given away....The amount of subscription (12 sen a year for one copy) is less than cost but with the Brooklyn donation it is sufficient.[115]

The missionaries also corresponded regularly with Japanese pastors and evangelists under the care of the mission who lived and worked in the towns and cities distant from the treaty ports where missionaries were permitted to reside. Once or twice a year for each region, the missionaries who were focused on evangelism and church-planting would obtain the government "passport" still required and make extended tours into the interior of the country to encourage the work there. In situations where the Japanese evangelist was not yet ordained, the missionary would also administer the sacraments. This became a pattern of missionary activity.

Especially in these early days of missionary touring, the visit of a foreigner to a community in the interior attracted a great deal of attention and could gather a large number of hearers. Excerpts from E. R. Miller's 1881 letter reporting on a tour to the region of Ueda and Komoro describe the work. While the details may not be of crucial importance, they picture an aspect of the life of an itinerant missionary and the realities of travel in Japan before the development of public transportation and proper roads.

> Last month Mrs. Miller and myself made a tour into the country of Shinano to visit Mr. Maki, our ordained assistant at Komoro, and the church at Ueda. We started early on the twentieth, taking very little with us as we intended to depend upon Japanese food almost entirely.
>
> As the Japanese stages [horse-drawn carriages] are still in a very primitive condition and the stage-houses badly cared for

---

[115]  MEM to JMF, Jan. 19, 1882.

or rather not cared for at all, we preferred to travel by *jinrikisha*, and so engaged them for the whole distance through to Komoro, about 108 miles; the two *jinrikisha* with two men each costing 15 yen or about $8.00 U.S. By doing this we secured comfortable *jinrikisha* for the whole journey and avoided the delay and trouble of having to change the men every few miles.

The second day out we were caught in a storm and had an uncomfortable experience in crossing streams where the bridges were down. At one place we had to make a detour of several miles and finally cross the swollen river in a small boat, which was so laden down with *jinrikisha*, the boatman, ourselves, and the men, that the gunwale was only a few inches above the water, and the angry current threatened to swamp us. We reached the other side in safety however, but had to find our way as best we could by the narrow muddy roads through the rice fields till we reached the [main road]....We intended to push on to Itahama, since we thought we could not reach Annaka before dark. However we had gone but a few miles beyond Takasaki when we heard that another bridge was down and we must make a detour and come in beyond Itahama. To make this detour we had to cross the river on a pontoon bridge and to climb a steep hill in a pour of rain, while the muddy roads were not improved by the two days rain. As it was rapidly growing dark and we were on a strange road our situation was not very pleasant. In going up the hill the road became so heavy that I put the four men to Mrs. Miller's *jinrikisha*, while I got out in the mud and pulled mine, and in a very few minutes came to the determination not to turn *jinrikisha* man. Before long we came to a stream where the bridge was washed away, but there was no time to do anything but get across in some way as quickly as possible. The men waded about till they found a ford and then pulled the *jinrikisha* over one at a time, although the water came in the bottom. After losing our way in the dark, we came to a house where we lit the lanterns and inquired the way. But we did not reach the hotel at Annaka till after eight o'clock.

Annaka is a place of considerable size and center for the silk trade, but there is only one respectable hotel in the place, that is, respectable in character [not functioning as a brothel], but very badly kept....

After a good rest we started off in good spirits as the day was bright. The roads however were very bad from the long continued rain, and before evening the men became quite discouraged with the mud and the hills. Being Tokyo men they could run all day on a level without feeling it, but they were not used to the hills and thought it very dangerous when they saw the country men running down hill in a good round trot.

The view in crossing the Usui Pass was magnificent, but the pass seemed much longer than usual and the men were quite tired when we got to the other side and we found it impossible to reach Komoro that night. Next morning it was raining again and one of the men was lame so we left him behind as it was only five or six miles further to go and set off with three men.

On reaching Komoro we hunted up Mr. Maki, he had about given us up on account of the rain, but he was delighted to see us and took us to the hotel, where we were accommodated with a very pleasant room. They were extremely kind and attentive to us during the whole of our stay, and as the food was very good we got along nicely in spite of the small amount of provisions we brought with us.[116]

Maki Shigeto had been the pastor of the Ueda Church, an organized congregation. However, when the congregation was unable to support him fully, he had come directly under the direction and support of the Reformed Church Japan Mission, serving as an evangelist, and moved to Komoro toward the end of 1880, thus expanding the mission's outreach. At the time of the Millers' tour, Pastor Maki and his family were the only baptized Christians in Komoro, but there were a number of interested or curious people attending his services or Bible study classes held in several places in the region each week, and he had also begun a Sunday school. During the time the Millers were in Komoro, meetings were held almost every night, lasting till after 10:30 and sometimes till almost midnight. Large numbers gathered because of the novelty of hearing a foreigner speak [in Japanese], and to see a foreign lady. Maki of course tried to capitalize on this opportunity to arouse the interest of more people in Christianity.

A unique characteristic of Japanese evangelistic outreach already evident in this period was also described in Miller's report.

When we reached Komoro, Mr. Uyemura [Uemura Masahisa], the pastor of the Shitaya Church, had been laboring for about one week in Ueda, and the church there was very anxious that while we were in Shinshiu we should hold a large lecture meeting, or *yensetsu-*

---

[116] ERM to JMF, Oct. 25, 1881.

*kuwai* [*enzetsukai*]. I call them lecture meetings for want of a better name, but they differ from our lectures at home in that there are nearly always a number of speakers and the subjects are taken from any department of learning. They are exceedingly popular in Japan at present and the name is very taking [appealing], as many will come to a lecture on some teaching of Christianity who would not come to a sermon on the same subject....The object of holding them in Ueda was to attract attention and break down prejudice.

We went on to Ueda and had two such meetings at each of which Mr. Maki, Mr. Uyemura working in connection with our Mission, and Mr. Kozaki of the ABCFM Mission, who came on from Annaka for the purpose, as well as myself spoke. One of the meetings was held in the town government school, as we should call it, which has never before been lent for that purpose. The attendance was large as the room was the place where their local assembly meets. The believers think that much good will come of the meetings.[117]

During the days at Ueda, Miller baptized six converts and administered the Lord's Supper. He noted that although there was at that time no resident pastor, Ueda Church was doing well and even growing under the diligent leadership of its lay leaders. Miller planned to tour the area once or twice a year. It had also been arranged with Tokyo Union Theological School that the students would go out not only during summer but also for a month's work in the field in the winter and again in the spring. Churches in the interior without a resident pastor such as Ueda could thus be nurtured and grow.

James Ballagh, freed from teaching preparatory school classes after Wyckoff's arrival, was able to give himself primarily to evangelistic work from the fall of 1881. The mission gave him responsibility for outreach and development of evangelism from Yokohama west and southwest, including the Hakone area and Izu Peninsula and as far southwest as Nagoya. Ballagh was noted for his enthusiasm for missionary touring. However, it was a daunting and exhausting task, as excerpts from his letters indicate. "I returned to this place [Yokohama] one week ago tonight, making the distance, 45 miles in from Hakone in a day. It required an early start, and a walk of three miles by aid of a lantern before break-of-day to accomplish it. The haste to return was owing to the meeting of the Daikwai being set for the next day."[118]

117   Ibid.
118   JHB to JMF, Nov. 7, 1881.

Ballagh had spent October of 1881 on an extended tour to the southwest, traveling much of the way on foot, circumventing Mt. Fuji, visiting believers and witnessing in villages along the way. At one point, he was a passenger on a river skiff down the rushing Fuji River for forty-five miles. He described a situation he encountered with believers in the Hakone region:

> This day and the Sabbath following were trying days. Our recent convert at Gotemba, the school teacher, under great pressure from debt, kindred & enemies, was about to renounce Christianity for a situation [employment] in a school requiring such a renunciation. This we felt could not be allowed, so with fasting & extraordinary efforts he was stayed from the fatal act. Our gracious God himself, and most loving Master prevented this sad failure and great disgrace from taking place. We induced the Christians themselves to employ him as their teacher & so save him. He hoped the opposition would withdraw when they found this stand was taken.

Ballagh went on:

> "I write this late at night as I start again tomorrow for a three weeks trip to Nagoya. I have had no rest for even a moment since return, & go forth tired to start with. I generally like to get rested a little, as with late nights and early mornings and long journies [*sic*] and the excitement of meeting people & continuous preaching, makes a preaching tour pretty fatiguing."[119]

Ballagh, however, seemed to thrive on such touring, and it became the hallmark of his long missionary career. He often wrote of his tours with great enthusiasm. Of a tour in the winter of 1882 to Mishima and the surrounding region, he wrote, "Eleven persons were baptized, and believers and inquirers visited & services held at twenty to thirty places. Our faithful Brother Ito Tokichi was with me in the visits to these places and was much encouraged by God's blessing upon his faithful labors.... The assembling seldom took place before 10 P.M. and exercises had to last till midnite. Journeying by day & preaching late at night exhausts one rapidly. I find I walked above 150 miles during the 18 days journey in the field."[120]

Guido Verbeck related a story of the perseverance of one of the very earliest converts. We noted previously the baptism of a young

[119]  Ibid.
[120]  JHB to JMF, March 13, 1882.

Buddhist priest named Shimizu by Verbeck in Nagasaki in June of 1868. In the fall of 1882, Verbeck wrote:

> The day before yesterday I had a surprise. In 1868 or so, I baptized a Buddhist priest, by name Shimidzu; while I was still in Nagasaki he suffered a good deal of persecution in a private way, but was not further molested in his person. Toward the close of the year I left Nagasaki, however, he was called to the government office in charge of these matters, examined & on his confession of having received baptism & refusal to recant, was put into the common prison. Thence he was after a time removed to a prison in Omura, & finally to another one in Higo, his native province. Altogether he was in prison about five years, promises being held out to him from time to time that he would be released if he renounced the Christian religion. But he persevered in the faith & was finally set free by express order of the government two years later than all the rest of the native Christians had been released. These latter were Roman Catholics. Shimidzu was kept in prison the last two of the five years at the instigation of the sect to which he formerly belonged. The priests of that sect offered to bear all the expenses if the government would still further keep him in confinement; but the offer was not accepted & he was at last let go. Prison life at that time was exceedingly hard; the accommodations, the food, & the company were all equally bad. No books of any kind were allowed the prisoners & all they had on entering were taken away from them. Thus the only spiritual comfort Shimidzu had during all the years of his imprisonment was his faith in the Saviour, private prayer & the few Scripture passages he had committed to memory. Since leaving the prison he has been engaged, he tells me, in teaching at a primary school in a poor village on the seacoast of Higo. On Sundays he used to gather the children & teach them from one of our catechisms, which he got for this purpose from Nagasaki. But the schoolhouse having since been burned during the Satsuma rebellion & the next time carried off by a flood, the funds for rebuilding it a third time were wanting. The Buddhists hearing of the state of things came forward & built a new school, but of course would have nothing to do with the Christian Shimidzu, who was thus left without employment. During all these years I had heard nothing of this man, except once through Bro. Stout; and I am sorry to say that Mr. Stout's report was not a satisfactory one. Mr. Stout suspected the man

of having taken some article out of his parlor on one of his visits to him. He had, however, no clear proof, I believe. Servants can easily purloin small articles themselves & then accuse a casual visitor. Such things are known to have been done by bad servants & might have been done in this case. I know that this same man came to my house for several years, being often left alone in my study or parlor, yet I never had reason to doubt his entire honesty. —However, the day before yesterday he surprised me by presenting himself in my study. I had a long interview with him & learned from him the above part of his history. Although now 38 years of age, he looks just about as when I left him at Nagasaki 13 or 14 years ago. This morning I had him interviewed by our oldest native pastor, Rev. Mr. Okuno, whom I had previously told all I knew about the man, not omitting Mr. Stout's suspicions; Mr. Okuno & other native pastors & Christians will soon know whether he is a true believer or an impostor, for they have means far superior to us in judging of their own countrymen's true character & the sincerity or insincerity of their professions. Mr. Okuno was quite satisfied with the result of his interview with Shimidzu & at the conclusion of it offered up a hearty prayer for & with his new acquaintance in the Lord. I have given Shimidzu an introduction to Rev. Mr. Yamamoto, pastor of our Koji-machi Church, & recommended him that he should join himself to that church. Here he has no friends, so I have taken him to live with me for the present. It will not be long before we know whether he is sincere or not. My prayer is that he may show himself a true disciple of Jesus, for the profession of whose blessed name he has apparently suffered and borne a good deal.[121]

As the 1880s progressed, the increasing openness of the Japanese people toward Christianity became apparent, not only in Tokyo and Yokohama but also in outlying areas. In the spring of 1884, E. R. and Mary Miller made an evangelistic tour to the north and northwest of Tokyo, accompanied by two seminary students and the wife of one of the students. In the area surrounding Wado Church, and in the region of Komoro and Ueda, during their twenty-three-day tour, numerous lectures and preaching services were held, and Mary Miller and the student's wife held services for women and children, all with good results. Candidates for baptism were examined at several of the regular meeting places, and many of them were baptized.

[121]    GFV to JMF, Oct. 16, 1882.

Transportation was beginning to improve, and the Millers were able to travel part way toward their northwest destination on newly opened train lines. Nevertheless, they still mostly traveled on foot or by *jinrikisha*, and occasionally Mary was carried in a palanquin. Having become accustomed to Japanese food and country inn lodging, they entered energetically into the daily meetings and activities with their Japanese fellow Christians. Excerpts from their report help us picture their experiences. The report includes references to what is called an "orguenette," which was evidently a small portable mechanical reed organ. It was operated by a hand crank that worked both the small bellows and the pinned wooden player roll. It functioned like the later player pianos in that it used a perforated paper roll or disk, and they must have had paper rolls or disks of hymns. Miller reported:

> Monday the 21st Mr. Hitomi and I went with Mr. Maki to Iwamurada, a town some six miles from Komoro where there are services nearly every week. I had a strange experience here and learned a new use to put the "orguenette" to. When we returned from America, three years ago, I brought two "orguenettes" with me and gave one to Mr. Maki and one to Mr. Ito, in Mishima.
>
> These have proved of great service in gathering the people together, as well as helping them in the singing. Lately Mr. Maki has used his for a different object: some of the young men who were baptized last year have used their spare time in selling Bibles and have found the "orguenette" very useful in drawing a crowd together, and since in Iwamurada the preaching day has not always been regular, they have used the little instrument in letting the people of the town know that there was to be a meeting: so after we had reached the town and rested a little we started off through the town, down the main street and up the side ones playing the "orguenette" and telling the people there was to be a preaching meeting as usual and inviting them to come to it. Mr. Maki thought that if the inventer [*sic*] of the "orguenette" could have seen the new use to which his instrument was put he would have been amused, to say the least, and if a Christian would certainly have rejoiced....
>
> While in Komoro we made a discovery, which I am surprised we never thought of before, namely, that we could always get bread when out in the country. The Japanese have a kind of cake called "man-jiu" [manju], which is made of a wheaten dough, filled with sweetened bean-paste and steamed; these are made in all towns of

any size, and at all seasons of the year. The dough is raised with yeast and if made well is very wholesome and palatable.

We ordered some made without the bean-paste, and had some very good bread, in forms like biscuits, but without any crust, being steamed instead of being baked. We shall certainly remember this in future....

The Japanese in the country have not yet learned the value of time and it is impossible to begin the meetings at the time fixed, they are always late: besides which the country-people are never satisfied if the meeting breaks up before ten o'clock at night, a much more usual time is after eleven.[122]

Reflecting on their recent trip, Miller wrote,

It seems to me that the people through the country are more anxious to hear the truths of the Gospel than ever before. Some of them are drawn out of curiosity, to be sure, but many have a real desire to know what is meant by Christianity.

We are always treated with great respect: and this time especially, I noticed that the "preaching-meetings" were just as well attended, if not better, than the so-called "lecture-meetings."

There are a good many Bibles and tracts sold to the country people;...I, myself, took more on this trip than on any previous one and the people were always glad to get them.[123]

By the end of 1884, church growth throughout the regions reached by the Reformed and Presbyterian Japan Missions and their Japanese partners appeared to be gaining momentum. Five new churches were organized during that year, and 425 adults and 43 children were baptized. Of the thirty-nine organized congregations, eleven were related to the Reformed Mission. Church membership had increased 20 percent in one year, reaching a total of 2,948 members. Furthermore, Amerman remarked, "The interest of the people in the matter of the support of their own churches is steadily increasing."[124]

Although his chief work was in relation to theological education, Amerman also took part in touring. He, too, visited Pastor Maki to encourage him in the work at Komoro, and shared in the ministry. He reported in part,

---

[122] ERM to HNC, May 5, 1884.
[123] ERM to HNC, May 16, 1884.
[124] JLA to HNC, Jan. 26, 1885.

In the evening the service was long but not less interesting. The room was <u>packed</u> full, as many being present as could find place either sitting or standing, and quite a large number outside the building but within hearing distance. Three sermons were preached, the first by one of our students who had been spending several days in the place, the second, a very animated and intensely earnest discourse by Mr. Maki, and the third by myself.

Maki also reached out to the area surrounding Komoro. Amerman reported,

Mr. Maki has 3 or 4 places within 30 miles, where he preaches at least once a month, and we visited one of these the next day, about 20 miles distant, and after climbing in the afternoon a mountain pass from which we had a view of wonderful grandeur, I spent the evening with a number of people who had come together to hear a Christian discourse. There were about 60 present, and of these only one had received baptism, and 10 or 12 are studying the scriptures as they have opportunity. Here was an audience very different from that which we have in Tokiyo, and certainly vastly different from the audience of students to whom I talk every day, and I felt that the Master was with me to help me in my address to them.[125]

The United Church's *Daikai* of 1885 reflected the church's growth. It opened with forty-four organized churches and more than four thousand communicant members and added several new churches at the synod. Ballagh expressed the growing optimism and confidence of the missionaries when he wrote.

Is not this a glad day in Zion? <u>Five</u> Missions conjoined in work for one church and that church now having <u>five</u> Classes or Presbyteries, with nearly 50 churches and soon with the blessing of God 5000 members! I feel so sanguine of results, with the blessing of God resting upon us, viz., that of His Holy Spirit, that instead of the 15 years assigned by some for the finishing of missionary work in Japan, or before the close of the 19th century, I see no reason why it may not be done in 7 years or before 1893, the Centennial of Missions.[126]

---

[125]  JLA to HNC, May 8, 1885.
[126]  JHB to HNC, Dec. 4, 1885.

Examples of the growing interest in and openness to Christianity were apparent everywhere. In Yokohama, Christians rented a theater to hold an *enzetsukai* (lecture meeting). Seven or eight speeches, ranging in length from thirty minutes to two hours each, were presented by Verbeck, Knox, and leading Japanese ministers from Yokohama and Tokyo. Despite inclement winter weather, attendance was eight hundred in the afternoon and six hundred at night.[127] Similarly, when Ballagh and Presbyterians Knox and McAuley went on an evangelistic tour north to the Sendai area and to Fukushima to assist in the work of Oshikawa, attendance at preaching services and lecture meetings regularly overflowed the meeting places. Ballagh remarked, "At present it is most marvelous how people will sit for hours listening to the discussion of religious and philosophical truth, and showing an aptitude for handling such themes no one would ever dream of."[128]

The United Church continued its rapid growth. In the eighteen months since the 1885 *Daikai*, eleven new congregations were organized so that there were now fifty-five, and church membership had grown from 4,100 to 7,094. Baptisms had been as follows: male adults—1,044, female adults—686, and children—288, for a net gain by baptism of 49 percent. Contributions had also increased considerably, but there was a notable shortage of ordained ministers. By the end of 1887, there were thirty-four ordained Japanese pastors and forty-eight Japanese evangelists (not yet ordained licensed preachers) in the United Church.[129]

During the spring of 1887, Ballagh and Miller made an extensive evangelistic tour through the area stretching from Mishima to Nagoya. Sometimes together and always in partnership with Japanese pastors or theological students, they held meetings in Mishima, Shizuoka, Okazaki, Tsugumura, Nagoya, Seto, Gifu, and Tsushima. In Mishima, where Ballagh had begun some years before by preaching in the street in front of a large Shinto shrine, there were now more than two hundred believers, including those in the surrounding villages. A convert, Mr. Hanajima, gave his brewery to Mishima Church, and its building was being remodeled into a church and mission school for girls. During this tour, there were baptisms of new converts in Gifu and Tsushima, the first Christian funeral in Tsushima, and a lecture meeting at the largest theater in Nagoya attended by more than one thousand people.[130]

---

127  JHB to HNC, Feb. 8, 1886.
128  SJHB to HNC, Apr. 12, 1886.
129  MNW to JMF, Jan. 2, 1888.
130  ERM to HNC, June 27, 1887; JHB to HNC, June 28 & Oct. 26, 1887.

The ministry at Mishima Church, meeting in the remodeled brewery building, grew to a membership of 250, and its private girls' school prospered. A Meiji Gakuin student who came to assist during his summer vacation reported, "At the first meeting I attended there were two hundred attentive men and women in the audience. Many visitors came to my room daily to have the Bible explained, and it was not until late in the night that I found time to rest." At Nagoya Church, founded by Ballagh, in 1884 there were fifteen members, but by 1888 there were hundreds of Christians. A Meiji Gakuin student who visited and preached in many villages in the vicinity of Nagoya reported, "All the people welcomed us with warm hearts."[131]

The Millers wished to live in the interior to do evangelistic work and had considered the possibility of moving to Kochi, on the island of Shikoku, but gave up the idea because Mary could not tolerate the summer heat there. From March of 1888, at the request of Oshikawa of Sendai, the Millers began a new venture. In partnership with the Reverend Miura Toru and Mr. Hayashi, a recent graduate of the theological school, E. R. and Mary Miller began a pioneer work in Morioka, a northern city half way between Sendai and Aomori. Hayashi, the licensed preacher, went ahead to do some preliminary work. Miller and Miura went in March to establish the evangelism outpost, and soon seven believers were baptized. Foreigners were not legally permitted to reside in the interior. To go there to live required at least part-time teaching, which allowed the government to issue a teacher's passport. After some delay by officials, Miller obtained a three-year passport permitting him to teach English and theology. To justify the residence permit, Miller initiated an English class for adult men with thirty to forty members.

In June of 1888, the Millers moved from their home in Tokyo to a rented thatched-roofed house on the edge of Morioka City. However, they needed a more substantial house that they could keep warm during the cold winters. Nothing suitable being available, they bought land in Miura's name, had a snug Japanese house built, and moved in before winter. Soon four more converts were baptized, and fifteen men from Miller's English class began attending his Bible class. With the help of Japanese colleagues, they soon had a Sunday school of seventy to eighty pupils. Miller, Miura, and Hayashi preached and lectured, not only at Morioka, but also in nearby towns. In connection with a community Ladies Association, Mary Miller was asked to teach a women's English

---

131   HH to HNC, Oct. 17, 1888.

class five days each week, out of which developed her Bible class and a prayer meeting for women. Enjoying good health, Mary was able to participate in evangelistic work, while at the same time continuing as editor of "Glad Tidings," the publication for children and women. In less than a year, there were fifteen converts in Morioka. The work of the Millers and their colleagues continued to prosper, and by the summer of 1889, there were already thirty-five baptized Christians and a number of seekers. They waited to seek formal organization as a congregation until they were better able to support themselves.[132]

### Nagasaki Station

Missionary itineration into the interior away from the treaty ports also became an integral part of the work of Nagasaki Station on the southwestern island of Kyushu. Henry Stout was limited in his movement, not only by the government's travel restrictions, but also by his responsibilities to the theological students in Nagasaki. Nevertheless, he made numerous trips to Kagoshima and Saga to resolve problems and encourage the evangelists in their ministry. An episode reported from one of these trips in 1883 portrays the life situation of the Japanese Christians on the island of Kyushu.

> I have just returned from a visit to Kagoshima. The steamer by which I went arrived on Monday night. I went immediately to find Mr. Tomegawa. He was at the chapel, where the church members were gathered to pray for a young woman lately baptized, who is being persecuted. Her history is briefly this. She was sent with some others a few years ago to Tokio to learn the duties of a teacher in kindergarten, and while there she heard something of Christianity. She felt drawn towards the truth, but in the frivolity of the life she led, the impressions faded away. She has now been three or four years teaching in kindergarten in Kagoshima, and has made something of a reputation as a teacher. Some months ago she happened to be passing the chapel as services were going on, and went in. From that time she became an earnest and diligent inquirer. Her mother, who is a widow, at first objected to her associating with Christians and studying their religion, and when she proposed to be baptized refused to give her consent. But in the end she yielded. The young woman was baptized about

---

[132]  ERM to HNC, Oct. 28, 1887; Jan. 17, March 20, and June 29, 1888; Feb. 25 and July 29, 1889.

a month ago, and all seemed going on well, except, perhaps, that her mother was not pleased with the idea of her daughter's being a Christian, and she herself had to endure a good deal of banter and ridicule from her associates in school, on account of her new religion. But a short time ago an uncle, who is a Shinto priest, returned from a long preaching tour, and when he heard what had been done, he became very violent. He is in some way in charge of his deceased brother's family, and has taken it upon himself to order his niece to give up her religion, threatening her with severe penalties in case of refusal, among which is that of taking her life. Of course in these days this can amount to nothing more than a threat. But he has confined her to the house, and will no doubt go to the extreme of what he dares to do. The mother of course seconds him, and former friends use their utmost influence to induce her to recant. But so far as was known, she yet stood firm. On the Sunday before I arrived, the church had decided to meet for the three following nights for prayer that she might be sustained in the trial....On Tuesday evening there were eight men who took part in the exercises.[133]

By the mid-1880s, more opportunities for the expansion of the evangelistic work in Kyushu began to open up. Stout commented, "A spirit of inquiry is abroad in the land. And I wish we had a large force to go up and possess it." One theological student studying under Stout and Segawa, Kurihara Kenmei, insisted on postponing the completion of his studies to reside in Saga and serve as the first resident evangelist there from the beginning of 1884. Early in the year he found interested people in Karatsu City, some thirty miles northwest of Saga. Kurihara began monthly services there, resulting in several baptisms, and found inquirers in other towns. Segawa, invited by an interested former schoolmate, spent several weeks evangelizing in the northeast part of Kyushu in Nakatsu, his hometown, with promising results.[134]

These new and hopeful prospects occurred despite new challenges, as related by Demarest in the 1884 Nagasaki Station report.

He (Kurihara at Saga) has experienced active and most determined opposition through the influence of a society, called *Kiu Kuwai*, which has been established extensively in the southern part of Japan for the express purpose of hindering the spread of

---

133    HS to JMF, Aug. 10, 1883.
134    HS to HNC, May 8, 1884.

Christianity. The Saga section was especially active during the year, involving the people in large numbers, making a house to house canvass, giving lectures to set forth the evils of Christianity and to incite the people to oppose its influence. They even intimidated those who went to hear preaching and attempted by the throwing of mud and stones to break up the services. They even went so far in their virulence as to incite the children to set upon the preacher's children on the street and do them harm, and to vent their spite upon "Christian dog" (as they called the preacher's dog) whenever he ventured outside the gate. This sort of opposition, however, became of such a shameful nature that many, who allowed themselves to be enrolled in the society, have been disgusted and withdrawn. A few have even acknowledged to Mr. Kurihara their folly in being inveigled into the ranks of the opposition. As a result the tide seems to be turning and the last reports from Mr. Kurihara are most encouraging, so that there is every reason to hope that good will come for the evil endured, although it was impossible to make progress while the opposition lasted.

Subsequent visits to Saga by the missionaries or public lecture meetings by the Japanese pastors resulted in repeated experiences of harassment, heckling, sand and stone throwing, and threats, sometimes instigated by the Buddhist priests.[135] This direct opposition and persecution in fact continued in the region of Saga for several years, and although in some cases the overt confrontation resulted in attracting serious inquirers, Saga remained a region known for its resistance to the spread of Christianity. Even so, remarkable instances of the working of God's Spirit offered encouragement, as related at length by Demarest.

Some months ago a young man named Wada became quite noted in central Japan because of his eloquence in addresses against Christianity. The Buddhist priests of Saga invited him to come thither and lecture in their interests against Christianity. Hand bills announcing his coming, and speaking of his eloquence, etc., were scattered throughout the city and his arrival was awaited with great rejoicing and expectation on the part of the Buddhists, but with forebodings on the part of the Christians. But as of old the Lord appeared to the persecuting Saul on the way to Damascus, the Spirit strove now with the young lecturer, Wada, on his way

[135] NHD to HNC, Apr. 23, 1886.

to Saga. Wada had some time before been quite interested in Christianity but rejecting it had given all his talent to subvert its influence. On his way to Saga his purpose to oppose Christ was shown to him in all its wickedness, and it was as a conscience-stricken man that he entered that city. He made his way to Mr. Kawasaki's house, but Mr. Kawasaki was yet at Chiukai. The next morning he returned home and his first visitor was this young Buddhist, who, though engaged to lecture against Christianity, with troubled soul and sorrowing heart is seeking for mercy at God's throne. For many days the conflict in Wada's soul would not allow him any peace, day or night, but the mercy of God then was revealed to him, and the cleansing power of Christ's blood was eagerly prayed for and we trust received by him. He is now daily studying the Scriptures and is quite a strong instrument in Saga for proclaiming the truth of Christianity from house to house.

Another like incident occurred near Saga. This time God's Spirit moved upon the heart of a Shinto priest over 70 years old. He gradually accepted the Bible as God's Word and has left the old Shinto temple and religion at quite some sacrifice, to earn his daily living on a farm. Though this is very arduous work for such an aged man, he does not complain but rejoices in the peace of heart which Christ gives His own.[136]

In connection with the Reformed Church Japan Mission annual meeting, which was held in Nagasaki for the first time in December of 1884, Stout and Verbeck made an extensive preaching tour into areas north of Nagasaki, including Kurume, several miles northeast of Saga, where work had been initiated. Twenty or thirty people had become interested in Christianity. Stout reported,

Dr. Verbeck and I spent three days with them, instructing them as opportunity offered....The last night we were in Kurume, we had a lecture service in the theater. It was most satisfactory, for about a thousand people listened to us quietly and attentively for three hours, as we reasoned with them upon some of the cardinal doctrines of Revelation.

In Saga our first attempt to lecture was not attended with good success. The house that had been secured for the purpose was too small for the numbers that gathered, and the crowding and confusion made it necessary to cut the meeting short. On our way back to our hotel we were met with some rudeness on the part of a crowd of boys, who apparently tried to emulate the spirit of their elders in their hostility to Christianity the last year. But our second lecture the following evening was well received. Nearly two thousand people assembled in a large theater, and but for a slight diversion created by one or two who had been drinking too freely, the attention was good and the lectures listened to for more than two hours. The Sunday morning service with the little band of Christians and a few brethren from the church at Yanagawa, was a delightful one. It was a great privilege to Dr. Verbeck to speak to and celebrate the Lord's Supper with a number of the family of Wakasa [first Christian in southwest Japan, baptized by Verbeck eighteen years before] who are among the believers.[137]

Stout's understanding of the missionary's role in evangelization was clear:

> Of all departments of mission work, evangelization is that which must most necessarily be done by the natives. Such services as Dr. Verbeck and I held in Saga and Kurume are useful in breaking down the old religions, but can do little towards building up the new. That will have to be done by hand to hand and heart to heart contact by the natives. Even this, however, the missionary may be useful in aiding and stimulating, especially in times of discouragement. And so the evangelistic work will need superintendence.[138]

Nathan Demarest made his first evangelistic tour away from Nagasaki in June of 1885. Traveling by *jinrikisha*, he visited the evangelists in Saga and Kurume, observing the devastation of recent floods along the way. He was encouraged by the work in Saga, where he celebrated the Lord's Supper with twelve believers, including a twenty-year-old woman baptized that morning. He reported, "In the neighborhood of Saga many calls for preaching have been responded to by Mr. Kurihara, and six or seven adults baptized on confession of faith, while as many men are under instruction as catechumens, awaiting baptism." Kurihara was to begin focusing his work in Karatsu, northwest of Saga. The work in Kurume also appeared promising, and Tomegawa was to move there from Kagoshima. Demarest added, "Our school work ended with June

---

[137]   HS to HNC, Jan. 19, 1885.
[138]   HS to HNC, May 2, 1885.

[summer break from theological study], and as we thought a trial of active work would help both us and the young men, we have sent them out by two's to various places, the more advanced in study to conduct the meetings, the other to assist him by colporteur work and visitation. Mr. Kawasaki and Mr. Yoshidomi finished their course of studies and have gone to their fields of labor; Mr. Kawasaki to Saga, Mr. Yoshidomi to Kagoshima."[139]

Evangelization and church formation progressed under the supervision of Stout and Demarest, through their periodic visits to pastors and evangelists, and by sending theological students out for firsthand experience and to extend outreach into new areas. In this way, not only in major cities, the centers of culture and power in Japan, but also in interior cities and towns, the Christian movement was slowly gaining momentum.

Demarest's letter in 1886 exuded faith and feeling for the work in Kyushu.

> Let me point out a fact in connection with our work which, though recognized generally, is not always realized—namely, whenever the church has tried to do what it could, God's blessing has been poured out upon the work, even before we expect it. Take for example this field—For a long time the church hesitated as to its duty concerning Nagasaki. Before I was accepted for the work God had put it into the hearts of the young men [Stout's theological students] to send one of their number to Saga, and thus occupy a new post for Christ, and <u>on the night of the day I landed in Nagasaki, this man left for Saga</u>. Again came a season of waiting. In Saga there was persecution, in Nagasaki indifference, in Kagoshima discord. The church again sends out those who shall help us. Saga's persecution stops very nearby the time the re-inforcements [sic] reach Nagasaki and a new work springs up the next fall in Kurume.
>
> Again comes times of discouragement & waiting. The work at Kurume seems unsuccessful. In other places only a moderate success attends our labors. Now the church determines to do with <u>all its strength</u> for this work, and notice how the blessing of God is poured upon us. Nagasaki, Kurume, Saga, Karatsu, Nakatsu, Hitoyoshi—<u>all our work is greatly blessed</u>, and calls come to us in such number that we have not men enough to fill them. My dear

---

[139]  NHD to HNC, July 1, 1885.

brother, these coincidences are not accidental. God may go before His church but "according to your faith" is still the measure.
Yours with joy in God's work, N. H. Demarest.[140]

Land for a church building in Saga was purchased in 1887 and the buildings on it used temporarily. Fordham Manor Reformed Church of the Bronx in New York City provided a large portion of the money for a building for Saga Church, which was eventually designed by Stout and completed in 1890. A church building was built and dedicated at Karatsu in the fall of 1888.[141] The church buildings served to ensure the permanence of the mission's work in these very resistant areas.

This blossoming of the evangelistic work of Nagasaki Station in many parts of the island of Kyushu continued. As theological students completed their preparation and passed their examinations by *Nishi Chukai*, they were sent out as resident evangelists to work under Demarest's supervision and encouragement. As the work expanded, Nagasaki Station requested an additional man to visit churches and preaching stations in the interior of the island with Demarest. Stout and his family were scheduled to return to America in February of 1888 for only their second furlough in nineteen years on the field. Once again, even as the Stouts prepared for a much-needed rest, disappointment struck Nagasaki Station. The life-threatening illness of Annie Demarest required her return to America. The Stouts left Nagasaki in April of 1888. In the resulting absence of both Stout and Demarest, Verbeck came down from Tokyo for extended touring in Kyushu in the spring and again in the fall of 1888. Of Verbeck's touring, Peeke wrote, "The good Dr., as he goes through the country, with no thought apparently but that of preaching Christ, comes as near the apostolic ideal as anything I ever expect to see."[142]

The Stouts returned to Nagasaki in March of 1889, and the Nagasaki missionaries were all relieved to learn of improvement in Annie Demarest's health.[143] Nevertheless, their return to the field being somewhat delayed, Verbeck once again came down from Tokyo in the fall of 1889 for a preaching tour of the churches in Kyushu.[144] The Demarests returned to Nagasaki in early November, after nineteen months in America, and Demarest resumed his supervision and evangelistic touring of the outstations.[145]

[140]  NHD to HNC, Aug. 13, 1886.
[141]  HVSP to HNC, Nov. 9, 1888.
[142]  Ibid.
[143]  HS to HNC, May 18, 1889.
[144]  AO to HNC, Aug. 26, 1889.
[145]  NHD to HNC, Nov. 18, 1889.

Sasebo Church, where work was begun in 1889
and this chapel was erected

During 1889, evangelism and church planting in Kyushu looked more and more promising. An outstation was opened in Sasebo, about thirty miles north of Nagasaki. The theological student who went there in the summer, Shiroishi Yaichiro, postponed the completion of his studies to develop the work there. Two new preaching places were opened in other parts of Nagasaki, with good results. At one of them, Elizabeth Stout assisted with the Sunday school and taught sewing classes to build relationships with neighborhood women. The outstation in Hitoyoshi, being isolated from other centers of Reformed Church-related work (two days' travel from the nearest at Kagoshima), was transferred to the Congregationalist based in Kumamoto, who had work nearby. This arrangement included an agreement with the Congregationalists not to interfere with development of Reformed Church-related work in Miyakonojo, which was closer to Kagoshima and could be served by the pastor there.[146]

The northwestern part of Kyushu offered encouraging signs as well. Stout described one situation there after a trip to Karatsu.

The occasion for the trip was to fulfill the duty of a member of a committee, appointed by the Chiukai, to go to Karatsu in response to a petition from the Christians of that place for a church organization. The work there has been under the care of

---

[146]  HS to HNC, Sept. 22, 1889.

Mr. & Mrs. Kurihara for the last two years, and has been carried on with good success. About a year ago the believers, then about twenty in number, made an effort to secure a church building. They canvassed the matter among themselves, and collected nearly a hundred yen. Then they applied to the church at Nagasaki and to the Mission for assistance. They thus secured about two hundred yen altogether. Their building has been completed and in use for some months. It is a plain, neat one, with seating for about a hundred persons. They have imitated the example of some churches in America, and have a debt—about thirty yen. But they have done better than some of those churches, for they have a definite plan for the liquidation of the debt by their own efforts, and are succeeding in accomplishing it. In the meantime they are paying all expenses for the work among themselves, except the evangelist's salary, and contribute to benevolent objects. It was the spirit of enterprise, more than the numbers—now about thirty in all—that influenced the Chiukai to accede readily to the request for a church organization, and the committee to proceed to carry out the plan. The church was duly organized under the name of the "Church of Matsuura," that being the name of the district, including Karatsu, in which the church members reside.... Sunday was a day of gladness to the little company of believers,... The officers of the church were ordained on Sunday, and we then gathered round the table of the Lord. The past history of the little Christian community augurs well for the future. And I think we may reasonably expect that a strong, self-supporting church will soon be found in Karatsu, with branches in all the surrounding villages.[147]

Through the cooperation of the Japanese pastors and evangelists and the itinerating missionaries, not only the work of the Tokyo-Yokohama Station, but also the outreach of Nagasaki Station began to bear fruit in the opening of new preaching stations and the growth of the several organized churches.

### Separation into North and South Japan Missions

As early as January of 1882, Stout had proposed that the Reformed Church work on the southwestern main island of Kyushu, for many years called Nagasaki Station of the Japan Mission, be treated

---

[147]  HS to HNC, May 18, 1889.

Members of the Japan Mission present at an annual
meeting of the mission in the late 1880s. First row, l-r:
James Amerman, Rebecca Amerman, Lizzie Harris, Mary
Brokaw, Emilie Booth, Eugene Booth, Mary (Kidder) Miller,
child, Anna Wyckoff; back row: Nathan Demarest, Martin
Wyckoff, Henry Stout, E. Rothsay Miller, M. Leila Winn,
Howard Harrris, Guido Verbeck, and James Ballagh.

as a mission in its own right, distinct from the Reformed Church work
centered in Yokohama and Tokyo. The two stations were 750 miles
apart, and travel time between them was still at least four or five days
each way by ship. The time and money expended (three weeks away
from the work and seventy dollars per person) to go from Nagasaki to
Yokohama or Tokyo for Japan Mission meetings seemed unjustifiable.
Furthermore, Stout saw little value in the unity of organization, since
the colleagues in Tokyo and Yokohama did not necessarily understand
the situation in Kyushu, and some of them had at times openly opposed
enlarging the work in Nagasaki. Stout believed that a meeting of all
the Reformed missionaries for fellowship at the time of the *Daikai* of
the United Church would be sufficient. He continued to advocate for
the division of the Reformed Church's Japan Mission into two separate
missions, and Demarest shared in urging this change.[148]

During the almost two decades since the Stouts first disembarked
in Nagasaki in 1869, to all intents and purposes, Henry Stout *was* the
mission there. Other missionaries came and went, but it was twenty
years before he had colleagues with enough experience and sufficient
acquaintance with the language and culture of Japan to give him

---

[148]   HS to JMF, Jan. 2, 1882; HS to HNC, Dec. 5, 1883; NHD and HS to HNC, Aug. 11,
1885.

any relief from the weight of responsibility for the work there. Not surprisingly, Nagasaki Station was sometimes referred to as Mr. Stout's mission. Those twenty years were a time of much anxiety and many disappointments, but at last the Reformed Church work centered in Nagasaki had firmly taken root and its continuance was assured.

The Yokohama and Tokyo missionaries had often appeared to give low priority to, or at least not to be in full sympathy with, the plans for Nagasaki Station advocated by Stout and his colleagues. They evidently were resisting what they perceived to be Stout's attempt to develop educational institutions in Nagasaki to rival in scale those in the Tokyo-Yokohama area. In reality, the Nagasaki Station plans were tailored to the situation, possibilities, and challenges faced in western Japan and were part of a valid vision. Fortunately, understanding and cooperation improved greatly from the beginning of 1887. An excerpt from a letter to Dr. Cobb reveals Stout's perspective on these breakthroughs.

> The experiences of the recent annual meeting were a surprise and a delight to us all. From certain premonitions that had reached us, I feared that there would be a fight over the plan for theological instruction here,—in fact there was privately a "feeling of the pulse." But everything went off pleasantly. The brethren say that since the Board has decided to go ahead, why of course we must go ahead. It is put this way by some,—"The Board has now said practically by sending Mr. Oltmans that it means to prosecute the work in this way, and that is the end of the controversy"—this, notwithstanding the same sort of action in sending Mr. Harris just about the time the controversy began! Some of them say they "never opposed school work,—what they opposed was an attempt to establish such a school as they have in Tokio." They insist upon it that they have misapprehended our aims throughout! But as Mr. Demarest put it,—"That was not our fault." And the Board has certainly not failed to get our idea. Well, it struck us that these were exceedingly small holes out of which to attempt to crawfish. But as far as we are concerned, we are happy whether there is an attempt to crawfish or not, so long as the brethren give us their countenance and support as they did at the last meeting. I am very glad that the meeting came off. There is a better feeling all round. There was a decided disposition on the part of the strong to help the weak. This has never been shown before in all the history of the mission. It was seen in the fact that there was hearty

support of such propositions as that for Dr. Verbeck & Mr. Miller to come down here to help in the evangelistic work and to get Mr. Demarest into the way of doing it, and of the propositions for Mr. Maki to come and locate in one of the Kiushiu outstations, and for Mr. Oghimi to come here to take up my work as far as possible while I should be away. It is true these propositions all came from us but they were heartily approved. This sort of thing tends to obliterate very greatly the bitterness of the past.[149]

Nevertheless, Stout and the other missionaries who worked in the south continued to feel that they always came out on the short end of things within the Japan Mission, which often seemed to have a Tokyo-centered mentality. When the Stouts returned to Nagasaki from their second furlough in the spring of 1889, there were twenty-six missionaries and associate missionaries in the Reformed Church Japan Mission, of which nineteen were in the north and only seven in the south. In hopes of gaining more recruits and higher appropriations for the work in the south, Stout and his colleagues requested of the mission board that the work of the missionaries in the north and the south be separated. With the enlargement of the missionary force in Nagasaki, the board concurred that it was more practical to separate into two organizations on the field, and the request was granted. By action of the board, in 1889 the work of the Reformed Church in Japan was divided into the North Japan Mission and the South Japan Mission, and the two organizations remained separate entities until 1917. During those years, the ratio of personnel in the two separated missions did in fact come more into balance.

### Great Expectations

The period of the pioneers, from 1859 to 1889, began in preparation and waited in expectation. It grew into a time of hopeful signs of new life in the form of courageous converts and a few gathered congregations with promising native leadership. It blossomed into an era of rapid growth of churches, multiplication of preaching outstations, and trained Japanese pastors eager to spread the gospel to their compatriots. All this took place despite the opposition of various religious and other elements in the society. It occurred through the commitment, partnership, and personal sacrifice of both the early Japanese Christians and the missionaries from the West.

[149]   HS to HNC, Jan. 24, 1887.

With regard to the early missionaries, one should not overlook the great personal cost involved. Living and working in Japan at that time required not only learning an incredibly difficult language and functioning within a very different culture but also adjusting to a different climate, unsanitary conditions, and exposure to numerous health hazards. Correspondence from the missionaries tells the story of repeated epidemics of cholera, small pox, dysentery, tuberculosis, measles, and malaria. It also reveals how vulnerable the missionaries were. Three families were bereaved by the death of a young child. Several missionaries were forced to return to America due to broken health. Most experienced times when it was necessary to retreat somewhere to recover from utter exhaustion or illness. Nevertheless, they persevered in their mission.

As the 1880s had progressed, the missionaries had become increasingly confident and optimistic that the evangelization of Japan might be completed and their work in Japan accomplished. In the spring of 1887, Amerman remarked, "You may have noticed in the minutes of our Annual Meeting a long preamble capped with a single resolution looking towards an effort to persuade the Board to increase its work in Japan with the hope of completing it in a few years."[150]

The year 1889 marked thirty years since the arrival of the pioneer missionaries. With hope and great expectations for the growth of the church and the evangelization of Japan, the mood was almost euphoric. In the words of Henry Stout:

> It is interesting to study the feelings which prevail almost everywhere, among both natives and foreigners, that affairs in Japan are upon the eve of a great change. The proclamation of the [Meiji] Constitution is no doubt one reason for this, the report that the American minister has concluded a treaty which will make a great change in the relations of citizens of our own country residing here, is another. Such a treaty, it is supposed, would be followed by similar treaties with other nations, whatever that may be. And so a new era is to begin, of advantage to all concerned. No one pretends to say just what the advantages are to be. There are a few croakers of course, but notwithstanding these, there is a general feeling of hopeful expectation. There is a boom in land in the foreign settlement. Every lot has been taken up by the foreigners, and more are called for. Property is really once more worth something in the market. As missionaries we also have our

[150]  JLA to HNC, Apr. 2, 1887.

hopes, one is that we shall have greater freedom of access to the people, and that a spirit of greater confidence, and less reserve, will characterize our intercourse.[151]

Howard Harris remarked confidently, "Today we can go to parts of this country where there are no churches, Sunday schools, Young Men's Christian Associations, preachers or anything of the kind, but in a very few years it will be hard to find such places in Japan."[152]

In 1889 such optimism seemed justified. The churches had seen remarkable growth, despite all obstacles, during the seventeen years since the organization of the first congregation on March 10, 1872. Beginning with the large public meetings of 1883, the evangelistic outreach of the Japanese ministers and theological students, accompanied by the missionaries' evangelistic tours, had resulted in many baptisms and the establishment of numerous preaching places and organized churches. The number of Japanese Christians grew by 450 percent during those six years. The very first Protestant congregation, the Kaigan Church in Yokohama, had continued to grow and was the largest congregation. In 1889, this one congregation baptized 103 people, and its total membership reached 704, consisting of 317 men, 347 women, and 40 children.[153] Similarly, Kochi Church, begun through the cooperative evangelistic outreach of Japanese pastors and Reformed and Presbyterian missionaries, had shown remarkable growth. From its organization with twenty-two members May 17, 1885, it had grown to a membership of 625 in 1890.[154]

However, during the same period there were also some ominous signs that seemed to suggest that the great expectations of the missionaries and their Japanese colleagues might not be so easily or soon realized. For example, Amerman reported,

> The government, apparently annoyed at the failure of the last Treaty Revision Conference, is coming to be very stringent in its construction or construing of the passport regulations. This bears most heavily on those who are living in the interior and on those who wish to travel in the interior from time to time on mission work. Some years ago we had the assurance of those in high position that the requirement of "health or scientific research" as

---

[151]  HS to HNC, May 11, 1889.
[152]  HH to HNC, Sept. 19, 1889.
[153]  JHB to HNC, Feb. 4, 1890.
[154]  James A. Cogswell, *Until the Day Dawn* (Board of Publications, Presbyterian Church U.S., 1957), 55.

the assigned reason for an application for a passport was a mere form of words and was understood by the government to cover everything except trade. Those now at the head of the Foreign Office however say that the form means just what it says and nothing else....I have not heard of any missionary who has been refused a passport on application, and none are interfered with in any of their work. But there are many who cannot conscientiously ask for a passport now who had no hesitation a few years ago.[155]

As if to substantiate this concern, Ballagh observed in a letter, "I fear a considerable difficulty in getting passports freely as they involve some equivocation and greater time to get them and stricter adherence to lines of travel. It required nearly two weeks to get a simple passport to visit Sendai."[156]

While Christianity had attracted a great deal of interest among the public, anything that could be called a mass movement toward the churches never developed. Response to the gospel was always by individuals, never by groups. The witness and teaching of the missionaries and early Japanese Christian leaders tended to touch the intellectuals and the upper middle class and never reached the common people. Even so, the missionaries and the Japanese Christians continued to feel very hopeful about the future of Christianity in Japan. They welcomed many of the social and political changes that were transforming Japan and continued to expect that these changes would facilitate the spread of the gospel. One of the key changes they hoped for was the relaxation of restrictions on travel and residence of foreigners in the interior of the country. However, it became clear that this issue would not be resolved without Japan achieving the revision of what its leaders felt to be the humiliating, unequal treaties with foreign countries.

The impact of the first thirty years of Japan's encounter with Protestant Christianity was summed up by Charles Iglehart in these words:

Perhaps never again in Japan's modern century was the church so close to the intellectual, the political and the social leadership of the nation, nor did it ever again attract quite such wide attention and interest. Never again was it so near to a mass movement in growth. It probably did not again register so high a level of

---

[155] JLA to HNC, Dec. 14, 1888.
[156] JHB to HNC, Jan. 16, 1889.

spiritual experience on the part of ordinary members of the churches. An imposing roster of names among both ministers and laymen was posted. Its accomplishments in proportion to its size were impressive. It offers an example of a normally developing Christian movement in a nation passing swiftly to modern statehood. Viewed across the tumultuous events that followed in the next decades, this period presents an idyllic scene, scarcely again to be repeated.[157]

---

[157]   Iglehart, *Century*, 84-85.

PART II

# Mission amid the Rise of the Japanese Empire

CHAPTER 6

# The Onset of the Period of Reaction

## The Meiji Constitution and a New Nationalism

We have noted many details of the experience of the missionaries and the early Japanese Protestant Christians during the first thirty years of the mission, and it is important to see them in the larger Japanese context. Beginning with the Meiji Restoration of 1868, Japan entered a period of socioeconomic and political transformation. Japan was intent upon developing into a modern state patterned after the leading Western powers with which it had come into contact. It faced questions such as how to develop a stable government, what would enable it to catch up with Western nations, and how to achieve wealth through industrialization. Slogans reflecting these concerns were used in intellectual debates of the day, e.g., *bunmei kaika* ("civilization and enlightenment"), *fukoku kyohei* ("rich nation, strong army"), and *shokusan kogyo* ("encouragement of industries").[1]

---

[1] David J. Lu, *Japan: A Documentary History, Vol. II: The Late Tokugawa Period to the Present* (Armonk, NY: Sharpe, 1997), 345.

Young men were sent to learn from the West, especially to England to study the navy and merchant marine, to Germany to learn about the army and modern medicine, and to the United States to imitate business methods. Western technology brought steamships, telegraph lines, and railroads. World trade led to an unprecedented exchange of consumer goods. Evidence of the early stages of an industrial revolution appeared, particularly in the development of a spinning industry, a nationalized railway, and a banking industry. New Japanese products appeared on the market, and distribution channels became more organized. An educational system modeled on those in Western nations was developed, providing elementary education for all, secondary education for some, and higher education for a few. An army and a navy were developed, initially to protect Japanese sovereignty, but gradually to advance Japanese interests in Asia.

Japan also soon began to catch the Western appetite for empire building. The Japanese government demanded control over all territories that were either inhabited by Japanese or that it considered naturally to belong to the group of Japanese islands. It claimed the Kurils, the Bonin Islands, and the Ryukyu Islands (Okinawa) as its territory. In 1875, by intimidation of the weak rulers of Korea, Japan obtained a favorable treaty and extended Japanese influence and trade opportunities there. The appetite for empire building also became apparent within Japan in the economic sphere. Middle- and lower-class farmers, small business owners, tradesmen, and manufacturers were suppressed as conglomerates, called *zaibatsu*, grew into powerful capitalist corporations (Mitsui, Mitsubishi, Sumitomo, and Yasuda) with not only economic but also political influence. In historian Tomonobu Yanagita's words, "A vulgar materialism swept over the people, and the major ambition among young people of the period was to become a success in the business world."[2]

In the mid 1870s, certain social changes seemed to favor the spread of Christianity. One example is the government's decree in 1876 making Sunday the official day of rest for the people. The government had no religious motive in this decision, but when offices, schools, and some businesses began to observe Sunday as a holiday, it was a boon to Christian work, in particular because of the emphasis by the missionaries on strict Sunday observance. Especially in the 1880s, Japan demonstrated a virtual craze for things Western and had become quite open to Christianity, even though incidents revealing a latent

---

[2]    Yanagita, *Short History*, 47.

antagonism sometimes broke out. While these underlying currents of hostility toward and fear of Christianity were no doubt rooted in part in Japan's earlier encounter with Roman Catholic mission, they were also intimately related to a deepening ethnic awareness and national pride. A growing sense of national power was emerging, accompanied by a resolve to reassert Japan's political independence and its unique cultural traditions. However, it was necessarily a period of flux and uncertainty during which both government and people felt their way toward stability amid the cultural and political challenges posed by Japan's encounter with the West.[3]

In any case, Japan's "westernization" process took some unusual turns. Some within Buddhism had become alarmed by the nationwide trend toward interest in Christianity. They organized to adopt aspects of Western culture in an effort to block the spread of the Christian movement, using lectures and the press. They translated and published works by Western agnostics and skeptics to undermine the Christian message and even claimed that Christian missionaries were part of a political plot to take over Japan.[4]

On the other hand, in the mid 1880s some government leaders and hitherto anti-Christian scholars encouraged a shallow, politically motivated "westernization" movement. Among these leaders was Fukuzawa Yukichi, founder of Keio University. According to Yanagita, these men "suddenly changed from their former bitterly antagonistic attitude toward things Christian to one of proposed alliance and cooperation. In 1884 Fukuzawa argued that Japan should officially become a Christian country." This proposal was of course purely utilitarian, and Fukuzawa himself had no intention of becoming a Christian. Yanagita added, "In spite of this wave of westernization, the government promoted a series of nationalistic policies which began to shape the base and structure for a totalitarian nation in such important fields as military power, public expression, and education."[5]

The 1868 Meiji Restoration of the emperor to a more prominent role as monarch never meant actual, direct rule by the emperor. Governance of the nation remained almost completely in the hands of an oligarchy, a group of former clan leaders from Satsuma (Kagoshima), Choshu (Yamaguchi), Tosa (Kochi), and Hizen (Saga), all regions in southwestern Japan. They had wrested control of the government from those who had supported the shogun. The struggle for political control

---

[3]  Drummond, *History of Christianity*, 196-97.
[4]  Cogswell, *Until the Day Dawn*, 45.
[5]  Yanagita, *Short History*, 45.

The Meiji emperor, Mutsuhito, in 1879, when he was twenty-seven years old

had continued among the former clan leaders, the *daimyo* (feudal lords) and their samurai, who had become the privileged class known as the *shizoku*. As early as the mid 1870s, some of the *shizoku* from Tosa and Hizen, who had been gradually squeezed out of the oligarchy, agitated for the formation of a constitutional monarchy. When some of them initiated the Freedom and People's Rights Movement and formed political parties in an attempt to affect the political process, they were suppressed and some were imprisoned. However, the pressure continued to build for a wider participation in the nation's governance.

On October 12, 1881, Emperor Meiji (Mutsuhito) promised the people that a constitution would be prepared and promulgated, and that in 1890 there would be elections to form a parliament. Under the leadership of Ito Hirobumi, who with his assistants had spent a year and a half in Europe in 1883-84 studying the governmental institutions of other countries, a constitution for Japan gradually was formulated. Austrian and especially German influence was apparent, but the Japanese governing institutions were not to be in imitation of those in Europe. Ito was determined to protect the imperial institution from popular radicalism and to insure that he and his oligarch colleagues would retain a central role in the power structures. Ito and his colleagues urged the bolstering of the imperial institution as the foundation of government but made sure that the emperor would not have public responsibility for governing. Actual governing authority and administrative power was to rest in the hands of a privy council and the cabinet. To separate the emperor from the common people, who were to be represented in the lower house of the Diet (parliament), they created a class of peers, and subsequently a House of Peers (upper house of the Diet). The 507 former feudal lords (*daimyo*) and 137 court nobles were given titles as peers (*kizoku*). In imitation of Europe, they initiated the practice of limiting imperial succession to a male heir, which had not been the case in the past in Japan. However, instead of emphasizing the primacy of the monarch as in European constitutions, the Japanese framers deliberately claimed and invoked the emperor's divinity in their constitution.[6]

In doing so, the framers of the constitution were making use of a blend of Confucian and native Japanese "scholarship" developed earlier in the nineteenth century. Aizawa Seishisai, writing in 1825, had claimed, "Our Divine Realm [Japan] is where the sun emerges. It is the source of the primordial vital force sustaining all life and order. Our Emperors, descendants of the Sun Goddess, Amaterasu, have acceded to the Imperial Throne in each and every generation, a unique fact that will never change. Our Divine Realm rightly constitutes the head and shoulders of the world and controls all nations."[7]

In framing a constitution, Confucianism was bent to emphasize imperial loyalty in such a way that Japan's uniqueness would no longer derive from samurai nobility but from the emperor's dynastic continuity, and myth and religion were to be in the service of, in fact united with, government and politics.[8] Japan was construed to be one great, unique family, with the emperor as its divine father.

With the Christian movement gaining momentum, another weapon came to be wielded against it, i.e., State Shinto. Shintoism was the primitive religion of Japan, predating the introduction of Buddhism. The name *Shinto* means "way of the gods." A primitive religion, it originally focused on the worship of nature, ancestors, and ancient heroes and emphasized by simple rituals the placating of evil spirits or seeking blessing from benevolent spirits. However, the forces behind the Meiji Restoration concluded that Japan's new nationalism needed a strong religious base in order to succeed in its goals. Consequently, in 1882, the Japanese government announced the classification of Japan's religions into four groups—State (or Shrine) Shinto, Sect Shinto,

<hr />

[6]   Marius B. Jansen, *The Making of Modern Japan* (Cambridge: Belknap Press of Harvard Univ. Press, 2000), 391-95.

[7]   Ibid., 204.

[8]   Ibid.

Buddhism, and Christianity. The critical point was the distinction between State Shinto and Sect Shinto. The government included in the first group the thousands of shrines of any size throughout the country whose ceremonies and myths could be used for the purpose of promoting nationalism, and among these the cult of emperor worship was to be central. Furthermore, the government declared that these shrines were primarily patriotic, rather than religious in nature.[9] In this way Japan's nationalism was provided with a religious ideology, while at the same time insuring that national loyalty and conformity trumped real religious freedom.

However, during the thirty years since the forced opening of Japan to the outside world, both westernization and Christianity had become so deeply rooted in the nation that additional forces were rallied against those influences. The Japanese Religious Principle Association was organized in 1888. It claimed "the intrinsic unity of Shintoism, Buddhism, and Confucianism, implying that Christianity was unfit for Orientals." Another organization, the Seikyo Association, was formed that held to the same point of view. Both organizations strongly opposed Christianity. At the same time, men of the legal profession actively promoted this form of nationalism.[10] Richard Drummond elucidates what was happening.

> During the 1880's Japan achieved a new national group consciousness and social cohesion. In place of the old divisive loyalty to feudal lords, the nation had come to develop a patriotism focused on the emperor, a patriotism that for the first time in Japanese history embraced the entire country. Both contributing to and expressing this unity were the new system of compulsory elementary education and the conscript army. The popular press often opposed the government and generally supported the Popular Rights Movement and a "progressive" stance toward modernization. But, it was also strongly nationalistic and backed without qualifications the government's efforts to secure revision of the unequal treaties. The conditions were ripe, therefore, for a reassertion of the traditional Japanese concept of the state as religiously absolute.[11]

The emperor's promises of 1881 were fulfilled February 11, 1889, with the official promulgation of the Meiji Constitution, and, in July of

---

9   Cogswell, *Until the Day Dawn*, 45.
10   Yanagita, *Short History*, 46.
11   Drummond, *History of Christianity*, 199.

1890, with Japan's first parliamentary election. The date carefully and deliberately selected for the promulgation of the constitution was the mythological date of the ascension to rule of the first emperor, Jimmu, grandson of the sun goddess, Amaterasu Omikami. It became a national holiday, called National Foundation Day. Modernity and change, in the granting of a constitution, were presented as if they were a renewal of antiquity. This is illustrated by the emperor's invocaton of mythology in the opening paragraph of the constitution, as follows:

> Having by virtue of the glories of Our Ancestors, ascended the Throne of a lineal succession unbroken for ages eternal; desiring to promote the welfare of, and to give development to the moral and intellectual faculties of Our beloved subjects, the very same that have been favored with the benevolent care and affectionate vigilance of Our Ancestors, and hoping to maintain the prosperity of the State, in concert with Our people and with their support, We hereby promulgate, in pursuance of Our Imperial Rescript [of 1881] a fundamental law of the State, to exhibit the principles, by which We are guided in Our conduct, and to point out to what Our descendants and Our subjects and their descendants are forever to conform.[12]

### Rising Imperialism and Missionary and Japanese Christian Naiveté

The missionaries and the Japanese Christians joined the general populace in celebrating the promulgation of the constitution. In Yokohama, on the day of its proclamation (February 11, 1889), they held a union prayer and thanksgiving service at Yokohama City Assembly Hall. Pastors and lay leaders of the four main local Japanese churches presided, played the organ, offered prayers, and gave addresses. James Ballagh reported, "You will see in the papers an account of the substance of the Constitution & its important article on freedom of conscience in religious matters. This is peculiarly satisfactory to the Japanese Christians."[13] In a letter later in the year, Ballagh referred to Emperor Meiji as the 72nd in succession and casually commented, "The 3rd of November was a great day in Japan this year. It was the Emperor's 38th birthday, and the festival of Jimmu Tenno's (Emperor Jimmu's) ascension to the throne of Japan 2,649 years ago."[14] In light

[12]   Jansen, *Making of Modern Japan,* 395.
[13]   JHB to HNC, Feb. 15, 1889.
[14]   JHB to HNC, Nov. 4, 1889.

of the fact that there was no historical basis for this "history" of the imperial dynasty, it is remarkable that the missionaries seem to have accepted the claims at face value. It must be remembered that Japan not only had no written language prior to the sixth century C.E., but it did not even possess quasihistorical literary documents prior to the mythological *Kojiki* (Record of Ancient Matters), compiled in 712, and the *Nihon Shoki* (Chronicles of Japan), compiled in 720.

The missionaries appear to have naively accepted the new government and the emperor system of Japan as comparable to the constitutional monarchies of Europe. They do not appear to have questioned the mythology or understood the religious implications of the emphasis on the divine origin of the emperors and the Japanese "race" as superior and unique. Reformed missionary Howard Harris described enthusiastically the ceremonies and celebrations in connection with the promulgation of the constitution, and he commented:

> The Constitution comprises 332 articles. The Emperor remains the source of all law. His subjects are entitled to freedom of religion, of public meeting, of speech and association. The concessions and privileges are much greater than had been hoped for. The people seem satisfied and begin to feel that Japan is now a truly civilized country.
>
> The heaven-born Ruler in abdicating his autocratic power admits that the people possess a right to share the functions of government with him. Henceforth the people of Japan are to enjoy the privilege of a representative form of government....Parliament will be established in 1890. We have bright hopes for the future.... It is now evident that by talk, by argument, by enlightenment, by every means brought to bear upon public opinion, Japan in the future is to be governed. If this is true, then under the new Constitution, the influence of Christian men and women, as it roots itself in the hearts and minds of the people, will have a much greater harvest of good to the nation than would have been possible under autocratic power.[15]

The year 1889 certainly marked a turning point, not only in the history of Japan, but also in the progress of the Christian mission movement in Japan. However, at the time neither the missionaries nor the Japanese Christians grasped the implications of the Meiji Constitution or anticipated the consequences of the intimately related

[15]    HH to HNC, Feb. 21, 1889.

resurgence of Japanese nationalism. Excerpts from the Constitution (in English translation), from "Chapter I: The Emperor" and "Chapter II: Rights and Duties of Subjects" help to clarify the situation.

> Article I. The Empire of Japan shall be reigned over and governed by a line of Emperors unbroken for ages eternal.
> Article III. The Emperor is sacred and inviolable.
> Article XXVIII. Japanese subjects shall, within limits not prejudicial to peace and order, and not antagonistic to their duties as subjects, enjoy freedom of religious belief.[16]

The missionaries and Japanese Christians celebrated what they saw as a granting of religious freedom, apparently without realizing the implications of the limitations placed on that freedom by the qualifying clause, "not antagonistic to their duties as subjects." Emperor Meiji issued the Imperial Rescript (official declaration) on Education on October 30, 1890. It was drafted by Confucian scholar Motoda Eifu, with assistance from others, and according to David Lu,

> It incorporated the neo-Confucian moral precepts in the garb of modern nationalism, and attempted to make them the foundation of education. Children were taught to hark back to "the glory of the fundamental character of Our Empire," and to "render illustrious the best traditions of your forefathers." There was an unmistakable reaction to the rapid pace of Westernization, and a desire to return to the purity of "Japanism." It served to indoctrinate generations of school children, through periodic public readings of the rescript and through required memorization.[17]

This Rescript on Education came to be accorded a reverence and awe beyond logical explanation. Numerous educational administrators, after making mistakes in its formal reading at public events, are known to have committed suicide to take responsibility for desecrating the divine emperor's sacred Rescript on Education. The following is an English translation of it.

> Know ye Our subjects:
>     Our Imperial Ancestors have founded Our Empire on a basis broad and everlasting, and have deeply and firmly implanted

[16]   George M. Beckmann, *The Making of the Meiji Constitution: The Oligarchs and the Constitutional Development of Japan, 1868 – 1891* (Westport: Greenwood, 1957), 151-52.
[17]   Lu, *Japan*, 343.

virtue; Our subjects ever united in loyalty and filial piety have from generation to generation illustrated the beauty thereof. This is the glory of the fundamental character of Our Empire, and herein also lies the source of Our education. Ye, Our subjects, be filial to your parents, affectionate to your brothers and sisters; as husbands and wives be harmonious, as friends true; bear yourselves in modesty and moderation; extend your benevolence to all; pursue learning and cultivate arts, and thereby develop intellectual faculties and perfect moral powers; furthermore advance public good and promote common interests; always respect the Constitution and observe the laws; should emergency arise, offer yourselves courageously to the State; and thus guard and maintain the prosperity of Our Imperial Throne coeval with heaven and earth. So shall ye not only be Our good and faithful subjects, but render illustrious the best traditions of your forefathers.

The Way here set forth is indeed the teaching bequeathed by Our Imperial Ancestors, to be observed alike by Their Descendants and the subjects, infallible for all ages and true in all places. It is Our wish to lay it to heart in all reverence, in common with you, Our subjects, that we may all attain to the same virtue.[18]

Decades later, Japanese church historian Yanagita summed up the implications of what had transpired in these words.

The Imperial Constitution and Regulations of the Imperial House, promulgated in 1889, and the Imperial Rescript on Education of 1890 were the climax of the nationalistic and totalitarian movement. In the Constitution and Imperial Rescript on Education the Christian view of God, of human beings and morality were strictly rejected. Both laws were remarkably clear expressions of the Japanese national will, which had been gradually antagonized and embittered by various western influences, particularly Christianity, ever since the opening of the country to the world in 1854. The basic concept of these fundamental national laws was that Japan was a Shinto country: it worshipped the emperor as a living god. Coupled with that concept was the corollary, the unconditional moral obligation of the subjects to their emperor which such a philosophy took for granted. This anti-Christian spirit was exactly parallel to Hideyoshi's purge

[18]    Ibid., 343-44.

directive in 1587, which had declared: "As Japan is the divine land, it is a matter to be much deplored that we have been given a heretical religion by Christians."[19]

An incident in 1891 illustrates the changed state of affairs that resulted from the new emphasis on the emperor's divinity. Uchimura Kanzo (1861-1930), son of a samurai, was converted to Christianity while a student at the new agricultural college in Sapporo, and he later studied in America. However, Uchimura, who became a leading Christian scholar and nationalist, reacted against the denominational divisions of the churches established by the Protestant missionaries. He eventually formed a movement called *mukyokai*, the non-church movement, which centered in informal Bible reading and study groups meeting evenings and weekends. This movement did not recognize church structures and generally neglected the sacraments. In any case, after he returned from study in America, in 1890, Uchimura accepted a teaching position at the preparatory academy of Tokyo University. Drummond describes the *fukei jiken* ("incident of disloyalty") that took place involving Uchimura.

On January 9, 1891, the teachers of the Tokyo school were compelled to participate in a ceremony which became standard procedure for all schools in the Japanese empire until the end of the Second World War. A personally signed copy of the Imperial Rescript on Education, which had been promulgated the previous fall, was placed on a pedestal; and as the students stood at attention, the teachers were expected to step forth one by one and make a low bow of obeisance. Some Christian teachers absented themselves from school to avoid the issue. Uchimura, however, was not the man to follow this course, and, as he described the incident in a letter..., "Hesitating in doubt, I took a safer course for my Christian conscience, and in the august presence of 60 professors...and over one thousand students, I took my stand and did not bow." The result was such consternation as almost to disrupt the ceremony.

Uchimura was assured by Christian friends that bowing in this case was not an act of worship....A newspaper, however, picked up the story and spread it across the country. It became impossible to confine the issue, and Uchimura was forced to resign his post.[20]

[19]   Yanagita, *Short History*, 46-47.
[20]   Drummond, *History of Christianity*, 203.

Uchimura Kanzo (1861 – 1930)

Uchimura was by no means a westernized or disloyal Japanese. His patriotism was unassailable. In fact, he was known as the man who loved the two "Js"—Jesus and Japan. Nevertheless, the incident in which he hesitated to bow before the Imperial Rescript stimulated renewed attacks against Christianity. Inoue Tetsujiro, an influential professor of Tokyo University, published a series of articles in 1891 and 1892 that attacked the loyalty of Christians and claimed that Christian faith was not compatible with the principles and duties of a Japanese citizen. Sociopolitical conservatives and Buddhists joined the renewed attacks against Christianity and its adherents, and these attacks were not limited to verbal abuse. "In the 1890s as in earlier periods the experiences of persecution in individual cases ranged from petty annoyances from government officials to community expulsion, disinheritance, and even stone-throwing."[21]

It is clear that neither the missionaries nor even the Japanese Christians grasped the implications of the reinterpreted role of the Japanese emperor. They apparently did not see the connection between the emperor system and the anti-western, anti-Christian reaction. In 1898, Ballagh spoke of the month of February as a "stirring and memorial month in Japan" and reported, "The 11th with 2,558th

[21]    Ibid., 204.

anniversary of Jimmu Tenno's ascension to the throne, and the 8th anniversary of the Promulgation of the Constitution was duly observed by a Christian lecture service in the Kaigan Church under the YMCA auspices."[22] They did not anticipate the impending manipulation of the nation by the nationalists and militarists that began already in the 1890s.

Ballagh often made references to the emperor, speaking not only with respect, but sometimes also with seeming admiration and reverence, despite his own reporting of episodes such as the following at Ueda.

> A principal of the large three-story Memorial Girls' School,... whose wife is a Methodist Christian, and who himself favored Christianity, a quiet & efficient teacher & generally esteemed, was so persecuted on account of his Christian principles that he was driven to commit suicide! The school building was burnt one Sunday night recently, the work of an enemy it is supposed, & he was charged with disloyalty <u>for not saving the Emperor's photograph!</u> The two papers there were filled with vituperation, a gunshot was fired at night near his house, & the treatment received at the distribution of diplomas such that immediately thereafter he took his life by a sword-cut across his throat.[23]

The missionaries, who quite naturally felt a love for the nation and the people of Japan, repeatedly revealed their naiveté regarding Japan's role among nations. In the Sino-Japanese War (1894-95), provoked by the Japanese, the intent of the Japanese government was to eliminate Chinese influence over Korea. It was clearly Japanese imperialism, with the goal of gaining economic primacy and political hegemony over Korea. The Chinese were defeated on land and their navy was destroyed by the more modern Japanese military. This war of aggression was settled by the Treaty of Shimonoseki, and the Chinese were forced to pay large indemnities and cede Taiwan to Japan.

Ballagh's reaction during these events is noteworthy. He joined the crowds along the railway hailing the emperor, whose train passed through Yokohama on its way to Hiroshima, the war headquarters. He also praised the patriotism of Japanese Christians, who held lectures and prayer meetings in support of the war.[24] When the emperor showed

---

[22]   JHB to HNC, Feb. 14, 1898.
[23]   JHB to HNC, Apr. 11, 1898.
[24]   JHB to HNC, Sept. 13, 1894.

displeasure at atrocities committed by Japanese during the war, Ballagh waxed eloquent, saying, "We have just reason to hope and believe that the prophecy concerning Cyrus of old is to receive a wider fulfillment in His Majesty Mutsuhito's case as the 'righteous man from the East' whose right hand the Lord has holden."[25]

Another example of this naiveté is the attitude of missionaries when the antiforeigner Boxer uprising broke out in North China in 1900. Many foreigners were killed and the legations of Peking were threatened. At that time Japan acted as one of the consort of "Western" powers to save the legations and safeguard foreign treaty rights, and almost half of the relief expedition of twenty thousand men that marched on Peking was made up of Japanese troops. Missionary response to the news of these events is revealing. Booth commented, "We who have given our best years to the people of Japan look with excusable pride upon the part which, in the providence of God, the Japanese have played in the relief of Peking. We trust it is only the beginning of a wide reaching humanitarian Oriental policy, which in the near future will become openly and aggressively Christian."[26] The missionaries, for the most part, did not foresee that Japan's participation in the defense of the colonialist foreign concessions in China was part of its policy of imperial penetration in Asia.

The extension of Japan's control over Korea led to the outbreak of the Russo-Japanese War (1904-05). Russia had challenged Japanese power in Asia, seizing the Liaodong Peninsula portion of Manchuria in 1898 and becoming a rival for influence and control in Korea. By February of 1904 Japan had decided to use force to secure its position in Korea and Manchuria and declared war on Russia. The war resulted in massive casualties on both sides, but the Japanese army prevailed in January of 1905, and in May of 1905 the Japanese navy destroyed the Russian fleet. However, both nations were exhausted and economically depressed by the war, and the Japanese secretly asked President Theodore Roosevelt to mediate. By the treaty of peace negotiated at Portsmouth, New Hampshire, and signed September 5, 1905, Japan gained recognition of its exclusive rights in Korea, as well as two Russian ports and the Russian railroads in Manchuria, but was awarded no compensation for the enormous cost of the war.[27]

Ballagh, who was scheduled for a much-needed furlough in

[25]  JHB to HNC, Jan. 17, 1895.
[26]  ESB to HNC, Aug. 21, 1900.
[27]  Andrew Gordon, *A Modern History of Japan: From Tokugawa Times to the Present* (New York: Oxford Univ. Press, 2003), 120-21.

America, declined to leave Japan because of the Russo-Japanese War, writing, "I cannot feel it right to be out of touch or sympathy a single hour. Have daily and hourly prayed for the success of the Japanese arms." He met with a small group of Japanese throughout the war to pray for its success.[28] In January of 1905 he wrote, "<u>The war, I trust, is truly over</u>. I have that faith, and God I feel is accomplishing that result and in answer to constant and united prayer."[29] When the Russian fleet was destroyed, Ballagh spoke of it as God's judgment, adding, "But Japan is far from being right with God. Happily she is, in her contention with Russia, and in general conduct of the war, but her reverence to God, and thankfulness to Jehovah's interposition is sadly deficient, if not provocative of His Holy displeasure."[30]

Comments in one of Stout's last letters to the board indicated awareness of the conflict with Russia from its early stages. Captured Russian ships were brought into Nagasaki harbor, and Russian consular personnel were evacuated through Nagasaki. However, the continuing naiveté of the missionaries regarding Japanese nationalism and imperialism was apparent in Stout's observation. "The Japanese are beaming over the news thus far received. May the good reports continue."[31]

In 1907 Japan forced the Korean monarch to resign and disbanded the Korean army. With its expanding colonial empire, Japan was becoming a recognized world power. Relieved of Chinese and Russian competition, Japan was able quietly to annex the entire Korean peninsula in 1910. When Japan took this final step in colonizing Korea, there was no protest from the Western powers. Nor was there any opposition from among the Christians in Japan. It may be that throughout this deliberate imperialistic progression both the Japanese Christians and the missionaries were in part misled by the information control of the Japanese government. Be that as it may, few Christian voices were heard passing judgment on the aggression and colonialist policies of the Japanese government.

Among the Japanese public, victory over China, participation in the suppression of the Boxer rebellion, and victory over Russia added to the prestige of Japan's military. Japan had gained a new confidence regarding its power and hegemony. Furthermore, in the words of Harvard's Andrew Gordon,

---

[28]   JHB to HNC, Sept. 26, 1904.
[29]   JHB to HNC, Jan. 23, 1905.
[30]   JHB to HNC, May 5, 1905.
[31]   HS to HNC, Feb. 15, 1904.

The Meiji Empire in 1910

Military and economic domination were two sides of a single coin. All of Japan's elites as well as the vigorously opinionated public saw Korea, and Asia more generally, as a frontier for Japan's expanding power and prestige. The move to empire was thus "overdetermined." That is, it was compelled by connected logics of military power, competitive geopolitics, expanding trade and investment, as well as nativist ideals of Japanese supremacy. These ideas were reinforced in turn by the racialist thinking so dominant in the West at this time.[32]

The Meiji Era came to an end in July of 1912 with the death of the Meiji emperor (Mutsuhito), whose son Yoshihito (1879-1926) became the new emperor in what was named the Taisho Era (1912-1926). The new emperor, however, was never well, and plagued by mental illness.[33] In Japanese history his role was virtually irrelevant. Nevertheless, the Taisho Era saw major changes and significant developments.

---

[32]   Gordon, *Modern History*, 123.
[33]   Three weeks after his birth, Yoshihito contracted meningitis, which left him in poor health both physically and mentally.

World War I (1914-1918) provided Japan with another opportunity to expand as a colonial power, and with little risk or effort. Having formed an alliance with Great Britain, Japan declared war on Germany. The outcome of the war in Europe was of little interest to Japan, but it provided the opportunity to take over the German colonies in Asia. In 1915, Japan also coerced China into conceding broad economic rights not only in Shantung, but also in Manchuria and the province of Fukien, the region of the Amoy Mission of the Reformed Church. Reischauer concluded,

> Thus only fifty years after the Restoration, Japan emerged from World War I as Britain's chief rival for domination in China. She went to the peace conference at Versailles as one of the Big Five among the victors and an accepted world power. The Meiji leaders, who had set out in 1868 to create a Japan that would be militarily secure from the West and fully equal to it, had, within the very lifetimes of their most long-lived members, done exactly that.[34]

World War I also proved to be an economic boon to Japan at no great cost in life or treasure, because it provided the nation with expanded markets for industrial products as well as increased access to raw materials. With a population that had doubled to 60 million in a little over half a century, Japan was poised for expansion and exploitation. Richard Halloran summed it up, "Of the few things that Japan learned well from the West, technology stood first. Military aggression and imperialism was a close second."[35]

---

[34]   Reischauer, *Japan: The Story*, 151.
[35]   Richard Halloran, *Japan: Images and Realities* (Tokyo: Tuttle, 1969), 43.

CHAPTER 7

# The North Japan Mission: 1889–1916

Beginning in 1889, for twenty-eight years the mission activity of the Reformed Church in America in Japan was carried out separately by its North Japan Mission and South Japan Mission. This period of mission involvement in Japan coincided with the rise of Japanese imperialism, i.e., the period from the promulgation of the first Japanese constitution in 1889 until World War I. Although both of these Reformed Church missions worked in cooperation with the United Church of Christ in Japan, their situations were different and their work and relationships developed along somewhat different lines. The work of the North Japan Mission encompassed parts of the northern half of Japan's largest island of Honshu. Three other Reformed and Presbyterian Missions cooperating with the United Church also had work on this main island, and in some cases the work overlapped. Most of the leaders of the United Church and most of its strong, self-supporting Japanese churches were also located there in the major cities.

## Mission amid the Rising Anti-Western and Anti-Christian Reaction

Evidence of the changed situation was almost immediately apparent in the central part of Japan, the seat of political and economic power and the area where the work of the North Japan Mission was primarily being carried out. On the very morning of the day the Meiji Constitution was promulgated, February 11, 1889, Mori Arinori, the minister of education of the government, was assassinated by a Shinto radical for the simple reason that he was a Christian and had supposedly shown a lack of proper reverence at the Ise Shrine.[1]

In the fall of 1889, the correspondence of some missionaries of the North Japan Mission began to report a strong antiforeign reaction in relation to the issue of revision of the unequal treaties with foreign nations. Increasingly the general populace, and especially many young men, had become hostile toward Western nations and foreigners on the one hand and impatient and unhappy with their government on the other. Japanese officials had negotiated revisions to the treaties, and these revisions were submitted to foreign governments for their approval in 1890. However, the newly proposed treaties were unpopular in Japan, seen as still unequal, as not recognizing and honoring Japan as a nation equal to nations of the West. Furthermore, these revised treaties were not actually ratified by the foreign governments, so there was no real progress in resolving the treaty issue.

The minister of foreign affairs, Okuma Shigenobu, though not a Christian, was a former student of both Verbeck and Stout and known to be a friend of missionaries. Okuma was for several years involved in trying to negotiate revision of the unequal treaties with foreign governments, but he was considered by the political opposition to be too conciliatory to the West. A young radical attempted to assassinate him by throwing a dynamite bomb. Okuma survived, but his leg had to be amputated. His would-be assassin slit his own throat and died on the spot. Amid such turmoil, inevitably, the work of the missionaries and of the Japanese Christians was affected.

Eleven Christians were among those elected to the Japanese Diet. One of them, Kataoka Kenkichi, was under consideration to become president of the Diet. To facilitate being chosen, he was urged by non-Christian compatriots to resign from his position as elder of Kochi Church. He replied that he would rather be an officer of the church than of the Diet. Needless to say, he was not elected to the post.[2]

---

[1]    Yanagita, *Short History*, 48-49.
[2]    JHB to HNC, Sept. 8, 1890.

The Reformed Church's mission schools in Yokohama and Tokyo at this time were well staffed and organized for a promising future. Ferris Seminary was led by Eugene Booth as principal and assisted in the teaching by Leila Winn, Anna Thompson, Mary Deyo, Julia Moulton, and Emilie Booth, as well as Japanese assistants. Leila Winn was preparing to return to the United States for furlough, and Mary E. Brokaw moved to Yokohama to take her place, transferring from Sturges Seminary in Nagasaki. The mission school for boys and young men in Tokyo, Meiji Gakuin, with academic and theological departments, had strong Japanese leadership and staff and was jointly supported by the Reformed Church and the Presbyterians. Administrative and teaching staff provided by the Reformed North Japan Mission included Amerman, Wyckoff, Harris, and Verbeck (part-time).

Nevertheless, at Meiji Gakuin, while student retention was good, there was in 1889-90 a noticeable drop in new student enrollment in the Preparatory School. At Ferris Seminary also, the impact was felt. Booth remarked, "Now that the reaction in public opinion has set in, means & ways must be devised to prevent disaster as much as possible.... our disappointment in not admitting more pupils is keener than we can express."[3] The enrollment at Ferris Seminary for the 1889-90 school year dropped from the previous 120 to 80 pupils.[4]

In answer to questions regarding the large expenditures needed to maintain the missionary staff at Ferris Seminary, Booth challenged the distinction between educational and evangelistic work, saying, "This school has always been, is now and will be, so long as I am connected with it, an evangelistic agency, and I regret that it is looked upon at home as something quite independent of Christian evangelistic work."[5] He also went on to point out that all the women missionaries who had recently taught at the school—Moulton (music teacher), Winn, Brokaw, Deyo, Thompson, and Emilie Booth—had also been active in outside evangelistic work among women and/or children.

The North Japan Mission had continued to press forward enthusiastically, despite challenges presented by the changing circumstances. At its annual meeting on February 1, 1890, it was decided to send an urgent request to the board for reinforcements. The missionaries asked that three men be sent to prepare for evangelistic work, and that two women be sent to learn the language and engage in work especially among women and children. At that time, in the North

---

3     ESB to HNC, Jan. 17, 1890.
4     ESB to HNC, June 24, 1890.
5     ESB to HNC, Oct. 15, 1891.

Japan Mission there were three men involved primarily in evangelistic work. Miller worked in the Tohoku (northeast) region, two hundred miles north of Tokyo, working out of Morioka. Ballagh and Verbeck covered an extensive area of central Japan, traveling as far southwest as Nagoya, as far northwest as Nagano and Niigata, and as far east as the Chiba peninsula, working out of Yokohama and Tokyo. No addition had been made to the mission for evangelistic work since Miller had joined the mission fifteen years earlier. Since the opportunities and urgency for such evangelistic workers was apparent, and since new men would need several years of language acquisition and experience before becoming useful, it was urged that reinforcements be provided as soon as possible.[6]

The women, too, were involved in evangelism. Mary Miller had demonstrated very early the ability of women missionaries to reach women and children effectively. Leila Winn, who had been drawn into teaching English at Ferris Seminary because of teacher shortages, had already shown great gifts in reaching Japanese women, as well as Japanese naval personnel, through her evangelistic work in Yokosuka. Many Japanese had become Christians through the witness and Bible teaching of these early women assistant missionaries, and the men urged the further implementation of female missionary potential.

The movement for union between the United Church of Christ in Japan and the *Kumiai* (Japanese Congregational Church) having failed, some Japanese Christians were a bit discouraged regarding the momentum and prospects of evangelistic outreach. They faced a nation distracted by political change and renewed antiforeign feeling, and of course Christianity in Japan was closely identified with the presence of foreign missionaries. Amerman remarked, "The political agitation this year incident to the election of members of the Imperial Diet, and the meeting of that Diet in the autumn, the formation of political parties, etc. takes away the attention of the people to a large extent from everything else, and they are not so easily accessible to Christian influences. This and some other items I might mention will perhaps retard the advance of Christian work during the year."[7]

Concerning the changing situation, Ballagh commented: "One thing is becoming quite clear, that there is an immense amount of anti-foreign and perhaps anti-Christian spirit brewing in the hearts of the student class. This perhaps is not to be unexpected if we consider that

---

[6]   JLA to HNC, Jan. 9, 1891.
[7]   JLA to HNC, Apr. 15, 1890.

most of this class are of the former *shizoku* or samurai class, and who have been accustomed to look upon themselves as the embodiment of chivalry and nobility, and who consequently feel the greatest umbrage at the superiority of western men and their civilization."[8] While Ballagh's assumption of "the superiority of western men and their civilization" may be judged inappropriate, the revitalization of Japanese national pride was doubtless a factor in the growing antiforeign and anti-Christian reaction that had so quickly resurfaced in the larger cities.

Booth    reflected on the situation. "The date fixed for the convening of the first Imperial Diet is Nov. 25th. The question now occupying the public mind is the 'Treaty Revision.' What the next six months may bring forth in the political field no one can say. Not a little anxiety is felt in many quarters. Still we have the promise 'As thy day so thy strength shall be,' and we can well afford to hold fast what we have, & see what the Lord will do in Japan, for we are certainly on the eve of a great crisis."[9] In fact, as we have observed, the revision of the unequal treaties with Western nations sought by the Japanese government in 1890 was not realized.

When sending the annual report of the North Japan Mission for 1890, Booth commented: "I could wish the Report were more encouraging, especially in view of the heroic efforts made last year to sustain the work; yet I cannot help but feel that there are more discouraging ones to follow. For the indications are that the retrogression that has set in has but begun, and that both the church at home and the missionaries in the field may yet be called upon to develop more of the grace of patient perseverance."[10]

James Amerman and his wife, Rebecca, had arrived in Japan in 1876. He had been recruited to help develop theological education and had served in the theological department of Meiji Gakuin from its inception. He not only taught theology but also published several theological works in Japanese. The North Japan Mission took advantage of his accounting skills, repeatedly appointing him mission treasurer. He was skillful in human relationships, a valuable member of the mission with many gifts. However, the family was frequently troubled by health problems. In the spring of 1891, Rebecca returned to America in precarious health. James Amerman's health was also deteriorating. In 1892 he, too, sought recuperation in America, and they did not return

---

8   JHB to HNC, May 23, 1890.
9   ESB to HNC, Oct. 16, 1890.
10  ESB to HNC, Feb. 23, 1891.

to Japan. James was eventually appointed to the position of treasurer of the Board of Foreign Missions of the Reformed Church.

Guido Verbeck, who had taught part time for many years, was appointed to Amerman's position in the theological school, teaching Old Testament exposition and homiletics, as well as Old and New Testament introduction and pastoral theology. However, Verbeck, the oldest member of the mission, preferred other work to teaching, and the mission hoped for a new missionary appointment for teaching in the theological department.

While not directly related to the anti-Western, anti-Christian reaction, the transformation taking place in public transportation in Japan contributed to the differences between life and attitudes in the cities and in the countryside. Gradually the major cities were connected by an expanding railway system, and local public transportation began to develop as well, increasing both mobility and the exchange of information. This transformation was a boon to missionaries in some of their itinerant work. For example, the rail line linking Tokyo and Osaka provided convenient access to cities along the way. Previously, when Ballagh had traveled the one hundred miles from Yokohama to Shizuoka, it had been a three-day journey by foot and *jinrikisha*. In 1891, the same distance could be covered in six hours, and there were four trains a day each way.[11]

Compared to the larger cities, countryside communication and transportation changed more slowly. Of course, paths had gradually become roads. Long distance transportation along Japan's coasts by small steamships had progressed, a slow but basic means of moving people and goods. But the impact of the antiforeign, anti-Christian reaction was not keenly felt immediately away from the larger cities. In the spring of 1891, when Ballagh and a Japanese evangelist visited scattered Christians on the Boso Peninsula, across Tokyo Bay, travel was by small ship, then by *jinrikisha*, and for many miles on foot. In this remote region, they found receptive inquirers and were able to gather appreciative audiences.[12]

Similarly, Verbeck had a very positive experience in the fall of 1892. At the request of Japanese Christians and missionaries (Southern Presbyterian) on the island of Shikoku for concentrated evangelistic outreach, additional evangelists were sent and a series of evangelistic tours carried out by experienced preachers through a plan of the *Daikai*.

---

[11]  JHB to HNC, June 12, 1891.
[12]  JHB to HNC, March 31, 1891.

Verbeck was the first experienced preacher sent. Without returning home from the synod he went to Shikoku, canceling some classes at the theological school in order to go. He reported that many of the roads were bad and "much of the travel had to be done on foot, sometimes for miles through soft sea-sand, often up and down steep mountain paths." For five weeks Verbeck preached extensively throughout much of the island of Shikoku, speaking twice each Sunday and once each evening the other days. His sermons or addresses always lasted from one to one and a half hours, and were delivered not only in churches, but also in private houses, hotels, halls, or theaters. "The meetings were invariably attended by deeply interested hearers. When time allowed, inquiry-meetings were held, showing real earnestness on the part of both young and old." Verbeck noted, "During my sojourn in the town of Kochi, I was also told, the Savior was burned in effigy. But it was reassuring to learn that the sensible people of the places where such outrages are perpetrated are far from regarding them with favor. On the contrary not a few cases were brought to my notice where such senseless demonstrations had led individuals to a serious inquiry into the true nature of Christianity and eventually to their conversion." Verbeck concluded that this tour had been "the most successful evangelistic campaign in my experience."[13]

Verbeck's preaching tours were of necessity limited by his teaching responsibilities at the theological department. The mission expressed to the board its desire that Verbeck be set free to engage in evangelistic work, that Miller teach in the theological school temporarily, and that "some good man be sent out to prepare for the theological school work."[14] Verbeck's own perspective was clear.

> I can do <u>three</u> kinds of work, viz. 1. educational; 2. evangelistic; and 3. literary.
>
> 1. For the <u>first</u> of these I am much less qualified than for either of the other two, while it taxes my strength and constitution most severely...
> 2. For the <u>second</u> I am best qualified, while it also best suits the present state of my constitution, is in fact rather conducive than otherwise to my health. My liberty of locomotion is beyond what any other missionary in Japan enjoys,[15] yet it has been

---

13    GFV to HNC, Jan. 30, 1893.
14    MNW to HNC, May 10, 1893.
15    Griffis, *Verbeck*, 327-30. Verbeck had no citizenship, having lost his Dutch citizenship and having been unable to meet residence requirements for U.S.

quite useless during the past two years. I continually receive most urgent calls from every part of the evangelistic field, all of which I shall henceforth have to decline and disappoint on account of my school work.

3. Of the <u>third</u> kind of work I might do a good deal in the intervals of the second, and not a little is required of me from time to time, while now I can do next to nothing in this department.[16]

In 1894, Wyckoff wrote, "Dr. Verbeck pressed his claims once more, saying that he is just as much dissatisfied with his position as he ever was, and urging that all the arguments in favor of his being set free for other work are still valid."[17]

Miller also pleaded Verbeck's cause, saying, "It does seem too bad that Dr. Verbeck should be confined to the school when he can do such splendid work in the field by visiting the churches to lecture and preach to them. There is no one his equal in this work in Japan, and if another person came out to do this work today it would take him more than ten or a dozen years before he could do it satisfactorily, and even then he could not begin to do the work that Dr. Verbeck can now do."[18] It is possible that no other missionary has ever matched Verbeck's combination of facility in both oral and written Japanese, spiritual depth, and evangelistic persuasive power.

In the fall of 1895, Miller moved to Tokyo alone (Mary Miller was loathe to leave her life and work at Morioka) to teach at the theological school temporarily. This freed Verbeck for evangelistic touring but still covered the needs at the theological school until a new person could be sent out to teach.[19] The need in the theological department at Meiji Gakuin appeared to be met in 1896. The mission board appointed the Reverend Dr. Jacob Poppen to the North Japan Mission. Poppen and his wife, Anna, arrived in Japan in the spring of 1896 and enthusiastically began language study. Jacob Poppen made unprecedented progress in learning the language during the first several months, but then his health broke down. After he had fulfilled only

---

citizenship. He was technically a man without a country, but in lieu of his service to the Japanese government, Verbeck was granted a "special passport" that allowed him unrestricted travel and residence anywhere in Japan, a kind of honorary Japanese citizenship. This meant that he was not subject to the travel restrictions placed upon other foreigners.

16    MNW to HNC, May 15, 1893.
17    MNW to HNC, July 23, 1894.
18    ERM to HNC, March 7, 1895.
19    ERM to HNC, March 7 and July 12, 1895.

minimal teaching responsibilities, doctors ordered Poppen to return to America, describing his condition as a state of nervous prostration. To the profound disappointment of all concerned, the Poppens left Japan after less than a year and a half, never to return.[20]

## North Japan Mission Evangelism in the Interior

Access to the north from Tokyo on the island of Honshu was also being transformed by the extension of the railroads. When the Millers began work there (in Morioka) in 1888, travel was by *jinrikisha* or on foot, but early in the 1890s the railroads were gradually extended through Sendai and Morioka all the way to the northern tip of the island at Aomori. The extension of railroads not only stimulated the development of towns along the way, but also facilitated evangelistic outreach into the region. Even so, the anti-Western, anti-Christian reaction was not immediately felt there as in the large cities.

When Wyckoff and Harris (both on the faculty at Meiji Gakuin) visited this northern region in the summer of 1893, they found evangelistic opportunities waiting to be implemented. Maki Shigeto, longtime associate of the Reformed Church missionaries, had been serving in Aomori for two years. He had gathered a nucleus of believers for a church there, described by Harris as "a wide awake company of believers." There were at that time no Reformed Church missionaries stationed north of Morioka, but through the Japanese evangelists working for the North Japan Mission, small groups of believers had been formed in Aomori and several other towns in the north of Honshu, as well as in six places in Hokkaido. Wyckoff and Miller visited and preached at numerous stops on their trip, and they found encouraging signs of interest and response to the gospel.[21]

Throughout the extensive territory served by the North Japan Mission, to the north, east, west, and southwest in the interior regions, the missionaries and their Japanese associates continued to be able to arouse considerable interest in Christianity. Such was not necessarily the case in the core cities of Tokyo and Yokohama. Worship attendance at many churches in Tokyo had shown a marked decline. Booth remarked in 1892, "Everybody is at work amid apparently growing indifference."[22] By the end of the year he reported the following ominous situation:

> Pray for us, dear brother, for the opposition apparently waxes stronger & stronger. To hear of Christ being burned in effigy is not

---

[20]   Jaccob Poppen to HNC, Aug. 25, 1897.
[21]   MNW to HNC, March 6 and Aug. 16, 1893; HH to HNC, Aug. 23. 1893.
[22]   ESB to John W. Conklin, March 17, 1892.

uncommon. And the indignities to which professing Christians are subject now-a-days are increasingly malevolent. A number of our pupils, I believe, are Christians, and have sought their parents' consent to being baptized, but they are told by their parents that the Christians in this neighborhood are very bad, and they could not think of allowing them under any circumstances to associate with them. And the poor girls having no opportunity of proving the contrary are obliged to take their word for it & say nothing. If they protest then at once a cry is made against the influence of foreign education, to which is attributed their lack of loyalty to parents.[23]

The renewal of anti-Western and anti-Christian feeling among the general public in Japan presented a challenge and temptation for many Japanese Christians. They quite naturally desired to be accepted as good and loyal citizens. However, according to Booth, it was well known among native Christians that some of the church leaders, including Uemura Masahisa, were covertly supportive of the public sentiment to expel foreigners and stated publicly that there was no need for more missionaries in Japan. Some church leaders cast aspersions on the Japanese evangelists who were in the employ of the missions. Booth stated, "If they have a place where the foreign missionary has succeeded in winning the confidence of their assistants, and they are working harmoniously, peaceably & efficiently, they take pains to arouse mutual distrust, & endeavor to break up the existing harmony."[24]

Of the general situation in Japan, Booth commented,

There is still a deep seated anti-foreign sentiment abroad arising, I think, from an unwarranted estimate of national strength and importance, as egotism bolstered up by ignorance and prejudice. Steam and electricity have been imported and applied to transportation and manufactories, but it is found that this one class of people, comparatively small in numbers, is being enriched rapidly. Another class, representing millions, are being impoverished.

The majority, therefore, and they are doubtless abetted by the Buddhists, feel that foreign intercourse has been an unmitigated evil to the country.[25]

[23]   ESB to HNC, Dec. 28, 1892.
[24]   ESB to HNC, Dec. 28, 1892.
[25]   ESB to HNC, Feb. 4, 1893.

A report of the North Japan Mission at the end of 1894 indicated that church membership statistics for the year showed a net loss. The evangelistic work of the North Japan Mission had resulted in three independent and self-supported churches, three organized but dependent churches, and sixteen preaching places, all of which, of course, were or were expected to become a part of the Church of Christ in Japan.[26]

Revision of the treaties between Japan and Western nations was an unresolved issue. Forty years had passed since Japan had been forced open by Commodore Perry, and thirty-five years had passed since the arrival of the first Protestant missionaries. Resentment against foreigners had resurfaced. In the resurgent nationalism, some government officials and even some Christian leaders advocated restriction of property rights of foreigners and continued restriction of their residency to foreign settlements. The extent of ill feeling was illustrated in the report that children in Tokyo had spit and thrown shoes at foreign children in Tsukiji (the foreign settlement in Tokyo).[27]

In 1896, in an insightful letter, Harris reflected on the changed situation for missionary activity in Japan.

Some few years ago the feeling prevailed among some of our workers here that, in some way, by the beginning of the next century millions of the inhabitants of this fair land would be gathered into the Church of Christ. That was talked of when interest in the Christian religion was very conspicuous, but in these days no one seems to think this will come to pass. No more need of missionaries after the close of this century! This is what some maintained in the days when large numbers were being drawn into the Church simply by the influence of the movement. But we find that the cry that the day of foreign missionary service in Japan is fast passing away is still heard. In former years it was believed that the Church would be so large and powerful as to require no more outside aid, while today it is said that the foreign worker is handicapped for personal work, and hence it is better to commit the work to the Japanese. All agree, I think, that the past two or three years have been years of scant progress.

When we come to look squarely at the matter we find this little advancement in divine things to be due first, to the state of things among the people. Consider how they live amid the noise

---

[26]    JHB to HNC, March 12, 1895.
[27]    JHB to HNC, March 3, 1894.

of the 19th century civilization. Innumerable railroads are being laid throughout the country; steamships carry the products of the land to all parts of the world; great buildings in which is cunning machinery are springing up on all sides. Business is the craze of the day. This wave is touching all classes, the Church as well as the world. The minds of the people are so absorbed in material things as to give but little attention to religious matters.

Secondly, the religious reaction is to a more perfect knowledge of Christianity. There was a time when the Christian religion was not fully understood by this people. To many it was a means simply to some ulterior object; to others it was a sort of dream. Some even thought that if they were baptized they were safe for heaven. They had but a faint idea of what is required of a follower of Christ. The people are beginning to learn that the Christian's pathway in most cases is rough and thorny, that persecution often follows open profession, that a Christian must delight to do the will of his God. This has tended to lessen the interest taken in religious matters.

Third, this reaction is due to the few missionaries at work outside the open ports. Out of five hundred missionaries, nearly three hundred are living in Tokyo, Yokohama, Osaka, and Kobe. In a few of the large cities in the interior there is one and, sometimes, two families living. What is needed is the presence and influence of educated Christian men and women. This people need, as well as the preaching of the Gospel, the varied beneficent living of Christianity.

The indifference spoken of is due to the lack of trained, manly, native preachers. Japan today is an open field, with willing listeners everywhere. But in large cities of fifteen and twenty and twenty-five thousand inhabitants there are only two or three evangelists at work. And most of these men are poorly equipped for the work they have in hand. In the face of this, some of the home societies [mission boards] talk of withdrawing from the field because the results do not come up to their expectation. I am glad to find Japanese young men springing up around us of great personal worth, but I cannot agree with those who claim that these young men are able to assume the responsibility for the conversion of Japan. They can preach, no doubt, but this is only a part of what is needed. Organizing and carrying on work is of vast importance in this day and many have failed in this. So, while the native preachers may work along certain lines, there is great need of foreign oversight and counsel. Surely we all need a double portion of the Holy Spirit. This will sanctify every man, body, soul, and spirit, and enable us to bring to this people the teachings of the everlasting Gospel in the most effective manner.[28]

The situation for Christianity in Japan had changed. While the national movement toward the civilization of the West had been on the rise, Christianity had been recognized as one of the elements of that civilization. But in the 1890s, the Christian movement could not avoid being deeply affected by the antiforeign feelings. The changed environment brought on an identity crisis, especially for many young Japanese Christians. Were being a true Japanese and being a sincere Christian inherently contradictory?

Presbyterian missionary William Imbrie summed up the situation. "A new attempt at treaty revision had failed; and the nation was irritated. Foreign customs, foreign ideals, foreign thought, were no more to the mind of the people as they had been; and Christianity, as something foreign, could not possibly escape the influence. The cry was raised that the spirit of Christianity and the spirit of Japan were antagonistic; that Christ was a rival of the emperor."[29]

At the same time some positive signs were apparent within the Japanese Christian community. Wyckoff summed it up saying, "There is much that is discouraging in the present condition of churches and Christians in Japan, but it is a hopeful sign that there are so many of the native brethren who deeply realize the unsatisfactoriness of present things, and who are earnestly wrestling with God in prayer, that he will awake both themselves and their fellow Christians to a realizing sense of what it means to be followers of Christ."[30]

### North Japan Mission Women in the Interior

Evangelistic work by women missionaries among women and children was on the whole warmly welcomed by many Japanese, and in the churches by both the pastors and the church members. Perhaps because even educated women were not seen as authority figures within Japanese culture, women missionaries were not threatening. And their love, selflessness, and Christian piety were transparent.

In 1891, Leila Winn moved to Morioka, where the Millers served, to take up evangelistic work among women and children. She took

---

[28]  HH to HNC, Sept. 10, 1896.
[29]  William M. Imbrie, *The Church of Christ in Japan* (Philadelphia: Westminster, 1906), 45.
[30]  MNW to HNC, Nov. 1, 1898.

over the work of Mary Miller while the Millers were on furlough. Winn, with a young Japanese Christian woman, a graduate of Ferris Seminary, as her colleague and housemate, became the first of the Reformed Church's single women missionaries to reside away from the core cities of Yokohama and Tokyo, where most foreigners lived. She remarked, "I knew I could be more useful in the country." From Morioka she wrote,

> So far as comforts and pleasures are concerned, Yokohama is far preferable to Morioka. There I could attend English preaching on Sunday. I could enjoy the literary society, etc. Here I shall be debarred of everything of the sort. But the question with me was, is it right? I could never get the language perfectly in Yokohama, hearing so much English and so little Japanese. Besides, with my perfect health, it seemed if it was anyone's duty to go off in the country, it was <u>mine</u>.[31]

Winn was happy in the interior. However, with the Millers about to return to Morioka from America, she considered what she should do next. She had hoped to expand her work with women and children to surrounding towns and villages. This plan had been stymied by the governor of the region. For ten months she had visited the town of Hanamaki weekly for meetings. But then, in her words, "the governor forbade my going out of Morioka limits even for a few hours without a traveling passport. Mr. Miura made many attempts to procure a 24 hours passport, such as the missionaries of Sendai have. Our governor would sanction no arrangement, and so I have been shut up here a <u>semi-prisoner</u>."[32] Consequently, since Mary Miller could continue the work in Morioka, Winn hoped to go to a different field. She was invited to go to Hakodate and Aomori. Winn wrote, "It would be far pleasanter to go to Hakodate. I should not have the worry of the residence-passport, it being a treaty port, and I could have foreign friends to associate with. But I visited both Hakodate and Aomori last summer, and feel convinced I am much more needed at Aomori. It is my wish to make the most of my life. God has given me perfect health and I have the language.[33]

After two and a half years at Morioka, and a brief stay at Yokohama while waiting for a residence-passport from the Japanese government,

---

[31]    M. Leila Winn to HNC, Oct. 10, 1891.
[32]    MLW to HNC, Nov. 8, 1893. Strictness in enforcement of treaty regulations governing residence and movement of foreigners varied depending on the whims of local authorities.
[33]    MLW to HNC, Nov. 8, 1893.

Winn moved to Aomori in the spring of 1894 to take up evangelistic work among the women and children there. A suitable house was found for her and she began her work there. Unfortunately, in October of that year a major fire destroyed much of the city. The parsonage of Pastor Maki, which also served as the preaching place, was burned down, and the Maki family moved in with Winn until a suitable house could be procured by the mission for the Makis.[34] The mission bought land and built a new church and parsonage in Aomori using funds realized from the rent of the church property in Yokohama. Winn continued her work, especially among women and children of the Aomori area. In contrast to most other areas where Reformed Church missionaries were at work, Aomori was noted for its severe winters. In December of 1897, Ballagh noted the winter conditions in which she worked. "Fourteen days and nights of continuous snowing, Miss Winn reports, with snow up to the second story requiring tunneling of one's way out is not an inviting prospect for the holidays, but she, faithful to her trust, will not avail herself of a holiday to warmer and brighter parts."[35]

Mary Brokaw, after teaching at the girls' schools in Nagasaki and Yokohama for ten years, was approved for evangelistic work by the North Japan Mission. Furthermore, Mary Deyo, who had been teaching at Ferris Seminary for five years and was on furlough in 1894, also desired to enter evangelistic work. In the spring of 1894 Brokaw visited several fields, conducting meetings for women and children and exploring possible places to settle. Brokaw reported, "As far as I have been able to judge from my itinerary there is much the same work to be done everywhere, building up churches and training 'workers' of which there is a sad lack. Everywhere the pastors and church members have shown me respect and kindness and each pastor begged me to locate in his parish."[36] Brokaw hoped that Deyo might be returned to Japan and that they might work as a team in the work. With plans still unclear, Brokaw wrote, "My feelings in this perplexing period are best described in the words of Moses found in Ex. 33:12-16."[37]

Brokaw moved to Ueda in Nagano Prefecture in the fall of 1894. Excerpts from a letter telling of her new work offer insights into life as a single woman missionary in the interior.

> Miss Hirano and I arrived here Oct. 25th and received a warm welcome from the women of the church and a more formal one

[34]   MNW to HNC, Oct. 10, 1894.
[35]   JHB to HNC, Dec. 30, 1897.
[36]   MEB to HNC, Aug. 24, 1894.
[37]   MEB to HNC, Aug. 24, 1894.

on Nov. 3rd when the Emperor's birthday and our coming were celebrated together....I am about settled, as nearly as one can be in a very old Japanese house. From Ferris Seminary to a thatched roof cottage is quite a change but I hope to be comfortable and more than all else, I pray God will permit me plenty of work for Him. There is much to be done but as you doubtless know some of the native brethren in certain localities are jealous of foreign oversight and power. The new pastor here who arrived two weeks after I did seems to have imbibed some of the independent spirit of the times. For my own personal comfort in my work I could wish for the pastor who was here last spring and is now in an American seminary. However, by God's Holy Spirit, I hope we shall be able to work together effectively and harmoniously.

What is the best way to work with, or not with, the native brethren—there is usually not difficulty with the sisters—is a very serious problem which we must confront, whether we like to or not. Sometimes I am inclined to think it would be very wholesome "all-round" to take them at their own estimation, for a season, & let them work entirely independently of men and means.

There are numerous villages in sight of Ueda & hundreds, I suppose, in the province, that are almost as dead to Christianity as if there were no Christian teachers in the land. Who shall do the work & how is the question....

I have meetings regularly in three of the adjoining cities which are so conveniently located that I can go and return the same day by R.R. Last week I began my English class of young men & beg your prayers especially for that work that God may teach me how to use this opportunity to lead them to Christ.[38]

Early in 1895, both Harris and Wyckoff visited Ueda, and they were pleased and impressed with Brokaw's beginnings and with the opportunities for evangelism there. Within a few months Brokaw could report,

I have been encouraged since the beginning of the year by being able to open two new S.S. in adjoining villages. So far they are very flourishing and hopeful. I also hold meetings for the women in the same buildings....The knitting class at which a Christian book is read and a Bible talk given is chiefly attended by young women from fifteen to twenty years of age. I am glad to reach them....

[38]    MEB to HNC, Dec. 6, 1894.

It is still difficult to entice the married women to meetings. It has not been customary for them to go out on the street, i.e., the better class of women, so their failure to attend is frequently excused by the ever ready phrase, "It is not the custom." One finds after <u>residing</u> in the interior that the Japanese are not as much emancipated from old customs as one sometimes supposes when only thrown in contact with people of the ports.[39]

Mary Deyo returned to Japan in the spring of 1895, and it was decided that Brokaw and Deyo should work together to carry out their evangelistic work based in Ueda in the large Nagano region (including Ueda, Komoro, Nagano, Matsumoto, Suwa, Iida, etc.). After repairs and alterations to the little house Brokaw had acquired, and the rental of a house across the street for their helpers and for a meeting room, they settled into the evangelistic work in the interior. Deyo was pleased to acquire an assistant, Miss Tanaka, who was willing to join her in evangelistic work. Tanaka, a graduate from the Grammar Department of Ferris Seminary, had been living at home for two years. Though an earnest Christian, she was too timid to do any aggressive work by herself. Deyo explained,

> She was very glad to come here as she has been entirely deprived of Christian influences since she left school. There were no Christians in her native place and none of her family sympathized in any way with her faith. She said she had not heard a prayer nor a hymn nor the Bible read aloud for nearly two years. She has however kept up her own Bible study and prayers and seems anxious to learn more of the Bible and how to teach others.[40]

Brokaw and Deyo worked well together, focusing on evangelistic work for women and children. However, when Brokaw left for furlough in the spring of 1898, she had become engaged to the Reverend William Jones, a Presbyterian missionary to Japan (a childhood friend). Brokaw returned to Japan in 1899, married Jones, and became a Presbyterian missionary. They took up evangelistic work together at Fukui. Deyo continued in Ueda, assisted by three Japanese young women, and was visited frequently by other members of the mission.

Harriet J. Wyckoff, the daughter of Martin and Anna, was appointed as a new missionary by the Woman's Board. She returned

---

[39]   MEB to HNC, Apr. 9, 1895.
[40]   Mary Deyo to HNC, Aug. 31, 1895.

to the land of her childhood in September 1898, in the company of her parents, who were returning from a furlough. Though slated for evangelistic work, Harriet was appointed to teach at Ferris Seminary (along with language study) during the furlough of Julia Moulton. Harriet next spent a year in Ueda, while continuing language study, living with and working alongside Deyo in evangelistic ministry with women and children.

Although Harriet Wyckoff subsequently taught English at Ferris Seminary during the furlough and later the illness of Anna Thompson, she took up evangelistic work for a time in Aomori in partnership with Leila Winn.

## Policy Shifts in the North Japan Mission

Several factors contributed to shifts in emphases in the work of the North Japan Mission. The antiforeign and anti-Christian reaction came to be felt everywhere, but it was most deeply felt in the mission's work in Yokohama and Tokyo. It affected the reception accorded the evangelistic outreach of the churches, but it also complicated relationships between the missionaries and some of the church leaders. The most independent of them sometimes seemed embarrassed to be associated with foreign missionaries.

The changed situation also had an impact on the mission schools. A significant decrease in enrollment had occurred at both Ferris Seminary in Yokohama (enrollment of eighty to a hundred students maintained for many years had decreased to about thirty-five) and the Meiji Gakuin in Tokyo (enrollment in the academic department had decreased from almost two hundred to about fifty-five). The expenditures required to support the number of foreign teachers that had been serving at the schools became difficult to justify and had been a factor in the decision to release Winn, Brokaw, and Deyo from work at Ferris for evangelism in the interior. Questions were also raised about the necessity or wisdom of sustaining a missionary family (the Booths) at Ferris, with Eugene Booth, a man, as head of a girls' school. During the Booths' furlough in 1896-97, Ferris Seminary was administered by Anna Thompson, assisted by the music teacher, Julia Moulton. It was concluded by the board and the mission that, while it was not necessary for a man to head Ferris, Booth was best qualified to carry out the school's reassessed aims and purposes.

Important changes were implemented. For many years the school had maintained three departments—primary, grammar, and academic. The primary department was discontinued, and the main course became the five-year grammar department, perhaps equivalent in level to the fourth through eighth grades. The academic department was suspended, but a special two-year course to prepare girls who had become Christians for Christian service was initiated. The intent was that some of the graduates of the grammar department would be given further training in order to serve as Bible women (lay evangelists, often working as helpers or literary assistants of the missionaries) or as Christian teachers.[41] A mission committee ruled that all assisted (tuition free) students in this Bible course would be required to serve the mission as assistants for two years after completing their studies. However, these changes in policy had the effect of further reducing enrollment, which dropped temporarily to sixteen students.[42]

Fortunately, under Booth's leadership, enrollment at Ferris Seminary gradually improved. Furthermore, on October 24, 1899, the school acquired official government recognition as a Christian private school. Mission schools for girls, such as Ferris Seminary, were of a lower grade level than the boys' schools at that time. They were recognized, but did not have academic accreditation. They did not face some of the issues confronted by schools for boys (e.g., military conscription, difficulty of admission to higher, male-only government schools). However, the school was responding to a growing appreciation for the importance of female education in Japan. Enrollment soon grew to about one hundred students, the higher, more academic course was resumed, and the reputation of the school as a leading institution was gradually restored.

At Meiji Gakuin, reorganization of the school with the reduction of the number of foreign teachers led to the decision to have only one Reformed Church missionary in the academic department. Howard Harris held this position while the Wyckoffs were away. Following their furlough, Martin Wyckoff once again took up his responsibilities in the academic department of Meiji Gakuin. During the mid-1890s, enrollment had declined to about fifty students as a result of the antiforeign, anti-Christian reaction, and because the missionaries and Japanese leaders of the school decided to decline government recognition rather than give up Bible teaching and worship. There was firm support from teachers and students for maintaining a strong Christian identity.[43] In fact, the school emphasized preparation for Christian ministry, and, as Harris pointed out, "An institution which has for its great purpose the building up of a theological school may

---

[41]   MNW to HNC, March 23, 1897; ESB to HNC, July 16, 20, and 22, 1897.
[42]   ESB to HNC, Jan. 27, 1898.
[43]   MNW to HNC, May 29, 1896; HH to HNC, Sept. 30, 1897.

do a good work, but must not expect a large number of students."[44] Later the school gained semiofficial recognition from the Tokyo City government as a *chu gakko* or middle school (a five-year course approximately equivalent to the seventh through the eleventh grades), without sacrificing its Christian character, and this recognition helped enrollment grow to about 125 students.

### Scattered Evangelistic Outreach

In 1896 the evangelistic work of the North Japan Mission was spread over a very extensive territory. At that time the missionaries involved primarily in evangelism lived and worked out of five places: Ballagh – Yokohama, Verbeck – Tokyo, Miller – Morioka, Winn – Aomori, and Brokaw and Deyo – Ueda. There were five independent (unaided) churches at that time directly affiliated with the mission.[45] Twenty-four additional churches and preaching places and twenty-three Sunday schools were maintained, and the Japanese staff employed by the mission included seven ordained ministers, thirteen male evangelists, and five Bible women.[46] Supervision and encouragement of this ministry required a great deal of correspondence and financial management, as well as extensive touring both by the missionaries and the mission's experienced Japanese pastors, Inagaki, Maki, and Ito. These Japanese ministers performed a crucial role in guiding and inspiring the younger workers. They were involved in preaching tours and meetings with the evangelists throughout the field, sometimes along with a missionary, but often independently on behalf of the mission.

No young men had been sent out specifically for evangelistic work since the arrival of the pioneers in 1859 and 1861. The Reformed Church Board of Foreign Missions' perennial shortage of funds precluded new missionary recruitment. In 1895 the Millers proposed a solution to this dilemma. E. R. Miller possessed private resources in America that had increased greatly in value, and the Millers had no children. They offered to become self-supporting, thus freeing their financial support from the mission board to be used for a newly appointed family.[47] Their offer was accepted with gratitude. In 1897 the board responded to the North Japan Mission's request for reinforcements, appointing new evangelistic missionaries. The Reverend Frank S. and Florence S. Scudder, as well

---

44    HH to HNC, Oct. 6, 1897.
45    Kaigan (Yokohama), Kojimachi and Shitaya (Tokyo), Mishima, and Yokosuka Churches.
46    MNW to HNC, March 30, 1896.
47    ERM to HNC, Sept. 3, 1895.

A group of believers in Miyako, a town on the Pacific coast
east of Morioka, where work was begun in 1909

as Jennie D. Schenck, Florence Scudder's mother, arrived in October.
Mrs. Schenck, a widow, was appointed as a missionary, but at her own
expense.

The Scudders and Jennie Schenck became the first missionaries
assigned to live in Nagano. There they began language study, and Frank
assumed supervisory responsibility for the Japanese evangelists in the
Nagano region who were employed by the mission. The cold winters
were a challenge for the Scudders (Frank had grown up in tropical India
as a missionary child), and they had some health problems. Nevertheless,
the next year Scudder could report, "We have encouragements. Two
baptisms this month, and three fine young men now preparing for
baptism, and besides [despite] all violent opposition from the Buddhists
on every hand. They break up our work a great deal, but I am glad to see
that they are regarding Christianity as a great menace to their faith."[48]

Scudder not only supervised evangelistic work in the area, but
he also immediately began his own ministry, preaching through an
interpreter. He also soon implemented his musical gifts, reporting, "I
am training young men to sing, not only for church but believing that
by this means I can keep up their interest in neighboring evangelistic
meetings where I want them to sing." Scudder also illustrated the
difficulty of witness in Nagano, as follows:

[48]    Frank S. Scudder to HNC, Nov. 26, 1898.

In my report for the year, I spoke of a man who had become very earnest and had opened his house for services, etc. He has been much persecuted by his brothers and tormented by the priests, for he is a prominent man. The priests recently came to him offering him a fine position and bringing him a valuable present. He refused to be moved by either entreaties or threats, affirming that he was now a Christian. At last the priests demanded back the present and left. His brothers call him "fool" and try in every way to break up his Sunday schools and services and lately they have managed to get some of his property away from him. Last Sunday they went to his house and trampled it full of mud,[49] then called him in and clubbed him over head, back, and legs till he was a sorry looking object. I called upon him to comfort and encourage him, but he was already radiant, praising God that he was able to offer up his body a living sacrifice, and saying that seven persons, including a sister and his wife, desired to become inquirers as a result of this affair.[50]

Reports by Scudder in 1899 illustrate the contrast between the lives of missionaries in large cities and those working in interior locations. Roads were still largely undeveloped. One day Scudder was holding his four-month old daughter Margaret in his arms riding in a *jinrikisha* when it overturned. He was thrown down an embankment with the baby in his arms, and wrote, "We praise the Lord for another safe deliverance; do not understand how we escaped with nothing more than slight bruises.[51] Another letter from Scudder indicated the challenge of living in a rented Japanese house poorly designed for the cold winters.

We have had a very severe winter, and that has interfered with our work....I have dreaded the time when we should come to zero weather, while living in a Japanese house. But this year it has come to pass....Water poured out a few minutes before breakfast froze in the glasses before we drank it; and food, set aside a few minutes froze, so that the things which came on at the end of the meal were frozen before they were served. This state of things lasted for several days. How I do pity the Japanese in such weather. They have almost no means to modify the terrors of the cold.[52]

---

[49]   Deliberately muddying the straw mat floors, where people never wear shoes in Japan, was an act of humiliation.
[50]   FSS to HNC, Feb. 14, 1899.
[51]   FSS to HNC, July 10, 1899.
[52]   FSS to HNC, Feb. 10, 1900.

Scudder gradually gained facility in the language to the point where he could preach in Japanese, and he began to explore different ways of reaching people with the gospel. The mission placed great hope in the Scudders, the first missionary family recruited to focus on evangelism in the interior.

With the idea of giving more emphasis to evangelism, Harris was transferred from teaching at Meiji Gakuin to the interior, and in October 1898 the Harrises moved to Ichinoseki, halfway between Sendai and Morioka. In his new role, Harris learned how hard it was to make an impression on people, remarking, "Like lifting a drowsy man out of sleep, they are continually dropping back into the old dull state."[53] Later he wrote, "After a residence of some months in the interior of the country I am more than ever persuaded that the evangelization of this empire calls for a good deal of hard so called drudgery on the part of the missionary. A man who takes up this work must consent to be nothing in name that he may be everything in helpfulness."[54]

Harris believed that if numerous young missionaries, "men of inspired life, were in all parts of the country, going from town to town, for the most part taking up their quarters with the poorer classes, and entering fairly into conversation with them on the concerns of their souls," good results would surely be realized. And he lamented,

> But as it is now the field work is being sadly neglected. Every cut of the Board falls heavily on this part of our work. This placing of native workers here and there throughout our fields and leaving them there to carry on their work for a number of years, with no encouragement except now and then a visit from a missionary is preventing the progress of the Gospel...and when a native goes forth fresh from his studies to enter upon evangelistic work, as is the case in many instances, hardly knowing what he believes himself, what may we expect of him after a sojourn of a few months in one of these towns. How long will he be able to preach and teach Jesus only. How necessary it is that all our helpers shall be enlarged, ennobled, and developed....So then, there is need to keep our ranks full of warm-hearted, inspired men who will not only go out among the people and preach the Word, but also be preparing the native helpers for the important part they must take in the evangelization of this great country.[55]

[53]    HH to HNC, Nov. 17, 1898.
[54]    HH to HNC, Dec. 26, 1898.
[55]    Ibid.

The North Japan Mission, because of recurring budget cuts, struggled to maintain financial support of its Japanese evangelists working in the interior. They were poorly paid, and, given the difficulty of evangelism and church development, self-support in most of the scattered small congregations remained a distant goal. The mission was too strapped even to provide literature to the workers. Of these evangelists, Wyckoff remarked, "The poor fellows have to struggle on, 'making bricks without straw.' They ought to be encouraged by visits from the missionary in charge, or someone representing the mission, at least three or four times a year, but under present conditions, the more distant places, where encouragement is most needed, are fortunate if they get one visit a year."[56] The situation was made worse by the fact that neither Ballagh nor Miller was in good health and could not be counted on to do much more than keep up on correspondence with the evangelists in the field.

The missionaries were desperate to provide funds for the evangelistic work. Some years earlier they had often paid some of the expenses out of their own salaries, but, despite continuing inflation and increases in the cost of living, their own salaries had remained virtually the same for forty years. When Booth was asked to teach English three hours each evening (on top of his full-time job as head of Ferris Seminary) in a "school" for postal clerks and telegraph operators at a good salary, with mission consent he agreed to do it. Wyckoff reported, "The income from this source is to be applied to alleviating the effects of the cut in our appropriations for evangelistic work."[57]

The next year, with mission consent, Booth became the interim pastor of Yokohama Union Church (English-speaking, for the foreign residents), while continuing his duties as principal of Ferris Seminary. He accepted the call because of the great need of the church itself, and especially because of the mission budget deficit. The money he received was turned over to the mission, in an effort to avoid having to discontinue some of the evangelistic work.[58]

Concerning the difficulty faced by the North Japan Mission, Ballagh wrote,

> For the first time, at an annual meeting, in the forty years of the mission's history has a whole day been occupied in trying to see how a full suit of clothes could be cut out of a deficient piece of

---

[56]  MNW to HNC, Feb. 3, 1899.
[57]  ESB to HNC, Jan. 23, 1899; MNW to HNC, Jan. 24, 1899.
[58]  MNW to HNC, Jan. 12, 1900.

cloth. By the utmost patching and piecing we came within two thousand yen, or one thousand dollars, of meeting our deficiency, and this by leaving the work at three stations uncared for, and not allowing one cent for contingencies or expansion. This is the darkest beginning of a new year...we have yet known.[59]

Despite the efforts of the missionaries, the financial problem persisted. The mission board faced serious deficits, and the annual appropriations sent to the mission were cut repeatedly.[60]

## The Final Days of Guido Verbeck

Ever since he had been relieved of teaching responsibilities, Guido Verbeck carried out numerous preaching tours to all parts of Japan. Griffis described this ministry:

> His first pleasure was preaching, for which he had talents that would have made him notable in any land. I should say that his chief powers were the graphic vividness with which he could portray a scene, being richly gifted in voice and gesture; then the resistless logic with which he forced truth home. His sermons abounded in illustrations, and were the delight of Japanese audiences. Wherever he went, the people came in crowds to see and hear.[61]

Leila Winn, involved in evangelistic work at the northernmost tip of the island of Honshu, reported on Verbeck's last preaching tour as follows:

> Though for many years a member of the same mission with Dr. Verbeck, I never felt that I really knew him until the autumn of 1897, when he came to Aomori to give us a ten days' series of lectures and sermons. The first thing that impressed me was what a student he was. He never preached at random. One could see at once that there had been thorough preparation beforehand. He called the little park at Aomori his "study room." As soon as breakfast was over he would go off to the park and not be seen again until noon. After dinner he did the same till evening. It was no wonder then that, evening after evening, he held his audiences spellbound.

---

[59]  JHB to HNC, Jan. 21, 1901.
[60]  MNW to HNC, Jan. 29, 1901.
[61]  Griffis, *Verbeck*, 364-65.

His self-effacement was another thing that impressed me. A compliment seemed to give him pain rather than pleasure. He always changed the subject. He wanted people to think of Jesus Christ, not about himself.

Dr. Verbeck swayed and governed those about him by his gentleness, rather than by words of fault-finding and criticism. His visit here made me wish to be a nobler, better woman, and to overcome all that was petty and belittling in my nature.[62]

Despite his activity, Verbeck's health was deteriorating, and members of the mission became concerned. In October, because of a serious kidney problem, his doctor forbade any evangelistic touring, and he had to cancel a scheduled two-month tour in Kyushu.[63] Verbeck had prostate and heart problems as well. Even so, his health seemed to improve, and he went out preaching again in the vicinity of Tokyo. In a letter written February 24, he wrote, "I feel I am now able to lay out plans for some near country work. The fresh air and exercise on country touring always benefit me much. And a little later I hope to be blessed with strength enough to respond to two calls to more distant fields: Kochi and our large field in Kyushu....And then there is our own Shinshu [Nagano Prefecture] field which is never off my mind."[64] Regaining confidence, and "growing restless to be again in the work of visiting the field," on March 3 he visited Ballagh at Yokohama to confer regarding his planned preaching tour to the Izu Peninsula.[65] Consequently, it was a great shock to both family and mission when on March 10, 1898, Guido Verbeck died suddenly of heart failure at the age of sixty-eight.[66]

Not long before his death, several leading missionaries had determined to present copies of the Bible in both Japanese and English to Emperor Mutsuhito (posthumously called Emperor Meiji). Verbeck was chosen to write the letter to accompany the Bibles.[67] As it turned out, preparing this letter was one of his last works.

No other missionary to Japan, before or since, has had as large an impact on that nation. His influence was deeply felt, not only in the Christian movement but also in Japan's modernization. The respect and admiration attained by Verbeck among the Japanese may be seen

---

[62]  Ibid., 362-63.
[63]  ESB to HNC, Nov. 20, 1897.
[64]  Griffis, *Verbeck*, 350.
[65]  Ibid., 352-53.
[66]  HH to HNC, March 14, 1898.
[67]  JHB to HNC, Dec. 10, 1897.

Guido and Maria Verbeck

in the fact that, nineteen years after he left the employ of the Japanese government, not only did top officials attend his funeral but the emperor presented a gift of 500 yen (about $250, a large sum at the time), the government provided a military escort to the cemetery, and the city of Tokyo presented the family with a receipt for a perpetual lease of the burial plot at Aoyama Cemetery in Tokyo.[68]

The greatest of the pioneers had fallen, sorely missed by mission and church. In a letter pleading for replacements for Poppen and Verbeck, Miller wrote the following on behalf of the mission. "We can never expect anyone to occupy the sphere filled by Dr. Verbeck, unique in so many ways, yet we sigh as we think of the long years, and the toil and laborious years, that would lie before anyone who came out to fill, in some small measure, the position once held by our beloved friend and father in mission work."[69]

**Treaty Revision**

The unresolved issue of the unequal treaties had been like a festering wound for the Japanese government and many of its citizens for many years. The Treaty of Amity and Commerce negotiated by Townsend Harris of the United States had been signed in 1858. The

---

[68]    Griffis, *Verbeck*, 356-57.
[69]    ERM to HNC, Aug. 17, 1898.

original treaty promised friendly aid to Japan by American ships and consular representatives, prohibition of opium importation, and the provision of technical experts to work for the modernization of Japan. However, the treaty had not recognized Japan as an equal with Western nations. It had been humiliating in both theory and practice.

To Japan's benefit, the treaty provided that Westerners residing in Japan be restricted to treaty ports. This protected most of Japan from foreign commerce, and it had limited the movement of foreigners, including missionaries, into the interior by requiring travel permits. On the other hand, it had permitted foreigners to lease land and build and own buildings in the treaty port concessions and had allowed foreign traders preferential tariffs. Japan's lack of tariff autonomy had retarded industrial development.

Furthermore, and most humiliating, the resident foreigners had been granted extraterritoriality, i.e., exemption from the legal jurisdiction of a country of residence. The Japanese legal system being considered inadequate to guarantee the human rights of Westerners, the treaty provided that foreign nationals could not be prosecuted under Japanese legal codes and courts and were subject only to their own nation's consular officials. For example, even if a foreign sailor at a port raped a Japanese woman or committed robbery or even murder, he could not be prosecuted by the Japanese authorities and could often escape punishment. Politically and economically, the 1858 treaty had made Japan legally subordinate to foreign governments, an imposed inferiority, a semicolonial status. Ironically, this national humiliation became a contributing factor in the transformation of the country from a collection of feudal territories into a united, self-conscious nation. It helped produce not only national pride, but ultimately ultranationalism.[70]

The unequal treaties had been a persistent irritant, and repeated efforts to achieve equal status with Western nations through treaty revisions had failed. Forty years passed without the issue being resolved. After agreements with the several key Western nations were at long last negotiated successfully, the emperor announced in the spring of 1899 that new treaties would go into effect July 17. These new treaties abrogated extraterritoriality and instituted more equal regulation of tariffs. The missionaries were delighted that the forty-year policy of restricting foreign residence and travel were abandoned. Missionaries could live, work, and move freely anywhere in Japan.

---

[70]    Lu, *Japan*, 288; Gordon, *Modern History*, 50.

On the other hand, all foreigners were henceforth subject to Japanese law and the Japanese courts. They were required to register with the government, clearly showing their name, place of residence, and their personal history (*rireki*), including place of birth, citizenship, education, vocation, employment history, and any criminal record. This was the beginning of what came to be called alien registration, which identified non-Japanese residents as outsiders. The foreign concessions in the treaty ports and cities were abolished. Rules regarding land changed, and foreigners were permitted the equivalent of owning land (a three-hundred-year lease) anywhere in the country and were allowed to construct buildings on it.

Additional regulations were also issued regarding religions and religious workers, to go into effect August 4, 1899. All religious workers (including Japanese) were required not only to register and submit a personal history, but also to report the nature of their religious activity, places of meeting, and any property held for religious purposes. This can only be described as a form of surveillance. Even so, to the missionaries, the new regulations also appeared to have a positive aspect. They seemed to imply a kind of recognition of Christianity by the granting of equal rights under the law to religions other than Shinto and Buddhism.

In accord with the emperor's proclamation, the new treaties went into effect July 17, 1899. Miller wrote, "I really think that the effect of the Emperor's proclamation will be widely felt, and that in the fall the people will be much more ready to come to church and listen to the preaching of the gospel."[71] However, the new treaties also held ominous possibilities. Wyckoff noted, "If this alone is done, it will be a gain for Christianity in many ways, but there may be other attentions added by this paternal government that will make us wish that Christianity had remained unrecognized."[72]

## Government Regulation of Education

In April 1899, it appeared that new regulations affecting the mission schools were in the offing. On May 1, Wyckoff reported the following ominous news: "The Department of Education is trying to take a backward step by trying to shut out Christianity by legislation to shut religion out of schools."[73]

On August 3, Japan's Ministry of Education issued new directives, two rules of which would have a profound impact on mission schools.

---

[71]   ERM to HNC, July 28, 1899.
[72]   MNW to HNC, Aug. 4, 1899.
[73]   MNW to HNC, May 1, 1899.

First, new regulations stipulated that no pupil could enter any private school until graduating from a government upper elementary school (*Koto Sho Gakko*). A second directive would especially affect schools such as Meiji Gakuin, which had gained semiofficial status as a five-year middle school (*chu gakko*), with accompanying privileges of student deferment from military conscription and admission of graduates to higher schools. The new directives stated,

> It being essential from the point of view of educational instruction, that general education should be independent of religion, religious instruction must not be given, or religious ceremonies performed, at Government Schools, Public Schools, or schools whose curricula are regulated by provisions of law, even outside the regular course of instruction.

Six of the prominent mission schools, including Meiji Gakuin, met to consider what course to take in view of these instructions. Missionaries of the North Japan Mission were deeply concerned for the future of Meiji Gakuin. However, on August 17, 1899, the school's board of directors, the majority of whom were Japanese Christians, unanimously passed the following resolution:

> Resolved that inasmuch as the Instruction recently issued by the Department of Education forbids the teaching of religion and the performance of religious rites in all *chu gakko* throughout the Empire, even in the case of those supported by private funds, the Meiji Gakuin, having been from its foundation a Christian institution, is constrained by its principles to relinquish the privileges of a *chu gakko*.[74]

As a result of this courageous decision, within a month the school lost about 25 percent of its students. Wyckoff noted, "We have been exceedingly gratified that our Japanese brethren have stood with us unwaveringly in this matter, even though the representatives of other schools have failed to take the same positive stand, and some have twitted our men as being 'too honest' or 'lacking in shrewdness.'"[75]

Since the Meiji Restoration, the Japanese had emphasized education as one of the keys to modernization. With remarkable speed basic education became universal throughout the country. Illiteracy was being eliminated among the younger generation. Under the

[74]    MNW to HNC, Aug. 22, 1899.
[75]    MNW to HNC, Oct. 30, 1899.

new regulations, however, in all accredited schools, whether public or private, every boy was to be given basic military training and was forbidden to receive religious instruction or to attend religious exercises of any kind. At the same time, it was claimed that Shintoism was not actually a religion but simply a system of ancient rites and ceremonies that needed to be preserved. Furthermore, school ceremonies to demonstrate and teach reverence for the picture of the emperor and the Rescript on Education were required. Wyckoff observed, "There is evidently a nationalistic spirit back of it all, which will not recognize any relation to be higher than that which all Japanese subjects must have towards the imperial family. It seems probable that Christianity is to meet its strongest opposition along this line."[76]

Nevertheless, as a result of joint negotiations by representatives of Meiji Gakuin and the other leading boys' schools with the Japanese government, a kind of recognition was achieved in 1900. These mission schools retained their right to teach and practice Christianity. Military training had to be incorporated into their curriculum, but because they regained the right of student deferment from army conscription, like the government schools, enrollment again began to increase. The following year additional privileges, such as admission of graduates to higher schools (albeit by entrance exam), were granted to private middle schools such as Meiji Gakuin, placing them on a footing similar to government schools. Enrollment at Meiji Gakuin soon reached 175, and religious activities among the students were thriving (more than sixty regularly attended weekly student prayer meetings).[77]

Early in 1902 Wyckoff could report that "there is good reason for believing that before long the Higher Course of the Academic Department will obtain government recognition similar to that already granted to the Middle School Course."[78] This "higher course" would be a three-year program approximately equivalent to the senior year of high school and two years of college, perhaps comparable to the European *gymnasium*.

Government recognition of the Meiji Gakuin academic department definitely helped the school's situation, but in 1903 the school was still handicapped by a kind of discrimination against nongovernment schools. Mission school graduates were required to pass an entrance examination for admission to higher government schools. In 1904, after a struggle of five years with authorities of the

[76]  MNW to HNC, Oct. 30, 1899.
[77]  MNW to HNC, May 22, 1901.
[78]  MNW to Board of Foreign Missions, Reformed Church in America, Feb. 6, 1902.

Japanese Ministry of Education, full privileges were granted to the recognized mission schools, "without any restriction as to religious training and exercises." Wyckoff remarked, "I think we may honestly claim that much of the credit belongs to the Meiji Gakuin because it was the leader in taking a firm attitude from the first, and has never for a moment turned aside from principle."[79] In September of 1904, enrollment at Mejij Gakuin had risen to 190 in the academic department and fourteen in the theological classes.

The Reformed Church had been unable to provide a full-time faculty member for the theological department at Meiji Gakuin since the departure of Jacob Poppen in 1898. Albert Oltmans, a member of the South Japan Mission since 1886, was deemed best qualified for this role. After a furlough in America that included further study, Oltmans was transferred to the North Japan Mission, taking up this teaching position in April of 1904.

In 1905, in addition to government recognition of its middle school, the higher and theological departments gained government recognition as *senmon gakko*, or professional training schools. Enrollment in Meiji Gakuin's middle school course continued to increase. By 1907 it had climbed to four hundred students, but the quality of the students had begun to deteriorate, many of the new entrants being those who had failed to pass exams to enter government schools. In any case, more teachers were needed. The Reformed Church provided an additional foreign teacher for the school in the person of Walter E. Hoffsommer, an educator who, with his wife, Grace, joined the North Japan Mission in the fall of 1907.[80]

Ferris Seminary had also gradually recovered from the detrimental impact of the general reaction against all things Western and Christian experienced in the 1890s. By the summer of 1904, Booth could report that the school was in a much improved situation. Four foreigners and seven Japanese made up the teaching staff. The school had four departments: a preparatory course of three years (38 pupils), a grammar course of five years (perhaps similar to fifth through ninth grades—81 pupils), an English normal course of three years (training English teachers—21 students), and a Bible course of two years (training Christian workers—10 students). Of this total of 150 pupils, 54 had become Christians.[81] Two-thirds of the students lived in the dormitory; the rest were day students.

[79]    MNW to HNC, Jan. 28, 1904.
[80]    Walter E. Hoffsommer to HNC, Sept. 18, 1907.
[81]    ESB to HNC, June 6, 1904.

Harriet Wyckoff, after some experience in evangelism in the interior, was again teaching at Ferris Seminary and also had charge of the evangelistic work of the school, which consisted of calling at the homes of the day pupils and guiding the meetings carried on by pupils. She trained some of the older girls to serve as leaders of devotional Bible study classes for the younger girls and supervised older Christian students in outreach into the community. They had charge of five branch Sunday schools in various parts of Yokohama, with two hundred children in attendance. Harriet met each week for prayer with a group of sixteen girls who hoped to go into Christian work. She also influenced two young men, new converts who had become members of Kaigan Church, to become involved in evangelism, conducting branch Sunday schools in their own homes. "They work together, having one Sunday school right after the church service on Sunday morning, at one house, and when that is over, they both walk out to a little fishing village outside of Yokohama, where the other young man lives, and have another Sunday school there in the afternoon."[82] However, after seven years as a missionary under the Reformed Woman's Board, Harriet resigned from the North Japan Mission to marry the Reverend John E. Hail, a missionary of the Cumberland Presbyterian Mission. Concerning Harriet, Booth remarked, "The girls simply worship the ground she walks on....Her influence in the school has been a tower of strength."[83]

Fortunately, the Woman's Board was able to send Jennie M. Kuyper of Pella, Iowa, as a teacher for the girls' school. At the beginning she taught only two days each week, giving most of her time to studying the language, going to Tokyo to a new language school opened by a Christian scholar named Matsuda. She took over supervision of the Sunday school work done by the Ferris girls and commented, "My ignorance of the language handicaps me necessarily in everything—but it's my greatest incentive to study to see these many open doors for work."[84]

The increase in enrollment continued. Total enrollment in 1905 was 185, and in 1907 it was 238, of whom only 84 lived in the dormitory. The dormitory/boarding students were under Christian influence day and night, and more of them tended to become Christians. The increase in day students, therefore, made it more challenging to lead the girls to Christian commitment.

82    Harriet J. Wyckoff to HNC, May 31, 1904.
83    ESB to HNC, June 27, 1905.
84    Jennie M. Kuyper to HNC, Dec. 5, 1905.

## North Japan Evangelism and Church Development in the Interior

The North Japan Mission hoped to capitalize on the newly acquired freedom of movement and residency in the interior for foreigners that resulted from the treaty revisions. The Harrises had joined the Millers and Leila Winn in the northern region. (The Harrises served in evangelistic work first in Ichinoseki, then later in Aomori during the furlough of Leila Winn.) Mary Deyo and the Scudders were serving in Ueda and Nagano City in the large Nagano Prefecture. Even so, with the loss of Verbeck and the recurring health problems of both Ballagh and Miller, the scattered evangelistic work was not being adequately cared for and opportunities for development were not being acted upon. On behalf of the mission, Miller pleaded for the appointment of two new evangelistic missionaries. His plea included his assessment of the immaturity of many Japanese Christian workers at that time.

> The continuance of the foreign missionary in Japan is necessary because the Japanese Church is not yet in a position where it can carry to a successful issue the different branches of church work without foreign care, advice, and supervision—to say nothing of foreign money. The Japanese are deficient in the inventive faculty necessary to inaugurate new work; and further they do not possess the patience and perseverance to carry on to fulfillment work once undertaken. They also lack the faith and hope necessary to retrieve failure and defeat, especially in the defection of an individual Christian, who, often in his own eyes as well as in the eyes of others, is given up as hopelessly irreclaimable.[85]

Winn also, writing from Aomori, pointed to some of the shortcomings of the evangelists working for the mission, saying, "Our native pastor is an able man, but like so many of the native pastors, is such a poor pastor, and _not_ fond of taking suggestions. The missionary to Japan needs so much _wisdom_, _discretion_, and _tact_."[86] It might also be said that the Japanese pastors working for a mission administered by foreign missionaries needed a great deal of patience, forbearance, and humility. While it was true that they often had little or no experience in a mature congregation and consequently little understanding of pastoral care or church administration, they were after all educated Japanese with a growing sense of national pride and a desire for independence.

[85]  ERM to HNC, Feb. 7, 1901.
[86]  MLW to HNC, Feb. 25, 1901.

Several of the mature Japanese pastors working for the mission were in fact not only very gifted and skillful, but also genuine colleagues and indispensable to the work of the missionaries.

The missionaries had an unusual experience in Aomori in early December 1901. E. R. Miller was there for special evangelistic services and stayed at the home of Leila Winn and Harriet Wyckoff, the resident missionaries. The chimney overheated and caught fire, and local Japanese firemen, assuming the house itself was on fire, "rushed in and proceeded to wreck everything in sight, quieting Mr. Miller by turning the hose on him whenever he remonstrated too loudly. So considerable damage was done, though nothing was destroyed by fire."[87] Despite protests to the local authorities regarding the outrageous behavior of the firemen, no one would take responsibility for the considerable cost of repairing the damage to the mission house. Even though the behavior of the firemen may have reflected antagonism toward the foreign missionaries, Leila Winn was concerned that things might be made unpleasant for her in the community if the matter were to be stirred up any more,[88] and the issue was dropped.

In the spring of 1902, the Harrises moved to Morioka to take responsibility for the evangelistic work in that region, replacing the Millers. The Millers had lived and worked there, with the help of their Japanese colleagues, for fourteen years, and 158 people had been baptized during that time.[89] The Millers moved back to Tokyo, and from there E. R. Miller took responsibility for oversight of much of the evangelistic work of the mission in the interior, as well as in nearby outstations. Mary Miller, with the help of her long-time associate, Pastor Miura, continued publishing periodical literature for women and children. *Glad Tidings* (circulation 3,100) and *Little Tidings* (circulation 4,500) were each issued twice monthly and were used in many churches and Sunday schools throughout Japan.[90]

Subsequently, in the fall of 1902, Leila Winn and Mary Deyo took over the evangelistic work in the Morioka region, and the Harrises moved to Aomori. The work there was making good progress, with new church members added, a class for forty or fifty older girls, women's and men's Bible study classes, and a Sunday school enrollment of 450. A Japanese evangelist (Mr. Hijikata) and a Bible woman worked with them. As it turned out, however, Howard and Lizzie Harris did not remain long in

87    MNW to HNC, Dec. 9, 1901.
88    ERM to HNC, Feb. 26, 1902.
89    ERM to HNC, May 8, 1902.
90    ERM to HNC, Jan. 1, 1903.

Aomori. Unable to tolerate the very severe winters, they resigned from the mission for health reasons, leaving Japan in November 1904, having served twenty-one years.[91] Furthermore, in 1905 Deyo, having served seventeen years, resigned from the mission and returned to America, feeling responsible to care for a family member in failing health.[92] In this way, the number of missionaries engaged in evangelistic work in the interior dwindled.

Ballagh, seventy years old and suffering from chronic diarrhea, went on evangelistic tours as his health permitted. In a letter of September 5, 1902, Ballagh told of riding a pack horse five miles and walking ten miles over a mountain pass to attend the funeral of Katsumata Shokichi, who died at the age of seventy-six. Ballagh had baptized him decades earlier, when the man was working for a Christian at Hakone. Katsumata had been for many years the only believer in the district were he lived, a place so isolated that Ballagh had visited him only two or three times in thirty years, and native pastors not much more often. Katsumata had very seldom been able to hear preaching or meet with other Christians, although he had come out for Christmas each year. He could neither read nor write, and yet he kept track of Sunday with a string of seven beads, moving one each day. On his death bed he said to visiting Pastor Ito, "I am hanging on to the hem of Jesus' garment." Many, including the leading men of the village, attended Katsumata's funeral. Ito gave an account of his early life, and of the persecutions he had endured from the Shinto priest and a rich man of his native village. The priest tried to force him to sign a recantation and promise to give up Christianity, but he refused, and he was expelled from the village. He had lived thirty years in another village, and he did not conceal his light. He made a crude cross, and he got someone to write on it, *Jujika Gumi*," which means "Company of the Cross." It was his sign that he belonged to the followers of Jesus. He put it up in his home and explained its meaning to inquirers. His lonely perseverance was rewarded in that at the time of his funeral both his widow and his son had become seekers.[93]

The Scudders experienced numerous difficulties in Nagano. Jennie Schenck, who had been a great help in the work with women and children, left Japan in the spring of 1901 in poor health and never returned. The Japanese pastor working with Scudder departed for another field. Embarrassing local scandals involving Christians erupted.

91    ERM & MLW to HNC, Jan. 28, 1904; HH to HNC, Feb. 10 and Oct. 12, 1904.
92    MD to HNC, Dec. 23, 1905.
93    JHB to HNC, Sept. 5, 1902.

Nevertheless, Scudder was able to report an encouraging response in the work there. He had found creative ways to engage people in the work and to reach out to find inquirers. Scudder prepared and published an Easter anthem in Japanese for use not only in Nagano but also by other churches. He inspired lay Christians to initiate two branch Sunday schools, and they raised the money themselves to carry on this work. He also reported:

> Another interesting thing has been the responses to an advertisement I put in the paper offering to lend Christian books. A single adv. brought over 80 applicants. The majority will undoubtedly prove to have no better motive than curiosity, but there are a number of very interesting cases of inquirers. It is too soon to tell what the result of the scheme will be, but I feel satisfied that already some have been led to be most earnest seekers, and, inasmuch as from the same town, in some cases, there have followed several requests, as though one person had told others, I believe that if we were in a position to go to these places and hold meetings we could get a foothold quite easily. One person said he had called at my house a year ago, and at that time received his first desire to know about God; he had purchased a Bible, but could not understand, and had become discouraged. Seeing my adv. he asked for books, and afterwards wrote to me telling me the steps by which he had been led into larger knowledge and finally true peace. Another recently wrote that he was very anxious to have Christianity taught in his town. He was so eager that he would like to have a preacher sent, Sunday schools opened, and meetings for the instruction of women. He talked like one who knew something of the methods of Christian evangelization.[94]

Scudder's report is the first evidence of such a creative use of advertising in the newspaper by a missionary in Japan. Ten years later this idea was implemented and further developed by Albertus Pieters in Kyushu.

In the spring of 1902 Scudder used music as a tool of evangelistic outreach. He trained church members and several normal school students in singing. Then the Scudders and the singing group put on a benefit concert for mine disaster relief. The program included not only singing, but also piano, reed organ, three violins, clarinet, flute, cornet, and Apollo harp, and the musically gifted Harrises, who were visiting

[94]    FSS to HNC, March 21, 1901.

at the time, also took part. The result was good publicity for the work of the church in Nagano.[95] The Scudders and their Japanese colleagues carried on ten branch Sunday schools, with total regular attendance of four hundred to five hundred pupils in the cool months. Florence Scudder carried the chief responsibility for this branch of the work.[96] Although the Scudders spent five years as the first resident missionaries in Nagano and saw progress in the work, the living situation and severe climate took its toll on their health. They went to America for a health furlough in October of 1902, and Miller gave guidance to the Nagano work in their absence.

The first years of the twentieth century were particularly frustrating for the missionaries because, while they believed that the time was right to expand evangelism and church development, the mission was subjected to repeated cuts in appropriations from the mission board. In 1903, unable to pare expenses further, the mission was forced to cut off support of two outstations and considered abandoning the support of partnerships of many years with the small groups of Christians in Mishima and Gotemba in Shizuoka Prefecture and on the Boso Peninsula (Chiba Prefecture). As it turned out, Leila Winn was moved by the mission to Mishima to guide and encourage the work there.

In a quandary as to how to act responsibly upon the opportunities before them with such a shortage of missionaries and funds, in 1905 the mission considered the possibility of transferring its work in Aomori and Morioka to the German Reformed Japan Mission.[97] Furthermore, with no relief in sight, the relationship with the work on the Boso Peninsula was cut off completely in 1906. Yoshioka, the pastor there, was dismissed and urged to find other work, and the believer groups were turned over to the Episcopal mission.[98]

Booth remarked, "The application of the 'cut' every year reminds me of the man who cut his dog's tail off an inch at a time so that it would not hurt him so much."[99] The cuts continued. In 1905 mission treasurer Wyckoff wrote, "I am just now struggling to cover the little foot of our evangelistic work with the smaller stocking of appropriations, and so far as I can see at present some of the toes will have to stick out in the cold."[100] He later noted that without more money from the board, some

---

95    FSS to HNC, Apr. 2, 1902.
96    FSS to HNC, July 1, 1902.
97    MNW to JLA, Apr. 6, 1905.
98    ERM to HNC, Aug. 16, 1906.
99    ESB to HNC, Jan. 27, 1903.
100    MNW to JLA, March 10, 1905.

Japanese evangelistic workers would have to be let go, because higher prices after the Russo-Japanese War made it absolutely imperative that workers' salaries be increased. Wyckoff added, "I suppose one can bring himself to part with some of his fingers, if it must be done, but it is hard to decide which ones must go."[101] Given this difficult situation, the mission began to consider the possibility of turning one of its fields over to others who might do justice to the possibilities.

The Reverend Douwe C. Ruigh (later known as David C. Royce, an Americanized form of his Dutch name) went to China in 1902 as a missionary serving with the Amoy Mission. He was married in 1904 and his wife, Christine, also became a member of that mission. However, Douwe became seriously ill with a persistent high fever, and the Ruighs went to Japan for his recuperation. Since it appeared that he could not tolerate the climate in China, in 1905 the board reappointed the Ruighs to the North Japan Mission. After a time of recuperation in the mountains at Karuizawa, the Ruighs spent a year in Tokyo, where he attended Matsuda's Japanese language school.[102] Ruigh toured the mission's work in the large Nagano field with Frank Scudder, and the northern fields centered in Aomori and Morioka with Oltmans, and stated,

> These two tours have given me a fairly comprehensive view of the evangelistic work, and still more of the needs, of the North Japan Mission. Would that God's people at home could see what we have seen and could realize how much of this history making and progressive people is still un-evangelized, then I am sure there would be no question of giving up one of our fields. Instead an extra effort would be made to supply both workers and means to thoroughly cultivate this great field. Much has been done in Japan, much is being attempted by the missionary body and the Japanese for which we ought to be profoundly grateful to God, but much remains to be done.[103]

In 1906 the Ruighs were assigned to Morioka, and Ruigh took charge of the northern field, including both Morioka and Aomori. Enthused about the potential for the work but concerned that the inadequate appropriations would limit the ability to respond to the opportunities, he commented, "The decision to maintain or at least

[101]    MNW to HNC, Nov. 17, 1905.
[102]    Douwe C. Ruigh to HNC, May 17, June 8, and July 31, 1905.
[103]    DCR to HNC, Oct. 24, 1905.

retain the field was perhaps more an act of faith than of judgment—faith in the Church that she would ultimately stand by us and give us sufficient support to carry on the work."[104] The Ruighs were happy in Morioka, and Miller, who had served there for fourteen years, reported, "The meetings are growing in attendance. The people are too [very] glad to welcome back the missionary."[105]

The mission's work in Morioka and vicinity prospered anew under Ruigh's leadership. A fine young Japanese pastor, Mr. Senoue, and two Japanese Bible women were his colleagues. A year after their move to Morioka, Ruigh could report:

> We now have four branch Sunday Schools. In these and in the main School there are considerably over three hundred pupils who <u>attend</u> regularly. The number of pupils enrolled is a little over three hundred and fifty, exclusive of the Bible classes which meet in our home and also exclusive of the Normal Class [teacher training class] conducted by the pastor....The two Bible Women who are helping us in this work are splendid teachers....The pastor in his normal class is doing fine work in teaching what and how to teach.[106]

Following their furlough in America, the Scudder family returned to Japan in 1904. They considered residing in Suwa, a city more centrally located for supervising the work of the mission in all of southern Nagano Prefecture. However, unable to find a suitable house there, their former Japanese house in Nagano City was repaired enough to make it livable. Besides oversight of the work in Nagano City, Scudder took up the task of itinerant evangelism. For example, during an eleven-day fall tour on his bicycle, he conducted eleven meetings at seven places. Besides preaching to more than one thousand people on this tour, he had many profitable personal encounters.[107] In addition to the work in Nagano City, Scudder gave oversight and encouragement through evangelistic touring to the widely scattered evangelists and Bible women working for the mission. By the end of 1905, the work in Nagano City, with Pastor Kimura as colleague, was flourishing once again. Scudder himself, despite suffering from a chronic sore throat, besides his larger work of oversight and itineration, was teaching four Bible classes and meeting with numberless enquirers and callers.

---

104    DCR to HNC, Jan. 2, 1906.
105    ERM to HNC, Oct. 31, 1906.
106    DCR to HNC, June 11, 1907.
107    FSS to JLA, Nov. 15, 1904.

The Scudders' third child was born December 3, 1905, and mother and child were well.[108] However, four months later Wyckoff reported, "Mrs. Scudder is in the hospital at Tsukiji [in Tokyo] and has today had an operation to remove an ulcerous growth in her breast. Fortunately, no signs of cancer were found, and the operation so far as can be known at present is successful and without reason to expect bad results of any kind."[109] She appeared to be recovering, but eleven days later she was taken with nausea and a persistent high fever.[110] Florence Scudder died April 23, 1906, at the age of thirty-two, in the ninth year of her missionary service. She left behind two elementary-aged children, her four-month-old daughter, and a devastated husband.

Frank and the children stayed temporarily with the Wyckoff family in Tokyo, but after several months Scudder returned to his work in Nagano. A wet nurse provided nourishment for the baby, and household help covered some of the childcare. However, Florence had not only managed the household but also home-schooled the older children. All of this became Frank's responsibility, on top of his regular work. He continued teaching four Bible classes and three singing classes each week and provided supervision and encouragement to the evangelistic workers.[111] However, it became impossible to keep going, and, although he was very sorry to leave Nagano, Scudder moved to Tokyo at the end of the year. He and the children moved in with the Oltmans family, Alice Oltmans taught his children along with her own, and Scudder was assigned to teach at Meiji Gakuin.[112] This appeared to be a workable solution until other issues made Scudder's situation impossible.

According to mission board policy, after several months Scudder's salary was reduced to that of an unmarried missionary. Despite the strictest economy, he was going into debt. Furthermore, the Oltmans family was leaving for a furlough, and there was no way to educate the children. With great regret, after only ten years in Japan, Scudder resigned from the mission. Although the board reconsidered the salary issue, when Scudder was called by the Hawaiian Evangelical Association to work among the Japanese in Hawaii, he accepted the invitation. He could continue to work among Japanese people, and he decided that it was the best for his children. Scudder left for Hawaii in September of

---

108   FSS to HNC, Dec. 20, 1905.
109   MNW to HNC, Apr. 5, 1906.
110   MNW to JLA, Apr. 20, 2006.
111   FSS to HNC, Oct. 18, 1906.
112   FSS to HNC, Jan. 21, 1907.

1907, taking with him not only his children but also little Ruth's wet-nurse.[113]

In the interior fields of the North Japan Mission—the regions of Aomori and Morioka, northern and southern Nagano Prefecture, and Mishima and the Izu Peninsula—doors appeared to have opened for evangelism as never before. However, the force of evangelistic missionaries had been seriously depleted. Not only had Verbeck died, but the Harrises, Deyo, and the Scudders had gone, and both Ballagh and Miller were aging and no longer in good health.

Under these circumstances, in 1907 the mission conferred with representatives (Uemura and Kiyama) of the *Dendo Kyoku* (domestic mission board) of the Japanese church with regard to the future of the mission's work in Nagano Prefecture. The mission proposed turning over its work in Nagano, Matsumoto, Suwa, Sakashita, and Iida to the care of the *Dendo Kyoku*, the mission providing gradually decreasing financial grants for their support. This plan was acted upon from March of 1907.[114] However, a few months later, due to an ongoing discussion on the nature of the cooperative relationship between the missions and the Japanese church, the plan of turning over the Nagano work to the *Dendo Kyoku* with financial support from the mission was rescinded.[115]

Ruigh wrote of his concern for the undermanned condition of the mission.

> In regard to the future of our mission, unless the board is in a position, financially and otherwise, to furnish at once the reinforcements asked for it seems to me that it would be wiser to close the evangelistic work here in the North and make the North Japan Mission a purely educational Mission. If this were done and the evangelistic strength, the little remnant that remains, be transferred to the South Japan Mission both Missions would, in my judgment, be greatly strengthened and put in a position to do better and more effectual work.[116]

Such a radical proposal was not likely to be welcomed by the senior members of the North Japan Mission, Ballagh, Miller, and Winn. They had given the best years of their lives to the development of the far-flung evangelistic and church-planting work of the mission. Yet, it

---

[113]  It was a comfort that Scudder had family in Hawaii, cousin Doremus Scudder, pastor of Central Union Church in Honolulu. FSS to HNC, May 27 & July 20, 1907.

[114]  ERM to HNC, Jan. 18, Feb. 26, and Apr. 2, 1907.

[115]  North Japan Mission Minutes, Aug., 1907.

[116]  DCR to HNC, July 6, 1908.

was clear that the personnel and funds available to the mission were completely inadequate to meet the opportunities and challenges in the regions where evangelistic work had been undertaken.

A letter over the signatures of Ballagh, Miller, Wyckoff, and Ruigh stated that the three evangelistic missionaries were not half enough to oversee the work under the mission's care. And it noted that there had never before been "such a wealth of opportunity to spread the Gospel. In every one of our fields the permanent residence of a foreign missionary would be welcomed, and the Christians would be greatly encouraged and strengthened by his presence, not to mention the evangelists."[117] Specifically, Japanese Christians and the mission were requesting the residence of missionary families, one each at Mishima and Aomori, and at least two in Nagano Prefecture, as well as three more women missionaries for evangelistic work. The letter went on to state, "If these demands cannot be met by us [the Reformed Church], then it is manifestly our duty to withdraw from such parts of the country as we can not properly evangelize."[118]

Another noteworthy event occurred in Aomori, the northernmost evangelistic center of the mission's work. In May of 1910 a great fire virtually wiped out the city of Aomori. Within two-and-a-half hours, everything but a few houses on the edges of the city was burned up. Fortunately, there was little loss of life, but almost nothing was saved. Houses, public buildings, businesses, and all three Christian churches were lost. The Christians and the evangelist working for the mission, Yamaguchi Shokichi, had lost all or most of their earthly possessions, but they continued the ministry, living and holding meetings in temporary quarters until the church and parsonage could be rebuilt.

As of the end of 1910, the Japanese in the employ of the North Japan Mission included four ordained ministers, five licensed evangelists, and several lay Bible women, who carried on outreach ministries with the missionaries in twenty-three small churches and outstations and numerous branch Sunday schools. A list of the missionary personnel at the end of 1910 and a map showing the extent of the mission's work clarifies the realities.

Evangelistic missionaries and their places of residence:

- James H. Ballagh – Yokohama
- E. Rothsay Miller – Tokyo
- M. Leila Winn – Morioka

---

[117]  ERM to HNC, Jan. 9, 1909.
[118]  ERM to HNC, Jan. 9, 1909.

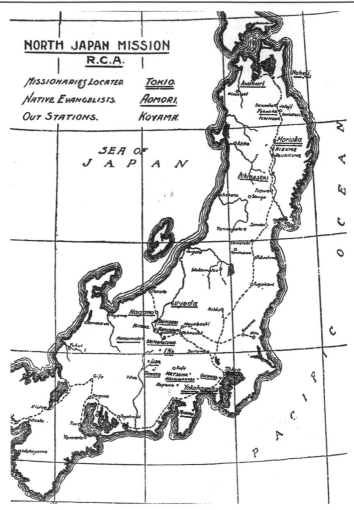

The area of Japan served by the North Japan Mission in 1910, showing the locations of missionaries, evangelists, and outstations

Educational missionaries and their places of residence and work:

· Eugene S. Booth – Yokohama, Principal, Ferris Seminary
· Anna Thompson, Julia Moulton, Jennie Kuyper – Yokohama, Ferris
· Albert Oltmans – Tokyo, Meiji Gakuin Theological Department
· Martin N. Wyckoff, Walter E. Hoffsommer, Douwe C. Ruigh – Tokyo, Meiji Gakuin

Associate missionaries (wives), who worked in education and/or evangelism as able:

- Anna Wyckoff, Emilie Booth, Christine Ruigh, Grace Hoffsommer
- Alice Oltmans – in America for education of children

CHAPTER 8

# The South Japan Mission: 1889-1916

As noted earlier, for twenty-eight years beginning in 1889 Reformed Church mission in Japan was carried out through two separate missions. The evangelistic work of the South Japan Mission was confined to the island of Kyushu, and it was the only mission cooperating with the Church of Christ in Japan working on most of the island, with its population of seven million people. The years of separate existence were years of fruition and fulfillment for the South Japan Mission, but for several years it was also a period of frustration, conflict, and disappointment.

## Evangelistic Outreach in Kyushu

In southwestern Japan, distant from the centers of political and economic power and social change, a delay in the impact of both the earlier westernization process and the later new nationalism was apparent. Excerpts from Demarest's report of his first evangelistic tour after returning from a furlough for his wife, Annie's, health pictures the Kyushu environment and realities of evangelism there in 1889.

I have now been entirely over my field and am rather surprised at the growth of the work. In many places the new faces outnumbered the familiar ones, and in all the work seemed to be going on very well—possibly with the exception of Saga....I took two separate journeys to go over the field—one to the north[1]...the other to the south visiting Kagoshima and Miyakonojo....

I started out on my first journey Dec. 27, '89, just six weeks after landing in Nagasaki....After a pleasant trip of twenty-two hours [by ship] Mr. Segawa & I arrived at Shimonoseki and took breakfast at the "Kimparo," a hotel kept by a member of our Shimonoseki Church. After this we crossed Shimonoseki Straits in a small steam-tug to Kokura where we took *jinrikisha* for Nakatsu. It was a cold windy ride of thirty-five miles but our men pulled it in a little over seven hours. The next day being Sunday we met our Christians, some of whom had come over five miles through the rain. Nor was this an unusual thing for these people to do, as they are always in their places Sunday morning if the road can be traveled—they generally walk both ways. Mr. Segawa took both services that day. The next day we separated, Mr. S going to Kurume to join in the effort to abolish the licensing of prostitute quarters....

About ten o'clock I took *jinrikisha,* but after two hours ride we ran into a hard storm and were glad to reach Tateishi at 5:30 P.M. and spend the night. This is twenty-two miles from Nakatsu and the last stopping place before climbing Hiji Mountain. That climb was left for the next day and were very glad to find on arising.... prospects of clearing. In the afternoon the sun struggled through and from the summit of Mt. Hiji gave me a beautiful view.

The beautiful blue bay surrounded by high hills lay directly at our feet 3500 feet below, and the houses of Hiji were seen shining in the sunlight two miles away, and the road thither wound around and around with many abrupt bends. We were very glad that the rain had softened the road [slowing the wheels of the *jinrikisha*], otherwise our descent would have been rather dangerous.

At Hiji I met Mr. Munakata who had been spending his holidays working here. He graduates from our theological department next June. He had for four successive nights given public lectures on Christianity to audiences increasing from

---

[1]     To Nakatsu, Usagun, Hiji, Kurume, Saga, Karatsu, and Sasebo.

100 to 200 & 300. I arrived Dec. 31st and that night answered some objections to Christianity which had been propounded the night before. Of the one thousand inhabitants of Hiji over 350 were present and gave us a very attentive and respectful hearing, though I believe I am the first foreigner who ever spoke to them. Before the meeting I examined and baptized a young man who had been led to Christ by the life and influence of a young woman at Hokkyoji, an outstation...[who] has been very diligent in telling her friends of Christ and as her father is the most wealthy & influential man of the Usa District, the people have quite a curiosity to learn what our Bible teaches....

The next morning our Christians assembled to partake of the Lord's Supper. We were just twelve believers and the service was somewhat remarkable from the fact that the ten Christians from Usa District came from six different villages. Of these the one from Hiji came 22 mi. through the rain the day before, while the others had come two to five miles that day....

This was my first visit to the Usa District and I was delighted with the people. The Christians although without any pastor meet in four villages, alternating, and every Sabbath, one of them acting as leader, they assemble, each bringing as many friends as possible. This gives us a good opening in four or five adjoining villages.... It is a grand opportunity for us and the field is so promising we hope to put Mr. Munakata in charge after his graduation next June.[2]

Sadly, these encouraging evangelistic tours by Demarest were his last. He returned to Nagasaki to find Annie seriously ill again. Her health had deteriorated, as she progressed from bronchitis to pleurisy and then to tuberculosis in both lungs. The doctor concluded she would not live if she remained in Nagasaki through the next rainy season. They left Japan in the spring of 1890.[3] However, before their departure from the field, Demarest reported the dedication of the Saga Church building on February 22, 1890. Designed by Stout, it included a main sanctuary said to accommodate 150 people and a tower with a small room to be used as a pastor's study or Bible study classroom. Demarest reported that the Japanese were pleased with the building, saying, "It is very simple and yet churchly." No missionaries attended

[2]   NHD to HNC, March 17, 1890.
[3]   Demarest served for twenty-two years as a Reformed Church pastor in Roxbury, New York.

the ceremonies, conducted by Japanese pastors Segawa, Tomegawa, and Nakamura, as well as Kurihara, the evangelist at Karatsu Church.[4]

Once again the plan for the evangelistic work of the South Japan Mission had to change. The Demarests were gone and Stout commented, "The condition of that department of our work, so long already with scarcely any superintendence, is really almost desperate." Someone else needed to assume this major responsibility.

Albert Oltmans, who had taught and served as principal at Steele Academy since his arrival in 1886, was appointed to evangelistic work by the South Japan Mission. Of this decision, Stout remarked, "We are persuaded that Mr. Oltmans has qualifications that fit him eminently for the work now proposed. To speak of nothing else the facility with which he acquires and uses the language seems to point him out as a man especially qualified to be an evangelist."[5] As a result of this change H.V.S. Peeke, the short-term teacher at Steele Academy, had to take over leadership at the boys' school for the time being. The mission once again pleaded for reinforcements, with the hope of eventually having three men and one woman engaged in evangelistic work.

Students of Steele Academy, not only those of the theological department but also some of the Christians in the academic department, took part in summer evangelistic outreach. Oltmans reported on his participation with them.

> I have just returned from visiting our students in their summer work. I think a great deal of good has been done. Especially at one place, Shimabara,...results are very promising. Quite a band of young men have been led earnestly to inquire the way of the Lord. Five of them have already expressed a desire to receive baptism. Among them are two of our students who live at Shimabara. At the house of the parents of one of them we had a preaching service....Not only the whole house but also the private yard was filled with quiet listeners...as many as three hundred. This for a meeting at a private dwelling, away from the city part and from all thoroughfares, is a very large audience. There were no chance listeners that happened to pass by and stop; all came with the definite purpose to hear Christian preaching, as it was advertised. An earnest request was made to have the work continued after the summer vacation.

---

[4]    NHD to HNC, Apr. 7, 1890. When the author began work as a cooperating missionary in Saga in 1961, this sanctuary was still in use, substantially unchanged.

[5]    HS to HNC, March 26, 1890.

Other places held similar efforts, but the men for the work are lacking. Earnest, faithful native evangelists is the great need. At Karatsu we had delightful meetings, and three received baptism after a very satisfactory examination. At other places baptisms are requested as soon as some ordained minister can come among them. The matter of traveling in the interior seems to become more difficult for us according to recent regulations. But if we can only have a sufficient number of native men trained for the work it will not so much matter.[6]

## Developments at the Mission Schools

Meanwhile, after Brokaw's departure from Sturges Seminary, under the leadership of Rebecca Irvine the girls' school was reorganized, with Irvine as principal and one of the teachers, Mr. Saito, as assistant principal. In the fall of 1889 the school's enrollment had shrunk to ten boarders and four day students. However, within a few months of the changes in leadership and organization the enrollment began to grow, with new students entering and unhappy students who had quit earlier asking to be readmitted. Irvine reported, "All this is an unlooked for success. The former prejudice existing against the school seems to have passed away, very much sooner than any of us had anticipated, and the future prospects of the school seem bright in spite of the reaction which has taken place in Japan the last year."[7] Both mission schools in Nagasaki were again understaffed. The mission sent urgent requests to the board not only for additional teachers but also for the appointment of another man for evangelism, and a woman to engage in evangelistic work, whose task would be to train and direct Japanese women in Bible work, especially through house-to-house visitation. This training and guidance of Bible women would of course require speaking ability in the Japanese language.

The South Japan Mission was at the same time negotiating with Presbyterian missionaries in Osaka about cooperating to develop the promising work in Kyushu, so long undermanned. The cooperation they were contemplating encompassed both educational and evangelistic work. The Presbyterian Church's West Japan Mission unanimously approved the proposal of the South Japan Mission and decided on the first of their missionaries to be sent to Kyushu. Communication also

---

6    AO to HNC, Sept. 8, 1890.
7    RLI to HNC, May 21, 1890.

took place between the Reformed and Presbyterian boards. However, while the Reformed mission board approved of the plan, the Presbyterian mission board balked and ultimately refused to allow it. The South Japan Mission was disappointed, and Presbyterian missionaries in Japan were not only disappointed but also embarrassed. In any case, the plan could not be realized.

In October 1890, Carrie B. Lanterman arrived to teach at Sturges Seminary. The mission had stressed how important it was that the new teacher for the girls' school be able to teach music. Consequently, there was some disappointment on the part of the mission upon learning that Lanterman, although a well-trained and experienced educator, had no musical ability. In any case, she entered the work, shared the English teaching responsibilities with Irvine, and taught calisthenics (physical education). Anna Stout, the nineteen-year-old daughter of Henry and Elizabeth Stout, returned in the summer of 1891 to live with her parents in Nagasaki after completing her studies in America. At the request of the mission, the mission board employed Anna, not as a regularly appointed assistant missionary like the older women, but as a part-time music teacher at Sturges.

The mission board also appointed a new couple for the South Japan Mission. The Reverend Albertus and Emma Pieters arrived in Nagasaki in September 1891, along with Anna Stout. Although he wanted to serve in evangelism, because of the need on the field Albertus Pieters was appointed to teach at Steele Academy. Peeke, with the assurance that his close friend and classmate at Hope College, Albertus Pieters, was coming to replace him at the school, had left Japan earlier in the summer after teaching three and a half years. He was eager to complete theological education and return to the South Japan Mission as a career missionary. Pieters began teaching the English courses for the preparatory and academic departments immediately, while Stout and Segawa taught courses in the theological department. During the ensuing year the mission board also responded positively to the request for a woman missionary to engage in evangelistic work. Sara Maria Couch was appointed to this new position, to arrive in the summer of 1892 to begin language study.

Meanwhile, the mission proposed major changes in the administration of the schools, which were approved by the mission board. A board of directors for each school, consisting of mission members, was formed. However, the role of principal at each of the schools was transferred to a Japanese Christian. Saito, who had served as assistant principal at Sturges Seminary, became its principal. The

Reverend Ohgimi Motoichiro, one of the two who had graduated from Hope College and New Brunswick Seminary, had come to Nagasaki to teach at the boys' school in the fall of 1890, and he took over the administration of Steele Academy in 1891. These changes were seen as an important step toward the time when the mission schools might become truly Japanese Christian schools.[8]

The change made in school administration was especially fortuitous for the girls' school. Saito proved to be a gifted and effective Christian leader at Sturges Seminary. Enrollment continued to grow. In contrast to the fourteen students in the fall of 1889, in November of 1891 there were forty-seven students. Eleven of these students were Christians and twelve more had asked for baptism. With Saito's leadership, the numerous comings and goings of the women missionary personnel that continued did not seem to impede the progress of the school. During the 1891-92 school year, there were briefly three missionaries, two of them full-time teachers and one a part-time music teacher.

However, in the summer of 1892 Irvine returned to America on leave to restore her health and did not return. Furthermore, tragically, on September 10, 1892, after an illness of but ten days, Carrie Lanterman died suddenly from complications of dysentery. She had served as a missionary teacher for less than two years. With Anna Stout, the part-time music teacher, as the only foreign teacher, the school faced a serious challenge. Sara Couch arrived in Nagasaki in October of 1892 and began language study in preparation for evangelistic work among women. Responding to the need at Sturges Seminary, she also taught English. The student body had grown to sixty-four students. Couch temporarily filled the gap until new women missionaries could be sent for teaching. This need was met with the arrival of Harriet M. Lansing and Martha E. Duryea in December, 1893.

Meanwhile, the mission had become increasingly certain that it had been a mistake to expect missionaries to be effective in their work at Sturges Seminary without language training. Proficiency in the Japanese language on the part of women members of the mission was seen as essential for effective work, whether they were involved in evangelistic work or teaching in a mission school, because the purpose of the school was not only education but also evangelism. Accordingly, when Stryker arrived as a missionary teacher to replace Duryea in 1897, she began language study along with part-time English teaching. However,

[8]   HS to HNC, Jan. 22, 1891.

Japanese study proved too much for Stryker, the stress causing intense and debilitating headaches. She wrote, "Japanese is very difficult for me and takes too much of my nervous force. The rest of my work I can do quite comfortably. I am afraid I am a disappointment to the Board, but not more so, I can assure you, than to myself. I know God sent me here, and so I can only believe that in some way or other He will make my being here a blessing to someone.[9] Stryker was excused from the language requirement, with the realization that her health would not likely permit a long career as a missionary, and she began to teach at Sturges full time.

With Stryker taking more responsibility at the girls' school, it became possible for Lansing to leave Nagasaki. Since the mission had concluded that the best way to learn Japanese was to study while living in the interior, away from the port city of Nagasaki, where many foreigners lived, in the summer of 1898 Harriet Lansing moved to Kagoshima for language study and a deeper immersion in the culture. Of her potential, Peeke remarked, "She is of Mohawk Dutch stock, and it shows....I will be greatly surprised if she does not become an effective all round worker as a result of a sojourn in the interior with all her time given to study."[10] As it turned out, Lansing remained in Kagoshima for many years, proving very effective in developing Sunday schools, working with women, and training Bible women.

The boys' school in Nagasaki seemed to be more affected by the general antiforeign reaction in Japan than the girls' school, as evidenced by a drop in enrollment in the lower classes at Steele Academy. Even so, during the four years after the new building was built and the school put on a firm footing in 1887, much good had been accomplished. Six students had already graduated from the theological department and were serving as evangelists, and eleven more were studying in that department. Of the forty-one students in the academic department in the spring of 1891, eleven were Christians and seven were awaiting baptism, and seven of the Christians were expecting to become ministers. Many students showed eagerness to engage in Christian work. Five theological students went on biweekly trips out from Nagasaki to Omura, Isahaya, and Shimabara to conduct preaching services. This involved riding in a *jinrikisha* for half a day on both Saturday and Monday, in order to serve all day Sunday. Furthermore, six boys from the academic department, four of whom planned to become ministers, were conducting Sunday schools at three different locations in Nagasaki every week.[11]

[9]    Anna K. Stryker to HNC, Sept. 12, 1898.
[10]   HVSP to HNC, Sept. 22, 1898.
[11]   HVSP to HNC, May 28, 1891.

Stout, Oltmans, and Pieters with theological students
in Nagasaki in 1893

After replacing Peeke and teaching four months at Steele Academy, Pieters spoke positively of what he had seen. "It is clear that the large number of theological students, about one fourth of the entire number, and the manly Christian life of the professed followers of Christ among the undergraduates is having an extremely good influence upon the school. We hope and pray that this favorable condition of affairs may continue."[12] Enrollment increased in 1892, with twenty-seven in the preparatory classes, thirty-two in the four-year academic department, and twenty-three in the theological department.[13] The large enrollment of students preparing for the ministry bode well for the plan of the mission to train men in Nagasaki and involve them in evangelizing southwestern Japan.

In 1892, the mission schools of the South Japan Mission also made name changes. The English name of the boys' school became Steele College, and it was given the Japanese name Tozan Gakuin— Tozan identifying its geographical location and Gakuin meaning educational institution. The girls' school retained its English name of Sturges Seminary and was given the Japanese name Umegasaki Jogakko—Umegasaki being its geographical location in the city and

12    Albertus Pieters to JWC, Jan. 23, 1892.
13    AP to HNC, Sept. 24, 1892.

Jogakko meaning girls' school. The mission requested a new man to teach at Steele College. Such an appointment would free Pieters from teaching responsibilities and allow him to study the language full time in preparation for fulfilling his hope of entering directly into a preaching ministry. Of Pieters's possible change, Stout said,

> He could then turn his attention to the evangelistic work, and, I am persuaded, would soon be able to do not a little in looking after it. This opinion has been formed more particularly because of the examination he passed in the language, at a session of our annual meeting last week. I must say that I was quite astonished at what he had been able to accomplish, especially in view of the regular work he has done in the school. Now, I do not pretend to say that he is prepared to go into the work in the field, and do all that should be done. But I do think he would be very useful in looking after the work in Oltmans absence, to say nothing of his being so much sooner prepared for thorough efficiency. And really, this kind of work is the crying need in our mission at the present time.[14]

Nevertheless, this goal of Pieters and the mission was not to be realized immediately. The mission had requested the appointment of two men, one for evangelism and one young man to teach. However, it became clear that the mission board in America had only enough resources to appoint one couple to the South Japan Mission. Peeke was completing theological training in the hope of an appointment for evangelistic work. Realizing that Peeke might be sent to a different field or not sent out at all, Pieters put the future of the South Japan Mission ahead of his personal desires. Pieters wrote.

> Now as far as I am concerned, if it is a choice between my going into the evangelistic work and Peeke coming to this mission I would by all means choose the latter. I am quite willing to remain where I am for an indefinite number of years and I am quite willing to sacrifice something for the sake of working along side of one in whom I have so much confidence. I do desire to study the language and prepare for preaching but if only one man can be sent out let it be Peeke for the field and not a stranger for the school.[15]

[14]    HS to HNC, Jan. 23, 1892.
[15]    AP to HNC, Jan. 24, 1893.

In the spring and summer of 1893, once again the possibility of cooperation in mission school education in southwestern Japan was raised. Plans were proposed for Steele College that encompassed not only union work with two other Japan missions but also the actual moving of the school away from Nagasaki to a new location. Although a small school, with its academic and theological departments Steele College was meeting the need for trained leadership for the churches and outstations of the mission on the island of Kyushu and had welcomed several theological students related to two Presbyterian missions. The proposed plan would enlist the partnership of these other members of the Council of Missions working in western Japan, the Presbyterian West Japan Mission, with its work in western Honshu, and the Southern Presbyterian Japan Mission, with its work focused on the island of Shikoku. However, since Nagasaki would not be a central location in the enlarged constituency field, it was proposed that the school be moved to a more convenient city. It appeared that there was some interest in union work in theological education on the part of these missions.

This proposal was strongly advocated by Ohgimi and Segawa, both employed by the mission for Steele College. It soon became clear, however, that their urging of the removal of the school from Nagasaki was not motivated purely by their concern for the future mission and prosperity of the school. Ohgimi and Segawa apparently assumed that the move away from the treaty port, the base for the South Japan Mission and its foreign missionaries, would facilitate the forming of a new administrative structure, one whereby "the control will naturally fall into their own hands." Ohgimi was clearly unhappy with the fact that mission members (missionaries) constituted the board of directors of Steele College, and he wrote a letter to the mission board stating his objections. Stout and Pieters were also surprised to learn that Ohgimi and Segawa favored introducing the teaching of Buddhism or Buddhist philosophy into the curriculum at Steele College.

The missionaries concluded that until Japanese Christians were able to demonstrate mature Christian leadership and contribute to the financial support of the school, the mission should retain supervision. Subsequently, the whole matter of union work in education was submitted to the mission board for consideration. The board did not sanction moving the college, and the movement for full-fledged union in mission education in western Japan faded away.

While Saito's fine leadership at Sturges Seminary provided stability for the girls' school, by the spring of 1896 it had become clear that Ohgimi's leadership at Steele College had proved detrimental to the school's progress. Oltmans explained.

> It has been found necessary to ask for the resignation of Rev. M. Ohgimi, President of Steele College. His connection with the institution has produced none of the benefits that were expected to result. The spiritual tone has not been deepened, its material prosperity has not been increased, it has not been brought into closer touch with its Japanese constituency, and its efficiency in scholarship has rather fallen. The low state of the school and the inefficiency of its head are common topics of conversation among the evangelists on the field....The students have for him neither love nor respect.[16]

Ohgimi resigned, and there appeared to be but one way forward for Steele College. Stout, Oltmans, and Peeke asked the mission board to appoint Pieters to the presidency of the college. Pieters's response was both understandable and admirable.

> I have always felt better at home in the pulpit than in the classroom, and still greatly prefer that kind of work. Nothing would suit me personally better than to have the Board at last grant my desire, and appoint me to the field, to reside in the northeast of Kiushiu.... My personal preferences are toward the proposal that I should enter the evangelistic work, but my opinion as a missionary of what the best interests of the work require, points in the opposite direction.[17]

Pieters took over as president of Steele College in the fall of 1896. A Christian foreign teacher named A. A. Davis, with experience teaching English in Japan, was hired to assist in the academic department. Under Ohgimi the college's enrollment had dropped, and Pieters began immediately to try to reinvigorate it. The mission hoped that not only enrollment but also Steele College's spiritual and academic quality would improve. Pieters was assured that if an appropriate Japanese leader could be found in the future, he might be permitted to enter the evangelistic work to which he aspired.

### Missionaries in the Interior

Missionary itineration into the interior of the island of Kyushu from their base at Nagasaki had remained the best way to do evangelistic

---

[16]    AO to HNC, Apr. 20, 1896.
[17]    AP to HNC, May 6, 1896.

outreach. Stout reported late in 1890, "The latest revised passports contain the following clause, 'Foreigners who travel on Passports are not allowed to permanently dwell in the houses of the Japanese in the interior.'"[18] Consequently, the missionaries found it necessary to apply for travel passports, and then to push the edge of legality in order to carry on this work.

The South Japan Mission, suffering such a long lack of sufficient personnel, had not experienced the great surge in church growth to the extent of other areas during the 1880s. On the other hand, it was apparently far enough away from the centers of power and influence not to be affected as immediately by the great reaction against Christianity that occurred in other parts of Japan from 1889. In some ways the mission seemed at long last poised to realize its objectives.

Signs of progress in evangelism and church growth continued. At Nagasaki Church, the preaching and pastoral care had been provided for by the mission, i.e., by the missionaries and Segawa Asashi, who worked for the mission as a teacher at Steele College in the theological department as well as assisting in itinerant evangelism. On November 2, 1890, Hirayama Taketomo was ordained and installed as pastor of Nagasaki Church, with primary support from the congregation.[19] On April 18, 1891, Kurihara Kenmei was ordained and installed as pastor of Matsuura Church in Karatsu. This church, which had its beginning seven years earlier through the itinerant monthly preaching of Kurihara when he was resident evangelist at Saga, had very early demonstrated a spirit of self-reliance and was endeavoring to be self-supporting. There was also evidence of vitality and growth in the work in Saga and Kurume.[20]

In the churches and outstations connected with the South Japan Mission, the report for 1891 indicated sixty-four baptisms for the year and forty-four more candidates for baptism. In the following months, in Oita Prefecture, there were six baptisms at the new outstation in Hiji and the first three baptisms in Toyotsu. Another young man there desired baptism, but it was deferred because of the "enmity of his relations," a not uncommon situation. On March 6, 1892, Nagasaki Church rejoiced in the addition of twenty-three new members, fifteen by adult baptism, three by confession of faith, and five by infant baptism.[21] When Nagasaki Church celebrated the sixteenth anniversary

18    HS to HNC, Nov. 28, 1890.
19    HS to HNC, Nov. 3, 1890.
20    AO to HNC, Apr. 30, 1891.
21    AP to JWC, March 12, 1892.

of its organization in December of 1892, it had grown to a membership of 233.

The work of the Reformed Church through the South Japan Mission was bearing fruit. By December of 1892, beginning with Segawa, fourteen men had been taught and trained and sent out to proclaim the gospel. Besides Nagasaki Church, there were twelve young churches and preaching stations where these pastors and evangelists were working. In the words of Pieters, "With the outstations, there are no less than thirty places under our auspices where the Word is regularly preached."[22] And by the spring of 1893, there were twenty men who had received their theological training in Nagasaki.[23]

In 1893 Henry Stout drew attention to an area of mission activity that no one had as yet addressed. He wished to begin a ministry among the outcasts of Japan, then known as the *eta* and in the twentieth century called the *burakumin*. These outcast people, though ethnically no different from other Japanese, were treated as subhuman and not only looked down upon but discriminated against and forced to live in isolation from the rest of Japanese society. Their occupations were limited to tasks such as slaughtering animals and working with leather, which were associated with Buddhist taboos. Stout appealed for funds to begin ministry among them, but there was no response, and Pieters took up the cause, writing,

> Their condition is truly pitiable and their need of the Gospel very great. We are very sorry no response has come to Mr. Stout's appeal. These people really ought to be reached and no Protestant missions are paying any attention to them at present. I ask permission, therefore, to do some private soliciting for this cause. Some friends in the West said to me before our departure that I should appeal to them if anything special were needed. How they will come up to their pledges I do not know but would like to try....I will even promise to ask not more than three men to contribute together the one hundred dollars needed. I hope to get it from one man.[24]

Later in the year Pieters reported that a Mr. Hospers had agreed to provide the one hundred dollars for work among the outcasts, and that the mission was seeking a suitable man for that work.[25] In January

22    AP to HNC, Dec. 14, 1892.
23    AP to HNC, May 27, 1893.
24    AP to HNC, Jan. 24, 1893.
25    AP to HNC, Dec. 12, 1893.

of 1896, Oltmans reported that ministry among these outcasts was actually being carried out at Usabara in Oita district by an evangelist of the mission named Tokunaga. This effort continued for about five years, but was ultimately discontinued. The mission reported that "it seems impossible to make any impression."[26]

During the first thirty years of Reformed Church mission activity in Japan, both the financial support of the work and its personnel came primarily from its churches in the eastern United States. During the 1890s this situation began to change as the so-called "western" churches (actually located in the Midwest and made up of fairly recent Dutch immigrants) grew and became engaged in world mission. In regard to denominational publications, Pieters drew attention to the fact of a language problem that restricted communication, and consequently support, and remarked,

> The last report of General Synod shows in the five Dutch classes of Dakota, Grand River, Holland, Iowa, & Wisconsin a total of 8442 families. It is safe to say that the heads of one half these families <u>cannot</u> read the *Christian Intelligencer* or the *Mission Field* on account of the language and that three fourths of them <u>do not</u> read the *Intelligencer*. It seems to me therefore that it would be a good thing if all official reports, appeals, statements etc. from the Board were published in *De Hope* [in Dutch] as well as in the *Intelligencer*.
>
> Arrangements could easily be made with the editors to reproduce such information in Dutch.[27]

The Reformed Church's South Japan Mission, in contrast to the situation of its North Japan Mission, bore almost exclusive responsibility for mission work related to the Church of Christ in Japan on the island of Kyushu, with its seven million people. However, this was not due to an exclusivist mentality. Stout and his colleagues were not only open to working with others, they repeatedly sought the cooperation and partnership of the other missions in the Council of Missions, especially the West Japan Mission of the Presbyterian Church and the Southern Presbyterian Japan Mission. However, with the exception of some temporary teaching help at Steele College, the educational and evangelistic work on the island of Kyushu continued to be the responsibility of the South Japan Mission.

[26]    HS to HNC, July 14 and Nov. 11, 1899.
[27]    AP to HNC, Jan. 24, 1893.

The Reverend Harman Van Slyck Peeke, having completed theological training, returned to Nagasaki and the South Japan Mission September 7, 1893, accompanied by his new wife, Vesta. Immediately, a step was taken toward Stout's long-cherished vision of placing missionaries in the interior to supervise the increasing number of young Japanese evangelists. The mission was concerned about what Pieters described as "the un-shepherded condition of our evangelistic work" as a serious drawback to progress.[28] It was arranged, therefore, that the Peekes reside during much of the year in Kagoshima. Peeke was to continue his language studies there, and he also would itinerate among the several churches and outstations in southern Kyushu. Pieters and Peeke went down to Kagoshima, found a house to rent that could be easily adapted for westerners, and within two weeks Harman and Vesta Peeke had moved to Kagoshima.[29] Consequently, in the fall of 1893, thirty-four years after Verbeck first arrived in Nagasaki, for the first time missionaries of the South Japan Mission actually resided in the interior, away from the treaty port. Kagoshima and Miyakonojo were cities within Peeke's new field where evangelists of the mission were already working, and ministry was being carried out at additional outstations in the region, for which Peeke would also have supervisory responsibility.

The Oltmans family returned to Western Michigan for a furlough in 1893 and were ready to return to their work in Kyushu in the summer of 1894. Their return to the field was postponed several months, however, due to the dangerous international situation in Asia. The trouble was armed conflict on the Korean peninsula, only a hundred miles from Nagasaki. This "dangerous international situation" affected the progress of mission work in ways large and small. For example, a Presbyterian missionary to Korea, W. L. Swallen, took refuge in Nagasaki during the fighting in Korea. He taught temporarily at Steele College while away from his own field. The Oltmans family, after a delay of several months and despite the ongoing conflict, returned to Nagasaki November 1, 1894.

The fact that Japan was engaged militarily nearby did not stop the mission from pressing ahead, nor did Japan's continued restrictions on the movement and interior residence of foreigners. The Peekes already resided in Kagoshima much of the year to work in the surrounding southern region of Kyushu. Upon the return of the Oltmans, another

---

[28]    AP to HNC, Nov. 18, 1893.
[29]    AP to HNC, Sept. 23, 1893.

step was taken in implementing the plan for evangelism. It was decided that they should be based in Saga, to provide supervision and encouragement for pastors and evangelists in the northern part of Kyushu. Oltmans wrote: "The people at Saga are trying to make the necessary passport arrangements for us to live there. A house has been rented, which is being readied for us. The prospects are that sufficient freedom of travel for my evangelistic work will be granted under the passport. We may be able to move this spring."[30] The Oltmans family did move to Saga in the spring of 1895.

**Efforts amid Instability**

Elizabeth Stout, though frequently ill and apparently unable to regain robust health, participated actively in the work in Nagasaki. Pieters said of her, "In spite of it all, however, she keeps up her Saturday morning Bible class for the women, and teaches a class from the theological seminary in Christian evidences."[31] Henry and Elizabeth Stout had returned to their homeland for rest and recuperation only twice during their twenty-four years in Japan. Elizabeth's bouts with illness gradually became more frequent (influenza, bronchitis, pneumonia, dysentery, and chronic sciatica), leaving her in chronically delicate health. Her doctor recommended an extended furlough in America.[32] The Stouts began to plan to take such a furlough from May of 1894, but the needs of the mission dictated the timing. Actually, Stout was very concerned about the situation in the mission and hesitant to leave at that time.[33]

As it turned out, Elizabeth's health improved, at least temporarily, and the Stouts returned to America in May of 1895. By that time it had been arranged that the Reverend R. B. Grinnan of the Southern Presbyterian Mission would come to teach in the theological department during Stout's absence. Furthermore, the Reverend Aoyama, a Japanese minister associated with the West Japan Mission of the Presbyterian Church, was sent to teach at Steele College. Consequently, while union in mission school education was never realized in western Japan, a measure of cooperation with these two Presbyterian missions was a great help to the work there for a time.

At first, the reaction against Christianity that began in 1889 did not seem to affect the work of the South Japan Mission significantly.

---

[30]   AO to HNC, Feb. 22, 1895.
[31]   AP to HNC, Nov. 18, 1893.
[32]   HS to HNC, Feb. 22, 1894.
[33]   HS to HNC, May 5, 1894.

However, signs of discouragement gradually appeared. In 1893 Pieters reported,

> The stations seem to be holding their own. But that is only a negative blessing. We are longing for progress. There are, indeed, sporadic cases in which the Holy Spirit's power and influence are plainly seen, and these cause us to thank God and take courage; but as a general thing, throughout our work on this island, there can be felt a sluggishness and coldness, which seem to indicate that the fires of spiritual life and zeal in the hearts of our evangelists (and perhaps also of the missionaries!) are burning low.[34]

Pieters continued to entertain the hope that he might be released from teaching English at Steele College and enter into the work of itinerant preaching and encouragement of the evangelists. The mission hoped to have two men teaching at Steele and three men to preach and encourage the many inexperienced pastors at the increasing number of preaching stations and outstations.

Japan had gradually expanded its economic interests in East Asia and had begun to flex its military muscles. Rivalry between China and Japan over control of Korea and commercial interests there had led to armed conflict, known as the Sino-Japanese War, which lasted from July of 1894 to April 17, 1895. In this conflict Japan destroyed the Chinese navy and captured several of China's cities. The Treaty of Shimonoseki brought hostilities to an end, granted Korea independence from China, ceded the island of Taiwan to Japan, and awarded Japan an indemnity payment of $150 million. This defeat weakened China, but in Japan the victory encouraged militarism and fanned the flames of nationalism.

With the arrival of the two women to teach at Sturges Seminary, Sara Couch, who had temporarily served as a teacher at the girls' school, was freed to take up the work for which she had come to Japan. It was arranged that not only the Oltmans family, but also Couch would reside in Saga. For the time being at least, Saga became the center for Couch's work in evangelism, as she trained Bible women to partner with her in mission to women. A house was rented, and she moved in September of 1895. Her plan was to have the Japanese Bible women she was training live in the same house with her.[35] The mission asked for another woman to assist in this new venture.[36]

---

34    AP to HNC, Nov. 18, 1893.
35    AO to HNC, Sept. 28, 1895.
36    AP to HNC, July 3, 1896.

As a next step in implementing its plan of evangelism, the South Japan Mission restructured, dividing the work into three stations based in Kagoshima, Nagasaki, and Saga. Each station was given a measure of autonomy, but engaging and dismissing native workers remained the prerogative of the mission. The new plan and rules for the function of the stations were communicated to the pastors in the field, and the long-term goal of the mission stated as follows.

> The first and chief aim of the mission—very much in common with other Protestant missions throughout the world—is to establish a church, and then by close and sympathetic association with those in the church, to foster it, till it shall become independent and give promise of stability in itself and of efficiency to do its part, with other churches, in the great work of evangelizing the land.
>
> In order to this, the missionary is a necessity. He has to be a teacher and leader at first, everything depending upon him, and then an advisor to and cooperator with the church, but in the end he must disappear. We are already at the beginning of a transition period between mission work pure and simple, and ultimate pure church work....The important thing is to adjust matters for the transition.[37]

The mission's plan called for three male missionaries to focus on evangelism. However, without the appointment of a new person to teach the English classes at Steele College, Pieters could not be released for his role as the third man. Both the mission and Pieters himself repeatedly pleaded to the board to send someone for the teaching position.[38] Pieters wrote, "Now if there is any reasonable hope that after one, two, or even three years, the Board will be able to grant us this solution, the best thing will be to wait for it. This I shall in such a case gladly and patiently do." However, Pieters went on to suggest that if he could not be released from teaching English to fulfill his calling to preach the gospel in Kyushu reasonably soon he would need to ask for a transfer to another field, such as India, China, or the North Japan Mission.[39] At the same time, Pieters's own words reveal his evangelistic passion for Kyushu.

> With all my heart I echo the prayer that "some way out" may be found. If I understand the situation at all, our wants will not stop

---

[37]   AP to HNC, April 13, 1895.
[38]   AO to HNC, Jan. 2, 1895.
[39]   AP to HNC, Jan. 22, 1895.

with three men in the field. My thoughts have lately turned to the great islands of the Goto and Amakusa lying right at our doors, visible on a clear day from the hill-tops that overlook Nagasaki. In these islands live at least a hundred thousand men, and there is no one to tell them a word about the Gospel....The question presses itself upon me. "What is to be done for Amakusa? What is to be done for the Goto?"...

We hear a great deal about the profound problems presented by work in Japan....But the one that overshadows all in Kiushiu is simple. Given 6,000,000 people who know nothing of Christ, and are dying without him, how shall we bring the good news to every ear in the shortest span of time?[40]

In Kagoshima, while continuing language study, Peeke gave oversight to five Japanese pastors and evangelists working at his station. Each of these workers, graduates of the theological department at Steele College, occupied one of the outstations and served two additional preaching places. As missionary in charge, Peeke gave oversight and encouragement to these men, but also paid their salaries, since they were under the employ of the mission.

Such a life necessarily involved a lot of travel, for Peeke not only visited native evangelists, he also needed to go to Nagasaki for mission business and family health care and to attend meetings there and elsewhere. In 1895 there was neither public transportation nor any real roads in southern Kyushu. Peeke reported that he traveled not only by steamboat, river skiff, *jinrikisha*, packhorse, and on foot, but also as much as sixty-five miles in one day by bicycle.[41] Peeke's work plan alternated extended periods of study and preparation at home in Kagoshima with trips further into the interior of six weeks to three months, visiting and working with all the preachers under his care. Extended trips of course affected the missionary family left at home. A humorous comment by Peeke hints at what the missionary wife had to contend with when her husband brought home "unwanted guests." "Fleas are the bane of my wife's existence, and I have been liming and carbolicing for two days [spreading lime and carbolic acid]. If the fleas bother your wife, she does not sleep well, and will likely make it hot for you the next day. I say 'Down on the fleas.'"[42]

After several years' experience, Peeke still found preaching in Japanese very challenging. But at the same time he pointed to a problem

---

40    AP to HNC, March 12, 1895.

41    HVSP to HNC, Apr. 11, 1895.

42    HVSP to HNC, Sept. 8, 1896.

often felt by the missionaries, the tendency for Japanese preachers to be too intellectual. I quote: "There is one thing that ought to be a continual source of encouragement to us foreigners, tho we often overlook it. I refer to the fact that nine-tenths of the preaching of the natives goes entirely over the heads of everything but the more than passably educated. The women and unlettered get but little."[43] Peeke observed that three years' study of the Japanese language should result in the ability to preach acceptably in the language. And he commented, "I will be very glad when Pieters gets his chance, for he can learn more in one year than I in two. He has a splendid mind, and will no doubt be our theological teacher some day, or at least he ought to be. For clearness of expression and thinking he is very hard to beat."[44]

Although the circumstances of the South Japan Mission did not permit Pieters to leave Steele College and enter into direct evangelism as he desired, he initiated a creative means to assist in that work that would seem to substantiate Peeke's judgment of him. Pieters modestly told of his new project.

> From time to time slight references have been made in my letters to a little sheet sent out to our evangelists. This was at first my private undertaking, and was sent free to all our preachers. Last month it assumed permanent form as the *Chinzei Dendo Geppo* (*Chinzei* being the name of the chukai or classis, and *Dendo Geppo* meaning evangelism monthly), to be a monthly magazine of news and theological discussion. Mr. Segawa and I are joint editors....It is a very little thing of ten pages, and boasts no great ambitions. But we hope it may serve as a medium of communication between the workers and help keep up an interest in study after young men leave the theological school. It has 25 subscribers at 50 sen a year, which, of course, does not suffice to pay the cost of publication, which is paid by the editors. It is to contain contributions by Japanese and foreigners, both originally written in Japanese and translated, the only rule being that nothing is to be copied from any other paper in print. If the sheet is to remain small, it shall at least be original.[45]

In January of 1896, Albert Oltmans began a very significant new venture in connection with the Saga station, which he called his "Winter

---

[43]    HVSP to HNC, Sept. 8, 1896.
[44]    HVSP to HNC, Apr. 11, 1895.
[45]    AP to HNC, Apr. 13, 1895.

Bible School." Pieters described this pioneering example of continuing education for pastors.

> Mr. Oltmans opened the year with an enterprise that, so far as I know, is quite new in Japan....He has held a special Bible conference for the evangelists on his district. There are twelve men working under his superintendence, and two others so closely associated with our mission that they are always counted in when something of this kind takes place. All of these men have studied theology at Nagasaki more or less. Two of them are ordained. Almost all the rest have been examined by Classis, and have been licensed to preach. The great majority of laborers in Japan have this standing. These men are isolated in their Christian lives, most of them occupying points where few or no believers are found. The supply of books to aid them in Bible study is extremely limited, as only a few valuable religious works have yet been produced here. Even if they know enough English to use books and magazines published in that language, it does not help them much, for they are unable to buy such works. Under these circumstances it is not surprising that Mr. Oltmans cast about for some means to help them to keep up their interest in careful and systematic study of the Bible. His plan seems to have worked very well. He invited all these men to assemble at Saga for a week or more of Bible study. They all gladly accepted the invitation, and from Jan. 15th, spent nine days together with great interest and profit. The sessions began daily at 8:30 A.M., with a prayer meeting. After that some topic was taken up for discussion until half past eleven. Then a recess was had until two o'clock. The afternoon meetings closed at four. Every other evening was occupied by a sermon. The alternate evenings were left open for anything that might be suggested, which was frequently a continuation of the discussion of the afternoon. The following are some of the subjects treated. "Christ and John the Baptist," "The Kingdom of God and the Church," "Christ and His Apostles." Mr. Oltmans very wisely excluded discussion on speculative philosophical subjects and on practical questions, such as methods of work. The result was that the attention of all was fixed and kept concentrated on spiritual truth. Distinct spiritual blessings were enjoyed during the conference. Mr. Oltmans wrote in a letter to me: "Our Bible school was a success, according to the testimony of each one concerned in the matter. There were no long harangues,

or ventilating personal opinions. In this respect the school improved each day as we went on. Day by day the men became less talkative and more studious, less desirous to give and more desirous to receive. Their being together in the same hotel was a wonderful help in a supplementary way. They talked over the lessons of the day, and never, they said, retired before midnight. Not a man missed even the least part of a prayer meeting or Bible study. Certainly we have much reason for gratitude to God. My fears were wonderfully put to shame. Throughout the meetings, the Holy Spirit's presence and power were subjects of prayer, and these prayers were answered, I verily believe."[46]

Regarding this Winter Bible School, Oltmans reported, "As it was an experiment I did not feel free to ask mission money for it, but I was helped by a personal friend and by Miss Couch in bearing all the expenses of traveling and lodging, as the men were not able to pay for themselves. It is the expressed hope of all that this first attempt may not be the last."[47] In fact, the following year twenty-four male evangelists, three Bible women, and Peeke attended this Winter Bible School led by Oltmans,[48] and it became an annual event.

Another example of creative work by Oltmans may be seen in his joint preaching tour in 1897 with five Japanese evangelists of the northern part of Oltmans's field.[49] They held evangelistic meetings two nights each in public meeting places at these towns and cities during ten days. Oltmans and the evangelists took turns presiding and preaching, with multiple speakers at meetings of two hours or more. It was a joint seed-sowing effort that also provided mutual insights and encouragement.[50]

## Reassessment of the Evangelistic Vision

Stout's vision for evangelizing the people of Kyushu had been based on the principle of giving potential evangelists biblical and theological instruction in Nagasaki, interspersed with practical experience preaching and teaching the Bible there and on trips into the interior. Upon completion of this preparation, the men were sent to work at preaching stations and their outstations. On the one hand,

[46]  AP to HNC, March 14, 1896.
[47]  AO to HNC, Jan. 26, 1896.
[48]  AO to HNC, Jan. 23, 1897.
[49]  Evangelists serving in Oita, Hiji, Kitsuki, Usa, and Nakatsu.
[50]  AO to HNC, Apr. 12, 1897.

Albert Oltmans (center) and H.V.S. Peeke (on Oltmans's right) with participants in the Winter Bible School for pastors and Bible women

Stout had shown an admirable willingness to trust Japanese colleagues and entrust them with responsibility. On the other hand, he never lived away from Nagasaki and perhaps could not adequately grasp the difficulty the evangelists faced or adequately appreciate their needs. The evangelists were all first-generation Christians who had grown up in a totally non-Christian environment, and they were sent to plant churches where there were usually no more than a handful of new converts and inquirers.

As Peeke and Oltmans began to live in the interior, they experienced firsthand the challenges faced by these marginally prepared evangelists. They traveled extensively in their respective fields, giving assistance and guidance, and they believed that there was a limit to how many of these inexperienced evangelists they could adequately supervise. Pieters also shared their concern, commenting to the board secretary, "Experience shows that the ordinary native preacher is of comparatively little value unless he can have the help, instruction, and direction of a missionary. It is therefore useless to multiply such native agencies indefinitely, for you thereby spread the missionary out so far as to be almost incapable of doing any effective work. There is a distinct limit to the capacity of missionaries. So we come back again to the old cry, 'Send us more men.'"[51]

[51] AP to HNC, Feb. 22, 1897.

The three younger missionaries were putting forth their several efforts to deal with the situation of the evangelists. They struggled to find the best form of cooperation between the missionary and the evangelists. Pieters wrote, "But this does not mean that 'No native preacher is to be trusted out of sight of a missionary.' That is a misapprehension of our position. We stand squarely upon this proposition. Under ordinary circumstances, only so many evangelists should be employed by the mission as can be effectively cooperated with by the foreign missionaries." He added, "By cooperation we understand moral, mental and spiritual companionship quite as much as superintendence in the ordinary meaning of the term."[52]

There were some signs of progress in the form of new converts in the evangelistic work, not only at the outstations but also in Nagasaki. While many of those baptized at Nagasaki Church were students at the mission schools, and often not Nagasaki residents, there were exceptions. Pieters tells the story of one of several people baptized at Nagasaki Church late in 1895. Her story underscores the ongoing challenge of the work.

> One of them was a girl, less than twenty years old. This poor girl has suffered a great deal of persecution. She has a stepmother, who never liked her, and took occasion to give vent to her spite when the girl became interested in Christian things. Her father, who had always been very kind to her, also acted very harshly, and repeatedly struck her, a thing very uncommon in Japan. They called her "Yaso!", a term of contempt, a corruption of "Jesus." Her father tried kindness as well as severity, and when he found that he could not move her, threatened that if she were baptized he would disown her. Nevertheless she was publicly received into the church shortly before New Years, with a most tender and affectionate welcome by the pastor, Rev. A. Segawa. Forbidden to return home, she went to visit relatives at Sasebo. It is to be hoped and expected that this storm will blow over, and that she will be received back again, but then will come the harder task of living a Christian life in her own heathen home.[53]

When the Stouts returned to America in 1895, it must have been with a keen sense of relief and satisfaction. For the first two decades of their missionary career, Stout had often been the lone warrior of

---

[52]   AP to HNC, Apr. 2, 1899.
[53]   AP to HNC, March 14, 1896.

Nagasaki, struggling to establish the Reformed Church's work on the island of Kyushu. Now they could leave for a time feeling that many of their dreams and plans were being realized. While there were differences of opinion on some mission policies, three missionary families and three single women missionaries committed to the overall goals of the mission were faithfully carrying on the work, and Japanese Christians were in administrative positions in the two mission schools.

The Stouts extended the normal one and one-half year furlough, hoping for a more complete recovery of Elizabeth's health. During their absence, the younger men of the mission gave fine leadership to the growing number of evangelists and preaching places throughout Kyushu. The work of the Peekes in Kagoshima was brought to a halt temporarily when Harman contracted typhoid fever, and it took five months to regain his health and strength sufficiently to work at all. As he gradually recovered, however, he laid out his plan for the Kagoshima district, making use of literature and public meetings.

> I plan to have about three short, simple tracts, probably getting them up myself. One will be used as a sort of dodger to advertise a meeting, another will be given out at the meeting. The meeting will have two or three pointed addresses. This armament will be discharged at as many places as possible between March 15th and June 15th or later. The aim will be to put a short resume of the plan of salvation where many people will be able to read it, to tell that same thing to many people, to let many people know where the evangelist lives who can tell them more, and to leave a general impression that something has come that did not used to be here, and people will do well to find out what it is.[54]

In an effort to build up a sense of community between the pastors and evangelists in the field and the missionaries under whose leadership they were working, the South Japan Mission prepared an extensive memorandum and sent it out to each of them. It affirmed the goal of the mission's work, "the building up and strengthening of the Kingdom of our Lord Jesus Christ in this land, in cooperation with that part of His church which is known as the *Nihon Kirisuto Kyokai*." It described the various aspects of the mission's ministry in education and training as well as evangelism and church planting. The evangelistic work was divided into three districts—northern, western, and southern Kyushu—with eighteen stations and numerous outstations. Besides

[54]    HVSP to HNC, Dec. 28, 1897.

the missionaries, the personnel of the mission at that time included four ordained ministers, seventeen licensed preachers, and five Bible women.[55]

The Bible women were trained by and worked with Sara Couch, who was the first single woman in the mission to learn to speak Japanese well. Peeke, praising her Japanese, observed, "Our Japanese brethren have certainly no need to blush when she takes her turn to speak."[56] The mission was pleased to learn of changes by the board that gave more rights to the women missionaries. Amendments to the missionary manual distinctly gave "all ladies actively engaged in work under the mission the right to vote on all matters relating to Woman's Work," whether educational or evangelistic.[57] Later, at its annual meeting in the summer of 1900, the South Japan Mission went on record favoring all full-time women missionaries (but not wives) being given full voting rights in the mission.[58]

With Pieters as president of Steele College, enrollment in the academic department immediately began to increase (from thirty in 1896 to eighty in 1897),[59] but the theological department could not recover quickly. Whereas there were twenty-three theological students in the 1892-93 school year, by the fall of 1897 one regular student in the senior class was all that remained in the theological department. Grinnan taught theology in place of Stout for two years, but with the change of circumstances at the school keeping him in Nagasaki could not be justified, and he left for other responsibilities in his own mission in 1897. While he was in Nagasaki, Grinnan, a widower, had married Martha Duryea, a Reformed Church missionary at Sturges. The couple's departure from Nagasaki also created a shortage in the teaching staff at the girls' school. These developments could not help but be a source of concern for the South Japan Mission.

Unfortunately, by the spring of 1899, Peeke's health had deteriorated to the breaking point. His digestive tract had evidently never been robust, and digestive problems had become more acute since his bout with typhoid fever two years earlier. The stress and intense labor of five and one-half years of language study and itinerant evangelism took their toll. By chronic indigestion and nervous exhaustion his weight had dropped to 130 pounds, and his doctor,

55   AP to HNC, Jan. 31, 1898.
56   HVSP to HNC, Sept. 22, 1898.
57   AP to HNC, Apr. 19, 1897.
58   HS to HNC, Aug. 7, 1900.
59   AP to HNC, June 5, 1897.

feeling he was malnourished and in danger of contracting tuberculosis, prescribed immediate and complete rest at a "health resort." Before the end of March, the Peekes departed for America, Vesta and the children to Minneapolis to stay with her sister, and Harman to Battle Creek, Michigan, to restore his health at the Seventh Day Adventist sanitarium there.[60] Peeke responded to treatment, and the Peeke family returned to its work in Kagoshima in September 1900.

In September 1899, during the absence of the Peekes, the Pieters family moved to Kagoshima, Stout became acting president of Steel College in place of Pieters, and Charles M. Myers arrived to teach English at the school. Pieters was finally able to focus on Japanese language study, while giving some assistance in the evangelistic work in that region. It was a temporary arrangement, since the Pieters family was to leave for its first furlough in 1900, after nine years in Japan.

The delayed impact of the reaction against Christianity and all things Western had become apparent in Kyushu by the middle of the 1890s. During the extended furlough of the Stouts, the modest church growth that had continued for a time had stagnated. In 1899, even Henry Stout recognized the discouraging situation faced by the mission. During the previous year six evangelists had left the employ of the mission, for a variety of reasons. One or two were dismissed for ineptitude. One retired, and several resigned out of discouragement or poverty and debt from inadequate income. In fact, during the period following the Sino-Japanese War, a pronounced inflation had seriously affected the livelihood of the pastors. Their low salaries from the mission had not been increased, and expecting progress toward self-support was unrealistic, given the lack of church growth. In the hope of preventing a further loss of evangelists, the mission raised salaries somewhat, but it was limited by the budget cutting of the mission board that had gone on for several years.[61]

The missionaries were further distressed by word from the board that due to its critical financial situation, appropriations for 1900 would be radically reduced. The missionaries were appalled when advised that, while missionary salaries would remain the same, funds for the work would be reduced to 57 percent of the budget requested by the mission. This could only mean deep cuts in the salaries of already poverty-stricken evangelists, if not their dismissal. The mission pleaded for additional funds. Pieters wrote, "To close up our evangelistic work,

---

[60]    Dr. M. E. Paul to AP, March 2, 1899; AP to HNC, March 11, 1899; HVSP to HNC, March 6 and May 6, 1899.

[61]    HS to HNC, Nov. 11 and Dec. 23, 1899.

that is, to discharge our evangelists, would be to commit suicide as a mission. To shut up Steele College would be not exactly that, but would not be far from it. It would sacrifice the labor of years." In the event of no further monies from the board, the missionaries contemplated using part of their own salaries for the work, even though their modest salaries had remained the same for forty years, despite inflation and new taxes.[62] The mission cut work budgets to the bone and postponed necessary property maintenance.

Debate continued on what to do about the financial crisis. The board did not wish to recall one missionary temporarily and suggested abandoning one of the stations, perhaps Kagoshima. The missionaries strongly opposed this idea. Stout wrote, "We are therefore at our wits end to know what to do to help along in this matter of cutting down expenses....Whatever else may have to go, the sentiment of this mission is decidedly against eliminating any part of the evangelistic work. That is considered vital."[63] Stout lamented the Reformed Church having undertaken support of the Arabian Mission when it could not adequately maintain the missions already initiated in India, China, and Japan, saying, "I am persuaded that undertaking to gorge herself with Arabia, when she had her mouth already full, was one serious cause of the trouble,"[64]

When the Pieters family returned to the United States for furlough in the spring of 1900, Albertus began intensive itineration among all the churches in the Midwest, most of which were Dutch speaking. Being fluent in Dutch, Pieters hoped to build support for missions in these churches. During two-month and six-week trips, he visited almost all of the churches west of Chicago and the Great Lakes. Then he wrote to the board saying, "I am ambitious to speak in every Dutch speaking church in the denomination."[65] In subsequent itineration he aimed to speak in all the Chicago area churches, as well as all the churches in Michigan, and the Dutch-speaking congregations in Cleveland; Rochester, Marion County, Albany, and New York, New York; and Patterson, New Jersey.

Concerned about the threat of drastic budget cuts and ministry cutbacks in the South Japan Mission, Pieters had voluntarily reduced his furlough salary, but it soon became apparent that funds were insufficient to send the family back to Japan, and it seemed the return to the field would be postponed. The fact of insufficient funds and

---

[62]  AP to Friend, Feb. 16, 1900.
[63]  HS to HNC, Feb. 20, 1901.
[64]  HS to HNC, Apr. 19, 1901.
[65]  AP to HNC, Nov. 6, 1900.

the board's decision not to send the Pieters family back in 1901 was published in the Reformed Church's *De Hope*, the Dutch-language magazine, and *Der Mitarbeiter*, the German-language publication. The result was protests and offers to raise the necessary funds.[66] With board approval, a subsequent movement among the western churches brought in enough contributions to permit the return of the Pieters family to Japan on schedule in the summer of 1901.[67]

Despite the grueling speaking schedule of that furlough, Albertus Pieters accepted the request of Western Theological Seminary to give a series of five lectures on missions. The themes of the lectures were as follows: (I.) the missionary purpose, i.e., "the Christianization of a country, defining this as the establishment of the institutions of Christianity in such a manner that practically the whole of each generation as it comes upon the stage of life will find itself in contact with the essential truths of the gospel"; (II.) the conditions under which this purpose is to be accomplished in Japan; (III.) the Japanese church as related to this purpose; (IV.) the educational problem as related to this purpose; and (V.) the missionary and the Japanese evangelist as related to this purpose.[68]

Meanwhile, after the return of the Peeke family to Japan and Kagoshima, Harman was once again in good health and good humor. He reported, "I am doing nicely as far as health is concerned....Last week I was out five days with three Japanese on our union Forward Movement. I rode 110 miles on my bicycle, walked ten, had pretty middling tough country hotels, native food, and fleas galore. Preached five times, made thirty or forty calls, distributed a few hundred tracts, got back Saturday at noon, and now on Monday morning am unconscious of having been putting forth any unusual exertion. (I resume after stopping to demolish a flea. The rascals can jump around a corner, making any angle they please during the jump. I just saw it done.)[69]

Anna Stryker, despite restful vacations in China, never achieved the robust health required for missionary service and returned to America at the end of 1900, after three and one-half years on the field. Sara Couch, who had returned to Nagasaki after a period of work in Saga, assumed the role of vice-principal of the girls' school, and Anna Stout increased her English teaching responsibilities.[70] However, Sturges Seminary was also affected by the budget limitations of the

66    AP to HNC, March 23, 1901. Pieters was approached by John Luxem, pastor of First Reformed, Muskegon, and Isaac Cappon, elder of Third Reformed, Holland.
67    AP to HNC, Apr. 27, 1901.
68    AP to HNC, Nov. 6, 1900.
69    HVSP to HNC, May 27, 1901.
70    HS to HNC, Dec. 11, 1900.

South Japan Mission. Principal Saito, a fine Christian leader and effective school administrator, had financial responsibility for his extended family and could not meet those obligations on his salary from the mission. Consequently, he resigned to assume a higher paid position in a government school. In his place, Hirotsu Tokichi, an evangelist trained by the mission, was brought in from the evangelistic work. He served as principal of the girls' school for many years.[71]

Following the return of the Pieters family to Japan in 1901, Albertus initiated Reformed Church evangelistic work in Kumamoto, the largest city in Kyushu at the time and an education center. No missionaries associated with the Church of Christ in Japan had previously resided there, but an organized church had been established by a pastor sent by the Japanese church's Board of Domestic Missions. The pastor and congregation welcomed the cooperation of the Reformed mission. Centrally located between the Reformed mission's southern and northern outstations, it was a logical location for an additional field missionary. After a little more than a year in evangelistic work there, Pieters reported, "I feel personally so happy over the fact that I am at last fully launched as a preaching missionary that I want all my friends to rejoice with me."[72]

From the beginning of the twentieth century, encouraging signs of interest in Christianity began to appear, and the missionaries noted a modest increase in baptisms. With renewed optimism, to facilitate property acquisition at the outstations, the mission devised a plan to raise necessary funds without adding to the requested budget. They negotiated a lucrative lease of part of the Nagasaki Church property, and asked for and received board permission to apply the income each year to building projects. With this income, the land on which the Saga mission house stood was purchased. Meanwhile, Fukuoka was becoming an increasingly important commercial city, and a national university with a medical school was to be located there. To develop mission work there, the Nagasaki property income was used to buy a very good property in the center of Fukuoka, in Tenjinmachi. An existing building served as parsonage and temporary meeting room on the back part of the lot, and there was space to build a church in front. The mission planned to continue to use the income from the Nagasaki Church lot for further church and parsonage construction in Kagoshima, Miyakonojo, and Oita.[73]

[71]    HS to HNC, July 12 and Sept. 17, 1901.
[72]    AP to HNC, Jan. 24, 1903.
[73]    AO to HNC, Dec. 26, 1901, and Jan. 14, March 28, and Aug. 6, 1902; HS to HNC, Aug. 19 and 24, 1903; HVSP to HNC, July 11, 1904.

By the end of 1901, it had become clear that under new government regulations, the private mission schools could apply for accreditation and acquire privileges associated with it. The boys' school, often spoken of as Steele College, though not actually college level, would by government recognition acquire a clear-cut academic level. It would thus become Steele Academy, a five-year course following elementary education. The most important advantages of accreditation would be student exemption from military conscription and the opportunity to compete in the examinations for entrance into government universities, thus providing incentive for retention of students until graduation. Necessary improvements in staff and facilities were provided for by an additional gift from the Steele family, the required building projects and application process were completed, and government approval was attained in 1907.[74]

In 1902, thanks to increased giving, the mission boards were able to pay off outstanding debts, and the next year they responded to pleas for new appointees. Two single missionaries, Grace Hoekje and the Reverend Garret Hondelink, were appointed and sent to the South Japan Mission. To everyone's surprise, almost immediately after arrival on the field in the fall of 1903, Hondelink announced his engagement to Grace Hoekje. Until their wedding in the summer of 1904, they immersed themselves in language study, Hondelink living with the Pieters family in Kumamoto and Hoekje living with Harriet Lansing in Kagoshima.[75]

Unfortunately, by the summer of 1901, it became clear that Elizabeth Stout once again was in precarious health. She died in Nagasaki at the beginning of March, 1902.[76] During the remainder of Henry Stout's career, his daughter Anna continued to live with him in the mission house in Nagasaki.

## Conflict in the South Japan Mission

The South Japan Mission had planned for some time to give its first and most faithful Japanese colleague, Segawa Asashi, an opportunity to study in America. This goal was realized in 1896 when Segawa was given a year's sabbatical from teaching theology and went to study at New Brunswick Seminary, while the Stouts were still on their extended furlough. As a result, when Grinnan left Nagasaki, there

---

[74]  HS to HNC, Dec. 23, 1901; H. R. Steele to HNC, Apr. 17, 1903; AP to HNC, May 21, 1903; AP to HNC, Sept. 7, 1906.
[75]  HVSP to HNC, June 17, 1903; Garret Hondelink to HNC, Nov. 24, 1903.
[76]  HS to HNC, June 14, 1901, March 4, 1902.

Segawa Asashi
in his study

was no one there responsible for the theological course. The mission sought guidance from the board, presenting several possibilities for training evangelists. With continuing uncertainty regarding Stout's return, two of the remaining theological students left for Tokyo to study at Meiji Gakuin. With only one student and the prospect of only a few recruits in the near future, even though the board had asked that theological education be continued in Nagasaki, it had to be temporarily suspended in the fall of 1897. Though unavoidable, this decision was undoubtedly a profound disappointment for Henry Stout. It might have been different if Stout could have gone back to Nagasaki, but in the summer of 1897 Elizabeth's health did not yet allow their return.[77] The theological department in which he had taught having been suspended, when Segawa returned to Japan in the summer of 1897, he embarked on an evangelistic tour for the North Japan Mission.[78] He later served again as pastor of Nagasaki Church.

Another matter further complicated the return of the Stouts to Nagasaki. Stout requested that his daughter Anna be provided employment with the South Japan Mission. The mission members on the field disapproved of missionary family members receiving full missionary appointments, and they also had reservations as to Anna's qualifications. However, recognizing the value for the Stouts of having their daughter with them, they suggested a solution: appoint Anna as a contract teacher for three years, so that she might accompany her parents.[79] Peeke remarked,

[77]  AP to HNC, Apr. 18, May 1 and 17, July 8, Aug. 14, 1897; HVSP to HNC, Apr. 19 and 22, 1897.
[78]  HVSP to HNC, Sept. 22, 1897.
[79]  AP to HNC, Sept. 7, 1896.

Three at least of us...repeatedly heard Dr. Stout say that he would never have a member of his family a regular member of the mission....The truth is that while we all like Dr. Stout immensely and wish him soon back, and find Miss Anna an excellent companion, we do not think it well to have another member of the Dr's family in the mission. There are chances enough for trouble with a man of the good Dr's bent, without inviting more by introducing more of a family nature. As to Miss Anna, if we had heard she had experienced some marked change of heart, had had a sort of second conversion, and wished to come out here and labor for the good of the heathen, it would be quite another matter. As far as we know her, she is not the kind of a missionary we want.[80]

Stout wrote to his colleagues in Japan to inform them that once Elizabeth's health improved sufficiently, they would return to Japan, but only on two conditions; not only must Anna have a position with the mission, but also there must be a promise that theological education would be resumed in Nagasaki as soon as circumstances allowed. The reaction of his younger colleagues suggests that, while they appreciated and respected Stout, the champion of the South Japan Mission, he had not always been easy to get along with. Peeke remarked,

Of course I suppose it behooves us all to try and shape the work so that Dr. Stout can have just what he wants, as he always has had. I do wish, however, that some plan could be devised whereby this field could get the work it is entitled to. Cannot the Dr. take a church and relieve the Board of his support, so that a new man can come to us the sooner. Of course this is not saying that he shall not come back to Kyushu as soon as family circumstances, and his *ultimata*, permit, but it seems a pity that year after year that much of our appropriation should be spent at home [Stout's salary].[81]

Regarding theological education, Pieters wrote,

We join in the hope that it will be possible to resume in some form next year, altho the prospect is not very encouraging in this respect. We earnestly hope that Dr. Stout will be able to come back early next year. Does this depend on the fate of theological

80    HVSP to HNC, Sept. 8, 1896.
81    HVSP to HNC, Oct. 23, 1897.

instruction, in such a way that if it were not wise to continue that, he would not be willing to come back for the ordinary kind of missionary work?[82]

The Stouts, with Anna, returned to Nagasaki in November 1898, after three and a half years away from the field. The board had evidently agreed to the two conditions Stout had demanded. Anna came as a duly appointed missionary, and Stout came counting on the resumption of theological instruction. However, a meeting of the mission revealed immediately the widening gulf between Stout and the younger men. Excerpts from a long letter from Peeke to the board clarify the issues.

> The future work of Dr. Stout and Mr. Segawa was discussed. Our discussion was very quiet and calm, but the cold logic of facts soon brought us to a most serious position...no prospects for theological instruction at present. No suitable candidates are offering from the field, and not for three years can a scattering few be looked for from the school [Steele Academy]....Mr. Segawa himself considers the resumption of theol. instruction at present not only impossible, but thinks the few men whom we may be called upon to train can be better trained in a single seminary in Tokyo.
>
> The next question was whether we really wanted to train more men for the ministry. I said that I had six men associated with me, that I tried to spend four weeks a year with each, but could do better if it could be six weeks....My experience has taught me that work by a native preacher unsupervised, unassisted by long visits and cooperation from the foreigner, was extremely unsatisfactory. The native and the foreigner must preach together, study together, and pray together several weeks in the year if our work was to have its proper results....
>
> Mr. Oltmans then spoke in a similar manner, somewhat to my surprise. He has about a dozen men under him, and this year has in several cases been able to try the experiment of a week or longer spent in calling and preaching with a single man. The men like to have the foreigner with them, their whole work is toned up, and a better feeling is worked up all around. Mr. Oltmans said that he had just twice too many stations....He and I both agreed that in view of the necessity of learning the language and the hindrances attendant upon sickness and furloughs, if the Board should grant

---

[82]    AP to HNC, Nov. 1, 1897.

us two new men for evangelistic work this moment, our mission would not be justified in increasing the number of its outstations or preachers. We would, it is true, need new men from time to time to fill up gaps. These men we could reasonably hope to come from our Kyushu constituency, though it is doubtful whether a regular theological plant is needed down here to train them.

You get from the above just where the three members of the mission continuously on the field the last four years, who have been closest in touch with the evangelistic work for the last ten years, stand....There is no theory about it. It is the logic of cold facts, as impressed upon the men who are out here trying to deal with the facts on the spot.

Dr. Stout heard the above, said he was surprised and disappointed, for while he had heard that some such views prevailed in Japan, he did not think they had gone to the lengths they had and that he was very much disappointed. He had always believed in a very different theory of missions. He believed in training young men, sending them out, giving them the best oversight you could. The more help and oversight the better, but to go on expanding. He had no use for any other theory, and could not work with any pleasure or satisfaction along the lines we had indicated, and the best thing he could do would be to "step down and out."[83]

Pieters reported, "Mr. Oltmans said to Dr. Stout in the meeting in which these things were discussed: 'We are sure that if you, Dr. Stout, were to reside in the field for one single year, and go in and out with our men as we do, you would think with us.'"[84] Oltmans spoke from personal experience. And one of his letters reflects the great sensitivity with which he worked with the Japanese evangelists.

There are two ways mainly in which the foreign missionary can make his influence felt with the men in the field. The one is that of oversight and direction as to details of work; manner of preaching, of visiting, of personal study, etc. This might be called "oversight proper," and is something with which I have but little sympathy. At times, however, aid of this kind can be rendered, and may be acceptable if given with patience, wisdom, and care. In general, the men should be trusted for the proper management of these things, and not only so, but we should let them know

[83]    HVSP to HNC, Nov. 28, 1898.
[84]    AP to HNC, Apr. 2, 1899.

that we trust them by falling in heartily with their plans, and by helping them to carry out these plans as far as possible.

And this suggests the other way in which we can make our influence felt with the men, namely, by being their <u>helpers</u> in the work. When I visit an outstation I go expecting to carry out the program proposed by the man in charge of the place, and I let him feel that <u>he</u> is in charge and not I. If consulted I give my best advice, and usually it is followed either from courtesy or from conviction....Our entire attitude towards our Japanese brethren frequently presents itself to me in one word, namely, <u>sympathy</u>.[85]

Pieters described the difficult situation of the Japanese evangelists. He insisted, "The thing peculiar to the Japanese evangelist is not the tendency to indolence, but the absence of ordinary checks to that tendency." Most of them worked in isolated situations, where there not only were no organized churches, no structured church life, and no responsible church elders, but also few or no believers. The Japanese evangelists had not grown up in the church and had no mental image of the role of a minister or evangelist. Pieters asked,

Now, if he simply does nothing but sit on his cushion by his little charcoal fire and read an interesting book or doze, or study English, instead of going about and seeking to find entrance for the gospel, who is to know it? Is it to be wondered at? If on the contrary, he bestirs himself, and conscientiously uses day after day in visiting people that had rather not see him, in exhorting people that turn a deaf ear, and in preaching to audiences that turn away in utter indifference, does it not betoken an unusual amount of native energy and push, combined with a deep conviction of the importance of his message?

Stout apparently could not accept what these men understood from experience. In a letter to the board, Peeke bluntly stated his feelings regarding Stout. "A man who cannot work unless his theories prevail in every branch of the work, even in those rather remote from his individual operations, is of little use out here."[86] Pieters wrote: "Dr. Stout's return is a bitter disappointment. We had hoped much from that, and now he is already talking of going home again on account of difference of opinion with the rest of us as to proper method."[87] The

---

[85]   AO to HNC, Apr. 14, 1899.
[86]   HVSP to HNC, Nov. 28, 1898.
[87]   AP to HNC, Nov. 28, 1898.

immediate crisis passed, since Stout did not carry out his threat to leave. The financial loss of the board in sending the Stouts back to the field notwithstanding, it might have been better if Stout had resigned. But in fact, this difficult mission meeting was only the beginning of a long, drawn out, and draining conflict in the South Japan Mission.

Years before, theological education in Nagasaki had been a key factor in the evangelistic outreach in southwestern Japan. Begun in a formal way in 1881 by Stout and Segawa, it had produced numerous evangelists. Conditions looked favorable for many years, but the situation gradually changed. The years from 1885 to 1890 were ones of great progress all over Japan. For the twelve years preceding 1890, the number of believers had doubled every three years. This success extended into the 1890s in Kyushu, and many expected the church's constituency to be multiplied many times in a few years. However, in this era of reaction against Christianity and all things Western, growth had come to a virtual standstill. Adult membership in 1902 was less than seven hundred in the entire *chukai*, hardly a constituency adequate to expect sufficient candidates to justify a theological course in Nagasaki.[88]

The board had agreed to Stout's condition that theological instruction was to be resumed as soon as it was feasible. The other missionaries conceded that, given the board's position, such training must begin again with even one pupil whenever Stout thought the pupil was ready for it. The reality was that no candidates came forward. Nevertheless, the issue remained unresolved. In 1899 Pieters stated his perspective.

> I believe that it is impossible ever to re-establish theological instruction here. I do not consider it necessary or wise, neither does Mr. Peeke, neither does Mr. Segawa, neither, I think I may venture to say, does Mr. Oltmans. Everybody concerned would be glad to see it definitely abandoned or indefinitely postponed, if that could be done with good understanding, and without offense to Dr. Stout or the loss of his valuable services to the work. This being so, it is, in my mind, only a question of time when this will be the result.[89]

Nevertheless, Stout continued to believe that theological education in Nagasaki could and would be resumed, and that his ideas

---

[88]  AP and HVSP to HNC, July 24, 1902.
[89]  AP to HNC, Apr. 2, 1899.

regarding the work of Japanese evangelists would prevail. From the summer of 1899, Stout reluctantly accepted the role of president of Steele College, with the hope of reinstating the theological course in connection with it. But by the summer of 1901, it had become clear that real rapport was lacking in the mission. Peeke described the situation.

> We have just had our Annual Meeting....Some years ago we used to have mission meetings in which a number of people with plans and ideas came together, talked, discussed, prayed, and then decided. No one man's ideas prevailed, but we generally managed to work out a line of action that we believed to be in accord with the mind of the Master of the work, and then returned to our work happy. There was some encouragement to initiative, we counseled together, and we felt that we were all directing the mission policy according to the best light that daily developments gave us.
>
> It is far different today. One member of the mission has plans and policies that were formulated years ago. They change but slightly. All plans must originate in that one mind, the most that can be hoped for is a slight modification that has to be wrested, and one constantly feels that if that one will is seriously set aside, it means an appeal home. It is a constant beating against a dead wall....A few years ago we tried to have our Annual Meetings a time of spiritual uplift. We endeavored to have all the families together. We planned for a devotional season daily, and the Lord's Supper during the session, but that is all gone now, and I doubt if anyone has a heart to strive for its restoration. Some things do not thrive in some atmospheres.[90]

At a meeting in December of 1901, it was proposed that the suspension of theological education in Nagasaki be made permanent. The rationale for this change was presented. Conditions in Japan had changed and required a more thorough education for evangelists than could be provided in Nagasaki, given the limitations of personnel and the unavailability of finances from the board. Kyushu was no longer the isolated place it had once been. Transportation to Tokyo had become faster and cheaper, due to the expansion of rail travel. And the indefinite suspension of theological instruction was having an unsettling influence on work plans. The proposal was rejected by a vote of four to three, those in favor being Oltmans, Pieters, and Peeke, the

[90]    HVSP to HNC, July 10, 1901.

men involved in evangelistic work, and those defeating the proposal being Henry Stout, Anna Stout, Sara Couch, and Myers, actually a contract English teacher.[91] The vote technically settled the matter, but no actual candidates for theological study presented themselves.

In the summer of 1902, it appeared that a few candidates for a theological course might be available at the beginning of the next school year, April 1903, and Stout proposed resuming theological education.[92] On the grounds that "such re-opening will be injurious to the work, doing in a less desirable manner, and at greater expense a work which could be better and more cheaply done by sending our students to the theological department of the Meiji Gakuin," Pieters and Peeke sent a letter of appeal to the board to change the policy and definitely abandon theological education in Nagasaki.[93] They also sent letters detailing the reasons for their appeal. Though of the same mind with Peeke and Pieters, Oltmans did not join in the appeal because of his changing situation. Asked repeatedly to join the theological faculty at Meiji Gakuin, he had finally requested the board's permission to accept the position and transfer to the North Japan Mission.[94] The Oltmans family left Saga in 1902 for furlough, following which they moved to Tokyo, and Albert began teaching in the theological department of Meiji Gakuin in 1903.

Stout of course insisted that the resumption of theological education in Nagasaki was not an open question. He assumed the board would uphold his perspective, but, in case the board took up the appeal of Peeke and Pieters, Stout intimated he was ready for battle.[95] He argued that Pieters and Peeke were obligated to approve the resumption because they had agreed to it in the past, and he refused to consider any change in policy. Stout also stated his rationale for reinstating theological education in Nagasaki in a lengthy letter to the board.[96]

Pieters argued, "Shall theological instruction now be reopened? That is a question of the present and of the future, not of the past. It must be decided, not on the ground of what I and others believed, said, and did at Kobe in 1893, at Nagasaki in 1898, or at any other time or place, but on the ground of the needs and resources of the South Japan

[91]    HS to HNC, Dec. 22, 1901.
[92]    South Japan Mission resolution, July, 1902.
[93]    HVSP to HNC, July 8, 1902.
[94]    AO to HNC, July 8, 1902.
[95]    HS to HNC, July 29 and Aug. 2, 1902.
[96]    HS to HNC, Oct. 28, 1902.

Mission at the present time."[97] Peeke remarked, "Differences of opinion are not always a bad thing. They are as often as not an undisguised blessing. And even if they were a bad thing, might not the responsibility and blame rest as well on those stubbornly clinging, perhaps for the sake of consistency, to the 'old path' that ought to be abandoned, as upon those striving to strike another path that present circumstances seem to them to indicate as the right one?[98]

Stout expressed his bitterness toward Pieters and Peeke, saying, "The crookedness of which members of the mission have been guilty is utterly repugnant to me."[99] A letter from the board, dated January 19, 1903, settled the question but did not resolve the conflict in the mission. The board determined that theological instruction in Nagasaki should be discontinued. However, an embittered Stout had already begun a series of letters of hair-splitting inquiry to Pieters and Peeke, demanding that they explain or justify various statements or positions taken in the past. It proved to be a very time-consuming and emotionally trying ordeal, the record of the resulting correspondence over the course of three months reaching thirty-six typewritten pages. Still unsatisfied, Stout concluded in a letter to Pieters and Peeke, "I cannot help feeling still that you have done me a great wrong. And therefore I have to say that after this, though I shall endeavor to conduct myself in all matters affecting the mission as if nothing unpleasant had occurred, that will have to be the extent, i.e., friendly, social relations between us will be impossible."[100]

Stout rigidly applied this stance, participating in mission meetings "as if nothing unpleasant had occurred," but outside of such business contacts refusing to speak to or even shake hands with Pieters and Peeke. They lamented,

> We are in this country trying to carry on, as representatives of the Board, a spiritual work, trying to interpret to this people God's purpose of salvation through the Messiah, and also the spirit of Jesus. With one of our number cherishing such feelings as are expressed in Dr. Stout's letter of Feb. 19th further interpreted by his refusal of the ordinary amenities of social intercourse, we believe it impossible for our mission to succeed, or for us to enjoy God's blessing upon it. We believe that endeavoring to continue

---

[97]  AP to HNC, Oct. 31, 1902.
[98]  HVSP to HNC, Nov. 6, 1902.
[99]  HS to HNC, Dec. 15, 1902.
[100]  HS to HVSP and AP, Feb. 19, 1903.

to work together under these circumstances means constant unhappiness and probably serious friction. We value our peace of mind and spiritual joy highly. This is seriously marred, and it is a constant grief to be associated so intimately with one who declares so unequivocally that he has withdrawn from us confidence and respect.[101]

Learning of the situation, Stout's most trusted Japanese colleague for many years, Segawa Asashi, offered to meet with Stout to try to bring about reconciliation. Of this offer, Peeke remarked, "It speaks volumes for the piety and faithfulness of Mr. Segawa, but what shall we say of a condition where a missionary of long years has to be besought by one of his own spiritual children to put away an unforgiving spirit!"[102] Segawa's effort was to no avail. Peeke concluded, "If Mr. Segawa's intervention had not taken place, I can imagine the Board's writing out and asking us to make another try at an adjustment, and we'd have done it, I'm sure. But since a thoroughly disinterested, thoroughly friendly party of this kind has intervened, and using every plea, has failed, I am sure the Board will not think of asking us to do more."[103] Pieters and Peeke decided that for the mission's work and their own peace of mind, a change in personnel was necessary, and they presented the alternatives: resignation of Stout, transfer of Pieters and Peeke to the North Japan Mission or a Presbyterian mission, or dismissal of themselves as missionaries.[104]

In a letter to the board of May 19, 1903, Stout stated that "adjustment of the difficulty is impossible, and as Messrs. Pieters and Peeke regard present conditions as intolerable, I agree with them that a change must be made, and upon one of the lines suggested by them." He then offered to resign from the mission and retire.[105] The board's response, received in July, was to accept Stout's resignation from the South Japan Mission and to offer him the possibility of transferring to the North Japan Mission, to take up evangelistic work. Stout refused this option.[106] It was later learned that the reason he declined this offer was that working in the North Japan Mission would include renewed contact with Oltmans, for whom he held the same feelings as toward

[101]    AP & HVSP to HNC, March 31, 1903.
[102]    HVSP to HNC, Apr. 5, 1903.
[103]    HVSP to HNC, May 2, 1903.
[104]    AP to HNC, May 2, 1903.
[105]    HS to HNC, May 19, 1903.
[106]    AP to HNC, Aug. 19, 1903.

Pieters and Peeke.[107] The mission asked Stout to remain as head of Steele College until March 31, 1904, which would allow eight months to work out arrangements for the work in the forthcoming post-Stout era.

Inexplicably, in December of 1903, the board suggested that Stout call a conference of members of the mission, including newly arrived Garret Hondelink, for the purpose of bringing about reconciliation between Stout and Pieters and Peeke. Accordingly, a committee of Couch, Lansing, Myers, and Hondelink met separately with Stout and then Pieters and Peeke, to hear their views, and then the full conference was held. Another unpleasant encounter ensued. Pieters and Peeke could not see or admit that they had wronged Stout, but asked to be forgiven if they had. Stout remained unwilling to forgive them and said that he had lost a great deal of confidence in them and respect for them, and he doubted their integrity. The committee of four concluded that Stout's cutting off of social relations was wrong. No real reconciliation was possible, but Stout expressed willingness to listen to the counsels of the committee and to resume friendly relations.[108]

Pieters and Peeke reported, "I know you will rejoice with us that this scandalous condition of affairs that has disgraced our mission for nearly a year, is thus terminated."[109] Remarkably, although they still undoubtedly harbored bitterness, Stout and Anna returned immediately to speaking terms with Pieters and Peeke and resumed hearty and warm social relations with all the members of the mission. Stout did not resign as of March 31, 1904, as contemplated, and he continued as head of Steele and secretary and treasurer of the mission. However, on June 23, 1904, both Stout and Anna sent letters of resignation to the board. To colleagues, Stout "inferred that it was because he was dissatisfied with the way that the whole difficulty was finally settled."[110] No doubt another important factor in their decisions was the engagement of Anna to marry a Scotsman named S. M. Officer, branch manager of the China and Japan Trading Company in Nagasaki.[111]

Both Henry and Anna Stout terminated their work with the mission as of the end of 1904. Stout remained in Nagasaki for a time, spending most of 1905 supervising construction of a Y.M.C.A. building.

---

107   HVSP to HNC, Apr. 14, 1904.
108   HVSP to HNC, Dec. 31, 1903, and Jan. 11, 1904; GH to HNC, Jan. 27, 1904; HVSP and AP to HNC, Jan. 30, 1904.
109   AP and HVSP to HNC, Jan. 30, 1904.
110   GH to HNC, July 9, 1904.
111   HS to HNC, June 23, 1904.

Anna married and remained in Nagasaki. Stout returned to America in the spring of 1906, where he served as a pastor in Reformed churches in New Jersey for three years. Thus ended the missionary career of Henry Stout, founder and stubborn advocate of the South Japan Mission for thirty-five years. And a difficult period of conflict in the South Japan Mission was over.

## A Peaceful Respite in the South Japan Mission

After the departure of Oltmans, Pieters, in addition to his work at Kumamoto, for a time made an effort to cover the entire northern field that included the Saga, Fukuoka, and Oita districts. However, in the summer of 1903, the Peeke family moved to Saga to take responsibility for the northern areas.[112] After their wedding in 1904, the Hondelinks settled in Kagoshima, where they continued language study and began to oversee the evangelistic work. Harriet Lansing also continued her work in Kagoshima. After an evangelistic trip in the area, Peeke remarked, "Miss Lansing is doing admirably. The last Sunday I was there, Easter, she had a round up of her Sunday schools, and about two hundred assembled on her lawn and in her parlor. I like her immensely, but I can never understand why all the Japanese should be so fond of her and especially why little children should so follow her around like flies. It must be that love begets love."[114]

In early 1905, Pieters left Kumamoto and moved to Nagasaki to become once again the principal of Steele Academy, as well as to take over as treasurer and secretary of the mission. Myers had concluded his teaching at Steele Academy and left Japan. Consequently, when Pieters took over the school, he had to carry not only its administration, but also the teaching of all English classes. Fortunately, his burden was alleviated by the arrival of Anthony Walvoord to teach at the school. Meanwhile, as a result of Anna Stout's resignation, and new missionary Grace Hoekje's marriage to Hondelink, Lansing and Couch were the only single women missionaries. Sara Couch, vice-principal of Sturges Seminary, was also its only English teacher. The women's board responded to this situation, sending Miss Grace Thomasma as a new missionary. She arrived in November 1904 and went to Kagoshima to stay with Harriet Lansing while studying the language.[114]

---

[112]   HVSP to HNC, July 21, 1903.
[113]   HVSP to HNC, Apr. 14, 1904.
[114]   HVSP to HNC, July 16, 1904; Grace Thomasma to HNC, June 29, 1905.

In an interesting development, it was planned that Jennie A. Pieters, the younger sister of Albertus, would come to Japan to be with her brother's family and to help school their children. She had taught school for six years in Michigan and Wisconsin but had not been physically robust. Albertus thought the change might be good for her, and other brothers in America agreed to pay Jennie's passage. When it turned out that Sturges Seminary needed an English teacher, the mission requested that Jennie Pieters be hired to teach on a three-year contract. From the beginning of 1905, she carried a full teaching load at the girls' school, living with Sara Couch. Jennie's health proved to be satisfactory, and the next year the mission requested she be allowed the same allowances as regularly appointed missionaries. Jennie Pieters became a regularly appointed missionary and served in Japan for thirty-five years.[115]

One of the challenges faced by the mission schools was finding well-qualified Japanese Christian teachers. Two key developments deserve mentioning. Tomegawa Jun was a graduate of Sturges Seminary and the daughter of Tomegawa Ichiro, one of the leading pastors. Realizing her promise, the Pieters family provided a scholarship for her to attend the advanced course at Joshi Gakuin, a Presbyterian mission school in Tokyo. In the spring of 1905, she came back to Nagasaki to teach at the girls' school.[116] Also at Steele Academy, Pieters was fortunate in acquiring a new, well-qualified Christian and licensed teacher, Kusano Yoshidachi, who had just returned from study in America. With this addition, the required number of qualified teachers for the school's accreditation was complete.[117] For many years, enrollment at Steele Academy had been about one hundred students. Pieters had hopes that, with accreditation, a good program, and well-qualified teachers, the school would grow to a student body of about two hundred.

The positive atmosphere in the South Japan Mission in 1905 was exemplified by the report of its annual meeting in July. Out of town mission members slept at the girls' school. Pieters described the scene.

> The weather was very warm, but in spite of that we had not only a successful business meeting, but a jolly good time together. Both the ladies at Sturges and we ourselves broke up our ordinary family arrangements, and loaded our servants and dishes, so that

---

[115]    AP to HNC, Aug. 2, 1904, AP to JLA, March 7 and April 7, 1905; HVSP to HNC, July 19, 1905.

[116]    AP to JLA, Apr. 7, 1905; AP to HNC, Apr. 26, 1905.

[117]    AP to South Japan Mission members, May 25, 1905; AP to HNC, June 9, 1905.

the entire mission became for the time being a boarding club. The children were all present and enjoyed it very much. They gave us a little entertainment one afternoon, by way of closing their school exercises, and on Sunday Mrs. Hondelink held with them a Junior Christian Endeavor Meeting, which was a great success.[118]

The mission appealed to the board, asking that missionary numbers be restored to their former strength by sending another family for evangelistic work.

A "Saga Exposition" was held for fifty days in April and May of 1906 to promote the business interests of the eight prefectures in Kyushu and Okinawa, and Peeke took advantage of this exposition as an evangelistic opportunity. He rented a lot near the exhibition entrance and put up a tent, where Bibles and tracts could be sold or given away, daily preaching meetings could be held, and Christians from near and far could gather. Pieters reported of this venture, "Mr. Peeke's special effort to do evangelistic work there has met with splendid success, so far as hearers are counted. The place is crowded all day." And Peeke himself remarked, "Our Exposition work has succeeded beyond my expectations."[119]

Garret and Grace Hondelink worked in the Kagoshima field from the fall of 1904. However, Grace continued to struggle with health problems (intestinal troubles) that had begun almost immediately after her arrival in Japan in 1903. She bore a healthy daughter in 1905. They took vacations in the mountains at Karuizawa each summer, in hopes that Grace would recover the good health she had known in America. However, her debilitating condition was not relieved. In September of 1907, while en route home from Karuizawa by train, Grace had a miscarriage. They got off the train in Saga, where the Peeke family lived, to seek medical help. Multiple complications and high fever persisted for several months. The Hondelinks lodged with the Peeke family in Saga from September to March. Despite the best medical care available in Saga and the tender care of her husband and Vesta Peeke, Grace remained weak and totally bedridden. It was concluded that the only option was resignation from the mission and return to America.[120]

In October of 1907, the Reverend Willis G. Hoekje, brother of Grace Hondelink, arrived in Nagasaki as the newest appointee to the South Japan Mission. Unfortunately, upon his arrival he learned of the serious illness that would lead to the termination of the missionary

---

118   AP to HNC, July 27, 1905.
119   HVSP to HNC, July 19, 1905 and Apr. 11, 1906; AP to HNC, Apr. 7, 1906.
120   GH to HNC, Oct. 14, 1907; Feb. 7 and Apr. 8, 1908.

careers of his sister and her husband. The Hondelinks left Japan in April of 1908, and they did not return. Once again the mission was shorthanded for evangelistic work.

Hoekje, after only five months in Japan, took time away from language study to accompany Peeke on a five-week tour of numerous outstations in Kyushu. Peeke was anticipating his upcoming furlough and hoped to introduce Hoekje to the work of an evangelistic missionary. He was impressed with his new colleague and reported, "He is a capable young man in every way....His knowledge of the language was already what it requires most men a full year to acquire, and he was able to devote himself to a study of the men he met and missionary methods and conditions. I did not spare him a bit. Japanese food and hotel arrangements were patiently borne with, and he came through with flying colors. During his short stay he has a stronger grasp of the general conditions than most men get after a stay of three or four years."[121] After his tour with Peeke, Hoekje was equally enthusiastic about the work, writing, "Whether from the standpoint of unexploited fields of labor, or of promise of work already done, or of cordial relations with Japanese Christians and ministers, even where our mission has no work of its own, there is a splendid future for our mission in Japan."[122]

In the fiftieth year since the beginning of Protestant mission, the missionaries remained positive despite the continuing challenge of the work. When asked whether he could cite an example from his twenty years of evangelism of any individual who had been ready to accept the gospel offer on its first presentation as the very thing looked for and longed for, Peeke responded as follows:

> I have hoped for many years that I might discover such a case as you describe, for it seemed to me reasonable that such should exist, but I have never met a person who could by any interpretations of terms be put in such a class. A person with such desires and longings could only be found among a meditative and deeply religious people, and the Japanese are not meditative and not religious. Life and its various problems sit very lightly upon them. Most of them do up a certain amount of "religious chores," and there religion stops with them.[123]

What Peeke called "religious chores" were nominal Shinto and Buddhist religious rites and practices observed for centuries by most

---

[121]  HVSP to HNC, June 19, 1908.
[122]  Willis G. Hoekje to HNC, July 18, 1908.
[123]  HVSP to HNC, Jan. 8, 1909.

Japanese. Peeke underscored the difficulty of communicating the gospel in the Japanese context. Nevertheless, Hoekje, involved in itinerant evangelism already while continuing language study, could express joy. A newly ordained Japanese pastor reported having administered the baptism of a convert for the first time. Of this young pastor's first convert, Hoekje commented,

> It is the old, old story in Japan of a lad of twenty, just through school, laid low by consumption [TB]. And it is the old, old story of seeking rest, and comfort in dying, which Buddhist priest and Shinto teacher know not how to bring. And the youth became almost violently insane in his grief, so that men almost feared to bring the Christian minister to him, even when such action was suggested. But....to know and to believe in Jesus Christ brings peace, and to be baptized on the bed in Christ's name brings a joy worth shouting out for when it comes. Who knows how often the story will be told in the country round about?[124]

The missionaries were convinced that a wonderful opportunity for growth was opening before them. Segawa had returned to the employ of the mission, after several years as a missionary to expatriate Japanese in China. His new role was as an itinerant evangelist-at-large in Kyushu. The mission again pleaded with the board for new personnel, both men and women, to expand evangelistic outreach in Kyushu. It planned to divide the work of the Saga station into two fields and locate a missionary in Oita. The missionaries hoped once again to base men in Kumamoto and Kagoshima. However, they were also fully aware that the right kind of person was required for this itinerant evangelist role. In Peeke's words,

> I doubt if it is realized at home just how trying the life of an evangelist in Japan is. It is especially trying to some natures, and to men who have led a fairly quiet and easy life, with "conveniences" and the regulation coffee, roll, and chop breakfast. The food is coarse and unattractive, sleeping on a hard mat floor, one must be largely in his stocking feet, must be up till midnight generally, must sit for days in rooms so cold as to show every breath, and at meetings often sit for a couple of hours, talking and singing in frosty outer air. Often the only chance for a week to get warm is when a bath is taken in a more or less open and drafty bath-room.[125]

[124]   WGH to HNC, May 25, 1909.
[125]   HVSP to HNC, May 28, 1909.

The mission requested the appointment of two additional single women for evangelistic work, and possibly locating them in Fukuoka. Hoekje noted,

> Experience in Kagoshima, to say nothing of Nagasaki and Saga, has demonstrated the value of such work, in aiding the pastor to interest and win and hold young men and women, especially those who are students; in training many of them in simple Christian work, in the Sunday School or the Christian Endeavor Society; in organizing Sunday Schools to attract hundreds of scholars; and in directing Bible women to reach and teach the mothers of such children. The conditions in Fukuoka for such work are distinctly promising....The work of our devoted pastor there, and the worthy nucleus of Christians, cannot but be benefited by the presence and assistance of foreign missionaries. The students, the children, and the mothers of Fukuoka, who need our church and whom our church needs—this is the field that invites the labors of two lady missionaries.[126]

The mission hoped not only to establish self-supporting churches, but also to implement the Japanese pastors and self-supported churches in a movement "to bring to the last man and woman and child in the entire region some intelligent conception of the message of the gospel." Underscoring this vision, Hoekje added, "We realize that the missionary must always be on the frontier, always a pioneer, always just ahead of the luxury of the convenient railroad and the comfortable hotel, always just beyond the leadership of the self-supporting church."[127]

The Reformed Church's missionaries in Kyushu were encouraged and enthused about the prospects for the advance of the work. Fifty years had passed since the arrival of Guido Verbeck in Nagasaki, and the foundational work of Henry Stout and others was already history. The dark days of the reaction against things Western and Christian appeared to be passing, and with mission rapport a brighter future seemed possible. However, the missionaries were convinced that reinforcement of their ranks was essential. Furthermore, progress in the work of the missions would require resolution of the issue of the nature of their cooperation with increasingly self-conscious Japanese church leaders.

As of the end of 1910, the Japanese in the employ of the South Japan Mission included twelve pastors and evangelists and several lay

[126]  WGH to HNC, March 8, 1909.
[127]  WGH to HNC, March 8, 1909.

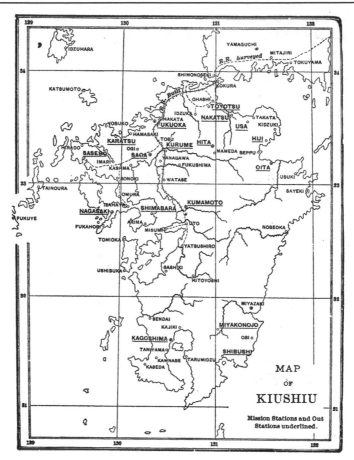

The area of Japan (Kyushu) served by the South Japan
Mission in 1910, showing the locations of missionaries,
evangelists, and outstations

Bible women, who carried on outreach ministries with the missionaries
in at least thirty small churches, outstations, and house meetings,
as well as through numerous branch Sunday schools. A list of the
missionary personnel at the end of 1910 and a map showing the extent
of the mission's work clarifies the realities.

Evangelistic missionaries and their places of residence:

· Harman V. S. Peeke – Fukuoka
· Willis G. Hoekje – Oita
· Harriet M. Lansing and Jennie Buys – Kagoshima
· Albertus Pieters – on furlough in America

Educational missionaries and their places of work

· Anthony Walvoord – Nagasaki, principal, Steele Academy
· Minnie Taylor – Nagasaki, Steele Academy
· Sara M. Couch, Grace Thomasma – Nagasaki, Sturges Seminary
· Jennie A. Pieters – on furlough in America, Sturges Seminary

Associate missionaries (wives – work in education and/or evangelism as able)

· Edith Walvoord - Nagasaki
· Emma Pieters – on furlough in America
· Vesta Peeke – in America for education of children

CHAPTER 9

# Relationships: The Missionaries and the Church

As of the end of 1890, twenty-seven Protestant foreign missions or churches had representatives in Japan, six of which were the Reformed and Presbyterian missions partnering with the United Church of Christ in Japan. The others, ranging from Episcopal, Baptist, Congregational, and Methodist to Unitarian and Universalist, had formed separate denominational organizations in Japan. The United Church was not only the original and thus oldest but also the largest Japanese church organization, with a growing sense of its own identity. The statistics for all Protestants in Japan for 1890 indicate 297 churches, 32,380 believers, of whom 4,431 were baptized in 1890, 129 native ministers, and 455 unordained preachers and helpers. Of these, the United Church had 71 churches, 10,611 members, of whom 1,077 adults and 153 children were added in 1890, and there were 45 native ministers and 91 unordained preachers and helpers.[1] Clearly, the Japanese church associated with the Reformed and Presbyterian missions had been the most effective in producing leaders and becoming a self-governing church.

[1]    JHB to HNC, Feb. 12, 1891.

### The Growing Independence of the Japanese Church

The leadership of the United Church of Christ in Japan, stung by the failure of the union movement with the *Kumiai* (Japanese congregational churches) in 1889, and also no doubt challenged and affected by the antiforeign and anti-Christian atmosphere around them, began to exercise more independence. At the *Daikai* held in December 1890, several important decisions were made. The church name, i.e., *Nihon Kirisuto Itchi Kyokai* ("United Church of Christ in Japan") was changed to *Nippon Kirisuto Kyokai* ("Church of Christ in Japan"). The change reflected the reality that the Protestant churches of Japan had been unable to form one truly united church, but it also affirmed that this church did not identify itself with any foreign denomination. The English acronym for the Japanese church name became NKK.

Another development at the 1890 synod was the preparation of a new Book of Government. It was a well thought out document, consisting of a constitution, canons, and an appendix, and arranged to distinguish clearly among fundamental principles, rules that may be adjusted to meet changing circumstances, and forms of procedure. Among many other changes, the new 1890 Book of Government provided for opening the office of deacon to women, and considerable support was expressed for the future opening of the office of elder to women as well. The office of elder was actually opened to women in 1905. These advances in recognizing the right of women to serve in church offices predated similar developments in the missionary sending churches by many decades.

Major developments also took place concerning the church's creeds. The influx of new theologies from Europe had awakened the church's leaders to the importance of articulating a clear expression of belief. At the time the original union was formed, the Japanese church had been in favor of a brief and simple creed, but under the influence of the missionaries it had adopted four creedal statements of the Reformed tradition as its standards: the Heidelberg Catechism, Canons of Dort, Westminster Confession, and Westminster Shorter Catechism. In the thirteen intervening years, the two catechisms had been widely taught, but the Confession and Canons had not. These Western documents were seen as not well suited to the needs of Japan as confessional standards. It was argued that the churches of Christ in every land and age should form confessions suited to their own situations.

The synod sought to clarify the characteristics of the creed the Japanese church needed at this juncture in its history. The *Daikai* concluded it should be brief and simple: not an elaborate theological document, but a confession understandable and usable by the whole church, a confession of the faith of the church. The church in Japan was face to face with Buddhism, Confucianism, agnosticism, and rationalism and needed a confession setting forth the essentials of Christian faith. The debate, however, appeared to be leading only to deep division and controversy, and it seemed at the end of a day of discussion that the synod would fail to resolve the issue. The next morning, a young elder and professor at Meiji Gakuin, Mr. Ishimoto, presented a new proposition. To the surprise of the assembled delegates, it was a brief statement of faith to which all could agree. The 1890 *Daikai* unanimously approved the following confession, here in English translation:

> The Lord Jesus Christ, whom we worship as God, the Only Begotten Son of God, for us men and for our salvation was made man and suffered. He offered up a perfect sacrifice for sin; and all who are one with him by faith are pardoned and accounted righteous; and faith in him working by love purifies the heart.
>
> The Holy Ghost, who with the Father and the Son is worshipped and glorified, reveals Jesus Christ to the soul, and without his grace man being dead in sin cannot enter the kingdom of God. By him the prophets and apostles and holy men of old were inspired; and he speaking in the Scriptures of the Old and New Testaments is supreme and infallible judge in all things pertaining unto faith and living.
>
> From these Holy Scriptures the ancient Church of Christ drew its Confession; and we, holding the faith once delivered to the Saints, join in that Confession with praise and thanksgiving. (Then follows the Apostles Creed).[2]

Ballagh reflected on this event at that 1890 *Daikai* after this unique Japanese confession of faith was produced.

> Many could but go over the articles contained in so brief a creed with joy again and again expressed. And whilst leaving no doubt as to its out and out evangelical teaching as the living faith of this body of believers, it had not sought to be disconnected from the great body of the historical church in its thankful and

---

[2]     William M. Imbrie, *The Church of Christ in Japan* (Philadelphia: Westminster, 1906), 105-06; Drummond, *History of Christianity*, 196.

devout adoption of the Apostles' Creed. This is a matter of great gratification. And another is that no regard has been had for what other churches may think or desire or we desire in regard to them. It is not even to antagonize error, or to preserve the purity or peace of the church, it is our own vital faith each and all.[3]

The 1890 synod also acted to clarify the relationship of missionaries of the six Reformed and Presbyterian missions in the Council of Missions to the Church of Christ in Japan. According to Reformed polity, ministers are members of a classis or presbytery. The earlier rules of the Japanese church had allowed missionaries to be recognized as members in full standing of the *chukai* in Japan in which they worked, though not under the discipline of the Japanese church, and while continuing membership in a classis in America. According to the new Book of Government, missionaries were required to choose. If they chose to remain members of a classis in America, they would be recognized as advisory members of a *chukai*, with the right to speak, to introduce resolutions, and to serve on committees, but without the right to vote.[4]

At the time of this synod meeting, Martin Wyckoff was still readjusting after a time of furlough in America. He reflected on the changes taking place in the Japanese church with words that exemplify the sensitivity required of cooperating missionaries.

> Some of our pet ideas and hopes have been entirely shattered, but when we get cool enough to judge without prejudice, we find that they were not the essentials we supposed them to be. I am not at all certain that we did not, and do not, need a little adversity....
>
> I am inclined to believe that our opportunities are as great and important as they have ever been, but we must have great carefulness and patience in using them. Though our words may not receive as much attention, or produce as great effect as they have seemed to in the past, the influence of Christ-like living has lost none of its power. Our desire now is to be "living epistles."[5]

At its *Daikai* in late 1892 the Church of Christ in Japan passed a resolution that resulted in a radical change in the administration of the evangelism and church-planting carried on under the direction of its Board of Domestic Missions. The change would place the conduct of

---

[3]   JHB to HNC, Dec. 4, 1890.
[4]   Imbrie, *Church of Christ*, 102.
[5]   MNW to HNC, Dec. 26, 1890.

this work entirely in the hands of a committee of six people, all resident in Tokyo, instead of in local committees in the field as before. The missionaries, at the Council of Missions, opposed the plan, but it was approved by the Japanese anyway. Since the several missions were still expected to provide most of the required funds, this did not end the matter. The several missions either protested or refused to appropriate the necessary funds. Consequently, lacking funds, the *Daikai* plan died a natural death. Pieters commented, "It is a very significant condition of affairs, as it is many years since the foreigners have refused to grant the funds for a plan of work carried in the *Daikai*. It seems to indicate something of a reaction against the idea of allowing the Japanese almost unrestricted control."[6]

Most of the missionaries connected to the Council of Missions attended a convention in Kobe in 1893 to discuss the nature of their future cooperation with the Church of Christ in Japan. Some believed the time had come to place all evangelism and church planting within the Japanese church structures at the *chukai* level, under joint committees of equal numbers of Japanese and foreign missionaries, supported financially by the missions, with the Japanese contributing as able. In the South Japan Mission, Oltmans favored this proposal. On the other hand, some suggested that the missions should withdraw from formal cooperation with the Japanese church. The idea was that the Japanese church should carry on its internal development and as much evangelistic work as it could handle with its own funds, while the missions should run the schools and do evangelistic work using their own funds, the two organizations working alongside each other in harmony but distinct. In the South Japan Mission, Pieters and Peeke favored this proposal.

Since it was clear at the Council of Missions convention that each of these approaches was too radical to be implemented at the time, a compromise was seen as the only possibility. In effect, the missionaries reaffirmed their policy of cooperation with the Japanese church organization, including three of the mission boards providing three-fourths of the financial support of the projects under the Japanese church's Board of Domestic Missions. Pieters remarked, "It was doubtless the best that could be done. But after all, it is only a compromise. It does not dispose of the questions involved. These will recur again and again and it is inevitable that either of the two diverging paths should finally be chosen."[7]

6   AP to HNC, Jan. 24, 1893.
7   AP to HNC, May 1, 1893.

Stout reiterated basic mission policy, the issues at stake, and his understanding of the situation.

> It has always seemed to me that one of the main objects had in view by the several missions cooperating with the Church of Christ in Japan, was to establish and foster a church, by close and sympathetic association and aid, till it should become independent, and give promise of stability in itself, and of efficiency to do its part with other churches in the great work of evangelizing the land. It has been the common practice to encourage the Japanese to engage in work in every possible way, in association with the missionaries, and in certain efforts by themselves, so that they might be prepared for this great work. In order that they might participate in the management of affairs, two things as a rule have been insisted upon, (1) the men must be of tried Christian character, proved such by faithful work done under mission direction or in the pastorate and (2) the church at large must show a willingness to bear some good part of the expenses of the work undertaken. There seemed to be an expectation that at no very distant future the church would be in a condition to assume the responsibility of the whole work, with aid, doubtless for a time, from the churches formerly cooperating with them through the missions. With such views I have been in hearty accord, and have been in the habit of presenting and explaining them to the Japanese connected with us, as occasion offered. I have considered them of prime importance, as stimulus on the one hand, and as a means of restraint against undue attempts at forging ahead, on the other hand. More than this, I have used my influence to adjust matters in the schools and on the field for the accomplishment of this very end, believing that we are already in the transition period between pure mission work and ultimate pure church work.[8]

However, in the matter of how to proceed in this transition period, maintaining unanimity was often difficult. In the case of the South Japan Mission, two small mission schools had been established and evangelistic outreach had spread to many parts of the island of Kyushu. However, financial responsibility by the Japanese for the two branches of the work was still only a distant hope. In the face of longstanding resistance to Christianity, not one congregation in Kyushu could be

8    HS to HNC, May 5, 1894.

described as truly independent and self-supporting. Stout thought the proposals of the younger missionaries were premature and reflected their inexperience. Given "Mr. Ohgimi's attempt to grasp after power in the college"[9] on the one hand, and differences of opinion among the four male members of the mission on the other, he believed the time was not right for major changes in policy and relationships with Japanese church leaders. Stout favored cooperation, but with a continuation of missionary guidance. His perspective exemplified worthy goals and a sense of responsibility to lead Japanese Christians and churches to self-support and self-propagation. However, it also reflected the reticence of the missionaries to relinquish authority, even though exceptionally gifted Japanese Christians had shown strong leadership.

Understanding the growing spirit of independence in the Church of Christ in Japan of necessity leads to a consideration of the role of one of Japan's exceptional Christian leaders, the Reverend Uemura Masahisa (1858-1925). Uemura was a member of the Yokohama Band, the group of gifted former samurai youth whose faith was nurtured under the teaching and preaching and prayers of James Ballagh, and whose theological perspective and acumen was formed under the teaching of S. R. Brown. Coming under Ballagh's influence, Uemura was baptized in May 1873, at the age of fifteen, and soon committed himself to the life of a Christian evangelist.

He had from the beginning a very independent spirit, preferring not to receive student financial support from the missionaries. In order to pay his tuition for Brown's theological class, he taught as many as fifty students privately from one o'clock in the afternoon to ten at night and also raised pigs, a profitable but humiliating task for someone of the former samurai class. He completed his formal training at the new theological school established in Tokyo in 1877 but remained a life-long, self-motivated scholar of theology and literature. In 1877, while still a student, he started a *dendosho* (preaching place) in Tokyo, at the age of nineteen, evidently the first example of formal Protestant evangelism initiated primarily under Japanese responsibility.[10]

Uemura's early ministry was carried out in connection with the Reformed Church missionaries in the Yokohama and Tokyo areas, his first pastorate being Shitaya Church from 1879 to 1884. Throughout the remainder of his long career, Uemura was pastor of a church in Fujimicho, Tokyo, at the time known as Ichibancho Church. He died

---

[9]   HS to HNC, May 5, 1894.
[10]   Drummond, *History of Christianity*, 209-10.

January 8, 1925, at age sixty-seven. Kyogoku Jun-ichi summed up the life of Uemura. "He was a nationalist who, while imbibing the spirit of 'civilization and enlightenment,' fought for an independent and self-sustaining church, and for the evangelization of Japan by Japanese."[11] He was unquestionably the most influential leader among the first generation of Japanese Protestant Christians. In the words of Iglehart, "Almost without a peer as pastor, preacher, theologian, author, editor and dominating personality, [Uemura] was viewed by his generation and by later ones as God's particular gift to the church during its formative years of crisis. He was relentless in his own standards of high quality, and impatient with anything less in others."[12]

Uemura's public life could be summarized by the word "evangelist," but his evangelizing activities transcended the usual role of a pastor. He traveled throughout Japan preaching, and his leadership in the Church of Christ in Japan was so energetic and pervasive that he was sometimes facetiously referred to as "the Protestant pope." He participated in the translation of the Old Testament and taught in the theological department of Meiji Gakuin, but he later founded a theological school independent of the missionaries, the Tokyo Shingakusha. Though without traditional academic credentials, he was widely read and a brilliant scholar and apologist for the Christian faith. He wrote for and edited journals throughout his life, which extended his influence throughout Japan. He authored six books on Christianity. However, he wrote authoritatively not only on religious subjects but also on literature as a critical essayist. He endeavored to make a Christian impact on the culture, and even on the politics, of Japan.

Drummond has stated Uemura's role in relations with the missions clearly.

> Of particular importance both for the career of Uemura and the history of Protestantism in Japan was his relationship with and developing policy toward the foreign missions in the land. Uemura . . . owed much to the early missionaries and never ceased to express his gratitude for their contributions as well as for those of their successors. He had intimate and warm relationships with several missionaries. He early came, however, to the conclusion that Christian witness in Japan after its first beginnings by foreign missionaries could be properly carried on only if Japanese

---

[11]   Kyogoku Jun-ichi, "Uemura Masahisa." *Japan Quarterly* 11, no. 2 (Apr.-June, 1964): 221.

[12]   Iglehart, *Century*, 123-24.

were primarily responsible. In the first two decades the number of missionaries, as of Japanese Christians, was small, but as the number of the latter notably increased from the late 1870s, so did the missionaries. The mission organizations were strengthened, and as their financial resources increased they came to constitute powerful, independent ecclesial structures alongside the Japanese churches. The missions were not denoted as churches, but exercised "the ecclesiastical functions of a presbytery or synod in founding, developing, aiding and directing local churches." Uemura became the foremost leader in the movement to rectify this imbalance and to establish an authentically independent Japanese Christian church.[13]

In a lecture presented as part of the fiftieth anniversary of the coming of Protestant missions to Japan, Dr. Ibuka of Meiji Gakuin noted four principles the Church of Christ in Japan had followed from the beginning: (1) independence of all foreign church organizations; (2) the spirit of unity; (3) a simple evangelical creed; (4) the spirit of evangelism.[14] The more influential Japanese Christians faced pressure from the increasingly nationalistic society around them to demonstrate their freedom from foreign direction. The issue for Uemura and other Japanese Christian leaders was not the presence of or cooperation with foreign missionaries, to which they did not object. They were concerned to establish the authentic independence of the Japanese church and the assumption by Japanese Christians of the primary responsibility for evangelizing their own nation.

However, it appears that there was sometimes a fine line between a wholesome and legitimate independent spirit and an unhealthy and questionable nationalism evident in the attitudes and actions of Japan's church leaders. This danger was exemplified in what may be called the Tamura affair. The Reverend Tamura, while on a visit to the United States in 1893, published a small book in English, entitled *The Japanese Bride*. He claimed that his purpose in publishing the book was to awaken sympathy and obtain help for evangelizing Japan. In fact, the book was not only poorly written but also inaccurate, unfair, and in poor taste in its portrayal of aspects of Japanese culture. Japanese church leaders were outraged and took action against him. He was deposed from the ministry by action of *Daikai*, judged unfit to discharge the offices and functions of a Christian minister. Tamura's statements and opinions in the book had no connection with the doctrine or standards in the

---

[13]    Drummond, *History of Christianity*, 212.
[14]    ERM to HNC, Jan. 10, 1910.

constitution of the Church of Christ in Japan. Missionaries could not see how his actions could be construed as immoral. Wyckoff stated, "While all foreigners are agreed that the sentence in Mr. Tamura's case is too severe, and such as would never be given for similar reasons at home, we are still obliged to face the fact that at the present time, and in the mind of almost every Japanese, there is no greater immorality than to be unpatriotic, and for us to say that Mr. Tamura's action is not immoral, is like shouting in the face of a hurricane."[15]

## Cooperation: Diverging Church and Missionary Perspectives

Clarification of the relationship between the Japanese church and the several missions proved to be difficult. It was a process that covered fifteen years. At the 1894 *Daikai* of the Church of Christ in Japan, Uemura proposed establishing an evangelism commission (*dendo kyoku*). It was to function under direction of the church's *Daikai*. The intent was to coordinate church extension activities at the national level, because evangelism without overall strategy, and primarily under the missions in cooperation with the separate *chukai*, was seen to cause proliferation of small preaching places unable to sustain growth or attain self-support.

Uemura's radical proposal was passed after strenuous debate despite some strong opposition. In effect, it severed the official organizational link between the Japanese church and the evangelistic work carried on by the missions. Congregations receiving aid from a mission and thus not independent were no longer recognized as members of the *Daikai*. As a result of the passage of Uemura's proposal, about one-fourth of the churches lost their former status. On the one hand, this decision meant that the missions actually had to assume greater control over pastors and churches under their care. On the other hand, it stimulated the spirit of independence among Japanese Christians. It challenged them to fulfill the rule requiring self-support by a congregation before becoming a full participant in the Japanese church. In contrast to the earlier Board of Domestic Missions, in the case of which three foreign missions provided three-quarters of the funds, the new *dendo kyoku*, or evangelism commission, raised funds from Japanese Christians. Consequently, it was not dependent on the missions. The new *dendo kyoku* began by selecting small potential congregations and leading them to self-support.[16]

---

[15]     MNW to HNC, July 16, 1894.
[16]     Ishihara Ken. *Nihon Kirisutokyo Shiron* (Tokyo: Shinkyo Shuppansha, 1967), 153-54; Drummond, *History of Christianity*, 214-15.

New rules established in 1895 by the Japanese church permitted limited cooperation with the six associated missions, under strict supervision. Under the new arrangement, Japanese itinerant evangelists were sent out by the *dendo kyoku* to strengthen small mission-related preaching places, as well as to witness to non-Christians. This evangelism commission also began the work of sending Japanese missionaries to Taiwan (Japanese colony from 1895), and later to Korea, Manchuria, and some cities in China, primarily to reach out to Japanese expatriates.[17]

These measures did not really solve the problem of cooperation with the missions, however. At the *Daikai* of 1896, Uemura introduced a further proposal calling for joint management of all evangelistic work. And on July 8, 1897, the *Daikai* issued a resolution defining the nature of its cooperation with the several Japan missions in the Council of Missions. It defined a cooperating mission as one that plans and executes *all* its evangelistic operations through a committee composed of equal numbers of members of a mission working within the bounds of a *chukai* of the Church of Christ and of members of that *chukai*.[18] The Council of Missions, meeting in the summer of 1897, reacted strongly to the resolution passed by the church's synod. Subsequent dialogue between representatives of the church and the several missions proved inconclusive, and misunderstandings threatened to undermine trust. The issue was control of the activities of the several missions heretofore under the control of the missionaries.

The disagreement in part reflected the difference between the situations faced by most of the Japanese pastors, churches, and missionaries, who worked in the outlying regions of Japan, and the Tokyo church leaders, whose experience centered in the big cities. Some city churches had grown into strong, self-supporting, self-propagating congregations. Uemura and other gifted Japanese ministers were taking leadership roles in the Church of Christ. However, the anti-Christian reaction and rise of nationalism had arrested the rapid church growth of the 1880s. Consequently, unable to grow sufficiently to become self-supporting, most pastors and their small, isolated, struggling churches in the rest of the country remained dependent on the several Japan missions and their missionaries.[19] Nevertheless, it would become

[17]    Drummond, *History of Christianity*, 216.
[18]    Pieters translation of letter from clerk of *Daikai*, July 8, 1897.
[19]    In 1905, in the Church of Christ in Japan, there were 78 churches and 110 preaching stations, of which 30 churches and 34 preaching stations were independent of mission aid. Average church membership per congregation was 37. There were 89 ministers and 90 licensed preachers or evangelists. ERM to HNC, Oct. 30, 1905.

increasingly crucial for all who represented the missions to find a way to relinquish authority where possible, while fulfilling their calling and carrying out their responsibilities.

The ecumenical General Conference of Protestant Missionaries in Japan, held in Tokyo October 24-31, 1900, indirectly demonstrated the inherent difficulty of the transition from missionary movement to cooperation with a self-reliant national church in mission. This all-inclusive Protestant missionary conference was attended by 435 Japan missionaries representing forty-two missions and agencies. Its proceedings were published in English in a volume of more than a thousand pages. The desirability of missionaries working in a foreign land to meet for fellowship and mutual edification need not be questioned. However, the fact that almost no provision was made for Japanese Christians to participate in the conference is suggestive. Forty-one years had passed since the arrival of the first missionaries. The total number of Japanese Protestant Christians in 1900 had reached about 45,000. Among them were many very intelligent and gifted leaders. So thoroughly foreign a conference discussing mission in Japan without significant Japanese input seems inconsistent with stated missionary goals.

Within the Church of Christ in Japan, efforts were made to bring the evangelists working under the guidance and with the support of the six Reformed and Presbyterian missions into closer ties with the Japanese church. In 1902, the *Chinzei Chukai* (classis in Kyushu) proposed a resolution that was then passed by the *Daikai* of the Church of Christ. It provided that all evangelists, i.e., not yet ordained licensed preachers, be seated at *chukai* as advisory members (nonvoting, but otherwise able to participate), virtually the same status as missionaries. This change brought evangelists, many of whom had worked for a mission for many years, into relationship with a deliberative body of the Church of Christ in Japan. As a result, in Kyushu, as Peeke reported, "instead of a meeting of classis with a beggarly seven or eight in attendance, we have had sixteen or so at every session....We met on Thursday and adjourned Monday night. I do not think I have ever attended a meeting that pleased me quite as much. The classis numbered only seven members, but with evangelists and Pieters and myself, we had quite a deliberative body." On a further positive note, Peeke added, "There seemed to be utter unconsciousness of any distinction between foreigner and native."[20]

However, the difficulty of the work in Kyushu was such that as of 1904 not one of the churches or preaching stations of the South

[20]    HVSP to HNC, Apr. 14, 1904.

Japan Mission had reached true self-support and independence.[21] The relationship between the South Japan Mission's work and the national church thus remained rather tenuous. In 1904, Peeke reported,

> Mr. Uemura recently toured these parts. In speaking of our Kyushu work, he at once put his finger on our weak spot. The policy of the mission has been for years to be sufficient unto itself, and to keep aloof from the church at large, as centered around Tokyo. The coming of men from those parts as pastors to Kyushu would have kept us in touch with the whole, and we would find ourselves in much different shape today. Our endeavor will be to correct the error of the past in these lines, but it will not be easy.[22]

In 1905 the Council of Missions proposed to the *Daikai* that organized churches under the care of the missions be transferred to the *chukai* when they reached one-half of self-support. The *Daikai* declined to approve this proposal. However, the synod reconfirmed its resolve not only to function as an independent church, but also to accept help gladly from the missions.[23] In the fall of 1905, Mr. Ishida, a close associate of Uemura and a representive of the *dendo kyoku*, visited Kyushu for extended visitation of the South Japan Mission's churches and preaching stations, encouraging them toward self-support. Peeke met for an extended dialogue with Ishida. As a result of the meeting, Peeke felt confident that a cooperative relationship between the mission and the assertively independent Japanese church leaders would be realized.[24]

The Uemura group of church leaders, however, was in fact encountering resistance among many Japanese Christians. Ruigh, of the North Japan Mission, observed,

> The leaders of the church who fathered the "Independence Resolution" and carried it through the last *Daikai* are not meeting with as much encouragement and success in putting these resolutions into practical operation as they had fondly hoped for. The good brethren are finding that resolving to do and the doing itself are widely differing things. Unfortunately they have mistaken centralization for independence and the church as a

---

[21]   AP to HNC, July 24, 1906. Pieters reported that on July 1, 1906, Nagasaki Church became the first self-supporting church connected with the South Japan Mission.

[22]   HVSP to HNC, March 9, 1904.

[23]   GH to HNC, Sept. 2, 1905; HVSP to HNC, Oct. 18, 1905; Iglehart, *Century*, 122.

[24]   HVSP to South Japan Mission, Dec. 7, 1905.

whole is too democratic a body to fall in with the ideas of the present leaders.[25]

Ishida again visited Kyushu at the time of the meeting of *Chinzei Chukai* in the spring of 1906. Pieters and Peeke were also in attendance. At this classis meeting, decisions of the *Daikai* meeting were reported, including that what had hitherto been called *kogisho* (preaching stations) were henceforth to be called *dendo kyokai* (mission churches), which were to be more directly under guidance by *chukai*, and that the Church of Christ no longer recognized any official "cooperating mission" status, but would henceforth receive "cooperating missionaries" who accepted the confession of faith, constitution, and canons of the Japanese church. These missionaries could be approved as *ingai giin* (advisory members) of *chukai*. Pieters and Peeke were approved as advisory members of *Chinzei Chukai*.[26]

Peeke stated the South Japan Mission's perspective.

> We are glad to accord autonomy to the Japanese church, and propose to do only those things they cannot do for themselves, and even those as far as possible as they wish them done; but on the other hand, the mission has its autonomy which must be respected, and until the American church passes over its funds in lump to the Japanese church with (_____) or permission to employ us, we are to be in full control of our own business. We cannot serve two masters. When we must obtain the consent of the Japanese church before doing or ceasing to do, we cease to be able to serve those who have commissioned us and are at present sustaining us.
>
> Our Kyushu men see this clearly and seem to approve our position. We on our part are more than ready to consult, tho it will be very inconvenient in many cases, and the Japanese are not in a position to be very helpful parties to some consultations yet.[27]

Regarding the independence movement, Pieters and Peeke insisted, "We must maintain the freedom of the church in determining the terms on which it will receive assistance, but we must equally maintain the freedom of the mission to determine the terms of the assistance which it is willing or able to give."[28]

[25]    DCR to HNC, Jan. 2, 1906.
[26]    AP & HVSP to HNC, Apr. 6, 1906.
[27]    HVSP to HNC, Apr. 11, 1906.
[28]    AP & HVSP to HNC, Apr. 6, 1906.

## Seeking a Workable Cooperative Relationship

In the spring of 1906, it was clear that some of the leaders of the Church of Christ were still not satisfied with the character of the cooperative relationship with some of the missions. Uemura apparently objected to cooperative arrangements worked out when his colleague Ishida visited Kyushu, agreements subsequently adopted by Chinzei *Chukai* and Naniwa *Chukai*.[29]

A letter was sent by a committee of the Japanese church to all the Reformed and Presbyterian foreign mission boards in February 1906, stating that in 1897 the Japanese church's synod had made clear that no cooperation in the proper sense of the word existed between the missions and the Church of Christ in Japan. It stated that since that time no change had taken place and lamented that there was no prospect of a change. The letter surveyed the history of attempts to cooperate, beginning in 1886. The several mission boards replied courteously to the Japanese church, but it was clear that extended dialogue would be required to resolve the issues. The several Japan missions once again faced the need to clarify their relationship with the Japanese church.

Pieters stated the South Japan Mission's position and expressed his opinion.

> The missions have no power and do not wish to have any power over the affairs of the Japanese church or any part of it. All they insist upon is when they give financial assistance to any branch of the church they shall have the right to fix their own conditions, which can be rejected by the negotiating body....
>
> But what the Daikai is after is not to secure the independence of the Japanese Church. That is already secured abundantly. The movement is partly directed to the encouragement of a spirit of self-support, so as to render appeal to the missions needless. In so far, we heartily approve and welcome the movement. But what is dwelt upon chiefly in the letter sent out is not this. It is an effort to destroy the independence of the missions by obliging them to submit all their operations to the decision of a committee composed of half Japanese and half missionaries. This has not been agreed to by a single mission. It would hamper them in every way, and practically destroy their independence and efficiency as evangelizing agencies....
>
> Perhaps I may be lacking in sympathy for what some call the "legitimate aspirations" of the Japanese church, but to me the

---

[29]   HVSP to HNC, May 21, 1906.

movement seems lacking in genuineness. It seems to originate rather in the little circle of ambitious men in Tokyo than in any real need of the church.

In another view, it is inevitable that such questions should come up for discussion, for the relations of the missions to a self-governing church have never been clearly defined.[30]

At its *Daikai* in October of 1906, the Japanese church officially approved its new definition of cooperation.

A cooperating mission is one which recognizes the right of the Church of Christ in Japan to the general care of all evangelistic work done by the mission as a mission within the church or in connection with it: and which carries on such work under an arrangement based on the foregoing principle and concurred in by the synod acting through the Board of Missions [*Dendo Kyoku*].

The several missions hitherto known as the missions cooperating with the Church of Christ in Japan are cordially invited to formulate plans for cooperation in accordance with the foregoing resolutions and to confer with the [Japanese] Board of Missions regarding them.[31]

Two of the six missions comprising the Council of Japan Missions accepted working under the Japanese church's revised definition of a cooperating mission.[32] The other four missions were not ready to work under that definition. Consequently, a protracted period of discussion and negotiation followed.

The Reformed Church's mission board in America gave its tacit approval to the proposals of the Japanese church, much to the consternation of most of the missionaries in both the North and South Japan Missions. In the North Japan Mission, an informal meeting of three members of the mission noted that the Reformed Church's mission board approved the Japanese church's right to control all work of the missions and decided to approve the church's proposal. However, when the implications of such a decision became clear, a meeting of the full North Japan Mission reversed the previous action.[33] The North and South Japan Missions held joint meetings to discuss the issues

---

30 AP to HNC, June 14, 1906.
31 AP to HNC, Sept. 15, 1906.
32 The West Japan Mission of the Presbyterian Church in the U.S.A. and the Japan Mission of the Reformed Church in the U.S. (German).
33 GH to HNC, Aug. 19, 1907.

and agreed in their opposition to the Japanese church's position. E. R. Miller alone would have accepted it.

The missionaries, knowing the meaning in Japanese of certain words used in the original proposal, believed that the English translation sent to the mission boards was misleading. *Kankatsu*, translated as "general care" (of all evangelistic work done by a mission), actually means "control, direction, or jurisdiction." *Kankoku*, translated as "cordially invited" (to formulate plans for cooperation), actually means "to advise, admonish, or exhort." Furthermore, the missionaries were no longer to be allowed to participate in *chukai* meetings as *ingai giin* (advisory members), and were no longer to attend its meetings.[34] However, most offensive to the missionaries was the requirement that in order to be accepted as "cooperating missions" they would henceforth be required to confer, not with their Japanese colleagues in their respective *chukai*, but with the *dendo kyoku*, a group of about six church leaders in Tokyo, two days' journey away. Peeke asserted that this amounted to usurpation of the legitimate powers of the *chukai* by "a clique in the church."[35] Peeke sensed these changes were part of an accelerating tendency toward the centralization of power in the Church of Christ in Japan.[36]

Pieters also expressed his view concerning evangelism responsibility clearly.

> The whole question may be briefly stated to concern the independence of the American churches in their missionary work. In my mind they are independent and sovereign no less in their missionary work in Japan than in any other department of their activity, and ought to remain so. They have not a secondary responsibility to the heathen in Japan, but a primary one, as primary and direct as that of the Japanese church itself. Let them do their work here until it is clear that they are no longer needed, or are needed more elsewhere, and when the time comes to withdraw, let them go bag and baggage, men and money together, and leave the Japanese church to do its own work in its own way.[37]

Peeke and Pieters were shocked to learn that there had even been discussion of turning over part of the evangelistic work of the Reformed

[34]   HVSP to HNC, Feb. 21, 1907.
[35]   HVSP to HNC, Aug. 9, 1906.
[36]   HVSP to HNC, Oct. 24, 1907.
[37]   AP to HNC, Sept. 15, 1906.

Church's North Japan Mission to the Japanese church's *dendo kyoku*.[38] Pieters remarked,

> If it were a plan to turn over absolutely a number of stations and let the Dendo Kyoku support them, there could be no objection. But it is a plan to turn over the mission evangelistic funds to them for administration. This is to create a subsidized denomination. We are getting rid of the evils of supported local churches, and shall we now go into the business of raising up a supported [Japanese] Mission Board? And that in the face of the experience we have, that a self-supporting Mission Board is so much better in every way than an assisted one?[39]

William Imbrie, a Presbyterian missionary teaching in the Meiji Gakuin theological department, was among those who promoted turning over the evangelistic work and its funding to the Japanese church's *dendo kyoku*, and who suggested that the work of the missions was nearly completed. Pieters objected on the basis of mission theology and the missionary calling. Referring to a letter from Henry Cobb, Pieters wrote,

> With your definition of the purpose of mission work,...I have no controversy. I understand you to say there that the church is not considered as fully established until it is strong enough in virtue of its own resources of men and means to complete, in conjunction with other native churches, and within a reasonable time, the work of evangelization....At that time I see that the purpose of missions is accomplished and that the work should cease. But the view that I am opposed to is contained in the unqualified statement: "The establishment of a native church, possessing full powers of self-government, maintenance, and extension, is the ultimate aim of Christian missions." This, in its unqualified form, is held by some. If so understood, it results that when a church can govern itself, can support itself, and can carry on so much evangelistic work as constantly to extend itself, that then the purpose of missions is accomplished. This leaves out of sight the un-evangelized mass, and makes no provision for them....Unless we keep our eyes turned to the un-evangelized, we

---

[38]   Such a plan had been initiated in March of 1907 and then rescinded several months later. ERM to HNC, Feb. 26, 1907; North Japan Mission Minutes, Aug., 1907.

[39]   AP to HNC, Sept. 15, 1906.

shall lose the fervor of our evangelism, and when that is gone the life of missions has departed.[40]

According to Peeke, the challenge of defining a workable cooperative relationship with the Japanese church was being made more difficult by Imbrie's role. In his colorful words,

> Things are moving on very nicely in Japan at present. The Japanese nation seems ready for a steady move forward, and the movement is taking place. Our principle anxiety is in regard to the Dendo Kyoku, fathered by Dr. Imbrie. I do abominate office missionaries that sit in their revolving chairs, plan out schemes from their inner consciousness and lack of practical experience in evangelistic work, with the result of making things difficult for the fraternity that swelter and are flea bitten part of the year and suffer from frost much of the rest, in order that the Gospel may be preached in what are practically the highways and byways of the empire.[41]

Pieters expressed his regret that the Reformed mission board had sanctioned the Japanese church's definition of cooperation without even consulting the missionaries on the field. Regarding what the board secretary, Henry Cobb, had written in a major presentation, Pieters agrees with most of it, but adds,

> When you say that a native church ought to have the right to supervise the work done for its benefit, i.e., the evangelistic work of the missions, I fail to follow your reasoning...such evangelistic work is not done primarily to extend the church, understood as a visible organization. It is done to extend a knowledge of the gospel and to bring men to Christ. Also to organize in each locality a permanent agency, but in my view the benefit accruing to that combination of local churches known as a denomination is altogether secondary and incidental....The idea that missionaries are no longer needed, for instance, is constantly found on the lips of such men as Dr. Imbrie, and finds a show of justification only in his theory of missions, whereby the perfected denominational organization is the object of the work....
>
> Neither can I agree with your view that the direction of such evangelistic work can be better done by natives than by foreigners,

---

[40]   AP to HNC, Dec. 5, 1906.
[41]   HVSP to HNC, May 8, 1907.

on account of their being better acquainted with customs, language, etc. It is certainly beyond question that these are advantages, but they are, in my opinion, more than overbalanced by other advantages which the missionary has over any native workers who can be induced to take part in the evangelistic work. He is...much freer from entanglements with the internal life of the church and consequently certain to be much more single-hearted in his devotion to the interests of the evangelistic work.... Certainly I could not consent that any Japanese known to me as available for evangelistic work would have the competence that Mr. Peeke has, all things considered. A man who has spent fifteen years studying this one problem is not so ignorant of the customs or language of the country that he is seriously hampered in that aggressive organizing work that he needs to do.[42]

In Booth's response to the question of whether new missionaries should be sent while the cooperation question is not yet settled, he urged that missionaries were needed because of the millions of Japanese not being reached by the Japanese churches under the leadership of that time. He wrote,

The *heimin* class, viz., the common people, of whom there are more than thirty-five millions, are as yet practically untouched by the gospel, and it is generally admitted that the ex-samurai leaders in the Japanese church of today have no adaptability for that work, and foreign missionaries are imperatively needed for that work.[43]

On behalf of the South Japan Mission, Pieters prepared a pamphlet, which was read to the Council of Missions in 1907 and sent to the mission board as the official position of the South Japan Mission. Of this thoroughly reasoned document, Hondelink reported:

Mr. Pieters' pamphlet is the best that has been written on cooperation. I do hope that all our Board will stand on the principle that the church and missions should be independent each in their own sphere. This is the best way to work in Japan. In this way the empire will be most speedily evangelized....there will be a minimum of friction and a maximum of peace and harmony.[44]

[42]   AP to HNC, Aug. 7, 1907.
[43]   ESB to HNC, Feb. 7, 1908.
[44]   GH to HNC, Aug. 19, 1907.

In his pamphlet, Pieters stated, "The right of the church to exercise control over all work carried on within its bounds is indisputable, and is gladly and fully recognized by this mission. Accordingly, in all such acts as the receiving and disciplining of church members, the organizing of churches, the ordaining of ministers, the licensing of evangelists, etc., etc., the church is supreme. The mission neither has nor desires to have any authority whatever in such matters." Referring to wording in the Japanese church's definition of cooperation, Pieters argued,

> The words "carried on within the church or in connection with it," are a real limitation upon the words "all the evangelistic work of the mission"; for a considerable portion of our work, all that portion, indeed, which aims to reach the wholly un-evangelized masses, is neither within nor in connection with the ecclesiastical organization as such. To this category belongs all the work of the Bible women, colporteurs, and other workers who do not conduct the regular services of an organization of the Church of Christ in Japan; all work done in places where no organization of that church exists; and at least nine-tenths of all work done by the ordained missionaries and single ladies.[45]

Ruigh, of the North Japan Mission, stated, "Now it must not be thought that I am opposed to cooperation with the Church of Christ in Japan. I do believe in it most heartily and emphatically. It is the cooperation as defined by the last synod to which I object."[46] The missionaries made clear that they had no reservations about granting full authority to the Japanese church but insisted that, while welcoming consultation regarding their own evangelistic activity, they needed a measure of independence in order to fulfill their calling and responsibilities.

The Council of Missions insisted that the missions welcomed consultation but denied the inherent right of the Japanese church's *dendo kyoku* to exercise complete control of the missions. The Church of Christ, however, at its fall meeting, pressed on with the plans put forth by Uemura and his colleagues. This 1907 *Daikai*, in the words of Pieters, "passed another very radical resolution, practically forbidding any 'mission church,' i.e., any partially or temporarily organized congregation to receive any assistance from 'non-cooperating' missions, on pain of being, as an organization, excluded from the Church of Christ in Japan."[47]

---

[45]   AP to Board of Foreign Missions, Sept. 9, 1907.
[46]   DCR to HNC, Aug. 24, 1907.
[47]   AP to HNC, Oct. 18, 1907.

Efforts by a small group of leaders in Tokyo to consolidate control of the Japanese church appeared to be gaining momentum. At the 1907 *Daikai*, Uemura "set forth an argument for entirely abolishing the *chukai*."[48] That suggestion was not acted upon, but the high-handed approach of the Uemura group aroused a reaction. Rumors of the possibility of churches separating from the Church of Christ to form a new denomination were heard. Of this matter, Pieters wrote,

> The missions have no desire to do such a "monstrous" thing as to enter into competition with the church they have founded. The danger lies in quite a different quarter, among the Japanese themselves, for not a few of them are exasperated at the action of the dominant party, and are ready to renounce their allegiance to the *Nihon Kirisuto Kyokai*....the present difficulties are not so much the result of any peculiarities of the Japanese mind as they are the outcome of an unsolved problem, viz.: "Has the native church any right to direct, or share in directing, the work done with mission funds?" This problem is troublesome only because unsettled.[49]

The problem of the relationship between the Church of Christ in Japan and the four missions of the Council of Missions who could not approve working under the Japanese church's definition of a cooperating mission was finally resolved in the fall of 1909. The Church of Christ approved an alternate mode of cooperation, for "affiliated missions." The North and South Japan Missions of the Reformed Church, as well as the East Japan Mission of the Presbyterian Church and the Japan Mission of the Southern Presbyterian Church, accepted this status as a basis for working in partnership with the Japanese church.

An "affiliated mission" was deemed one that agreed to conduct its evangelistic work according to several conditions, including the following:

> The mission shall sincerely accept the Confession, Constitution, and Canons of the Church of Christ in Japan, and shall regard the same as suitable and sufficient for the ministers, evangelists, *dendo kyokai*, and *kogisho* in connection with the mission.
>
> Persons engaged in evangelistic work in connection with the mission shall be those who have received licensure or ordination from a *chukai*, and those who are ministers shall be eligible to become associate members of *chukai* and *daikai*.

[48]     HVSP to HNC, Oct. 24, 1907.
[49]     AP to HNC, Dec. 28, 1907.

Mission *dendo kyokai* and *kogisho* shall have no organic connection with the Church of Christ in Japan. However, they shall be included in the statistics of the Church of Christ in Japan in a separate column. They shall report to the *chukai* once a year their financial and spiritual condition, and shall, as far as their circumstances permit, exert themselves to promote the interests of the Church of Christ in Japan as a whole.

The mission shall organize no churches. When mission *dendo kyokai* or mission *kogisho* wish to be churches, they shall make application to the appropriate *chukai*, and when organized as churches they shall be Churches of Christ in Japan.[50]

On the plus side, this agreement with "affiliated missions" provided a place within the Japanese church structure for any Japanese ministers or evangelists working for one of the missions. However, mission-assisted *dendo kyokai* and *kogisho* were no longer an organic part of the Church of Christ in Japan. Membership of the Japanese Christians in the mission churches and preaching places thus became nebulous, since it was not technically church membership. The South Japan Mission was not pleased that the affiliation plan severed relations between the Church of Christ in Japan and the mission-assisted congregations, believing such action was "unnecessary, un-Reformed, and un-Christian."[51] Even so, the plan was accepted by both the North and South Japan Missions. Wyckoff observed, "It offers a practical scheme for working harmoniously."[52] Under this arrangement Reformed Church missionaries remained free to carry on pioneer evangelistic outreach and to contribute to the growth and development of independent churches.

In the South Japan Mission, Peeke and Segawa arranged to meet with the ministers and evangelists working under its guidance and support and to clarify the principles of their working relationship.[53] The missions were obliged to assume an awkward, quasiecclesiastical responsibility for mission-assisted congregations until they could reach a state of self-support, at which point they would be transferred to the

[50]    AP to HNC, Oct. 18, 1909. Plan of affiliation document translated from the Japanese by Albertus Pieters. A *dendo kyokai* ("mission church") was a small congregation of ten or more members, partially organized, but under the supervision of the mission. A *kogisho* ("preaching place") was a small group of believers with the simplest form of organization.
[51]    AP to HNC, Dec. 13, 1909.
[52]    MNW to HNC, Jan. 12, 1909.
[53]    WGH to HNC, Nov. 16 and Dec. 24, 1909.

Church of Christ in Japan. Fortunately, schism and the formation of a new denomination by the Japanese pastors of mission-assisted churches were avoided.

The resulting two modes of cooperation, though somewhat different in nature and nuance, both worked well, and a relatively stable cooperative relationship between the six missions in the Council of Missions and the Japanese church continued for many years. At the same time, the Church of Christ in Japan continued to be characterized by the spirit of independence exemplified by Uemura, and the requirement of full self-support remained as a condition for full membership of a congregation in the church's assemblies.[54]

Throughout the first fifty years of Protestant mission work in Japan, the missionaries had emphasized two types of activity, education and evangelism. The evangelistic work had resulted in the formation and development of an independent and increasingly self-reliant Japanese church with which they had to reformulate a working relationship. The educational work had resulted in the development of growing and respected mission schools. However, the original missionary vision of a Japanese church with the will and strength to take responsibility for further development and support of these schools proved unrealistic. The schools remained *mission* schools, dependent upon the mission organizations for support and unable to become true Japanese church schools.

## Uemura Masahisa: Theologian and Theological Educator

Uemura Masahisa came to be recognized not only for his leadership in the Japanese church, but also for his role in clarifying Japanese evangelical Protestant theology. The introduction of new theological perspectives had begun to affect the Christian movement in Japan. German missionaries Wilfred Spinner and Otto Schmiedel had come to Japan. According to historian Yanagita Tomonobu, through their journal they "introduced the study of Biblical criticism, something completely new to Japanese Christians. Sneering at belief in the supernatural and the orthodox interpretation of the Anglo-American missionaries, in the name of science they inspired a spirit of liberalism...in the Japanese churches which destroyed faith in the inspiration of the Bible."[55] One of the most prominent leaders of the Japanese Congregational churches, Ebina Danjo (1856-1937), was deeply influenced by this new theology.

---

[54]    Drummond, *History of Christianity*, 216-17.
[55]    Yanagita, *Short History*, 51.

What came to be called the Uemura-Ebina Controversy of 1901-1902 proved to be a watershed experience in the career of Uemura Masahisa. This debate, which has been described as "the most vehement and significant one on record since the introduction of Protestant Christianity to Japan in 1859,"[56] attracted the attention of the entire church in Japan. The controversy or dialogue was carried on primarily in the pages of two well-known periodicals, the *Fukuin Shimpo* ("Gospel News") and the *Shinjin* ("New Man"), of which Uemura and Ebina were the respective editors. Ebina, in his subjectively oriented thought, "emphasized the role of Christ as teacher and example rather than as redeemer through his sacrifice on the cross. His theological position might be described as theistic philosophical idealism."[57] Ebina did not believe in the incarnation of Christ and consequently denied Christ's divinity and the doctrine of the Trinity. He saw Christ "as man's ultimate religious experience of the God-man relationship."[58] By contrast, according to Drummond,

> The position in this controversy of Uemura...was staunchly on the side of classical Protestant orthodoxy. While recognizing the historical and human elements in the development of Christianity, he preferred to see its origin in divine revelation. He stressed the work of God. Over against Ebina's tendency to an adoptionist view of Jesus as the Christ, Uemura stoutly believed in his deity, in a literal incarnation. He saw Christ as a proper object of worship, as one to whom men may properly pray. He saw Jesus Christ as Savior, as the worthy object of all trust, as the one to whom we are united in life and in death.[59]

Uemura accused Ebina of "opening the way for man to confess God as Father without first being liberated from his sins."[60] In a series of thirteen articles in *Fukuin Shimpo*, Uemura published what became his comprehensive treatise on Christology, entitled *Kirisuto to Sono Jigyo* ("Christ and His Work"). This series of articles, concluded on July 2, 1902, not only ended the Uemura-Ebina controversy but also established Uemura as the preeminent evangelical Christian leader and scholar of his time. Uemura's theology was not simply a repetition of

---

[56]   Ishida Yoshiro, "The Uemura-Ebina Controversy of 1901-1902," *Japan Christian Quarterly* 39, no. 2 (Spring, 1973), 64.

[57]   Drummond, *History of Christianity*, 218.

[58]   Ishida, "Uemura-Ebina Controversy," 66.

[59]   Drummond, *History of Christianity*, 218.

[60]   Ishida, "Uemura-Ebina Controversy," 65.

Uemura Masahisa (1858 – 1925)

doctrines and arguments from the West but included a serious effort by a self-conscious Japanese to indigenize his theological position. The two theological perspectives, represented by Uemura and Ebina, continued to exist within the Christian movement. However, by the clear, forceful expression of his views, it was Uemura who helped most to form and strengthen the mainstream of Japanese Protestant theology.

Uemura also had a notable impact in the area of theological education in Japan. In addition to his prodigious work as preacher, pastor, writer, and church leader, Uemura served for many years on the faculty of the theological department of Meiji Gakuin, where he had completed his own formal theological studies. In 1903, when he learned that an objection had been raised to his use in class of what one missionary considered liberal textbooks, Uemura resigned from Meiji Gakuin. Then, in 1904, with the help of several other pastors, Uemura founded the first theological school independently administered and financed by Japanese Christians, called the Tokyo Shingakusha. Uemura's reputation and leadership is reflected in the fact that this new theological education venture was able to begin with more than thirty students enrolled. The school was conducted at the church in Ichigaya, Tokyo (Fujimicho Church), at which Uemura was pastor. The Japanese expression *te bento de* was often used to describe the manner in which Uemura and his colleagues carried on theological education. This Japanese expression may be literally translated "carrying one's own lunch," and it meant that the pastors who taught at this school received no salary and even brought their own lunches when they came to teach. Uemura and his colleagues not only taught, they also mentored their students and served as role models for Christian ministry. Uemura's theological school, the Tokyo Shingakusha, exemplified the spirit of independence, financial and otherwise, from the several missions working in relationship with the Church of Christ in Japan.

In a letter in 1907, Oltmans, a professor in the theological department of Meiji Gakuin, noted that at the recent *Daikai* of the Church of Christ, approval had been granted for graduates of Uemura's school to be examined for licensure and ordination. Oltmans commented, "For my part, I wish that the theological work of Mr. Uemura and that of Meiji Gakuin could be united. There is no call for two seminaries of the Church of Christ in Japan right here in Tokyo. And I am sure such a union could be effected if some of our Japanese brethren were not so hopelessly out with Mr. Uemura.[61] In a joint 1913 letter regarding theological education addressed to the Reformed and Presbyterian mission boards, Oltmans and Imbrie remarked, "The union that ought to be effected is one between Meiji Gakuin and Mr. Uemura's school; but though Mr. Uemura has been approached several times on the subject his replies have afforded little encouragement."[62]

In 1919, the Reformed and Presbyterian Japan Missions, which jointly supported Meiji Gakuin, and the Board of Trustees of Meiji Gakuin, expressed the conviction that the interests of the Church of Christ in Japan, of theological study in Japan, and of the evangelistic work of the various missions working in relation to the Church of Christ would be best served by a union of the Japan School of Theology (Uemura's school) and the theological department of Meiji Gakuin. They urged the forming of this one high caliber theological school in Tokyo, linked directly to the *Daikai* of the Church of Christ.[63] Representatives of the Reformed and Presbyterian missions and the Meiji Gakuin board took the initiative in promoting this union in theological education. However, negotiations with Uemura proved unproductive. Nevertheless, the Meiji Gakuin theological department was separated from the parent school and relocated to a different site in Tokyo, in the hope that this would facilitate progress toward union.[64]

Uemura Masahisa died suddenly on January 9, 1925. His was a very strong personality, and he had made a profound impact on the Christian movement in Japan. His emphasis on the independence and self-reliance of the Japanese church had left its positive mark, but he had sometimes found it difficult to cooperate with other Christian leaders,

[61]    AO to HNC, Jan. 30, 1907.
[62]    AO to William I. Chamberlain, Feb. 18, 1913.
[63]    Luman J. Shafer to WIC, March 25, and Aug. 1, 1919.
[64]    LJS to WIC, Oct. 4, 1921, July 29, 1922, June 7, Aug. 3 and 6, and Dec. 6, 1923.

both Japanese and missionary. Both of the Japan missions involved with Meiji Gakuin, as well as the respective mission boards in America, strongly favored and repeatedly urged the unification of theological education in Tokyo. However, the Reformed Church's Japan Mission also made it clear that it would be necessary to be patient and wait for Japanese church leaders to take the next step toward an eventual union theological school.[65]

Both the Tokyo Shingakusha and the Meiji Gakuin theological department continued producing ministers for the Church of Christ in Japan until 1929. Those ministers who studied in Uemura's school, however, were especially imbued with the spirit of independence characterized by its founder. Since some of the missionaries and Japanese church leaders had jealously guarded a measure of control of theological education at Meiji Gakuin, and because Uemura's school represented in part a protest of independence, during the twenty-five years of their coexistence inevitably a spirit of competition was created. Even so, the magnanimity of Japanese Christians was apparent in that graduates of the two schools worked together in the churches without disruptive rivalry or friction.[66]

In 1929, the Church of Christ accepted the offer of the missions of the Reformed Church and the Presbyterian Church to unite the theological department of Meiji Gakuin with the Tokyo Shingakusha. The resulting union school was called Nihon Shingakko (Japan School of Theology). The two missions made "a congratulatory gift"[67] to this new school, which would be needed to absorb the expanded student body and faculty. The Reformed Church Japan Mission's gift, 6,000 yen, or $3,000 in 1930, was to continue for five to ten years on a decreasing basis. In addition, each mission agreed to provide a missionary teacher for the school. The Japan School of Theology welcomed the services of the Reformed mission's Henry Stegeman as professor of New Testament but did not accord him official status as a full member of the faculty. The founding of the Nihon Shingakko marked the end of the era of missionary control over theological education.[68]

---

[65]    AO to WIC, May 29, 1925; Stephen W. Ryder to WIC, July 25, 1925; WIC to WGH, June 30, 1928.

[66]    Drummond, *History of Christianity*, 217-18.

[67]    This is an English translation of a euphemistic Japanese term used for financial assistance or subsidy in deference to Japanese sensitivities and independent spirit.

[68]    Ryder, *Historical Sourcebook*, 70-71.

# CHAPTER 10

# Mission amid the Rise of Japanese Colonialism

## Power Shifts, Colonial Expansion, and International Tension

During the 1890s and the early twentieth century, Japan realized its declared goal of achieving *fukoku kyohei*, i.e., becoming a rich nation with a strong army. Not only had industry and commerce developed remarkably, but also the army and navy had become disciplined and well-equipped military forces. Expansion of influence in and hegemony over northeast Asia were realized in part through clandestine activities and armed conflicts. Japan clearly demonstrated its newfound military might in its conflicts with China (1894-95) and Russia (1904-05).

Emulating the West, Japan aspired to become a colonial empire. As a spoil of victory in the Sino-Japanese War, in 1895 Japan gained Taiwan as a colony to the south and extended its influence on the Korean peninsula, beginning the process of establishing a colonial empire. As a result of the Russo-Japanese War, in 1905 Japan gained full control of the Kuril Islands and Karafuto to the north and procured the leasehold of southern Manchuria. Furthermore, the military victories over China and Russia effectively ended competition with them for

413

hegemony over the Korean peninsula. Japan gradually extended its influence and control over Korea, culminating in its annexation and colonial occupation in 1910. In August 1910, an imperial rescript was issued, stating,

> We, attaching the highest importance to the maintenance of permanent peace in the Orient and the consolidation of lasting security for our Empire and finding in Korea constant and fruitful sources of complication....have now arrived at an arrangement for permanent annexation....All Koreans, being under Our direct sway, will enjoy growing prosperity and welfare, and with assured repose and security will come a marked expansion of industry and trade.[1]

Japan's victories over China and Russia added to the domestic prestige and influence of the military. In both the popular press and in the schools the military's valor and commitment were stressed.[2] "In turn, these triumphs furnished the Japanese nation with a new set of heroes as well as instilling an undeniable sense of national pride."[3] Even the mission schools for boys capitulated to the government requirement and included military drill in their curriculae.

Social and economic pressures were also factors in the development of Japan's colonialism. The population began to grow more rapidly, mostly in urban industrializing areas stretching along the eastern coast from Kobe to Tokyo. Estimates indicate a Japanese population of 35 million in 1873, 41 million in 1891, and 52 million in 1913. Emigration from Japan to Hawaii and the west coast of the United States provided some relief, but by 1900 Japan was no longer able to produce enough food for its people, and it needed additional natural resources and markets for its industries. Japanese expatriates in large numbers went to Taiwan, Korea, and southern Manchuria. They built railroads and extended communication and commerce networks. Such developments brought only limited advantages to the colonized peoples but served the purposes of the Japanese occupiers well.

Emperor Meiji (Mutsuhito) died in 1912, after a reign of forty-four years. During the Meiji Era, the nation had become the self-assured Japanese Empire. It had been controlled by the *genro*, the elite ruling

---

[1]     Jansen, *Making of Modern Japan*, 445.
[2]     Ibid., 452.
[3]     James Crowley, "Creation of an Empire, 1896-1910," in *Imperial Japan: 1800-1945*, ed. Jon Livingston, Joe Moore, and Felicia Oldfather (New York: Random House, 1973), 228.

oligarchy, for several decades. However, by the end of the Meiji Era, that control had given way and a balance of power had evolved. Not only elected officials, but also elite bureaucrats (mostly graduates of Tokyo and Kyoto Universities), the tycoons of the capitalist conglomerates, officials of the imperial household, and elite military leaders shared control of the several aspects of government. The nation was becoming prosperous, but Japan's newfound wealth and power were felt primarily in its cities.

Meanwhile, the standards of living and resulting customs of the general populace were also changing, albeit at a much slower pace.

> In the countryside, among ordinary people, things went on much as before for much of the Meiji period. Life for Japan's tenant farmers remained difficult and penurious, and...for many life was lived at its lowest possible level: simple houses with dirt floors, bare feet or straw sandals, and a diet that featured coarser grains than rice and little or no fish or meat. For independent, land-owning farmers conditions of life changed noticeably only by the turn of the century....Houses became better, mat floors were raised above the dirt, wide eves swept around the building, and sliding paper panels, sometimes upgraded to glass, made for a brighter and cleaner home. Tiles [for the roof, instead of thatch], long forbidden for commoners, brought color in the monochrome villages of earlier times. Around the turn of the century oil lamps, and then gradually electricity, made it possible to be up after dusk. Hulled rice became the staple of every diet that could afford it, and soy and other sauces to supplement its taste became common. Fish, and sometimes meat, became more common in the diet of ordinary people. In the cities horse trams appeared along with swarms of rickshaws, and by late Meiji, streetcars and rail made it possible to travel to the cities to work and shop. By mid-Meiji years a Tokugawa-style top-knot was a rarity in cities, and by late Meiji men all over Japan wore their hair short. The head then began to be covered, with cap or hat. Leather shoes were expensive and frequently uncomfortable, but the straw-shod and bare-footed commoners of early Meiji turned to wooden clogs.[4]

In contrast to feudal times, when the samurai were an elite class superior to the other four classes in Japanese society—farmers, artisans,

---

[4]   Jansen, *Making of Modern Japan*, 454-55.

merchants, and laborers—the armies of imperial Japan were largely recruited from among common people and indoctrinated to serve as the loyal soldiers of the emperor. Behind all the elements of the obvious transformation of Japan during the Meiji Era, an almost hidden coup had occurred. Japan's conservative intellectuals had succeeded in laying the foundations of a new ideology of imperial divinity and national superiority that would facilitate the control and manipulation of the people.

The Meiji emperor was succeeded by his only surviving son, Yoshihito, on July 30, 1912. Yoshihito had actually been born not to the empress, but to a lady in waiting at the palace. In any case, he was the biological son of the emperor. Unfortunately, due to the meningitis he contracted shortly after his birth and other possible causes, Yoshihito, the Taisho Era emperor, was never healthy, physically or mentally. Always poor in matters requiring higher thought, and as a result of his disabilities and eccentricities, the Taisho emperor became known as the *Baka Tenno*, or the Mad Emperor.[5] He undertook no official duties after 1919, and his oldest son, eighteen-year-old Prince Hirohito, carried out official duties as regent until the death of the Taisho emperor in 1926. It goes without saying that his was an undistinguished career. Nevertheless, during his career certain events affected Japan's place in the world as well as the Christian movement in Japan.

The Taisho Era was marked politically by the liberal movement that came to be known as Taisho Democracy, which suppressed the power of the privileged classes typical of the Meiji Era. Political power shifted from the clique of elder statesmen to political parties and the parliament. As a result, Japan progressed toward a democratic system of government during this period, and universal male suffrage was achieved in 1925. However, the democracy movement soon lost momentum, and the Taisho Era (fifteen years) was rather distinguished by the consolidation of Japanese influence in northeast Asia and the Pacific, and by the strengthening of Japan's self-image as a world power. During the latter half of the Taisho Era, Japan participated in the formulation of treaties intended to preserve peace and gave the impression of being a good neighbor in the western Pacific region.

---

[5]    Yoshihito's four older brothers suffered early deaths, and he was designated crown prince in 1888. Because of his maladies, he was generally kept out of public view. In one infamous episode, at his official opening of the Diet in 1913, he is said to have rolled up his prepared speech into a telescope and stared at the gathered assembly through it.

However, extremist elements in the government, the military, and the civilian population remained committed to the use of military force to expand Japan's territory. Economic, social, and political factors also facilitated the growth of the influence of the militarists, who were bent on empire building.

Based on the Anglo-Japanese Alliance of 1911, when World War I erupted, Japan participated as one of the Entente Powers, even though it had officially declared neutrality. It played an important role by securing the sea-lanes in the south Pacific and Indian Oceans against the German navy, and by troop transport escort and antisubmarine operations in the Mediterranean. Despite its only limited direct involvement in World War I (1914-1918), Japan was able to seize Germany's Asian possessions, i.e., the Mariana, Caroline, and Marshall Islands in the Pacific; German New Guinea; and Germany's settlement at Tsingtao in China's Shandong Province. Participation in treaty negotiations in 1919 resulted in European recognition of the extension of Japan's hegemony in Manchuria and Inner Mongolia. Japan also profited greatly by industrial expansion, providing war materiel to Europe, and exports quadrupled from 1913 to 1918. Japan sat in at the Paris Peace Conference after the war, and when the League of Nations was formed in 1920, Japan was granted a permanent seat on the council. Japan thus emerged from the war recognized as a great power in international politics.

During World War I Japan seized with particular fervor the opportunity to expand its influence in China. Manufacturing and trade increased dramatically, but the Japanese islands were lacking in natural resources. Due to unprecedented population growth in Japan, the nation needed both an outlet by emigration for its unsustainably large population and a source of raw materials for its industries. Japan looked to expand into China's northeastern province of Manchuria, where it had already stationed ten thousand soldiers, the Kwantung Army, to protect the South Manchurian Railway and related extensive commercial interests.[6]

A popular uprising against Japanese imperialism arose in Korea in 1919. Following the annexation of Korea in 1910, the Korean people had been oppressed and forced to assimilate as Japanese. Education was in the Japanese language, and Koreans were even required to take Japanese

---

[6]    As a result of Japan's victory in the Russo-Japanese War (1904-05), it had gained possession of leased territories in southern Manchuria, as well as control of the South Manchuria Railway.

names. These policies, which not only trampled on human dignity but also took away Korean culture, resulted in an independence movement in line with the concept of national self-determination espoused by President Wilson in January 1919 at the Paris Peace Conference. A Declaration of Korean Independence was drawn up and signed by thirty-three leaders in the Korean nonviolent resistance, many of whom were Christians. On March 1, 1919, the declaration was read publicly at a peaceful demonstration in Pagoda Park in Seoul. This demonstration in Seoul was ruthlessly suppressed by Japanese military police. However, the movement had already spread throughout the country, eventually involving two million people in nonviolent resistance demonstrations. During the suppression of the next several months, Japanese forces killed about 7,500 Koreans and wounded more than 15,000.

One example of the Japanese atrocities aimed at subduing the independence movement was an infamous massacre April 5, 1919, in the village of Suwon. Japanese soldiers ordered thirty men of the village to assemble in the village's Christian church, ostensibly for instructions, and proceeded to seal up the building and set fire to it. Those inside were burned alive, and women and children who attempted to rescue them were shot. The soldiers then burned down thirty-one houses in the village and hundreds more in surrounding villages. Missionaries visited the scene two days later to investigate, and they reported these atrocities to the outside world. Of course, this information was suppressed in Japan.

This period in Japanese history also was distinguished by increasing tension between Japan and the United States, in the form of acrimonious relations over Japanese aggression in China and Korea and competition for influence in the Pacific region. This tension was not unrelated to gradual changes in America's posture in the world. Despite a long-standing treaty recognizing the independence of Hawaii, in 1898 the United States annexed the islands by force. Furthermore, as a spoil of the Spanish-American War, from 1898 the United States took possession of the Philippines. Although this was historically uncharacteristic of America, by these acts it became a colonial power. The takeover of Hawaii particularly irritated the Japanese government, which saw it as an expansion of American hegemony in the Pacific. On the other hand, the United States made it known that it did not approve of the way Japan extended hegemony over Korea and then annexed it in 1910.

Later, relations between Japan and the United States were affected by American racial discrimination. A law passed by the

California legislature, called the Alien Land Law of 1913, prohibited ownership of land or property by those ineligible for citizenship, i.e., by Asian immigrants. Asians were at that time the only immigrants ineligible for naturalization under U.S. immigration laws. Prohibiting land ownership by Japanese immigrants was seen by Japan for what it was, racial discrimination. The Emergency Quota Act of 1921 placed restrictions on immigration. Then the Immigration Act of 1924, passed by the U.S. Congress under political pressure from California in an election year, seriously aggravated relations between the two countries. This last law, which included the National Origins Act and the Asian Exclusion Act, while restricting immigration of southern and eastern Europeans, totally prohibited immigration of East Asians and Asian Indians. These immigration policies remained the law of the land in America until the 1950s. Understandably, these developments affected the image of Christianity in Japan as well as relationships between the missionaries and Japanese Christians.

## Missionary Observations on Japan's Ultranationalism

As early as the summer of 1894, Eugene Booth had observed, "Great excitement prevails over the prospect of war with China....The war spirit is running very high through all classes of people; what will be the outcome no one can prognosticate. The Japanese have not counted the cost; every one of them is sanguine of success. Japan is ambitious to show the world how she can fight, and now that the opportunity has come she will not let it pass un-embraced."[7] Booth remarked in 1895, "Japan is hot blooded and feels big enough to whip the world just now."[8] Yet during the Sino-Japanese War neither missionaries nor Japanese Christians appear to have questioned Japan's actions seriously, i.e., seen them as acts of aggression. Capitalizing on the situation, they sought and sometimes gained permission to distribute Bibles to soldiers and sent evangelists to work among them.[9]

Early in 1896, however, missionaries in Japan learned from missionaries in Korea of Japanese atrocities that had occurred there. Japan had taken advantage of the fact that the Korean government was weak and sent its military into that sovereign country. On October 8, 1895, Korea's king, a virtual hostage in his own palace, watched helplessly while the queen was assassinated by a man he could identify.

---

[7]    ESB to HNC, Aug. 2, 1894.
[8]    ESB to HNC, March 8, 1895.
[9]    ERM to HNC, March 7, 1895.

Two Koreans were later executed for the murder, but that had been arranged as a cover for an act that was actually planned and carried out by the Japanese.[10] When he received this information from a missionary to Korea named Gage, E. R. Miller commented, "It looks as if the government was badly implicated."[11]

On October 19, 1899, Booth wrote the following observations in a letter to the mission board, observations that would prove to be remarkably prophetic.

> Japan's wonderful "progress," as described by a few superficial observers, and assented to with reserve by many, has been phenomenal. A people, whose land, fifty years ago, was a *terra incognito* to all the world, has fallen into step with the civilized Christian (?) nations of the world. How has it been done? What have been the forces at work to cause so great a change? The forces have been varied and numerous, and all more or less marked by the characteristic of superficiality.
>
> In public the official and well-to-do commercial classes are clothed in tailor-made suits after the styles of the latest Parisian fashion plates, from top-hat to pointed-toed shoes....
>
> They have clothed themselves also in the utilitarian thought of this utilitarian age. They are dressing their cities and towns with a network of poles and wires—telegraph, telephone, electric lighting, and the trolley. They are clothing themselves too in all the appliances of steam upon land and water.
>
> And they say to you over there "look at us, we can do all the same as you, and we expect to go you one better."
>
> They have ransacked the schools and universities, the manufactories and industries, the judicial, legislative, and executive practice and policies of every respectable country in the world, and, judging from what has been brought forth, some that are not so respectable.
>
> The American public school system has been Germanized and Japanned, and every boy is taught the manual of arms, but is forbidden to receive religious instruction or to attend religious exercises of any description.
>
> The institutions, laws, and inventions which have cost the West centuries of effort, the highest and noblest effort

---

[10]    Okamoto Ryunosuke, a member of the Japanese legation in Korea, was observed killing the queen, and two other Japanese men took part in the atrocity with him. Japanese troops withdrew from the palace immediately after the assassination.

[11]    ERM to HNC, Jan. 30, 1896.

the human race is capable of, have been copied, imitated, with and without modification and, one would suppose, without comprehension....Character with us is fundamental, with them it apparently is external. When art, dress, and adornment cease to give expression to character but are used to hide the real nature they become nothing more than a masque, and they who do them are merely masqueraders upon the stage, playing the significance of which they know nothing and apparently care less, so long as the audience is pleased with the spectacle.

The Japanese is the same in native characteristics that he was while in his isolation, clothed in the light of modern material civilization. He is destitute of the moral qualities and religious experiences which have in the past safeguarded that feature of civilization in the West and which continue to do so at the present. But they will none of it. They shout with the rabble that surrounded the Christ before Pilate, "away with him." This is clearly seen in the recent action of the Shinto cult. They have declared themselves a "secular body whose function shall be to preserve the ancient rites and ceremonies of the land, and to file or record petition made in heaven." This latter must not be understood as a form of prayer. For "the Japanese never pray." This action has been called "astute" and rightly, for it is now rumored that a bill is to be introduced in the next Diet making the performance of so-called ancient rites and ceremonies obligatory upon all Buddhists, Christians, and whatnot alike. In other words they will by this act ask that "Caesar shall reign over them" and they will render unto Caesar the homage and worship that is due unto God alone. And this will be made the test of patriotism.

Christianity has indeed been formally recognized by the state by means of an Imperial Ordinance. All missionaries, ministers, pastors, evangelists, churches, and preaching places throughout the Empire are duly registered, together with the methods of propagandism pursued. Will the proposed Board for the preservation of rites and ceremonies require His Imperial Majesty's Picture and Rescript to be exposed in the churches, before which on stated occasions the "ancient rites and ceremonies" shall be performed? If so, what if the Christians object, indeed, refuse? Are they for a matter of conscience to be apprehended, and condemned as traitors to their most beloved sovereign?

I do not wish to pose as an alarmist, and yet the situation is pregnant with possibilities such that the history of this people in the early part of the twentieth century may be but the re-writing of that which has already been recorded in the seventeenth century.

Liberty of conscience, as an individual, God-given right, is unknown except to a comparatively few Japanese, and perhaps many of the few who have convictions are more willingly led by expediency and policy than by conscience. As a result of centuries of official espionage, it has become habitual, perhaps, to perform outwardly acts which the moral sense condemns, and for the sake of peace to keep the conviction of right hid in the heart.[12]

Concerning the treaty revisions and subsequent issuance of new regulations governing religions and education issued in 1899, Martin Wyckoff commented,

There is evidently a nationalistic spirit back of it all, which will not recognize any relation to be higher than that which all Japanese subjects must have towards the imperial family. It seems probable that Christianity is to meet its strongest opposition along this line, and strangely enough one of the steps taken to strengthen themselves for this opposition is the recent paradoxical action of making Shintoism no longer a religion, but a system of rites and ceremonies. At first sight that would seem to be the removal of a competitor, but since the time of that action I have more than once seen intimations that every loyal Japanese ought to conform to these rites and ceremonies, WHATEVER HIS RELIGIOUS BELIEF. In this I think I see the wisdom of the serpent, though the harmlessness of the dove is not equally conspicuous.[13]

Even James Ballagh, who always showed great respect for the emperor and royal family, revealed his concern after the developments of 1899, saying, "A shadow is cast suddenly over the landscape...in the steps being taken to foster worship of the Emperor in order it is asserted to strengthen nationalism. This is the most regrettable in view of the recent edicts against teaching religion or holding religious services in schools of any kind."[14]

Eugene Booth observed that since the revision of the treaties with Western nations in 1899, many people in America seem to assume "that now Japan has come into the comity of nations" and that "she is fully redeemed from the tradition of the past, and stands open handed and open hearted to receive the truth." Booth responded to that assumption:

[12]   ESB to HNC, Oct. 19, 1899.
[13]   MNW to HNC, Oct. 30, 1899.
[14]   JHB to HNC, Nov. 3, 1899.

Yes she is ready to receive truth of a materialistic, utilitarian sort; truth that can be converted or perverted into diplomatic prestige, national glorification, and dollars, but truth in its Altruistic, Christian, and Divine sense, she would have none of it. It is just because of the existence of this inverted or perverted sense that the missionaries are here, or that the kingdom of God has a struggle for existence in the world. I am well aware that the Japanese have no monopoly of this perversion of the <u>absolute</u>.[15]

After the conclusion of the Russo-Japanese War in 1905, Albert Oltmans wrote,

O what deep streams of thought have been set in motion by this war, that will go on flowing and deepening day by day and month by month and year by year. And not the least significant of these streams is the one that runs in the channel of religious thought. You can already see some flashes and hear some mutterings in papers and magazines and from the rostrums that presage a great conflict in the not very distant future, and to speak my honest conviction, I do not think the Church of Jesus Christ in this land is ready at this time to meet the conflict that will specially be coming upon her very soon. There never was, it seems to me, a more critical time for the church than this. But instead of truly girding herself for the strife, she is occupying herself with things of second and third importance, and fails to show the united front that is necessary.[16]

D. C. Ruigh, who of course had a special interest in China because his first three years as a missionary had been with the Amoy Mission there, in 1907 offered his insights on China.

What she sees in Korea and Manchuria is not at all calculated to put her at ease with reference to her future relations with Japan. The future is pregnant with unknown possibilities and we can only hope and pray that God will overrule all things for the good of his people and his own glory. The Christian people and the Christian church in China have not much to hope for from the Christian nations as matters now stand.[17]

---

[15]  ESB to HNC, Jan. 30, 1900.
[16]  AO to HNC, Dec. 30, 1905.
[17]  DCR to HNC, June 11, 1907.

Shortly after Japan annexed Korea in 1910, Ballagh noted, "There are evidences that the military authorities are making it more difficult for soldiers to become Christians, or the Christians to attend worship." And he commented, "I cannot feel satisfied with the way Korea has been treated—saved out of one despoiler's hand to fall into that of another.[18]

In 1911, Booth wrote,

> The government school system, having been found utterly inefficient in its ability to afford its pupils satisfactory moral training, the department of education has recently ordered the government school teachers to require their pupils to worship at ancestral or Shinto shrines at stated times, which is exceedingly embarrassing to children of Christian parents. It is a deliberate effort to revive the ancient superstitions, and to make their frightful mysticism the basis for developing the moral sense in the children.[19]

In February of 1912, the minister of home affairs of the Japanese government convened a religious conference of several days, which was attended by fifty-two Buddhist, thirteen Shinto, and seven Christian religious leaders. According to Booth, at this conference resolutions were passed to the effect that each of the religions proposed to propagate their respective beliefs "with all possible zeal and diligence, and in this way to render the State all the help it could to maintain the integrity and security of the Imperial Dynasty." Opinions were mixed regarding this apparent attempt to "mingle politics and religion" or perhaps use religion.[20]

In a letter dated March 7, 1912, Pieters observed, "The general situation here these days is intensely interesting." Pieters referred to an article, published in English by a Japanese professor of Japanese literature at Tokyo University, and noted that it may not have been translated into Japanese and made public. He noted that some minor points had been criticized, but added,

> The main contention of the article remains unshaken, viz., that the Japanese government is assiduously cultivating an artificial and religious reverence for the Imperial line. There is much grumbling among Japanese at the restrictions placed upon scholarship, for they are not at liberty freely to investigate

[18]   JHB to WIC, Sept. 28, 1910.
[19]   ESB to WIC, Oct. 31, 1911.
[20]   ESB to WIC, March 11, 1912.

the origins of their religion and history and to publish their conclusions. For instance, the other day some were discussing in my hearing the "sacred emblems"[21] supposed to be preserved, and it was said that no Japanese scholar, of whatever rank, was permitted to examine them, that their antiquity and even their very existence was doubted, etc.

Whither this kind of repression is going to lead in an educated country is clear, it is only a question of time.[22]

At that point, Albertus Pieters appeared confident that intelligent Japanese would soon reject such manipulation and deceit, but his confidence soon faded. In July 1912, Pieters was asked by Dr. S. A. Moffett, a Presbyterian missionary in Korea, to consult with him and Methodist missionaries to Korea in Kyoto. The subject was the so-called "Korean Conspiracy case." One hundred twenty-three Koreans, mostly Christians and church officers, were accused of conspiracy against Japanese rule. Pieters reported,

> The evidence brought by the brethren certainly deepened my sense of the gravity of the situation, along two lines. (1) They have evidence that the use of torture etc. and the general effort to work up a case against the accused involves the highest officials far more directly than I had expected. In common with most Japan missionaries I was quite willing to believe such things of the lower police and prison officials, but confident of the good intentions and justice of those higher up. The evidence in the hands of Dr. Moffett & others goes far to shake such confidence. (2) Next, they showed me a statement made by released prisoners describing the tortures in detail, a statement that bears strong internal evidence of genuineness, for uneducated Korean boys could not have imagined or described such things unless they had experienced them....It looks black for the poor Koreans—confessions extorted

---

[21]    The "sacred emblems" here refers to the Imperial Regalia called the Three Sacred Treasures, consisting of a sword, a mirror, and a jewel, representing valor, wisdom, and benevolence. Traditionally, these three items were symbols of the emperor's divinity as a descendant of Amaterasu, the sun goddess, from which lineage the emperor derived legitimacy as the supreme ruler of Japan. According to legend, the three artifacts are located at the Atsuta Shrine in Nagoya, the Grand Shrine of Ise, and the Imperial Palace in Tokyo respectively. It is claimed that they are presented before the emperor by certain Shinto priests as part of the imperial enthronement ceremony. However, they have never been made public, and no drawings or photographs exist.

[22]    AP to WIC, March 7, 1912.

by torture are apparently the only evidence the prosecution has, but the defense is not allowed to call witnesses and apparently the verdict is a pre-determined one. It is a great shock to our confidence in Japanese courts of justice.[23]

In the second stage of the trial, most of the Koreans were released for lack of evidence, only six being convicted and punished, but the whole affair suggested that the cruelty of the Japanese police in occupied Korea was a reality.

Emperor Mutsuhito, subsequently called the Emperor Meiji, died July 30, 1912. During the next month Pieters held a conference in Beppu for those who had become interested in Christianity through his newspaper evangelism project. He had planned to emphasize Christian music there, but learned that, because of the emperor's death, all singing and use of musical instruments was forbidden for a month, further evidence of the cultivation of religious veneration of the emperor.[24]

Harman Peeke described the impact of the cult of veneration of the emperor being cultivated by the leaders of Japan. The Japanese evangelist in Saga had had occasion to visit numerous public school principals and officials, and he took the opportunity to urge the claims of Christianity privately. Peeke noted, "He found sympathy and approval, a genuine conviction of the need of religion in the national life, and a respect for Christianity, but when it came to any step beyond that, it was 'Excuse me.'" Peeke tried to explain the basis of this feeling of reticence on the part of Japanese people to open their hearts and accept Christianity.

> In Japan we hear a great deal about Christianity being contrary to the National institutions. Simmered down this means that theoretically at least, the orthodox Japanese belief is that the Emperor is *quasi* divine, descended from wholly divine ancestors, and that it is disrespectful to believe or express a belief in the existence of any being or power above him. Any act that can be interpreted as being disrespectful to the emperor, or failing in devotion to this extreme idea, may in a moment cause the loss of position to an official or teacher, and serious difficulty to almost any other man. It is a subject that must be treated with utmost delicacy. An accusation is almost equivalent to condemnation. In old New England times an accusation of witchcraft was almost

---

[23]     AP to WIC, July 30, 1912.
[24]     Ibid.

impossible of defense. Similarly if the enemies of a school-teacher or principal can make it out that his words or actions have been lacking in punctiliousness, the most that can be said will seldom suffice to remove the stigma or avert calamity.[25]

In 1915, during World War I, D.C. Ruigh expressed concern over the possibility of war between the United States and Japan.

> Do I believe there will be a Japanese-American War? No I do not. The Japanese Government does not want such a war and will in every way do all in its power to prevent such a war, not withstanding the popular idea that such a war is inevitable....
> The California land question and kindred questions are aggravating to the Japanese but these are questions over which the Japanese will not go to war. The real danger lies in China. What Japan needs more than anything else is commercial expansion and she is bound to secure it. The logical field for such expansion is China. If you review the history of American-Japanese relations since the Japanese-Russian war you will recall that a very disturbing element was introduced by Secretary of State Knox when he tried to secure the neutralization of the Manchurian Railway. This was deeply resented by the Japanese and has made them distrust our Government. Any move on the part of our Government to restrain or curb Japan's activities in China will be resented.[26]

Referring to Japan taking possession of German territories in Asia and the Pacific during World War I, Peeke remarked, "It is getting rather late in the world's history to play the grab game, and it could not be done at all if the great powers were not so busily engaged in the Occident. However, when one group of rowdies is engaged in stripping the clothes off another's backs, it would be only passing strange if one of their number with more leisure than the others should be inspired to strip the clothes off a neighboring unprotected clothesline."[27] Referring to Japan's early aggression in China, he commented, "Japan certainly did go about the matter in a bungling manner, and she certainly has hurt herself considerably in the eyes of her fellow nations, to say nothing of her nearest neighbor."[28]

[25]  HVSP Quarterly Letter, Apr. 15, 1914.
[26]  DCR to William B. Hill, March 19, 1915.
[27]  HVSP Quarterly Letter, Apr. 15, 1915.
[28]  HVSP Quarterly Letter, July 10, 1915.

The Japan Mission Report for 1919 to the board suggested, "The real solution of the Korean problem and of Japan's Chinese relations is to be found in the overthrow of militarism in Japan. It is always necessary in thinking of this country to make a distinction between the people and the military clique, which is practically in control of the foreign relations of the Government."[29]

Luman Shafer was hopeful after World War I, saying, "We cannot help but feel that the victory of the Allies will have the effect in Japan of tempering the ultra-nationalistic attitude of the Japanese and thus removing much of the present opposition to Christianity."[30] But in 1920 Shafer noted that missionary work in Japan was being negatively affected by anti-Japanese agitation in America.[31]

At the time when anti-American feeling was high in Japan as a result of the Asian Exclusion Act, on July 6, 1924, the Japanese government organized a meeting of one hundred leaders representing the Shintoists, Buddhists, and Christianity. The missionaries seem to have seen this naively as a positive thing, despite the fact that it was a blatant example of using religion for nationalistic aims. Shafer wrote, "The calling together of the representatives of the three religions on the part of the authorities will again have its good effect in bringing Christianity forward.... The more thoughtful people are deeply concerned about the moral conditions and, while to be sure the emphasis will be placed on nationalism, on the other hand the real longing for moral purity is bound to give a wide opening for our message."[32] At that point in history, however, moral purity in Japan meant subservience to Japan's ultranationalistic goals.

The Japan Mission's report for 1926 noted, "The Government has been preparing a new religious control bill and many are pleased at its purpose of indicating Christianity as one of Japan's three leading religions instead of including it in the vague class of "others."" But among its numerous provisions the new bill looks toward a certain bureaucratic control of religion just as the Government controls education, charity, business, agriculture, and almost everything else."[33]

## The North Japan Mission under the Plan of Affiliation

In 1911, the Council of Missions held its usual summer conference in Karuizawa. The council had become simply an opportunity for

---

29   Board of Foreign Missions Report to General Synod, RCA (BFMR), 1920, 44.
30   LJS to WIC, Dec. 9, 1918.
31   LJS to Abbe L. Warnshuis, June 26, 1920.
32   LJS to WIC, Apr. 5, 1924.
33   BFMR, 1926, 52.

mutual enrichment, since its negotiations with the Japanese church leaders were no longer necessary. Relationships with the Church of Christ had been clarified, and the Reformed and Presbyterian missions looked forward to a new era of pleasant cooperation.[34] In the North Japan Mission, however, capitalizing on the situation was frustrated by the shortage of evangelistic missionary personnel. Miller lamented in 1910, "Our message is, give us men for our evangelistic work. Dr. Ballagh, who came out in 1861, and I who joined the mission in 1875, are the only evangelistic missionaries on the field, though we hope Mr. Ruigh will come back next year [from furlough]. This has been our cry for years and it does not seem any nearer of fulfillment now than when Mr. Scudder left us [in 1907]."[35]

The North Japan Mission also experienced loss of members by illness and death. Margaret Ballagh died in Yokohama March, 16, 1909, having served along with her husband for forty-eight years. Mary Miller died in Tokyo June 29, 1910, after a prolonged illness, at the age of seventy-seven. Her notable missionary career of forty-one years included her role as founder of Ferris Seminary and her literary work, publishing the Christian education periodicals *Yorokobi no Otozure* and *Chiisai Otozure* in partnership with Pastor Miura, for almost thirty years. James Ballagh and E. R. Miller continued to serve after the loss of their wives, although both were in declining health.

Jennie Kuyper contracted TB and moved to a rented cottage by the sea at Hayama to recover her health. Another loss was the death of Henry N. Cobb April 26, 1910. He had served as the board secretary and as advocate and confidant of the missionaries for thirty years. Then, on January 27, 1911, Martin Wyckoff died suddenly at his home in Tokyo at the age of sixty-one. It was a terrible loss not only for the Wyckoff family but also for the mission. Although a layman, primarily an educational missionary at Meiji Gakuin, Wyckoff had sometimes assisted in the evangelistic work, going into the interior on speaking tours during breaks in his teaching schedule, and he had carried major administrative responsibilities in the mission. The year 1911 proved to be one of repeated tragedies in the Wyckoff family. Not only did Anna Wyckoff lose her husband, but in July her son-in-law, John Hail, Harriet's husband, was killed on a mountain in a volcanic eruption, leaving Harriet with four small children, and in September both the Wyckoff's younger daughter and her newborn child died. Anna moved temporarily to the city of Tsu to live with Harriet.

[34]   WGH to WIC, Sept. 1, 1911.
[35]   ERM to SMZ, Jan. 29, 1910.

The mission found it necessary to appoint Ruigh to replace Wyckoff as teacher in the academic department at Meiji Gakuin, and consequently the Ruighs moved from Morioka to Tokyo. Despite his new responsibilities, Ruigh had to remain in charge of the distant Aomori-Morioka field and guide work at three preaching places in Tokyo.[36] Jennie Kuyper, still in precarious health after fifteen months, returned to America to recover. In 1912 Ballagh, eighty years old and often too ill for speaking tours, and Miller, sixty-nine years old with recurring health problems, were the only ordained missionaries involved primarily in evangelistic work. Leila Winn was the only missionary residing in the interior, for a time in Mishima and from 1909 in Aomori. Anna Thompson, who taught at Ferris Seminary for twenty-six years, resigned from the mission to marry a widower, a member of the German Reformed Mission. So much illness and loss of personnel made this a very discouraging period for the North Japan Mission.

The missionaries had long pleaded with the board for new recruits, not only to restore but to enlarge their ranks. Ruigh stated bluntly, "Unless such reinforcements come very soon we will be forced to turn over a big portion of our territory to others or let it go by default."[37] The missionaries were convinced that a very important role that the Japanese church could not fill had devolved upon the missions. In their newly recognized roles as affiliated missions, they were free to evangelize those not being reached by the very limited number of independent churches of the Church of Christ in Japan. Three-fourths of the population of Japan was rural and had never heard even an inadequate presentation of the gospel. The mission envisioned new missionary recruits meeting this need by living in the interior and laboring in the towns and country villages, where they would be welcomed as mentors by the small groups of scattered Christians.[38] This approach to reaching the unevangelized millions of Japanese stood in contrast to the original vision of Brown and Stout, which was to train Japanese evangelists and simply send them out to do the evangelizing. The original ideal had proven to be inadequate for the real situation faced by the Christian movement in Japan, especially after the antiforeign, anti-Christian reaction.

Ballagh and Miller, as well as Oltmans and other younger missionaries, met periodically with groups of evangelists working in the interior. These conferences usually included not only study and

36    DCR to WIC, Aug. 25, 1911.
37    DCR to WIC, March 8, 1911.
38    ERM to WIC, Nov. 25, 1910.

E. Rothsay Miller, meeting with Japan Mission workers in the interior on the Izu Peninsula field. Front row: seminary students doing summer field work evangelism and unidentified child. Second and third rows: Miller surrounded by resident pastors and evangelists and Bible women working in the region.

prayer, but also guidance in practical matters given by the missionaries and experienced Japanese pastors. They were meant to encourage and strengthen pastors and evangelists who often labored in lonely and difficult circumstances, but these periodic conferences had proved insufficient. Oltmans, during his years with the South Japan Mission, had pioneered an annual program of continuing education for pastors in Saga called "Winter Bible School," beginning in 1896. Once again, as part of the theological faculty of Meiji Gakuin, he developed a program of continuing education to meet the needs of pastors and evangelists working in the interior. As Oltmans noted,

> Most of these men are thrown entirely upon their own rather meager resources in the way of keeping fresh in their thoughts and in the methods of their studies and their practical work. Nearly every one of them graduated poor in worldly goods, with not a very large stock of books to take along to their fields, and with but few facilities to exchange ideas on the subjects concerning which they have to constantly speak and preach."[39]

[39]  AO to WIC, Dec. 1, 1910.

Ibuka, president of Meiji Gakuin and Oltmans's colleague on the theological faculty there, first broached the subject of holding a summer school at Meiji Gakuin for pastors and evangelists, noting the need of the men in the field to restock their mental and spiritual storehouses. After enthusiastic approval of the school's faculty and the receipt of financial support from the Reformed and Presbyterian mission boards, this new venture was initiated in 1911.

Ibuka, Oltmans, and Imbrie planned the eight-day summer school. It was held in early June, after the theological students had left for summer work. That way, the pastors could stay in the student dormitory, and, since the school's academic department was still in session, they could eat with the college students. Virtually all the mission-associated pastors and evangelists took part, and it was a great success. This continuing education program was an annual June event for several years. It attracted participants not only from the interior but also from Tokyo and Yokohama and included some Bible women. By the second year attendance had grown to fifty or sixty each day, and the well-prepared presentations were greatly appreciated. This study conference not only provided mental and spiritual nurture and practical training, it also helped develop a sense of community.[40]

Meanwhile, the financial situation of the mission board had improved, and it was prepared to recruit missionaries for Japan. However, perhaps partly because the turmoil regarding the nature of cooperation between the missions and the Japanese church was widely known, volunteers had not come forth. Eventually, strenuous recruiting by both the board staff and the missionaries resulted in some new appointments. The appointees were sent by the board specifically to develop evangelistic work in the interior, away from the larger cities.[41]

The first recruit to arrive was the Reverend Hubert Kuyper, a native of Orange City, Iowa, and a recent graduate of Western Theological Seminary at the age of thirty-four. Kuyper arrived in Japan in October 1911 and immediately began language study. Then, in January of 1912, the Woman's Board appointed Anna Wyckoff, the widow of Martin Wyckoff, to do evangelistic work. The mission assigned Wyckoff to live in Matsumoto, to work there as well as in Suwa, Nagano, and Ina, among women and children, assisted by three young Japanese Bible women.[42] During five years of work centered in Matsumoto, Wyckoff and her assistants carried on eleven Sunday schools, with an average attendance of fifty-five pupils each.

[40]    AO to WIC, June 24, 1912.
[41]    WIC to ERM, March 15, 1912.
[42]    ERM to WIC, March 4, 1912.

The personnel of the North Japan Mission were further augmented in 1912. Nathan Demarest had been a missionary of the South Japan Mission from 1883 to 1890 and had left Japan because of the serious illness of his wife. He then had served as pastor of the Jay Gould Memorial Church in Roxbury, New York, for twenty-two years. Some time after the death of his wife, Demarest reapplied to the board and was again sent to Japan, accompanied by his daughter, May Demarest, who was appointed as a missionary by the Woman's Board. Florence E. Dick was also appointed by the Woman's Board, with the expectation that she would enter evangelistic work. The board also appointed two young men, both freshly graduated from New Brunswick Seminary, along with their wives, for evangelistic work. The Reverend David Van Strien, with his wife, Eleanor, and the Reverend Luman J. Shafer, with his wife, Amy, as well as Nathan and May Demarest and Florence Dick all arrived on the field in the fall of 1912.

With this influx of new workers, the North Japan Mission appeared poised for a great advance in evangelism in the interior. The new missionaries delved into the task of acquiring a working knowledge of the language while the senior missionaries endeavored to keep the mission's evangelistic work going and planned for its expansion. Ballagh did what he could, although he was in his eighties and had chronic health problems. And during breaks in the Meiji Gakuin and language school schedules, Miller, Oltmans, Ruigh, and Kuyper toured the several fields of the mission, visiting Aomori and Morioka and most preaching stations there, as well as the scattered stations in Nagano Prefecture and the Izu area.

On these tours, the missionaries found the evangelists greatly encouraged by an increasing number of inquirers and larger audiences at church services. However, despite an improvement in facilities for travel into the interior, missionary tours could still be taxing. For example, on a return trip from Aomori to Tokyo, Miller and Kuyper had to spend twenty-seven continuous hours in a stagecoach, followed by two nights and a day on a coast steamer. Providing adequate support and encouragement of the Japanese workers in the interior from Tokyo and Yokohama was impossible.

The mission was trying to maintain churches and outstations in three distinct regions—the Izu area, Nagano Prefecture, and the Morioka/Aomori region.[43] The mission members looked forward to the

[43]  In Izu: Mishima, Koyama, Gotemba, Shuzenji, Kashiwakubo, and Yugashima; in Nagano: Nagano, Matsumoto, Kami Suwa, Shimo Suwa, Ina, Iida, and Kiso Fukushima; in Morioka/Aomori: Morioka, Ichinoseki, Hizume, Kogawa, Iwaizumi, Miyako, Aomori, Hirosaki, Kominato, and Noheiji. ERM and WEH to Board, July 10, 1913.

implementation of the new recruits and felt assured that their arrival boded well for brighter days ahead. After one year of language study in Tokyo, Hubert Kuyper moved up to Morioka, where, while continuing language study, he could provide supervision of the mission's work with help and guidance from the mission's very experienced minister there, Ito Tokichi.[44]

In 1912 Leila Winn, who had served for thirty years very effectively, for many of those years the only single woman of the mission living in the interior doing evangelistic work, felt obliged to return to America. She had been summoned home to care for her sister Eva, who was said to be dying of tuberculosis. Excerpts from her letter to the board secretary tell of her dilemma.

> For no other member of my family would I have even <u>thought</u> of leaving my work to go home, but I am under especial obligations to <u>this</u> sister. For almost thirty years she has made it possible for me to be in Japan. Things were such in my home that either she or I had to stay home, i.e., to take care of an aged father and an elder sister. She took care of them both until they died. Now she herself is dying and is so alone in the world. She wrote me she had reached the place where she could no longer care for herself, that she hated so to call me from my work. I spent several days & nights thinking and praying over it, and it seemed to me I <u>ought</u> to go. So here I am on the *Nippon Maru*, speeding away! It was the hardest problem I ever had to solve. The work at Morioka was <u>so</u> interesting and <u>encouraging</u>. It was like cutting my heart strings to have to pick up and leave. You know how very much we need workers for the <u>evangelistic</u> field. Nothing else appeals to me so much.

Feeling it unfair to burden the board with the cost of her passage, since it had been less than three years since her furlough, she paid her own way out of her meager savings. She mentioned how glad she was that new missionaries had come, adding, "And oh, may they see their way clear to leave the charms and attractions of Yokohama and Tokyo and go out into the <u>needy</u> country and rural work! So many thousands are still living in darkness, knowing not of Christ and his love."[45]

Eleven months later, aboard ship en route to Japan, Winn could write,

44    ERM to WIC, Jan. 31, 1913.
45    MLW to WIC, Nov. 20, 1912.

"I feel <u>so glad</u>, so <u>very</u> glad to be going back to Japan! God has been <u>good</u> to me. I came home to see my sister die, but God has been good to spare her & make her better. While she is far from well, she is much better, & I was able to make better arrangements for her. I left her cheered up & in better spirits altogether. I am so <u>grateful</u> and want to make this term of service my <u>very best</u>, God helping me."[46]

Incredibly, once again the hopes of the mission were dashed as unexpected personnel losses occurred one after the other. The North Japan Mission expected that Nathan Demarest, after a refresher study of Japanese, would become a great asset to the evangelistic work, since he had previously served seven years in the South Japan Mission and had many years of pastoral experience in America. However, Demarest had a very difficult time adjusting to this new stage in his life and almost immediately plunged into a serious depression.[47] Mission members did their best to help him through the crisis. After a summer in the mountain air in Karuizawa, Kuyper took him with him to Morioka, hoping for a further recovery. Meanwhile, Hubert Kuyper and May Demarest announced their engagement, although their plans remained uncertain because of her father's health.

Unfortunately, Demarest's health remained precarious, and he left Japan in November 1913, accompanied by Albert Oltmans, who hastened his furlough departure to care for Demarest on the way to America. May Demarest, after a year of language study, taught for a year at Ferris Seminary, where she was highly appreciated. But May was caught between calling and duty. Relatives insisted that it was her first and paramount duty to return to America to care for her father. May felt obliged to set aside her work, postpone her marriage to Kuyper, and return to America, which she did in July 1914.[48]

Losses continued. The mission planned that after language study in Tokyo, the Van Striens would be assigned to Matsumoto in the fall of 1914. Tragically, Eleanor Van Strien, expecting her first child and apparently in perfect health, suffered a "premature detachment of the placenta with concealed hemorrhage," resulting in the death of both mother and child on October 9, 1913.[49] In May 1914, E. R. Miller, after repeated surgeries and in very poor health, departed Japan for a much-

---

[46]    MLW to WIC, Sept. 13, 1913.
[47]    Hubert Kuyper and AO to WIC, Sept. 1, 1913.
[48]    ESB to WIC, May 5, 1914.
[49]    DCR to WIC, Oct. 11, 1913.

needed furlough. Unable to regain his health, he died of heart failure in America on August 7, 1915, at the age of seventy-one. Florence Dick, who had arrived in Japan in 1912 with the new recruits, apparently lacked the necessary mental and physical toughness required for missionary work. Overwhelmed by language study and the adjustment to life in Japan, after some teaching at Ferris Seminary, she left the mission in the spring of 1915.

Meanwhile, David Van Strien and Luman Shafer, having successfully completed the prescribed two-year language course, were assigned to evangelistic work in 1914. Van Strien was sent to Nagano City, from which he would oversee the work of several outstations in Nagano Prefecture. The Shafers moved to Morioka, where they lived temporarily with Hubert Kuyper because there was no suitable house at Aomori, where Shafer was to be in charge of the evangelistic work. Regarding Aomori, Shafer wrote, "We hope and pray that it may be the purpose of Providence that we should remain at Aomori for the rest of our missionary life, and that we may be able to do something toward bringing this Ken [prefecture] to Christ."[50]

In the spring of 1915 Luman and Amy Shafer and their newborn child moved into a rented Japanese house in Aomori, and the board gave Shafer permission to raise the money from their home churches in Roxbury and New Paltz, New York, to build a good mission house. Evangelistic work in Aomori was promising, but the rented house was, according to Oltmans, "absolutely unsuitable for occupancy during the cold winter season."[51] Although the building funds had not yet been raised, the mission borrowed money to build a house before the severe winter weather set in. The new mission house was completed and ready for occupancy in December. Unfortunately, Amy Shafer had in the meantime become ill, and the family was unable to move into its new home.[52] Shafer was assigned to teach at Meiji Gakuin as a substitute for Ruigh, who was recovering from tuberculosis, and the Shafer family stayed at a cottage on the seashore in Hayama for Amy's recuperation. She had been diagnosed with nervous fatigue or neurosis.[53] When she did not respond to treatment, doctors advised a return to America for recuperation, and the family left Japan for what was hoped to be a temporary furlough in June 1916.[54]

---

50    LJS to WIC, Apr. 9, 1915.
51    AO to WIC, Aug. 16, 1915.
52    AO to James Cantine, Dec. 30, 1915.
53    LJS to JC, March 28, 1916.
54    AO to JC, May 11, 1916; LJS to JC, May 13, 1916.

In the midst of these discouraging losses experienced by the North Japan Mission during the course of three years, two additions were made to its personnel. Two of the daughters of Albert and Alice Oltmans, Evelyn and Janet Oltmans, returned to the land of their birth and childhood as duly appointed missionaries of the Woman's Board in 1914. Meanwhile, the mission continued to insist that to do justice to its opportunities, far more missionaries would be necessary. Hoping that the church in America would be in a spirit to provide for a great advance in evangelism, the mission boldly asked for the appointment of fourteen new families and seven new single women.[55] The missionaries were convinced that the time was right for expansion, citing a more positive attitude among the people toward Christianity.[56]

With the Booths and the Hoffsommers on furlough in America, the assignments of the members of the mission in Japan for 1916-17 were as follows:

| | |
|---|---|
| Ballagh | Evangelism, Yokohama and Nagano Prefecture |
| H. Kuyper | Charge of Morioka field, oversight of Aomori field |
| Ruigh | Meiji Gakuin, Higher Department |
| A. Oltmans | Meiji Gakuin Theological Department, Tokyo evangelism |
| Van Strien | Charge of Izu field, residence at Mishima |
| A. Wyckoff | Matsumoto, women's work |
| Winn | Aomori, women's work |
| J. Kuyper | Ferris Seminary |
| Moulton | Ferris Seminary |
| E. Oltmans | Ferris Seminary |
| J. Oltmans | Ferris Seminary |

**The South Japan Mission under the Plan of Affiliation**

In the fall of 1909, a feeling prevailed in the South Japan Mission that the work was on the verge of a forward surge. Furthermore, mission members were encouraged by the promise of new personnel for evangelistic work. Upon his return from furlough, Harman Peeke visited all the evangelists throughout Kyushu and took up residence in Fukuoka. The church in Fukuoka achieved self-support and independence, and Peeke returned to Saga as his base of operations. Willis Hoekje moved to Karatsu for one year, the first missionary to reside there, to develop outreach in partnership with the evangelist

---

55    WEH to WIC, Oct. 24, 1914.
56    ESB to WIC, May 21, 1914.

and Christians of the region. Hoekje next was assigned to Oita for one year, the first Reformed missionary to reside there. Additional young evangelists were engaged by the mission for the Oita region, and the mission hoped at long last to be able to advance the work there.

In the summer of 1911, Willis Hoekje visited the mountain resort area of Karuizawa to attend the Council of Missions meeting and for a vacation. During his recreational climb up nearby Mount Asama with two missionary friends, the mountain's volcano erupted. One of the companions, John Hail, the husband of Harriet Wyckoff, was killed, the other was quite seriously burned. Hoekje was fortunate to escape with superficial burns. John Hail and his sister, Annie N. Hail, were second-generation missionaries, children of pioneer Presbyterians serving in Osaka. In the fall of 1911, Willis Hoekje and Annie Hail announced their engagement, and they were married in April 1912. Annie Hoekje was transferred to the South Japan Mission, and they moved to Nagasaki, where Willis was needed to teach at Steele Academy during the Walvoords' furlough.

Albertus Pieters, on the eve of his departure for Japan after a furlough, conveyed the following thought-provoking words to the board's corresponding secretary that remind us of realities that can accompany the separation of missionaries from their loved ones:

> I am leaving three children in this country, whom I commend to the kindly interest and care of the Committee [Japan Committee of the board] in case anything should be necessary. Only do not cable us if one of them should be seriously ill or die. It is bad enough to hear such things when full details accompany the intelligence. A mere telegram is worse than useless in such cases.[57]

Peeke reported in 1910, "Pieters has a plan for using the newspapers for carrying the gospel message. He presents it in most convincing fashion and I hope he finds backers at home."[58] The Pieters family returned to Japan in the fall of 1911 and moved to Oita, once again taking up evangelistic work. Pieters was on the verge of launching his creative new approach to evangelism. During the furlough, Pieters had gained support for his plan, and within days of arriving in Oita he was preparing to realize his goal.[59] Despite roadblocks, the project began to take form. On February 3, 1912, Pieters noted, "The repairs to the building I have rented for an office are completed, and I moved in this

57    AP to WIC, Sept. 26, 1911.
58    HVSP to HNC, Apr. 4, 1910.
59    AP to WIC, Nov. 20, 1911.

week. Have the first advertisement ready for insertion, but the necessary authorization from the provincial authorities has not yet come, though I started the red tape to unwinding two months ago. I hope the matter may be gotten through now without much more delay."[60] The project was indeed launched, and a letter from Pieters a month later clarifies its character and the response.

During the month of February we got over one hundred replies to our advertisements, although we did not at first go into the matter of actual Christian doctrine. The first ad. as an announcement of the opening of my office, called the "Ei Sei Kwan" or Hall of Eternal Life, and of the business we were prepared to transact, viz. to furnish information of all kinds in regard to the Christian religion, to send a portion of the Scriptures and a brief explanation free, to hold public meetings wherever desired, to sell books and tracts at the regular price, etc.

The next advertisement was a very brief promise to send literature free. This is made a standing order with the papers, so that whenever no larger or other ad. is handed them, they are to put this in. This arrangement enables me to keep the monthly expense within the limits of what I can afford to pay and yet keeps me before the public all the time. The third advertisement was written by our local preacher, and was an exhortation to study the Christian religion, giving the names of all the preachers of our church in Oita Ken, with their addresses. This seems to have had considerable effect in one or two places in the way of increasing audiences and stimulating inquiry.

This morning the fourth advertisement appears. It consists of a brief announcement in very large type on the front page that the column in which it stands has been reserved for the presentation of reasons for the study of Christian truth and for the insertion of Christian teaching for the rest of the month, with a request to give it a careful perusal.[61]

Pieters's newspaper evangelism project was a breakthrough that clearly provided great satisfaction. After he had received about seven hundred inquiries in the first six months, Pieters reported,

I have rarely been quite so busy in my life as during the past six months, and never quite so happy....I feel that God has at last

---

[60] AP to WIC, Feb. 3, 1912.
[61] AP to WIC, March 7, 1912.

given me such an opportunity to get into touch with the hearts of men and of ministering to their spiritual needs as I never have had before. The routine correspondence is, of course, attended to by my Japanese clerk, but I have to dictate all special letters and to prepare on the type-writer in Roman letters all my articles, which are then transcribed by him in proper form for the printer.... Including the Japanese, English, and Dutch correspondence, I mailed something like 2000 letters and cards during the last six months."[62]

The first year of the newspaper evangelism project had been approved by the board as an experiment. After the first six months, at the annual meeting of the mission, the project was evaluated and deemed to have turned out well. The mission requested full underwriting in the budget for the next year.[63] This creative method of evangelistic outreach attracted attention in the North Japan Mission as well. When Hubert Kuyper set out for Morioka to begin his work there in 1913, he planned to make use of the newspapers in a similar way. Pieters offered Kuyper the use of the articles and other materials he had developed. Kuyper was convinced that this method of evangelism would be an effective way to reach people not only in Morioka but throughout the surrounding towns of Iwate Prefecture and even Aomori farther north. He planned also to ask Miller to write appropriate articles, since he had intimate knowledge of and experience in evangelism among the people of Morioka and Aomori.

Though Kuyper himself was still young and inexperienced, with the materials from Pieters and the assistance of a Japanese pastor, he could do effective work immediately. His plan was not only to offer himself as a contact, but also to introduce the Japanese pastors and evangelists working in the surrounding towns as contacts.[64] He published a series of thirty articles in a Morioka newspaper between May 3 and July 9, 1914, offering to answer questions in person or by mail, and sent Christian tracts and a copy of one of the gospels. In September he began a series of articles on the life of Christ, written by Pieters. As of November 10, he had received 145 requests for literature and had sold twenty-one Bibles. Newspaper evangelism was clearly effective.[65]

Peeke was most pleased at the return of Pieters to evangelistic work, and he commented on their very special relationship. Peeke's words also offer insight into the character and gifts of Albertus Pieters.

---

[62]  AP to WIC, July 30, 1912.
[63]  AP to WIC, Aug. 9, 1912.
[64]  HK to WIC, Sept. 12, 1913
[65]  HK to WIC, Nov. 10, 1914.

It is a great pleasure to me to have my friend of long, long years, Mr. Pieters, with me again. I sometimes wish he would not feel obliged to marshal absolutely all the arguments for what seem sometimes like self-evident propositions, but yet there is a great gain in having someone who can so skillfully master the pro's and con's when a really serious matter comes up. We first met in the Grammar School in Holland twenty-five years ago, and our relations have been most harmonious and intimate ever since. We greatly enjoy visiting together and sparring with wit and repartee, but our tastes and abilities are very different.[66]

Peeke himself was a man of remarkable energy and dedication. His work for many years required incessant travel for evangelistic preaching, and for the encouragement and supervision of twelve Japanese evangelists. He saw himself as primarily an evangelist, rather than as a scholar. Yet he also persisted in polishing his language skills, and in 1912 he published a book on how to study and learn the characters used in written Japanese, as well as a pamphlet for younger missionaries on how to pray in Japanese.[67] By the summer of 1915, Peeke had to his credit five publications designed to assist foreigners in the study and mastery of the Japanese language, including a dictionary indexing six thousand Japanese characters.[68]

In a letter, Peeke offered insightful observations on evangelism in Japan.

The task is a hard one. Pieters...recently sent out by post 1,500 invitations to Oita city people to come to a Bible class that he intended to open. It is almost incredible that he should not have had fifty or a hundred responses of one kind or another, and yet he did not have a single one,—and that in a city in whose newspapers he has been publishing Christian matter for nearly a year. I suppose that in India or China there is any amount of opposition to the gospel, but in Japan there are forces at work binding the entire population into a unit of conservatism as far as religion is concerned, of whose nature no one seems to be altogether certain....

Mission work in Japan calls for a prodigious amount of patient, untiring work, by men of a rare combination of abilities.

---

[66]    HVSP to WIC, Feb. 8, 1912.
[67]    HVSP to WIC, Sept. 27 and Dec. 26, 1912.
[68]    HVSP Quarterly Letter, July 10, 1915.

 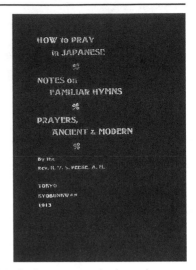

Two of Peeke's publications designed to help young missionaries
become functional in the Japanese language

It cannot be done in a hurry any more than you can graft trees
and pick the fruit therefrom in a single season.[69]

Peeke persisted in that task, reporting, "I have been busily engaged
of late traveling and preaching, and most heartily enjoy it. It is annoying
when administrative work takes time and care....Things are rather thick
for me just now, but I think the principles according to which I am
working are correct, so long as I work in kindness and humility, I need
fear no evil."[70]

The women of the Reformed Church, through the Woman's
Board, continued to recruit and support single women to serve in the
North and South Japan Missions. Their living situations sometimes
became a problem. In both Yokohama and Nagasaki, those appointed
to teach at the girls' schools generally lived together in mission housing,
and it was usually a convenient and mutually beneficial arrangement.
However, the missions were sometimes obliged to put people together
who were uncongenial, and personality differences between the women
led to trying circumstances.

The South Japan Mission developed a pattern of sending all
new single women missionaries to Kagoshima to study the Japanese
language. The mission had produced a required two-year language

[69]    HVSP to WIC, Nov. 26, 1912.
[70]    HVSP to WIC, June 14, 1912.

course, the content of which served as a basis for exams before the rest of the mission. While in Kagoshima the young women lived with Harriet Lansing, who was also a wonderful role model. In 1904, Grace Thomasma arrived on the field and went to study in Kagoshima, after which she moved to Nagasaki and taught at Sturges Seminary. In Nagasaki, Thomasma lived with Sara Couch, as had other young, single women who taught at the school. This living arrangement did not prove to be a positive one for either Thomasma or Couch. In Peeke's words. "They wear on one another, or one wears on the other, when both of them are trying hard to do the right thing."[71] Thomasma left Japan for furlough in July 1911 and did not return.

Jennie Pieters began her work in Japan in 1905 as a contract teacher at the girls' school. After receiving regular appointment as a missionary in 1908, she went to Kagoshima to study Japanese. In 1909, while Lansing was in America on furlough, Jennie Buys arrived as a regularly appointed missionary and went immediately down to Kagoshima, where she studied the language while living with Jennie Pieters. Lansing returned to Kagoshima after her furlough, and Pieters returned to Nagasaki to teach at Sturges Seminary. She lived with Sara Couch, a happy combination. Peeke reported, "Miss Couch is very fond of Miss Pieters, and what with the relief from the past arrangement, a restful summer, and anticipation of life with a most congenial person, she seems to have turned time back a few years in his flight."[72] Buys worked with Lansing in Kagoshima in evangelistic work. Jeane Noordhoff was the next appointed missionary, arriving in 1911. Noordhoff, too, was sent immediately to Kagoshima to study Japanese,

*Reminiscing*, written by Noordhoff, reveals both how much travel was changing with the extension of the railways and yet how life in rural Japan remained a world apart. Her words picture that unique life in 1911.

> Mr. W. put me on the train for Kagoshima. I was the only American aboard. In the car ahead was an attendant of the visiting Prince saying goodbye to his master and then he came into the car where I sat. He took off his silk hat and put it into a hatbox. Then vest and coat, next trousers, putting each carefully into the suitcase. I looked the other way when I learned it was all to be changed and sure enough when I looked back a few minutes later, there he sat in a kimono reading the paper telling of the great doings of the day before....

[71] HVSP to WIC, Oct. 4, 1911 and March 8, 1912.
[72] HVSP to WIC, Oct. 4, 1912.

Our train passed through many tunnels, I believe 75 of them, and the scenery was constantly changing—mountains, sea, fields of grain, cities, country homes with thatched roofs, and more tunnels all the way from 7:00 a.m. to 9:30 p.m. when we reached Kagoshima. Miss Lansing was there to meet me, and a teacher in the city schools, Mr. Schartz, and we soon set out for the house in *jinrikisha*. I could not be sure the men knew where we were going as Miss L. had gone on ahead to finish the dinner, but Mr. S. assured me the men knew where we were going and sure enough we arrived safely.

The two small maids were at the door kneeling and bending their heads to the floor to welcome me. They were absolutely green and did not understand a word of English so I was to have many a struggle to understand and be understood.

After dinner I was shown to my room and I shall never forget how far I seemed from anyone when I got there. Miss L's room was at one end of the house, and upstairs, while mine was at the other end and downstairs. There were slatted doors to let in some air (and mosquitoes) and street sounds! And the street seemed to be right beneath the windows. I could hear the feet in geta [wooden clogs] and the insects in the hedge, so I soon extinguished the kerosene lamp as it drew mosquitoes and I got into bed under the mosquito net. Then began a greater noise. The rats were having a real field day over my head and as the boards of a Japanese ceiling are loosely laid I had visions of them catching their toes and falling down on the net. Weary with the trip I soon slept but when asked the next day about my rest, I ventured to say, "Did you know there were mice in my room?" She laughed loudly and said, "Japan has no mice, we have rats!" and sure enough I learned wherever I went there was a battle with rats ahead.

The very next morning Language study began when I was introduced to a Japanese lady teaching in the Kagoshima schools. She had been engaged to teach me two hours daily from 8 to 10 o'clock every morning, at which time we stopped for a cup of hot chocolate after which she went to her school while I went on studying all we had gone over by myself. In the afternoon a man came to teach me grammar but here I had to do the preparation myself. He knew little English and there were endless exercises which he corrected, but he scarcely understood any of it, so it was sink or swim by myself.

The first Sunday as we were walking to the church Miss L.

Jennie Buys in a *jinrikisha*

explained as there was no one to play the organ I would likely be asked to play. Never having had organ lessons I was troubled, but I made out and the next week I played every hymn in the book so as to be ready for what might come anytime. And that about spells one's duties and attitudes on the mission field—you do what you are told to do and improve it as you go along. I spent my evenings reading books on Japan...so as to get used to attitudes and situations that might turn up.[73]

When Noordhoff went to Kagoshima, Jennie Buys moved to Miyakonojo to engage in evangelistic work in connection with Miyakonojo Church. She worked among the women and children, primarily through Sunday schools. Buys was not only gifted with an ability to attract young people, but she also found her musical ability to be a great asset. Each summer she traveled to Gotemba, a resort area in the mountains southwest of Yokohama. There, through her musical gifts, she assisted Uemura Masahisa in his summer evangelistic meetings. Unfortunately, heart disease and goiter so weakened her that she had to leave Japan after only four years. She was not able to return to the field and never fully recovered her health. She died four years later (in 1917) at the age of forty-two.

Missionary wives as well as the single women contributed greatly to the evangelistic work. For example, Emma Pieters, within weeks of their arrival in Oita, initiated outreach. Albertus reported, "My wife has succeeded in re-opening the Sunday School, and in spite of many

---

[73] Jeane Noordhoff, *Reminiscing*, Joint Archives of Holland.

difficulties, has now a fairly good organization, with three teachers besides herself, and a regular attendance of thirty or forty children after the holidays, and nearly sixty before."[74]

In response to repeated pleas, two new missionaries were appointed to the South Japan Mission in 1913, the Reverend Stephen W. Ryder and Hendrine E. Hospers. Ryder was assigned to language study in Tokyo. In September 1914, Ryder married Reba C. Snapp, a Methodist missionary in Japan, who then became a member of the South Japan Mission. The Ryders moved to Kyushu and became the mission's first resident missionaries in Kurume, an outstation where the mission's most experienced pastor, Segawa Asashi, was working.

Hendrine Hospers went to Kagoshima to study while living with Harriet Lansing. The city is situated on a large ocean bay, and three miles across the bay stands Sakurajima, a beautiful volcanic island five miles in diameter. The volcano, dormant for centuries, erupted violently in January 1914. The booming could be heard in Saga, 150 miles away, and an enormous amount of ash fell. Lansing and Hospers were safe, although accompanying earthquakes toppled chimneys and stone garden walls and brought down some plaster in their house. Nevertheless, they remained in Kagoshima, continuing to work under continually falling ash from the rejuvenated volcano.

In October 1916, the Reverend Alexander and Helena Van Bronkhorst were also appointed and sent as reinforcements for the South Japan Mission. They took up residence in Nagasaki and began language study. With the new missionaries on the field and increased attendance at church services and public meetings, the missionaries believed that the evangelistic work had entered a very promising period. Through its mission churches and preaching places (not counting independent churches in Nagasaki, Kagoshima, and Fukuoka) there were 100 new converts in 1915 and 106 in 1916, the most in the history of the mission.

### Steele Academy

The city of Nagasaki had changed gradually during the first fifty years of Protestant mission. As one of the first three ports open to foreigners, Nagasaki had served as a crossroads of commerce and culture. It had attracted many promising young people seeking Western education. However, times had changed. Tokyo/Yokohama and Kyoto/Osaka/Kobe had become the academic and cultural centers of Japan.

---

[74] AP to WIC, Feb. 3, 1912.

And in Kyushu, the center of commerce, industry, and trade had shifted to Fukuoka and the northern cities of Kokura and Moji, as well as Shimonoseki, across the straits on the western tip of the island of Honshu. Public transportation had developed. Steamship routes linked all the major coastal towns and cities. But even more important was the system of railroads expanding throughout the country. The regional mission schools had become five-year schools equivalent to seventh through eleventh grade, and they could now only hope to attract local and regional youth.

The boys' school in Nagasaki, Steele Academy, had made progress under the leadership of Albertus Pieters. Government accreditation had been achieved. Not only the facilities, but the academic and spiritual levels began to improve, and the enrollment stabilized at about two hundred. The addition of qualified Japanese Christian teachers, as well as Anthony Walvoord as an effective English teacher, contributed to the progress of the school. When the Pieters family returned to America for furlough in 1910, Walvoord was prepared to take over as principal of the school. Education throughout Japan had made great progress by the early twentieth century. Prior to taking over, Walvoord was given an opportunity to make a four-week observation tour of twenty-five schools throughout Japan to gain insights for his administrative role. He reported, "As I went on this trip I could not help but conclude that the reason why mission schools have no better reputation is because they do not deserve it. We ought either bring our schools up to the standard, or else go out of business."[75] Subsequently, he gave good leadership. Despite limited funds, the school's facilities were improved and expanded, the quality of the school improved, and enrollment increased.

The need for a foreign English teacher at Steele Academy led to an unusual development. Minnie Taylor had been employed temporarily by the Methodist girls' school in Nagasaki, but she had been told she was too old to be appointed as a permanent member of that mission. Taylor was an experienced teacher, and the Reformed mission decided to hire her on contract to teach at the boys' school, even though the idea of a woman teaching at a boys' school was at that time extraordinary. Taylor not only proved to be an effective English teacher, but she also exerted a fine Christian influence on the boys. Peeke remarked of her, "She is a little scrap of a woman, with just health enough to keep going, but grit enough to come up to the line every time. She improved in

---

[75]    Anthony Walvoord to HNC, March 18, 1910.

health steadily in Nagasaki, but while she did not miss a day in her work, there were weeks in the early part of her service when she went from school to bed, and staid there till she returned to school next day, but yet with her head held so high and her spirit so strong that none would suspect it."[76] Taylor was later appointed a regular missionary and served for twenty-seven years, sometimes without salary.

The Walvoords were away for a furlough from August 1912 to February 1914. While in America Walvoord completed an M.A. degree at the Divinity School of the University of Chicago and also, with board permission, raised $2,500 for construction of better facilities for Steele Academy. From 1914 to 1917 improvements were made, including the erection of a lab, special classrooms, a gymnasium, a students' common room, and dormitories, as well as innovative curriculum changes. With its reputation enhanced, Steele Academy continued to grow. By 1916, enrollment had increased to 386 students.

### Sturges Seminary

Sturges Seminary had functioned well and gained a good reputation under the leadership of its Japanese principal, Hirotsu Tokichi, with Sara Couch as vice-principal. However, the school had remained small, with about seventy-five students, while Kwassui, the Methodist girls' school next door, had received significant financial support and personnel from America and grown much larger. Kwassui needed land and buildings for expansion and hoped to add a higher level academic department for women in Nagasaki. At the same time, the Methodist girls' school in Fukuoka had not prospered, being inadequately equipped and staffed. Walvoord favored the idea of an exchange of property between the Reformed mission and the Methodist mission. He urged that Reformed mission property, the Sturges Seminary land and facilities and adjacent mission house, be exchanged for the Fukuoka Methodist school property. This would mean that Sturges Seminary would move to Fukuoka, the prospering commercial center of Kyushu.

However, another possibility was also presented. The West Japan Mission of the Presbyterians had founded a mission school in Yamaguchi named Kojo Jogakuin that had remained small. It had formulated a plan to move this school to a more promising location in the port city of Shimonoseki at the southwestern tip of Japan's main island of Honshu. The Presbyterian mission proposed to the Reformed South

---

[76]    HVSP to WIC, March 8, 1912.

Japan Mission that the Presbyterian girls' school and Sturges Seminary (*Umegasaki Jogakko* in Japanese) amalgamate to establish a union school in Shimonoseki. Of course, both the Reformed and Presbyterian missions were affiliated with the Church of Christ in Japan. At a special meeting on January 25, 1912, the South Japan Mission voted in favor of the Presbyterian union proposal, with the understanding that the necessary funds could be provided if the Methodist mission would consent to purchase the Nagasaki property.[77] The Methodists were, in fact, clearly interested in purchasing the property. The Reformed missionaries were enthusiastic about the possibility of union work in education for young women, and a well-thought-out Basis of Union document was prepared jointly with the Presbyterians.[78]

Both the Presbyterian and the Reformed denominational mission boards favored the union proposal.[79] Consequently, it came as a great surprise to the South Japan Mission when a letter was received from the Reformed Woman's Board flatly rejecting it.[80] Peeke addressed each of the issues raised by the Woman's Board in a carefully composed letter.[81] Pieters, as secretary of the mission, wrote a reasoned response (eighteen pages and twenty pages of supporting documents), persuasively arguing the mission's case.[82] As a result, the Woman's Board reversed its decision, approving the establishment of a union school for girls in Shimonoseki, pending the sale of the Nagasaki property to the Methodists.

The Methodist mission did purchase the Nagasaki property, and the union of the *Umegasaki Jogakko* and the *Kojo Jogakuin* was consummated. The new school was named *Baiko Jo Gakuin*, a name formulated from a combination of the Japanese characters in the original schools' names, and the new school retained the English name of the Nagasaki school, Sturges Seminary. *Baiko Jo Gakuin*, a five-year high school, opened its doors in newly constructed buildings on a hill overlooking the harbor of Shimonoseki in April of 1914. The new school's facilities included the main building—with thirteen classrooms, three smaller rooms, a science hall (for sewing, cooking, and etiquette lessons), and small rooms for reed organ practice—as well as a dormitory for fifty girls, a gymnasium, and a home for the foreign

[77]    WGH to WIC, Jan. 29, 1912; AP to WIC, Feb. 3, 1912.
[78]    VSP to WIC, Apr. 29, 1912.
[79]    Robert E. Speer to WIC, March 9, 1912; HVSP to WIC, Apr. 13, 1912.
[80]    Olivia H. Lawrence to WIC, May 7, 1912.
[81]    VSP to WIC, June 4, 1912.
[82]    AP to WIC, Aug. 5, 1912.

The new Baiko Jo Gakuin (Sturges Seminary) school
buildings completed in 1914 for the
jointly supported school

women teachers. The beginning student body consisted of eighty-nine students, forty-nine of whom were transfers (twenty-eight from the Nagasaki school and eleven from the Yamaguchi school) and fifty were new students.

The goal was to have an enrollment of two hundred, of whom one hundred were to reside in dormitories. Both the cost of land and buildings and the financial support of the union mission school were to be shared equally by the Reformed and Presbyterian missions. Besides the principal, Hirotsu Tokichi, the faculty included twelve Japanese teachers, most of whom were Christians, and four women missionaries (two provided by each mission). Sara Couch chose not to move with the school but to remain in Nagasaki, where she carried on evangelistic work with women and children for the rest of her career. However, Jennie Pieters moved to Shimonoseki, where she served as the much-loved music teacher at the union school. Jeane Noordhoff, having completed her language study in Kagoshima, moved to Shimonoseki to teach English and Bible, joining Pieters there as the second teacher provided by the Reformed Church. The union school was an immediate success, with 149 students by the end of 1916, and many students were becoming Christians. Sturges Seminary (*Baiko Jo Gakuin*) continued to grow and prosper in Shimonoseki under the leadership of Principal Hirotsu, and the two missions each continuously maintained two foreign teachers at the school.

### Reunion of the North and South Japan Missions

As early as January 1912, the North Japan Mission suggested to the South Japan Mission that they form a joint committee to consider the possibility of reuniting,[83] and initial discussions took place. The subject of reunion was again broached in 1915 by both Pieters and Ruigh, and there appeared to be a growing sentiment in its favor among the missionaries. The board's financial limitations and its inability to provide adequate personnel to responsibly meet the needs and opportunities of both missions were cited as reasons for consolidation of their efforts. Ruigh stated, "I am fully convinced that we could do better work and make a more substantial contribution to the evangelization of Japan if our evangelistic forces were united and concentrated either here or down in Kyushu. It would probably be better to concentrate in Kyushu because there is more of a field there that is not occupied by other missions." And he added, "The work of both missions, the North and the South, is spread out too much. It is impossible for a man to give enough of his time to any one station to do really constructive work."[84]

A deputation from the Reformed Church Board and Woman's Board visited Japan in 1915.[85] After they had toured both fields, representatives of the North and South Japan Missions met with the delegation. Among the subjects discussed at this Shimonoseki Conference was the possibility of cooperation and consolidation of the work of the two missions. The board secretary urged formation of a joint committee of the two missions to explore the pros and cons of a possible reunion.

A cooperation committee, with representatives from the North and South Missions, met for almost a week in 1916. The result was a reunion proposal, which was then submitted to each mission and approved. The two missions petitioned the board to reunite the two missions, with the understanding that all four mission schools would continue to be supported and that the subject of concentration of the evangelistic work would be left to the deliberation and decision of the reunited Reformed Church Japan Mission.[86] Most of the missionaries had already come to believe that the only solution to the perennial problem of inadequate personnel and financial means was concentration of evangelistic work in one region, most logically on the island of Kyushu, where the South Mission had always worked.

Ballagh and Winn favored reunion, but not the concentration of evangelistic work in Kyushu. They had both invested their lives in the

---

83    North Japan Mission Annual Meeting, Dec. 2, 1911, Jan. 29-30, 1912; WGH to WIC, Jan. 29, 1912.

84    DCR to WIC, Apr. 23, 1915.

85    The delegation consisted of W. I. Chamberlain, secretary of the board, W. B. Hill, and their wives, who were vice-presidents of the Woman's Board.

86    AO to WIC, Aug. 16, 1916.

interior evangelistic work of the North Japan Mission. Ballagh felt so betrayed that he took it upon himself to write bitter letters of protest to prominent Reformed Church ministers in America.[87] In any case, the reunion was approved by the mission boards, and the two missions once again became one Japan Mission on January 1, 1917.[88]

At the Shimonseki Conference, the missionaries had continued to advocate for an ongoing and strong missionary presence in Japan. It was argued that

> the conviction of late has grown in the minds not only of the missionaries but also of leading Japanese Christian workers that the end of foreign mission work in Japan is not nearly as close at hand as was supposed twenty-five years ago. There is also much more than a lurking suspicion in the minds of not a few of us that certain things that are from time to time set forth as positive signs of an amazing desire on the part of the Japanese people to be evangelized, either as individuals or as a nation, are subject to an alarming discount when put to the test of careful scrutiny. There is a good deal of opposition to the Gospel here....
>
> As for the Japanese Church doing the work of evangelizing or Christianizing the nation, though a real beginning has been made for which we are truly thankful, her strenuous effort at self-support as an organized church, and her laudable efforts, especially in the outlying territories of Japan proper [Taiwan and Korea] is at present taking all her strength and resources, leaving the great task of evangelizing the country as a whole practically untouched.[89]

Following organization of the reunited Japan Mission, it became clear that in the face of the limited resources available from the two Reformed Church mission boards, establishing priorities was essential. Consequently, in 1917 the mission decided to continue its relationships as before with the four mission schools, but to concentrate its evangelistic activities in Kyushu. Negotiations were initiated for the transfer of all work of the former North Japan Mission in Iwate and Aomori Prefectures (centered in Morioka and Aomori cities) to the Japan Mission of the Reformed Church in the United States (German Reformed).

---

[87]    JHB to pastors Bruce, Fagg, and Gowen, Aug. 23, 1916.
[88]    WIC to AO, Nov. 24, 1916.
[89]    AO Notes on Shimonoseki Conference, Nov. 29-30, 1915.

The transfer was agreed upon, and it began January 1, 1918. The arrangement provided that the receiving mission assume responsibility for the twenty-six mission churches and outstations, with a total membership of 186 and a total Sunday school enrollment of 1,350 children. The receiving mission also assumed support of the transferring mission's Japanese workers, consisting of two ordained ministers, seven evangelists, and two Bible women. On the other hand, the mission church properties were transferred to the receiving mission at no charge, with the understanding that they would be given to the respective churches as they gained independence.[90] The transferring mission sent Hoekje to Morioka to oversee the work until June 1920, to allow for a smooth transition.

Leila Winn remained in Aomori, working there until her return to America for retirement in the autumn of 1919. Winn had served thirty-eight years. A pioneer in evangelistic work especially for women and children, she had willingly served alone year after year in isolated outposts in humble devotion to the spiritual welfare of all, especially the poor and suffering.[91]

The missionary residences of the North Japan Mission in Morioka and Aomori were sold to the German Reformed mission, with the understanding that funds realized would be used to purchase land and build missionary residences in Kyushu. Thus ended more than thirty years of the North Japan Mission's involvement in evangelism and church-planting in the Iwate and Aomori Prefectures of northern Japan.

Concentration of the evangelistic work of the reunited Japan Mission also resulted in the termination of the North Japan Mission's evangelistic and church-planting work in Nagano Prefecture. Some of the churches, such as those in Ueda and Matsumoto, had already become independent of mission support, although through Anna Wyckoff Reformed Church mission activity among women and children in and around Matsumoto had continued. As late as the summer of 1917, at age eighty-four and in declining health, Ballagh made a ten-day tour, preaching thirteen times in the Matsumoto area.

In any case, the Japan Mission, convinced that it was unable to provide adequate personnel to do justice to the opportunities in the region, proposed to hand over all its remaining work in Nagano Prefecture directly to the *Somu Kyoku* ("General Board") of the Church

[90]  AP to WIC, Jan. 25, 1917.
[91]  LJS to WIC, Aug. 1, 1919.

of Christ in Japan. The four mission churches, in Nagano, Suwa, Ina, and Iida, were to be transferred, along with the four evangelists serving there. The proposal provided that the transferred work be subsidized on a declining basis over the course of six years by the Japan Mission, and it arranged for gradual transfer of mission church property to the Japanese church. The plan was intended to encourage progress toward self-support while providing time for the Japanese church to prepare to give any necessary support. The Japanese church's *Somu Kyoku* accepted the proposal February 22, 1917, and, after approval by the board, it went into effect January 1, 1918.[92]

Nevertheless, the decision to make this transfer was not taken lightly by the Japan Mission. Pieters noted,

> I regret to say that this resolution was not carried by a unanimous vote. Miss Winn, Mrs. Wyckoff, and Dr. Ballagh could not bring themselves to vote in favor of the motion to transfer to others the work in Shinshu [Nagano Prefecture] with which they have been so long and so intimately connected. Their feelings in this respect are entitled to receive, and are accorded by the rest of the Mission the highest respect. They did not, however, vote against the proposed action, much less record any formal protest against it, so that this has been resolved upon with a greater degree of unanimity than can usually be expected in so difficult and important a matter.[93]

The only evangelistic work of the former North Japan Mission retained by the reunited mission was that on the Izu Peninsula and in Tokyo and Yokohama. The Japanese staff of the mission on the Izu Peninsula in Shizuoka Prefecture included two ordained ministers and a licensed evangelist.[94] The mission maintained preaching places at Gotenyama and Osaki in Tokyo, as well as at Choja Machi in Yokohama. An ordained educational missionary in Tokyo was made responsible for the oversight of this evangelistic activity. With these exceptions, the ministry of the former North Japan Mission region was limited to work related to the educational institutions, Ferris Seminary and Meiji Gakuin, and the church-related evangelistic activity of the Japan Mission came to be focused in Kyushu.

The blending of the two missions, the transfer of most of the evangelistic work of the North Japan Mission to others, and the

---

[92]    DCR to Uemura Masahisa, Jan. 13, 1917; WIC to AP, July 13, 1917.
[93]    AP to WIC, March 23, 1917.
[94]    Serving in Gotemba, Mishima, Kashiwakubo, and Yugashima.

concentration of evangelistic activities in Kyushu resulted in the relocation of many of the missionaries. The widowed Anna Wyckoff, after five years of work with women and children in Matsumoto, was assigned to Tokyo for children's and women's work at the mission church in Gotenyama. The Peekes moved up from Saga to Tokyo to teach at Meiji Gakuin and to take responsibility for the remaining evangelistic work on the Izu Peninsula and at Tokyo and Yokohama.

James Ballagh remained in Yokohama without regular assignment, carrying on such evangelistic activity as strength allowed.[95] In declining health and feeling unable to go on, he left Japan for America in June 1919, after fifty-eight years of service. Eight months later, James Ballagh, the last of the pioneer missionaries, died January 29, 1920, at age eighty-seven. He was known throughout his long career as a passionate itinerant preacher and a man of prayer. The mission suffered another loss October 17, 1920, in the sudden death of Anna Wyckoff at her home in Tokyo after thirty-nine years of missionary service, much of it focused on women and children. Excerpts from her letter, written four days before her death, convey her spirit.

> These are busy days here in Tokyo during the World's Sunday School Convention...I have my house full and enjoy it, and what is more lovely than having your friends about you. It has been a great feast of meeting old friends both Japanese and foreign....a great joy to meet them and see how they have appreciated the little we have done for them. Our prayer is that the children's parents will understand and the children will be allowed to come to Sunday School and be taught the right way.[96]

The Japan Mission continued to provide three teachers or professors for Meiji Gakuin in Tokyo, and in Yokohama to provide the principal and three single women teachers for Ferris Seminary. The Booths had been on furlough, and in July 1917, shortly before their planned return to Japan, Emilie Booth died suddenly. The Japan

---

[95]   AP to WIC, Jan. 11, Aug..14, 1917; Aug. 3, 1918. Ballagh had postponed his furlough repeatedly, preferring to stay in Japan. By his mid-80s, he was in fact unable to carry regular responsibilities but was receiving a full salary. The South Japan Mission had already in 1916 proposed adopting a retirement age for missionaries. The reunited Japan Mission also urged the board to establish a retirement age and policy. Ultimately it was agreed that missionary retirement should be at seventy, that retirees would receive two-thirds salary, and that they should be free to remain on the field or return to America.

[96]   LJS to ALW, Oct. 25, 1920.

Mission's tribute to her pictures the often unrecognized multifaceted role of the missionary wife, the associate missionary. Emilie Booth

> for thirty-eight years was a member of our Mission, and during thirty-six of these years was connected with Ferris Seminary, where, as the devoted wife of the Principal, as the loving mother of her children, as the sympathetic friend and wise counselor of teachers and pupils, as a faithful and efficient teacher, as a hospitable and genial hostess, she, in humble and sincere piety lived a life of service that leaves the sweet memory of one who "walked in her house with a perfect heart."[97]

Eugene Booth returned to his post at Ferris Seminary alone later in 1917. Two years later, Florence Dick, who had earlier taught at Ferris for three years, was reappointed to the Japan Mission and married Booth in Yokohama.

In the educational work in Nagasaki, with Anthony Walvoord as principal, Steele Academy grew into a very respected and well equipped boys' school of four hundred students. In the summer of 1919, Walvoord expressed his hope of transferring the role of principal to a Japanese Christian and to focus his energies on evangelistic work among the students. However, on September 5 Walvoord noticed a small sore above his left elbow, possibly caused by an insect bite. Serious infection set in. Lancing and even amputation proved insufficient to arrest the spread of infection, and he died of apparent blood poisoning September 16, 1919, at the age of forty-one. Edith and their three daughters returned to the United States. Luman Shafer, released temporarily from evangelistic work, served as acting principal of Steele Academy. Subsequently, in 1921, Ruigh was appointed principal.

To implement the comprehensive plan of evangelism in Kyushu, evangelistic missionary personnel were reassigned and new recruits added. Hubert Kuyper and the Shafers moved to Kyushu, and later the Hoekjes returned there. The Reverend Henry Van Eyke Stegeman and Gertrude (Hoekje) Stegeman (sister of Gerrit Hoekje) arrived to join the mission in 1917, and Lillian Orbison, a Presbyterian missionary to China, married widower David Van Strien and joined the Japan Mission. In response to the pleas of the mission, the board appointed a trained and experienced stenographer, Ann M. Fleming, to relieve the burden of office work. Based in Nagasaki, Fleming was assigned the role of assistant secretary and assistant treasurer of the Japan Mission.

---

[97]    AP to WIC, July 24, 1917.

In another new development, Harriet Lansing moved from Kagoshima to Fukuoka to work with women, children, and students, in connection with the self-supporting Fukuoka church.

Following the reunion of the Japan Mission, evangelistic missionaries were stationed in Nagasaki, Kagoshima, Saga, Oita, Kurume, and Fukuoka. During those first years after reunion, the women doing evangelism with the help of their Japanese Bible woman assistants were Sara Couch, Harriet Lansing, Hendrine Hospers, and Evelyn Oltmans, working in Nagasaki, Kagoshima, Saga, and Fukuoka. The ordained men who, with their wives, served at the several stations were Peeke, Pieters, Hoekje, Kuyper, Van Strien, Shafer, Ryder, Van Bronkhorst, and Stegeman. Unfortunately, once again attrition occurred in the mission's ranks. In 1920 Hoffsommer, who had earned a doctorate in education, accepted appointment as principal of the Tokyo School for Foreign Children (later called the American School in Japan), and the Hoffsommers resigned from the mission.[98] As a result, Peeke was needed at Meiji Gakuin. The Van Striens resigned from the mission while on furlough during the same year.

Hubert Kuyper and May Demarest had been engaged to be married in 1913. Obliged to care for her sick father, May had broken off the engagement and returned to America. Reappointed to the Japan Mission after her father's death, May taught at Ferris Seminary from 1918. Kuyper and May once again became engaged in 1921, were married in 1922, and served many years in evangelistic work in Kyushu. In 1919, Kuyper took over responsibility for the newspaper evangelism and Christian book loan library begun in Oita by Pieters in 1912.

Based on his experience and success with newspaper evangelism in Oita, in 1919 Pieters prepared a plan to develop an interdenominational, nationwide newspaper evangelism project in association with other missions in the Federation of Christian Missions in Japan. Although this broad project proved impracticable, the Reformed Japan Mission strongly supported the plan[99] and gained board approval for its regional implementation on the island of Kyushu. Pieters returned from a furlough in 1921 and launched the program, based in the city of Fukuoka, with support not only from the Reformed Church, but also from Presbyterians and Lutherans. The program involved not only paid newspaper articles, but also a literary club that provided loan of Christian books by mail, a monthly bulletin, and messages that could

[98]  On December 22, 1922, Walter Hoffsommer, while on a school business trip, died of asphyxiation from escaping coal gas in a hotel room in Peking, China.

[99]  LJS to WIC, Aug. 2 and Nov. 20, 1919.

be read as sermons in small, home meetings of interested persons in remote places. Serious inquirers nearer churches were introduced to the Japanese pastors, and numerous baptisms resulted. Branch offices of the program were to operate in the other cities where the missionaries resided.

Unfortunately, the comprehensive project lost its visionary leader. Two Pieters daughters living in America became seriously ill, and, due to the long convalescence they required, in August of 1922 Emma Pieters returned to America to care for them.[100] Because of this family crisis, Albertus also left Japan in February 1923, taking an early furlough without salary. He was invited to teach Bible and serve as college pastor at Hope College for one year, and this arrangement was later extended. The health issues of the daughters not being adequately resolved, Albertus and Emma Pieters resigned from the Japan Mission in September 1925, ending their thirty-four year missionary career.

However, the work at what had been expected to become the branch offices and loan libraries related to the comprehensive project continued. Newspaper evangelism and its follow-up ministry through the Eiseikan office in Oita, the work of the Tanshinkan reading room and book store in Kagoshima, and book loan and Bible sales in Saga were maintained for many years by the resident missionaries. Later, a similar media ministry was initiated in Kurume. Extensive use of literature distribution, a Christian book loan library, and reading rooms open to the public became a mainstay of evangelism at the stations of the Japan Mission in Kyushu.

Julia Moulton, who had taught music at Ferris Seminary for thirty-four years, was in poor health and nearing retirement age. An appeal had already been made for her replacement in this important role at the school when, in May of 1922, Moulton's heart failed in the very midst of the work she loved. Her death occurred in a dramatic manner, while directing a performance of the girls' school chorus and accompanying them at the piano. Moulton had made a fine contribution in the field of music, for which the school had gained an excellent reputation.

Eugene Booth served as administrator of Ferris Seminary until his retirement at age seventy. Jennie M. Kuyper had served with distinction as a teacher at Ferris for many years, and most recently had for two years been involved in evangelistic work for women and children in Kagoshima. She succeeded Booth as principal of Ferris on September

---

[100]    AP to WIC, July 26, 1922. Elizabeth contracted TB and Dorothy had a nervous breakdown. The Pieters sold their piano to pay for Emma's travel back to America, it being less than a year since returning from a furlough.

1, 1922. To maintain the desired numbers of foreign teachers at the four mission schools, as well as to provide the promised personnel for evangelistic work, the board sent numerous reinforcements in 1921 and 1922. These were a great encouragement to the mission after the recent losses.

Two single men were sent to teach at the boys' schools, George W. Laug (Meiji Gakuin) and Gerald A. Mokma (Steele Academy). Due to Laug's fine Christian impact upon his students, the mission affirmed him in his declared calling to pursue theological study and return to Japan as a career missionary. Seven newly appointed single women arrived during 1921-22: J. Gertrude Pieters (daughter of Albertus and Emma), Edith V. Teets, Gladys W. Hildreth (temporary music teacher at Ferris), Florence V. Buss (to become music teacher at Ferris), Dora Eringa, Flora Darrow, and Florence C. Walvoord. The Reverend John and Amelie Ter Borg were the one new family appointed, John being the only ordained minister among the new recruits. Gertrude Pieters and Edith Teets served four years, and the two short-term male teachers three years. With the ongoing need to maintain the foreign teaching staff at the four mission schools, the board again recruited short-term missionary teachers. Henrietta Keizer (Sturges Seminary), Cornelius A. Dykhuizen (Meiji Gakuin), and Martin Hoeksema (Steele Academy) arrived in 1925 for three-year terms.

Although as short-term English teachers these latter missionaries did not have the opportunity for thorough language study, they made valuable efforts in evangelism both among and with their students. They taught English Bible classes for some of the more advanced students and found ways to assist in Sunday schools or to encourage the students who had become Christians. By way of example, Martin Hoeksema related a story from his experiences in Nagasaki.

> Three students and I held a little service at a TB sanitarium not far from the Nagasaki R.R. depot. Eiichi Komori, a 5th year student, was our preacher, another read the Scripture, another led in prayer, we sang some hymns. One hymn selected by a patient was, "I would not live always."
>
> Hanging on to the straps in the streetcar as we bounced our way home one student remarked, "Christmas means more to me this year now that I am a Christian." During those years about one fourth of the students became Christians by the time they graduated. Our enrollment was 500. That Christmas vacation the same group met for Bible study and at one session decided

to hold a street meeting. Komori, who was in the habit of street preaching by himself, secured a drum from the YMCA. I had my slide trombone. As we approached a street through which ran a canal one student said, "I want to jump first." "You'll get wet," I replied. "I mean," he continued, "I want to be the first to give my testimony."[101]

In an example of the mission's appreciation of the contributions of the short-term missionaries, Hoekje reported, "In addition to his excellent work in the classroom with our large classes of active boys, Mr. Hoeksema has assisted wonderfully with the music of the school, particularly as organist for chapel services and for the teaching of hymns to the first year. I do not know of anyone else in the station who can take up the work when he goes."[102] When short-term teachers Keizer, Dykhuizen, and Hoeksema completed their terms of service, the mission recorded, "All of our schools, without exception, have enjoyed and profited by their presence. Their work has contributed to the evangelistic purpose of the schools, as well as to the provision of necessary teaching hours. Their spirit of enthusiasm for the Mission's work, and their sympathy with its various enterprises, have encouraged and helped us all."[103]

Advance and regression alternated in the evangelistic work of the Japan Mission throughout the Taisho Era (1912-1926). The vicissitudes of financial support from the boards in America were a contributing factor. Cuts in appropriations particularly affected evangelistic work. The problem was exacerbated by extreme inflation in Japan in the period after World War I.[104] Salaries of the missionaries and the Japanese pastors, evangelists, and Bible women employed by the Japan Mission for mission churches, preaching places, and women and children's evangelism, already inadequate, could not be reduced. Consequently, when budget cuts were made, insufficient funds for itineration, evangelistic meetings, and literature reduced the effectiveness of the work. The resultant frustration was apparent in a letter from the mission's secretary, Ruigh.

Surely if we starve our evangelistic work, the real purpose for which we are in Japan is, to a considerable degree, taken away. It is natural that in the distribution of funds the needs of our

---

101  Martin Hoeksema. *Our Pilgrimage*, 11, Joint Archives of Holland.
102  WGH to WIC, March 7, 1928.
103  WGH to WIC, July 27, 1928.
104  Cost of living doubled from 1914 to 1922.

educational institutions should be considered from the viewpoint of maintaining that work without interruption, that is to say, certain needs exist and must be met if the schools are to continue to function. This sometimes in the past has made it impossible to give to our evangelistic work the funds this work is entitled to.[105]

The mission boards made great efforts to publicize the mission's work and to increase support, and their evangelism budgets were sometimes augmented. Thanks to these efforts, despite difficult financial times further evangelistic missionaries were eventually sent out. A case in point was the appointment of the Reverend Boude C. and Anna Moore. Both had been born in Japan, the children of Presbyterian missionaries, and Anna was the granddaughter of James and Margaret Ballagh. The Moores were appointed as missionaries to Japan by the Reformed Church board, but there was no money to send them. Desiring to leave for the field as soon as possible, they proposed to travel at their own expense and to support themselves by teaching English for the first year. Just before their departure in 1924, the First Reformed Church in Catskill, New York, undertook their full support. The Moores began their work in Japan in Nagasaki.[106]

In accordance with the retirement age set for all missionaries, Albert Oltmans and his wife Alice formally retired after thirty-eight years of service on Albert's seventieth birthday, November 19, 1924. Under the newly clarified policy, as emeritus missionaries they were entitled to two-thirds of the regular salary and housing. They chose to remain in Japan and continued serving as volunteers. H. V. E. Stegeman had been appointed to replace Oltmans on the theology faculty at Meiji Gakuin after a furlough and additional study. Consequently, Oltmans actually continued teaching at Meiji Gakuin until the return of the Stegemans in 1926. After retirement, Oltmans served as general secretary for the Japan ministry of the American Mission to Lepers[107] and frequently assisted in the mission's evangelistic activities.

## The Changing Role of the Mission and Missionary

Stephen Ryder's insightful report after attendance at the annual meeting of the Conference of Federated Missions in 1923 points to the increasingly delicate and changing role of the missionary in Japan.

---

[105]  DCR to WIC, Oct. 1, 1924.
[106]  WIC to LJS, May 10, June 20, July 2, 1924.
[107]  DCR to WIC, Aug. 12, 1924; AO to WIC, March 23, 1926.

I was forced to recognize that for better or for worse, the missionaries have recognized the claims of the Japanese brethren that the time has come for missionaries to step out of many of their positions held heretofore, especially those of an administrative nature, and turn them over as cheerfully as may be possible to representatives of the Japanese church. Happy is the missionary who can do this wholeheartedly, and show his faith in the leaders of the Japanese church whom God has raised up for this age, by prophesying well for them, and doing his utmost to make the prophecy come true.[108]

Due to its "affiliated mission" relationship with the Church of Christ in Japan, the mission had retained a good deal of independence in the oversight of its mission churches and preaching stations, as well as of the Japanese evangelists employed by the mission. When mission churches achieved self-support, they were of course transferred to the Japanese church, and their pastors acquired full membership in the church organization. However, most of the small churches could not achieve this status and remained dependent on the mission and in a nebulous relationship with fellow Japanese Christians in the Church of Christ in Japan.

After the Reformed Church Japan Mission's reunion, its evangelistic work as an affiliated mission was concentrated on the island of Kyushu, the region of the *Chinzei Chukai* ("Classis") of the Church of Christ. The mission and *Chinzei Chukai* had maintained a good relationship, but it became apparent that local Japanese church leaders desired more involvement in decision-making. At their request, in 1920 the mission began reporting its evangelistic plans to the *chukai*, and in 1921, at the urging of the mission's Japanese evangelists, a plan for participation of the Japanese in the administration of the evangelistic work of the mission was formulated and adopted.[109]

By the end of 1921 many national Japanese church leaders and foreign missionaries had come to believe it was time for closer coordination between the work of both the "cooperating" and "affiliated" missions and the Japanese church. Ibuka remarked, "It is the men who were most bitter in the old discussion who are now coming to see the need of better cooperation."[110] In 1922 the Joint Committee of the Church of Christ and the missions proposed

---

[108]    SWR to Japan Mission, Aug., 1923.
[109]    LJS to WIC, Aug. 3, 1921, Feb. 4 and July 29, 1922.
[110]    LJS to WIC, Dec. 9, 1921.

formation of a united evangelistic board, composed of an equal number of representatives from the missionaries and from the church, to carry on all the evangelistic work being done by both the missions and the native church.[111]

However, interestingly, most of the evangelists in Kyushu who worked for the Reformed Church mission were opposed to what they saw as the centralization of power in Tokyo. They were concerned that it would result in neglect of the work in the interior. Representatives of the four missions[112] associated with the Church of Christ in Japan met and prepared amendments to the original proposal to allow for representatives on the sixteen-member Joint Evangelistic Board from the interior and for the direct involvement of local committees. The four missions and many leading Japanese churchmen favored the new plan of cooperation, and, after a counter proposal from the *Daikai* and discussion, a compromise proposal was submitted and tentatively approved. It appeared that the new plan only required negotiation on some detailed rules of operation before final approval. Both the Japanese church and the missions had basically approved the plan, with the understanding that it would be implemented beginning January 1, 1925.[113]

However, in October of 1924 it all came to nothing when the *Daikai* voted to postpone the operation of the joint evangelistic plan, in effect killing the very proposal the Japanese church leaders had initiated. Uemura had come out in opposition, no doubt fearing that the strong, independent, self-respecting spirit of the Church of Christ in Japan would be jeopardized. As a result, the Japan Mission of the Reformed Church retained full control of its evangelistic work and mission churches. It had no choice for many years but to concentrate on strengthening its relationship with the evangelists in its employ, share authority with them increasingly, and develop closer cooperation on the regional level with *Chinzei Chukai*.

A correlation may be seen between Japan's international relations and consequent Japanese attitudes toward the West and the relationship of the missionaries with the Japanese church. By way of example, when the United States passed the Japanese Exclusion Act in the spring of 1924, it was a great shock to Japanese Christians and resulted in a

---

[111]  LJS to WIC, Feb. 4, 1922.
[112]  The four missions related to the Church of Christ in Japan at that time were those of the Reformed Church in America, the Presbyterian Church in the USA, the Reformed Church in the United States, and the Presbyterian Church in the U.S.
[113]  LJS to WIC, Feb. 13, 1924.

nationwide reaction among the general public against America. Peeke wrote, "The nation is dazed, grieved, indignant, and angry."[114] Oltmans stated frankly,

> Judging from statements in the home papers, many people there seem to think that the main cause for dissatisfaction on the part of the Japanese is with the <u>manner</u> in which the immigration bill was carried through Congress, lacking in courtesy and in due consideration. But I think that is a great mistake our people are making. The dissatisfaction lies far deeper: it is "racial discrimination" pure and simple, and that is a far more serious question with modern Japan than mere diplomatic courtesy for which suitable apology might be made.[115]

Numerous Christian organizations in America, including the Reformed Church board, spoke out against the new law. Board Secretary Chamberlain wrote, "We are sensitive to the whole situation and realize how seriously the great task of establishing the Kingdom and Spirit of Christ in Japan has been shocked if not jeopardized by the hasty action of some politicians."[116] The Japan Mission sharply and publicly protested against the Asian Exclusion Act. The Joint Evangelism Board plan met its untimely end in the poisonous atmosphere of the immigration bill.[117]

To make the most of the situation, despite the challenge of working with very limited financial resources, the evangelistic missionaries incorporated new methods of attracting and nurturing inquirers and bringing them into contact with the mission churches and their pastors. The missionaries not only distributed literature, but also used a stereopticon[118] for projecting pictures at public meetings. Public transportation had improved, but infrequent train service was limiting, and many places in the interior had no rail service. Some missionaries had begun to use motorbikes for itineration. However, these means of transportation did not allow for taking much equipment along. In the 1920s, there were no paved roads on the island of Kyushu, but rough, two-track roads with crude bridges over streams and gullies linked most cities and towns. The time had come to incorporate the automobile into their work.

---

[114]  In an article submitted to the *Atlantic Monthly*, but not accepted for publication. Rejected article, in Reformed Church Archives, sent to Chamberlain July 17, 1924.

[115]  AO to WIC, June 27, 1924.

[116]  WIC to AO, Aug. 8, 1924.

[117]  LJS to WIC, Oct. 17, 1924.

[118]  A slide projector designed to allow one view to fade out while the next is fading in.

At Van Bronkhorst's instigation, the Japan Mission in 1923 sought and received board approval to solicit from the churches in America the necessary funds "for the purchase of an outfit consisting of an automobile fitted up with bookshelves and a moving picture machine [stereopticon], to be installed in the machine [automobile], for use in widespread outdoor evangelism and Bible selling in connection with our stations in Kyushu."[119] This dream was realized, as evidenced by Van Bronkhorst's story in the mission's report for 1925.

> The automobile as an evangelistic agency is not a luxury, but a necessity. At any rate it is not the missionary's idea of luxury to drive a Ford over the Japanese mountain roads. He would much prefer to ride comfortably in a train....
>
> During the year we were able to hold 13 meetings, at which stereopticon pictures, on some religious subject were shown. At these 13 meetings the aggregate attendance was approximately 4,000. Several of these meetings would have been impossible without an auto, and the rest were much more conveniently and economically attended because of the auto. We were able to make two trips for Bible and book selling, at some of which street preaching was also done. On these trips, and also at the house and in other ways, 625 Bibles, Gospels and portions, 90 hymnbooks, and about 400 books were disposed of, the sales amounting to about Yen 400. In addition we were able to distribute about 20,000 tracts of all kinds. While doing this work we traveled about 2,000 miles by auto.
>
> Perhaps the most interesting of all the meetings was that held in the little town of Mori on the evening of December 26th. This was a village Christmas engineered by our evangelist there, at which he had asked us to show our pictures of the book, "Ben Hur, a Tale of the Christ." This town is about 40 miles from Oita, but we were advised to go around by another road, about twice as far, because the direct road was very bad on account of heavy snows. When we were about six miles from our destination, the road was being repaired and we could not go on. The last bus had just left the other side of the break, and there was no direct telegraph or telephone from this mountain hamlet. The only thing to do was to go back six miles and then detour, just a slight matter of thirty-five miles, over mountain roads to get to Mori. We left Kakizaka, where the detour began, at 5 P.M. over narrow, tortuous, rough,

---

[119]   LJS to WIC, Apr. 26, 1923; WIC to LJS, June 30, 1923.

The Van Bronkhorsts and the first mission car

muddy, steep mountain roads, entirely unfamiliar, with a car-sick twelve-year-old boy as an extra passenger, and reached Mori at 8:30 P.M., where we found an audience of nearly one thousand patiently and anxiously awaiting our coming. We had driven almost continuously from 10:30 A.M. to 8:30 P.M., 110 miles to keep this engagement, then stayed up till 11:30 P.M. to finish the meeting, and spent the night in a Japanese bed in a Japanese hotel. But it was worthwhile just to be able to sow the seed of the Gospel in the hearts of those 1,000 people.[120]

When the Van Bronkhorsts left the mission in 1926, the automobile was transferred to the Kagoshima station, where John Ter Borg used it for widespread outreach to remote areas of the district. Ter Borg reported, "Everywhere we had crowds to listen to our message, songs, and prayers. Truly a great opportunity for sowing the Gospel seed in the field of human souls in Kagoshima Prefecture lies before us and there is no other Protestant missionary to do it."[121]

The Moores, after their initial service and language study in Nagasaki, began work in Kurume. Due to the shortage of funds for evangelistic outreach, Moore sought and received permission to teach English four hours per week, the income to be used for "the conduct of tent evangelism and for expenses of upkeep of the motorcycle used in the work." Moore added, "I have requests from all our men in Kurume

[120]    BFMR, 1925, 56-57.
[121]    BFMR, 1927, 57.

The 1927 Japan Mission annual meeting participants
Front row (l-r): Caroline Ryder, Betty Ryder, Jennie Hoekje, Catherine
    Shafer;
seated: Sara Couch, Harriet Lansing, Alice Oltmans, Albert Oltmans,
    Willis Ryder (standing), Harman V. S. Peeke, Vesta Peeke, Luman
    Shafer, Shafer child, Amy Shafer;
third row: Anna Moore, Evelyn Oltmans, Bessie Shafer, Louise
    Muyskens, Florence Walvoord, Reba Ryder, Gertrude Stegeman,
    Jennie Pieters, Janet Oltmans, Rachel Hoekje, Amelie Ter Borg;
back row: Boude Moore, Eugene Duryee, Dora Eringa, Willis Hoekje,
    Annie Hoekje, Stephen Ryder, Henry Stegeman, Cornelius
    Dykhuizen, Henrietta Keizer, Martin Hoeksema, John Ter Borg

Station for a trial of this form of work, and as the tent in Saga (used for evangelism at festivals) and the lantern [stereopticon] are to be had for this purpose, I am asking permission to do some experimental work along this line."[122]

Harriet Lansing, upon her return from furlough in 1924, left evangelistic work with the church in Fukuoka to take up a new work in Tokyo. At the invitation of a Mr. Obara, one of her former students who had become the principal of the new Sawayanagi School, Lansing and her assistant, Miss Uchida, took up Christian ministry among the students. This meant working not at a mission school but at a Christian school initiated by the Japanese. In a letter to the board reporting this change, Ruigh remarked, "The mission is watching this new departure with great interest. As the doors to work in and with the church are more and more closed it may be that not only Miss Lansing but others as well will find new avenues of activity opened up for them."[123]

---

[122]   WGH to WIC, Feb. 9, 1926.
[123]   DCR to WIC, Nov. 17, 1924.

## The Great Kanto Earthquake

A natural disaster in the 1920s proved to be a pivotal event not only for Japan but also for the Japan Mission. Japan is one of the most earthquake-prone regions of the world, and the missionaries had shared with the Japanese the anxiety of frequent tremors of varying intensity. In June 1894, an earthquake had toppled most chimneys in Tokyo, and the building of the theological department at Meiji Gakuin had been ruined. And in another earthquake March 23, 1909, chimneys at Ferris Seminary in Yokohama were broken off. However, one of the worst such events in history, the Great Kanto Earthquake, struck the Tokyo and Yokohama areas at noon on September 1, 1923. It destroyed a third of Tokyo and most of Yokohama, and the quake and ensuing fire killed an estimated 143,000 people. The Church of Christ in Japan sustained great losses of life and property. Ten of its churches in Tokyo and its theological school were destroyed. The churches in Yokohama and Kamakura were also completely lost.

Most of the Tokyo and Yokohama missionaries were planning to return to their posts from summer vacations within a few days and were not in the cities. Only Jennie Kuyper, the principal of Ferris, had returned early to prepare for the opening of the new semester. Peeke was one of the first missionaries to get to Tokyo after the earthquake and to report to the other missionaries the extent and nature of the devastation in Tokyo and Yokohama. While the earth was still shaking and the fires still burning, Peeke walked by night from Tokyo to Yokohama, about twenty-five miles. At the scene of destruction in Yokohama he hastily noted his observations and then went to a ship in the harbor, where he mailed his notes on the tragedy to the mission board, the first detailed report to reach America.

In Tokyo, the buildings of Meiji Gakuin sustained some damage. However, in Yokohama, Ferris Seminary was totally destroyed. Shafer relayed the story of Jennie Kuyper's death in the earthquake, one year to the day after she assumed the role of principal of the school.

> At the time the building fell down Miss Kuyper was in her office, and apparently jumped up from her desk, which was in the middle of the room, and reached the door of the office which led out to the back hall, where she was caught by the falling timbers. The clerk of the school, who was in the other building, rushed out and as he passed her office called, but receiving no reply went on to the gate to extricate his own wife and children from the ruins of the gate house. Then he went back and was able to approach

near enough to Miss Kuyper to converse with her. It seems that he could not see her, but she could see him. Her arms were either pinned under the timbers or else were broken so that she could not use them. She said her body was free, but she could not move her arms. She was in a crouching position with heavy timbers all about her. The gate keeper tried to get several people to assist him but there were only a few men on the place and at first they were busy with their own families and when they did reach the spot the timbers were so large that nothing could be done. After about an hour the fire came up from the street below and reached the building. The clerk stayed by Miss Kuyper until he was in danger of catching fire and she told him to go. He told her that the fire was coming and asked if there was any message she wished to leave and she said, "Remember me to the friends in America and to the Japanese friends." She said that whatever is His will is alright, and then sent the clerk away.[124]

In a memoriam to Jennie Kuyper, the Japan Mission noted, "Those who talked with her before she died speak of her faith and fortitude in the last moments of life. This has been an inspiration to her associates in the Mission and amongst the Japanese. In the hour of approaching death she was as calm, serene, strong in her faith and trust in the Lord, as she had always been in life."[125]

The other missionaries were all safe. Those residing in Yokohama and some living in Tokyo lost all their possessions in the fires. Young missionaries attending Japanese language school in Tokyo were sent to Kyushu to continue their studies. In Yokohama there had been severe loss of life among the students and staff of Ferris Seminary, and many were left homeless. The mission felt responsible to continue to provide for the education of the more than four hundred girls who had survived the disaster. Several Ferris teachers and Jeane Noordhoff went about inquiring as to the welfare of the students, visiting them where they could be found.

Albert Oltmans, sixty-nine years old and thus one year from retirement, was elected by the mission to serve temporarily as principal of the school for the critical period of recovery. The two Reformed Church boards and the Ferris Seminary Alumnae Association each raised half of the funds necessary to continue, and arrangements were made to erect temporary quarters for the school. Ferris was able to

---

[124] LJS to WIC, Sept. 29, 1923.
[125] LJS to WIC, Nov. 14, 1923.

Jennie M. Kuyper (1872 – 1923)

reopen in these facilities four months after the earthquake, in January of 1924, with 350 students. Furthermore, despite its own difficult financial situation, the board appropriated emergency funds not only for repairs at Meiji Gakuin but also for the earthquake relief work of the Church of Christ in Japan.

In the summer of 1924, Luman Shafer was elected by the mission to serve as the new principal of Ferris Seminary, and he soon began to make long-term plans. The temporary school building was expected to provide classroom space for three to five years, but a more permanent structure would be required. Missionary residences and a student dormitory would also be needed. During a Shafer furlough, Jeane Noordhoff served as acting principal, and Peeke purchased land near the school site and supervised construction of a dormitory, a residence for four single women missionary teachers, and a residence for the principal, all of which were completed in 1926. These missionary residences in Yokohama came to be known by their address, #37 Bluff.

By the end of the Taisho Era in 1926, the four mission schools had grown into substantial institutions. Although linked closely to the missions rather than to the Japanese national church, they were administered by boards of trustees in which Japanese Christians played a prominent role. Each school had gained in reputation and increased its enrollment. Meiji Gakuin in Tokyo remained a boys' school affiliated with the Reformed and Presbyterian missions. Its president was a Japanese Christian, and it included three departments, with enrollment of 1,071: academy, 768; college, 247; and theological department, 56. Steele Academy, the Reformed Church affiliated boys' school in Nagasaki, with Ruigh as principal, had almost 500 students. Sturges Seminary in Shimonoseki, supported by the Reformed and Presbyterian missions and ably administered by Principal Hirotsu, enrolled about 350 students. And Ferris Seminary in Yokohama, supported by the Reformed Japan Mission, with Shafer as principal, had about 400 students. The two girls' schools had developed into five-year middle- and high-school-level programs, and each maintained a two-year advanced or postgraduate course for a limited number of students. The Japan Mission justified these schools not only as a means of education according to Christian principles but also as a means of evangelism.

CHAPTER 11

# The Mission, the Church, and Militarist Japan

## The Era of Ultranationalist and Militarist Japan

Upon the death of the Taisho emperor in 1926, his eldest son, Hirohito, succeeded him, initiating the Showa Era. The parliamentary government of the Taisho Era had not established deep enough roots to withstand the economic and political pressures of the 1930s. During the reign of Hirohito, Japanese militarism and aggression reached its zenith. In the words of Andrew Gordon, "The most crucial features of politics in the 1930s were continued turbulence within the military and the rising power of the army over the bureaucracy, the court, and the parties."[1] The period was marked by the breakdown of civilian control of the government, with repeated assassinations of civilian political leaders, seizure of control of foreign policy, and ultimately manipulation of the entire government of Japan by military extremists. The twenty years ending with the World War II surrender on August 15, 1945, may rightly be dubbed the era not only of colonialist, but also of ultranationalist and militarist Japan.

[1]    Gordon, *Modern History*, 197.

A series of actions taken by radical elements in the increasingly powerful military framed the escalation of Japan's aggression in China and beyond. When Chinese nationalists began an attempt to unite all of China's widespread regions under Chiang Kai-shek's Kuomintang (Nationalist Party) between 1925 and 1928, Japan's militarists feared their plans for territorial expansion in Manchuria would be stymied. Japan attempted to block formation of a unified China, sending additional troops[2] to prevent a union of Manchuria with the Chinese Nationalist cause. But Manchuria embraced Kuomintang nationalism, hoping to reduce Japan's role to a commercial presence, and began to develop Chinese-owned private railways that competed with Japan's South Manchurian Railway. The result was conflict between Chinese nationalists and Japan's powerful bureaucrats and Kwantung Army in Manchuria. Extremist Japanese army officers assassinated the Chinese warlord ruler of Manchuria in 1928, but his successor was an even stronger supporter of Chinese nationalism. Meanwhile, in Japan, the extreme nationalists branded moderate bureaucrats, politicians, and military leaders as un-Japanese.

In 1931, military leaders began to take the initiative in Japan's national affairs. They sought an excuse for a thoroughgoing military action against Manchuria. The resulting Manchurian Incident[3] of September 18, 1931, marked the start of Japan's invasion of northeastern China. Evidence suggests that extremist elements in the Japanese Army created the excuse, exploding a bomb on the Japanese-owned South Manchuria Railway. There was no loss of life and little damage, but supposed Chinese terrorists were blamed. With this as justification, Kwantung Army troops seized the Manchurian city of Mukden. Claiming the necessity to protect Japanese life and property, the army embarked upon the conquest of all of Chinese Manchuria. These acts were carried out without prior consent from the Japanese civilian government in Tokyo, and when Prime Minister Inukai attempted to bring the military aggression in Manchuria to a halt, military officers assassinated him in May of 1932.

The intensifying relationship between Japan and China is reflected in the cautious comments of Willis Hoekje. "We are grieved over some of the developments in the disturbed regions of China; grieved, too, that despite the need of the sufferers from flood and famine [in China]

---

[2]   Prior to this action, Japan's Kwantung Army had maintained a little more than ten thousand troops in Manchuria to protect commercial interests there.

[3]   The Japanese government publicly described its aggressive activities in Manchuria and China as *jihen*, or incidents, rather than as war, trying to avoid being accused of violations of international law and treaties renouncing war.

the ship bearing gifts of sympathy from Japan is said to be returning with its burden unaccepted."[4]

Japan's aggression against China in the fall of 1931 was widely covered in the press in Europe and America. The Reformed Church board secretary noted

> the distressing conditions in China, accounts of which are filling our daily papers and weekly magazines, and for which Japan seems so largely responsible....Japan is being brought under severe criticism. The last straw is the ruthless bombing of large native areas of the International City of Shanghai and the killing of multitudes of innocent people and the destruction of their homes....The general sentiment is very strong, involving bewilderment and surprise and stern criticism, as also among Christian people who have done so much to promote good relations with Japan, a feeling of deep regret at the course which Japan is appearing to take through its army and its navy.[5]

Growing international notoriety notwithstanding, when the Kwantung Army had completed its conquest of Manchuria in September 1932, it proceeded to transform this vast region of China into a puppet state it named Manchukuo. It enthroned the last Manchu emperor of China, Henry Pu Yi, as nominal ruler. China complained to the League of Nations regarding Japan's aggressive actions, and the League sent an international team of nine people (called the Lytton Commission) to investigate the Manchuria Incident. As a result of the conclusions of the Lytton Report, the League of Nations urged member nations to withhold recognition of Manchukuo. With this reprimand as an excuse, Japan withdrew from the League of Nations and immediately invaded areas of northern China adjoining the former Chinese Manchuria. China's Jehol Province was incorporated into Japan's puppet state of Manchukuo in 1933.

Shafer's observations in 1933, while based on Japan's controlled news coverage, reveal a growing sense of impending crisis among the missionaries. "One gets terribly impatient with the militaristic nationalism which has gained control of the situation. It is very hard to see how a fascist government can be avoided, ultimately, in which case our Christian movement might come in for a rather hard time."[6] A few months later he wrote to supporters in America,

[4]    WGH to WIC, Sept. 30, 1931.
[5]    WIC to WGH, Jan. 30, 1932.
[6]    LJS to WIC, Aug. 8, 1933.

The political situation is giving us all a good deal of concern. In company with other nations, Japan is engulfed in a strong wave of nationalism. Liberal opinion is practically quiescent. Much is being made in the press of a Soviet menace, but it savors a good deal of propaganda designed to unify public opinion behind an increased budget for military expenditures—a not uncommon practice in other countries. An open fascist dictatorship is unlikely since the same results can probably be secured by maintaining a semblance of the forms of parliamentary government.[7]

On February 26, 1936, the *Ni Ni Roku* incident occurred, in which young army officers assassinated seven key civilian government leaders. From the time of this coup until the end of World War II, the Imperial Army was the controlling power in Japan's political life. The military government aligned itself with Nazi Germany and Fascist Italy in the Anti-Comintern Pact of 1936. By the beginning of 1937 Japan had invaded additional northern territories of China and occupied all areas north, east, and west of Peking. Japan viewed the Communist Soviet Union as a threat to its conquests on the mainland of Asia, particularly Manchukuo.

Subsequently, the Marco Polo Bridge Incident of July 7, 1937, triggered the war between China and Japan called the Eight Year War. Using a minor conflict at the bridge near Peking as an excuse, Japan launched all-out war against China, capturing Peking and invading China's northern provinces. Both the Chinese army and Communist guerrillas who had established strongholds in northwestern China gave strong resistance, despite the Japanese army's superior numbers and weapons. While fighting continued in the north, the Japanese also attacked Shanghai on China's eastern coast. Chinese nationalist troops were defeated and Shanghai was captured in November 1937. From Shanghai, the Japanese moved up the Yangtse River and attacked Nanking, the capital of Nationalist China.

The fall of the capital in December 1937 was accompanied by what came to be known as the Nanking Massacre. Japanese soldiers executed thousands of Chinese soldiers who had surrendered to them, and then, with encouragement from their officers, proceeded to loot the city and slaughter Chinese civilians with horrifying brutality. Foreign observers were invited to witness the indescribable atrocities carried out against Chinese civilians—men, women, the elderly, and children. These terrible acts were widely reported by foreign observers in the world press but

---

[7]    LJS to Dear Friends, Oct., 1933.

never reported to the Japanese public. China's Nationalist government had no choice but to abandon the coastal cities. It established a wartime capital in the interior at Chungking, from which it carried on its resistance. Japan never succeeded in capturing all the interior provinces of China, but the fighting provided Japanese soldiers with combat experience that prepared them for later warfare.

The invasion of China, the brutal treatment of civilians by Japanese troops, and Japan's unrelenting pursuit of aggression against China contributed to the souring of relations with the United States, which responded with economic measures. It denied Japan access to certain war-related raw materials, terminated trading privileges, and assisted China's Nationalist government in Chungking. The economic measures hardened the attitude of Japan's militarists and increased their hostility toward the United States, which they considered to be meddling in Japan's sphere of interest in East Asia. The Japanese government declared that it intended to establish a new order in Asia, the Greater East Asia Co-Prosperity Sphere, a Japan-centered, Japanese-controlled group of countries that would supply Japan with raw materials for its industries and buy its exports. Japan's grandiose plan for hegemony in Asia included Australia, Burma, the Netherlands's East Indies (Indonesia), Malaya (Malaysia), New Guinea, New Zealand, the Philippines, and Thailand, and any country that resisted inclusion was considered an enemy.

Tensions increased with the United States, and Japan sought allies who would support its aggressive plans. On September 27, 1940, Germany, Italy, and Japan signed the Tripartite Pact, an agreement that not only recognized Japan's self-assumed right to establish virtual control over all of East Asia but also provided for mutual assistance by the three axis powers. When Japan seized French Indochina (Vietnam) in July, 1941, President Roosevelt imposed an embargo on the sale of American oil to Japan and froze Japan's assets in the United States. Subsequently the British government and the Dutch government-in-exile also imposed economic sanctions on Japan. By August 1941, resource-starved Japan faced an almost total embargo of military-related imports, including the iron ore, steel, oil, and rubber necessary to continue its undeclared war in China.

In ongoing negotiations to resolve conflicting positions, America insisted that Japan withdraw troops from China and abandon the plan to force countries to join its Greater East Asia Co-Prosperity Sphere. Faced by the embargo, Japan was forced to choose between economic collapse and withdrawal from territories gained through aggression on the Asian mainland, with attendant loss of face, and war with the Western powers. Hardliner militarists in Japan were unrelenting in the pursuit of their aggressive goals and made the decision to wage war. When Prime Minister Konoe appeared willing to work toward a diplomatic settlement with the United States, he was summarily replaced as prime minister by hard-line militarist Tojo Hideki on October 17, 1941. Japan had developed the largest, most modern navy in the western Pacific by 1941, and by naval dominance hoped to facilitate takeover of U.S., British, and Dutch possessions in Southeast Asia and thus gain access to the resources Japan lacked.

Due to the increasing tensions, the United States had moved its Pacific fleet from California to Hawaii, to act as a deterrent to Japanese aggression against the American, British, and Dutch possessions in Asia. This proved to be a strategic mistake that played into the hands of Japanese militarists. Japan sent a special envoy to Washington to engage the attention of the United States in diplomatic maneuvering, while at the same time completing preparations for an attack on the U.S. Pacific fleet based at Pearl Harbor, Honolulu, Hawaii. Japan's surprise attack was carried out December 7, 1941, from six of Japan's largest fleet aircraft carriers and supporting warships. Almost simultaneously, Japanese forces attacked Hong Kong and the Philippines. The attack on Pearl Harbor brought about the U.S. entrance into the Pacific theatre of World War II.

## Mission Efforts in Militarist Japan

In the context of gradually increasing international tensions during the late 1920s and 1930s, the Japan Mission carried on as best it could. As the world situation deteriorated, the position of the missionaries in Japan became more precarious and their relationships more delicate. They were caught between their calling to Christian mission, their love for Japan and the Japanese, and their loyalty and commitment to the Japanese church on the one hand and their growing awareness of Japan's ultranationalism and militarism and their identity as Americans on the other. With regard to evangelism, the Japan Mission came to realize more and more both the necessity of relinquishing its authority and the difficulty of retaining initiative in the mission's work.

### Church Cooperation Reconsidered

In 1927 once again the character of the cooperative relationship between the Japan Mission and the Japanese church came under review. During almost twenty years the mission had remained an "affiliated mission" in its official relationship to the Church of Christ in Japan. On the island of Kyushu, where the evangelistic work was concentrated, the missionaries had frequently conferred on matters of mutual interest with leaders of the Japanese church's classis, *Chinzei Chukai*, but administrative responsibility for the mission's work had never been shared. A monumental new plan was proposed in 1927, adopted in 1928, and implemented January 1, 1929, by which the church-planting work of the mission in Kyushu was to be conducted under the management of a Committee on Church Extension Work in Kyushu.

The plan provided that this new administrative committee be composed of ten members—five members of the mission and five Japanese, two of whom were to be nominated by the classis and three of whom were to be nominated from among themselves by the evangelists working for the mission. These nominations were then to be approved by the mission. While each station manned by the mission would continue to have a resident missionary in charge, the joint Committee on Church Extension Work in Kyushu was to exercise general management of the work. The committee was given considerable authority: to employ, locate, transfer, pension, and dismiss evangelists; to open or close outstations; to organize or disband mission churches; to make recommendations regarding the scale of salaries, allowances, and pensions; to arrange for summer work by theological students; to appoint evangelists to attend the *Daikai*; and to determine the form of monthly reports.[8]

Veteran missionary Peeke spoke positively of this development, saying, "The future should be very bright for our mission." However, he also noted, "The men sent out to us [missionaries] should be of the hard-headed and strong-bodied kind that can surely learn to swing the language. This closer cooperation with Japanese means that the missionary must be equal to holding his own in a meeting where the language is principally Japanese, and it is surely the whale of a language."[9] In fact, when the mission's new Committee on Church Extension in Kyushu held its first meeting, January 17, 1929, minutes were kept in both English and Japanese, but the committee chose Japanese for its language of discussion and deliberation, a departure for the missionaries.

This joint administration of evangelistic work was advanced further in 1933. The membership of the mission's Committee on

8    WGH to WIC, Aug. 2, 1927, Apr. 21, 1928.
9    HVSP to Wm. B. Hill, Apr. 11, 1928.

Church Extension in Kyushu was reduced from ten to eight: four missionaries elected by the mission and four Japanese pastors elected, not nominated, by *Chinzei Chukai*, two of these to be evangelists working for the mission. The election of the Japanese committee members by the Japanese church transformed the Committee on Church Extension in Kyushu from a mission-centered committee into a joint committee of the mission and the church for the administration of the mission's church-planting work.[10]

Subsequently, in the fall of 1933, the *Daikai* of the Church of Christ in Japan adopted a new fundamental policy with regard to cooperation with missions or missionaries. Interestingly, in substance it was the same as the policy for joint administration of the mission's evangelistic work already put into practice by the Reformed Church's Japan Mission and the *Chinzei Chukai*, the Committee for Church Extension in Kyushu. In agreeing to the new national church policy, however, it is significant to note that the Japan Mission accepted a new relationship. Shafer noted, "To be sure, technically, it is a joint committee, but in setting up this committee the mission has abandoned its traditional position as an 'Affiliated Mission' and it now becomes a mission in cooperation with the Church of Christ. In other words the mission has now recognized the right and duty of the organized church to share in the administration of our evangelistic work and this step puts our work under the control of the church, within the limitations specified in the rules."[11] This constituted a major change in the relationship.

As missionaries, however, a related issue had necessarily to be faced. A meeting of mission board representatives in America and the National Christian Council of Japan had begun to stress that the initiative for the work in Japan must now come from the church in Japan. Shafer raised serious questions.

> The sense of responsibility for the evangelization of Japan that went with the initiative heretofore exercised by the boards, must still be maintained after initiative is no longer exerted. Nearly all agree that this must not result in diminution of effort for the evangelization of Japan, but I must confess to considerable misgiving with regard to the actual result. Can this sense of responsibility for the work be maintained on the same level when it is definitely agreed that the home churches no longer need to take the initiative with regard to it? The actual situation in

[10]    LJS to WIC, Aug. 14, 1933.
[11]    LJS to WIC, Oct. 19, 1934.

Japan is in a critical condition; the church to which initiative is to be transferred is staggering under a terrific burden; it has great difficulty to maintain itself and has very little energy left for broad extension of its borders —. And yet it is perhaps more important for the history of the world what happens to Christianity in Japan than in any other nation in the Far East. While this is all true and pretty clearly understood, we are being pushed, as though by an inexorable fate, into a position where it seems inevitable that the actual effort of the American churches will be on a gradually diminishing scale rather than otherwise.

We [the Japan Mission] do not wholly agree that the initiative must rest entirely with the church here. We feel that our commission is from Christ and while we will always be prepared to cooperate with the existing church on the field, we do not feel that in doing so we should refuse to express our opinions, or to take responsibilities upon ourselves. We cannot but feel that the principle laid down long ago which made it the aim of missions to establish a self-governing, self-supporting and self-propagating church is being carried to a doctrinaire conclusion which ignores the fact that, while a church may be all of these things, it may still be unable alone to carry the burden of evangelization of the millions yet unreached by the Gospel.[12]

The circumstances faced by the Japanese church in increasingly militaristic and nationalistic Japan made the very impression of dependence upon foreign missions and missionaries an increasing embarrassment. Certainly, Japanese church leaders desired deeply not only to become truly independent, but also to win their compatriots to Christ and to grow as a church. But it was no doubt difficult to accept the reality of the situation. That reality included the following facts as of the end of 1933: of 442 churches, mission churches, and preaching places of the Church of Christ in Japan only 158 had achieved self-support; of 501 Japanese pastors, 282 were ordained ministers and 219 were licensed preachers; only eleven churches had an average Sunday morning worship attendance of 100 or more; and out of a total of 54,006 church members, 22,572 were regular contributors.

The "independent" Nihon Shingakko, or Japan Theological Seminary, was the one educational institution supported directly by the Church of Christ in Japan. And yet, regarding the seminary, the church could only give the appearance of financial independence. The Japanese

---

[12]    LJS to WIC, Nov. 20, 1934.

church declined to accept "subsidies" from the missions, but it saved face by taking a stated grant each year as a "congratulatory gift," which by mutual understanding had been spread over a number of years. Even so, the seminary was faced with an annually increasing deficit. The worthy goal of true independence remained elusive.

### An External Irritant

Beginning in 1930, an unexpected distraction from America presented itself. The mission was informed that an interdenominational Laymen's Foreign Missions Inquiry was being initiated, funded by John D. Rockefeller, Jr., and guided administratively by John R. Mott of the International Missionary Council. This "inquiry" planned to set up an Appraisal Commission to review the activity of missionaries of seven American denominations in India, China, and Japan. The missionaries were informed that the purpose behind this movement was not criticism, but "a sincere purpose to ascertain the facts with a view to promoting the great cause of foreign missions."[13] The announced objective of the inquiry was "the beginning of a new creative era in the initiative, intelligent participation and effective leadership of laymen in the world mission of Christ."[14]

The Reformed Church's Japan Mission appointed Hoekje, Stegeman, and Shafer to cooperate with the fact-finding representatives of the inquiry, who were to visit Japan. When the representatives visited Kyushu for several days in 1931, however, Hoekje noted, "The brethren are happy to find lodging and fellowship at missionary homes, but the greater portion of their time is spent in direct contact with Japanese. Evidently they are not concerned most with what the missionaries think or be doing."[15] Most of the representatives did not in fact speak Japanese and were not especially knowledgeable regarding the culture.

The commission submitted its report, based on six or seven volumes of reports of the surveys taken abroad, which was then formally approved by the Laymen's Foreign Missions Inquiry in November 1932. The Reformed Church Board of Foreign Missions secretary, William Chamberlain, reported that representatives of the seven boards whose mission work had been surveyed were invited to a conference to receive a formal report of the inquiry's work. In advance of the conference, before the mission agencies had received any report, the Appraisal

[13]  WIC to WGH, Sept. 25, 1930.
[14]  WIC to WGH, Nov. 25, 1932.
[15]  WGH to WIC, Feb. 24, 1931.

Commission provided copies of its extremely critical appraisal and recommendations to a publicity agency. Chamberlain reported,

> This, however, was done in a way to command great publicity by the use of one of the best known publicity agencies of the United States. Twenty-three successive "press releases" were distributed to the newspapers of the United States, copies being sent to the members of the Boards especially interested, and these appeared with more or less conspicuous and misleading headlines in the papers throughout the country. The selections from the Report constituting the press notices were made by the publicity agency, but distinctly approved by the Chairman of the Directors of the Inquiry. The selections were naturally made, in the circumstances, from those parts of the Report...most critical and would consequently attract the most attention. The conspicuous headlines, for which the newspapers alone are responsible, added to the critical nature of the extracts.

Chamberlain went on to point out that this publicity attracted wide attention not because it criticized methods and personnel but because it called into question the very aim of foreign missions and the place of the Christian message. He added, "This we had not at all anticipated; much less did we anticipate that the great basis and warrant of the Foreign Missionary Enterprise of the Christian Churches of America and Europe would be attenuated into a purpose of goodwill and that the place of the Christian Message of the Gospel of Jesus Christ would be reduced to a syncretism, each religion, including Christianity, to make its contribution to the ultimate 'spiritual unity of the human race.'"

The only role of the board in this whole matter had been to encourage the missionaries to cooperate with the inquiry, and the mission board had not been in any way responsible for the inquiry's method or findings. Chamberlain continued, "The purpose of the Inquiry was so admirable, in endeavoring to bring about the revival of missionary interest among the laymen of our churches, that we are disappointed and disturbed by this conspicuous feature of the Inquiry to which I have just referred." Chamberlain was unequivocal. "The Reformed Church in America is committed to the purpose of making Jesus Christ known to all men as Redeemer and Master, both for the saving of their souls and for the rectifying of their lives personally and socially. The Board of Foreign Missions has this mandate from the great Head of the Church. No other basis can be considered."[16]

---

[16]   WIC to WGH, Nov. 25, 1932.

In light of the fact that the original invitation to the mission boards to participate in the inquiry had stated, "It is understood, of course, that there are certain things that must abide, chief among them, the central Christian message as expressed by the International Missionary Council at its meeting at Jerusalem,"[17] the most significant conclusions and recommendations of the inquiry amounted to a betrayal of its stated purpose. They reflected the liberal theological bias of its leaders against evangelical Christianity. The publicity accorded the inquiry in the press in Japan aroused anti-American sentiment among some Japanese, and Japanese Christian leaders spoke up, not only against the manner of release of the conclusions of the report, but also in opposition to its basic assumptions. The executive committee of the National Christian Council in Japan unanimously supported a proposition stating that, although it recognized the values of non-Christian religions, it emphatically held the conviction that Christianity has a distinctive message.[18]

Following the publication of the book, *Rethinking Missions*, based on the Laymen's Foreign Missions Inquiry, the Japan Mission responded with its own report on the inquiry and the book, beginning with these words:

> While feeling utterly out of sympathy with the theological bias of *Rethinking Missions* and feeling that many of its criticisms result from this bias and that others are due to insufficient knowledge of conditions, nevertheless, we feel that this report is a call to personal examination in the light of God's Word and by the aid of His Spirit. We desire to be more truly filled with that Spirit, and to come to a fuller recognition of the failures in our work, and to a truer consecration of ourselves to our Master.[19]

The missionaries showed willingness to learn from any valuable suggestions made in the report, while at the same time critiquing its inadequacies. They reasserted their convictions regarding the fundamental purpose of missions and reaffirmed their commitment to building up an independent Japanese church. The board secretary remarked after a letter from the Japanese church, "It has been to us quite impressive that all of the official bodies in Japan, as far as I can recall, have expressed themselves so definitely upon the fundamental

[17]   WIC to WGH, Dec. 19, 1932.
[18]   WGH to WIC, Dec. 29, 1932.
[19]   Japan Mission Report, July, 1933.

inadequacy of the point of view assumed by that Report in the opening chapters. The Japanese Christian leaders, especially of the N.K.K. [Church of Christ in Japan] and the N.C.C., seem to be very clear in their conviction as to the uniqueness of Christianity in its relation to the other religions in Japan and the absoluteness of Christ."[20] From the missionary perspective, Shafer stated, "It is our considered conviction that mission work can be carried on successfully only by those who are convinced that men are lost without Christ and who consequently long to share Him and His salvation with those who do not know Him. We have no other message for Japan."[21] Even so, the Laymen's Foreign Missions Inquiry proved to be a distraction and was undoubtedly detrimental to the cause of missions and its support from the churches in the United States.

### Economics and Mission

The economic problems the mission schools faced were different from those faced in direct evangelism and church-planting. The Japanese church and its leaders had never exhibited either the ability or the will to take financial responsibility for operating the schools, although many Christians were happy to serve on the faculties or with the missionaries on the boards of trustees administering the schools. In 1926, in the case of the four mission schools of the Japan Mission, from one-half to two-thirds of the cost of running each school was covered by fees paid by the students. The remainder of the operating expenses, as well as salaries and housing for the American teachers and the cost of property and buildings, had generally to be borne by the mission. In 1927, the mission reported, "As yet the church is, for the most part, dependent upon mission schools to educate its leaders. She being unable to help to any large extent financially is thus also unable to take any large share in Christian education."[22]

Serious inflation and a depression in Japan in the late 1920s contributed to the challenges faced by the schools, and the mission boards could not absorb increased costs. Large student tuition increases were untenable under the circumstances. The alternative, an increase in the number of students, became the oft-repeated solution to the budget dilemmas of the schools. The resultant challenge was how to provide a quality education and make a significant Christian impact on the lives of an increased number of students.

---

[20]  WIC to LJS, Jan. 30, 1934.
[21]  LJS to WIC, Nov. 20, 1934.
[22]  BFMR, 1927, 48.

The new Ferris Seminary building, completed in 1929. The auditorium of the building was named Kuyper Memorial Hall.

A significant capital investment was necessary if the mission schools were to continue. As a result of gifts from the Reverend Dr. and Mrs. William Bancroft Hill, major buildings were provided for the girls' schools, Sturges and Ferris. It was the very large gift from the Hills that made possible the construction of Ferris Seminary's Kuyper Memorial Building in 1928. This reinforced concrete structure replaced the main school building destroyed in the 1923 earthquake. A newly formed Japanese support society and the school's alumni association raised a considerable sum toward the project. However, more than 85 percent of the almost $300,000 required for the reconstruction of the school was provided by the Reformed Church's Woman's Board (Hill gift included). By way of comparison, the total expenditure of the Board of Foreign Missions for the operation of the Japan Mission for 1928 was $97,046. Without exceptional capital investment gifts of well-to-do and generous individuals such as the Hills, the construction of these substantial permanent buildings for mission schools would have been impossible. Providing such facilities contributed greatly to the eventual development of the schools into self-supporting educational institutions.

Investment in land and houses for the evangelistic missionaries at each station had long been an issue and a goal, because having appropriate housing had proven important for the health and efficiency of the missionaries. Residences for missionary families had gradually been provided in Nagasaki, Saga, Kagoshima, and Oita, and in 1927 a

Tomegawa Jun and Sara Couch on the veranda
of the Nagasaki mission house

new mission house was constructed for a family in evangelistic work in Kurume (first residents, the Moores). These provisions had been made possible in part from the sale of the mission houses in Morioka and Aomori.

In 1927, also as a result of a gift from the Hills, a fine Japanese house was purchased for use by Sara Couch and her work in Nagasaki. Her new home was strategically located in a part of the city where there was no church, in a good location for developing her evangelistic ministry, along with her Bible woman colleague, Miss Tomegawa Jun. Their work included operating four branch Sunday schools, with an average of eighty children each, three regular meetings for women, an English Bible class for students, and a Japanese Bible class. They built their ministry around contacts with mission school alumnae and friendships developed during their more than three decades of living in Nagasaki.[23]

Income from rent to commercial businesses of portions of the land acquired by missionaries in Yokohama and Nagasaki for the first church buildings, augmented by legacy gifts from missionaries and modest additions from the annual budget, had established the James H. Ballagh Fund in Japan. The income from this fund over the course

[23]    BFMR, 1927, 58-59.

of many years made it possible to buy land and build churches and parsonages for congregations being developed through the mission's church-planting work. It was often the case, however, that the long-term cost of maintaining the less tangible direct evangelistic work of the mission, i.e., evangelistic missionary travel, evangelistic outreach activities, support of the evangelists, and development of the mission churches, suffered the most when periodic cuts in appropriations from the mission board were made. Due to these cuts in the late 1920s and early 1930s, many of the evangelistic missionaries sought and received permission to teach English or music part time to raise funds for their evangelistic activities.

The mission board did not have the resources to respond to all the Japan Mission's requests for missionary reinforcements, but it put forth extraordinary effort to raise at least the funds necessary to provide personnel replacements for recent losses in the mission.[24] Numerous recruits were sent out in the late 1920s, but some of their careers became casualties of the Great Depression.

The Reverend Eugene C. Duryee, a graduate of Rutgers College and Hartford Seminary, was appointed as a career educational missionary in 1926, with the understanding he would fill the need for a teacher at Meiji Gakuin. He was well prepared for and attracted to work with students. His five years of service were highly regarded by the mission. Louise S. Muyskens was appointed by the Woman's Board in 1926. She was the widow of Dr. John M. Muyskens, a doctor who had hoped to become a medical missionary. Louise offered to teach music at a mission school, and she served at Ferris Seminary for five years. George Laug returned to America after service as a short-term teacher at Meiji Gakuin with the intention of completing his seminary studies and returning to Japan as a career missionary, a plan enthusiastically endorsed by the mission. Laug and his new wife, the former Miss Hubbel, who had served as a missionary in South America, were appointed and sent to Japan for evangelistic work in 1927. Laug was put in charge of the Saga station but chose to live in the city of Takeo, which was more centrally located for developing Saga outstations in Takeo, Imari, Arita, and Kashima. The Laugs served five years, until 1932. James McAlpine was appointed as a short-term teacher at Steele Academy and asked to serve as assistant mission treasurer. McAlpine was a brother of Anna Moore and a grandson of James and Margaret

---

[24]   Van Bronkhorsts resigned in 1926, Ruighs in 1927, and the mission needed to replace teachers who had completed teaching assignments at the mission schools.

Ballagh. He returned to America in 1932 to attend Western Theological Seminary, from which he graduated in 1935. His hope, shared by the mission and tentatively approved by the board, of appointment as a career evangelistic missionary of the Reformed Church could not be realized.

Despite the Great Depression, some newly appointed career people were able to serve many years. The Reverend John C. de Maagd applied to the board for appointment to Japan in 1927 but was advised to do additional study with the hope that his support could be raised later. He went to the field in 1928, met and married Marian Morris, a Presbyterian missionary teaching at Sturges Seminary, and the De Maagds took up evangelistic work at Beppu in Oita Prefecture. Also in 1928, the Woman's Board appointed and sent Helen Ruth Zander as a career missionary. Zander taught one year at Sturges Seminary in Shimonoseki and studied Japanese in Tokyo before taking up career-long teaching at Ferris Seminary. Zander postponed furlough in 1933 to accommodate the teacher shortage at Ferris Seminary, but unfortunately she soon became ill with tuberculosis. After almost a year at the Episcopal mission's sanitarium at Obuse in Nagano Prefecture, she recovered enough to return to America for furlough. The Reverend Bruno and Regina Bruns were appointed and sent out in 1930. After language study in Tokyo and Nagasaki, they took up the evangelistic work of the Saga station, where they served faithfully for many years. And the Reverend Barnerd M. Luben was appointed as a career missionary for teaching in the college departments at Meiji Gakuin, after language study. In 1932, Luben married Edith Erickson, a missionary of the Southern Presbyterian Church's Japan Mission.

Unfortunately, the Japan Mission continued to experience attrition in its ranks during this period. Harriet Lansing, after a period of student evangelism work in Tokyo, was forced by failing health to retire two years early. She returned to America in October of 1928, where she died January 22, 1933. During her thirty-five years of ministry in Japan, Lansing had been noted for her remarkable impact on Japanese young men. Leila Winn, who had retired from the mission in 1920, returned to Asia in her retirement to carry on evangelistic work among ex-patriot Japanese in Seoul, Korea. She left that work in 1928. The Ryders, veterans of sixteen years and involved in evangelistic work, citing insurmountable difficulties in educating their children, requested a leave of absence and left the field in 1929. They resigned from the mission in 1930.

The Peekes, because of the ill health of Harman, took an early furlough in January 1929. Examination and surgery at Detroit revealed inoperable cancer, and they were informed they would not be able to return to Japan. Despite his serious condition, Peeke prepared and delivered a series of lectures on Japan at Western Theological Seminary. The Japan Mission's senior missionary died in Holland, Michigan, December 27, 1929, ending prematurely forty-two years of exemplary missionary service. His extraordinary career included the publication of several books on learning the Japanese language that assisted numerous younger missionaries in that daunting task. The final such contribution, a brochure on how to conduct meetings in the Japanese language, was published in 1927.[25]

Like all mission schools for boys in Japan, Steele Academy was required by the Japanese government to include military drill in its curriculum. This duty was properly fulfilled, and periodically military officers were sent to the school to observe and approve the drill. However, the intensity of militaristic feeling building up among Japan's youth was evident in an episode at the school in the spring of 1928. The mission reported that the third-year students "undertook by agitation as a group to compel the removal of one of our Christian teachers, alleging use of language in the classroom unfavorable to the Imperial military and naval establishment and so the Imperial family itself. As newspapers gave the incident various degrees of publicity, the school will have to live down a somewhat blemished reputation."[26] This may have been a factor in declining school applications.

In any case, fundraising limitations of the Reformed Church's mission board, and to a lesser extent of its Woman's Board, combined with radical inflation within Japan to force the reevaluation of mission priorities. By the spring of 1930 it had become clear that over the long term it would not be possible to continue to support the entire existing program of the Japan Mission. Adjustments and further concentration would be necessary. The mission, in consultation with board representatives, concluded that Steele Academy, the boys' school in Nagasaki, should be closed.

Though the school had been doing valuable work, and many of the boys had become Christians, it faced circumstances that made a contribution to the mission's purpose commensurate with the cost to the mission of its continuance impossible. In addition to the board's financial issues, those circumstances included a declining student enrollment, with consequent deficits due to less tuition income, and

---

[25]   WIC to WGH, Sept. 29, 1927.
[26]   BMFR, 1928, 58.

the increased provision for Christian education for boys in Nagasaki by a Methodist mission school. Consequently, under the guidance of the principal, Willis Hoekje,[27] Steele Academy was fazed out. Beginning in 1931, no new students were admitted; in the spring of 1933 the remaining lower classes of students were transferred to the Methodist school, Chinzei Gakuin; school land and buildings were sold to the Roman Catholic diocese; the school's records, library books, equipment, and assets were transferred to Meiji Gakuin for its maintenance and redevelopment; and when the school closed in March 1933, Steele Academy was officially amalgamated with Meiji Gakuin.

It was understood that the mission would concentrate on Meiji Gakuin in its educational mission work for boys and young men, and that the closure of Steele Academy also meant a reaffirmation of the commitment to evangelistic work in Kyushu. Flora Darrow, after several successful years of teaching boys at Steele Academy in Nagasaki, was transferred to the academy level at Meiji Gakuin in 1931. Dora Eringa, who had carried out very effective evangelistic work in Kurume with women and children for many years, was transferred to Ferris Seminary in 1934 due to the foreign teacher shortage there. In 1935 she became seriously mentally ill and had to be escorted to the United States for treatment. Sadly, she died of pneumonia February 11, 1936.

In 1934, the Kyushu evangelistic work by missionaries, with their Japanese associates, was being carried out by three women in Nagasaki (Couch, Noordhoff, and Taylor [emeritus]), and by four families— Kuyper in Oita, Ter Borg in Kagoshima, Moore in Kurume, and Bruns in Saga. Not only itineration for support and encouragement of the mission's Japanese workers, but varied evangelistic efforts by the missionaries were bearing fruit under sometimes trying circumstances. Through Bible classes, branch Sunday schools, street meetings, meetings in homes, house to house visitation, newspaper ads, literature distribution, reading rooms, Christian book loan, Bible and hymn book sales, and a Bible exposition, a broad witness was continuing at each of the stations. Several churches had achieved independence, and self-support of the mission churches was also increasing. However, a cloud hung over the mission's work. Bruns reported from Saga, "We everywhere run up against this ultra-nationalism. There seem to be many who would like to approach a little nearer to the study of Christianity, but because of the strength of public opinion they fear

---

[27]    D.C Ruigh had served with distinction as principal of Steele Academy from 1921 until the Ruighs left the mission in 1927. Hoekje succeeded him as principal.

that their position will be compromised if they associate too closely with the foreigners."[28]

The Japan Mission planned to continue to maintain six evangelistic missionary families in Kyushu, as well as one part-time evangelistic worker in Tokyo, and to furnish them with reasonably adequate provision for carrying on effective evangelism of various types. It was further hoped that a moderate advance in evangelistic work for women and children might also be possible.[29] However, the Great Depression in America frustrated these goals.

While it is generally acknowledged that the crash of the U.S. stock market on September 29, 1929, marked the onset of the Great Depression in America, it was several years later, after the failure of the banks, the onslaught of massive unemployment, and the bankruptcy of many farm families in the Midwest that the Depression seriously affected the Reformed Church's foreign mission enterprise. When the mission board reluctantly cut appropriations in 1931, the missionaries in Japan accepted the reality that reinforcements would not be possible until conditions improved, and they sought ways to work within their appropriations. The mission postponed its plans to deal with urgent property needs, and the missionaries voluntarily reduced their own already woefully inadequate salaries by 7 percent.[30] Even so, the board's financial situation continued to deteriorate.

As the impact of the Depression deepened, various measures were taken. Aware of the financial situation of the board, Duryee, who was on furlough in America, voluntarily extended his furlough without salary and continued his graduate studies while working part time as an assistant pastor. To save the heavy cost of travel to and from the field, the board decided to detain missionaries on furlough in America (not only Duryee, but also the Laugs)[31] and also asked that the furlough of the De Maagds be postponed. In 1933, all the missionaries, as well as the board staff in America, were required to forego one month's salary because of a 27 percent decrease in contributions from the previous year. Then, in the summer of 1933, Chamberlain wrote,

> I did not find it easy to tell our [furloughing] missionaries whom
> I met in Grand Rapids last week what I had been charged by

---

28    BFMR, 1935.
29    WGH to WIC, May 19, 1930.
30    WGH to WIC, Dec. 28, 1931.
31    Unable to send the Laugs back to Japan, the board arranged with the Reformed Church Women's Board of Domestic Missions for their appointment to work with native Americans in Macy, Nebraska.

the Board to say to them: that, while we are making every effort to return to the fields those of longer service and experience, the return of those of but a single term simply could not be provided for from the diminished resources which the Reformed churches had placed and are placing in these difficult days in our stewardship for the continuance of the Foreign Missionary Work of our Denomination. This meant not permanent severance, in our hopes, but it did mean their early entrance upon other forms of remunerative service, facing the facts of the present year.[32]

The impact of the Depression became ever more severe, and the gifts of Reformed churches for foreign missions continued to decline, resulting in still more reductions in appropriations for the work in Japan. Because of the austere mission budget, the Japan Mission turned over its remaining mission churches in the Tokyo/Yokohama region (Gotenyama in Tokyo, Kashiwakubo, and Gotemba, together with its outstation in Koyama) to the Church of Christ in Japan, even though these mission churches were not yet self-supporting. Boude Moore, representing the mission, visited each church to preach and offer parting respects. Moore's report expresses the deep meaning of maintaining these Christian outposts, despite the difficulty of reaching self-support.

It was very interesting to me to visit these churches with which Dr. Ballagh had such intimate contact. In Kashwakubo I found three elders baptized by Dr. Ballagh over 47 years ago and still faithful to the church. There were several families in which there were third generation Christians and one in which a young man was fourth generation, this young man being present at the service. In Gotemba also we found third generation Christians. We have no reason to be anything but happy over the work that has been done there. In every case the separation of our support from the church has been accomplished in an atmosphere of cordial understanding. It is our hope that though we cannot help them in a financial way, still we may be of further use in a spiritual way.[33]

## The Final Days of the Reformed Church's "Japan Mission"

The Japan Mission summed up its position in a resolution passed at its annual meeting in July of 1934.

---

[32]    WIC to WGH, June 13, 1933.
[33]    Boude C. Moore to WIC, Aug. 10 and Oct. 17, 1934.

RESOLVED, that in these times of financial distress, when appropriations to the work of the Kingdom in Japan are still being drastically cut and comparatively large numbers of workers are being detained in America, with no replacements, that the Mission draw the attention of the Board to the fact that in all these financial exigencies the Mission has always closely cooperated with the Board, suffering without complaint these reductions of funds and personnel, to make possible everywhere the continuance of the great work of the Church in evangelizing the nations of the world. The Board is further reminded that the Japanese workers, faithfully giving themselves to the cause of Christ, have cheerfully accepted reductions in allowances that have placed them on salaries the very lowest possible minimum for a decent living and anything like effective service....

For seventy-five years the church has sacrificed to send its sons and daughters as missionaries in Japan. In trials many schools have been built and evangelistic stations established. A wonderful and large work has been and is being done in a most difficult field. The Mission is today in the thick of the battle, not only bravely holding entrenched positions, but ever advancing under the banner of the Cross to new victories for Christ and His Church.

The Mission would impress upon the Board the urgent necessity of conserving these gains of the past. We feel thankful for the development of the Church in Japan, but the powers of this Church are still far too inadequate to carry the whole burden of the evangelization of sixty millions. In this tremendously important enterprise, in which the Mission regrets that in its depleted condition it is unable to take full advantage of the opportunities which are the fruits of past efforts, the home Church cannot now afford to withdraw further. The forward look and the laying of foundations by the pioneers, the tears and the prayers and the lives of the many who have builded, the gifts and the hopes and the interceedings of the thousands at home who have for three quarters of a century envisioned a Christian Japan—the Mission is not merely sentimental when it pleads with the Board in view of all this, that there be no more retrenchment, and that, when possible, the Mission be strengthened with replacements in personnel and greater financial backing.

The Mission pledges its continued cheerful cooperation with the Board in whatever of further trials may await the church, but this should not be interpreted to mean that the Mission considers the policy of further curtailment in Japan a sound missionary policy. We regret the desperate measures that have been necessary and prayerfully look for a better day, for we firmly believe that our work is far from finished, that we are urgently needed in the evangelization of this country, and that any further reductions in personnel or funds would be disastrous. We believe that large sacrifices on the part of the home constituency are necessary to build up an indigenous church in Japan capable of holding its own against overwhelming odds. The strategic position of Japan in the present world condition, with her rapid strides in industry and science and learning, with her untouched millions, and with her present dangerous nationalism, is an unprecedented challenge to the Christian Church, making imperative increased efforts on the part of the faithful lest their greatest opportunity in modern missions be lost. The Mission would urge upon the Board its absolute conviction that the limit of retrenchment has been reached and that we should look forward in the future to advance and increased effort in mission work in Japan.[34]

However, despite the pleas of the missionaries, full restoration of mission personnel was not to be. By the summer of 1935, the number of active missionaries on the field was reduced to sixteen (compared to thirty-two in 1927), and the majority of them were engaged in maintaining the work in the three mission schools. The De Maagds went on furlough in 1934, but, with no funds to send them back to Japan, John served two years as a pastor in Hopewell Junction, New York. Only the more experienced personnel—Jennie Pieters, the Stegemans, Annie Hoekje (on extended furlough for children's education), and Helen Zander (having recovered from TB)—were able to return to the field in 1935.

In the spring of 1935, in ill health, William Chamberlain resigned as corresponding secretary of the board after having served twenty-five years. The board treasurer, Francis M. (Duke) Potter, was appointed in his place, and the board asked Luman Shafer to return to America to become associate secretary. Shafer had served twice previously in the board's offices during furloughs in America and was well acquainted not only with its work but also with the home churches. He resigned as principal of Ferris Seminary in April 1935, and H.V.E. Stegeman was

---

[34]     Flora Darrow to WIC, July 27, 1934.

appointed principal. Meiji Gakuin also experienced a major change in leadership. Tagawa, long-time president of the school, resigned, and Willis Hoekje, who had been serving as treasurer of the school in addition to teaching, was appointed by the board of trustees as acting president. He held this position in a time of difficult changes at the school until a new president, Yano Tsuraki, took over administration in 1939. In April 1940 the Nihon Shingakko (Japan Theological Seminary) welcomed Hoekje as a part-time lecturer in New Testament exegesis.

Meanwhile, as the Depression began to ease, churches responded sacrificially. At least some of the missionaries on furloughs were able to return to the field, and the Woman's Board sent replacement teachers for the schools for girls. For evangelistic work, in 1936 Hubert and May Kuyper returned to Oita and Jeane Noordhoff to Nagasaki, and in 1937 the Bruns family returned to Saga and the De Maagds were reappointed and assigned to Kurume. In 1936 Flora Darrow returned to Meiji Gakuin, and F. Belle Bogard and Priscilla Bekman were newly appointed for the girls' schools, and in 1937 Florence Walvoord returned to Sturges Seminary and the Luben family to Meiji Gakuin. The next year Mary E. Liggett was appointed as a short-term teacher.

Following Japanese military activities in Manchuria and beyond in the early 1930s, the fortified ports of western Japan in Kagoshima, Nagasaki, Sasebo, and Shimonoseki became increasingly sensitive areas, especially for male missionaries. In 1935 the Ter Borgs were transferred from Kagoshima, where they had served for many years, to Tokyo. Moore continued for a time to give oversight to the Kagoshima work from distant Kurume.

At the time of the synod meeting of the Church of Christ in Japan in November 1937, the missionaries in attendance had their usual meeting with the church officers. Hoekje reported that it seemed clear that the church leaders were eager to continue and make more effective the method of cooperation that had been put into practice earlier. He added, "At this gathering, too, voices were heard advising the missionaries to show in this crisis their understanding of and identification with the Japanese people, as aloofness and criticism will prove a hindrance to their influence."[35] Furthermore, arrangements were made for a clearer relationship between the missionaries and the Japanese church. The ordained missionaries were invited to become members of the *chukai* ("classis") of the Japanese church within whose bounds they worked, without losing their membership in the home

---

[35]    WGH to LJS, Nov. 17, 1937.

church. With the approval of the mission board in America, this was done.

However, after the outbreak of war with China in 1937 and the strong international reaction to Japan's aggression, the situation of the missionaries changed radically. They experienced great obstacles to their work of evangelism. Tent meetings and street preaching were forbidden in many places. Tract distribution was officially banned or voluntarily curtailed, and in some towns and villages the missionary was no longer welcome. The impact of the changed situation was felt first and most strongly at fortified ports. In 1938 Hoekje explained why the Ter Borgs could not return to Kagoshima after furlough.

> The city and prefecture of their former residence are so located with reference to present activities that the location of a missionary there is out of the question. While the pastors of the two small churches in the prefecture outside of the prefectural capital city are extremely cordial to us and our group, they have felt it necessary to request the missionary specially concerned not to visit their churches, as it involves questionings and embarrassments harmful to their work. On occasion, they prefer to make a long journey to the missionary's place of residence, and there consult with him about their work....
>
> It should be said too very clearly that the present situation calls for a very unusual degree of circumspection on the part of every missionary, not only as regards methods and places of work, but also in regard to practically every detail of the life of the missionary and all his possible contacts with the constituted authorities. It is fortunately true that the great mass of the people are still very friendly and approachable. Yet there is a certain section of the public, and among those in authority, which looks upon all foreigners with suspicion, and with disapproval of the teachings which it is our desire to bring to the people. Should we give this minority occasion, it may be within their power to make it practically impossible for us to function, and greatly to hamper the work of the churches and pastors and schools with which we are associated.[36]

The missionaries found it increasingly necessary to be very cautious in their personal activities and to carry on their work less publicly. At the same time, Kuyper's report for Oita and Kagoshima

[36]   WGH to LJS, May 24, 1938.

Stations for 1937 was able to include the following evidence of energetic evangelism by the mission's Japanese pastors:

> One of the pastors has a circuit of five places outside of the town in which he lives. He visits each of them regularly, having both Sunday Schools and meetings with groups of older people. He also has regular meetings for the patients in a large government hospital, having 150 to 300 in attendance.
>
> Another pastor, situated in an industrial city, has found an entrance into the dormitory of one of the factories. He presents the message to from 30 to 50 of the workers, the Christmas program bringing out nearly 200. Still another pastor goes from house to house in the country districts in which he is located, distributing tracts, finding many opportunities for personal work with individuals. An Exposition in the city of Beppu, open for 50 days, gave a good opportunity for broadcast seed-sowing, both through preaching and tract distribution.[37]

The next report stated, "The year 1938 was one of strain. The future for the Christian cause has been uncertain and while wishing to push as vigorous and loyal a campaign for the spread of the Gospel as possible, it has been inadvisable to do anything that would merely raise opposition without accomplishing anything."[38] Reporting on the mission's annual meeting in the summer of 1938, Hoekje observed, "I think we were aware as we met that the last year has been full of unanticipated tensions, and that we were in the midst of circumstances of insecurity."[39] The next month he reported that they had just been through five days of air defense drill, further reflecting the disquiet in international relations.

The increasingly delicate situation confronting the missionaries became eminently clear in the experience of Boude Moore in the period leading up to the family's furlough in 1938. Moore had incurred the suspicion of the authorities to such an extent that during the last months before departure he was subjected to extremely severe surveillance, such as no other member of the mission ever had to experience. After the Moores left Kurume, city authorities notified the mission that it would be very undesirable for the mission to appoint any ex-serviceman to work in that city.[40] The mission concluded and

37    BFMR, 1938.
38    BFMR, 1939.
39    WGH to LJS, Aug. 3, 1938.
40    Moore had served several years in the U.S. Army before becoming a missionary.

informed the board secretary that after furlough the Moores could not be reassigned to Kurume, or even to anyplace in Kyushu, and the De Maagd family was sent to Kurume in 1938. The Japanese government had revised the rules regarding registration of foreigners in 1938, requiring reregistration annually and adding the requirement to report "rank and kind of service in Army, Navy, or Air Force, if any." However, there was also an intimation of a possible indiscretion on the part of Moore that had brought on the severe surveillance, and the board asked for an explanation. Hoekje, the mission secretary, reluctantly replied as follows:

> The party concerned frequently called on and was very intimate with consular officers of his own country, something perfectly legitimate and natural in itself, and yet we believe it to have been the chief cause of the troubles to which he was subjected. The continuance of these relations after it was evident that they caused misapprehensions was one of the things characterized as imprudent....The case probably lay in the local official mind something like this: "Here is a person born in this country, able to talk easily and freely to people of all classes, and to understand what they say. He also has many foreign friends in various walks of life whom he visits and from whom he gets information. The information that he gathers from various sources, he transmits to the officials of his own country. Being an ex-service man, he is much more able than an ordinary person to sense matters that bear on the present situation." This is our interpretation of the situation....
>
> It is natural and legitimate that one should want to know as much as possible about affairs in the country where one is working, yet we feel that the anxiety of the authorities is caused by the fact that they think the party concerned knows too much about certain affairs. In order therefore to allay this feeling, we think it necessary that there should be a voluntary limiting of the field of inquiry to such things as can cause no suspicion, and to do this so wholeheartedly that all thought of ulterior motives will disappear....
>
> We feel that, especially as the situation became more difficult, there was an undue brusqueness in his dealing with those who look after us, his attitude being provocative rather than conciliatory. This was another of the things characterized as imprudent. We realize the provocation and we know that

The 1939 Japan Mission annual meeting attendees

it takes a special measure of the grace of God and the firmest determination to keep sweet under grilling repeated ad nauseam and ad infinitum. Yet, the attitude of the authorities being what it is, we feel that in order to win back confidence it is absolutely necessary to adopt a different attitude, and to do all that can be done to conciliate them and to remove misapprehensions.[41]

The Moores were permitted to return to Japan in January of 1940, but they were assigned to evangelistic work in Tokyo. In light of the fluid international situation, it was also decided that Shafer, associate secretary of the board, should visit Japan in an effort to thoroughly appreciate Japanese feelings and attitudes. Shafer arrived in Japan in early August, in time to meet with the mission at its annual meeting. Hoekje noted, "Dr. Shafer's presence in our midst for these weeks before and after, as well as during the Mission meeting, in view of far-reaching adjustments in missionary work that seem imminent seems providential and significant."[42] During Shafer's visit policies were put in place to deal with the emerging realities.

Most of the missionaries, as long as they acted with discretion and showed their sensitivity to the situation faced by their Japanese associates, were able for a time to carry on their work much as before. However, an abrupt change of atmosphere was apparent in the fall of 1940. Special Higher Police visits to missionaries' homes for inspection

41    WGH to LJS, Nov. 20, 1939.
42    WGH to Francis M. (Duke) Potter, Sept. 6, 1940.

became common. Mission school administrators where missionaries taught were held accountable for the missionaries' movements and activities. Missionary travel from the cities to interior towns was increasingly subject to surveillance. And for the pastors and churches in towns or villages visited by the missionaries, the presence of a Westerner attracted the attention of the authorities and became an embarrassment. Formerly, when a missionary moved about among the people, he had often overheard the word, *Yaso* (derogatory colloquial for Jesus). In 1940 and 1941, on the street or on buses and trains, the missionary would commonly overhear the mumbled word, *supai* ("spy").

It was in the autumn of 1940 that the relationship between the United States and Japan reached a crisis and began to affect seriously the relationships of the missionaries to the Japanese church. The Japan Mission, agreeing with Stegeman that the time had come for transferring Ferris Seminary to Japanese leadership, endorsed his resignation as school principal, effective immediately. The chair of the board of trustees of the school, the Reverend Tsuru Senji, became the new principal. Hoekje, Kuyper, De Maagd, and Stegeman, representing the mission, along with Shafer, met with leaders of the Church of Christ to consider future relations with the church. They were told that a revision in relations was clearly necessary but that they needed to confer and study the matter before responding.

Subsequently, the missionaries working in Kyushu were notified by the officers of the *Chinzei Chukai* that in the near future the classis desired to withdraw from connection with the mission, abrogating the cooperative agreement, and to have all mission-supported churches transferred to the jurisdiction of the classis. This meant that the mission would no longer be connected with church extension in Kyushu, a very abrupt reversal with consequences, since at that time there were ten ordained Japanese ministers and several licensed evangelists and Bible women in the employ of the mission. Stegeman noted, "The proposal was presented as a healthy movement for independence within the classis, merely an expression of the spirit that has become a tradition in the Church of Christ....We understand that the central officials of the denomination have been notified and that the Kyushu attitude may in some measure form part of a policy to be taken by the Church of Christ as a whole to related missions."[43]

At its *Daikai* in October of 1940, the Japanese national church did in fact take action to discontinue all existing forms of cooperation with

---

[43]   Henry Van Eyck Stegeman to FMP, Sept. 30, 1940.

foreign mission groups and to declare that missionaries as individuals no longer had any standing within the church organization. The Japan Mission was notified to that effect but also received from the Church of Christ in Japan a letter of thanks for the labor of past decades, noting that the mission's work had laid substantial foundations for the Christian movement in Japan. On October 17, 1940, in light of the advice of the American consuls in Japan that United States citizens be prepared to leave Japan for their safety, the board sent the following telegram:

> MISSION AUTHORIZED AT DISCRETION ARRANGE MOVEMENT MISSIONARIES WHERE INDIVIDUAL OR FAMILY CONSIDERATIONS INDICATE ADVISABILITY STOP DECISION ANY INDIVIDUAL ACCEPTED WITH FULL CONFIDENCE.

An emergency meeting of the Japan Mission was held October 16, with Shafer present, to consider proposals regarding personnel and property to be submitted to the board for approval. Given that the mission's field for organic cooperation with the Japanese church for the evangelization of Kyushu had come to an end but that the three affiliated mission schools still welcomed and needed missionary participation, principles were established for action in the deepening emergency. These included possible immediate furloughs for families in evangelistic work, earlier furloughs for other families or individuals, and permission for members of families in educational work to leave the field whenever it was deemed advisable by the mission.

Missionary departures began almost immediately. The Bruns family left November 13. Although he worked in education, in the anxiety of the times Barnerd Luben's health had deteriorated, and the Luben family sailed November 20. The De Maagd family moved from Kurume to Tokyo to replace Luben at Meiji Gakuin. On December 24, Secretary Potter sent the following telegram:

> SITUATION SERIOUS UNCHANGED CONSIDER RETURN CHILDREN.

The mothers departed with their children—Anna Moore in December 1940 and Amelie Ter Borg and Marion de Maagd in January 1941—leaving no missionary children in Japan. The remaining missionaries faced the hard choice of whether to go on furlough or to stay in Japan under increasingly difficult conditions for missionary work and in a deteriorating international situation. Stegeman noted, "The tension between America and Japan, in particular, has been increased by the strong utterances of America's political leaders and by the reaction they called forth here."[44] In fear of impending war, shipping companies were discontinuing trans-Pacific service. One by one the missionaries came to the conclusion that it was time to leave. Departures continued: the Kuypers, John de Maagd, Belle Bogard, Helen Zander, Jeane Noordhoff, Janet Oltmans, Mary Liggett, and Gertrude Stegeman sailed in March; Florence Walvoord went directly to India in March, transferring to the Arcot Mission; and Willis and Annie Hoekje left in April 1941.

Under these difficult circumstances, the matter of mission-owned properties had to be dealt with. School properties originally acquired and held by the mission had previously been transferred safely to school ownership. Following the cutting off of cooperative relations with the Japanese church, arrangements had already begun for church extension properties of the mission to be transferred to legal holding bodies of the Japanese church. It remained to arrange for constructive disposal of the missionary residences in Kyushu. The Kagoshima residence had been unoccupied for several years, and the Bruns family (Saga) and De Maagd family (Kurume) had left Kyushu. Properties were given as congratulatory gifts as follows: the Kagoshima property to Sturges Seminary to help it become self-supporting; the Kurume property to Meiji Gakuin to help it become self-supporting; the Saga property to *Chinzei Chukai* to facilitate its plan to assume indigenous support of all church extension in Kyushu; and, a bit later, the Oita missionary property to Ferris Seminary, to help it attain self-support.

The assumption, of course, was that the properties would be sold and the proceeds used for the designated purposes. The euphemistically labeled "congratulatory gifts" reflected the fact that both Japanese churches and Christian schools were required by the government to be independent of foreign support and, further, that the mission churches in Kyushu would need help to survive the sudden withdrawal of mission funds. Hoekje and Moore also negotiated a contract with the Mitsui Trust Company, successfully arranging for the payment of pensions for the mission's retired Japanese pastors for the next five years. The Nagasaki missionary residence (of Jeane Noordhoff) was sold to the Methodist mission school, Kwassui Jo Gakuin. In this manner, the missionaries made every effort to be responsibe in its divestment

---

44   HVES to LJS, Jan. 22, 1941.

of mission properties, several properties in Yokohama being the only exception. The mission was satisfied that property matters had been so disposed of that there was assurance of continuing benefit to Christian bodies and institutions.

Following the missionary departures between December and April, the Japan Mission as an organization was reduced to a skeleton contingent, with offices assigned to each of the four members: Darrow, president; Ter Borg, vice-president; Moore, treasurer; and Stegeman, secretary. They endeavored to carry on the mission's business and prepare for an uncertain future. Darrow, Ter Borg, and Moore taught at Meiji Gakuin but were limited to classroom contact, as it had become unacceptable to invite student groups to missionary homes. Darrow also taught one day a week at Ferris Seminary. Stegeman taught New Testament at both the Japan Theological Seminary and Kyoritsu (Women's) Bible Training School. Emeritus missionary Couch remained in her personal work in Nagasaki. On April 16, 1941, Stegeman gave a bleak appraisal of the abruptly changed situation of the mission.

> We have great reason to think that, even if no violent crisis develops, the abnormal state of things will continue for several years. This refers not only to the international situation, but also to the relation of the Japanese church and the missionary. A large welcome into cooperation with the church is hardly to be expected for a long time to come. It seems necessary to expect a long period of uncertainty, and our problem is to discover what values lie in and beyond that period, and how best to meet the present conditions....
>
> We must not be afraid to ask ourselves whether enough remains to warrant the strain that the coming days and years seem to hold in store.[45]

Ter Borg and Moore left Japan June 26, with the idea of visiting their families during the summer and possibly returning alone to their teaching in Tokyo. By the end of the summer, however, the situation of missionaries remaining in Japan had deteriorated further. Meiji Gakuin discontinued all teaching by foreigners. Stegeman informed the board that he had decided to leave Japan as soon as he could arrange passage. Shafer acknowledged, "I do not see any important service now to be rendered by remaining in Japan."[46] Leaving proved challenging,

---

[45]    HVES to LJS, Apr. 16, 1941.
[46]    LJS to HVES, Sept. 12, 1941.

however. Stegeman left Yokohama September 14 and shared the story
of his experience.

> My definite desire to return home dates from the time of the
> reciprocal freezing between America and Japan. This, with the
> suspension of steamship connections, was for me definitely a new
> situation, and I at once felt it my duty to try to join Gertrude
> as soon as possible. I soon realized that relations had suddenly
> worsened, and that the situations of Americans in Japan, cut
> off from avenue of return to America, and subject to constant,
> detailed supervision with reference to finances and properties,
> with financial dealings governed in the utmost detail by permit
> requirements, and with freedom of travel in the country curtailed,
> and with domestic censoring of foreigners' correspondence, had
> become decidedly uncomfortable. In fact, one had the feeling of
> being interned, or of being an "open prisoner."
> At first I hoped that direct shipping connections between
> our two countries would soon be resumed, and I planned to
> return by that route. Disappointed in this, I switched to the idea
> of catching an American steamer at Shanghai. My first effort to
> get to Shanghai was frustrated when on the very day of sailing we
> were informed that the ship would not call at Shanghai. N.Y.K.
> boats are subject to government control for military purposes,
> hence their movements are secret and uncertain. Finally, it
> appeared that the only way of exit from Japan toward Shanghai
> was to take the train to Nagasaki, and go by boat from there. Mr.
> Tsuru accompanied me all the way to Nagasaki, and made the
> train trip and the preparations for embarkation easier than they
> would otherwise have been. Alumnae friends financed his way, as
> they were very eager that I should be able to get away and rejoin
> Gertrude.[47]

Henry Stegeman saw Sara Couch in Nagasaki and learned that
she was not in the least inclined to leave Japan or Nagasaki. Flora
Darrow had also manifested no desire to leave Japan and was living
in Yokohama. Before departure, Stegeman made arrangements with
them for the days ahead. Darrow readily consented to take over the
mission's affairs, becoming not only president but also secretary and
treasurer. She was to submit the mission's detailed monthly reports
to the Japanese government. The balance in the mission's account and

[47]   HVES to LJS, Oct. 8, 1941.

Yokohama property rental income would be very adequate to provide for Darrow and Couch for several years.

The climactic Japanese attack on Pearl Harbor on December 7, 1941, brought out the dilemma of Japanese and American Christians who, on both shores of the Pacific, heard the news with shock and sorrow. Japanese leaders and friends of the missionaries in deep solicitude mediated with the police, as the round-ups for detention of the few still on the field took place. In California and New York furloughed missionaries spent hours calling, comforting, and reassuring Japanese residents who were awaiting in terror the visit of federal agents. Then the tides of war eliminated all communications, and the Christian communities of Japan and the West went on their separated ways, with their people.

Even after the outbreak of the war between the United States and Japan, Flora Darrow had chosen to remain in Japan, preferring to carry on quietly in whatever ministry was possible. However, when all foreign nationals were put into internment camps, Darrow was unable to carry on any work. She was later repatriated in an exchange of foreign nationals, arriving in Mozambique aboard the Japanese ship, *Asama Maru*, along with approximately eight hundred other civilians from Japan, Southeast Asia, and the Philippines. There they were met by the U.S. State Department chartered ocean liner *M.S. Gripsholm* of the Swedish America Line and were exchanged for 1,083 Japanese nationals deported from the United States and bound for Japan. Darrow and the other Western passengers spent two months at sea during their voyage from Asia, arriving in New York August 25, 1942. With the departure of Flora Darrow, the Reformed Church's Japan Mission ceased to exist as an organization.

Sara Couch had reached the retirement age of seventy in 1937 and had chosen to remain in Japan to continue her evangelistic ministry as an emeritus missionary in Nagasaki in partnership with her long-time Bible woman colleague and friend, Tomegawa Jun. Even after the war broke out, Couch had no desire to return to America and repeatedly declined offers of repatriation. Interned at first in Nagasaki, in December of 1942 she was moved eight hundred miles northeast to Camp Sumire, an internment camp for foreign civilians in the outskirts of Tokyo. When she became very ill, she was sent to a hospital in Tokyo, where Tomegawa was permitted to minister to her, but upon recovery Couch was sent back to the internment camp, where she remained throughout the war, and Tomegawa returned to Nagasaki. A letter from Couch to Shafer from the camp written November 16, 1943, included the following: "I am very well this autumn, and have much cause for thankfulness. According to God's promise, all my needs are supplied. His Word and the privilege of prayer are more precious than ever." Couch was the only Reformed Church missionary to remain in Japan throughout the war.

During the war, many furloughed missionaries took up useful work in interim or new roles: Bruno and Regina Bruns undertook work in the Virgin Islands under the Board of Domestic Missions; Luben became a field secretary for the Board of Foreign Missions; De Maagd served as a stated supply pastor; Noordhoff served for a time with a Japanese Presbyterian Church in California; Zander worked among Japanese Americans in New York, then took a leave of absence to work for the U.S. government; Janet Oltmans took up work in Annville, Kentucky, under the Board of Domestic Missions; Bogard worked in the office of the Woman's Board of Foreign Missions, then became a short-term missionary in the United Mission to Mesopotamia; Kuypers worked among Japanese Americans being assembled at Stockton, California, for internment, then taught Japanese in Boulder, Colorado; Moore took a leave of absence to accept a commission with the United States Army; and Stegeman joined the faculty of Northwestern College in Iowa.

## Japanese Christianity under Militarist Japan

In order to understand the radical changes in the work and relationships of the Japan Mission that resulted in its sudden virtual demise in the period leading up to World War II, it is essential to clarify the nature of the situation faced by all the Japanese churches at that time.

Ecumenical cooperation in the Christian movement in Japan developed very early. Both missionary and Japanese Christian cooperation crossed denominational lines, as exemplified by the formation of the Federation of Christian Missions in 1902 and of the Japan Federation of Christian Churches in 1911. The latter was superseded by the National Christian Council of Japan in 1923. The Federation of Christian Missions responded to the changing situation. In light of the growing maturity of the church, its desire for independence, and the need for foreign personnel and influence to be less prominent, the federation transferred most of its functions to the National Christian Council and restructured itself into the more informal Fellowship of Christian Missionaries.[48] Confronted by

---

[48]  Drummond, *History of Christianity*, 252.

the increasing impact of the military ideology, with its emphasis on veneration of the emperor and state Shintoism, in 1930 the National Christian Council of Japan issued "A Statement Regarding the Problem of State Shintoism." In its English translation, it read in part as follows:

> It is our judgment that in the social consciousness of the nation the all-prevailing consensus recognizes State Shintoism as a religion. While it is true that since the middle of the Meiji Era the traditional policy of the Government in its administrative treatment of State Shintoism has been to put it outside of the religious sphere, still the shrines of State Shintoism are actually engaged in religious functions. This has given rise to much confusion.
>
> Not only so, but recently the Government in its effort to foster religious faith has not only promoted worship at the shrines of State Shintoism but has made it compulsory. This is clearly contrary to the policy that State Shintoism is non-religious. Moreover, the question has often been raised as to whether it had not interfered with the freedom of religious belief granted by the Constitution of the Empire.[49]

The statement went on to request clarification as to whether State Shintoism is religious or nonreligious. It noted that if its nonreligious nature is asserted, then intercessions, prayers, distribution of charms and emblems, offering up of offerings, conducting of funerals, and all religious functions at such shrines should cease. It stated that if State Shintoism is placed within the religious realm, any religious functions at shrines ought not to be compulsory for Japanese citizens. However, nothing positive resulted from this courageous challenge to government policy. The government preferred ambiguity, which allowed the maintenance of the forms of the constitution while promoting the national policy and ideology. "Its purpose was to make the Christian church, as all other religious organizations, a fully compliant and cooperative tool of this policy."[50]

Already in the Meiji Era, the government had integrated emperor-centered Shinto beliefs into the power structure by giving its priests and institutions privileged status and financial support. In the 1930s, State Shinto was made a government institution and its priests government officials. The obvious conflict with the religious freedom clause of the

---

[49]    WGH to WIC, June 21, 1930.
[50]    Drummond, *History of Christianity*, 254.

constitution was side-stepped by claiming that State Shinto was not a religion. It was asserted that the ceremonies associated with the shrines were obligatory upon all loyal Japanese subjects. By the mid 1930s, the impact of militarism was being felt at all levels of Japanese society. Mission schools and Christian churches were no exception. The mission schools for boys had been required for many years to provide for military drill as part of the curriculum. As the militarists gained power, military drill was given more prominence, and active or retired military officers were sent to the mission schools to conduct the military drill, as well as to provide ultranationalistic "moral education."

Already in 1932 Sturges Seminary, located in very nationalistic Shimonoseki, had faced the issue of whether or not to allow students to participate in excursions to Shinto shrines honoring war dead, and where Shinto ceremonies were conducted. Soon all the mission schools felt pressure to introduce a practice required for many years at all public schools, namely, prominently displaying the picture of the emperor of Japan, observing related ceremonies of veneration, and reading the emperor's Rescript on Education. Learning of the issue, the mission board secretary suggested that the question of whether to accept the emperor's picture for display and to observe related ceremonies was a delicate matter requiring the considered judgment of Christian Japanese.[51] Hoekje wrote of the action taken in the matter in 1935 by Sturges Seminary.

> With regard to the Imperial Portraits, Principal Hirotsu had, with the consent of the Board of Directors, made application for them as well as for a copy of the Rescript on Education, and received word that he was to appear at the Prefectural Office in Yamaguchi City on the 20th to receive them. The ceremonious manner in which they were to be carried and escorted to Shimonoseki from that city and deposited in the school was also prescribed in some detail. In order that this might be done without flaw, so far as possible, regular school exercises were largely suspended on the 25th, and the pupils drilled in their duties on the morrow. At the chapel services Mr. Hirotsu addressed the students briefly and clearly on the significance of the reverence paid to the Imperial House and the bowing before the Imperial Portraits, and the distinction to be maintained between such expression of deep reverence and Christian worship of God.[52]

[51]  FMB to LJS, Sept. 24, 1934.
[52]  WGH to WIC, May 16, 1935.

An artist's depiction of the reading of the
emperor's Rescript on Education
by the principal of a Japanese
elementary school

Subsequently, both Ferris Seminary and Meiji Gakuin followed suit in 1936, applying for the portraits and following the prescribed practices. This compromise was seen as inevitable, as it appeared impossible for mission schools to continue as educational institutions without compliance with the government under whose Ministry of Education they functioned. Nevertheless, a description of the prescribed practices is suggestive. The principal had to hold the emperor's Rescript on Education with white gloves, to show his respect for the emperor, and intone each word with great reverence at the ceremony when he read the document before the students. A slip of the tongue in reading it was considered a virtually unforgivable sacrilege. Furthermore, the portrait of the emperor was required to be kept and displayed in a specially built sacred cabinet in the school. These practices undoubtedly caused painful internal conflict for many devout Japanese Christians.

From the mid-1930s, the Japanese government's monitoring of perceived dissidence gradually increased. The Peace Preservation Law of 1925, amended in 1928, provided the basis for what became more and more repressive measures. Ostensibly seen by the government as necessary to restrain any tendencies to Marxism or anarchy, this law became the means for control and suppression not only of labor movements, farmers' co-ops, and writers' groups, but also of religious organizations. The law prohibited even discussing altering the *kokutai*, which meant questioning the imperial system, an offence that could be punished by imprisonment or death. In all police precincts throughout the country "Special Higher Police" carried on surveillance of suspect groups, including Christians. Any prosecution of suspects was carried out by special "Thought Prosecutors" under the Justice Ministry. Actual incarcerations were limited, and death penalties rare, as control of information, education, and thought proved effective to bring about compliance and inculcate reticence to give even the appearance of disloyalty or unpatriotic behavior.

Once the army solidified its control of the government in 1936, its increasing controls over the civilian population began to affect every phase of life with escalating degrees of intensity. Virtually every major element in society—politicians, intellectuals, religious leaders, those in the financial sector, labor, and farmers—capitulated to the rule of the military. Christians felt the hostility of the military regime to their belief in a transcendent God, which by implication suggested superiority over the emperor, who was worshiped as a living god. Furthermore, the Christians' international relationships and perspectives and their emphasis on peace also made them suspect.[53]

The increasing tension is illustrated by the experience of a church near Kurume related to the Reformed mission. In connection with completion of a new church building for Hainuzuka Church, local authorities became rigid in enforcement of regulations affecting the activities and meetings of Christian churches. Pastor Narasaki was called to the police station and informed that meetings could not be held in the new church building until further notice. Several times in past years requests for permission to gather as a religious organization, as required by law, had been submitted, but authorities claimed there was no record on file. The pastor was told that the permission he had received to build a church building did not carry with it permission to use it for Christian services. The issue was resolved, but it revealed the tenuous situation the churches faced.[54]

Under the circumstances, individual Christians tried to live in a way consistent with their faith while at the same time showing themselves to be patriotic Japanese, an effort that proved increasingly

53 Drummond, *History of Christianity*, 250, 252.
54 WGH to LJS, Jan. 22, 1937.

difficult. Among the general public the attitude toward Christians and the church had become more hostile, influenced by the propaganda of the right-wing nationalists and militarists. Drummond noted, "Japanese Christians had always been loyal citizens and considered civil obedience and service to the state their divinely prescribed duty." While some individuals had indeed expressed grave misgivings with regard to the policy of military expansion, "once the nation as a whole was committed, apparently without power of retrieval, to war with China from 1937, almost all Christians felt that they had no alternative but to cooperate with national policy."[55]

In 1937, the Church of Christ in Japan, as well as most other denominations, actually passed resolutions of patriotic support. At a meeting with cooperating missionaries, held at the time of the Church of Christ's *Daikai* in the fall of 1937, the missionaries were advised "to show in this crisis their understanding of and identification with the Japanese people, as aloofness and criticism will prove a hindrance to their influence."[56] The government had cleverly included Christian representatives in called meetings with religious leaders, giving the impression of official recognition of Christianity. In reality, the government's purpose was to make the Christian church, along with all other religious organizations, the fully compliant and cooperative tool of its policy.[57] Christians were enlisted in the indoctrination of the people in the government's so-called Spiritual Mobilization Movement, which claimed noble aims and complete moral justification for the war. It also urged thrift, savings, contributions to the war effort, diligent work, strict observance of wartime regulations, strong family morale, and personal discipline.

In 1938 the National Christian Council, in complete subservience to the government, issued a pamphlet entitled *The People's Spiritual Mobilization and Christianity*, which clarified the action expected of the churches. The duties of church leaders stated there included: to pursue service to the troops and to society, to help correct public opinion toward Japan overseas, to re-educate ministers and laity regarding the national goals, and to use Christian periodicals for patriotic action. These injunctions served two purposes: they spurred people on to follow the government instructions, and they served as a warning against failures that might get Christians into trouble. Despite such

55    Drummond, *History of Christianity*, 255-56.
56    WGH to LJS, Nov. 17, 1937.
57    Drummond, *History of Christianity*, 254.

compliance, government control over religion became increasingly stringent.

In contradiction to the Japanese Constitution, laws to regulate religions had in the past been proposed repeatedly by ruling governments, but opposition, not only from Christians but also from liberal elements in the society, had succeeded in preventing passage. However, by the end of the decade the situation had completely changed, and in 1939 a compliant Diet easily passed a Religious Bodies Law. This law settled the question raised by the National Christian Council in 1930. "One of the measures of the bill served to place all State Shinto shrines outside the category of religious bodies and therefore not subject to the other provisions of the act. By this means the religious absolutism of the regime was technically removed from the category of religion, and shrine worship, the 'Peoples' Rite' (*Kokumin Girei*), and the like could be made constitutionally legal and compulsory for all Japanese."[58]

### Formation of the Kyodan

The Religious Bodies Law of 1939 permitted the government to supervise all religions and granted authorities the right to exercise censorship, require detailed reports, and refuse permission to carry on activities. The law crushed the sense of religious liberty and, little by little, broke down any antinationalistic sentiment remaining among the people. According to the Religious Bodies Law, to continue in existence every religious organization was required to fulfill certain conditions and be approved as a legitimate religious body by the Ministry of Education and then function under its jurisdiction. Furthermore, since the government, to facilitate its control, would not recognize small denominational groups, it became apparent to all Protestants that church union was necessary for the survival of Japanese Protestantism. After serious deliberation, the Church of Christ in Japan, or *Nihon Kirisuto Kyokai*, with which the Reformed and Presbyterian churches cooperated, decided to participate in a larger, organic church union. Drummond expressed the irony of the situation, "The great desire of most Japanese Protestants over long years, which they were not able to fulfill of themselves, was now to be realized under the pressures of a totalitarian government seeking primarily the reorganization of religious bodies into units of a size it could more conveniently control."[59]

[58]  Drummond, *History of Christianity*, 256.
[59]  Ibid., 257.

Interchurch discussions began August 15, 1940, and on September 2, 120 representatives of the various Japanese Protestant groups met to consider church union. The conferees "took action in the light of the contemporary international situation to urge the Japanese Christian churches to sever all ties with foreign missions and to commit themselves to self-support and independence."[60] Diverse groups, even the many small groups closely tied to and financially dependent upon Western denominations that had never related to the other more independent Japanese Christians, almost all agreed to church union as the only possible means of survival. Not only self-support, however, but creed and polity became crucial issues. As to a creed, diversity prevented immediate agreement on a confession of faith, so a simple, general statement of Christian doctrine was decided upon. As to polity, every conceivable form of church government was represented in the various groups, so it was agreed that within the new united church there would be a federated system with eleven unofficial blocs, allowing considerable autonomy in mode of worship, creed, and evangelistic work. Structures were formulated and a constitution drawn up for the establishment of a united Protestant church. The Church of Christ simply gave the Japan Mission notice of the planned new policies of the united church being formed. Examining the unilateral declaration, Stegeman observed bleakly, "For the time being at least, there is hardly any place for missions and missionaries within the working framework of the church."[61]

The last communications between Japanese Christian leaders and those in America were in the spring of 1941. A nine-member Japanese Christian delegation, most of whom had studied in America and were internationally minded, went to the United States in hopes of gaining a mutual understanding between the two countries. They met April 20-25 in Riverside, California, with representatives of the Federal Council of Churches of North America and the Foreign Missions Conference. Shafer represented the Reformed Church. Through discussion and prayer this "Riverside Fellowship" developed a sense of unity and common concern. The delegation then moved on to Atlantic City, New Jersey, where it met with representatives of the Reformed Church board and more than thirty other mission boards and Protestant agencies to discuss future possibilities within the reality that relations between their two governments seemed to have reached an impasse. The Reformed

60    Ibid., 258.
61    HVES to LJS, May 6, 1941.

board agreed with three conclusions regarding future relations with the Christian movement in Japan that came out of the Atlantic City Conference.

    a. The church in America should not completely resign all initiatives in the matter of the evangelization of Japan.

    b. The new church will welcome the continued cooperation of Christians from other lands in the work of the evangelization of Japan.

    c. In the future missionaries on the field will need to work under the direction of the church in Japan.[62]

The application of conclusions of these conferences would mean the end of mission-to-Japanese church relationships and suggested a possible future church-to-church relationship. The American representatives determined to face changes and new ways of thinking, and also to respond to the invitation of the Japanese visitors to form a delegation to visit Japan as soon as possible. In fact, the Japanese sailed on one of the last ships to leave an Americam port for Japan.

    The founding General Assembly of the *Nihon Kirisuto Kyodan*, or United Church of Christ in Japan, was held June 24 and 25, 1941, at Fujimicho Church in Tokyo. The three hundred delegates in attendance, representing thirty-four denominations and Christian organizations, voted unanimously to approve the constitution, elected the Reverend Tomita Mitsuru as the church's *torisha*, or director, and applied to the government for registration. The Kyodan was organized with eleven synods, including those for Taiwan and Korea, and one mission, Manchuria. The role of *torisha*, a title designated by the Religious Bodies Law for the head of a religious organization, was a unique characteristic. Although he answered to the Ministry of Education, he was deemed to hold all authority within the church. The government expected him not only to represent the church but to rule over it. Consequently, the new church structure was monolithic and authoritarian, unprecedented for a Protestant church.

> The structure of the church was that most suited to the forms of control which the government wished in order to meet wartime needs. At the same time, considering the military dominance of government, the Ministry of Education was not in general, in the context of the time, unreasonable; it did protect the churches... from what might have been much worse treatment. It may seem

---

[62]  LJS to HVES, May 23, 1941.

upon retrospect that Tomita and his headquarters staff at times overplayed the role of compliance with government directives, but his action and that of the churches must be viewed in the context of this relationship with the Ministry of Education. In any case, these men worked zealously to create an organic unity out of the Kyodan, a church in heart and life as well as name.[63]

The Public Order Preservation Law of 1941 had been added to the Religious Bodies Law, permitting state authorities to threaten, harass, and arrest people thought to have made protests against the government and its policies, or who were perceived as being at odds with State Shinto. Although the Christian churches remained publicly active in evangelism as long as they could, eventually they too were compelled to submit to the control of the military, and their actual role eventually became that of a tool of the government's program of thought control. During the course of the war the "Special Higher Police," similar to the Gestapo in Germany, monitored the Christian teachings and sermons in the churches and mission school chapel services. Not only were sermon manuscripts submitted to censorship, but also content to be included was prescribed. In every sermon pastors were required to justify Japan's national military policy, instruct people as to their duties as patriotic citizens, and exhort Christians to be models of conduct in society. Special Higher Police officers attended worship services to ensure compliance.

The psychological impact of the ordeal faced by Japanese Christians cannot be overestimated. When pastors or church members were suspected of disloyalty and taken for interrogation, overt torture was avoided, but clear and rapid responses to trick questions were demanded in an effort to harass and incriminate, and consequently to suppress. Examples of questions asked and their implications reveal the insidious nature of the surveillance and harassment: What is the Christian's idea of deity? (innumerable Shinto gods); What view of the emperor do Christians hold? (Who is higher, Christ or the emperor?); What are the views of Christians regarding Imperial Rescripts and Pronouncements? (authority of the Bible); and What is Christianity's attitude toward worship of the Japanese national gods? (attendance at shrines).[64] After such interrogations, some ministers and Christian students were arrested, sentenced, and later suffered and died in prison.

[63]    Drummond, *History of Christianity*, 261.
[64]    Iglehart, *Century*, 219.

The wife of a pastor friend (the Reverend Inoue Kenjiro) of the author related the following experience of harassment: Two officers of the Special Higher Police appeared at her door and abruptly challenged her, saying, "Who is superior, Emperor Hirohito or the Christian God?" Without answering their question, and with inspired wit she responded, "How dare you so lightly speak the name of the emperor!" Fear in their eyes, they glanced at each other and quickly fled the scene. Mrs. Inoue lived out the injunction of Jesus, "See, I am sending you out like sheep in the midst of wolves; so be wise as serpents and innocent as doves" (Matt. 10:16).

The government also at first urged (1938) and later ordered (1940) that in every household, Shinto tablets from the central imperial shrine at Ise be placed on a god-shelf for veneration, a requirement particularly offensive to Christians. Evidence suggests that most Christians quietly ignored this demand. Japan's defeat in the Battle of Midway in June of 1942, only six months after Pearl Harbor, was understood by many thoughtful Japanese as a sign of impending doom for Japan's military exploits. Many Christians doubted the veracity of the government's reports of unceasing glorious victories. However, expressing such doubts was virtually impossible in Japan's wartime atmosphere, since repression of even the hint of dissidence became increasingly severe. Many were arrested and imprisoned for the slightest word or act suggesting criticism or noncooperation. Even so, there is evidence that at the Kyodan's Annual Meeting in the fall of 1942, the church resisted government pressure to change its name to Japanese Christian Church. It insisted that the name United Church of Christ in Japan be retained, indicating a determination to maintain the universal character of Christianity.

Despite harassment and interrogations, incidents of outright persecution and torture were quite limited. Christians were certainly treated as a potential threat, as possibly unpatriotic and disloyal Japanese, or even as spies on account of their long-time relationships with Americans and British, but no general, widespread persecution occurred. As long as resistance to government policies could be suppressed, the authorities chose to refrain from actions that might result in diversion from the goal of unifying the nation to fight the war. The fact that the official leaders of the United Church of Christ in Japan, the Kyodan, compromised and cooperated with the government no doubt helped prevent extensive persecution.

It is true that in the later days of feverish patriotism officials of the Christian churches did visit the Ise Shrine, and offered there before the altar to the Sun Goddess petitions for the well-being of the Emperor, and for success in the nation's conflict. They said that their prayers were of course addressed to the Christian God. The act, however, seemed to meet with disapproval among the main body of Christians.[65]

The sinister extent to which the military government went in using the church for its own purposes is illustrated by the following description:

> In order that Christian ministers might be thoroughly equipped for their national service of morale-building, as well as exemplary in their own attitudes, a series of "processing meetings" was set up. In the districts and at the national level they were conducted as seminars or workshops. For long hours the text of the *Basic Principles of the National Structure* would be studied, and lectures upon it listened to. The various rescripts, including the Declaration of War on the Allies, would be expounded by government commentators, and the ministers quizzed. Exercises in writing, over and over again, the lyrical poems of the Emperor Meiji or of the present ruler were carried out. The term "brainwashing" had not then been coined, but it must have been some such processing which the authorities had in mind in putting Christian leaders through this tedious course of indoctrination. The pastors were instructed to conduct similar courses for members in their local churches.[66]

The churches, despite the circumstances and the other demands made upon the people's time, tried at least to continue regular Sunday worship services and weekly prayer meetings during the war. However, gradually the worship and spiritual life of many Japanese Christians changed. Many pastors were drafted into the army, leaving churches without trained leaders, but some groups of believers continued to meet privately in homes for Bible study and prayer. The sad truth is that at most churches actual Sunday worship became a casualty of the war, an instrument of emperor-worship and nation-worship.

As the war progressed church activity became more and more difficult to maintain and almost ceased when regular bombing raids

---

[65]    Ibid., 220.
[66]    Ibid., 250.

began in the spring of 1945. From 1944 pastors under forty-five years of age were mobilized to serve fulltime in various war production capacities. Biblical preaching or authentic religious teaching was almost completely transformed into exhortations to service the war effort. The People's Rite, at first a simple moment of silence with head bowed in memory of the war dead, came to include a turning toward the imperial palace in Tokyo, singing of the national anthem and the reading of some imperial rescript. The ceremony became a compulsory part of every service of worship or public religious meeting.[67]

<hr />

[67]   Drummond, *History of Christianity*, 266.

PART III

# Mission in Japan after World War II

CHAPTER 12

# The Changed Context of Mission in Japan

## Christians in Japan amid War's Devastation

On August 14, 1945, the Japanese people were informed that the emperor would broadcast a special message on the radio the next day. A direct speech by the emperor was unprecedented, and the people no doubt expected him to urge them on to a supreme effort for final victory in the war. What they heard instead was the following:

To our good and loyal subjects:

After pondering deeply the general trends of the world and the actual conditions obtaining in our Empire today, we have decided to effect a settlement of the present situation by resorting to an extraordinary measure. We have ordered Our Government to communicate to the Governments of the United States, Great Britain, China and the Soviet Union that Our Empire accepts the provisions of the Joint Declaration. To strive for the common

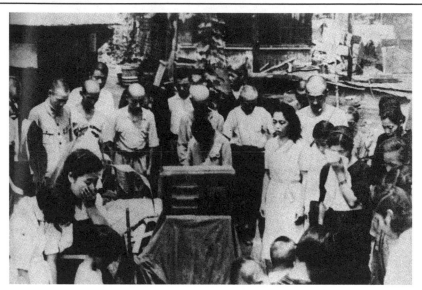

Mainichi newspaper photo of Japanese civilians listening to the emperor's radio address at noon, August 15, 1945

prosperity and happiness of all nations as well as the security and well-being of Our subjects is the solemn obligation which has been handed down by Our Imperial Ancestors and which we lay close to the heart.[1]

The message was delivered in the grandiose style of all imperial rescripts, and it was not until later in the day, when the government gave the facts in plain language, that common people began to understand that the emperor had announced an unconditional surrender. For eight years the people had been urged to bend all energy toward an assured ultimate victory. Most people knew few facts of the war's progress. Even the devastating bombing of Japan had been rationalized and the public assured that retaliation would bring victory. When the reality behind the emperor's announcement soaked in, the nation was stunned. The war was over. Japan lay in ruins. "For literally millions of the people the shock of defeat and the wearing years of privation left no capacity for much beyond a dull sense of rescue."[2]

Following the announcement of the surrender on August 15, allied occupation forces began arriving in Japan August 28, and Japan's formal surrender to the Supreme Commander for the Allied Powers (SCAP) Douglas MacArthur took place aboard the USS Missouri in Tokyo

[1]     English translation from *Nippon Times*, Aug. 15, 1945.
[2]     Iglehart, *Century*, 260.

Harbor on September 2, 1945. Among MacArthur's first orders were that no Allied personnel were to assault Japanese people or to eat any scarce Japanese food. While the Japanese people, even elementary-aged children, had been taught to fight to the last person against invaders and trained to use sharpened bamboo spears if necessary in a final effort to defend themselves, in fact the occupation soldiers encountered no resistance at all.

The Japanese people had been led to believe that an Allied occupation would mean savagery, rape, pillage, oppression, and hatred. Consequently, men in the cities who were able to do so sent their wives and daughters away to remote country villages for refuge with relatives or friends and then braced for the expected ordeal. No savagery occurred, and there was no sign of retaliation. Stories circulated of occupying soldiers handing out chocolate bars to hungry children and sharing their own rations with destitute people. Wives and daughters soon began to return to their families in the cities to face together the challenge of life amid the ruins.

Meanwhile, friends and long-time colleagues of Sara Couch, as well as the mission board staff, continued to be concerned for her welfare. After Japan's surrender, the few remaining internees were evacuated to America in early September, but Couch declined to go on the first ship. In a note sent with fellow internee, Lois Kramer, who was evacuating, Couch wrote,

> Doubtless you know that Nagasaki has been destroyed. I have no word about Tomegawa San, and do not know whether she is alive or dead. I feel I cannot leave until I find out, so decided to stay for the present. I may return later if she and all friends there are gone. I am trusting our loving Father to guide me. We were burned out May 25th and I lost the most of my belongings, but had no physical harm. Since then we have been at Seibo Hospital and Convent. I do not know where I will go from here, perhaps the Miyoshis will take me temporarily, they were not burned out.[3] I am pretty well....Of course we rejoice that peace has come, but oh, it is all so terribly sad.[4]

In a note sent to Shafer with Couch's note, Kramer, a missionary of the Evangelical Mission, wrote about Sara Couch: "She has been such

---

[3]    Miyoshi was a prominent Japanese minister in Tokyo, at that time pastor of Fujimicho Church, and his wife had been Couch's student many years before at the Reformed Church girls' school in Nagasaki.

[4]    Sara M. Couch to LJS, Sept. 1, 1945.

a blessing to us in our internment camp in Tokyo ever since she came to us from Nagasaki in 1942....After we were burned out she read me a quotation which she had written in her own Bible many years ago. 'We can afford to lose anything and everything except faith in the God of truth and love.' We are finding out how true it is."[5]

In a letter to Emma Pieters dated October 5, 1945, Couch wrote, "Here I am in devastated Nagasaki, in a badly damaged house, but so thankful that peace has come and that I am at home again." Tomegawa had indeed survived, though she was very thin. Couch and Tomegawa faced severe privations, food being extremely scarce, but Couch remained positive. "The experiences of long internment have done much to fit me for living under present conditions." The house windows were broken and the roof leaked badly, but although it was only a mile from the scene of the utter destruction of the atomic bomb that destroyed Nagasaki, the house had remained standing, sheltered from the direct impact of the blast by a high intervening hill. Tens of thousands had been killed, many were ill, and there was destruction everywhere. With so many homeless and destitute people all around and not one undamaged house in the city, Couch and Tomegawa took in burned-out families, and fourteen people were sheltered under their roof. Couch affirmed, "Beyond praying, I believe just now the most I can do for the people of this city is to love them and suffer with them."

On January 27, 1946, Sara Couch died of pneumonia in Nagasaki, at the age of seventy-nine, after more than fifty-three years of missionary service. Couch had spent most of her first twenty-two years in Japan in teaching and administration at Sturges Seminary, the girls' school in Nagasaki, as well as in mentoring young Bible women. When the school had moved to Shimonoseki in 1914, she had chosen to remain in Nagasaki and had spent the rest of her life in evangelistic work with children, youth, and women. She was originally from Schoharie, New York. Albertus Pieters said of her, "She was a true daughter of the Reformed Church in America, reared in one of its churches, holding earnestly and intelligently its doctrines, and devoted to its work." Pieters went on to relate from his own experience:

> One incident of that work lives on in my memory. One Sunday I happened to be in the city and Miss Couch asked me to go with her to one of her little Sunday Schools. As we approached the place, the children recognized her and began calling to each

5    Lois F. Kramer to LJS, Sept. 3, 1945.

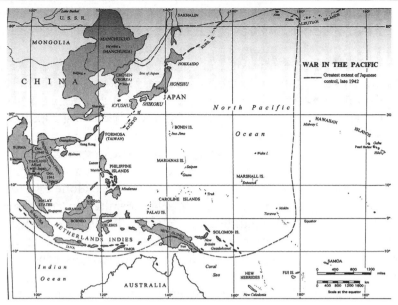

The greatest extent of Japanese control in the war
in the Pacific, late 1942

other, "Isoide, isoide, Yaso ga kita." "Hurry up, hurry up, Jesus has come!" Of course, I know that the children meant that the Christian teacher had come, but what they actually said was, "Jesus has come," and I thought to myself, they speak more wisely than they know. Where this dear missionary comes, it is true that Jesus has come.[6]

*Japan's Devastation*

The Pacific War was a tragedy for all concerned. Japan had for a time extended by force what it euphemistically called its Greater East Asia Co-Prosperity Sphere to include not only its first colonies, Taiwan, Korea, and Manchuria, but also a large section of China, Hong Kong, the Philippines, French Indochina, Thailand, Burma, Singapore, Malaya, the Netherlands East Indies, most of New Guinea, and a large number of South Pacific islands. Japan's brainwashed soldiers had proved to be not only well trained, intensely loyal, and ready to die for their emperor, but also in many cases incredibly ruthless and capable of horrendous atrocities.

---

[6]    AP, In Memoriam, Sara M. Couch.

The year 1942 had been frenetic with Japanese victories, and the nation had appeared totally captivated by a messianic sense of national destiny. Despite the beginning of Japanese defeats in 1943, the rallying cry in Japan had been "Awake Asia," a call to resist Western power and influence in Asia. Only rosy reports of success had been communicated to the people. Nevertheless, the national mood had changed in 1944 with the gradual realization that the homeland was becoming a battlefield. In 1945, incessant fire-bombing of sixty-seven of Japan's cities during the last seven months of the war resulted in the destruction of most of them, leaving five hundred thousand civilians dead and some five million homeless. The incendiary bombing of Tokyo alone by 279 B29 bombers on the night of March 9-10, 1945, resulted in an estimated 97,000 killed, 125,000 wounded, and almost 285,000 buildings and homes destroyed. Despite the widespread sense of impending doom among the populace, the call continued to go out to "Resist the Invader Unto Death."

Specifically, the tragic Pacific War resulted in the deaths of approximately 100,000 Americans, mostly military personnel, while Japan suffered about 2,100,000 military and 580,000 civilian deaths. Nevertheless, it was the loss of other Asian lives, though not widely publicized, that was particularly dramatic. It has been estimated that 3,884,000 military and more than 24,000,000 civilians of other Asian countries died as a result of the war. Of the civilian loss of life, some were indirect fatalities, some were killed in massacres, many died from starvation.

Japan's aggression had resulted in its virtual destruction, not only by the atomic bombs dropped on Hiroshima and Nagasaki, but particularly by the fire-bombing of Japan's cities. An estimated 210,000 people died when the two atomic bombs were dropped, but in Tokyo alone 80 percent of the city was destroyed, from either conventional bombs or firebombs and the resultant devastating fires. American Christian visitors who arrived in Japan in late October 1945 gave the following report:

> Air raids burned or destroyed nearly two and a half million buildings in Japan, including two million structures classified as residences. Bombs completely wiped out three hundred and thirty thousand military, governmental, industrial, and commercial buildings. In addition, ten thousand were partially burned or wrecked and a hundred thousand more dwellings partly destroyed.

The charred remains of a Tokyo residential district

Life amid war's destruction, Tokyo, 1945

We were told that one hundred and sixteen cities had been destroyed; but none of them fared worse than Tokyo itself. There, on the night of March 9, 1945, one hundred thousand people are said to have been roasted to death or, if they took refuge in shallow pools, boiled to death or, if they leaped into the canal, as they did by the tens of thousands, crushed or drowned.[7]

[7]   Douglas Horton, et al. *The Return to Japan: Report of the Christian Deputation to Japan: October – November, 1945* (New York: Friendship Press, 1945), 9.

Civilian deaths on the mainland would have been significantly higher had school children and some family members not been evacuated from the cities to rural villages for their safety. The devastation of Japan's cities was so complete and so catastrophic as to defy description, a scene of scattered broken chimneys protruding from the ashes and rubble. In Tokyo, the bombing raids had avoided some specific targets, such as office buildings saved for use by the occupation. However, not only most of the homes and businesses, but also the nation's infrastructure and industries had been destroyed, resulting of course in pervasive unemployment and lack of income for masses of people. The people had already been malnourished and on the verge of starvation at the time of the surrender.

The farms, while lacking fertilizer, could still produce food, but the distribution system was broken. Furthermore, the food shortage was soon to be exacerbated by the gradual return to Japan's main islands of some eight million Japanese military personnel and destitute expatriate civilian workers and their families from Taiwan, Korea, Manchuria, China, Southeast Asia, and Pacific islands. Drummond described the situation:

> For a time an exchange economy existed as city dwellers went out into the countryside to give of their most precious belongings in return for food. Many had died in the bombing raids; many had been burned or disabled without adequate medicine or care. Literally millions had been made homeless, and everywhere in the burned-out cities shacks began to appear built from the tin or corrugated iron roofing left over from the fires.[8]

However, there was another dimension to Japan's loss. What the people had been indoctrinated to believe was a kind of holy war on behalf of their divine emperor had ended in failure. Their spiritual world had collapsed. Iglehart writes:

> They profoundly believed in the uniqueness of Japan's land and people, of her culture and her faith, and particularly in the Emperor who formed the center of the national life and destiny, the channel for fulfilling the purposes of the ancestral gods in the new age. In the hour of humiliation to whom should they pray? Were the gods, indeed, angry; and if so, who or what was

---

[8]    Drummond, *History of Christianity*, 270-71.

the greater power to which they had bowed? Many a Japanese paused before the further bleak question: were there, after all, any such ancestral gods, or had their faith been a dream ending in a nightmare of despair? Had they awakened to a world in which only simple old women pray?[9]

It goes without saying that this devastation had a profound impact on Japan's Christian movement. Countless numbers of Christians had lost their lives. About one-third of Japan's church buildings had been totally destroyed. Of a total of 1,184 Protestant churches in Japan, 507 were destroyed or severely damaged. Of 163 churches in Tokyo, 154 were destroyed, 4 were damaged but usable, and only 5 were wholly undamaged. Of the 111 churches in Osaka, Japan's second largest city, 57 were destroyed. Many ministers had lost their entire libraries; surviving Christians had lost their Bibles and hymnbooks in the fires.[10]

On the other hand, after long years of repression, a new age of freedom appeared to be opening for the Christian movement. The goal of the Allied occupation, under the leadership of General MacArthur, was to disarm and democratize Japan, so that it might become a peaceful and cooperating member of the community of nations. As a part of that transformation, under the occupation, on October 4, 1945, the Religious Bodies Law of the Japanese government, by which the Japanese church had been rigidly controlled and manipulated, was repealed. In its place the Occupational Directive of December 28, 1945, which became the Religious Juridical Persons Law, was established. It brought about a change in the relationship of the government to religious organizations, which no longer required government authorization but only registration according to simple rules. It was a significant step toward real freedom of religion as a basic human right.

Furthermore, a proclamation by the emperor, issued January 1, 1946, included the following significant paragraphs:

> The devastation of the war inflicted upon our cities, the miseries of the destitute, the stagnation of trade, shortage of food, and the great and growing number of the unemployed are indeed heart-rending, but if the nation is firmly united in its resolve to face the present ordeal and to see civilization consistently in peace, a bright future will undoubtedly be ours, not only for our country but for the whole of humanity....

9  Iglehart, *Century*, 260.
10  Horton, et al. *Return to Japan*, 33.

We stand by the people and we wish always to share with them in their moment of joys and sorrows. The ties between us and our people have always stood upon mutual trust and affection. They do not depend upon mere legend and myths, they are not predicated on the false conception that the Emperor is manifest deity, and that the Japanese people are superior to other races and fated to rule the world.[11]

The emperor, by this proclamation, disavowed his divinity. This dramatic step prepared the nation to accept the new role of the emperor in a more democratic Japan. He was to be a symbol of the state and of the unity of the people; that role would be clarified in a new constitution. However, as Drummond observed,

By this statement the traditional spiritual foundation of Japanese government and society, the doctrine of the divinity of the emperor, which had been developed with increasing explicitness for over half a century, was at one stroke demolished. For many Japanese the act was psychically more shattering than military defeat and surrender, and it left literally millions to reconstruct their spiritual foundations and standards of value, a task for which most Japanese were hardly prepared by previous experience.[12]

### The Restoration of International Christian Fellowship

The Reformed Church in America played a leading role in restoring working relationships between Christians in Japan and America. In the spring of 1941, when the crisis in relations between Japan and the United States was growing and cooperative relationships were breaking down between the missions and Japanese church organizations, a delegation of Japanese Christian leaders had visited America. They met with representatives of American churches and mission agencies to discuss possible future relations and cooperation. The plan for representative American Christians to reciprocate with a visit to Japan had been rendered impossible by the outbreak of the war.

Nevertheless, throughout the four years of separation, the American members of the so-called "Riverside Fellowship" kept in contact. Furthermore, during the war the Japan Committee of the Foreign Missions Conference of North America, of which Luman

---

[11]     Lu, *Japan*, 467. Quoted from *New York Times*, Jan. 1, 1946.
[12]     Drummond, *History of Christianity*, 273.

Shafer of the Reformed Church served as chair, had been considering a united approach to possible future work in cooperation with the Japanese church. As soon as the war ended, the American members of the Riverside Fellowship arranged for a gathering at Buck Hill Falls, Pennsylvania, on September 12. Providentially, three days before their meeting, a Radio Tokyo broadcast was picked up that included the following encouraging words of the Reverend Miyakoda Tsunetaro, formerly a leader of the National Christian Council of Japan:

> The new situation has given rise to many new problems in the life of the Japanese churches that require an intelligent study from the broader point of view of the world mission of Christianity as well as of international relationships. For this purpose the wider experience of the older churches of the West will form an invaluable aid to the Japanese Christian movement. It will be recalled in this connection that the American church leaders promised in 1941 that they would send to Japan a deputation in return for the aforesaid visit of the Japanese deputation. That promise, however, has remained unfulfilled due to the outbreak of the Pacific War. Should they carry out their words at the earliest opportunity, it would be the most timely aid to the Christian forces in this country and should receive the warmest and heartiest welcome from Japanese leaders.[13]

The church leaders gathered in Buck Hill Falls decided to send a four-member deputation to Japan as soon as feasible, with the purpose of reestablishing face-to-face contact with fellow Christians in Japan, to strengthen spiritual unity in Christ, and to explore avenues of ecumenical cooperation. Luman Shafer, still chair of the Japan Committee of the Foreign Missions Conference, was one of the four members appointed to the deputation, the only one who had been a missionary to Japan and spoke Japanese fluently.

The Buck Hill Falls meeting appointed an arrangements committee, chaired by Dr. A. L. Warnshuis of the Reformed Church. Extraordinary efforts by Warnshuis resulted in winning the necessary priority status from the State Department, the Army, and the Air Transport Command for an almost immediate departure by this civilian deputation to occupied Japan. Amazingly, they arrived in Japan October 23, 1945, just weeks after the end of the war, the first westerners to arrive there in civilian clothes. Their traveling expenses were paid by

---

[13]   Horton, et al. *Return to Japan*, 4.

the Christian churches of America through the Federal Council and the Foreign Missions Conference. The deputation reported its perspective, in part, as follows:

> We went to Japan in the belief that the one supreme need of the world is devotion to Jesus Christ and that we cannot be united in our devotion to Him and not united to each other. We went with a confidence born of a personal affection for Japanese Christian friends which the war had altered not in the slightest degree. We went as seekers in Jesus' name, fully conscious of sin, denominational, national, and racial, in which we had participated. We asked now for the privilege of joining with the leaders and people of the Christian Church in Japan in the planning for a better future in Christ.
>
> We went ready to discuss any matter which our Japanese friends cared to bring up, our great desire being for the solidarity of the Christian Church throughout the world....

With gratitude to God that "the night of war has passed," the report went on,

> During these years of conflict our fellow Christians in many parts of the world have endured privations grievous to be borne. Their lot has been that of peril and of pain. They have seen the carnage and catastrophe wrought by war. Many have walked through the valley of the shadow of death. Others have been persecuted for Christ's sake, and not a few have sealed with their blood the faith that was theirs.
>
> Through no merit of our own we have been spared the devastation of our cities and countryside, the destruction of our churches, the desecration of our altars. Nor have we been required to eat of the bitter fruits of tyranny and oppression. We are for this reason the more eager to share the grief and suffering which have befallen our brethren in other lands. We are bereaved in the loss of our soldier dead, as are the peoples of other lands in the loss of their soldier dead. May it please the Christ of Calvary to make us ministers of his compassion in a world tortured by the travail of war's desolation....[14]

The American deputation met six of the eight original Japanese members of the deputation that had visited America in 1941, as well as

---

[14]    Horton, et al. *Return to Japan*, 6-8.

a number of current leaders of the *Nihon Kirisuto Kyodan* (United Church of Christ in Japan, hereafter Kyodan), and reported, "We shook hands briefly and said very little. Feelings ran too deep for words, but in that moment we knew that our fellowship in Christ remained unbroken, and that the cleavage in our relations occasioned by the war could be repaired and would be."[15] Following a shared Communion service, the four American churchmen entered into a conference with about thirty Japanese counterparts in Tokyo. After five days of meetings in Tokyo and a day in Nagoya, the deputation spent six days visiting Kyoto, Kobe, and Osaka, before returning to Tokyo for the remainder of their visit.

As a result of Shafer's participation in the deputation, the situation of some of the Reformed Church's former Japan Mission's institutions became clear. It was reported, "Of the three schools with which we were related, only one was destroyed: the Sturges Seminary in Shimonoseki. The Ferris Seminary buildings are intact, but looted and badly run down. The Meiji Gakuin in Tokyo is also safe, but the buildings are in need of repair. We do not yet know in detail what happened to the different church groups with which we were especially related."[16]

Former missionaries to Japan were among those serving on the staff of the Occupation. Outside of their official duties, these men were able to establish contact with Christian groups, which was important for the recovery of morale among Japanese Christians. Boude Moore of the Reformed Church was one of the army officers who was able to renew relations with Japanese Christians.

The attitude of the Japanese toward their late enemies proved quite remarkable. From the Japanese perspective, many negative factors had been at work. Given the exclusion laws of the United States against the Japanese, American munitions exports to China and trade embargo against Japan, Japanese military propaganda stating that Japanese soldiers captured by Americans were decapitated and their skulls sent home as livingroom ornaments, and the questionable morality of the air raids that had destroyed not only residences but even hospitals filled with patients and doctors, it is natural that the people of Japan, including the Christians, should have felt resentment against the Allied powers, especially the United States. However, only five weeks after the beginning of the occupation, the deputation members were welcomed warmly, not only by the Japanese Christians but also by the

---

[15]    Ibid., 13.
[16]    BFMR, 1946, 3.

general populace. They found that popular anger was instead directed toward the Japanese military, as the people had begun to discover that their military had deceived them, that Japanese soldiers had actually committed horrendous atrocities, and that the army of occupation was made up not of monsters bent on revenge but primarily of disciplined men who walked about unarmed, were kind to children, and were respectful of the Japanese.

The American deputation, which was not an official missionary delegation, was on a fact-finding mission and had no administrative responsibilities. Nevertheless, as a result of the three weeks of conferences between the deputation and Japanese church leaders, possibilities for future cooperation became clear. At a conference with Kyodan leaders on November 6-7, 1945, needs and requests of the Japanese church were considered. It was apparent that, in the future, missionaries would again be welcomed by Japanese Christians, but that the unsettled condition of the church precluded an immediate influx of missionaries. The deputation concluded:

> A majority of Christian leaders believe that there will be opportunity for large missionary service in the new situation that is developing in Japan. It is clear that so far as the schools are concerned, a number of missionary teachers will be desired as soon as the schools are in full operation and living conditions permit. It is our opinion that this generally favorable attitude toward missionary work will tend to grow stronger as the months pass and a new pattern of missionary relationships develops.[17]

More than anything else, the immediate need of the Christians and of all the people in Japan's cities was prevention of looming starvation, and Japanese church leaders asked for the help of North American churches. Furthermore, the need to get Japanese scriptures into the hands of Christian people who had lost theirs in the devastation of the war was impressed upon the four members of the American deputation. The deputation returned to America and presented a report of what it had seen and heard, including the observation that, given the unsettled condition of the Japanese churches and the fact that the nation faced radical transformation under strict military occupation, an immediate influx of missionaries was not practicable. The deputation concluded, "We therefore recommend that steps be taken for a few well qualified missionaries to proceed to Japan at the earliest possible moment, one

---

[17]    Horton, et al. *Return to Japan*, 55.

of these to be especially qualified to develop a relief program and one to act as a liaison between the church groups and the Allied authorities."[18]

## Immediate Postwar Challenges of the Japanese Church

In the immediate postwar period, the Japanese church faced the dual challenges of responding evangelistically to the spiritual needs of the nation and maintaining Christian unity. The restoration of church life in Japan began immediately after the end of the war, but many obstacles had to be overcome. With the repeal of the Religious Bodies Law, government restrictions and control ceased, and Christians were free to carry on genuine worship. However, congregations had been scattered, some pastors and many church members had died, many believers were without Bibles or hymnbooks, numerous churches had been destroyed or damaged, and most of the people were weak and malnourished. In some cases, services were held in the one or two rooms in which a refugee pastor and his family had found space with some household that had escaped the flames. These Christian gathering places also became centers of relief work as people shared what food and clothing they had. Some pastors died in the first years following the war as a result of malnourishment and overwork.[19]

The Kyodan had been formed under duress in 1941 to facilitate Japan's militarist government program of surveillance and control of all elements of society. It was a united church combining all Protestant churches. With the repeal of the restrictive Religious Bodies Law, Kyodan leaders immediately began the process of revising the church's constitution and bylaws, in an effort to preserve unity while carrying out a democratic reform of the church. Drummond described the complex situation.

> A mood of resentment toward the leadership and organizational structure of the Kyodan was growing, especially among the younger pastors and laymen. Essentially three major foci of thought existed in the church at this time. One group frankly advocated dissolution of the Kyodan as an unnatural union forced by government pressure. Another preferred a return to the bloc system characteristic of the first year of the Kyodan's life. A third, probably the majority, while acknowledging the impertinent role of government, saw also the hand of God at work in the process leading the church to its proper state of unity.

[18]   Ibid., 64.
[19]   Iglehart, *Century*, 280.

This group, however, was also determined to press for reform of the Kyodan in keeping with the demands of the new situation.[20]

The first postwar General Assembly was held June 7-8, 1946. In the midst of the physical devastation and spiritual confusion of the early postwar years, non-Christians who had lost their spiritual moorings had begun to visit the churches, not only to attend worship services but at any time of day or night, to seek meaning for their lives. The widespread spiritual vacuum of the time created an unprecedented openness to Christianity in Japan, an opportunity for evangelism that could not wait. Interestingly, Japanese church leaders estimated that what they sensed to be a new openness to Christianity might continue for only about five years. The united church leadership worked to redevelop its organization, with the hope of preserving its unity, but at the same time it vigorously pursued an evangelistic campaign. Recognizing the need and opportunity before them, delegates at the 1946 Kyodan General Assembly approved a proposal to initiate a three-year evangelistic plan, called the Christian Movement to Build a New Japan.

The period of openness to which this movement endeavored to respond continued from 1945 to 1951, and it came to be called Japan's "Christian boom." The most prominent figure in the resultant postwar evangelistic movement was the Reverend Kagawa Toyohiko, who might be dubbed the apostle of postwar Japan. The early developments in the Christian movement in postwar Japan are inseparable from the life and ministry of this man.[21] Kagawa was the remarkable man of the hour, uniquely prepared to seize the moment for the evangelization of his country. Through his prewar activities he had gained a nationwide reputation for positive social transformation, and he was possessed by a passion to preach the good news of Jesus Christ. In the first two years of the evangelistic campaign, Kagawa reported that he had spoken to more than 400,000 people and that 60,000 had signed cards at his meetings signifying their desire to become Christians. Iglehart describes Kagawa and the nationwide evangelistic campaign.

> The campaign was led by Toyohiko Kagawa who risked his health week after week, holding great meetings in public halls or in the open air, traveling from city to city, standing or sitting on the floor of crowded third-class railroad cars....The common people

---

[20]    Drummond, *History of Christianity*, 274.
[21]    Regarding the life and work of Kagawa, see Drummond, *History of Christianity*, 227-41.

he loved were never in such dire need. Labor circles and rural areas called for his counsel and help. To every call he gave attention, and he extended some sort of help to every case of need. No amount of disaster could dismay him. His vibrant voice could still ring out in laughter. The skill with which he set up temporary measures for emergencies was amazing, but always at the center was his Christian message, burning for utterance.

Crowds of people would gather for any kind of a meeting. There was not much regular employment as yet, and...curiosity led many persons to stop to listen. But deeper than these surface causes was the spiritual perplexity and the sense of inner shock of multitudes of earnest people....Japan was ready as never before in history to give a hearing to Christianity. Kagawa saw this and rushed to the encounter. During the three years of the campaign nearly two hundred thousand cards of inquiry and decision were handed in.[22]

Other speakers participating in the evangelistic campaign were also given a wide hearing. Of course, a high percentage of the initial respondents did not actually become active church members, but many did. This "Christian boom" bore great fruit in conversions to Christianity during the first five postwar years, and young men and women with a sense of call to Christian ministry entered theological schools in unprecedented numbers.

It may seem remarkable that so many Japanese people would become open to the gospel almost immediately after a devastating defeat and under foreign occupation. It has been noted that, when the occupation forces first entered Japan, they encountered virtually no resistance, despite decades of indoctrination and the inculcation of hatred toward America, which was seen as a Christian nation. In this regard, Shafer observed, "The favorable attitude of the Japanese is partly the result of the Japanese characteristic of bowing gracefully to the inevitable. It is also due to an honest recognition of the fact that their militaristic program was wrongly conceived and something else must be put in its place." Shafer further noted that people felt gratitude for food provided by the occupation to prevent starvation and that they realized that the occupation policy was not one of vengeance and retaliation.[23] These factors, in addition to Japan's distress and

---

[22]   Iglehart, *Century*, 290-91.
[23]   Luman Shafer, "Letter from Japan," *Church Herald*, March 14, 1947, 10.

disillusionment as a nation, may have contributed to the temporary openness of the Japanese people.

Meanwhile, however, continuation of the Kyodan as a united church after the termination of government control had become very challenging. In the months following the first postwar General Assembly of the Kyodan in 1946, dissatisfaction began to grow, not only with regard to the manner in which the church had been formed under government pressure, but also with the wartime administration of the united church, which was seen by some as having capitulated under pressure and cooperated too willingly with the militarist government. The situation was complicated further by the return to Japan of missionaries of denominations that had never been sympathetic with the idea of one united and independent evangelical Protestant church in Japan. These missionaries reconstituted foreign mission organizations in Japan and encouraged that denominational churches be re-formed. Evidence suggests that at least some of them influenced the withdrawals of churches from the Kyodan, as well as the subsequent reconstitution or formation of denominational churches, by promises of financial support and church reconstruction.

The result of the internal dissatisfaction and outside and inside emphasis on denominationalism was the withdrawal of about two hundred congregations from the Kyodan and the organization of various denominational churches between 1946 and 1948.[24] "However justifiable the reasons were from one point of view, the loss of these groups was a severe blow to the Kyodan as an organization and to those who continued to hold high the ideal of catholicity in a united church."[25] The majority of Kyodan ministers and churches clearly desired to continue as a united church. However, two related issues remained to be resolved as the church reorganized. When the Kyodan was formed in 1941, a bloc system, whereby varying traditions and forms of worship might be maintained by groups of churches within a larger fellowship or federation of churches, had been initiated. Under government pressure, this bloc system had been eliminated after one year. One issue, therefore, was whether in a reorganized Kyodan the bloc system should be reinstated.

---

[24]    These early withdrawals included a small group who desired a strong emphasis on Reformed theology and formed a Reformed Church in Japan (these were not churches that had been related to the Reformed Church in America missionaries), as well as almost all of the Episcopal churches, the Lutheran churches, most of the Baptist churches, and some of the Holiness congregations. Each of these groups organized Japanese denominational churches.

[25]    Drummond, *History of Christianity*, 276.

A second issue was the formulation of a creed, the Apostles' Creed being the church's only creedal statement since the formation of the Kyodan. During the war, church leaders had worked on but never completed a creed, because the government refused to allow the church to emphasize the lordship of Christ above loyalty to the emperor. However, in the Kyodan's postwar reorganization, a new problem emerged. There was disagreement about having a creed. A committee was established to prepare a creed, but its task proved difficult. "Some, especially those of the Presbyterian and Reformed tradition, held that a church is not truly a church without a creed. Others, of Congregational or Baptist background, preferred freedom in this area and no binding statement of faith, leaving the matter of clarification of the content of their Christian faith up to the individual congregation. A third group, of Methodist or kindred orientation, had no objection to a creed, but did not feel pressing need to take immediate action."[26] Consequently, in the immediate postwar period, even while trying to respond to unprecedented evangelistic opportunities, the Kyodan continued to be disturbed by this vexing internal problem.

The Kyodan General Assembly of 1950 passed the church's revised democratic constitution, which provided for a modified Presbyterian structure that refrained in practice from interference with the freedom of local congregations as much as possible. In other words, the form of the church's polity appeared Presbyterian, while authority rested primarily in the local congregation, a characteristic of Congregational church polity. The Kyodan thus became more democratic, compared to its authoritarian form under the government during the war, but also more Congregational. Furthermore, the unresolved issues of the formulation of a creed and whether to restore the bloc system led in 1950 to the secession from the united church of one more group, this time without influence from denominational missionaries. This group of about fifty churches withdrew from the Kyodan and formed the *Shin Nihon Kirisuto Kyokai*, or New Church of Christ in Japan.[27] Nevertheless,

---

[26]  Ibid., 276.

[27]  Ibid., 284-86. Led by the Reverend Onomura Rinzo of Sapporo, a group of pastors and laymen who had been part of the former Church of Christ in Japan, the Reformed-Presbyterian related group in the Kyodan, had campaigned for a return to the bloc system and for the recognition of the use of other confessions of faith besides the Apostles' Creed. When the Kyodan decided not to give formal recognition or ecclesiastical status to the old blocs, the decision was made to withdraw and form a new church. This was the last and most painful group secession, especially for the majority of those of Reformed-Presbyterian background who remained as part of the Kyodan. Almost all of the churches that had prewar ties to the Reformed Church's Japan Mission remained within the united church.

a majority of the Protestant churches and their leaders remained in the Kyodan, held together by the feeling that, given the opportunities confronting Christianity, there was strength in a united approach.

The Kyodan did eventually formulate its new Confession of Faith, as well as a set of Guidelines for Christian Living. Both were enacted October 28, 1954. Though relatively brief, the confession is a clear evangelical statement of faith, followed by the Apostles' Creed, and the accompanying guidelines set exemplary goals for Japanese Christians. The confession's limitations may be seen not in its content but in the fact that a certain freedom of interpretation was to be allowed, and that it was to serve as a confessional statement and not to be understood as a juridical formula.[28]

28    (Official English translation).The Confession of Faith: We believe and confess that: The Old and New Testaments, inspired of God, testify to Christ, reveal the truth of the Gospel, and are the sole canon upon which the Church should depend. By the Holy Spirit the Holy Bible is the Word of God, which gives us full knowledge of God and salvation, and is the unerring standard of faith and life.

The One God, revealed by the Lord Jesus Christ, and testified to in the Holy Scripture, being Father, Son and Holy Spirit, is the triune God. The Son, who became man, for the salvation of us sinners was crucified and made our redemption by offering Himself to God as the perfect sacrifice once for all.

God chooses us by His grace, and by faith in Christ alone He forgives our sins and justifies us. In this unchangeable grace the Holy Spirit accomplishes His work by sanctifying us and causing us to bear fruits of righteousness.

The Church is the Body of Christ the Lord, and is the congregation of those called by grace. The Church observes public worship, preaches the Gospel aright, administers the sacraments of Baptism and the Lord's Supper, and being diligent in works of love, waits in hope for the coming again of the Lord.

Thus we believe, and with the saints in all ages we confess the Apostles' Creed: (Here the Apostles' Creed follows.)

Guidelines for Christian Living:

Having been baptized by the grace of God in the name of the Father, Son and Holy Spirit, and admitted to the Church, which is the Body of Christ, we put aside all iniquities and superstitions, maintain with one another the close fellowship of brothers and sisters in the Lord, and make the following pledge:

We will respect the order of the Church, obey its teachings and discipline, emphasize the importance of Lord's Day worship, prayer services and other meetings, observe Holy Communion, be diligent in evangelism, and labor for the support and development of the Church by giving our time, treasures and talents.

We will study the Scriptures daily, be constant in prayer, and maintain a life of piety, purity, temperance, and diligence.

We will serve God, our whole family together, by emphasizing the importance of family worship, maintaining harmony in the home, and leading our children into the faith.

We will strive for the realization of Christ's justice and love throughout the world, by respecting each other's personality, loving our neighbors, and laboring for the welfare of society.

We will endeavor, following the will of God, to uplift the morality of the state, to realize international justice, and to attain world peace.

May God be gracious to us, and enable us to accomplish these intentions. Amen.

## The Resumption of Missionary Activity in Postwar Japan

The encounter of the four-member American deputation with Japanese Christians in the fall of 1945 clarified the situation, including immediate needs and future possibilities. The Reformed Church's Board of Foreign Missions reported to the General Synod in May 1946 as follows:

> The new situation in Japan offers an unparalleled opportunity for preaching the Gospel. The Church in Japan will vigorously press forward in this task, but it is also clear that missionaries will be welcomed and have rich opportunities for service. Lack of housing facilities and food will limit the number for a time, but our Board, in association with the other Boards cooperating in the Japan Committee of the Foreign Missions Conference, is engaged in developing the program....it is anticipated that some of our own missionaries will be on the field by this time next year.[29]

In response to the need of Japanese Christians for Bibles and hymnbooks, and in light of the fact that publishing facilities in Japan were destroyed in the war, the American Bible Society embarked on a major publishing project. Within two years two and a half million Japanese New Testaments were produced in America with funds raised by American Christians and sent to Japan for the Japanese Christians and their evangelistic outreach. In addition, Church World Service printed and sent out 100,000 copies of a Japanese hymnal for use in the churches and mission schools. Everything being under the tight control of occupation authorities, arrangements were made to admit the shipment of the books as chaplain's supplies.

Shafer's Japan Committee of the Foreign Missions Conference prepared to develop permanent cooperative relations with the Japanese church by sending out a Commission of Six, made up of representative and experienced missionaries. Religious favoritism was prohibited under the occupation, so Christians were not to receive preferential treatment. Missionaries could not make use of army facilities for food, housing, or transportation. At the same time, they would not be permitted to consume local goods in impoverished Japan, where thousands were on the verge of starvation. Following negotiations, permission was granted for the six missionaries, each of a different denomination, to proceed to Japan to make provision for the maintenance of others who would

---

[29]    BFMR, 1946, 5.

follow later. Housing would need to be secured, and food supplies would need to be taken from America.

The first official link with American Christianity was established in April of 1946 with the arrival of the first two of the six representatives. One of them, a Christian social worker, began to organize relief from overseas Christian sources to help meet the humanitarian emergency. The other became the contact person with occupation authorities for Japanese churches, opening channels for the return of prewar missionaries. In June the remaining four arrived and took up their several roles. Among them, the Reverend Henry G. Bovenkerk,[30] a son of the Reformed Church who had served twelve years in Japan under the Presbyterian board, took up responsibility for relations with the Japanese church and evangelistic work.

Church World Service, as well as several other smaller Christian relief organizations, soon went into action to help deal with the humanitarian crisis. Relief was administered through a central agency of the occupation and distributed through the Social Welfare Ministry of the Japanese government. The churches of America exhibited an outpouring of Christian compassion. Of about seven million pounds of food, clothing, medical supplies, and other essentials distributed within the first two years, about half were contributed by the Protestant churches of the United States. This work aided more than two million people and thirteen hundred institutions, including hospitals, clinics, orphanages, nurseries, and leper hospitals.

In addition to this North American Christian contribution to general relief, a special program was developed for Japanese Christian workers. Many pastors were malnourished, weary, and harassed by financial problems. Congregations had been scattered and decimated by the war and could provide only a fraction of what was needed by pastor's families for subsistence. While these pastors were engaged in manual labor to survive, they could only minimally carry on desperately needed Christian ministry. From the summer of 1946, the mission boards began providing relief for Japanese pastors. At first surplus naval food supplies were bought and distributed. Subsequently, relief funds from American

---

[30]    Bovenkerk, a graduate of Hope College and Western Theological Seminary and son of the Reverend John Bovenkerk, a Reformed Church pastor, had served as a missionary in Japan from 1930 to 1942, had been interned in Japan for a time early in the war, and had served as chaplain at a relocation center for interned Japanese in California during the war. He later served as secretary and treasurer of the Reformed Church Board of Foreign Missions. Incidentally, the author was baptized by John Bovenkerk in 1934.

churches provided a steady flow of food for Japanese Christian workers for several years in a program administered by Church World Service. This aid permitted pastors whose destitute congregations could not provide even a subsistence salary the opportunity to give themselves to the work of ministry instead of to manual labor for physical survival.

The physical needs of Christian workers remained a priority for five or six years. As Reformed Church prewar missionaries returned to Japan, they all also actively participated in relief work through the distribution to and through pastors, mission school teachers, and church members of clothing and nonperishable food received in packages mailed to them by Reformed Church members.

Luman Shafer, who visited Japan in December of 1946, reported,

"The situation is profoundly sobering. The opportunities are unlimited, but the Church is ill prepared to meet them and the force of older missionaries is greatly depleted, due to retirements and other causes. Furthermore, only those among them in the best of health should be sent out, due to the rugged conditions of the life. Children are not yet permitted by SCAP and this makes it difficult for missionaries with children to establish a home there. New missionaries require years for language study and preparation."[31]

Rebuilding churches, schools, and missionary residences was one of the first requirements after the war, and the Reformed Church actively participated in this rehabilitation. North American mission boards joined forces quickly to provide $200,000 to build fifty temporary church buildings in strategic population centers. In addition, Church World Service purchased and sent out twenty quonset huts to be used as relief and church centers. In this way seventy congregations whose buildings had been destroyed were at least provided with temporary facilities. The Reformed Church played a significant part in this postwar Christian relief. As noted in the Reformed Church board's report to General Synod in 1949,

> What this means can be judged by recalling in detail the story of one of the churches founded by our mission. When Mr. de Maagd returned to Japan in 1947, one of the first things he did was to visit the site of this church in Tokyo. The church building had been burned in one of the incendiary bombings of the city. For a while the church met in the parsonage, some miles further out in the suburbs, and later in a public hall in the neighborhood,

---

[31]    LJS, "Plans for Our Missionaries in Japan," *Church Herald*, Apr. 11, 1947, 9.

but through the carelessness of a homeless refugee who had been sheltered there, the parsonage was burned just as the war ended. So the church had neither house of worship nor parsonage. However, out of their poverty, they scraped together enough money to build a tiny shack for the pastor, his wife, and two sons.

Now the new church building has been erected. It is a prefabricated building sent out from America, with an entrance hall and a tower added by the congregation. It is twenty feet wide by sixty feet long. Two-thirds of it is the church auditorium; the other third was to be used as a parsonage, but the pastor and his wife have decided to stay in their little shack, and to use this room for a Christian kindergarten. At the dedication of this building, whose clean walls seem so bright and cheerful in contrast with the drabness of life in Japan today, the Rev. M. Tomita, speaking for the Japanese Church, emphasized the fact that this was Christian love in action. He said that when people without pressure from government or other source send this kind of gift, that the people of a former enemy country may also have the Gospel, that is real Christian love.[32]

Following upon the preparatory work and reports of the Commission of Six, representatives of eight Protestant churches[33] met in New York January 9, 1947, to create a structure for cooperation to meet the needs and opportunities offered by the situation in Japan. Subsequently, in August, representatives of this group went to Japan and held extensive deliberations with 150 leaders of the Kyodan and of Christian schools and Christian social agencies. The result was the formation by the North American churches of the Interboard Committee for Christian Work in Japan (IBC) to represent and coordinate the activities in Japan of the mission boards of the eight North American denominations. The Kyodan then set up a Council of Cooperation to deal with the Interboard Committee and supervise all cooperation with overseas churches and missionaries.[34] This meant that in principle the representatives of the several North American denominations would

---

[32]  BFMR, 1949, 9. This church was the former Gotenyama Mission Church, begun and nurtured by the Japan Mission. It had become self-supporting and independent before the war and been renamed Yukigaya Church.

[33]  The eight denominations were the Congregational Christian Churches, the Disciples of Christ, the Evangelical and Reformed Church, the Evangelical United Brethren Church, the Methodist Church, the Presbyterian Church in the U.S.A., the Reformed Church in America, and the United Church of Canada.

[34]  Drummond, *History of Christianity*, 278-79.

no longer limit their church associations and support in Japan to the churches and church leaders with whom they had been affiliated before the war, but instead they would relate through the Interboard Committee and the Council of Cooperation to the Kyodan, Japanese mission schools, and Japanese Christian social work centers.

This new plan went into effect in 1948. The eight North American denominations thus no longer maintained their respective Japan Missions. The post-mission era of Reformed Church mission in Japan had begun. John de Maagd of the Reformed Church, who had returned to Japan in 1947, played a key role in working out the new relationships between the Interboard Committee in America and the Japanese church leaders. He served as a liaison between occupation authorities and the Japanese Christian leaders and in an advisory capacity in the Council of Cooperation during its formative stages. He also worked to help prevent the exodus from the Kyodan of churches with historic connections to the prewar Reformed Church Japan Mission.[35]

Even before these formal structures for cooperation were in place, some of the former missionaries to Japan began to return. Each returnee had to receive military clearance to reenter Japan. Requirements for permission from occupation authorities to return included availability of housing, provision for food without consuming Japan's meager resources, and an invitation from a Japanese Christian institution. The mission schools were the first and best prepared to welcome back former missionaries. The missionary housing in Yokohama next to Ferris Seminary had survived the war, so five prewar Reformed Church missionaries were able to receive clearance, arrange passage, and return to Japan in 1946-47. Each returning missionary was required to take along not only clothing and necessary personal effects to last several years, but also one ton of nonperishable food.

Janet Oltmans was the first to arrive, returning to Ferris Seminary in Yokohama the beginning of November 1946. In the midst of devastation and social dislocation, she found even basic perishable food in short supply and rationed. However, as an American civilian, she was permitted to purchase limited amounts of some staple foods, such as salt, sugar, vinegar, potatoes, flour, and cooking oil. Milk, eggs, and meat were unknown quantities. Oltmans immediately began to work at the school.

Despite a great deal of destruction from the war in Yokohama, Ferris Seminary was very fortunate in that not only the missionary

---

[35]  John C. de Maagd to LJS, Jan. 10, Feb. 14 and 27, Apr. 1 and 12, 1948.

residences there but also the substantial main school buildings built in the 1930s survived intact. However, because the school facilities had been taken over and used by the Japanese military police during the war and by the occupation forces immediately after the war, equipment had been looted and the buildings were in bad repair. In April of 1947, Oltmans described the conditions: "We still sit uneasily on chairs which might collapse....Most of the class rooms are not provided with chairs for the teachers in case they should want to sit down. Glass or pieces of wood have been put into most of the broken places in the window frames."[36] Despite the lack of even basic educational materials such as textbooks and paper, the girls studied diligently, grasping at the opportunity to once again have a genuine education.

Florence Walvoord arrived February 3, 1947, arranging passage on a troop ship directly from India. When the missionaries were evacuated, Walvoord had been so eager to go back that she had volunteered to work in the Arcot Mission in India in order to be closer to Japan when the way should open again. Helen Zander was the next returnee. Oltmans reported, "Miss Helen Zander arrived at Yokohama, with her mountain of luggage, on April 12. Two of the Japanese teachers and I managed to get passes to be on the pier to welcome her, and Col. B. C. Moore took us in his jeep to the dormitory; he also secured the use of an army truck to bring up her trunks and boxes."[37] Zander immediately returned to her much-loved teaching role at Ferris Seminary. Before long she had also begun a Bible class at the Japanese church she attended, organized a class for public school teachers, and was developing branch Sunday schools in several places along with members of the church and Christian girls from Ferris.

Jeane Noordhoff, who had been involved in evangelistic work among women and children in Nagasaki before the war, returned to Japan in the summer of 1947 at the age of sixty-three. She responded to the strong appeal for the assistance of a missionary from Kawai Michi, a prominent Japanese Christian educator who had founded a Christian school for girls in Tokyo. From a beginning of nine girls, and despite government oppression during the war, Kawai had brought her school, called Keisen, to an enrollment of five hundred students.[38] It was arranged for Noordhoff to live with a Japanese couple. Being already fluent in Japanese, she was able to teach effectively immediately at the school and, during school vacation, to hold a three-day Sunday

---

[36]    Oltmans, *Church Herald*, Apr. 18, 1947, 13.
[37]    Oltmans, *Church Herald*, May 30, 1947, 9.
[38]    *Church Herald*, July 11, 1947, 6.

school teachers' institute, attended by forty teachers, in which she taught Sunday school songs and demonstrated the use of the flannel graph.[39] By the summer of 1950, with transportation facilities gradually improving, Noordhoff was able, during the Keisen school vacation, to travel to Kyushu to spend the summer in evangelistic work and in Sunday school teacher training.[40]

John de Maagd returned to Japan in the fall of 1947, leaving his family behind temporarily. He was the first male Reformed church missionary to return, and he set about visiting the churches and arranging for the provision of food and clothing for destitute pastors and their families. Permission for De Maagd's family to join him was later granted, but they were unable to return to Japan until the end of 1948, delayed by a shipping strike in America.

Walvoord related her experience at Shiloh Church at Christmas time in 1947.

> On one of the main thoroughfares in Yokohama stands what is left of a once beautiful church. Everything of wood and glass was eaten up by the flames following the bombing of May 29, 1945. Now, two and one half years later, the main auditorium is not yet being used. But the congregation, the soul of the church is still heroically carrying on.
>
> The pastor with his wife and four children live in the basement, in a space about twelve feet square that has been rudely partitioned off from the rest. The cooking is done in another corner. Still another part of the basement has been partitioned off for their church services. In one corner of this room is a slightly raised platform for a little [reed] organ and the pulpit. The rest of the floor is of uneven cement that is almost impossible to sweep clean. It was once covered with wood, but of course that also was burned. The seats are of every imaginable description, from a few chairs with high backs like pulpit chairs to backless benches. There is as great variety in the clothes people wear. A very few of the women wear kimonos, but most of them, as well as the men, are now dressed in western style clothing, and many of the women wear a sort of trousers that became the national dress during the war, something more appropriate to the stern reality of the times than their graceful kimono.
>
> But though outwardly things are ugly, yes, even depressing, for a time one forgets the ugliness because of the brave smiles of

---

[39]   *Church Herald*, June 18, 1948, 8.
[40]   *Church Herald*, July 28, 1950, 4.

the people. The little bouquet of flowers on the pulpit is a symbol of their attempt to keep beauty alive and to make the best of things.

And how did this little heroic group celebrate the coming of the world's first and greatest Christmas Gift? The Christmas worship service ushered in a day of fellowship. It was especially impressive because at this service twelve adults were baptized and taken into the church. One of them was a teacher in our school whose wife has been a member of the church for some time. Their faces were radiant when I congratulated them. One was a young man who had lost his mother in the bombing of Yokohama. A girl had come from Nagasaki, the only one of her family left after the dropping of the atom bomb on that city. Then there were three who were very young, so young that the pastor was inclined to ask them to wait. But the principal of the school they attended assured him that they were quite ready for the step. They were children of people whose only home is in a small boat, and for whom an earnest Japanese Christian conducts a school.

After the service the benches became tables and the motley array of chairs were put around them for the Christmas dinner! Each person unwrapped his little box of cold rice and vegetables, and the "Christmas turkey" came in the form of a bowl of Lipton's chicken noodle soup supplied by a missionary regularly attending the services. We all, children, young people and older folk, ate together in satisfying Christian fellowship, glad that Christmas could be celebrated without the fear of bombs, and that there is now a chance to rebuild even on the ruins of the old.[41]

Even though Sturges Seminary in Shimonoseki had been almost wholly destroyed, the students were eager for an education and returned to classes held at the principal's house and one undamaged building on the campus. A report in the fall of 1947 indicated the resilience and dedication of this mission school's Japanese Christian leaders.

Sturges Seminary now has eight hundred students and it is expected that next year there will be nine hundred. There are twenty-six teachers. Mr. Hirotsu, the former principal, is now serving as acting principal. He is seventy-seven years old. For a year and a half after the destruction of the school he lived in a little house in the country, but when Mr. Fukuda, his successor

---

41   Walvoord, "These Thy Brethren," *Church Herald*, March 5, 1948, 8.

in the principalship, resigned, he was asked to return. Besides being acting principal, he is president of the alumnae association, chairman of the board of trustees, and chairman of the reconstruction committee. He still finds time to do evangelistic work, and about ten people come to him each week for instruction in the Christian faith.[42]

Walvoord's return to Sturges Seminary awaited the arrival from America of a prefab missionary residence, since not only the school buildings but also the missionary house had been destroyed in the war. After teaching one year at Ferris Seminary, Walvoord returned to her much-loved work at Sturges in the spring of 1948. The mission boards of the Reformed Church and the Presbyterian Church contributed emergency funds toward construction of temporary structures set up to serve as classrooms for the school, and plans for the reconstruction of the school were soon set in motion by Hirotsu.

Belle Bogard returned to Japan in the summer of 1948, after a furlough following wartime service as a Reformed Church missionary in Baghdad (United Mission in Mesopotamia). Back in Japan, she began a new role, teaching at the Tokyo Woman's Christian College. Like all the returning missionaries, besides her college teaching, she taught Bible classes among the students and in two neighboring churches and shared care packages from Reformed Church members in America with the needy people around her.

Due to the extent of Japan's devastation, rehabilitation occupied a significant role in postwar missionary activity. John de Maagd, in addition to evangelistic preaching in the surviving congregations in the Tokyo and Yokohama region, played an important part in planning the program being developed by the newly formed Interboard Committee for Christian Work in Japan to place missionaries with the Japanese churches and mission schools. At the same time, he participated in the ongoing rehabilitation work. He developed a Christian Service Center in Yokohama to serve the needs of pastors and their families, church members, mission school staff, and through them the larger community around them. Excerpts from De Maagd's report of this work give insights into the continuing necessity and importance of this ministry three and a half years after the end of the war.

I wish you could see people come into our Christian Service Center, so hesitant, only half believing that we can give them

---

[42]    *Church Herald*, Oct. 17, 1947, 13.

such precious things as clothing and food, and see them go out later with their eyes lit up in joy, as they think what they have received will mean to their loved ones. They keep stopping me in churches I visit, and at other meetings, to make their second or third bow of thanks, and say again how grateful they are. Since last November some two hundred boxes have come in; there was life-saving woolen clothing in most of them, and life-saving food in the others. We have taken care of family after family, and of many orphans....

Congratulations to the Women's Personal Service Committee [of Reformed Church women]; the pastor's aid packages have begun to arrive. They are a wonderful lift to ministers who are still struggling desperately just to keep going. In the last three months, the wives of two pastors have become very ill with tuberculosis.... Two other pastors are about to give up their churches because they cannot hang on any longer without more food and clothing; you can guess what these boxes mean to them.

The soap and bandages sent from the Board offices finally arrived; one box was taken to the Center and is already in the hands of very grateful people. Soap is still about the most appreciated gift one can give; it is so scarce, so poor and so expensive....

We have lots of cold weather in the Spring, with fires burning to the end of April. Though the thermometer is seldom below thirty degrees above zero, it is damp and penetratingly cold. When there is no heat in your house you can only be a bit comfortable if you have on very warm clothes. We wear much heavier clothes than we did in New York or in Michigan, because it is so cold inside, not just out of doors. One of the pastors who is receiving a package almost died of pneumonia last year, but says, "The Lord miraculously saved me so that I could go on with this work." He is very conscientious and is building a good strong church of earnest Christian people. They are now meeting in a rented building....he is carrying on under many difficulties. Not the least of these is the almost starvation salary which is all the people can afford to give him, which leaves him physically weak.... The gifts from America will be a great help to him.[43]

In 1949, Luman Shafer, board secretary and chair of the Interboard Committee for Christian Work in Japan, was asked to

---

[43]    De Maagd, "The Christian Service Center in Yokohama," *Church Herald*, May 6, 1949, 4.

spend six months in Japan to assist the Japanese churches with their evangelism program. During his six-month visit he had opportunities to preach in many churches and public meetings and also to assess the needs and opportunities for missionary participation in postwar evangelistic work. Shafer's reports suggest that despite the large crowds at evangelistic meetings and the many new inquirers at the churches, the euphoria and optimism of some that Japan might quickly become not only a democratic but also a Christian nation were premature. Shafer noted, "We have tended to think that the casual surface interest of the Japanese in Christianity, which indeed has been remarkable, could be immediately converted into a strong and dominant Christian community. This attitude has underestimated the difficulties of rooting Christianity in an ancient and alien culture which still remains in Japan."[44] Nevertheless, Shafer urged:

> The field is wide open for preaching the Gospel. This does not mean that the country is going to become Christian at once. A lot of the same old difficulties stand in the way of acceptance of Christ—the stern demands of the Gospel, the fear of social discrimination, especially in matters of marriage, a fear the Buddhists are making the most of, and the natural stubbornness of the human heart. But the way to present the claims of Christ is open, and what more should one ask for?[45]

The last of the Reformed Church missionaries with prewar experience to return to Japan for regular appointment was the Moore family. Boude had served as an officer in the U.S. Army during the war and in the early stage of the occupation of Japan. The way having opened up for return to the field, the Moores were reappointed as missionaries in 1949 and returned to Japan early in 1950 for evangelistic work. They were assigned to work in Fukuoka, the principle city on the island of Kyushu, where Reformed Church missionaries had concentrated their evangelistic work in the years before the war.

Anna Moore also carried on work in Fukuoka, especially teaching English and Bible classes for students. She also sometimes spoke for women's groups. For example, she was asked to speak at the mothers' meeting of mostly non-Christians at a Christian kindergarten. She began by telling them it was like old times to gather with them and their children, for her own five children were born in Japan, and she used to

---

[44]    *Church Herald,* Jan. 27, 1950, 3.
[45]    Shafer, "Presenting the Claims of Christ in Japan," *Church Herald,* Dec. 2, 1949, 22.

bring them with her when her husband preached. And then, "In my grandfather's day in Japan [James Ballagh], ninety-two years ago, there was no Bible in Japanese, but today is a good day for us, for now we have it in Japanese. Let us read it together." Anna then read the story of the sheep and the shepherd, sang the solo, "The Ninety and Nine," and told the women that God loves us first, in the same way that earthly parents love their infants first. She then urged them to seek God's power for the raising of their children, and encouraged them to come to the church service the next day, when her husband would be preaching.[46]

Boude Moore had immediately begun evangelistic touring, finding broad interest and enthusiasm, especially among young people. By the fall of 1951, he had completed a series of extended evangelistic trips, visiting about one hundred of the churches on the island of Kyushu. Moore reported that everywhere churches were full, and in many places people were standing throughout the service. Messages were received with keen interest, and numerous reports came in of people who had begun to attend church regularly, ten here, twelve there, and in one case twenty-two people who were continuing to study the life of Christ. Moore emphasized that these were not mere card-signers at mass meetings, nor was there any pressure put on at the meetings, only the introduction of Jesus Christ as welcoming Savior.

At Fukuoka, Moore reopened the *Shin Sei Kan*, the center for carrying on newspaper evangelism, a program developed by Albertus Pieters in Oita and then Fukuoka, and carried on by others before the war. In 1951, Moore found that, in response to a single advertisement placed in three major newspapers, he could receive as many as two thousand requests for Christian literature. And more than twenty letters a day were coming in asking for personal guidance. Moore explained, "The Japanese like to write letters, and find it much easier to ask questions in writing than in personal interview. This is one of the great facts in presenting the Christian message through correspondence.... Thus newspaper evangelism is the most thrilling way to hunt out and reach those isolated souls who are searching for light, most of whom would never hear the message otherwise."[47]

The returning missionaries found that, even five or six years after Japan's defeat, a certain openness to Christianity continued. Shafer wrote,

> This offers a unique challenge to the Christian churches. Where it was difficult to get an audience before the war, people now crowd

---

[46] *Church Herald*, Sept. 26, 1952.
[47] *Church Herald*, Oct. 5, 1951, 5.

into the churches and public halls to hear Christian speakers. This doesn't mean that church membership is rapidly increasing. The gain last year in our own Church [Kyodan] was only a little over 11,000, but the Church leaders are very careful not to take people into the Church on merely casual interest. They are very much concerned lest people come into the Church for ulterior motives and there is a careful process of instruction and preparation for Church membership. This means that those who do come are solidly grounded in the faith.[48]

The context for missionary involvement in Christian work in Japan had clearly changed, but the need and opportunity for participation with the Japanese Christians in the Christian mission in Japan had been reaffirmed. The Reformed Church response to this need and opportunity was made clear in a resolution passed by the Board of Foreign Missions in the fall of 1948.

> VOTED: That the Board, remembering our great historic interest as a Reformed Church in the Japan Mission and viewing the great opportunities for proclaiming the Gospel which providence has opened in Japan in the post-war years and mindful of our part as Americans in the destruction and disruption of that country, declare its determination to continue to expand the work of the Reformed Church in Japan.[49]

The eight North American mission boards that had formed the Interboard Committee in order to work in cooperation and partnership with the Kyodan clarified the new structures under which they would henceforth function. These eight mission boards channeled and administered all finances and personnel to Japan through this Interboard Committee, a revolutionary ecumenical missionary strategy. The Kyodan had established the Council of Cooperation to deal with the Interboard Committee and supervise cooperation with overseas churches and missionaries. A Field Committee of eight missionary representatives was created to handle logistical matters of the missionaries, and the office of the field treasurer for the Interboard Committee provided missionary maintenance services in Japan.

The Council of Cooperation consisted of ten direct Kyodan representatives, eight representatives of the Association of Interboard

---

[48]   Shafer, "Bibles for Japan" *Church Herald,* July 28, 1950, 5.
[49]   LJS to JCD, Nov. 5, 1948.

Committee-related Schools, six representatives of the Japan Christian Social Work League, and the ten missionary members elected by the Interboard Committee. De Maagd served the Reformed Church board as its first field representative and was also the Reformed Church representative on the Council of Cooperation. Missionaries appointed by the mission boards served in Japan in evangelistic work, in mission schools, or at Christian social work institutions at the invitation of the Japanese church, and all cooperative relationships were arranged through the Council of Cooperation.

Furthermore, important principles were established for missionaries' working relationships within Japan. The mission boards, as sending agencies, would continue to carry the responsibility for the maintenance of all missionary personnel. However, it was agreed that neither the mission boards nor individual missionaries would supervise or employ Japanese ministers or coworkers directly or subsidize Japanese congregations. While the missionaries might assume initiative or carry responsibility in certain evangelism projects or centers approved by the Council of Cooperation, the dignity, self-reliance, and independence of the Japanese Christian movement was to be respected. Although individual churches or pastors were thus no longer directly supported by foreign mission funds, not only church and mission school building projects, but also the salaries of some pastors, the church building fund, theological education, scholarships for overseas study, administrative costs, and numerous other programs of the Kyodan continued to be subsidized by the mission boards through the Interboard Committee and the Council of Cooperation.[50] This policy of subsidizing the work indirectly continued for more than twenty years.

The role of the missionary within Japan had changed. No longer an authority figure, no longer an employer of Japanese ministers and evangelists, and no longer part of a denominational Japan Mission, postwar missionaries faced new challenges. They retained a certain independence and security by virtue of being appointed, sent, and supported by a foreign mission board. However, having no authority or status beyond that of cooperating missionary, it was understood that each missionary needed to find a way to implement his or her gifts while exercising a high level of cultural sensitivity. The cooperating missionary's roles had to become those of witness and faithful servant, friend and colleague, enabler and mentor, modeler of ministry, and unobtrusive source of wise counsel and insight.

---

[50]    LJS to JCD, March 2, 1948.

The roles of missionary wives also changed in the postwar era. No longer classified as assistant missionaries, they went through the same recruitment and appointment process as their husbands and were given equal opportunities for orientation and language study. While consideration was given to time and energy for child-bearing and nurture, as well as home-making, it was understood that as situations and opportunities permitted, they would also participate actively in mission through the home and in the churches, mission schools, and communities.

Financial support also changed. Rather than receiving a salary in the usual sense of the term, Reformed Church missionaries received a living expense stipend, housing, medical expenses, vacation allowance, and work funds. The stipend for families was given as a family unit, approximately double that for single missionaries, and families also received children's allowances, and the children's educational expenses were covered. In 1948, an attempt was made by the Interboard Committee to work out a common "salary" arrangement for all eight of the participating mission boards,[51] but in this they were not successful. The salaries and allowances of the eight mission boards involved varied considerably, and the attempt was complicated by the fact that each mission board tried to maintain equanimity between financial arrangements for its missionaries in Japan and those serving in other places.

[51]   LJS to JCD, Jan. 16, 1948.

# CHAPTER 13

# Mission under the Interboard Committee for Christian Work in Japan: 1948–1972

### The Reformed Church's Postwar Role at the Mission Schools

At the time the Interboard Committee was formed in 1948 it was agreed that, in contrast to the arrangement with Japanese churches, support of the mission schools would resume after the war on the traditional denominational basis. This difference resulted from the fact that from their inception the mission schools had been directly linked to the various North American denominations' Japan Missions, and the Japanese churches had never been able to take responsibility for them or incorporate them organically into the independent Japanese churches' structures. Even so, the schools had not only served an evangelistic purpose as a part of the work of the several Japan missions, but they also provided a Christian education for many who became members and leaders in the churches. Van Wyk noted,

> When war-time pressures brought all the churches together into the Kyodan and contact with the supporting boards in America was cut off, these schools found themselves divorced from both

church and mission and forced into an independent existence. The way they did it and the price they paid to stay open have had far-reaching effects on the whole nature of post-war Christian education.

One immediate result was seen in the nature of the IBC-Kyodan structure as it was worked out following the war. The church-to-church relationship that was envisioned was found to be practicable when it came to matters like evangelism; but it was quite another matter to fit independent, non-church, institutionalized projects such as schools and social work centers into the system.[1]

Consequently, the mission schools and Christian social work centers in Japan formed their own organizations, the Education Association of Christian Schools and the Christian Social Work League. These organizations were represented on the Council of Cooperation set up by the Kyodan but maintained their autonomy. For the mission schools, the Council of Cooperation functioned as a mere rubber stamp to approve the appointment of missionary teachers. The mission schools continued to make their appeals for financial support directly to the mission boards.

Accordingly, the Reformed Church not only contributed to the immediate rehabilitation needs after the war at Baiko Jo Gakuin (Sturges Seminary, the Girls' school in Shimonoseki), Ferris Jo Gakuin (Ferris Seminary, the girls' school in Yokohama), and Meiji Gakuin (the boys' school and college in Tokyo), but it also provided annual subsidies to these three schools and actively participated in their reconstruction. Contributions to reconstruction after World War II were made possible in part by the fact that world mission postwar recovery projects received a significant portion of the monies raised by the United Advance Fund, a two-year fundraising effort of the Reformed Church initiated in 1946. Another Reformed Church fund drive in the 1950s also provided major contributions to the mission schools. Enrollments grew at all the schools as they endeavored to move toward self-support primarily from tuition, but in the postwar years the Reformed Church mission board not only contributed toward reconstruction and additional facilities, it also sent significant subsidies toward operating costs.

In the case of Baiko Jo Gakuin, where the buildings had been almost completely destroyed in the war, the Reformed Church was able

---

[1]     Gordon J. Van Wyk, "The Schools, the Kyodan, and the I.B.C." *Japan Christian Quarterly*, Apr., 1961, 88.

Baiko Jo Gakuin buildings constructed in 1951 on the site
of the school destroyed in the fire-bombing
of Shimonoseki during World War II

to contribute one-fourth of the cost of reconstruction of the main school
building. One-fourth was contributed by the Presbyterian mission
board, and half was raised by the school within Japan. The value Baiko
placed on its relationship to the Reformed Church was demonstrated
in that, when the buildings' foundations were laid in 1950, Principal
Hirotsu brought out for inclusion in the cornerstone the small bell that
Sara Couch had kept on her desk when she was principal of the small
Reformed Church mission school that had eventually become part of
Baiko.[2]

In the 1950s, Ferris and Meiji Gakuin also benefited from
the generosity of the Reformed Church. It contributed land and
$50,000 of the $110,000 required for the construction of the new
Ferris Junior College building and eventually raised $200,000 toward
the reconstruction of the Meiji Gakuin University and High School
buildings in central Tokyo.

Perhaps more important than Reformed Church contributions
to the restoration and reconstruction of the physical plants of the three
mission schools were the reinforcements provided to their teaching
staffs. In the period immediately before and during the war, the Japanese
government had at first discouraged and later virtually prohibited the
teaching and use of English, the language of the enemy, but with the
end of hostilities and subsequent occupation came once again a great
surge in interest in learning the language. The highly regarded prewar

---

[2]    BFMR, 1950, 10.

English-language programs at the mission schools were reinstated after the war and attracted many new students.

In addition, new post-war school structures established by the Japanese Ministry of Education replaced the prewar system—which had consisted of a six-year elementary, five-year secondary, and a two- or three-year advanced course system—with a six-year elementary, three-year junior high, three-year senior high, and eventually two- or four-year college course system. Mission schools followed the new structure. Meiji Gakuin maintained junior and senior high schools for boys, a coeducational four-year college, and a college level night school, with a total enrollment in the early 1950s of more than four thousand students. Ferris and Baiko had junior and senior high schools and later developed two-year junior colleges and eventually four-year colleges for girls and young women. Enrollments at the girls' schools also increased significantly, and more teachers were required.

In response to this opportunity, one important aspect of missionary reinforcement became the program for infusion of numerous young American Christian teachers into these schools. Whereas they were needed mainly to teach English, they were accorded excellent opportunities for Christian witness and influence. Many such teachers were sent as short-term missionaries, appointed for three-year terms, and came to be called J3s (Japan three years).

The first of these newly appointed short-term missionaries to arrive after the war—even before some of the career people had been able to return—were Eunice Noda, the first *Nisei*, or Japanese American, to be appointed as a missionary to Japan, and Ronald G. Korver. They were sent out in 1948 and served at Ferris and Meiji Gakuin, respectively. Noda taught not only English but especially home economics. Korver, without a prior opportunity for formal language study, immediately took up his work, teaching English as many as seven hours a day, and began part-time study of Japanese. His quarters not yet ready at Meiji Gakuin, he at first lived with John de Maagd and commuted from Yokohama, but he soon moved to Tokyo and began to build close relationships with the Meiji Gakuin boys by directing their sports activities. He also taught English Bible classes at as many as three different churches. Theodore E. Flaherty was sent in 1949 to teach at Meiji Gakuin for three years, with the understanding that after his term he would return to America for further study and then go back to Japan as a career missionary. Like the other newcomers who had not yet learned Japanese, Flaherty primarily taught courses in English conversation and composition. He also taught English Bible for the more advanced students and an English Bible class at a neighborhood church.

In 1950 three more new recruits arrived. Helen J. Vander Meer, A. Burrell Pennings, and Louis P. Kraay were appointed as short-term missionaries (J3s) for service as English teachers at mission schools. Vander Meer went to Ferris in Yokohama, Pennings went to Meiji Gakuin in Tokyo, and Kraay went to a school in Matsuyama on the island of Shikoku, the first to be sent to a school not formerly associated with the Reformed Church's Japan Mission. The J3s all found many opportunities to relate to non-Christians, but they also realized that they could be an encouragement to young Christians. Pennings reported,

> Bible classes conducted in English are very popular among Japanese Christians, and the two which I have are a constant source of inspiration to me personally. One of these classes is with the college Y.M.C.A. and the other is in the Ushigome church here in Tokyo where I worship on Sunday mornings. Both of these classes are made up of wide-awake young folk who take their Christianity very seriously and who appear anxious to deepen their lives spiritually. In both of the classes we are studying the Gospel of John, and it is proving to be a rich experience to explain the truths in that book in the simplest English possible.[3]

The influence of these short-term missionaries is illustrated by stories shared by Helen Vander Meer and William H. Estell, who arrived in 1952. One of Vander Meer's students, Miss Seki, had become a Christian through Vander Meer's English Bible class. As she tells her own story, she helps clarify the patient witness needed to win Japanese to Christ. Seki wrote, in part,

> My ideas about religion were quite strange. Religion was what mankind sought to fulfill his own heart's desire. It was for bad people, those who failed in love affairs or those who had some unhappiness. I thought Christians were spiritually sick people. I never thought about studying Christianity, although I thought that when I got old I might need religion. When I heard that the Bible was interesting, I doubted it and thought it was false. But now I believe that there is no other book as interesting as the Bible.

---

[3]   Burrell Pennings, "At Home in Japan," *Church Herald*, Feb. 16, 1951, 21.

The time when I began to have faith was when I wanted to learn English conversation....I went to the church and heard you speak. It did not matter whether I understood or not. I began to read the Bible but I did not like it. But I read it, anyway, and went to hear the explanation, and then I began to see in you what I hadn't seen before. Your faith and your attitude were very beautiful, and I admired them from my innermost heart. As I began to understand the conversation, your lectures took hold of my heart.[4]

Bill Estell told of his after-school English Bible class with a group of Meiji Gakuin High School boys.

Today I sat in a small dark, dingy classroom, the Hi-Y room in the attic of the senior high school. There was the familiar triangle on the wall, but the words are in Japanese. There were other signs and notices tacked up, also in Japanese. There was no speaker's podium, no piano or organ, no curtains at the windows, or shade on the one light bulb in the room. There was only the usual classroom desks and benches....

After the class bell rang, the students started to go home; I could see many leaving the school. In a few minutes I heard some boys on the stairs. Only a handful of boys entered the room, some fifteen of the eight hundred, but somehow or other, the room changed; it was not now just a room of printed Japanese signs, but a room of Christian lives embodied in Japanese boys. One look at these boys and you have seen Christ in Japan.

This is the meeting conducted in English; there is another during the lunch hour on Fridays conducted in Japanese. These boys also come to school early daily for a short prayer before school begins.

After our worship service and Bible study, the boys adjourned to my house and gathered around a small reed organ to learn some of the great hymns of the Church in English. They are eager and interested, and sincere Christians.

I was impressed at a recent service by the baptism of seven into the Christian faith. This by itself was cause for rejoicing, but what impressed me most was the fact that three were members of my Bible class. Of course, I had very little to do with this, but still I was very thankful. These students were able to stand before us all

[4]    Helen Vander Meer, "Thy Word—a Lamp—a Light," *Church Herald*, Aug. 28, 1953.

and confess Christ because of many Christians who had worked with them. I am aware of three short-term missionaries who influenced them, Ted Flaherty, Ron Korver, and Burrell Pennings, along with the minister, and their fellow students at Meiji Gakuin who are witnessing Christians.[5]

It was clearly understood that while the J3s, who were not provided the opportunity to spend much time in language study, made valuable contributions as teachers and role models, career missionaries with facility in the language and greater immersion in the culture would also continue to be needed at the mission schools. Career missionary teachers were of course able to engage students and Japanese colleagues on a deeper level, but they were also valuable for the integration of the J3s. Accordingly, the Reformed Church mission board proceeded to augment the long-term missionary staff for the mission schools.

In an unusual and related development, Luman Shafer resigned as secretary of the Board of Foreign Missions in the spring of 1951. The Shafers hoped to spend the last years of their active service in Japan, where they had begun their careers, and the board reappointed them as missionaries there. Meiji Gakuin's President Murata and its Board of Trustees had invited Luman to assist in the desperately needed reorganization of the school, which had increased its enrollment during the war in order to survive, but to the school's great detriment. Shafer's work at the school was primarily administrative; he served as advisor to the president. After several months in this role, Shafer observed,

> We are gradually getting to understand their problems, which are many, but which, as you would expect, come down to matters of personnel and finance. Good leadership is rare anywhere but the supply of Christian teachers and real Christian leadership is critical here. The Church is too small to produce enough people to carry on the work that needs to be done. Our task here is to help produce the Christians needed for the Church and for the community, but to produce Christians you need Christians.[6]

It was hoped that part of the solution to this dilemma would be an increase in the number of committed missionaries on the school's staff. Shafer served in his advisory capacity at Meiji Gakuin for only a year before returning to America at the urging of the board. The critical

---

[5]    William Estell, "Enriching Experiences in Japan," *Church Herald*, July 3, 1953.
[6]    Shafer, "Word from the Shafers in Japan," *Church Herald*, Jan. 4, 1952, 9.

illness of the board secretary, Duke Potter, Shafer's close friend and colleague of many years, left a serious vacuum in the administrative staff of the mission board, and Shafer was asked to return as executive secretary. The Shafers reluctantly left Japan, and Potter died very soon after their return.[7]

As secretary, Shafer continued to build up the staff of Meiji Gakuin. Two families forced to leave China in 1950 because of the Communist takeover were reappointed to service in Japan. Dr. Everett and Edith Kleinjans, in 1951, and the Reverend Gordon J. and Bertha Van Wyk, in 1952, joined the faculty at Meiji Gakuin. Kleinjans, who had attained a doctorate in linguistics, worked to revitalize the English language program at the Meiji Gakuin schools. Van Wyk, an ordained minister with a strong commitment to evangelism in the academic setting, taught in the Meiji Gakuin University English Department and played an influential role on the school's faculty and board of trustees. He also led Bible classes for students at the Van Wyk home and at a local church. As family responsibilities permitted, Bertha (Birdie) taught English at Meiji Gakuin High School.

Ronald Korver, after completing his short-term service at Meiji Gakuin and a year in America, was married to Ruby Barth. The Korvers were appointed as career educational missionaries and returned to Japan and to Meiji Gakuin in 1952. When Meiji Gakuin later added a new junior and senior high school at Higashi Murayama in the western suburbs of Tokyo to its program, Korver played a key role, getting to know students well by teaching the same group English, physical education, and Bible. Ruby taught English at her alma mater, Keisen, a Christian high school and college for women.

Following Flaherty's marriage to Mary Watt, Mary was appointed as a missionary and joined Ted on his return to Japan in 1953, and after language study they began teaching at Meiji Gakuin as well. Henry M. and Carol Schaafsma were appointed as educational missionaries in 1958, and after they took up teaching at Meiji Gakuin, the Flahertys were appointed to teach at the high school and junior college at Ferris and moved to Yokohama.

The practice of appointing short-term missionaries, supported by the Reformed Church through the mission board, to work in the mission schools alongside the career people continued until the early 1960s. Theoretically, personnel sent to Japan through the Interboard Committee might be assigned through the Council of Cooperation

---

[7]    *Church Herald*, Oct. 3, 1952, 13.

on the field to any of the many mission schools associated with the Japanese church. Nevertheless, in practice, the new missionaries sent out by the several mission boards tended to be sent to schools traditionally affiliated with the former denominational Japan Missions.

Accordingly, most of the Reformed Church's short-term missionaries were assigned to Meiji Gakuin, Ferris, or Baiko. The board's policy of appointing and supporting short-term educational missionaries to supplement the work of the career missionaries at the mission schools continued until 1965. During the first twenty postwar years these young teachers, despite the language barrier, made valuable contributions, not only by teaching English but also as vibrant Christian witnesses in the schools, local churches, and the broader community.[8] The Reformed Church's contribution to the postwar reinvigoration of the mission schools may be seen in that in 1954 five young missionary couples and seven single missionaries were serving in mission schools attended by more than six thousand students.

During the 1950s the Reformed Church raised a significant portion of the capital funds needed for rebuilding and expansion projects at Baiko, Ferris, and Meiji Gakuin. However, with inflation, rising personnel costs, and the necessity of additional new facilities, the mission schools could no longer expect the mission board and American churches to provide a major portion of their financial resources. The Reformed Church provided annual subsidies to its three related mission schools into the 1960s, but as school enrollments and budgets continued to grow, these contributions became very small portions of the schools' total budgets.

Because secondary and college education functioned as the means to a secure future and upward mobility in postwar Japan, parents were willing to make great sacrifices for their children's education. Mission school alumni and parents worked hard to raise capital funds, and the schools' boards devised means to achieve self-support, primarily through increased student enrollments. This policy added tuition income, but it also tended to diminish the Christian impact of the schools on the students, both because there were never enough qualified Christian teachers to staff them and because the large student bodies

8    Subsequently appointed short-term missionary teachers: Marcella M. Poppen (1951-54), William H. Estell Jr. (1952-55), Carol Van Zoeren (1952-55), Verlaine R. Siter (!953-56), Fenita M. Harmelink (1955-58), Elaine Buteyn (1956-59), Aileen I. McGoldrick (1958-62), Jeneva K. Breed (1959-62), Carroll de Forest (1959-62), John D. Hood (1959-62), Barbara Bosch (1960-63), Eileen Fredriks (1960-63), James P. Rozeboom (1961-64), and Beth Bonnema (1962-65).

tended to produce an impersonal and secular environment. Already in 1960, Bovenkerk noted that neither the Interboard Committee nor the Council of Cooperation had arrived at a course of action to stem the tide of increasing size and secularization of Interboard Committee-related Christian colleges.[9]

Following the pattern developed by other Japanese private schools, the mission schools' capital funds came to be acquired through charging the applicants significant entrance examination fees,[10] and from required one-time parental contributions to the schools' building and maintenance funds at the time of matriculation. In this way, the mission schools became self-supporting, and by the early 1960s the Reformed Church's contribution became primarily providing Christian missionary personnel and all their maintenance costs. Until the mid-1960s, the Reformed Church sent and maintained on average about fifteen missionary teachers for the three Reformed Church-related mission schools.

By the mid-1960s, then, it had become clear that the most valuable contribution the Reformed Church could make to mission schools in Japan was dedicated Christian personnel to serve on their faculties. However, the role of missionary educators in the independent mission schools was not always clear. Did the schools only expect missionaries to be good English teachers, or were the schools serious about implementing the missionaries' Christian witness as well? Gordon Van Wyk expressed his concern in this regard as early as 1963, when he wrote, "Until Meiji Gakuin faces up to what it really wants out of a missionary and why it wants him and what it really plans to do with him when he does come, we missionaries cannot encourage any further recruitments."[11] In fact, no new career missionary was again appointed for college level teaching at Meiji Gakuin.

When Florence Walvoord reached retirement in 1960, Baiko Girls' School pleaded for a single woman missionary to replace her. However, the mission board was not successful in recruiting a career single woman missionary to serve there, and Shimonoseki was considered too isolated for the assignment of a short-term teacher without language training. A candidate was eventually found in the person of Alice Elzinga, formerly a missionary to South America and a Dutch-Canadian member of the

---

[9]    Henry G. Bovenkerk to RCA Missionaries in Japan, Feb. 18, 1960.

[10]   Because of competition for secondary and higher education, many more students took entrance examinations than could be admitted. Consequently, the examination fees became a significant source of school income.

[11]   Gordon J. Van Wyk to James J. Thomas, Oct. 1, 1963.

Christian Reformed Church who was already in Japan as a dorm parent at an international school. Elzinga was hired by the Reformed Church to serve as a contract teacher at Baiko in 1963, and, after meeting with personnel staff of the Reformed Church, was appointed as a career missionary in 1966.[12] Despite limited opportunity to learn the Japanese language and little occasion to relate to other Western people, Elzinga served faithfully on the faculty at Baiko for many years, not only by teaching English at the high school and junior college, but also through encouraging her colleagues in their Christian ministry and holding Bible classes in her home and at a local church.

## Resurgence of Postwar Reformed Church Evangelistic Work

Of all the missionaries' work, evangelism was particularly affected by postwar occupation policies and the eventual reestablishment of Japanese sovereignty. Several significant factors may be noted. Under the administration of the supreme commander for the Allied Powers, General Douglas MacArthur, early in the almost seven-year occupation of Japan only missionaries of mission organizations with prewar work in Japan were allowed to resume their activity. The North American churches that reestablished cooperative work with Japanese Christians through the Interboard Committee all fit this category, and they were distinguished by a sincere effort to respect the integrity and independence of the Japanese church.

In 1948, however, MacArthur modified occupation regulations to permit representatives of churches and mission agencies without prewar activity in Japan to enter as missionaries. The result was a rapid influx of mostly American, nonecumenical, fundamentalist, and independent missionaries with no connections to established Japanese churches and with little appreciation for Japanese sensitivities and culture. Many lacked a cooperative spirit. They soon outnumbered the mainstream Protestant missionaries who worked in cooperation with the already established Japanese churches, and they formed small, independent, missionary-controlled churches. One result was the proliferation of tiny denominations. The exclusivist attitudes and actions of many of these new missionaries and the churches and organizations they established tended to confuse and complicate the already challenging situation of the Christian movement in Japan. Furthermore, the almost universal use of English or English Bible classes by these new missionaries as a tool to attract people tended also to accentuate the image of Christianity as a foreign and a foreigners' religion.

---

[12]    JJT to GJV, Oct. 30 and Dec. 20, 1962.

The Treaty of Peace with Japan, commonly known as the San Francisco Peace Treaty, between the Allied Powers and Japan was signed September 8, 1951, and went into effect April 22, 1952. This treaty signified the official end of World War II, formally ended Japan's position as a world power, and provided for the allocation of Japanese overseas assets to compensate Allied civilians and former prisoners of war who had suffered Japanese war crimes, the allocation to be carried out through the International Red Cross. In signing this treaty Japan also accepted the judgments of the war crimes trials and agreed to carry out sentences imposed on Japanese nationals imprisoned in Japan.

The postwar Constitution of Japan, written under MacArthur's direction and approved with modifications by the Japanese government in November 1946, went into effect May 3, 1947. The new constitution was characterized by its provisions for universal suffrage (including women for the first time), the symbolic role of the emperor, the prominence of guarantees of civil and human rights, and the renunciation of the right to wage war (Article 9). Because of this last provision, the document has often been called Japan's Peace Constitution. However, the onset of the Korean War on June 25, 1950, and its relationship to the Cold War, brought about a change in the U.S. perspective on the post-World War II role of Japan in Asia, seeing Japan as an important ally. During the Korean War, Japan in fact served as a strategic base of operations for United Nations forces, and, ironically, the Korean War became an economic boon to Japan, stimulating the reconstruction of Japan's industries, which supplied goods to sustain the war effort.

Furthermore, while Japan's Constitution forbade the organization of Japanese Armed Forces, the American government, with its forces deeply engaged in Korea, began to encourage Japan to develop structures for its own defense. What was at first called a police reserve was developed into the Japan Self-defense Forces. On the day that Japan's peace treaty was signed, September 8, 1951, which was at the height of the Korean War, a separate security treaty between the United States and Japan was mutually approved. It granted the United States the right to maintain land, sea, and air forces in and around Japan and permitted them to be used to maintain peace and security in East Asia. There were more than seven hundred military bases, large and small, in Japan at the time. In addition, the treaty provided that the United States retain sovereign control over Okinawa (the Ryukyu Islands) indefinitely.[13] This amounted to unrestricted use of Japanese

---

[13]   Japanese sovereignty over Okinawa was restored in 1972.

territory by the United States, but the resultant provision of the security of Japan at modest cost to Japan while the United States and other allies dealt with the Cold War provided Japan the opportunity to give priority to its own economic recovery and growth.

The security treaty was at first well received by the majority of the Japanese public.[14] However, the presence of tens of thousands of American military personnel in numerous bases on Japanese soil, bases which monopolized hundreds of thousands of acres of prime real estate in the land-limited nation, also functioned as an irritant. While the end of the occupation and restoration of Japanese sovereignty were naturally welcomed, whenever immoral or criminal activity by U.S. military personnel in Japan became public, it exacerbated the irritation of the presence of foreign bases on Japanese soil, especially when Japanese courts were denied jurisdiction for prosecution. Nevertheless, since most of their political leaders were former supporters of imperialist Japan, many Japanese, tired of war and eager for peace, accepted the foreign bases as preferable to the potential resurgence of militarism.

Unfortunately, the gradual restoration of national pride was soon accompanied by signs of a resurgence of nationalism. True to the trend of Japanese history, the rise of nationalism led to a decrease in general interest in Christianity and things Western, and the crowds at Christian gatherings began to wane. While prewar antagonisms to Christianity had been greatly modified, most people were preoccupied with their economic recovery. Nevertheless, some were open to hearing the gospel. Those who were coming to the churches, influenced by the mission schools, or reached by the gospel in other ways were more earnest and more promising as potential church members, and freedom to carry on evangelistic work openly had been assured. Furthermore, many Japanese church leaders had come to recognize missionaries more fully as valuable associates in furthering the church's evangelistic activity.

As the occupation ended, John de Maagd was well positioned to help lay the groundwork for expansion of missionary activity in cooperation with the Kyodan through the Interboard Committee. He played a prominent role in developing this postwar cooperative relationship within Japan until 1959, when he returned to the United States to assume leadership of the New York headquarters of the Interboard Committee. Boude Moore prepared the way for enhanced postwar participation by missionaries in the evangelistic work of the Japanese churches on the island of Kyushu, where the Reformed

---

[14]  Lu, *Japan*, 499-503; Iglehart, *Century*, 310.

Church had concentrated its evangelistic work for three decades before the war. The Reformed Church accepted the challenge not only to reinvigorate the mission schools with new missionary personnel, but also once again to send a substantial number of young missionaries to learn Japanese, assimilate Japanese culture, and participate with the Japanese Christians in the evangelization of Japan.

Suzanne H. Brink was the first to be appointed as a career evangelistic missionary after the war, arriving in Japan in 1950. Following study at a Japanese language school in Kyoto, Brink was assigned to evangelistic work in cooperation with churches in the Kumamoto district on the island of Kyushu. Her long ministry there, until her retirement in 1977, focused on outreach to children, high school and university students, and women, teaching numerous English and Bible classes. She also called on hospital patients as a form of evangelism. In contrast to the prewar women missionaries, she did not have Japanese Bible women working under her; instead, she served as a coworker with Japanese pastors and lay leaders in the churches of the Kumamoto region. Although not an ordained minister, Brink was eventually accorded the status of a licensed preacher, and she was often invited to preach in the several small churches in the Kumamoto district. Sue Brink had a heart for rural people, the most unreached group in Japan. An example of her ministry follows:

> With Japanese pastors, I regularly visit mountain villages where there are no churches, and where we meet in the homes of Christians. Since we need something special for the children who attend, we always include a children's hymn in the services, and I always prepare special talks for the children, using pictures or any other aid, so that they have a feeling of participating with their elders in the services.[15]

Brink also told the story of the humble beginnings of a Japanese rural church.

> I have known some good fighters who have and are succeeding in making a *dent* for Christ in the country of Japan. Six or seven miles out of Kumamoto City, on a beautiful well-paved road, which the early Japanese samurai used to travel, is the turn-off to a narrow dirt road. If you follow this road for about a mile

---

[15]    Suzanne Brink, "Diversities of Gifts But the Same Spirit," *Church Herald*, July 23, 1965, 4.

you come to a small country church just off the side of the road. We know it to be a church because of its white cross which is visible to all who pass. This church, now ten years old, was begun because of the vision, faith and hard work of a Christian layman, Mr. Saburo Ushijima, whose home is on the opposite side of the road. Actually, it had its beginnings during the war when Mr. Ushijima was caring for war orphans in a building he had put up on his own land. After the war the government took over the orphans and the building was used for a meeting place for young people. Sons and daughters of farmers met here twice a month on Saturday evenings for simple Bible study, singing of hymns, etc. Also, every Saturday afternoon Sunday-school teachers from the city church of Reformed/Presbyterian background came out here to have Bible school for the children.

In September 1952 it was officially recognized as the outlying evangelistic center of the city church, and the pastor came out once a month to hold evening services. The location of the building out in the field, though ideal for war years, was not good for normal times as it was too difficult to reach. So it was decided to move it to its present location. This was done at no little expense, most of which was borne by the dairy farmer, Mr. Ushijima himself....

This church is a living testimony to the way in which God blesses and honors the faith, prayers and hard work of those who are *good fighters*.[16]

The patient witness of this faithful layman slowly began to bear fruit. Leaders of the Japanese church's Kumamoto District requested Sue Brink to assist regularly in the rural village work of the Koshi Toyo-oka Preaching Station. She preached regularly, helped develop a Sunday school, and worked especially with the women and young people. The preaching station was eventually able to call a young pastor. Brink reflected on the role of the missionary in this type of rural evangelism.

What qualifications do you need to be a country evangelist for country evangelism in Japan? Physical, mental and spiritual health and vitality; the ability to drive a car; ability to type; competence in music, if possible; a love for adventure; and a deep desire to make Christ known, that hungry hearts may be satisfied and that through you God may call those whom He has chosen to become heirs of salvation.

[16]   Suzanne Brink, "Barely Been Scratched," *Church Herald*, Aug. 18, 1961, 12.

Suzanne Brink

No, you will not have an easy life. You will need to be able to adjust yourself to an unpredictable schedule, to endure frustrations, to suffer almost unbearable loneliness at times, but it will all be outweighed and overcome in the joy you will experience in serving your Lord and King.[17]

At Fukuoka in Kyushu, Boude Moore not only reestablished the newspaper evangelism center, but also began to enlarge its work significantly. The Reformed Church mission board sent a short-term (1951-54) missionary couple, William and Bonita Sheets, to assist in the outreach ministry of the Shin Sei Kan. Bill Sheets, a veteran who had entered Japan in September 1945, and as part of the early occupation army for six months had seen the devastation of the country, responded to a new opportunity for a layperson to share in the evangelistic work. Funds were raised, and a new Dodge panel truck was shipped to Japan to be used for itinerant audiovisual evangelism. The truck was equipped with a movie projector, large screen, loudspeaker system, and a portable generator (electrical current was weak and unreliable in many rural areas at that time).

To carry out this audiovisual evangelism, Moore arranged for the Shin Sei Kan staff to make contact with the scattered churches and groups of Christians throughout the island of Kyushu to plan audiovisual evangelism meetings. Following the prearranged schedule,

---

17    Suzanne Brink, "Diversities of Gifts But the Same Spirit," *Church Herald*, July 23, 1965, 5.

despite minimal Japanese language skills on the part of Bill and Bonnie Sheets, the staff made extended trips of several weeks duration. The evangelists enlivened the outreach of Japanese Christians by showing a movie of the life of Christ, called *The King of Kings*, with a Japanese sound track to several hundred thousand people, most of them non-Christians. John de Maagd, after visiting Kyushu and attending one of these meetings, remarked,

> This is indeed a method of presenting the Gospel that does not have to overcome the usual guards people put up against speeches which they suspect to be propaganda. It is a deeply moving experience to be in a tense crowd of non-Christians—some of whom have hardly more than heard the name of Christ before—and feel they are "for" Him as the children applaud and the elders smile approvingly when He heals a cripple or cleanses the temple. And it is sometimes almost intolerably moving to watch with them the crucifixion, for you stand surrounded by those for whom Christ died, and for whom this may be the best, perhaps the only occasion, to catch that glimpse of His purpose which shall set them seeking till they find. How you pray then!
>
> Before the meeting is over, cards are passed out to all, with the offer to help anyone who wishes to know more about Jesus' life and message by sending them free literature from the Shin Sei Kan, our Literature Evangelism Center in Fukuoka.[18]

Bill and Bonnie Sheets conducted this audiovisual evangelism ministry for three years. When they completed their term in 1954, William Estell, a short-term missionary who had been teaching at Meiji Gakuin High School for two years, spent the third and last year of his term continuing itinerant audiovisual evangelism in western Japan. Estell related a story that shows how this method provided opportunities to witness to unreached people. Accompanied by a Japanese pastor, he visited a village in Oita Prefecture where there were no Christians. There being no other suitable meeting place, the minister persuaded the local Shinto priest to allow the use of the local Shinto shrine for their meeting.

> For quite some time before the meeting, the people in the village had seen posters announcing our meeting..., so they were prepared—some curious, some expectant, and others very critical.

---

[18] John de Maagd, "The Good News for Those in Darkness," *Church Herald*, Sept. 11, 1953.

The evening came like any other. We had the usual trouble trying to get the portable electric generator started in the cold night air....After I had started it and had gone inside the shrine, the people also began to wander in. Since there was only one place to put up the screen we put it right in front of the shrine. The Shinto gods had to give way for the screen on which we would present the one true God....Then...put our loudspeakers in front also, and after checking all the wires and connections, we were ready to begin.

At first we played many hymns on the tape recorder, sung in Japanese....There followed the usual announcements and introductions, and then we had the "children's feature"; slides and filmstrips especially for young folk. Every one of these was strictly evangelistic....At the end of this we showed a slide of Christ with arms outstretched, asking them to follow Him.

It was at this point that there were loud shouts of protest from the audience. This was not good, they cried, for us to show and preach Christ in their beloved Shinto shrine. It was not sure just what would happen. I felt like a Daniel in a den of lions ready to tear us and the equipment to pieces. But it seems as though God stepped right off the screen and shut their lips tight.

The meeting continued without further annoyance. We showed the film, *The Calling of Matthew*. At the end of the film, another evangelistic talk was directed at them. This time they were all silent; there were no comments. At the intermission, we gave each of them a copy of the newspaper which Boude Moore gets out at the newspaper evangelism center in Fukuoka and asked them to sign our cards, which would signify that they wanted to learn more about Christianity. The cards would put them on the mailing list of this monthly newspaper.

After filling the gas tank of the generator again, we showed the film, *The God of Creation*, concluding with another evangelistic talk by the minister, and with more recorded hymns. To our amazement, we found that about one third of the people present had signed the cards and turned them in to us.[19]

In 1953 the Reformed Church took the initiative, under Moore's leadership, to construct a Protestant evangelistic center in Fukuoka, and other churches related to the United Church of Christ in Japan,

---

[19]    William Estell, "Daniel in a Shinto Shrine," *Church Herald*, Feb. 18, 1955.

Nishi Nihon Shin Sei Kan ("West Japan New Life Building"), also called the Albertus Pieters Evangelistic Center

Boude Moore, preaching for the Japanese radio broadcast

as well as the United Lutheran Church, worked together to develop its evangelistic program. With considerable support from Reformed churches, land was purchased on a prominent corner in the city of Fukuoka and a four-story ferroconcrete building constructed for the work of the Nishi Nihon Shin Sei Kan (West Japan New Life Building, also called the Albertus Pieters Evangelistic Center). Included in this new center were a Christian bookstore, offices for the newspaper and audiovisual evangelism programs, a loan library for inquirers, a pastors' library, a small prayer room, a chapel for evangelistic meetings, and rooms for special meetings of the churches and Christian women's organizations in the city.[20]

With the dedication of the evangelistic center, a new phase of evangelistic outreach was initiated—the Japanese radio broadcast of the Reformed Church's *Temple Time*. Of course, in Japan the title *Temple Time* could not be used, as the word *temple* would suggest a Buddhist temple. The broadcast, begun in June 1953, was called *Shin Sei Time*, i.e., "New Life Time," and since most Japanese homes had radios, while only

[20]   BFMR, 1953, 12.

a few owned televisions, this additional means of outreach provided the opportunity to offer the gospel message in virtually every city, town, and village in the broadcast areas, which were gradually expanded to stations reaching much of southwestern Japan. The content or themes of the American *Temple Time* broadcasts were presented in Japanese by Moore (a virtual native speaker by virtue of his birth and upbringing) or by Japanese pastors, accompanied by a female Japanese Christian announcer and an eighteen-voice radio choir. Moore continued to head this ministry until his retirement in 1962.

By the early 1950s, with the ravages and dislocations of the war years and the focus on rehabilitation that followed largely behind them, it became possible for the Japanese churches to give greater effort to developing programs directly related to the evangelization of the country. With structures for cooperative work in place, the Kyodan encouraged the postwar participation of missionaries in the evangelistic outreach of the churches. De Maagd noted, "There are still 6,000 villages in Japan which have no congregations. Our sister church—the Church of Christ in Japan—is inviting more missionaries today than the boards in North America can possibly send."[21] Each of the fifteen synods of the Japanese church had a long roster of missionaries it wished to invite.

The pattern that was established provided that invited missionaries of the North American churches related to the Interboard Committee, following completion of a two-year language study course, were assigned through the Council of Cooperation to one of the fifteen synods or districts, called *kyoku*, of the Japanese church. Assignments by the Council of Cooperation were made after consultation with the missionary being assigned and the field representative of his or her denomination. Once the assignment to a synod was made, leaders of the receiving synod arranged for the missionary's cooperative relationship with the pastors and churches of one of its subdistricts.

In Japan, churches with prewar relationships with the eight North American denominations were all part of the Kyodan, but in North America the denominations remained separate entities. This reality limited the functional ecumenicity of the Interboard Committee. Theoretically, under the new ecumenical arrangement, evangelistic missionaries might expect to be assigned impartially to work anywhere in Japan where they were invited and/or needed by the churches.

However, in practice, prewar denominational ties tended to affect assignments, and it appeared that unless the Reformed Church provided

---

[21]    J. C. de Maagd, "Across a Century—in Japan," *Church Herald*, Feb. 15, 1957.

them, the churches of Kyushu Kyoku, the synod where Reformed Church evangelistic work had been concentrated before the war, were unlikely to receive newly assigned missionaries. As a result, Boude Moore became a champion for bringing in new Reformed Church missionaries for Kyushu. Moore envisioned once again stationing Reformed Church evangelistic missionaries in Kyushu's key cities to work in cooperation with the churches.

The Reformed Church mission board responded to the Japanese church's invitation by beginning to rebuild its career evangelistic missionary work force in Japan. Four new young families were appointed and sent out during 1952 and 1953: The Reverend Glenn and Phyllis Bruggers, the Reverend Russell L. and Eleanore Norden, the Reverend I. John and Etta Hesselink, and the Reverend Paul H. and Marjorie Tanis. Following language study in Kyoto or Tokyo, each missionary couple received a specific evangelistic assignment through the Council of Cooperation.

Through Moore's encouragement and his long-standing relationship with Japanese church leaders of Kyushu Kyoku, three of the couples were assigned to work on the island of Kyushu. In 1953 the Bruggers family moved to Kagoshima, where they became cooperating missionaries working with the Kyodan churches in that district. Similarly, in 1954 the Norden family moved to Kyushu to work in Kurume and to serve as cooperating missionaries with the churches of that district. And in 1955 the Hesselink family moved to Fukuoka, assigned to do evangelistic work among university students and to carry responsibility at the evangelistic center, Nishi Nihon Shinsei Kan, as well as serve in local churches. In the same year the Tanis family was assigned to evangelistic and audiovisual work in Atsugi, near Yokohama.

The postwar district evangelistic missionary's situation contrasted sharply with that of prewar times. Formerly, the Reformed Church Japan Mission had been a decision-making body, with authority to execute plans, assign missionaries, and employ Japanese workers. That structure and authority no longer existed, and the missionaries needed to formulate new roles and relationships with their Japanese Christian colleagues, a task that required not only a functional level of Japanese language but also cultural sensitivity and understanding. In Japanese culture, the role of the "go-between" often facilitates the building of good relationships, as is illustrated by the arrangements for the Bruggers family's assignment to Kagoshima. Glenn Bruggers reported from Kagoshima.

The three young families in
evangelistic work in Kyushu
in 1955 (l-r): Hesselinks, Nordens,
and Bruggerses

About two years ago, the pastors in this area of Japan asked for a missionary. When, on leaving the language school, we began evangelistic work in this prefecture, we consulted the Rev. Boude C. Moore on the type of work we would probably be doing, the men we would be working with, and the things we should and should not do. Moore spent many hours with us, telling us all he knew of the local situation. He told us then that when the ministers asked for a missionary, he sat down with them on several occasions, discussing what type of thing they thought a missionary could or should do with or for them.

As a result of this preparation, when we arrived on the scene the ministers were ready for the coming of a missionary; they had thought about it and prayed about it. Consequently, when we came to Kagoshima, we were told that we would have about two weeks to get unpacked and settled, after which, on an appointed day, all the pastors in the prefecture, six in number, would gather for a day of personal welcome and to plan our work for the year. Thus it would as far as possible be a cooperative venture with all the churches in the prefecture, and not a case of working with only one pastor and one church.[22]

A similar pattern was followed a year later when the Norden family arrived in Kyushu and began to work in the district with Kurume at its center. Moore, who had served to develop several of the churches in Kurume and the surrounding region before the war, introduced the Nordens to the work, and soon they were deeply involved in its evangelistic outreach. Itinerant preaching in the several small congregations, some of which had no resident pastor, administering the sacraments where the pastor was not yet an ordained minister, and

---

[22]   Glenn Bruggers, "Our Witness In Evangelism," *Church Herald*, Feb. 19, 1954.

meeting regularly with the pastors' group helped nurture the struggling congregations, and teaching English Bible classes at numerous locations provided evangelistic opportunities.

Bruggers and Norden were among the pioneers of a redefined postwar district missionary role, one in which the missionary was no longer a supervisor and had no authority over Japanese Christian workers. In contrast to Boude Moore, they were not missionary father figures within the Japanese church. As cooperating, ordained, evangelistic missionaries, they endeavored to serve in the roles of faithful witness and servant, friend and colleague of Japanese Christian workers, and unobtrusive source of wise counsel and insight, as models for ministry. Furthermore, their work was ecumenical. The churches in the districts in which they served were all part of the Kyodan and therefore included not only the congregations formerly associated with the prewar Reformed Church Japan Mission but also churches of Methodist or Congregational background.

The work of the Hesselinks from 1955-58 centered around the Shinseikan, or Albertus Pieters Evangelistic Center, in Fukuoka and included Etta's direction of the radio ministry choir and John's oversight of the center's work during the Moores' furlough. Moore had envisioned Hesselink succeeding him as manager of the Shinseikan. However, during his time in Fukuoka Hesselink's interest in Calvin's writings led not only to his partnering with Japanese pastors in the formation of the Japan Calvin Translation Society, but also to his goal of pursuing Calvin studies in Europe. During three years in Basel, Switzerland, Hesselink acquired a doctorate, and the possibility of a future in theological education in Japan began to open up. Consequently, the Hesselinks did not return to Fukuoka but were assigned in 1961 to residence in the Tokyo area, given six months for a refresher course in Japanese, and given time for their assignment to be clarified. Hesselink was invited to teach part time at both the Tokyo Union Theological Seminary and Meiji Gakuin University, and Etta directed the seminary choir. Hesselink soon became a full-time faculty member at the seminary and exerted a strong influence among the students. Furthermore, he soon gained recognition in Japan as a Reformed theologian and Calvin scholar. The Hesselinks served at the seminary until 1972, at which time they returned to America, where John became president of Western Theological Seminary.

Meanwhile, the Moores' retirement was approaching, and the future leadership of the Shinseikan was under consideration. Moore wanted Bruggers to move to Fukuoka to take over the role of manager, but Bruggers declined Moore's offer, believing that the Shinseikan Board of Trustees, made up mostly of Japanese church leaders, should make such a decision. However, the Bruggers family, which had been happily engaged in life and work in Kagoshima, acquiesced when the Japanese leaders decided that Glenn was needed at the Shinseikan. The Bruggers family moved to Fukuoka in the summer of 1961.

The Shinseikan continued its programs of evangelism through radio, literature, a Christian loan library, and a Christian book store. During his thirteen-year tenure as manager of the Shinseikan, Bruggers worked assiduously to transform it from a missionary-centered project into a ministry of the Japanese church, and he gently prodded Japanese colleagues to assume responsibilities and to decide what roles they wished missionaries to play. He also continued a weekly ministry among death-row prisoners that Moore had initiated and regularly taught a Bible class at the Bruggers home for people related to Kyushu University. During the latter part of their work in Fukuoka, Glenn was asked to assume responsibility for a *dendosho* (Japanese preaching place not yet organized as a church). Phyllis, who had home-schooled her children in Kagoshima, taught in a small school organized in Fukuoka to provide education in English for her own and other missionary children. She later taught English at a local mission school for Japanese girls.

The Norden family served in district evangelism centered in Kurume until the time of their second furlough in 1964. Russell Norden was asked by the district church leaders to take responsibility as pastor of one of the congregations, the Setaka Church, in which capacity he served for more than eight years. He also visited patients at a tuberculosis sanitarium regularly, and the Nordens both taught numerous Bible and English classes at the several churches or at their home in Kurume. In 1965 the Norden family moved to Yokohama, where Russell had been invited to serve as chaplain and professor of Bible and English literature at the newly formed four-year college of Ferris Girls' School, and Eleanore began part-time teaching in Ferris High School as family responsibilities permitted.

## The Challenge and Limits of Ecumenical Cooperation

John de Maagd lived in Yokohama and was closely associated with the establishment of the work of the Interboard Committee and its offices and structures at its Japan headquarters in Tokyo. He had also become the Reformed Church's field representative, and thus was a member of the Field Committee and on the Council of Cooperation.

Under the Interboard structures, the role of the field representative was to carry on correspondence with the board secretaries and represent the mission board on the field. Technically, he did not represent the missionaries in those roles, although the Reformed Church field representative met periodically in an unofficial capacity with two or three other Reformed Church missionaries who functioned as advisors and also sent out information in the form of a circular letter to the other missionaries. De Maagd and the board secretaries he represented (first Shafer, then Bovenkerk) had been prewar missionaries. They all strongly advocated the cooperative approach through the Interboard Committee and ostensibly showed deference to the Japanese church leaders. However, in actual practice they and the missionaries serving as Interboard Committee office staff in Tokyo wielded considerable power and influence.

Boude Moore, having returned to Kyushu, where he had served before the war, reestablished relationships with key older church leaders in the Kyodan's Kyushu Kyoku and worked with them to develop a vision and plan of evangelism for the region. Moore, who was not only a returning prewar missionary who had had Japanese pastors working under him but also a former American army officer who had carried administrative responsibility during the occupation of Japan, tended to take strong leadership. The synod in Kyushu had welcomed the return of evangelistic missionaries (the Moores) to work cooperatively with them, as well as new missionary personnel. Bill and Bonnie Sheets had gone to Kyushu for audiovisual work, and Sue Brink had entered district evangelism at Kumamoto. However, the assignment process for the four new ordained missionaries and their families began to bring out the issues involved in actually functioning ecumenically and in a changed missionary role. Moore had no hesitation about working ecumenically, but at the same time, since other Interboard denominations were sending their evangelistic missionaries exclusively to the areas where they had worked before the war, he strongly advocated the assignment of Reformed Church evangelistic appointees to Kyushu.

Henry Bovenkerk had returned to Japan as one of the Committee of Six American church representatives sent to reestablish relations with Japanese Christians in 1946-47. He subsequently served from 1947 to 1952 as executive secretary in New York for the Interboard Committee and worked closely with Luman Shafer of the Reformed mission board. These two were key architects of the Interboard Committee and strongly advocated its ideals. Bovenkerk became Reformed Church board treasurer in 1952 and succeeded Shafer as the board's secretary for

Japan in 1955. Tension between the prewar men regarding assignment of missionaries—between Moore on the one hand and De Maagd, Shafer, and Bovenkerk on the other—was inevitable. Several examples exemplify the tensions.

During De Maagd's furlough in 1953-54, Kleinjans, as interim field representative, wrote a letter to the board secretary, and Shafer reported Kleinjans's question and his own response.

> Is it the Board's thought that all of our evangelistic missionaries go to our former field in Kyushu, or should they be sent anywhere? The Secretary answered in his December 11th letter that the place of greatest need and greatest opportunity for service should be given precedence; that we are members of a larger group and while it was necessary to keep our Reformed Church fellowship, it did not seem necessary to have us all in one geographical area to maintain fellowship.[23]

Shafer was not only leery of guidance by Moore regarding the assignments of the new recruits, but he was also suspicious even of the motives of the Reformed Church missionaries on the field, when they wanted to meet for fellowship. Shafer tried to restrict the gathering of twenty or more Reformed Church missionaries as a group to a few hours once a year at the time of the annual conference for all 350-400 missionaries cooperating with the Kyodan. He expressed his concern about a planned fellowship meeting in the summer of 1954 for all the Reformed Church missionaries in Japan, and his words reveal his irritation at Moore's advocacy for Kyushu.

> The IBC Manual allows for one meeting a year for fellowship and prayer on the part of any group of missionaries, and I take it that is what you are planning at Nojiri. At the same time, if a meeting is held where you organize and constitute yourselves as advisors to the field representative on location of missionaries and other policies that you think ought to be followed, that is another matter. The location of missionaries, it would seem to me, would need to be considered in the larger context of the whole field and not in the context of one small group....I would like to see the Council of Cooperation challenge our young people with various fields where there is opportunity for work, give them an opportunity to see those fields and then, after that has been done, let the matter

---

23    Agenda for the meeting of the Japan Committee of the Board of Feb. 1954.

of location be discussed in the group if it is necessary when the Japanese committee has made representations on the matter. But let us not go ahead in our eagerness and make our own decisions and present them to the Japanese as something that we think would be well to do....We must not under any guise revive the old mission group where we meet in an enclave and decide our matters apart from Japanese advice and contemplation.[24]

All the Reformed Church missionaries did in fact gather for an overnight fellowship meeting that took place in late summer, 1954.

As it turned out, of the four young families recently appointed for evangelistic work, after language study the Bruggers (1953), Norden (1954), and Hesselink (1955) families all accepted appointments in Kyushu. Only the Tanis family (1955) accepted an assignment elsewhere. They served three years in Atsugi in Kanagawa Prefecture and did not return to Japan after their furlough. Ecumenical cooperation was not an issue for the missionaries. Moore and the other Reformed Church missionaries who began postwar evangelistic work in Kyushu did not limit their work to relations with the former congregations of the Church of Christ in Japan with which the Reformed Church Japan Mission had worked before the war, but were gladly cooperating with the synod in Kyushu of the Kyodan. Nevertheless, Moore's actions in encouraging the young Reformed Church missionaries to accept assignments in Kyushu was interpreted as working counter to the ecumenical principles of the Interboard Committee. Clearly De Maagd and Moore, the two prewar ordained missionaries, did not always see eye to eye, and not only De Maagd but also Shafer and Bovenkerk frowned on Moore's advocacy for Kyushu.

The idealism of the cooperative structures set in motion by the Interboard Committee notwithstanding, several realities soon became apparent. Japanese church leaders for the most part appreciated having missionaries once again cooperate with them in their overwhelming task of evangelizing the Japanese people, but they did not feel qualified to and were not interested in making many of the decisions regarding the missionaries' maintenance and assignments. Van Wyk observed, "Of course, it is the Church, not the missionaries, which does the appointing, but they won't touch it until after missionary politics have been satisfied."[25] Accordingly, it was the board secretary, his field

---

[24]   LJS to BCM and Everett Kleinjans, May 4, 1954.
[25]   GJV to John Fairfield, Dec. 30, 1961.

representative, and the Interboard Committee office bureaucracy in New York and Tokyo that actually controlled the cooperative relationship with the Japanese church and mission schools. At the same time, it was only at the local level that meaningful cooperation between missionaries and their Japanese colleagues could be developed and lived out.

Another reality was that the new missionaries of the other denominations related to the Interboard Committee were also being guided into assignments at locations where their missions had worked before the war. Furthermore, the missionaries of the other boards affiliated with the Interboard Committee did not hesitate to gather for denominational group fellowship and maintained their denominational identities. Suspicions of the board secretary to the contrary, the Reformed Church missionaries in Japan all served gladly within the Japanese United Church, and they understood the value of cooperation through the Interboard Committee. At the same time, most of them saw value and validity in forming a Reformed Church missionary group, which could provide a kind of pastoral care, i.e., a shared concern that each Reformed Church missionary be placed in an appropriate assignment and experience mutual encouragement. The problem was exacerbated by the Interboard Committee principle by which the field representative was designated as the representative in Japan of the mission board and not of the missionaries on the field.

Administration without missionary participation (except for the field representative) not only continued but became more extensive after Bovenkerk became the board's Japan secretary in 1955. Missionary frustration blossomed into criticism of the secretary and board at the furloughing missionary conference in the summer of 1958. Bovenkerk reported to missionaries on the field, "One of the important issues is, in areas where a national church has been established can RCA missionaries meet to give group judgments to the Board?"[26] At a follow-up meeting on August 28, 1958, Mrs. Wagner, chair of the board's Japan Committee, Bovenkerk, and three furloughing missionaries (G. Bruggers, G. VanWyk, and I. J. Hesselink) met to review the issues raised, and each participant wrote a statement after this discussion. In effect, these three young missionaries challenged the high-handed manner in which the board secretary functioned. Regarding the statements of the several participants, Bovenkerk conceded, "These papers recognize the necessity of not interfering with the integrity of the Church of Christ but seek some avenues of group expression as Reformed Church missionaries."[27]

[26]   HGB to RCA Missionaries in Japan, Oct. 27, 1958.
[27]   BFM Meeting, Japan Agenda, Feb. 11-13, 1959.

At the Reformed Church mission board meeting in May of 1959, the Japan Committee raised the question, "Is it possible for RCA missionaries in Japan to have a group consultative voice in the issues faced by the Church of Christ in Japan and the Reformed Church in a church to church relationship as it now functions through the Interboard Committee?" The secretary had not prepared any suggested action, and, at the board's subsequent meeting, it did not even take up the issue, saying that its position had already been made clear in paragraph 19 of the revised document titled, "The Role and Relationships of the Missionary."[28] In any case, the missionaries had not asked for a "group consultative voice," but only for the right to gather freely to share information, fellowship, and mutual encouragement. Clearly, an element of mistrust had developed in the relationship between the board's secretary and the missionaries on the field.

Meanwhile, in 1954, as the Japanese Protestant movement approached its centennial celebration in 1959, the Kyodan launched a five-year evangelism plan. Japan's metropolitan areas, such as Tokyo/Yokohama and Osaka/Kobe, had a number of larger, more prosperous churches well positioned to carry out such a plan in their regions. The outlying regions, with large unreached populations, were less well situated to sustain an aggressive evangelism campaign on their own. The Kyodan appealed for the appointment of more evangelistic missionaries.

On the regional level, Japanese church leaders on the island of Kyushu hoped to initiate a major expansion of evangelistic outreach among the island's ten million inhabitants. There were at least eighteen cities of more than thirty thousand people on the island with no Christian church at all. Most of the 122 Kyodan congregations on the island were small, and although 106 of them were officially self-supporting, their pastors' salaries averaged less than thirty dollars per month. Nevertheless, these ministers and evangelists were going out on foot, by bicycle, or on public transportation to an additional one hundred preaching places.

At the 1957 annual meeting of the Kyushu Synod of the Kyodan, the leaders advanced a plan for evangelistic outreach in which they hoped to enlist the cooperation of additional ordained missionaries. The plan, which Moore had no doubt played a part in developing, envisaged capitalizing on evangelistic and church extension opportunities on the island of Kyushu. First, the plan would place ordained missionaries in

28    HGB to RCA Missionaries in Japan, May 20, 1959.

Saga, Miyazaki, Nagasaki, Oita, and North Kyushu, supplied with funds to carry on extension work, then it would eventually place resident ordained missionaries in all eighteen of the cities that were without established churches. Hoping within ten years to have thirty ordained missionaries cooperating with them, Kyushu Synod pleaded for these evangelistic missionary reinforcements.[29] Application was made by the synod to the Council of Cooperation for these assignments, with the hope that not only the Reformed Church but also the boards of other denominations affiliated with the Interboard Committee would send evangelistic missionaries to Kyushu.

The De Maagds left Japan for a furlough in the spring of 1959. Gordon Van Wyk had been chosen to serve as the next field representative, but since he would not return to Japan from furlough until late summer, Ted Flaherty served as interim field representative. Flaherty's correspondence indicates the ongoing pattern of board secretary and field representative paying lip service to allowing the Japanese church to decide matters related to the assignments of the missionaries while in fact manipulating outcomes, as well as the animosity toward Moore and his advocacy for Reformed Church evangelistic work in Kyushu.

In a letter to the other Reformed Church missionaries in Japan, Flaherty told of the arrival of short-term appointee Carroll de Forest and remarked, "Mention has been made to him that previous short termers have driven an audio-visual truck in Fukuoka and environs. We do not know whether this audio-visual service of the Shinseikan can be renewed, and since we are quite concerned that Carroll de Forest has a pleasant and successful experience as a short-term missionary in Japan we urge that the Council of Cooperation give considerable attention to his assignment."[30] And in a letter to Bovenkerk, Flaherty stated, "In a letter I have just addressed to John de Maagd, I discussed the new appointees, and especially our mutual concern that Mr. de Forest be placed where he can confront the real challenge of the cooperative work here in Japan. I'm sure we are all three agreed on what the problem is; I'm merely seeking advice from John and you on the wisest and most tactful way to work it out."[31]

In reporting to Bovenkerk concerning a Field Committee meeting (not the Council of Cooperation, which would have included the Japanese), Flaherty wrote, "We discussed Mr. de Forest's assignment at

---

29   "The United Church of Japan Pleads For More Evangelistic Missionaries," *Church Herald*, Jan. 17, 1958.

30   Theodore E. Flaherty to R.C.A. Friends, June 3, 1959.

31   TEF to HGB, May 27, 1959.

great length. Most of the members agreed that if it is your hope and the hope of the R.C.A. Board that Carroll get the best possible impression of the cooperative work here in Japan, that Fukuoka is <u>not</u> the place to recommend that the C.O.C. send him! They thought the suggestion (of yours) that he be sent to Rakuno Dairy College is a good one."[32]

Since neither the church leaders nor the school's administrators on the northern island of Hokkaido had requested such a missionary assignment, a member of the Tokyo Interboard office staff, Frank Carey, agreed to write to ask that such a position be arranged. This was a deliberate ploy to keep De Forest from being assigned to Kyushu. A letter a month later to Van Wyk, soon to be the field representative, suggests a certain deviousness on Bovenkerk's part. He wrote, "No decision has been made on the appointment of Carroll de Forest. It now looks as though the Council of Cooperation is likely to make a decision between two possibilities: assignment to the audio-visual service at Fukuoka, assignment to agricultural work in Hokkaido in connection with the Rakuno Dairy College. This is all I know at the present time."[33] Bovenkerk already knew that De Forest's assignment to Hokkaido was virtually assured by Flaherty's actions on behalf of Bovenkerk at the Field Committee meeting.

With some reluctance, because of the time-consuming nature of the role, Gordon Van Wyk took over responsibility as Reformed Church field representative in September of 1959. Van Wyk fulfilled his role as the board's correspondent and representative on the field, but at the same time he consistently advocated for the validity of mutual support and interpersonal communications among the Reformed Church missionaries in Japan. In his words, "I'm all for cooperation, but the cooperative principle must never lose sight of the danger that everybody's business easily becomes nobody's business—hence my constantly harping on the legitimacy of the platoon identity within the larger fellowship of 400 missionaries."[34]

During the next several years, Van Wyk resisted inappropriate interference in the missionary assignment process on the field by the board secretary or anyone else. Negotiations for subsequent Reformed Church missionary assignments were handled with openness and honesty, and with concern that each missionary find a niche where his or her calling might be fulfilled. During the two years of language study,

[32]   TEF to HGB, June 5, 1959.
[33]   HGB to GJV, July 10, 1959.
[34]   GJV to JJT, May 3, 1962.

new career people were interviewed, provided opportunites to explore possible fields of service and consider the requests for missionaries from Japanese church leaders, and given adequate time to come to a decision. Regarding his role in the assignment of missionaries, Van Wyk, with typical clarity, famously said, "My operating principle which I've announced to all is that I'll fight anyone who says they must go somewhere and I'll fight anyone who says they can't go somewhere."[35]

The tendency of the board secretary in America not only to attempt to manipulate the assignments of the missionaries within Japan but also to dictate regarding their relationships was interpreted by the missionaries on the field as both a lack of trust in the missionaries and an inadequate understanding of their situation. In the perhaps unavoidable tension between the ideal and the real, the missionaries did get a hearing, and positive results were realized. The ordained evangelistic missionaries working in Kyushu in 1959 (Moore, Bruggers, and Norden), out of a desire for better understanding and as an outgrowth of discussions in the Kyushu Cooperative Evangelism Committee, prepared a paper on the missionary evangelist entitled, "The Role of the Missionary in Japan."

A draft of this twenty-page paper was sent March 1, 1960, to each of the missionaries in Japan at the time. When the annual Kyodan-Related Missionary Conference met at the end of March, under Van Wyk's leadership the Reformed Church missionaries gathered at a hotel the day before the conference and spent most of twenty-four hours in study, discussion, and reworking of the paper. The group of about twenty missionaries endorsed the principles enunciated in the amended paper and recommended that it be sent to the board for its information and consideration. This document was also enthusiastically endorsed by the present and two former moderators of the Kyodan.[36] After stating basic points of mission theology and a careful analysis of some unique challenges of mission in Japan, the paper draws out a number of conclusions, including the following:

> Once the primacy of the missionary task of the Church is accepted, there will be little cause for concern in the relations between nationals and the missionary, methods, processes and other aspects of the implementation of missionary work. There may be personality clashes on occasion. The mission of the Church may be misinterpreted by those outside of the Church. However, the

[35]    GJV to Mrs. Howard Schade, July 26, 1961.
[36]    The Reverends Shirai Keikichi, Muto Takeshi, and Kozaki Michio.

Church as such will move on with the task in great cooperation and expectation.

This seems very evident from the situation in Japan where the majority of Church leaders continually repudiate the idea that it would be more effective for the American Church to send money instead of missionaries. Continually they ask for more missionaries. They find it hard to understand why the need for missionaries is continually debated by both missionaries and the various sending Boards. Their quiet, continued requests exemplify a very high degree of patience and vision.

But this leads directly into another problem. If the Church in Japan is considered to be the body to take the lead in making plans, and if the missionaries are to work under and through this Church, why are its requests repeatedly questioned or even side-tracked? The task of mission in Japan is beyond the capacity of the Church, both in means and personnel. This is through no fault of its own. The Church in Japan feels led to ask the Church abroad for missionaries in order to be able to get on with the task. The reason for these requests is the fact that God has opened doors to all who feel called of Him to do mission work in Japan.

At this, the beginning of the second century of modern Christian work in Japan, a moratorium should be called on such useless questioning of the need for missionaries. A firm commitment to get on with the task should come to the fore. Similarly, when a missionary has made his adjustment with the Church at the working level, his every move should not be held in question. He should receive the backing of his sending Board the same as he receives the backing of the Church in Japan. If the policies determined in America are contrary to and out of step with the working policies hammered out through the sweat and tears of actual field experience, the missionary will be placed in an impossible situation. If he makes the necessary adjustments to the local situation which permit him to carry on evangelism in a manner in keeping with the expressed needs of the Church in Japan and in keeping with his vows of ordination, he will find himself at variance with policy declared in America. If he follows the policies decided in America, his position on the field will become untenable.

It seems logical to feel that the policy which should be followed is the time-proven policy of appointing men to do missionary work in whom the confidence of the Board, as representing the Church, can rest. For such a missionary, a rigid set of do's and don'ts will not be necessary. Ample freedom will be granted so that adjustments on the field can be made in order to facilitate the ongoing work of the Kingdom. Men and women who do not warrant such confidence should not be appointed to missionary service.[37]

The efforts of Van Wyk and the other missionaries evidently were beneficial. Bovenkerk responded positively to the paper, saying, "The paper on evangelism prepared by B. C. Moore and his colleagues is very well written and I have discovered that it contains many trenchant quotable paragraphs."[38] In regard to Reformed Church missionaries meeting together, which Van Wyk had strongly advocated, Bovenkerk wrote, "I am sure that the Board will consent to meet the cost of one Fellowship Meeting annually, such as you had earlier this year."[39] In any case, in November of 1960, Bovenkerk unexpectedly resigned from his position as executive secretary of the Board of World Missions, effective January 15, 1961.

During the next thirteen years, several individuals served as the board's Japan secretary. The first (1961-1968) was the Reverend Dr. James J. Thomas, who made a sincere effort at communication, despite being hampered by the fact that he had not had any firsthand experience of life and work in the complex and challenging missionary situation in Japan. Under Van Wyk's leadership on the field, and with mission board approval, communication and understanding between board staff and missionaries, as well as among the Reformed Church missionaries, was enhanced.

A Reformed Church Fellowship, with annual overnight gatherings, was officially sanctioned. Furthermore, formation of an Advisory Council and Business Committee on the field was officially approved and activated. It consisted of four people (some from Tokyo/Yokohama, as in the past with informal advisors, but at least one from Kyushu), who were to meet periodically with the field representative to discuss matters of particular concern to Reformed Church missionaries, and news of the meetings was shared regularly with all those related to the Reformed Church. The formation of the fellowship and of the committee, and the resultant improved communication, provided a firm basis for a working-sharing relationship within Japan, and of one

---

[37]    "The Role of the Missionary in Japan," March 31, 1960.
[38]    HGB to RCA Missionaries in Japan, July 22, 1960.
[39]    HGB to GJV, July 22, 1960.

not of opposing factions, i.e., New York vs. the missionary group.[40] As a further result, the Reformed Church field representative in Japan became not only the board secretary's representative but also the representative of the missionaries on the field.

The Reformed Church's mission board and staff on the one hand and missionaries on the field on the other all remained committed to the principle of cooperating in the Japanese Christian movement by working along with the boards and missionaries of other North American denominations through the Interboard Committee. And it gradually became clear that, for missionaries on the field, what mattered more than the denominational affiliation of missionary colleagues was their commitment to the basics of evangelical faith. However, there were also drawbacks to this cooperative arrangement. Working cooperatively meant endless hours spent in committees, and some Interboard missionaries became professional office staff and formed a kind of Tokyo bureaucracy. Although cooperation took place in many realms, some of the policies of the several mission boards were never able to be reconciled. At the same time, while the Interboard Committee provided a cooperative, joint approach to a united Japanese church by a group of North American denominations and eliminated some of the paternalism of the prewar Japan missions, it continued to be basically mission as a one-way street, from North American denominations to the Japanese church and mission schools.

## The Second Century of the Protestant Christian Movement in Japan

The year 1959 marked the one hundredth anniversary of the beginning of Protestant missionary activity in Japan. Japanese Christians marked the occasion with large celebrations in Tokyo and other cities around Japan during the first week in November. In Tokyo, ten thousand Christians gathered to worship and celebrate and to pledge themselves to ongoing witness and service. Representatives of the world church, such as the Reverend Dr. Willem A. Visser 't Hooft, secretary general of the World Council of Churches, and Dutch theologian and missiologist Dr. Hendrik Kraemer, came to offer their congratulations and present special lectures.

During the fourteen years since the end of World War II, Japan had passed through a period of foreign occupation and gradual recovery from the devastation of the war. At first, amid the shock of

---

[40]    JJT to GJV, June 6, 1962.

defeat and loss of national identity, a sense of relief under a relatively benevolent foreign occupation, and the generosity of Americans in rehabilitating Japan, the Christian movement had enjoyed a period of openness, the so-called "Christian Boom." While the almost euphoric interest waned in about seven years, many churches had been rebuilt and rejuvenated, numerous new churches had been started, and in the late 1950s perhaps as many as 70 percent of the church members were young people. The Kyodan had grown to include 1,548 churches and preaching stations, 2,621 pastors and evangelists, and 175,500 believers. Japan's population had grown to more than ninety million. While the percentage of Christians remained small, the foundations had been laid and the Japanese church's future appeared bright.

On the other hand, it had become clear once again that the rapid evangelization of all of Japan would not occur. At the beginning of the 1960s, Japan entered a stage of unprecedented rapid economic and social change. Industrialization on a scale not seen before was leading to rapid urbanization, as many of the younger generation left the countryside for employment opportunities or higher education. Traditional three-generation households were being replaced by nuclear families, who often lived in cramped apartments in the cities. Personal values were becoming increasingly materialistic and hedonistic. A new generation of Japanese clergymen, many of whom had been converted during the "Christian boom," had emerged from the theological seminaries, and these young men and women were realistically facing the challenge of building up and extending the church in Japan's rapidly changing society, with its unique religious environment.

A Reformed Church mission board deputation to Japan presented a report on Japanese religious life at the end of the 1950s as in general taking three forms.

> First, there is a continuation of the traditional forms of Buddhism and Sect Shinto in the small towns and villages; in general the Shinto shrines and Buddhist temples in the villages were not destroyed during the war by bombing and village life was not as deeply affected by the defeat as urban life was, and therefore, village thought and religion continue somewhat along the traditional patterns and were not fundamentally affected. The second form of religious life in Japan is a general renunciation of all traditional forms of religion and the assumption of the *modern mind* on the part of the intellectual and successful business leadership in the country. These who form the leadership of the aggressive *New Japan* may formally conform to some of the

outward aspects of traditional religion but their faith is in science as the solution to the human problem. They are devotees of scientism and humanism as the religions which offer the greatest promise for the future and are intellectually defensible. The third element in the religious life of the country are the followers of the *New sects* who have lost their confidence in the traditional religion and who by virtue of illness, economic adversity or for some other reason cannot place their confidence in the human efforts, such as the humanist does, but respond to the newer religions which are for the most part a mixture of Christianity, Buddhism and Shintoism. This is the segment of society that places its trust in the fast growing sects.[41]

Suzuki Yoshi, of the Tokyo Woman's Christian College, noted that the rapid growth of the syncretistic new religious sects might give the impression that religion held an important place among Japanese people. However, these religions and their adherents focused on physical and material blessings. Such sects were often described as *go-riyaku shukyo*, i.e., benefit religions, by many thinking Japanese. Suzuki stated, "Few religious bodies are concerned with the human soul in the correct sense. Those who belong to the intelligentsia are liable to consider religion as no more than superstition; they have a general inclination to despise and ignore any religion whatsoever. Under such circumstances the difficulties of spreading Christianity are beyond imagination."[42]

The "Christian boom" was over, and Japan's complex historic resistance to Christianity had once again asserted itself. Such a challenging environment for evangelism and church growth notwithstanding, Japanese Christians and their leaders remained positive. Furthermore, regarding the continuing participation of missionaries in the church's evangelistic task, they were unequivocal. Through the Council of Cooperation, the church especially requested the appointment of ordained missionaries for service in district evangelism.

### Enlargement of the Evangelistic Missionary Force

The last short-term Reformed Church missionary teacher was appointed in 1962. Given the growing financial independence of the mission schools, it had become difficult to justify using limited mission

---

[41]  Board for the Christian World Mission Report to the General Synod of the Reformed Church in America, 1960, 20-21.

[42]  Suzuki Yoshi, "Christian Students in Japan," *Church Herald*, Feb. 28, 1958, 5.

resources to send board-supported missionaries primarily to teach English. However, the Reformed Church did endeavor to respond to requests from the church in Japan for career missionaries, sending six new families for evangelistic work between 1959 and 1963. As a result, the number of board-appointed Reformed missionaries reached a post-war peak of thirty-six in 1964 and averaged thirty throughout the 1960s. Under the guidance of the Reformed Church field representative, already during the period of language study of the several newcomers efforts were made to acquaint them with opportunities for moving toward their future placements in appropriate assignments.

The Reverend Gordon and Evon Laman arrived in Japan in August of 1959, and they were soon followed in February of 1960 by the Reverend Rudolf and Trina Kuyten. During their period of language study in Tokyo, Van Wyk facilitated the objective consideration of possible work assignments by the new families. Accordingly, toward the end of their first year of language study, the Lamans were presented with the many aspects of evangelistic work. Various possible assignments were suggested, among which were spots in Kyushu. Van Wyk, with reference to past discord regarding assignments, commented, "I hope the day is near when we all will be able to discuss the claims of Kyushu more objectively."[43] In turn, the Kuytens, who had expressed interest in urban ministry, were given ample opportunity to explore and consider where best to implement their calling and gifts.

During the summer vacation of language school in July of 1960, the Lamans and Kuytens traveled together by overnight train to Kyushu, where they had accepted the invitation of the Shinseikan to spend a month doing audiovisual evangelism. Despite limited language skills after less than a year in Japan, the two couples traveled throughout all seven prefectures on the island in the old Dodge panel truck, conducting film evangelism meetings in twenty-one different churches. It proved to be not only an opportunity for service but also an excellent introduction to district evangelism in general and the Kyushu field in particular. Subsequently the Lamans and Kuytens spent the month of August together on a vacation camping trip on Japan's northern island of Hokkaido, and in the process also gained some acquaintance with that field.

Following two years of language study, the Lamans responded to an invitation to work in Kyushu and were assigned to district evangelism centered in Saga. Laman cooperated with four Japanese pastors in the

---

[43]     GJV to HGB, Apr. 30, 1960.

The old Dodge panel truck used by the Lamans and Kuytens in
1960 to visit twenty-one churches in Kyushu to conduct
film evangelism meetings. L-r: Anna Moore, Evon Laman,
Trina Kuyten, Rudy Kuyten.

evangelistic work of the six small churches in Saga Prefecture, initially focusing on itinerant preaching and English Bible classes. Feeling that, at least in Saga, English Bible classes were not a very effective means of outreach, in addition to his itinerant preaching and pastoral care at churches without a pastor, Laman sought other means to reach out to people outside the churches. He experimented with ads in local newspapers and singing in solo gospel concerts in churches and public halls.

In partnership with the Japanese pastors of the district, he developed a local media evangelism project, beginning in 1966. For outreach they used films, concerts, literature, and, three times per week, a local radio program aimed at students. A Saga Mass Media Evangelism office was set up, using the name *Yoake* ("Daybreak"). A logo not immediately recognizable as Christian was used on all mail and literature, in order to provide anonymity for seekers concerned about the prevailing anti-Christian prejudice of relatives and neighbors. During the six years of this outreach project, more than 350,000 evangelistic leaflets and 35,000 evangelism newspapers were distributed, and 4,000 New Testaments were sent to those who requested them. Follow-up of this seed-sowing ministry was carried out through literature and a Bible correspondence course designed for seekers.

Laman also served as a chaplain at a Christian home for cognitively disabled young adults. While living in Saga, Evon Laman provided an English education for their children early each morning before sending them off to Japanese school. In addition to family responsibilities, she joined a woman friend at Saga Church in organizing and leading a branch Sunday school.

The Kuytens considered a number of possibilities in Kyushu and elsewhere but ultimately requested and received assignment in 1962 to Japan's northernmost island of Hokkaido. The first Reformed Church missionary family to live and work on Japan's second largest island of Hokkaido, they settled in the city of Asahikawa as district missionaries. Working in cooperation with pastors and churches of that area, Kuyten traveled to the widely scattered churches, visited isolated Christians, and considered the evangelistic needs and opportunities in the region. During their second term, in addition to preaching and teaching in the churches of the district, the Kuytens pioneered methods of evangelistic outreach to young working adults in the urban center of the city of Asahikawa who had no relation to the churches.

With a koinonia ("fellowship") group as a nucleus, they organized bold outreach projects in the city (for example, a Christian movie at a public theater and a folk music concert) and eventually, in December of 1966, established a gathering place, called "The Room," or also the Koinoinia Center, located on the second floor of a business building in the entertainment district in the center of the large city of Asahikawa. An attractive place, it was decorated with Rudy's art work.[44] Furnished with a counter and comfortable chairs, this "upper room" became a place where young working people or students could gather to eat lunch, read, listen to music, work on hobbies, drink tea or coffee, or just talk, and feel at home. It was also a place of informal witness, Bible study classes, and Koinonia meetings, a new approach for reaching young people with the gospel.

[44]    Rudy Kuyten, the son of a Dutch painter and an artist himself, became a wood carver through an interesting encounter with an *Ainu* (aboriginal Japanese) carver. On an evangelistic tour to the man's village of Akan, Kuyten asked the man to carve a head of Christ. When the carver hesitated, asking if Rudy had a photograph of Christ and indicating he didn't know what Christ would look like, Rudy gave him a Gospel of John. On a return trip months later, when Rudy asked again about it, the man picked up a chisel, thrust it into Rudy's hand and said the equivalent of "man, do it yourself." Thus began a unique dimension of the Kuyten ministry, as Rudy applied his artistic gifts to the medium of wood carving. In subsequent years, he gathered logs or panels from a variety of species of trees wherever he traveled, and each piece yielded itself in its own special form to his chisel, mallet, and stain, expressing themes such as invitation, comfort, compassion, trust, and new life.

Agatha (Gae) Tigelaar was appointed in 1962, the first Reformed Church missionary sent to Japan as a Christian social worker. Following language study, Tigalaar served one year at the Hiroshima Christian Social Center as interim director during the furlough of the Thompsons, who were Methodist missionaries. Subsequently, Tigelaar was assigned to serve at the Nagasaki Christian Yuaikan, a Christian community center, where she was active in group work and became administrative assistant to the director and then director of the center. These two Christian social work centers had been established by Methodist missionaries after World War II in the cities devastated by the atomic bombs, and they were associated with the Kyodan. After her fruitful work at Hiroshima and Nagasaki, Tigelaar was granted a leave of absence for graduate study, after which she hoped to return to Japan. She completed her two-year program of study at Wayne State University but unfortunately, due to ill health, was unable to return to Japan and died a premature death of cancer.

In 1963, once again the Reformed Church through its Board of World Missions acted decisively to respond to the challenge in Japan. In its report to General Synod in 1963, the Board of World Missions reported,

> A recent urgent request from the United Church of Christ in Japan asks for fifteen missionary couples to do general evangelism in cooperation with existing churches and for twelve missionary couples to do pioneer evangelism in areas where no church exists. The question is sometimes asked, "In a highly developed nation such as Japan, with a mature, stable Church, are mission funds and missionaries from abroad necessary?" The request from the United Church of Christ in Japan gives a clear and concise answer. But even clearer are the facts. Christians in Japan are a small minority—700,000 in a country of 94,000,000 people. For every Christian there are nearly 200 non-Christians. How enormous is the task for this small number to attempt to make known to all the Good News![45]

The Reformed Church made a sincere effort to respond to this need and request. In 1963 four more new missionary couples for evangelistic work were sent to Japan: the Reverend Thomas J. and Barbara Harris, the Reverend George and W. Joyce Magee, the Reverend William M. and Sarah Unzicker, and the Reverend John E. and Helene Zwyghuizen.

---

[45]    Board of World Missions Report, 1963, 41.

Gathering in 1963 of many of the Japan missionaries during a
    field visit of the Reformed Church's stated clerk, Marion de
    Velder, and mission board secretary, James Thomas.
Front row (l-r): Helen Zander, Joyce Magee with Martha,
    Suzanne Brink, De Velder, Thomas, Judson Hesselink,
    Rudy and Trina Kuyten with Dan;
second row: James Rozeboom, Alice Elzinga, Helen Post,
    Belle Bogard; third row: Barbara Bosch, Beth Bonnema,
    Eileen Hendriks,  Helene Zwyghuizen with Ardeth, Ronald
    Korver;
back row: George Magee, Gordon and Bertha VanWyk,
    Russell Norden, John Zwyghuizen, unknown, Ruby Korver
    with Kathy, John and Etta Hesselink, Evon and Gordon
    Laman with Tim.

During their period of language study in Tokyo or Yokohama, the new
couples were given opportunities to explore the possibilities for their
future assignments and invited to choose from among the priority posts
approved by the Council of Cooperation. They eventually proceeded to
their several assignments in the spring and summer of 1965.

The Zwyghuizen family moved to Japan's southwestern island of
Kyushu, to take up work in Tsuyazaki in Fukuoka Prefecture, about an
hour away from the large city of Fukuoka. They were expected to partner
with Japanese church leaders in the planning and development of a
rural evangelism center, with lay training institutes for strengthening
rural churches. Numerous house meetings were conducted in rural
farming villages. Meanwhile, in the area between Fukuoka and
Tsuyazaki, large tracts of farm land were being transformed into new
residential neighborhoods with hundreds of apartment buildings and
small homes, a fresh evangelistic opportunity. Besides his work of
preaching and teaching Bible classes in the churches and the home-
based evangelistic meetings in the district, Zwyghuizen partnered with

Pastor Moriwake of Tsuyazaki Church in beginning a preaching station in the new housing development. Helene shared the Christian education work of the local church and Christian kindergarten. After eight years of evangelistic work centered in Tsuyazaki, the Zwyghuizens returned to America for urgent medical care for their youngest daughter, who was ill with acute leukemia. The child was miraculously spared, but circumstances did not permit the family's return to Japan.

The Magee family accepted assignment to Tomakomai, an industrial and port city on the southern coast of Japan's northern island of Hokkaido. They were assigned to evangelistic work in and around this lumbering, pulp, and paper manufacture area. There were eight partner churches, most of them small and scattered throughout the large district, and there was also a need to establish work in towns without any church. The Magees settled in for the long term.

The Harris family moved to Japan's second largest city, Osaka, a center of industry and trade, where Tom's interest in occupational evangelism had led to his assignment to the Kansai Labor Evangelism Fellowship. However, despite continuing efforts, Tom found learning the Japanese language to the point of effective usage to be impossible and the language limitation prohibitive of full-time work in labor evangelism. While continuing an informal relationship to labor evangelism, he took an assignment to teach English and work with students at Kansei Gakuin University for the remainder of the Harrises' five-year term, and subsequently they returned to the United States to enter the pastorate.[46]

The Unzicker family chose to go to Otaru, a port city on the northwest coast of Hokkaido known for its extremely heavy snowfalls, which sometimes reached a depth of more than fifteen feet. There they began to serve in district evangelism among the eight congregations of Otaru and the surrounding towns. Their ministry was representative of the evangelistic missionaries who served faithfully and patiently, in difficult fields and sometimes among ineffective or unappreciative colleagues, to help continue the witness and sustain the small, struggling churches of Japan's outlying districts. Bill preached and taught English and Bible classes in the churches, working alongside Japanese pastors. Sarah worked with the women, as well as with the children and youth in the Christian education programs of the local churches.

Carroll de Forest, who completed his three-year term as a teacher at Rakuno Dairy College in Hokkaido in 1962, had returned to the

---

[46]    Ronald G. Korver to JJT, March 26, 1966; JJT to RGK, March 30 and 31, 1966.

United States to attend seminary. In 1966, the Reverend Carroll and Betty de Forest were appointed to Japan as evangelistic missionaries. Reflecting his love for marginalized people, after language study Carroll de Forest served on the staff of the Asian Rural Institute, a Japanese Christian ministry designed to train leaders for third-world countries. The De Forests returned to America in 1970 and subsequently served under the Reformed Church Board of Domestic Missions at Annville Institute and in the Reformed churches of Jackson County in Kentucky.

After almost ten years in Saga, the Lamans were invited to work with the churches of Nagasaki District and moved to Sasebo City. Laman was asked by the Japanese church leaders there to take responsibility for evangelistic outreach in the northern part of Nagasaki Prefecture and to serve as pastor of a preaching station on the off-shore island of Hirado. A church building was needed to advance the Hirado evangelistic work, and all the churches in Nagasaki District contributed to the project, making possible the building of a chapel. Gordon preached in Japanese at Hirado every Sunday, and Evon played the reed organ for services. The region had been one of the focal points of the persecution of the Christians in the seventeenth century, and deeply rooted anti-Christian sentiment still prevailed. Door-to-door literature distribution was carried out to twelve hundred homes monthly in an effort to witness and break down the prejudice. Evangelistic work in this very challenging setting led Laman to pursue research into the historical roots of Japanese resistance to Christianity.

Laman also continued to be responsible for the seed-sowing mass-media evangelism ministry begun earlier in Saga. In addition to literature distribution, a late-night disc-jockey format evangelistic radio broadcast was carried out, aimed at the teenagers of Saga and Nagasaki Prefectures. Funds were raised among the churches of Nagasaki District for the purchase of radio time. Soejima Akiko, a widow and member of Sasebo Church, worked part time in follow-up work for this outreach ministry. During the years of such seed-sowing evangelism in the region, thousands of Bibles and tens of thousands of evangelism-oriented newspapers were distributed.

The Kuyten family moved from Asahikawa to Sapporo, the largest city (more than one million people) and key urban center on the island of Hokkaido, in 1971. With a vision of reaching out to those living in the anonymity of a large urban setting who would have little inclination to relate to a church, they experimented with an outreach model not yet tested in Japan, coffee house evangelism. Acting upon experience gained in their efforts at the Koinonia Center in Asahikawa, with several

Japanese Christians as partners in the venture, the Kuytens opened a commercial coffee shop in downtown Sapporo on July 1, 1971. The shop was called the Good Hour, with the hope and prayer that many would come through having a good hour to their best hour, when they came to know and follow Christ. With good coffee and tea, homemade pie, and other light food offered, the shop soon became a commercial success, with about fifteen hundred patrons a month. More important, the coffee house ministry in that modern urban center proved to be an effective means of evangelism, as informal conversations often led to interest in a discussion group or a Bible study group. The goal was to give hope to the discouraged and introduce people to the Way.

This enlarged force of postwar missionaries encountered an increasingly difficult environment for evangelism. Japan, in the 1960s, included a confusing multiplicity of religions and cults; the tendency to a nominal and shallow, but nevertheless obligatory, connection to one's family's religion; and the prevailing assumption among educated Japanese that science relegates all religious belief to the level of superstition or wishful thinking on the part of the weak. The influence of the legacy of persecution of Christianity and the persistent tendency to view commitment to Christianity as aberrant behavior for a Japanese person continued to be encountered by missionaries and Japanese Christians alike. And more than ever before, as nationalism surged once again, a deep level of cultural sensitivity and assimilation into Japanese church and society became essential for missionaries. A statement at the 1964 Reformed Church General Synod recognized this requirement: "In our century the church has come to see that the proclamation of the Gospel by the missionary can best be done—or perhaps can only be done—within the context of the society to which the Word has been carried; that is, by someone who will identify with that society, will set himself within its context and relate fully to it and to particular members of it."[47] The level of sensitivity and commitment required by the situation soon became abundantly clear.

## Mission in a Distracted Environment

The 1960s were a time of social and political upheaval led by the younger generation not only in Western nations, but also in rapidly industrializing and economically developing Japan. An idealized form of Marxism, abetted by Marxist economic theory popular in some Japanese academic circles for decades, began to have political implications, even

[47]  BWMR, 1964, 41.

though neither Russian nor Chinese communism had been highly regarded. A student radical movement influenced by Marxist ideology became prominent in Japan already in 1960, when students rioted in opposition to renewal of Japan's security treaty with the United States. This movement gained momentum during the 1960s amid media coverage of segregation, racial discrimination, and the human rights movement in America, intensification of the cold war, and escalation of the Vietnam War. During that war, the United States used its military bases in Japan as staging areas, which was seen as inconsistent with the peace clause of the Japanese constitution.

Many Japanese Christians increasingly came to see themselves in the role of "watchmen" and as "the salt of the earth" in their society. Through small or informal groups, some Japanese Christians expressed their views publicly or took action on behalf of world peace, nuclear disarmament, opposition to the Mutual Security Treaty with the United States, preservation of the postwar national constitution with its prohibition of offensive military capability, opposition to moves by conservative political forces to restore state support of Shinto, opposition to the Japanese government's participation in ceremonies at Yasukuni Shrine where Japanese military war dead were "deified," and opposition to American military action in Vietnam.[48]

In 1966, during the celebration of the twenty-fifth anniversary of the founding of the United Church of Christ in Japan, the Reverend Suzuki Masahisa was elected moderator of the General Assembly. The theme of the assembly was Tomorrow's United Church, and Suzuki set forth three goals for the Japanese church: self-reliance, consolidation, and extension. Self-government in the Japanese church had been present almost from the beginning, and most of the individual congregations had been basically self-supporting since the war, although many pastors' salaries were so low that they were forced to take other part-time work to support their families. However, the Kyodan's administration in 1966 was still largely subsidized through the Interboard Committee. Under Suzuki's leadership the Japanese church pledged to wean itself from this dependency. Through a mutually agreed-upon phased withdrawal of North American mission board support by a 10 percent reduction each year, the Japanese church assumed financial responsibility for its own administrative structures.

Suzuki urged moving the church toward this financial independence from the North American churches, "from a lively

---

48    Drummond, *History of Christiaity*, 291.

sense of responsibility for the evangelization of Japan." He promoted consolidation and simplification of the national church's organizational structure for economy and efficiency and urged the Japanese churches to carry on a vigorous program of evangelism. At the same time, the need for help in this task of evangelization in the form of personnel from abroad was reiterated.[49]

Glenn Bruggers, who represented the Reformed Church as a fraternal delegate at the 1966 General Assembly, observed that the motto, "Tomorrow's United Church," pointed positively to the future, and that the three goals—self-reliance, consolidation, and extension—indicated necessary stepping stones for the church's future. He saw self-reliance as leading to greater power for cooperation with the churches of the world in facing the unfinished task in Japan and the world, consolidation as a pulling together of all the various arms of the Japanese church in facing the common task, and extension as Japanese Christians taking an active part in evangelization, moving forward in the best sense of the word. The General Assembly also expressed its continuing concern over the Vietnam War. In this regard, Bruggers noted, "For the most I feel that this is an honest concern born out of honest motives. Although the various churches in the United States naturally must act according to their best knowledge and understanding, they must receive the reports of actions and communiqués from sister churches such as the United Church as honest attempts of mature Christians living in different settings to face the problems of our age. In this spirit, both can learn, grow and progress."[50]

The mid-1960s appeared to be a very positive time for the Kyodan. Suzuki was, however, also among those Japanese Christians concerned that the Kyodan had never acknowledged publicly its own compromise and complicity in Japan's war of aggression, and who were convinced that this failure to acknowledge responsibility hindered the church's witness to the people of Japan. Over his name and in his role as the church's moderator, on Easter Sunday, March 26, 1967, Suzuki issued the "Confession on the Responsibility of the United Church of Christ in Japan During World War II."[51] Since Suzuki undertook this public action without approval of the General Assembly or even its executive committee, the validity of the "Confession" as representing the voice of the whole church remained in question. Strangely, there were some who subsequently treated the statement as a foundational

---

[49]   BWMR, 1967, 8-9.
[50]   Glenn Bruggers to Marion de Velder, Oct. 27, 1966.
[51]   Drummond, *History of Christianity*, 291.

church confession of faith, rather than supplemental to the church's confession of faith, thus reflecting little appreciation for Christianity's creedal heritage. Others, while aware of the seriousness of the issue of war responsibility, objected to the way it was presented without due process in the church. While the failure of the Kyodan to admit, honestly and publicly, its weakness and cooperation with the militarist government during the war had no doubt hampered its witness after the war, issuing the "Confession," and also the manner in which it was promulgated, proved divisive in the life of the Kyodan.

The issues of war and peace were of particular concern among Japanese youth, especially those influenced by Christianity. Van Wyk clarified the element of Christian idealism in the context of those turbulent times.

> World War II was a terrible lesson to the Japanese people; the atomic bombs that fell on Hiroshima and Nagasaki left their scars not only on buildings and bodies but on the national conscience as well. Beyond the deep repugnance to war and to the use of arms by their own country, there is also, especially among Christians, the prayer that their national example may be used of God to influence the other nations of the world to abandon the suicidal arms race. Article 9 of the Constitution, in which Japan renounces recourse to arms, is a matter of national faith and pride.[52]

Unfortunately, radical student organizations at some of the universities were not only informed by Marxist ideas, they had also adopted Trotskyite methods, resulting in barricaded campuses, kangaroo courts, and violence both verbal and physical. The influence of the radical student organizations spread, as they formed cells on each campus, and the movement gained a foothold even among groups of students in the mission schools, especially at the university level. Radical student activity eventually brought Japanese higher education to a standstill amid mass demonstrations. The radicalism escalated to the point of interrogation sessions by students to oppose and demean administrators, faculty members, and church leaders. Students barricaded and occupied school buildings, where radicals conducted ideological teach-ins. Verbal and sometimes physical violence erupted not only at government universities, but also at private Christian mission schools such as Meiji Gakuin University, and even at Tokyo

---

[52]    Gordon J. Van Wyk, "The Japanese Church and Expo 70," *Church Herald*, Apr. 17, 1970, 12.

Union Theological Seminary. Ultimately, the only recourse open to the universities, including the Christian universities and the seminary, was to call in the government's riot police to remove barricades, evict the radicals who were illegally occupying school buildings, and restore facilities to the custody of school authorities, thus permitting the resumption of educational activity.

It is important to understand certain factors behind the crisis that developed not only in the mission schools but also in the Japanese church. Increasingly divergent theological perspectives on mission and the basic priorities of mission work among the North American denominations partnering in the Interboard Committee affected both their cooperative relationship and also the ministry of the Japanese churches and mission schools to which they were related.

Of course, there had always been differences of theological viewpoint or emphasis among the missionaries of the several mission boards. The Reformed Church missionaries in Japan, and many others working with the Kyodan, always understood their primary mission to be to communicate the evangelical Christian faith through evangelism and Christian education and to help nurture the churches with which they were in partnership. Some missionaries of other denominations had focused more on the social application of the gospel. The Interboard Committee-related missionaries had all nevertheless united in the postwar period in their efforts to assist the Japanese in rebuilding and extending the devastated Christian movement. However, in the 1960s the ecumenical idealism of the postwar period in North America had come unraveled. Fundamental differences in the purpose of mission and the role of the church in society had become more apparent. The origin of this changed mission theology is clear.

Especially during the 1960s and continuing until about 1975, many mainstream European and North American Protestant churches, influenced by such theologians as Hoekendijk, Van Leeuwen, and Cox, embraced a very secularized missiology. In this theology, the understanding that God's mission to the world is carried out through the agency of the church, in accordance with Christ's commission as recorded in scripture, was replaced by the insistence that God addresses the church through the world. According to this new way of thinking, it is neither the Bible nor the mission entrusted to the church by Jesus Christ, but the world, i.e., contemporary human society, that sets the agenda for the church's mission. By the end of the 1960s, this agenda was reduced to three major issues: hunger and political oppression, racial and other discrimination, and revitalized world religions. The third of these issues reflects the same liberal theology that came to the fore in some mission circles in the 1930s, at the time of the so-called Laymen's Foreign Missions Inquiry and the publication of Hocking's *Re-thinking Missions*.

From the 1960s this thought pattern was apparent among many in their acquiescence to religious pluralism, in their naïve promotion of dialogue or even partnership with other religions, in their treatment of all other religions as simply additional spheres where God is at work, and in their prevalent lack of conviction concerning the uniqueness of Jesus Christ. However, the main emphases of this secularized mission theology in Japan were issues related to political oppression and discrimination, and it was the acceptance of the identification of these issues as *the* Christian mission by certain elements in the Japanese church that functioned as a kind of cancer that came to torment the Christian community in Japan.

The theological problem was not that the struggles for justice, liberation, and human development became a *part* of mission, for these concerns have always belonged to mission, although in different forms in different periods. The problem was that for those captivated by this radical liberation theology these issues were given precedence over people's need to be converted, baptized, nurtured in the faith, and incorporated into the life and ministry of the church. Building up the church and evangelism were denigrated, and, in their place, issue-oriented action was glorified. Commitment to mission was measured by the level of involvement in such issues as opposition to the various forms of discrimination and the struggle for justice in society. The result soon became clear. Where this secular missiology was fully implemented, the church faltered, became confused, was derailed from its Christ-given mission, and began to lose membership.

In the Kyodan, a politically astute minority embraced this secular missiology. This group also generally adopted a diluted or distorted Christology (e.g., Jesus as the ideal liberator and revolutionary, rather than Jesus Christ as crucified and risen Savior and Lord) and assumed an attitude of indifference toward Japan's religious pluralism. Through the challenges brought upon it by this left-wing minority, the Japanese church entered a period in which it was distracted from its primary mission to Japan and the rest of the world, and its energy was sapped by endless internal strife and the struggle for hegemony, i.e., control of the leadership positions in the church.[53]

[53]   Gordon Laman, "The Challenge of Mission in Japan Today," *Reformed Review*, vol. 55, no. 3, 2002.

The United Church of Christ in Japan, which had never clarified the authority of its Confession of Faith nor required its acceptance for ordination, had remained poorly defined as a church and without theological consensus. Furthermore, because the Kyodan had never resolved the differences inherited from former denominational identities in matters of the nature of church government or the church's authority, genuine exercise of discipline beyond the individual congregation had been precluded. The Kyodan was thus especially vulnerable to external theological influences in matters of scriptural authority, Christology, and the nature of the church's mission. Inevitably, the radical movement within Japan's universities and the influence of external ideologies together affected, to varying degrees, not only all the mission schools but also many Japanese pastors and seminary students. It led both to serious conflict and division within the Kyodan and to strained working relationships for some of the missionaries.

In the case of the Japanese churches, the growing conflict reached a climax in the fall of 1969 in relation to the government-sponsored Osaka Exposition of 1970, usually referred to as Expo 70, the first international exposition to be held by an Asian nation. Naturally, Japan's national pride and disciplined energy were focused on this festival. However, the Vietnam War was in progress, and 1970 was also the year for reconsideration of Japan's security pact with the United States, which brought to the fore questions of Japan's international position in relation to both West and East, as well as questions of domestic peace and prosperity. These two events, i.e., Expo 70 and the reconsideration of the security pact, converged upon the Christian church in Japan and caught it up in implications far beyond expectations.

The immediate issue was a Christian pavilion at the exposition, which was to be planned and funded jointly by leaders of the Catholic and Protestant churches of the nation and was designed to serve as a striking Christian witness amid the materialism and paganism of such an exposition. The 1968 Kyodan General Assembly voted to participate in the project, and many church members shared the vision of an interdenominational Christian pavilion to witness to the millions of attendees. In the fall of 1969, however, as the pavilion plans proceeded, there were unanticipated developments. Van Wyk reported as follows:

> Sensitive Christians—especially young ministers, seminarians, and university students—began to have second thoughts about the propriety of the Church's participation in the Exposition.

Frustrated in their attempts to make themselves heard in the official councils of the church, they resorted to the violent tactics of "people's democracy" that have proved so effective in recent days, not only in Japan but around the world, as a technique for gaining a hearing for those heretofore denied a role in decision-making.

The United Church of Christ in Japan, by far the largest and most influential church participating in the project, was forced to call a special meeting of its General Assembly in late November for the express purpose of reconsidering its commitment to the Pavilion. But the session was barely called to order before seminary students commandeered the microphone and took control of the two days of debate, harangue, and intimidation. The Assembly finally adjourned without voting on the issue. The Pavilion is up, the exhibits are prepared, and the expenditures must be met, and so there seems to be little more the protesters can do than arrange further demonstrations or possibly picket lines.[54]

The radical and politically astute left-wing minority among the seminary students and young ministers in the Kyodan strongly opposed participation in the Christian pavilion project on the grounds that Expo 70 was a capitalist festival designed to uphold the political status quo and distract the populace from the government's policy of extending the Mutual Defense Treaty with the United States. These radicals became firmly committed to continuing their opposition. Using strong-armed tactics, which included holding the church's leaders captive for long hours while conducting kangaroo-court style interrogations, they fomented rebellion and antiestablishment action both in the churches and against Tokyo Union Theological Seminary.

The radicals not only blocked the functioning of the steering committee of the Kyodan but also disrupted worship services in some of the city churches. Furthermore, they contended that when the seminary faculty ultimately brought in the riot police to remove barricades and evict the occupying students from the school buildings, it had violated the principle of separation of church and state and shown support for a misguided and oppressive government. Thus began a decades-long internal struggle within the Kyodan for control of the church and its agenda between a radical left-wing minority with antiestablishment and political motives and the evangelical mainstream of believers,

---

[54]  Gordon J. Van Wyk, "The Japanese Church and Expo 70," *Church Herald*, Apr. 17, 1970, 12.

pastors, and theologians who continued to insist that the church must evangelize and be built up in order to fulfill its calling to witness to Christ's saving power and ultimately transform society.

The immediate result at Tokyo Union Theological Seminary was the division of the student body into three groups: one-third sided with the radicals and eventually left the seminary; one-third supported the faculty, remained committed to their calling, and continued to prepare to serve in and build up the churches; and one-third were confused by the conflict, became disillusioned, and many of them dropped out of seminary or even left the church. The result was the breakdown of youth and young adult ministry and the loss of at least a generation in many of the churches, as well as a reticence to become involved in political or even social issues on the part of many evangelical Japanese Christians.

The Kyodan became fundamentally polarized between those who saw mission only as solidarity in anger, opposition, agitation, and struggle for "justice" along with some in the secular world, and those who saw mission as the proclamation of the gospel of salvation in Jesus Christ and the formation and nurture of Christ's church, a church that as Christ's body could continually serve as the light of the world and the salt of the earth. Because of this polarization, a balanced, holistic implementation of a mission of the church rooted in winning people to Christ, nurturing them in the evangelical Christian faith, molding them into partners in Christ's ministry to and for the world, and sending them into mission with a Christian social witness was largely jeopardized and undermined. Ironically, the scars this era left on Christianity in Japan were largely escaped by the Christian churches in Western nations where the radical movements originated. In the West the radical confrontations were soon mostly forgotten, but they continued to have a positive impact, in the form of an aroused social consciousness, among many Christians.

In Japan the activities of the radicals were concentrated in metropolitan areas and larger cities, and church life in many congregations away from those areas was not directly affected—at least not immediately. The vast majority of Japanese church members were solidly evangelical Christians who longed to be upheld in their effort to live as Christians in a very secular and materialistic culture. Most of the churches continued to welcome the partnership of missionaries in evangelistic work, although there were cases of strained relationships with some of the younger pastors. In some districts it was the Reformed Church missionaries and some other evangelical missionaries who provided a stabilizing influence and reassurance in troubled times.

Gathering in 1970 of missionaries working in the Tokyo/Yokohama area, with prominent postwar Japanese Christian leader Muto Tomio and Reformed Church secretary of Adult Volunteer Services Beth Marcus. Front (l-r): Marcus, Helen Zander, Muto; second row: Betty de Forest, Etta Hesselink, Ruby Korver, Mary Flaherty, Eleanor Norden, Russell Norden; back row: Theodore Flaherty, Ronald Korver, Carroll de Forest.

In the late 1960s and early 1970s, the cry, "Missionary, Go Home!" was raised by certain Christian leaders from third world countries, and this attitude received wide publicity in the Reformed Church. Such words no doubt reflected a reaction against paternalism or condescension on the part of some missionaries serving in increasingly nationalistic nations where the national churches were moving toward independence and self-reliance. The element of a nationalistic spirit was also clearly present in the Japanese church's internal conflict, and the long since independent Japanese church was of course striving to achieve greater self-reliance. While the "Missionary, Go Home!" motif was not prominent in Japan, the issue of whether or not to continue to receive missionaries for evangelistic work was reconsidered during a moratorium period of two years from 1969 to 1971. Ultimately, the Kyodan's conclusion in the matter was clarified in a statement adopted by the Council of Cooperation in Japan in April of 1972, as follows: "We believe that the presence in Japan of missionaries from abroad will continue to be important in the future, both as a witness to the nature of the church as transcending nation, race, and class and as an implementation of mission in Japan."

CHAPTER 14

# Mission under the Japan-North American Commission on Cooperative Mission: 1973–2004

## An Experiment in Mutual, Cooperative Mission

The Interboard Committee for Christian Work in Japan was superceded by the Japan-North American Commission on Cooperative Mission in January 1973, with the purpose of facilitating cooperative Christian mission in both Japan and North America. This change was intended to better reflect and implement church-to-church relationships and mutuality in mission, with the understanding that not only North American but all churches ought naturally to become both sending and receiving churches. In contrast to the activity that led to the formation of the Interboard Committee, the Reformed Church did not play a leading role in the establishment of the Japan-North American Commission. This development occurred during the brief tenure of Dr. Choan-Seng Song as the Reformed Church's Asia secretary, and Song had had no firsthand experience of mission in Japan or of the Reformed Church's role in it.

Several significant changes were effected in the new cooperative format. Whereas the Interboard Committee had consisted of a group of

613

North American church representatives organized to cooperate jointly with the United Church of Christ in Japan (Kyodan), the new Japan-North American Commission on Cooperative Mission (JNAC) included not only representatives of seven North American denominational mission boards but also of the Kyodan and the United Board for Christian Higher Education in Asia as constituent members, as well as representatives of the Korean Christian Church in Japan and the Presbyterian Church in Canada as associate members.

The Kyodan was represented by members chosen by the Council of Cooperation, which included representatives not only of the Kyodan but also of the Council of Cooperation-related Schools Council (formerly the Interboard Committee-related Schools Council) and the Japan Christian Social Work League, Christian organizations associated with but not part of the Kyodan. Furthermore, the United Board for Christian Higher Education, a member of the commission, was also not a church. Consequently, the function of the Japan-North American Commission could not truly be described as church-to-church relations. The commission was meant to foster or emphasize the ideal of mutuality. However, the imbalance in size and strength between the Japan and North American organizations, the ongoing internal struggle of the Kyodan, and denominationalism in North America made realization of that goal of mutuality and true two-way mission difficult and perhaps unrealistic. Several issues may be cited.

Three representatives from Japan, two Japanese and one Korean, were included in the Executive Committee. However, the office of JNAC was in New York, its executive secretary-treasurer was a North American, and while the annual meeting of the commission was later sometimes held in Japan, the quarterly Executive Committee and Long Range Planning Committee meetings were all held in North America. According to the JNAC Constitution, the commission was to be involved in cooperative mission in Japan primarily in response to plans developed in Japan, and in North America primarily in response to plans developed in North America, while any member might suggest cooperative mission projects. In theory, the Japan side had an equal role, but in practice the North American representatives tended to take most of the initiative. The very language of the JNAC Constitution revealed the imparity when it stated that in cooperation with appropriate bodies in Japan and in North America the commission was to coordinate the *sending to Japan* and *receiving in North America* of missionaries and other workers appointed for cooperative projects.

In place of the Field Committee of the Interboard Committee structure, the Japan Missionary Maintenance Committee, with members from each participating North American denomination, was established. Ostensibly the members were no longer the representatives on the field of the mission boards, but essentially this new committee represented a change in name only. A unified support plan, which the Interboard Committee had been unsuccessful in working out in 1948, was agreed upon in 1973, resulting in a common basic salary and benefits plan for North American missionaries of five denominations serving in Japan, including the Reformed Church. This unified support plan was implemented for several years but ultimately abandoned in 1978 as impracticable because the cost was apparently prohibitive for some of the missions. In any case, it had never been truly unified, because several North American denominations had provided a variety of different additional benefits in accordance with their own denominational policies.

Japanese representatives on the commission strongly urged the continued sending of missionary personnel to Japan and, in the face of rising costs, promised to promote a policy of shared support, whereby missionaries would be partially supported financially from the Japan side. This policy was carried out from 1973, to the extent that it proved feasible. The mission schools had become financially independent and participated in the shared support program, gradually increasing their contributions toward the salaries of missionary teachers. In the case of missionaries working in evangelistic work, however, the reality was different. Due to the extreme difficulty of evangelism and resultant limited church growth in Japan, the Kyodan churches as a whole had difficulty maintaining self-support and did not have the wherewithal to contribute to the shared support program. The most that local Japanese partner churches where evangelistic missionaries were serving could manage was to provide the missionaries' work funds. Salaries of evangelistic missionaries continued to be provided by the North American sending churches.

Especially since the 1970s, there have been Japanese Christians with the desire and sense of calling to participate in mission outside of their homeland. Sending them out with adequate financial support has been the great challenge. A number of Japanese Christians have gone as missionaries to serve in Southeast Asian countries or on Pacific islands, and others have gone to serve in ministry among expatriate Japanese in Asia, Europe, or the Americas. However, although support groups in Japan were formed and endeavored to provide backing, the Japanese overseas missionaries have been primarily sustained in their work by the inviting groups, by self-support, or by North American mission boards.

The ideal of mutuality in mission, of two-way mission, of mission not only from West to East but also from East to West, was one that the Reformed Church and its missionaries wholeheartedly embraced. However, the Reformed Church did not play a defining role in establishing the policies and programs emphasized by the new Japan-North American Commission. It gradually became clear that many of the North American leaders involved in the formation of the new organization were influenced by a rather extreme form of liberation theology. These proponents of issue-oriented mission exercised a strong influence over the direction and main agenda of the JNAC organization and program from its inception, and they pressed for mission cooperation primarily in the form of projects advocating opposition to discrimination and engagement in the struggle for justice in society.

In the early years following the inauguration of the cooperative relationship under the Japan-North American Commission on Cooperative Mission, Japanese members on the commission opposed the issue-oriented mission emphasis. This was made clear in a paper prepared by the Council of Cooperation's acting general secretary, Saeki Yoichi, and approved by the 1975 General Meeting of the Council. Saeki stated the case with deep insight, in part as follows:

> With the increased dialogue with JNAC a difference in thinking about policy has become clear. The North American side emphasizes mission through lifting up issues and carrying out projects to deal with them. For example, they would like for the Japanese side to organize projects that deal with issues like the world food crisis, development of peoples, social justice, minorities, hunger, or multi-national corporations. Then they could cooperate with us in mission through these projects. In the discussions with JNAC this is called "issue-oriented, project-centered mission."
>
> Over against this, the mission policy emphasized by the Japanese is first securing strategic positions for mission. This means establishing new churches or building up churches which are beachheads of mission, so they can come to grips with the issues of society, and upgrading and strengthening schools and social work agencies. The second emphasis is personnel. This means personnel development and training, improving the pension fund for retired ministers, and securing missionaries. In the discussions with JNAC the first is called "institution-centered mission" and the second, "person-centered mission."

The first emphasis, institution-centered mission, might be called position warfare in a battle. You dig a trench, establish your position, and then plan how to move forward. In our case the battle lines do not change easily, and it looks like a long struggle. Japanese society is changing rapidly physically and technologically, and at first glance it seems that the entire society is going to change. However, the spiritual makeup of Japanese people, their value systems and life attitudes, stubbornly refuse to change. Since the gospel mission is to influence and change these Japanese people at the deep level of their personality, it is not a simple task. It calls for a strategy of establishing positions in the midst of society, then from these positions encountering people and challenging their way of living, and penetrating society. Evangelism in Japan does not mean to go chasing after every issue that makes the headlines, but rather to get at the roots of problems and work away at them in everyday mission activities.

The second emphasis on person-centered mission has the same basis. The way to change the spiritual makeup and value systems of the Japanese people who stubbornly refuse change in these aspects is through person-to-person relationships. Using one of the strategic positions as one's point of operation, one settles in for a long period of time, seeks interpersonal contacts, and through evangelism, education, and service deepens interpersonal encounter. This is the only way mission in Japan can be accomplished....

Person-centered mission is particularly important from the standpoint of the gospel message and the doctrine of the church. The church is the body of those called together by Christ, and the ultimate goal of the gospel is the establishment of a new people of God. This is the starting point for the discussion about missionaries within the CoC. In other words, the question of whether missionaries are needed or not is not considered only on the utilitarian basis of whether they are helpful or not, nor whether their work is effective or not. Rather it is considered in relation to the distinctive nature of the church itself and from the standpoint of Japan's person-centered mission policy.[1]

At the time of the inauguration of JNAC in 1973, the Kyodan had been for several years immobilized, engaged in the struggle between

---

[1]   Saeki Yōichi. "Historical Survey and Problem Areas in Cooperative Relationship with North America," 8-9, Joint Archives of Holland, Hope College, Laman file of Japan Field Representative correspondence copies on CoC Structure.

radicals and mainstream evangelicals for control of the church, and the radicals had not been among the representatives of the Kyodan on the commission. However, several years later, and for many years afterward, the positions of leadership in the United Church of Christ in Japan all came under the control of the radical left-wing minority in the church. They bought into the issue-oriented mission ideology and, as a result, instead of the church emphasizing evangelism, nurture, and growth, the resources and energy of the church at the national and synod level came to be focused almost exclusively on several sociopolitical issues, which were treated as *the* mission of the church.

Under the control of these leaders, involvement in the struggle over politicized issues became the test of Christian mission commitment in the Kyodan. To be more specific, the fight to eliminate discrimination against Japan's minorities, i.e., the outcaste community people (*buraku-min*), Korean nationals in Japan, and the *Ainu* people (Japan's aboriginal remnant in Hokkaido); opposition to nationalization of the Yasukuni Shrine (where Japanese military war dead, i.e., those who died on behalf of the emperor in World War II, are enshrined); protests against U.S. military bases in Japan; and opposition to the Japanese government's indirect support of the Vietnam War were some of the issues emphasized. For many years, by clever political maneuvers, the left-wing minority leaders maintained a majority in the Kyodan's Steering Committee and coerced and controlled the deliberations at the biennial General Assembly Meetings. The radicals were thus able to control or prevent the advance of the evangelical agenda of the Japanese church at the national level for many years. Even so, at the local church level and in some of the mission schools, many Japanese Christians continued their faithful witness and worked toward the day when the evangelical majority might eventually regain control of the national church organization and elect evangelicals to leadership roles in the Kyodan.

The disconnect between the leaders of the Kyodan and their policies and priorities at the national level on the one hand and the struggles of most congregations and mission schools on the other continued for several decades. Reformed Church missionaries sometimes felt discouraged at the apparent inability of the Kyodan to find reconciliation within its ranks, but at the same time they identified with the struggle of the evangelicals. They came to realize that, from the perspective of the church's evangelical majority, compromise of foundational Christian beliefs and reducing Christian mission to political and social activism was untenable.

At the Kyodan General Assembly of 1996, at long last representatives of the evangelical majority were able to elect evangelical ministers to leadership roles in the church, including the moderator, vice-moderator,[2] and a majority in the Executive Council. The new leaders and their successors eventually brought about a reorientation of the stated priorities and mission goals of the Kyodan. Evangelism and the church's growth and nurture once again came to be emphasized. However, the left-wing minority continued to agitate and to advocate its agenda, and true unity in the Kyodan remained elusive.

Aside from the Kyodan's internal struggles, which undoubtedly contributed to the stagnation of church growth, the last quarter of the twentieth century did not offer a favorable environment for the Christian movement in Japan. The nation's prosperity reached new heights as Japan's became the world's second largest economy. The pursuit of wealth and all the material symbols of success became the all-consuming obsession of many among the general public. The accelerated pace of urbanization contributed to the breakdown of the traditional values of family and society. Japan's majority religions, Buddhism and Shinto, held little appeal for post-modern Japanese. Activities of cults associated with Christianity—such as the Jehovah's Witnesses, the Mormons, and the Unification Church of Sun Myung Moon—had a negative impact on the image of Christianity, since many Japanese did not know enough about Christianity to make a distinction between the cults and the mainstream faith. At the same time, the minority Japanese church struggled to gain a hearing among the younger generation with a more contemporary message.

The religious environment became even more complex and challenging as a result of the activities of a Japanese cult called Aum Shinrikyo, often translated as Supreme Truth. Founded in the mid 1980s by *Asahara Shoko*, the cult combined elements of Yoga, Buddhism, Hinduism, and Christianity and became obsessed with the idea of the apocalypse. Asahara declared himself to be "Christ" and the first "enlightened one" since Buddha, claimed he could take upon himself the sins of the world, transfer to his followers his spiritual power, and remove their sins and bad Karma. He predicted the end of the world, used the term "Armageddon," and taught that humanity would end, except for an elite few, meaning those who joined Aum and became his followers. Remarkably, this cult attracted some of the ambitious students and graduates of Japan's top universities. In 1995, Aum Shinrikyo claimed to have nine thousand members, and the cult gained great wealth by operating electronics businesses and restaurants, as well

---

[2]   As moderator the Reverend Ojima Seiji and as vice-moderator the Reverend Yamakita Nobuhisa.

as by extortion and by requiring members to turn over their assets to the group.

After Asahara failed to gain a political foothold in the general election for the House of Representatives in the early 1990s, Aum became increasingly antisocial, carrying out clandestine kidnappings and assassinations of opponents, gathering weapons, and secretly manufacturing the nerve agents sarin gas and VX gas. A team of young Aum scientists experimented with biological toxins, such as botulin, anthrax, cholera, and Q fever, but when attempted biological attacks failed, the cult transitioned to the use of chemical weapons. Asahara's obsessions led to a bizarre attempt to destroy the world in order to save it. In Robert Lifton's words:

> On March 20, 1995, Aum Shinrokyo, a fanatical Japanese religious cult, released sarin, a deadly nerve gas, on five subway trains during Tokyo's early-morning rush hour. A male cult member boarded each of the trains carrying two or three small plastic bags covered with newspaper and, at an agreed-upon time, removed the newspaper and punctured the bags with a sharpened umbrella tip. On the trains, in the stations where they had stopped, and at the station exits, people coughed, choked, experienced convulsions, and collapsed. Eleven were killed and up to five thousand injured. Had Aum succeeded in producing a purer form of the gas, the deaths could have been in the thousands or hundreds of thousands. For sarin, produced originally by the Nazis, is among the most lethal of chemical weapons. Those releasing it on the trains understood themselves to be acting on behalf of their guru and his vast plan for human salvation.[3]

Asahara was arrested and charged with twenty-three murders and other offenses. He was found guilty of masterminding the attack, and he and some other senior members of the cult received death sentences.

As a result of the terrorist acts of Aum Shinrikyo, Japanese government surveillance of all religious activity became more intense, and new laws were enacted governing the activities, properties, and finances of all religious organizations, including churches. While no Christian churches were accused of doing anything illegal, the government's actions and new policies exacerbated the already difficult task of Christian evangelism. Non-Christian parents became very

---

[3]    Robert Jay Lifton, *Destroying the World to Save It: Aum Shinrikyo, Apocalyptic Violence, and the New Global Terrorism* (Holt: New York, 1999).

suspicious of all religion and were extremely reticent about allowing even their young adult children to have anything to do with religion in general, and any religious organization they did not fully understand in particular.

## The Reformed Church Mission Role under the Japan-North American Commission on Cooperative Mission

Despite so many years of challenge in the Japanese church and society, despite newly erected stumbling blocks, the Reformed Church and its missionaries in Japan neither compromised their foundational beliefs nor abandoned the mainstream of courageous evangelical Christians who had always made up the majority in the Japanese churches. The Reformed Church and its missionaries, perhaps more than any others cooperating with the Kyodan, consistently concurred in and implemented the basic approach to mission that had been spelled out in 1975 by Saeki as the Japanese understanding of mission. They labored beside Japanese colleagues to establish or strengthen those beachheads of mission, the small churches and preaching stations, and worked to elevate Christian witness at the mission schools, where most of the students and many of the teachers were not yet Christians. Person-to person mission.

This evangelistic task remained daunting in a culture in which outwardly there is freedom of religion but where in practice commitment to Christian faith is still considered aberrant behavior. Interestingly, Christians were often accorded a certain respect because of their integrity and wholesome contributions to society. Yet, every missionary could relate stories of courageous Japanese who embraced the Christian faith despite family opposition, community ostracism, discrimination at school or workplace, or subtle, and sometimes not so subtle, persecution. Many young Christians faced being disinherited or disowned by parents and siblings for refusing to give up being baptized or pursuing a call to become a Christian minister. It was and still is not unusual for women who had become Christian believers to be forbidden to attend church services on Sunday by their husbands. The Reformed Church's missionaries partnered with these courageous Christians.

In the summer of 1974, the Reverend Glenn Bruggers was appointed as the new secretary for Asian Ministries for the Reformed Church, and the Bruggers family returned to the United States. While the missionaries in Japan were sorry to lose these experienced and valued colleagues from the field, they were happy to have gained a well-qualified advocate with a deep understanding of the complexities of the situation in Japan at mission headquarters in America and representing the Reformed Church within the Japan-North American Commission. Bruggers served with distinction in this role until his retirement in 1989. Under his leadership, despite the high cost involved and a challenging financial situation in the Reformed Church, efforts were made to continue sending missionaries to Japan.

The Reverend John and Marilyn Koedyker were appointed to Japan as evangelistic missionaries in 1977. Following language study at Kyoto they accepted appointment to serve as district missionaries in Morioka, in Iwate Prefecture, an area about three hundred miles north of Tokyo, where Reformed Church missionaries had established the first Protestant evangelistic work in the region in 1888. During their initial two years, the Koedykers served primarily at the *Zenrinkan*, the Good Neighbor Christian Center in the city of Morioka, where John acted as chaplain and they both taught English and Bible classes. Subsequently, the Koedykers became involved more directly in evangelistic and pastoral activities in the churches of the Morioka district. In 1982, following a furlough, they were also given responsibility in a new church start in Takizawa, in the suburbs of Morioka, where John served as pastor.

Under the JNAC structure, career educational missionaries of the Reformed Church continued to play important roles at the three mission schools historically related to the Reformed Church Japan Mission. Helen Zander, the last remaining prewar Reformed Church missionary, whose enthusiasm for Ferris Girls' School, Christian witness, English teaching, the Japanese people, and all things Japanese spanned almost five decades, reached retirement in 1977. Alice Elzinga served faithfully at Baiko Jo Gakuin until her retirement in 1979. Unfortunately, the Reformed Church proved unable to send a career person in her place. Ted and Mary Flaherty continued to teach at Ferris Girls' School, and Ted was chosen to serve for several years as principal of Ferris High School. He taught English and Bible at Ferris until his untimely death in 1982. Mary returned to the United States for a time but went again to Japan to teach at Ferris until her retirement in 1988.

While most educational missionaries no longer played significant roles at the organizational level, each made unique contributions. Russell Norden assisted at a local Japanese church while continuing as chaplain and professor at Ferris Women's University. In his teaching role, he was able to implement his special interest in John Bunyan's writings, especially *Pilgrim's Progress*. Eleanore had begun her work at Ferris High School as a part-time teacher of English and Western cooking, but she later taught full time, when the family situation allowed. Eventually she was asked to serve as a homeroom teacher, the only foreigner to be given that responsibility since World War II. She thus carried responsibilities equal to those of her Japanese colleagues, and as a result she was particularly influential in the lives of many promising Japanese young women. The Nordens retired in 1991.

Beginning in 1976, the Flahertys, the Nordens, and Helen Zander had joined with others to restore worship services and to reestablish the ministry of an English-speaking congregation ministering to the international community, the Yokohama Union Church. This congregation had been established by Japan's pioneer missionaries to serve the foreign residents of Yokohama. It flourished before the war, but its sanctuary had been destroyed by American bombs in 1945. Eleanore Norden, as chair of the board of Yokohama Union Church, played a key role in the restoration of this international church's ministry, and three Reformed Church couples subsequently served the congregation: the Reverend John and Ann Piet (1987-89), the Reverend Delbert and Trudy Vander Haar (1989-91), and the Reverend Eugene and Joyce Vander Well (1992-94).

Gordon Van Wyk's Christian witness at Meiji Gakuin University was implemented not only in Bible classes for students taught at his home but also in his college courses in American cultural history, Puritan literature, and church history. At the same time, he also carried considerable weight behind the scenes in the faculty and administration, making a concerted effort to insure the school's Christian impact on the students, and he led in the formation of sister college and exchange programs between Meiji Gakuin and Hope College. The Van Wyks retired in 1985.

Ronald Korver, always an advocate for mutuality in mission, promoted programs for international exchange at Meiji Gakuin's Higashi Murayama High School. He initiated, guided, and/or provided orientation for Japanese and American high school exchange students, the school's summer home stay in America program, and the concert tours in America of the school's highly acclaimed bell choir. As one result, hundreds of Japanese youths were exposed to Christian witness and home life in America. Ruby Korver not only taught at Keisen Girls' School throughout her career, but she also became a very influential leader in the evangelical national women's movement of the United Church of Christ in Japan. The Korvers retired in 1992.

Already in the 1970s, financial support for sending North American missionaries to Japan was becoming an issue for the several cooperating boards. Negative factors included not only the rising cost of living in Japan and accompanying high personnel costs, but also excessive mission property maintenance costs. These factors were the result of Japan's unprecedented prosperity, which made the yen-dollar exchange rate extremely unfavorable for North American mission boards. However, there were also positive factors that favored a continuing missionary involvement, such as the assets of many trained personnel on the field, the ownership of valuable mission property, and the program of shared support of missionaries provided primarily by the mission schools.

Land purchased to build homes for missionaries in the first fifteen years of postwar mission activity multiplied many times in value in Japan's growing economy. Wise management of these valuable mission property assets eventually proved to be one key to ameliorating the high cost of missionary housing. Kami Osaki in Tokyo, near Meiji Gakuin, was the site of two aging missionary houses on a large lot. In a plan suggested and worked out by Van Wyk and Korver, half of this valuable land was sold and the proceeds used to build a five-unit townhouse complex on the remaining land in 1981. Such redevelopment provided smaller but better quality homes for one or two missionary families, and the rental income from the remaining apartments covered the cost of the complex's taxes, insurance, and maintenance, thus eliminating the need for the Reformed Church to budget money for housing the missionaries living there. Later, under Gordon Laman's leadership, a similar project was carried out in Koganei in the western part of Tokyo. In place of one deteriorating mission house on mission-owned land, three houses were built, one for a missionary family and two to rent out.

Nevertheless, the high cost of sending and maintaining missionaries in Japan was an inevitable consideration for mission boards, and the Reformed Church board was no exception. Given the ability of the Christian schools to be financially independent and the comparative economic weakness of the Japanese churches, the Reformed Church found it necessary to focus its limited financial resources on personnel for evangelistic work and training church leaders. Even though the shared support contributions of mission schools toward the cost of maintaining missionary teachers proved helpful, the Reformed Church was not able to appoint new career educational missionaries. All career people serving in educational work were sustained until retirement, but their replacements were not recruited.

To fill their need for oral English teachers, mission schools had begun to hire nonmissionary foreign residents as English conversation teachers. However, the mission schools strongly desired to have Christian native speakers of English to assist them in their foreign language programs. Karin Granberg, a member of the Reformed Church, a graduate of Hope College, and high school teacher in New Jersey, spent two summers teaching in the International Summer Session of Hope College. Her acquaintance with Japanese students she had taught in the summer program led to a desire to go to Japan to teach English and share her Christian witness. In 1972 Granberg traveled to Japan at her own expense in order to serve as a short-term contract teacher at a mission school in Sendai, Miyagi Gakuin. The teaching contract was arranged through Reformed Church auspices.

In 1973 Gordon Van Wyk proposed the idea of recruiting such contract teachers through the Reformed Church's Adult Volunteer Services office, which was then headed by Beth Marcus. Van Wyk pointed out, as an example, that Meiji Gakuin could pay a living wage once a teacher is in Japan, but that arrangements would be necessary for such matters as travel and health insurance. Van Wyk suggested that if committed Christian contract teachers could be recruited, screened, given some orientation, and sent to Japan, and then paid a salary by the mission school, it would be "mutually rewarding to the school, to the individual, and to our church."[4]

The Reformed Church responded to this challenge,[5] and, under the direction of Marcus, by 1975 there were ten such volunteers in Japan. The teachers were sent through Adult Volunteer Services, not as appointed missionaries under the direction of the secretary for Asian Ministries. A program was subsequently formalized whereby the mission boards of several denominations in North America recruited, screened, and sent out short-term contract teachers, for whom the recruiting denominations provided transportation to the field and the mission schools provided small apartments and a living stipend, generally on a two-year contract. These contract teachers, whose assignments were worked out through the Council of Cooperation, came to be called missionary associates. Most of these teachers served well, but in the case of denominations that did not screen candidates adequately, some were sent who were non-Christians or nominal believers and who came not to participate in mission so much as to experience living in an Asian country and to travel in Asia during school vacation times.

The Reformed Church faithfully and responsibly recruited and introduced more missionary associates than any other North American

4    GJV to Arie R. Brouwer, Oct. 13, 1973.
5    ARB to GJV, Oct. 25, 1973.

denomination associated with the Kyodan. This became a valuable contribution to mission work in Japan through the recruitment, careful screening, and orientation efforts of Marcus and her successors at Adult Volunteer Services.[6] The missionary associates sent by the Reformed Church, mostly young people right out of college, went as oral English teachers. They gained a fine reputation and performed a valuable service for the mission schools. Despite the lack of opportunity to attain fluency in the Japanese language, many of them proved to be effective Christian witnesses among the faculty and youth in the schools, as well as in many local churches. As of 2010, the Reformed Church had sent more than two hundred missionary associates to serve in Japan through its Adult Volunteer Services program.[7]

During the 1980s and 1990s, a gradual decline of interest in and commitment to mission in Japan occurred among several of the North American denominations participating in the Commission on Cooperative Mission. Financial considerations were clearly a significant factor. Not only the high cost of mission in Japan but also the decline in contributions for mission from their North American congregations had an effect. A lack of concern for evangelism among non-Christians, for leading them to faith, and for building up the church contributed to the decline. So did the continuing exclusive emphasis on issue-oriented mission on the part of the boards of these denominations, which in Japan meant focus solely on political action against various forms of discrimination. The priority placed on relatively less expensive mission in third-world countries was an additional element in the decline in commitment to mission in Japan.

The Reformed Church, however, while also facing financial challenges, remained committed to maintaining missionary personnel in Japan to work in partnership with the Japanese church. With its long-held understanding of holistic mission, the gospel spoken and lived out in both word and deed, the Reformed Church has consistently encouraged not only the ministry of the Word, but also acts of love and mercy and the promotion of justice in society. Reformed Church mission has appreciated the importance that Japanese Christians place on dealing with issues of discrimination within their church and in Japanese society toward the outcaste community people (*buraku-min*), the Korean minority in Japan, the *Ainu* people in Hokkaido, and other marginalized people. Acts of love and mercy in the larger community

---

[6]     Successors include Charlotte Ten Clay, Amy DeKruiter, and Jay Harsevoort.
[7]     See appendix II for complete list of missionary associates.

have also been part of the ministry of all Reformed Church missionaries. However, the Reformed Church, in its mission involvement in Japan, has not placed primary emphasis on the social and political issues. It understands that, especially in a place like Japan where Christians are such a small minority of the population, the priority must continue to be placed on evangelism, church extension and revitalization, and leadership training for the Japanese church. There is evidence that this perspective has been appreciated and has served as an encouragement among the evangelical leaders of the Kyodan.

The ministry of Reformed Church missionaries has reflected this priority, but at the same time it has demonstrated a balanced approach. While working with Japanese colleagues in evangelism for the enlargement of the church or in maintaining a Christian witness within the mission schools, missionaries have also labored to nurture Christian expressions of God's love and justice. While they did not get involved in political activism, examples of holistic mission work by Reformed Church missionaries abound. For instance, Boude Moore, Glenn Bruggers, Gordon Laman, Tom Vande Berg, and others engaged in prison ministries for many years. Ron and Ruby Korver became the legal guardians—the virtual parents—of a war orphan, who eventually graduated from college and theological seminary and served as a pastor. Birdie Van Wyk was involved in a telephone counseling ministry, a program that helped prevent many suicides. Rudy and Trina Kuyten worked among the *Ainu* people in Hokkaido. And virtually all of the missionaries served at various times as loving friends and advocates of members of the outcaste community, minority Koreans in Japan, the disabled, the elderly, and the abused, and worked for equality for women, or for the education and welfare of small children.

The Magees, along with their efforts in district evangelism and pastoral work in the churches of the district surrounding Tomakomai, gave leadership to two pioneer projects in their larger community. A Christian seamen's center, which enlisted volunteers from all the churches in the area, was established under Joyce's inspiration and guidance to provide hospitality and serve the needs of the thousands of seafarers of many nationalities whose ships call at the industrial port of Tomakomai. In another project of service expressing the love of Christ in their community, under George's leadership as prime mover and head of its board of directors, a unique care center to minister to the needs of a forgotten element in Japanese society, emotionally handicapped adults, was established in Tomakomai.

Joyce Magee, making use of several furlough periods for study at Western Theological Seminary as well as courses by correspondence, completed the necessary requirements and was ordained as a Reformed Church minister in 1995. Both George and Joyce carried significant responsibilities in the preaching and teaching ministries of the Japanese churches of the district in which they served. The Reformed Church missionaries continued to give priority to sowing and nurturing the seeds of the gospel, to building up the churches for living a life of witness in their challenging situations, and contributing to the training of the church's leaders. Their ministries have sometimes attracted attention but often consisted of quiet, undramatic, faithful Christian witness.

The Unzickers served unobtrusively with the eight urban and small rural churches of the Otaru region in Hokkaido for twenty-eight years, until their retirement in 1993. Their witness and hospitality touched numberless lives. Bill worked alongside Japanese ministers in preaching, teaching Bible classes, and, for several years, as a copastor. He modeled the role of a mature Christian pastor among his Japanese colleagues. Sarah taught English Bible classes, was active in women's ministries, and played the reed organ for church or church school. Sarah has described one example of effective outreach in Japan in which they participated, a house meeting. Her observations were of a scene such as has been experienced by most district evangelistic missionaries.

> The house meeting we attended that night was in the town of Zenibako, which has a population of several thousand. There are no churches within fifteen miles. The Christians who live there travel by train or bus to churches in Otaru or Sapporo, which are large cities on either side of Zenibako. Many fishing villages and farming communities have no Christian pastors, and only by house meetings do the people have chances to hear the good news.
>
> House meetings are important also because Japanese people often find it difficult to enter churches. They have no idea what to expect because they are not accustomed to communal worship in a public place. When they visit Shinto shrines they simply stand outside and clap their hands to ask for blessings. They visit Buddhist temples only for funerals. It's easier to respond to an invitation to a meeting in a home, public hall, or other familiar place, so these meetings have proved to be an effective tool even in areas where there are established churches....
>
> Our house meeting in Zenibako was ready to begin. Of the dozen or so people gathered there, four were not Christian, but

they all joined in singing hymns and listened as Pastor Oikawa read from the Bible and spoke about Jesus. There was very little discussion, but that is not unusual in such a group. Many Japanese feel rather shy about asking questions in new situations. They want to think things over and perhaps talk privately with a Christian friend. They may attend such meetings many times before deciding to attend a church service or to think seriously about what it would mean to them to become Christians. After the pastor finished speaking, we chatted over our tea and got better acquainted with each other.

The growth of the church has been slow in Japan, but that is no excuse for not giving everyone a chance to hear the gospel. Young people, parents, grandparents, and people in all walks of life are being touched by these house meetings.[8]

The Kuytens' unique effort in evangelism through coffee house ministry bore fruit, and out of it grew the vision of a new central city church uniquely trained for urban evangelism. A group of twelve leaders committed to this vision was formed, including Rudy and Trina and ten Japanese Christians, and in 1979 the Church of the Twelve Apostles was organized as a congregation. This church emphasized team ministry and, following up on experience gained in coffee house evangelism, continued to reach out to many who had come to feel the loneliness, meaninglessness, or emptiness of their lives, as well as to individuals who had experienced some kind of brokenness or failure. Among the new Christians baptized were divorcees, alcoholics, those rescued from cults, and the disabled. The Good Hour Coffee Shop remained part of the ministry, but a warehouse was remodeled into a church building and part of the building was developed into a second coffee shop. Called Ecclesia Coffee Shop, it incorporated a small Christian book store. A multifaceted program of evangelism evolved. Creative evangelistic outreach, music, art, and drama, reflecting the special gifts and charisma of Rudy and Trina, always played a significant role in the church's life. The Kuytens retired in 1994 after thirty-four years on the field.

After twenty years of involvement in evangelism and pastoral work in partnership with churches on the island of Kyushu, in 1981 the Lamans moved to Tokyo, where Gordon joined the faculty of the Tokyo Union Theological Seminary. Gordon, while never seeing himself as a scholar, had continued graduate study for many years with a focus on

---

8   Sarah Unzicker, "God's Houses in Japan," *Church Herald*, Feb. 4, 1983, 17.

The main building of Tokyo Union Theological Seminary

A seminary chapel service

mission studies, especially Japan's mission history and the reasons for Japan's resistance to Christianity. This represented an effort to remain hopeful amid the difficulty of evangelism in Japan and to grow as an evangelist, but in the process he acquired master of theology and doctor of ministry degrees. This study, along with many years on the front lines of evangelism, was judged by the Japanese as preparation for service as a professor of practical theology and director of field education for the seminary.

Wado Church, north of Tokyo, where Laman conducted
weekend evangelistic services

Laman with the
Reverend Miwa Zenji
at Wado Church

During twenty-one years at the seminary, in addition to his
teaching responsibilities, Laman developed a more adequate program
of supervised student field education and pioneered an annual program

of overseas study tours with seminary students to Korea, Taiwan, the Philippines, or China in order to build bridges and foster mutuality between Japanese and other Asian Christians.    Weekends offered opportunities to conduct evangelistic services at churches throughout the country. Evon taught oral English at the seminary, tutored Japanese preparing for study abroad, and served at West Tokyo Union Church on the steering committee and as a church school teacher. The Lamans retired in 2002 after forty-three years in Japan, at which time Gordon was named professor emeritus of Tokyo Union Theological Seminary and awarded a Doctor of Divinity degree.

As the postwar career missionary couples began to retire in the 1980s and 1990s the Reformed Church, unique among North American churches associated with the Kyodan, made a concerted effort to provide long-term personnel. Cornelia Roghair, who had taught in Japan as a Reformed Church adult volunteer for about ten years, was appointed as a career missionary in 1987 to serve primarily in educational ministry. Roghair accepted assignment to San-ai High School, a mission school in Ebetsu City, near Sapporo, on Japan's northern island of Hokkaido. The shared support of the school helped alleviate the financial burden for the Reformed Church. Roghair also served actively in the local Japanese church's Christian education program and worked with youth and women.

Under the leadership of Glenn Bruggers and Elaine Tanis,[9] who succeeded him as secretary for Asia in 1989, three couples were appointed to service in Japan. The first couple sent, in 1989, was the Reverend Thomas D. and Barbara Vande Berg. Following language study, Barbara, who was trained as an educator, was appointed to Meiji Gakuin's Higashi Murayama High School, where Ron Korver had served for many years. In addition to teaching, she assisted the director of the school's renowned bell choir with orientation and arrangements for the summer concert tours to American churches. Tom worked in cooperation with churches of the western Tokyo area in evangelistic work, especially among young people, and developed an effective prison ministry.

Wayne A. Jansen first went to Japan in 1983 as one of the missionary associates sent by the Reformed Church to teach English at a mission school, Yokosuka Gakuin. During his four years there, while attending Yokohama Union Church, he met and eventually married

---

[9]    Elaine Tanis served as a Reformed Church missionary, teaching at Ferris Girls' School, from 1956-59.

Sato Miho, a Christian from Yokohama who was teaching English at Keisen High School, a mission school. They went to America, where Wayne prepared for the ministry at Western Theological Seminary and then spent a year in an internship in clinical pastoral education at Pine Rest Christian Hospital. During that period Miho served on the faculty at Hope College, teaching the Japanese language. The Reverend Wayne and Miho Jansen were appointed as missionaries and sent to Japan in 1992.

Following Wayne's completion of language study, the Jansens accepted assignment to the district centered around the city of Hamamatsu in Shizuoka Prefecture. Wayne pioneered a hospital chaplaincy ministry at Seirei Hospital, earning the respect and cooperation of hospital staff, Christian and non-Christian alike. At the same time, he worked as a cooperating evangelistic missionary with the churches of the district, especially as a preacher. Miho taught at Shizuoka Eiwa, a mission school for girls.

Okazaki Sayuri was born in Tokyo and raised in the Christian faith by her mother, who had been baptized as a teenager. Sayuri studied theology at Japan's Rikkyo University. Encouraged by her Japanese pastor, the Reverend Takasaki Takeshi, who had studied at Western Theological Seminary, she went to America to pursue advanced study at the same institution. Abraham Kist, born and raised in Wisconsin, majored in music at Hope College, after which he went on to prepare for the ministry at Western Seminary. Sayuri and Abraham met in a summer Greek course at the seminary in 1987 and later married. During his senior year at the seminary, Abraham took part in the Seminary Consortium for Urban Pastoral Education in Chicago and felt called to ministry in the crowded urban world filled with people in need of God's love.

After Abraham's graduation, the Kist-Okazakis moved to New York City, where Abraham served as pastor of Queensboro Hill Community Church in Flushing and Sayuri pursued the remaining studies necessary for ordination in the Reformed Church. In 1994 the Reverends Abraham and Sayuri Kist-Okazaki were appointed as missionaries and arrived to begin language study (Abraham) and urban ministry in Japan. Subsequently, they were assigned by the Kyodan to work in urban evangelism and church revitalization with Kyodan churches in *Minami Shiku* of *Tokyo Kyoku* (South District of Tokyo Synod), and they soon found ways of implementing their musical gifts and relational skills to partner with Japanese Christians for the strengthening of the ministry of city churches.

Typical Japanese church buildings of the late 1980s and 1990s. Japanese congregations today are usually small, reflecting the difficulty of evangelism and church growth, but they are self-reliant and independent of foreign financial support.

CHAPTER 15

# Mutual Mission of Equal Partners in the Gospel

## The Clarification of Cooperative Mission

It eventually became clear that the Japan-North American Commission on Cooperative Mission structure had outgrown its usefulness. The world mission policies of some of the related North American churches had changed, following trends of the times and differing perspectives on theology and mission, and there had been a resultant steady decline in the number of missionaries dispatched to Japan. Some denominations had discontinued sending new missionaries to Japan or even withdrawn those on the field. At a mission conference held in Tokyo October 27-30, 2003, the decision was made to dissolve the JNAC cooperative structure, effective January 1, 2005. It was agreed that from among the hitherto JNAC partners, interested parties would agree to meet biennially as a consultative (not decision-making) body. They would act as a forum "to continue, flexibly, cooperative mission in Japan, with each denomination accountable to its own governing structures and to the groups that all or some of them agree to form to work together on common mission priorities."[1]

[1] "Consultation Leads to Dissolution of JNAC, New Proposal," *Kyodan Newsletter*, No. 325, Dec. 2003.

For almost sixty years, from the formation of the Interboard Committee in 1948, responsibility for such matters as the paperwork for visa applications, missionary orientation, work assignments, and oversight of foreign personnel within Japan had been handled by the Council of Cooperation, consisting of representatives from the Kyodan, the Council of Cooperation-related Schools Council, the Christian Social Work League, and the mission boards.[2] At the 85th General Meeting of the Council of Cooperation in Japan held May 10, 2007, the council was also officially dissolved. Mission cooperation within Japan was provided for in a new agreement between the Kyodan, the Christian Schools Council, and the Christian Social Work League. Responsibilities formerly fulfilled by the Council of Cooperation regarding all missionaries sent to the church in Japan were assumed directly by the Nihon Kirisuto Kyodan. The Kyodan had established a Commission on Ecumenical Ministries in 2006 to facilitate church-to-church relations, and with the dissolution of the council, a Committee on Mission Personnel and a Committee on Missionary Concerns were formed under the commission. By means of these changes, the Kyodan itself took over responsibility for personnel procedures related to receiving and assigning foreign missionary personnel, missionary orientation, an annual missionary conference, assurance of appropriate working conditions, and pastoral concern for personnel from overseas.

In 2008, in anticipation of the celebration of the 150th anniversary in 2009 of the beginning of Protestant mission in Japan, the leaders of the Kyodan initiated an unprecedented action. The church's moderator (equivalent to the Reformed Church's president of General Synod), the Reverend Yamakita Nobuhisa, and the general secretary, the Reverend Naito Tomeyuki, led a group of Japanese Christians on a visit to the United States with two purposes. The first was to travel to several locations to meet with former missionaries in order to thank them for their contributions to mission in Japan. The missionaries were honored with a dinner and time of fellowship. The second purpose was to clarify and emphasize the special relationship the Japanese church leaders believed existed between themselves and the Reformed Church in America and the Presbyterian Church (U.S.A.). The result was the

---

[2]   Under the Interboard Committee structure (1948-1973), the mission boards appointed missionary members of the Council of Cooperation, but after the formation of the Japan-North American Commission, the council consisted only of representatives of the Kyodan, Schools Council, and Social Work League. Nevertheless, the three Japan-based constituents generally included related missionary colleagues among their chosen representatives.

following agreement, signed by the two Japanese leaders and the Reformed Church's president of General Synod, the Reverend Dr. Carol Bechtel, and general secretary, the Reverend Wes Granberg-Michaelson.

Covenantal Partnership-in-Mission Agreement
Between the Reformed Church in America
And the United Church of Christ in Japan

With a vision toward strengthening the church of Jesus Christ in both Japan and North America, and in order to give witness to the unity of the body of Christ, the Reformed Church in America (RCA) and the United Church of Christ in Japan (UCCJ) renew their commitment to a mutual ministry. We enter this agreement fully recognizing that we have much to receive from, as well as to give to, each other through mutual ministry.

We agree first and foremost that our ministry together will be guided by the principles which provide the foundation for both of our mission programs, especially these:

1. That our mission together will be HOLISTIC, that is, that we will seek to bring the whole gospel, in word and deed, through our mutual endeavor, ministering to the spiritual, physical, intellectual, emotional, and relational needs of those with whom we interact.
2. That our PARTNERSHIP in mission will be reciprocal, both in our relationship with one another, and with the Christians with whom we share ministry, and further, that as the church in Japan further develops and our relationship deepens, we will seek to strengthen our partnership through different expressions of ministry and fellowship.
3. That we will seek out opportunities by which the churches in Japan can minister to and strengthen the RCA through visits, exchanges, or actual placement of mission personnel in North America.
4. That our mutual goal is to strengthen the UCCJ in its mission and vision. As the number of Christians in Japan is extremely low, evangelism and church formation are the most important issues.
5. In order to accomplish the above objectives, both the RCA and the UCCJ must mutually acknowledge each other's confession, ordination, ministry and polity.

In matters of missiology and philosophy, the two partners in this agreement will be equal. If matters arise that reflect differences in mission philosophy, they will be addressed through dialogue, seeking to reach resolution by consensus and agreement.

Given the history of the RCA's involvement in Japan, the main concern and thrust of this covenant will be to strengthen a church-to-church relationship that will enable both communions to fully engage in mission, learn from and encourage each other, while seeking for new and relevant avenues to fulfill the Great Commission.

The General Synod of the RCA, through its supervisor of mission programs in East Asia will be responsible for nurturing the relationship with the United Church of Christ in Japan. The UCCJ's General Secretary, or its designated agent, will be the body through whom all RCA agreements will be channeled. Both the RCA and the UCCJ should meet at least once every other year to evaluate the covenantal relationship and make any necessary adjustments.

Each partner will make its expertise and, as appropriate, its resources available to the other for the benefit of the ministry. For example, the RCA may invite the UCCJ to its annual assembly or to other national or regional events where they may be able to share their expertise. At the same time, the UCCJ will invite RCA leaders to its biennial general assembly, its district meetings or to events for pastors, youth, women, etc.

This partnership will be reviewed biennially. It shall remain in effect and/or be modified at the mutual agreement of both partners.

Participating in such a mature relationship of mutuality in mission requires an unusual depth of cultural understanding and requires openness on both sides to learning from each other. It is particularly difficult for outgoing, enthusiastic Westerners to make the distinction between apparent inefficiency and lack of decisiveness and a culturally determined form of forbearance and perseverance. Japanese Christians remain open to the contributions of missionaries from the West, and welcome their unique gifts, but also expect sensitivity to their situation. The Reverend Munesue Isamu, chair of the Japanese church's Missionary Personnel Committee, in a reaction to pressure from Reformed Church staff calling upon Japanese church leaders and missionaries on the field to evaluate the work of the missionaries according to North American ideas, made the following response (author's translation from Japanese):

In evangelistic work in Japan, I believe that establishing sharply defined goals and measuring a missionary's ministry according to specific "marks" does not work. Japanese ministers themselves are having a difficult time finding a way to evangelize effectively. For us, the matter of having missionaries work along with us is an enormous blessing. In the present situation in Japan, we do not need to be taught something or have something provided for us. We seek and rejoice in missionaries who struggle alongside us.[3]

## Reformed Church Participation in Redefined Mutual Mission

The Reformed Church has continued to partner with Japanese Christians in the unfinished task of offering the good news of Jesus Christ to their people. Every year vibrant young Christians, many of them graduates of Reformed Church colleges, have been recruited, screened, prepared, and sent out through the work of Jay Harsevoort, coordinator for volunteers, to teach English and make a Christian witness in the mission schools of Japan. Furthermore, seven career missionaries uniquely prepared by the Spirit for their ministries have continued to live out the calling to mutuality through their several creative forms of service in Japan.

Wayne Jansen, following his years of experience in evangelism and hospital chaplaincy in Hamamatsu, and after completion of a doctor of ministry degree with a focus on counseling and the roots of Japanese mentality and spirituality, was invited to join the faculty of the Tokyo Union Theological Seminary in the spring of 2002 in the field of pastoral theology. In addition to other teaching responsibilities, he directs the seminary's Clinical Pastoral Education program. He also established and heads the seminary's Pastoral Care Center, through which he helps many seminarians who come to him for counseling become better prepared for the challenge of ministry within the non-Christian and often anti-Christian Japanese context. The Jansens find opportunities to work with not only theological students but also pastors, who often feel as if they are salmon swimming upstream in Japan's secular society. Miho Jansen, who attained a master of education degree in TESOL (Teaching English to Speakers of Other Languages), teaches English at Jiyu Gakuen, a Christian high school and college. Her students are predominantly nonbelievers, and Wayne and Miho make time to get to know and witness to these students.

---

3    Munesue Isamu to Gordon D. Laman, Jan. 7, 2010.

The Kist-Okazakis work together in evangelistic training for congregations of the Kyodan, teaching churches how to incorporate worshipful contemporary music in Japanese and other "seeker friendly" elements into worship services in order to more effectively reach non-Christians, who make up 99 percent of Japan's population. Abraham composes, arranges, and plays music, and Sayuri often sings, as they teach and encourage creative ways to worship and witness. They are both called upon to preach and to lead seminars or retreats for youth or church leaders. Sayuri has also been active in a national organization for women founded in 1930 by a Japanese Christian woman, Hani Motoko, called *Tomo No Kai* ("Association of Friends"), which publishes a magazine on home life and child rearing called *Fujin no Tomo* (*"Woman's Friend"*). Although this organization is not directly related to the church, due to the influence of Mrs. Hani, many local *Tomo no Kai* chapters have established Bible study groups, where Sayuri is called upon to teach and share the gospel.

Cornelia Roghair, after teaching English at San-ai High School for twenty-one years, took up a new assignment in the same region. Her ministry included teaching at three church-related preschools and reaching out to the parents, working with Sunday schools and youth groups, and partnering with Nopporo Christian School to develop ministries throughout the island of Hokkaido. Her little known witness and service touches the lives of many, from the cradle to the grave, as may be seen in excerpts from one of her letters.

> The last Christmas celebration for 2009 was held yesterday for the youth with a time of worship followed by lunch, fellowship, skits, and games. Many of the youth who attended I taught in the preschool Sunday school class, so it was wonderful to see how they have grown.
>
> Christmas Eve I spent making tree shaped cookies to go with the cards a former student helped me make. On Christmas morning I got up early and walked to the train station with my 120 cookies and cards, being careful not to slip on the ice. I caught the 8:17 train, the 9:11 bus, and arrived a little before 10:00 at the Christian Nursing Home. I went from room to room with one of the caregivers and visited each of the residents. This is the 26th time I have visited during the Christmas season and I look forward to it every year.[4]

---

4    RCA Missionary Update from Cornelia Roghair, Jan., 2010.

Nathan Brownell, a native of Michigan, first felt called to mission in Japan in the sixth grade while reading a book about Hiroshima. During his studies at Hope College, where he majored in religion and minored in Japanese, he participated in an exchange program at Meiji Gakuin University in Tokyo. He went on to graduate from Western Theological Seminary in 1997. Ito Nozomi, daughter of a Japanese pastor, graduated with a degree in English literature from Ferris Women's University in Yokohama in 1990 and served there as an assistant to the college chaplain, Russell Norden. Nathan and Nozomi met in Japan and were married in 1996 at Western Seminary, where she completed her master of religious education degree. From 1998 Nathan served as pastor of the Japanese American United Church in New York City for eight years. Nozomi was also very involved in this ministry, especially in Christian education and among the wives of Japanese businessmen working in New York.

The Reverend Nathan and Nozomi Brownell were sent as long-term Reformed Church missionary appointees to Japan in 2007. The Brownells live in Yokohama, and their work in cooperation with the church in Japan is focused on the renewal of youth ministry, through development of a program of relational evangelism at the Green House Youth Center, a place to plant the seeds of Christian faith and see them sprout and grow. The center gathers students from four local mission schools and involves them in an after-school program in which, under the Brownells' leadership, missionary associates who are teaching English in these schools share the gospel through fellowship times with the students. Nathan teaches English part time and regularly preaches at Ferris Girls' School chapel services.

Nozomi Brownell, who is qualified as a Children and Worship trainer, joined two other Japanese Christians in translating the book, *Young Children and Worship*, into Japanese, and this manual was published in 2009.[5] Nozomi has conducted seminars at Tokyo Union Theological Seminary and at several churches and has established a Children and Worship Center at the Green House for conducting seminars and workshops there. At the Green House she has also developed a ministry that includes Bible study for mothers of children attending the pre-school of Yokohama Union Church.

The Reformed Church, out of all proportion to its size, has witnessed and served faithfully in Japan and has contributed to the

---

[5]   Nozomi joined forces with the Reverend Sacon Mieko and Nishibori Kazuko to translate this monumental work by Sonja M. Stewart and Jerome W. Berryman.

birth, growth, and strengthening of the church there for more than 150 years. Regarding the sending of Reformed Church missionaries to Japan, the Hesselinks have noted,

> Albertus Pieters' call for the importation of men and women who were "highly educated, deeply spiritual, intensely evangelistic, and firmly rooted in Christian conviction," the most costly gift to give but by far the most precious gift to receive, has been wonderfully answered.
>
> Whereas some denominations appear to have given up on Japan for either financial or theological reasons, the RCA's commitment to that powerful but spiritually needy land remains firm. Because of Japan's great resistance to the gospel, that commitment is as important as ever. Even if the age-old question, "Do missions pay?" is even legitimate for Christians, the record of the RCA's mission to Japan speaks for itself. In every generation the Spirit raises up men and women who answer the call to witness to Christ's saving work to the uttermost parts of the earth. The cycle is ongoing and mantle has been passed. The "mission churches" formed in the pioneer days of the missionary enterprise have now become "sending churches." To God be the glory![6]

Japanese Christians celebrated the 150th anniversary of the beginning of Protestant mission in Japan in the fall of 2009, and the Kyodan planned and carried out three commemorative events in Tokyo. At a June gathering, ceremonies included a message by the moderator, Yamakita Nobuhisa, entitled, "Make Disciples of All Nations," as well as special commendation for sixty-one pastors who had served fifty or more years in ministry. On November 22, Tokyo Yamate Church was packed with more than 950 people for a Laity Rally under the banner, "Giving Thanks for 150 Years and Aiming for 200 Years Together With Our Lord," and Moderator Yamakita encouraged all with his message, "Entrusted with the Gospel." The following day, 1,500 people came together at Aoyama Gakuin University under the banner, "Christ, Our Salvation." Messages included "The 'Foolishness' of Evangelism" by the Reverend Ojima Seiji, "The Role of the Layperson in Evangelism" by Hashimoto Toru, and "Lift Up Your Hearts" by the Reverend Kato Tsuneaki. These and commemorative gatherings in other parts of Japan

---

[6]     John and Etta Hesselink, "Reformed Church Witness in Japan: A Brief History," *Reformed Review*, Spring, 2002, vol. 55, no. 3, 205-06.

not only gave thanks for the 150-year history of Japan mission, they also expressed the recommitment of Japanese Christians to their part in the evangelistic task of the biblical and apostolic church.[7]

Japanese Christians and the Japanese churches continue to express a need for non-Japanese partners in the extremely challenging task of witnessing and in building up the body of Christ in twenty-first century Japan. They do not need paternalistic foreigners but consider having missionaries to work along with them a great blessing and encouragement, and they seek and rejoice in missionaries who struggle alongside them. The urgency of the invitation to become partners in mission with Japanese Christians among one of the largest unreached populations in the world remains. We together continue to be, in the words of Eugene Booth in 1891, "called upon to develop more of the grace of patient perseverance."[8]

[7]    Naito Tomeyuki, "The Kyodan's Commemorative Events for the 150th Year," *Kyodan Newsletter*, Feb. 2010, no. 356, 358.
[8]    ESB to HNC, Feb. 23, 1891.

APPENDIX 1

# Missionaries Appointed to Japan by the Reformed Church Mission Board, with Dates of Service

| | |
|---|---|
| Samuel R. Brown | 1859–1879 |
| Elizabeth G. (Bartlett) Brown | 1859–1879 |
| Guido F. Verbeck | 1859–1898 |
| Maria (Manion) Verbeck | 1859–1898 |
| Duane B. Simmons | 1859–1860 |
| James H. Ballagh | 1861–1920 |
| Margaret T. (Kinnear) Ballagh | 1861–1909 |
| Henry Stout | 1869–1905 |
| Elizabeth (Provost) Stout | 1869–1902 |
| Mary E. (Kidder) Miller | 1869–1910 |
| E. Rothesay Miller | 1875–1915 |
| Charles H. H. Wolff | 1871–1876 |
| L. (Buboc) Wolff | 1871–1876 |
| S. K. M. Hequembourg | 1872–1874 |
| Emma C. Witbeck | 1874–1882 |
| James L. Amerman | 1876–1893 |
| Rebecca (Ely) Amerman | 1876–1893 |
| Elizabeth F. Farrington | 1878–1879 |

| | |
|---|---|
| Mary J. Farrington | 1878–1879 |
| Harriet L. Winn | 1878–1887 |
| Eugene S. Booth | 1879–1922 |
| Emilie (Stella) Booth | 1879–1917 |
| Carrie E. Ballagh | 1881–1885 |
| Martin N. Wyckoff | 1881–1911 |
| Anna (Baird) Wyckoff | 1881–1920 |
| M. Leila Winn | 1882–1920 |
| Nathan H. Demarest | 1883–1890, 1912–1914 |
| Anna (Strong) Demarest | 1883–1890 |
| Howard Harris | 1884–1905 |
| Lizzie (Disbrow) Harris | 1884–1905 |
| Mary E. Brokaw | 1884–1899 |
| Clara B. Richards | 1885–1885 |
| Albert Oltmans | 1886–1939 |
| Alice (Voorhorst) Oltmans | 1886–1939 |
| Anna DeF. Thompson | 1887–1913 |
| Rebecca L. Irvine | 1887–1893 |
| Henry Van Slyck Peeke | 1888–1892, 1893–1929 |
| Vesta (Greer) Peeke | 1893–1929 |
| Mary Deyo | 1888–1905 |
| Julia Moulton | 1888–1922 |
| Carrie B. Lanterman | 1890–1892 |
| Albertus Pieters | 1891–1925 |
| Emma (Kollen) Pieters | 1891–1925 |
| Anna B. Stout | 1891–1895, 1898–1905 |
| Sara M. Couch | 1892–1946 |
| Harriet M. Lansing | 1893–1928 |
| A. A. Davis | 1896–1898 |
| Jacob Poppen | 1896–1898 |
| Anna (Van Zwaluwenburg) Poppen | 1896–1898 |
| Anna K. Stryker | 1897–1900 |
| Frank S. Scudder | 1897–1907 |
| Florence (Schenck) Scudder | 1897–1906 |
| Jennie D. Schenck | 1897–1902 |
| Harriet J. Wyckoff | 1898–1905 |
| Charles M. Myers | 1899–1904 |
| Garret Hondelink | 1903–1908 |
| Grace (Hoekje) Hondelink | 1903–1908 |
| Grace Thomasma | 1904–1912 |

| | |
|---|---|
| Jennie A. Pieters | 1904–1939 |
| Douwe C. Ruigh | 1905–1927 |
| Christine (Carst) Ruigh | 1905–1927 |
| Anthony Walvoord | 1905–1919 |
| Edith (Walvoord) Walvoord | 1905–1919 |
| Jennie M. Kuyper | 1905–1923 |
| Walter F. Hoffsommer | 1907–1920 |
| Grace Hoffsommer | 1907–1920 |
| Willis G. Hoekje | 1907–1941 |
| Annie (Hail) Hoekje | 1912–1941 |
| Jennie Buys | 1909–1914 |
| Minnie Taylor | 1910–1937 |
| Hubert Kuyper | 1911–1946 |
| May (Demarest) Kuyper | 1912–1914, 1918–1946 |
| Jeane Noordhoff | 1911–1952 |
| Florence (Dick) Booth | 1912–1915, 1919–1922 |
| David Van Strien | 1912–1920 |
| Eleanor (Orbison) Van Strien | 1912–1913 |
| Lillian (Orbison) Van Strien | 1917–1920 |
| Luman J. Shafer | 1912–1935 |
| Amy (Hendricks) Shafer | 1912–1935 |
| Stephen W. Ryder | 1913–1930 |
| Reba (Snapp) Ryder | 1914–1930 |
| Hendrine E. Hospers | 1913–1926 |
| F. Evelyn Oltmans | 1914–1933 |
| C. Janet Oltmans | 1914–1956 |
| Alexander Van Bronkhorst | 1916–1926 |
| Helena (DeMaagd) Van Bronkhorst | 1916–1926 |
| Henry V. E. Stegeman | 1917–1941 |
| Gertrude (Hoekje) Stegeman | 1917–1941 |
| Anna M. Fleming | 1918–1924 |
| A. L. Harvey | 1920–1921 |
| Edith V. Teets | 1921–1925 |
| J. Gertrude Pieters | 1921–1925 |
| George W. Laug | 1921–1924, 1927–1932 |
| Mrs. (Hubbel) Laug | 1927–1932 |
| Dora Eringa | 1922–1935 |
| John Ter Borg | 1922–1944 |
| Amelie (Sywassink) Ter Borg | 1922–1944 |
| Gerald A. Mokma | 1922–1925 |

| | |
|---|---|
| Florence C. Walvoord | 1922–1941, 1947–1960 |
| Flora Darrow | 1922–1942 |
| Florence C. Buss | 1922–1930 |
| Gladys W. Hildreth | 1922–1923 |
| Boude C. Moore | 1924–1941, 1950–1962 |
| Anna (McAlpine) Moore | 1924–1941, 1950–1962 |
| Henrietta Keizer | 1925–1928 |
| Cornelius A. Dykhuizen | 1925–1928 |
| Martin Hoeksema | 1925–1928 |
| Bessie J. Shafer | 1926–1928 |
| Eugene C. Duryee | 1926–1931 |
| Louise S. Muyskens | 1926–1931 |
| John C. de Maagd | 1928–1934, 1937–1941, 1948–1959 |
| Marion (Morris) de Maagd | 1928–1934, 1937–1941, 1948–1959 |
| Helen R. Zander | 1928–1974 |
| Barnerd Luben | 1929–1941 |
| Edith (Erickson) Luben | 1932–1941 |
| James A. McAlpine | 1929–1932 |
| Bruno Bruns | 1930–1941 |
| Regina (Buss) Bruns | 1930–1941 |
| Alice D. V. Buchanan | 1931–1933 |
| Virginia Reeves | 1932–1937 |
| Priscilla Bekman | 1936–1940 |
| F. Belle Bogard | 1936–1943, 1949–1974 |
| Mary E. Liggett | 1938–1941 |
| Ronald G. Korver | 1948–1992 |
| Ruby (Barth) Korver | 1952–1992 |
| Eunice Noda | 1948–1951 |
| Theodore E. Flaherty | 1949–1982 |
| Mary (Watt) Flaherty | 1953–1982, 1984–1988 |
| Suzanne H. Brink | 1950–1977 |
| Louis P. Kraay | 1950–1953 |
| A. Burrell Pennings | 1950–1953 |
| Helen J. Vander Meer | 1950–1953 |
| Everett Kleinjans | 1951–1966 |
| Edith (Klaaren) Kleinjans | 1951–1966 |
| William F. Sheets | 1951–1954 |
| Bonita T. Sheets | 1951–1954 |

| | |
|---|---|
| Marcella M. Poppen | 1951–1954 |
| Glenn Bruggers | 1952–1973 |
| Phyllis (Voss) Bruggers | 1952–1973 |
| William H. Estell, Jr. | 1952–1955 |
| Carol Van Zoeren | 1952–1955 |
| Gordon J. Van Wyk | 1953–1985 |
| Bertha (Vis) Van Wyk | 1953–1985 |
| I. John Hesselink | 1953–1972 |
| Etta (Ter Louw) Hesselink | 1953–1972 |
| Russell L. Norden | 1953–1991 |
| Eleanor (Short) Norden | 1953–1991 |
| Paul H. Tanis | 1953–1958 |
| Marjorie (Greving) Tanis | 1953–1958 |
| Verlaine R. Siter | 1953–1956 |
| Fenita M. Harmelink | 1955–1958 |
| Elaine J. Buteyn | 1956–1959 |
| Aileem I. McGoldrick | 1958–1962 |
| Henry M. Schaafsma | 1958–1962 |
| Carol (Armey) Schaafsma | 1958–1962 |
| Jeneva K. Breed | 1959–1962 |
| Carroll M. de Forrest | 1959–1962, 1966–1970 |
| Betty (Dodd) de Forrest | 1966–1970 |
| John D. Hood | 1959–1962 |
| Gordon D. Laman | 1959–2002 |
| Evon (Southland) Laman | 1959–2002 |
| Rudolf Kuyten | 1960–1995 |
| Trina (Vander Eems) Kuyten | 1960–1995 |
| Barbara Bosch | 1960–1963 |
| Eileen Fredriks | 1960–1963 |
| James P. Rozeboom | 1961–1964 |
| Beth Bonnema | 1962–1965 |
| Thomas J. Harris | 1962–1969 |
| Barbara Harris | 1962–1969 |
| Agatha C. Tigelaar | 1962–1969 |
| George Magee | 1963–2005 |
| W. Joyce (Tysen) Magee | 1963–2005 |
| William M. Unzicker | 1963–1993 |
| Sarah (McClain) Unzicker | 1963–1993 |
| John E. Zwyghuizen | 1963–1974 |
| Helene (Bosch) Zwyghuizen | 1963–1974 |

| | |
|---|---|
| Alice Elzinga | 1966–1979 |
| John C. Koedyker | 1977–1987 |
| Marilyn (Rathbun) Koedyker | 1977–1987 |
| Cornelia Roghair | 1977– |
| Wayne A. Jansen | 1991– |
| Miho Jansen | 1991– |
| Thomas D. Vande Berg | 1988–2001 |
| Barbara Vande Berg | 1988–2001 |
| Abraham D. Kist-Okazaki | 1994– |
| Sayuri Kist-Okazaki | 1994– |
| Nathan Brownell | 2007– |
| Nozomi Brownell | 2007– |

APPENDIX 2

# Missionary Associates Sent to Japan through Reformed Church Adult Volunteer Services

*Most missionary associates went out to serve for two years. However, some extended their service for additional years, and a few accepted repeated assignments.*

| Directory Year | Name |
| --- | --- |
| 1974 | Fliris, Rachel |
| 1974 | Luben, Deborah |
| 1976 | Beran, James |
| 1976 | Blauwkamp, Christi |
| 1976 | Hillier, Robert |
| 1976 | Kale, Karmen |
| 1976 | Riksen, Michael |
| 1976 | LaFave, Steven and Beth |
| 1976 | Roghair, Cornelia |
| 1976 | Stuit, Elaine |
| 1976 | Henseler, Sarah |
| 1976 | Wiedemann, Ellen |
| 1977 | Johnson, Karen |

| 1977 | Brana, Wayne and Kathleen |
| 1977 | Hoyt, Suzanne |
| 1978 | Zuverink, Timothy |
| 1979 | Vogelaar, Ted |
| 1979 | Fry, Kent and Joyce |
| 1980 | Roghair, Cornelia |
| 1980 | Voorhorst, John |
| 1980 | Weener, James |
| 1980 | Van Dam, Arlyne |
| 1980 | Drake, Mark and Barbara |
| 1980 | Jager, Calvin |
| 1981 | Vande Lune, Linda |
| 1982 | Bruggers, Carolyn |
| 1982 | Burt, Barbara |
| 1982 | Hagan, Susanne |
| 1982 | Rothermel, Mark and Patricia |
| 1982 | Buurstra, Todd |
| 1982 | Tuinstra, Rebecca |
| 1982 | Roghair, Cornelia |
| 1983 | Dykstra, Janelle |
| 1983 | Navis, Kathleen |
| 1983 | Soeter, Mary |
| 1983 | Brooks, Marisa |
| 1983 | DeKreek, Anne |
| 1983 | Kobza, Kenneth and Susan |
| 1983 | Larink, Marilyn |
| 1983 | Jansen, Wayne |
| 1984 | Eshuis, Sonya |
| 1984 | Smit, Nancy |
| 1984 | Eggebeen, Deborah |
| 1984 | Courson, Kimberly |
| 1984 | Edwards, Manna |
| 1984 | White, Susan |
| 1984 | Flaherty, Robert and Rachel |
| 1984 | Smith, Carol |
| 1984 | Reece, Richard |
| 1985 | Prochnow, Sheila |
| 1985 | Roghair, Cornelia |
| 1985 | Londo, William |
| 1986 | Brooks, Marisa |
| 1986 | Halversen, Deborah |
| 1986 | Le Poire, Debera |
| 1986 | Nielsen, Phillip |
| 1986 | Weisiger, Beth |

| | |
|---|---|
| 1986 | Laug, Lise |
| 1987 | Harrington, Phil |
| 1987 | Aug, Virginia |
| 1988 | Boertje, Barbara |
| 1988 | Courson, Kimberly |
| 1988 | Lankamp, Joan |
| 1988 | Scholtens, Lynn |
| 1988 | Van Swol, Diane |
| 1988 | Hakken, Mary |
| 1988 | Tysen, Kevin |
| 1988 | Timmer, Kyl |
| 1989 | Beran, Gail |
| 1989 | Germeraad, Renee |
| 1989 | Marple, Betty |
| 1989 | Moore-DeLaguardia, Kari |
| 1989 | Rienstra, John |
| 1989 | Harthoorn, Sheri |
| 1990 | De Groot, Thea |
| 1990 | Gandre, Nancy |
| 1990 | Hoogland, Jane |
| 1990 | Kennedy, David |
| 1990 | Skinner, Michelle |
| 1990 | Veldheer, Diane |
| 1990 | Jongerius, Rachel |
| 1990 | Smith-Sasaki, Carol |
| 1991 | De Prenger, Susan |
| 1991 | Dykstra, Crystal |
| 1991 | Ten Hor, Susan |
| 1992 | Beran, Gail |
| 1992 | De Prenger, Susan |
| 1992 | Dykstra, Crystal |
| 1992 | Lewicki, Beverly |
| 1992 | Caldwell, Mary |
| 1992 | Renes, Brenda |
| 1992 | Ten Hor, Sunni |
| 1992 | Bras, Harris |
| 1992 | Chang, Grace |
| 1992 | Purvis, Tena |
| 1992 | Boraas, Vincent |
| 1993 | Ratering, Mark |
| 1993 | Van Swol, Diane |
| 1993 | Harder, Hans |
| 1993 | Harris, Kathleen |
| 1993 | Terpstra, Wynette |

| | |
|---|---|
| 1993 | Vold, John |
| 1994 | Kennedy, David |
| 1994 | Raymond, Erinn |
| 1994 | Van Oort, Phil |
| 1994 | Courson, Kimberly |
| 1994 | Moore, Jim and Jan |
| 1995 | De Boer, Melanie |
| 1995 | Perry, Brent |
| 1995 | Kolk, Janelle |
| 1996 | Hanousek, Rebekah |
| 1996 | Bush, Jerre |
| 1997 | Kennedy, David |
| 1997 | Shibe-Davis, Susan |
| 1997 | Van Voorst, Vic and Ruthanne |
| 1997 | Tysen, Kevin |
| 1997 | Fowler, Stella |
| 1997 | Freilink, Carolyn |
| 1997 | Lang, Kathy |
| 1997 | Peters, Marti |
| 1997 | Zylstra, Brian |
| 1998 | Wallingford, Denise |
| 1998 | Chen, Melody |
| 1998 | Green, Jason |
| 1998 | Driese, Anita |
| 1999 | Boraas, Vincent |
| 1999 | Bush, Jerre |
| 1999 | Bentley, Ken and Erinn |
| 1999 | Grabill, Jodie |
| 1999 | Yue, Sorrell |
| 2000 | Maldonado, Kathy |
| 2000 | Brunink, Betsy |
| 2000 | De Koster, Luke |
| 2000 | Faulkner, William and Amanda |
| 2000 | Ryan, Colleen |
| 2000 | Terpstra, Wynette |
| 2000 | White, Judith (Taylor) |
| 2000 | Driese, Anita |
| 2000 | Bavin, Ruth |
| 2000 | Marvel, Jana |
| 2000 | Victor, Susan |
| 2001 | Wayman, Shaun and Julie |
| 2001 | Johnson, Karla |
| 2002 | Bosch, Matthew |
| 2002 | De Pree, Curtis |

| | |
|---|---|
| 2002 | Dorn, Katharine |
| 2002 | Blakeslee, Nathan |
| 2002 | Carowitz, Dawn |
| 2002 | Koedyker, Joel |
| 2002 | Smit, Jessica |
| 2002 | Roberts, William |
| 2002 | Bey, Zachary and Juli |
| 2003 | Admiraal, Phil and Judy |
| 2003 | Do, Tyler |
| 2003 | Nielsen, Angie |
| 2003 | Braaksma, Carol |
| 2003 | Chee, Ivan |
| 2003 | Hathaway, Jaime |
| 2003 | Marshall, Ryan |
| 2003 | Belote, Benjamin and Jeralyn |
| 2003 | Cubos, Myra |
| 2004 | Bavin, Ruth |
| 2004 | Cichocky, Mary |
| 2004 | Elder, Justin |
| 2004 | Thompson, Amanda |
| 2004 | Roberts, Maudie (Marti) |
| 2004 | Bolinder, Jesse and Megan |
| 2004 | Voss, Maribeth |
| 2005 | Nearpass, Angela |
| 2005 | Oosting, Kevin |
| 2005 | Blakeslee, Nathan |
| 2006 | Marshall, Ryan and Athonei |
| 2006 | Shepherd, Kimberly |
| 2006 | Boyes, Nicholas |
| 2006 | King, Elizabeth |
| 2007 | Rensink, Christopher |
| 2007 | Herzog, Anna |
| 2007 | Nelson, Tonya |
| 2007 | Kimura, Josephine |
| 2008 | Ekvall, Tabitha |
| 2008 | Appelgate, Travis and Angie |
| 2008 | Anderson, Robyn |
| 2009 | Herbert, Katharine |
| 2009 | Oosting, Kevin |
| 2009 | Van Antwerpen, Donald |
| 2010 | Hashimoto, Rachel |
| 2011 | Willems, Jeremiah |

# Bibliography

Archives of the Reformed Church in America, Board of Foreign Missions: Japan Files.

Ballagh, Margaret Tate Kinnear. *Glimpses of Old Japan: 1861 - 1866.* Tokyo: Methodist Publishing House, 1908.

Bartholomew, Allen R. *Won By Prayer, or The Life and Work of Rev. Masayoshi Oshikawa.* Philadelphia: Reformed Church Publishing House, 1889.

Beckmann, George M. *The Making of the Meiji Constitution: The Oligarchs and the Constitutional Development of Japan, 1868 – 1891.* Westport, Conn.: Greenwood, 1957.

Cary, Otis. *A History of Christianity in Japan,* Vols. I and II. Tokyo: Tuttle, 1909.

Chamberlain, Mrs. W. I. *Fifty Years in Foreign Fields; China, Japan, India, Arabia: A History of Five Decades of the Woman's Board of Foreign Missions of the Reformed Church in America.* New York: Woman's Board of Foreign Missions, R.C.A., 1925.

Cobb, Henry N. *A Century of Missions: Reformed Church in America, 1796-1896.* New York: Board of Foreign Missions, 1900.

Cody, Billy J. "Unifiers of Japan: Nobunaga, Hideyoshi, and Ieyasu," *Great Historical Figures of Japan*. Tokyo: Japan Culture Institute, 1978.

Cogswell, James A. *Until the Day Dawn*. Presbyterian Church, U.S.: Board of World Missions, 1957.

Corwin, Edward Tanjore. *A Manual of the Reformed Church in America (Formerly Reformed Protestant Dutch Church): 1628 – 1902*. New York: Board of Publication of the Reformed Church in America, 1902.

Craig, William. *The Fall of Japan*. New York: Dial, 1967.

*De Gereformeerde Kerk in Het Oosten: 1916*. New York: Board van Buitenlandische Zending, Gereformeerde Kerk in Amerika, 1916.

Drummond, Richard Henry. *A History of Christianity in Japan*. Grand Rapids: Eerdmans, 1971.

Ellison, George. *Deus Destroyed: The Image of Christianity in Early Modern Japan*. Cambridge: Harvard University Press, 1973.

Fairbank, John K., Edwin O. Reischauer, and Albert M. Craig. *East Asia: Tradition and Transformation*. Tokyo: Tuttle, 1973.

Gasero, Russell L. *Historical Directory of the Reformed Church in America: 1628 – 2000*. Grand Rapids: Eerdmans, 2001.

Gordon, Andrew. *A Modern History of Japan: From Tokugawa Times to the Present*. New York: Oxford University Press, 2003.

———, ed. *Postwar Japan as History*. Berkeley: University of California Press, 1993.

Griffis, William Elliot. *A Maker of the New Orient: Samuel Robbins Brown*. London: Revell, 1902.

———. *Hepburn of Japan and His Wife and Helpmates: A Life Story of Toil for Christ*. Philadelphia: Westminster, 1913.

———. *The Mikado's Empire*. New York: Harper, 1876.

———. *Verbeck of Japan: A Citizen of No Country*. New York: Revell, 1900.

———. *The Rutgers Graduates in Japan*. New Brunswick, New Jersey: Rutgers College, 1916.

Harrington, Ann M. "The Kakure-Kirishitan and Their Place in Japan's Religious Tradition," *Japanese Journal of Religious Studies*, Dec., 1980.

Horton, Douglas, Chmn, James C. Baker, Luman J. Shafer, Walter W. VanKirk. *The Return to Japan: Report of the Christian Deputation to Japan, October – November, 1945*. New York: Friendship, 1946.

Hori Ichiro, ed. *Japanese Religion: A Survey by the Agency for Cultural Affairs*. Tokyo: Kodansha International, 1972.

Howes, John F. *Japan's Modern Prophet: Uchimura Kanzo, 1861 – 1930*. Vancouver: UBC, 2005.

Iglehart, Charles W. *A Century of Protestant Christianity in Japan*. Tokyo: Tuttle, 1959.

Imbrie, William M. *The Church of Christ in Japan: A Course of Lectures.* Philadelphia: Westminster, 1906.

Jansen, Marius B., *The Making of Modern Japan.* Cambridge: Harvard University Press, 2000.

Kuroki Goro. *Baiko Jo Gakuin Shi.* Shimonoseki: Baiko Jo Gakuin, 1934.

Latourette, Kenneth Scott. *A History of Christianity.* New York: Harper, 1953.

Lifton, Robert J. *Destroying the World to Save It: Aum Shinryikyo, Apocalyptic Violence, and the New Global Terrorism.* New York: Holt, 1999.

Livingston, Jon, Joe Moore, and Felicia Oldfather, eds. *Imperial Japan: 1800-1945.* New York: Random House, 1973.

Lu, David J. *Japan: A Documentary History: Volume II: The Late Tokugawa Period to the Present.* Armonk, New York: Thorpe, 1997.

McAlpine, J.A. "The Rev. James Hamilton Ballagh, D.D." *Japan Christian Quarterly*, April, 1955.

Nishi Yutaka. *Nagasaki Kyokai no Sosoki (Jo): Shiryo to Kaisetsu.* Shizuoka: Kirisutokyo Shidankai, 2003.

Oltmans, A., ed. *Meiji Gakuin Semi-Centennial: 1877 – 1927.* Tokyo: Meiji Gakuin, 1927.

*Open Gates: A Handbook on Foreign Missions.* New York: Board of Foreign Missions of the Reformed Church in America, 1952.

Pieters, Albertus. *Mission Problems in Japan: Theoretical and Practical.* New York: Board of Publication of the Reformed Church in America, 1912.

———. *Seven Years of Newspaper Evangelism in Japan.* Tokyo: Kyobunkwan, 1919.

*Proceedings of the General Conference of Protestant Missionaries in Japan: Held in Tokyo October 24-31, 1900.* Tokyo: Methodist Publishing House, 1901.

*Proceedings of the Osaka Conference of Missionaries in Japan, 1883.* Yokohama: Meiklejohn, 1883

Reischauer, Edwin O. *Japan: The Story of a Nation.* Tokyo: Charles E. Tuttle, 1970.

Reischauer, Edwin O. and Albert M. Craig. *Japan: Tradition and Transformation.* Tokyo: Tuttle, 1978.

Ritter, H. and George E. Albrecht, trans. *A History of Protestant Missions in Japan.* Tokyo: Methodist Publishing House, 1898.

Ryder, Stephen Willis. *A Historical Sourcebook of the Japan Mission of the Reformed Church in America: 1859 – 1930.* York, PA: York Printing, 1935.

Sangster, Margaret E., ed. *A Manual of the Missions of the Reformed (Dutch) Church in America*. New York: Board of Publications of the Reformed Church in America, 1877.

Sansom, G. B. *The Western World and Japan*. Tokyo: Tuttle, 1950.

Schaff, Philip. *The Creeds of Christendom: With a History and Critical Notes, Vol. III: The Evangelical Protestant Creeds*. Grand Rapids: Baker, 1998.

Stout, Henry. "First Christian Funeral at Nagasaki." *Sower and Mission Monthly*, April, 1881.

———. *Sketch of the South Japan Mission*. New York: Board of Foreign Missions, RCA, 1899.

Suzuki Norihisa. "Christianity." *Japanese Religion: A Survey of the Agency of Cultural Affairs*. Tokyo: Kodansha, 1972.

Takaya Michio, ed., trans. *S. R. Brown Shosekishu*. Tokyo: Publishing Department of the United Church of Christ in Japan, 1965.

———. *Verbeck Shosekishu*. Tokyo: Publishing Department of the United Church of Christ in Japan, 1978.

Thomas, Winburn T. *Protestant Beginnings in Japan: The First Three Decades, 1859–1889*. Tokyo: Tuttle, 1959.

VanHoeven, James W. ed. *Piety and Patriotism: Bicentenniel Studies of the Reformed Church in America, 1776-1976*. Grand Rapids: Eerdmans, 1976.

Van Wyk, Gordon J. *Eighty Years of Concern: Meiji Gakuin, 1877 – 1957*. Tokyo: Meiji Gakuin, 1957.

Verbeck, Guido F. "History of Protestant Missions in Japan." *Proceedings of the Osaka Conference of Missionaries in Japan, 1883*. Yokohama: Meiklejohn, 1883.

Wheeler, W. Reginald. *The Crisis Decade: A History of the Foreign Missionary Work of the Presbyterian Church in the U.S.A., 1937 – 1947*. New York: Board of Foreign Missions of the Presbyterian Church in the U.S.A., 1950.

Wyckoff, M. N. "Rev. Guido Fridolin Verbeck, D.D." *Japan Evangelist*, Vol. 16, No. 9, Sept., 1909.

Yanagita Tomonobu. *A Short History of Christianity in Japan*. Sendai: Seisho Tosho Kankokai, 1957.

Young, John M. L. *The Two Empires in Japan*. Tokyo: Bible Times, 1958.

# INDEX

This index is a combined name and subject index. In many cases name entries for individuals refer to quotations and excerpts of letters. For brevity, some references to missionary wives (as part of couples) and children (as part of families) are included under the male missionaries' entries.